WARREN COMMISION 6 OF 26
HEARINGS VOLUME 6

INVESTIGATION OF
THE ASSASSINATION OF
PRESIDENT JOHN F. KENNEDY

I0482849

HEARINGS
Before the President's Commission
on the Assassination
of President Kennedy

PURSUANT TO EXECUTIVE ORDER 11130, an Executive order creating a Commission to ascertain, evaluate, and report upon the facts relating to the assassination of the late President John F. Kennedy and the subsequent violent death of the man charged with the assassination and S.J. RES. 137, 88TH CONGRESS, a concurrent resolution conferring upon the Commission the power to administer oaths and affirmations, examine witnesses, receive evidence, and issue subpenas

Volume

VI

UNITED STATES GOVERNMENT PRINTING OFFICE
WASHINGTON, D.C.

U.S. GOVERNMENT PRINTING OFFICE, WASHINGTON: 1964

For sale in complete sets by the Superintendent of Documents, U.S. Government Printing Office Washington, D.C., 20402

PRESIDENT'S COMMISSION
ON THE
ASSASSINATION OF PRESIDENT KENNEDY

CHIEF JUSTICE EARL WARREN, *Chairman*

- SENATOR RICHARD B. RUSSELL
- SENATOR JOHN SHERMAN COOPER
- REPRESENTATIVE HALE BOGGS
- REPRESENTATIVE GERALD R. FORD
- MR. ALLEN W. DULLES
- MR. JOHN J. MCCLOY

- J. LEE RANKIN, *General Counsel*

- *Assistant Counsel*

- FRANCIS W. H. ADAMS
- JOSEPH A. BALL
- DAVID W. BELIN
- WILLIAM T. COLEMAN, Jr.
- MELVIN ARON EISENBERG
- BURT W. GRIFFIN
- LEON D. HUBERT, Jr.
- ALBERT E. JENNER, Jr.
- WESLEY J. LIEBELER
- NORMAN REDLICH
- W. DAVID SLAWSON
- ARLEN SPECTER
- SAMUEL A. STERN
- HOWARD P. WILLENS

- *Staff Members*

- PHILLIP BARSON
- EDWARD A. CONROY
- JOHN HART ELY
- ALFRED GOLDBERG
- MURRAY J. LAULICHT
- ARTHUR MARMOR

- RICHARD M. MOSK
- JOHN J. O'BRIEN
- STUART POLLAK
- ALFREDDA SCOBEY
- CHARLES N. SHAFFER, Jr.

Biographical information on the Commissioners and the staff can be found in the Commission's *Report*.

Λ Mr. Willens also acted as liaison between the Commission and the Department of Justice.

☐

Preface

The testimony of the following witnesses is contained in volume VI: Drs. Charles J. Carrico, Malcolm Oliver Perry, William Kemp Clark, Robert Nelson McClelland, Charles Rufus Baxter, Marion Thomas Jenkins, Ronald Coy Jones, Don Teel Curtis, Fouad A. Bashour, Gene Coleman Akin, Paul Conrad Peters, Adolph Hartung Giesecke, Jr., Jackie Hansen Hunt, Kenneth Everett Salyer, and Martin G. White, who attended President Kennedy at Parkland Hospital; Drs. Robert Roeder Shaw, Charles Francis Gregory, George T. Shires, and Richard Brooks Dulany, who attended Governor Connally at Parkland Hospital; Ruth Jeanette Standridge, Jane Carolyn Wester, Henrietta M. Ross, R. J. Jimison, and Darrell C. Tomlinson, who testified concerning Governor Connally's stretcher; Diana Hamilton Bowron, Margaret M. Henchliffe, and Doris Mae Nelson, who testified concerning President Kennedy's stretcher; Charles Jack Price, the Administrator of Parkland Hospital; Malcolm O. Couch, Tom C. Dillard, James Robert Underwood, James N. Crawford, Mary Ann Mitchell, Barbara Rowland, Ronald B. Fischer, Robert Edwin Edwards, Jean Lollis Hill, Austin L. Miller, Frank E. Reilly, Earle V. Brown, Royce G. Skelton, S. M. Holland, J. W. Foster, J. C. White, Joe E. Murphy, Roger D. Craig, George W. Rackley, Sr., James Elbert Romack, Lee E. Bowers, Jr., B. J. Martin, Bobby W. Hargis, Clyde A. Haygood, E. D. Brewer, D. V. Harkness, J. Herbert Sawyer, and Gerald Dalton Henslee, who were present at the assassination scene; William H. Shelley, Nat A. Pinkston, Billy Nolan Lovelady, Frankie Kaiser, Charles Douglas Givens, Troy Eugene West, Danny G. Arce, Joe R. Molina, Jack Edwin Dougherty, Eddie Piper, Victoria Elizabeth Adams, Geneva L. Hine, and Doris Burns, employees of the Texas School Book Depository; Mary E. Bledsoe, William W. Whaley, and Mrs. Earlene Roberts, who gave testimony concerning Oswald's movements following the assassination; and Domingo Benavides, and Mrs. Charles Davis, who were present in the vicinity of the Tippit crime scene.

☐

Contents

Joe E. Murphy	256
Roger D. Craig	260
George W. Rackley, Sr	273
James Elbert Romack	277
Lee E. Bowers, Jr	284
B. J. Martin	289
Bobby W. Hargis	293
Clyde A. Haygood	296
E. D. Brewer	302
D. V. Harkness	308
J. Herbert Sawyer	315
Gerald Dalton Henslee	325
William H. Shelley	327
Nat A. Pinkston	334
Billy Nolan Lovelady	336
Frankie Kaiser	341
Charles Douglas Givens	345
Troy Eugene West	356
Danny G. Arce	363
Joe R. Molina	368
Jack Edwin Dougherty	373
Eddie Piper	382
Victoria Elizabeth Adams	386
Geneva L. Hine	393
Doris Burns	397
Mary E. Bledsoe	400
William W. Whaley	428
Earlene Roberts	431
Domingo Benavides	44

4

EXHIBITS INTRODUCED

7

TESTIMONY OF DR. CHARLES J. CARRICO

The testimony of Dr. Charles J. Carrico was taken at 9:30 a.m., on March 25, 1964, at Parkland Memorial Hospital, Dallas, Tex., by Mr. Arlen Specter, assistant counsel of the President's Commission.

Mr. SPECTER. May the record show that Dr. Charles J. Carrico is present in response to a letter request for him to appear so that his deposition may be taken in connection with the proceedings of the President's Commission on the Investigation of the Assassination of President Kennedy in connection with the inquiry into all phases of that assassination, including medical care rendered at Parkland Memorial Hospital.

Dr. Carrico has been asked to testify relating to the treatment which he rendered the President at Parkland Hospital. With that preliminary statement of purpose, Dr. Carrico, would you please stand up and raise your right hand.

Do you solemnly swear the testimony you will give before the President's Commission in this deposition proceeding will be the truth, the whole truth and nothing but the truth, so help you God?

Dr. CARRICO. I do.

Mr. SPECTER. Would you state your full name for the record, please?

Dr. CARRICO. Charles James Carrico.

Mr. SPECTER. What is your profession, sir?

Dr. CARRICO. Physician.

Mr. SPECTER. Are you duly licensed by the State of Texas to practice medicine?

Dr. CARRICO. Yes.

Mr. SPECTER. And would you outline briefly your educational background, please?

Dr. CARRICO. I attended grade school and high school in Denton, Tex.; received a Bachelor of Science in Chemistry from North Texas State College in 1957, and an M.D. from Southwestern Medical School in 1961, and served an internship at Parkland Memorial Hospital from 1961 to 1962, and a year of Fellowship in Surgery at Southwestern, followed by my residency here.

Mr. SPECTER. Are you working toward any specialty training, Doctor?

Dr. CARRICO. I am engaged in a general surgery residency which will qualify me for my boards in general surgery.

Mr. SPECTER. And what were your duties on November 22, 1963, at Parkland Hospital?

Dr. CARRICO. At that time I was assigned to the elective surgery service and was in the emergency room seeing some patients for evaluation for admission to the hospital.

Mr. SPECTER. And what were you doing specifically around 12 o'clock noon?

Dr. CARRICO. Approximately 12 noon or shortly thereafter I was in the clinic and was called to come into the emergency room to see these people and evaluate them for admission and treatment.

Mr. SPECTER. Were you notified that there was an emergency case on the way to the hospital at approximately 12:30?

Dr. CARRICO. Yes.

Mr. SPECTER. In which President Kennedy was involved?

Dr. CARRICO. At that time I was in the emergency room seeing these patients and the call was received that the President had been shot and was on his way to the hospital.

Mr. SPECTER. What is your best recollection as to what time it was when you received that call?

Dr. CARRICO. This was probably shortly after 12:30.

Mr. SPECTER. And how long after that call was received did the President's party actually arrive at Parkland?

Dr. CARRICO. An estimation would be 2 minutes or less.

Mr. SPECTER. Describe what occurred upon the arrival of the President's party at Parkland, please.

Dr. CARRICO. We were in the emergency room preparing equipment in response to the call we had received when the nurse said over the intercom that they were here. Governor Connally was rolled in first and was taken to one of the trauma rooms.

Mr. SPECTER. And what identification was given to the trauma room to which Governor Connally was taken?

Dr. CARRICO. Trauma room 2.

8

Mr. SPECTER. Who was present at the time that Governor Connally came into the emergency area?

Dr. CARRICO. As I recall, Dr. Richard Dulany, myself, several of the nurses, Miss Bowron is the only one I can definitely remember. Don Curtis, oral surgery resident, and I believe Martin White, the intern, was there. These are the only people I remember being present at that time. We had already sent out a call for Dr. Baxter and Dr. Perry and the rest of the staff.

Mr. SPECTER. Did Dr. Dulany take any part in the treatment of President Kennedy?

Dr. CARRICO. No, no, sir; he didn't.

Mr. SPECTER. Did Dr. Martin White take any part in the treatment of President Kennedy?

Dr. CARRICO. I believe he was in there and did the—he helped Dr. Curtis with the cutdown, the initial cutdown.

Mr. SPECTER. What did Dr. Dulany do?

Dr. CARRICO. Dr. Dulany and I initially went to see the Governor, as I said, and he stayed with the Governor while I went to attend to the President, care for the President.

Mr. SPECTER. Who was the first doctor to reach President Kennedy on his arrival at Parkland Hospital?

Dr. CARRICO. I was.

Mr. SPECTER. And who else was with President Kennedy on his arrival, as best you can recollect it?

Dr. CARRICO. Mrs. Kennedy was there, and there were some men in the room, who I assumed were Secret Service men; I don't know.

Mr. SPECTER. Can you identify any nurses who were present, in addition to Miss Bowron?

Dr. CARRICO. No, I don't recall any of them.

Mr. SPECTER. What did you observe as to the President's condition upon his arrival?

Dr. CARRICO. He was lying on a carriage, his respirations were slow, spasmodic, described as agonal.

Mr. SPECTER. What do you mean by "agonal" if I may interrupt you for just a moment there, Doctor?

Dr. CARRICO. These are respirations seen in one who has lost the normal coordinated central control of respiration. These are spasmodic and usually reflect a terminal patient.

Mr. SPECTER. Would you continue to describe your observations of the President?

Dr. CARRICO. His—the President's color—I don't believe I said—he was an ashen, bluish, grey, cyanotic, he was making no spontaneous movements, I mean, no voluntary movements at all. We opened his shirt and coat and tie and observed a small wound in the anterior lower third of the neck, listened very briefly, heard a few cardiac beats, felt the President's back, and detected no large or sucking chest wounds, and then proceeded to the examination of his head. The large skull and scalp wound had been previously observed and was inspected a little more closely. There seemed to be a 4–5 cm. area of avulsion of the scalp and the skull was fragmented and bleeding cerebral and cerebellar tissue. The pupils were inspected and seemed to be bilaterally dilated and fixed. No pulse was present, and at that time, because of the inadequate respirations and the apparent airway injury, a cuffed endotracheal tube was introduced, employing a larynzo scope. Through the larynzo scope there seemed to be some hematoma around the larynx and immediately below the larynx was seen the ragged tracheal injury. The endotracheal tube was inserted past this injury, the cuff inflated, and the tube was connected to a respirator to assist the inadequate respiration. At about this point the nurse reported that no blood pressure was obtained.

Mr. SPECTER. Dr. Carrico, with respect to this small wound in the anterior third of the neck which you have just described, could you be any more specific in defining the characteristics of that wound?

Dr. CARRICO. This was probably a 4–7 mm. wound, almost in the midline, maybe a little to the right of the midline, and below the thyroid cartilage. It was, as I recall, rather round and there were no jagged edges or stellate lacerations.

Mr. SPECTER. You said you felt the President's back?

Dr. CARRICO. Yes.

Mr. SPECTER. Would you describe in more detail just what the feeling of the back involved at that time?

Dr. CARRICO. Without taking the time to roll him over and look or to wash off the blood and debris, and while his coat and shirt were still on his arms—I just placed my hands at about his beltline or a little above and by slowly moving my hands upward detected that there was no large violation of the pleural cavity.

Mr. SPECTER. Why did you not take the time to turn him over?

9

Dr. CARRICO. This man was in obvious extreme distress and any more thorough inspection would have involved several minutes—well, several—considerable time which at this juncture was not available. A thorough inspection would have involved washing and cleansing the back, and this is not practical in treating an acutely injured patient. You have to determine which things, which are immediately life threatening and cope with them, before attempting to evaluate the full extent of the injuries.

Mr. SPECTER. Did you ever have occasion to look at the President's back?

Dr. CARRICO. No, sir. Before—well, in trying to treat an acutely injured patient, you have to establish an airway, adequate ventilation and you have to establish adequate circulation. Before this was accomplished the President's cardiac activity had ceased and closed cardiac massage was instituted, which made it impossible to inspect his back.

Mr. SPECTER. Was any effort made to inspect the President's back after he had expired?

Dr. CARRICO. No, sir.

Mr. SPECTER. And why was no effort made at that time to inspect his back?

Dr. CARRICO. I suppose nobody really had the heart to do it.

Mr. SPECTER. You had begun to describe some of the action taken in order to endeavor to revive the President. Will you continue with that description, please?

Dr. CARRICO. I believe we were to where the endotracheal tube had been inserted. After this, the President—his respirations were assisted by the Bennett machine. We again listened to his chest to attempt to evaluate the respirations. Breath sounds were diminished, especially on the right, despite the fact that the endotracheal tube was in place and the cuff inflated, there continued to be some leakage around the tracheal wound. For this reason Dr. Perry elected to perform a tracheotomy, and instructed some of the other physicians in the room to insert chest tubes, thoracotomy tubes. At the beginning of the resuscitation attempt intravenous infusions had been started using polyethylene catheters by venesection, lactated renger solution, and uncross-matched type O Rh negative bloods were administered and 300 mg. of hydrocortisone were administered. Shortly after the completion of the tracheotomy, Dr. Bashour arrived and had connected the cardiac monitor. Although I never saw evidence of cardiac activity, electrical cardiac activity, Dr. Clark stated that there was a perceptible electrical beat which shortly thereafter disappeared, and closed cardiac massage was instituted. The cardiac massage was successful in maintaining carotid and radial pulses, but the patient's state rapidly deteriorated and at approximately 1 o'clock he was pronounced dead.

Mr. SPECTER. What, in your opinion, was the cause of death?

Dr. CARRICO. A head injury.

Mr. SPECTER. Have you now described all the treatment which was given to the President as best you recollect it?

Dr. CARRICO. As I recall; yes, sir; that's all—I'm sorry.

Mr. SPECTER. Did you have any occasion or opportunity to examine the President's clothing?

Dr. CARRICO. We did not do that.

Mr. SPECTER. And was no examination of clothing made, Dr. Carrico?

Dr. CARRICO. Again, this was a matter of time. The clothes were removed by the nurses, as is the usual practice, and the full attention was devoted to trying to resuscitate the President.

Mr. SPECTER. On the examination of the President's back which you described that you performed, did you note any bleeding from the back?

Dr. CARRICO. There was considerable blood on the cart and on his back. I could not tell if this came from his back or had fallen down from the head injury. There was also some cerebral tissue there.

Mr. SPECTER. What did your examination by feeling disclose with respect to whether he had any back wound?

Dr. CARRICO. I did not feel any. Now, this certainly wouldn't detect a small bullet entrance. All this examination is designed to do is to establish the fact that there is no gross injury to the chest posteriorly.

Mr. SPECTER. Is that a routine type of examination, to ascertain whether there is a gross injury to the chest posteriorly?

Dr. CARRICO. Yes, sir.

Mr. SPECTER. What did you observe as to the President's clothing with respect to the presence of a back brace, if any?

Dr. CARRICO. There was, on removing the President's shirt and coat, we noted he was wearing a standard back support.

Mr. SPECTER. Would you describe that back support, please?

10

Dr. CARRICO. As I recall, it was white cotton or some fibrous support, with staves, bones and if I remember buckled in the front.

Mr. SPECTER. How wide was it?

Dr. CARRICO. How wide?

Mr. SPECTER. Yes, sir.

Dr. CARRICO. I don't know; I didn't examine below—you see—as I recall, it came about to his umbilicus—navel area.

Mr. SPECTER. Was there any Ace bandage applied to the President's hips that you observed?

Dr. CARRICO. No; I didn't remove his pants.

Mr. SPECTER. Did you have any opportunity to observe that area of his body when his pants were removed?

Dr. CARRICO. I had the opportunity, but I didn't look.

Mr. SPECTER. What doctors were involved in the treatment of President Kennedy?

Dr. CARRICO. Well, of course, Dr. Perry, Dr. Clark, Dr. Baxter, Dr. McClelland, Dr. Peters was in the room, Dr. Bashour, Dr. Ronald Jones, Dr. Curtis, I believe, Dr. White was there—initially, at least, I don't recall right offhand anyone else. There were other doctors in there, I just can't specifically remember—there were 10 or 15 people in the room before it was over.

Mr. SPECTER. Do you have an opinion, Dr. Carrico, as to the cause of the punctate wound in the President's throat?

Dr. CARRICO. No; I really don't—just on the basis of what I know. We didn't make an attempt, as you know, to ascertain the track of the bullets.

Mr. SPECTER. I can't hear you.

Dr. CARRICO. As you know, we didn't try to ascertain the track of the bullets.

Mr. SPECTER. And why did you not make an effort to determine the track of the bullets?

Dr. CARRICO. Again, in trying to resuscitate the President, the time to do this was not available. The examination conducted was one to try to establish what life threatening situations were present and to correct these.

Mr. SPECTER. Was there any discussion among the doctors who attended President Kennedy as to the cause of the neck wound?

Dr. CARRICO. Yes; after that afternoon.

Mr. SPECTER. And what conversations were there?

Dr. CARRICO. As I recall, Dr. Perry and I talked and tried after—later in the afternoon to determine what exactly had happened, and we were not aware of the missile wound to the back, and postulated that this was either a tangential wound from a fragment, possibly another entrance wound. It could have been an exit wound, but we knew of no other entrance wound.

Mr. SPECTER. Was the wound in the neck consistent with being either an entry or exit wound, in your opinion?

Dr. CARRICO. Yes.

Mr. SPECTER. Or, did it look to be more one than the other?

Dr. CARRICO. No; it could have been either, depending on the size of the missile, the velocity of the missile, the tissues that it struck.

Mr. SPECTER. Dr. Carrico, assume these facts, if you will—first, that President Kennedy was struck by a 6.5-mm. missile which entered the upper-right posterior thorax, just above the scapula, being 14 cm. from the tip of the right acromion, a-c-r-o-m-i-o-n (spelling) process, and 14 cm. below the tip of the right mastoid process, and that the missile traveled between two strap muscles, proceeded through the fascia channel without violating the pleural cavity, striking the side of the trachea and exiting in the lower third of the anterior throat. Under the circumstances which I have just described to you, would the wound which you observed on the President's throat be consistent with the damage which a 6.5-mm. missile, traveling at the rate of approximately 2,000 feet per second, that being muzzle velocity, with the President being 160 to 250 feet away from the rifle, would that wound be consistent with that type of a weapon at that distance, with the missile taking the path I have just described to you?

Dr. CARRICO. I certainly think it could.

Mr. SPECTER. And what would your thinking be as to why it could produce that result?

Dr. CARRICO. I think a missile of this size, traveling in such a direction that it had very little deformity, struck nothing which would cause it to begin tumbling, and was slowed very little by passing through this relatively easy traversed planes, would not expend a great deal of energy on exit and would very likely not tumble, thus producing a small, round, even wound.

Mr. SPECTER. What has been your experience, if any, with gunshot wounds?

Dr. CARRICO. In working in the emergency room at Parkland, we have seen a fairly good number of gunshot wounds, and with .22 and .25 caliber weapons of somewhat, possibly somewhat lower velocity but at closer range, we have seen entrance and exit wounds of almost the same size, especially the same size, when passing through superficial structures.

Mr. SPECTER. And what superficial structures did those missiles pass through to which you have just referred?

Dr. CARRICO. The ones I was referring to in particular were through the muscles of the leg superficially.

Mr. SPECTER. Approximately how many missile wounds, bullet wounds, have you had an opportunity to observe in your practice, Doctor?

Dr. CARRICO. I would guess 150 or 200.

Mr. SPECTER. Would you describe as precisely for me as possible the nature of the head wound which you observed on the President?

Dr. CARRICO. The wound that I saw was a large gaping wound, located in the right occipitoparietal area. I would estimate to be about 5 to 7 cm. in size, more or less circular, with avulsions of the calvarium and scalp tissue. As I stated before, I believe there was shredded macerated cerebral and cerebellar tissues both in the wounds and on the fragments of the skull attached to the dura.

Mr. SPECTER. Did you notice any other opening in the head besides the one you have just described?

Dr. CARRICO. No, sir; I did not.

Mr. SPECTER. Specifically, did you notice a bullet wound below the large gaping hole which you described?

Dr. CARRICO. No, sir.

Mr. SPECTER. What is your opinion, Doctor, if you have one, as to how many bullets were involved in the injuries inflicted on the President?

Dr. CARRICO. As far as I could tell, I would guess that there were two.

Mr. SPECTER. Prior to today, have you ever been interviewed by any representative of the Federal Government?

Dr. CARRICO. Yes, sir; the Secret Service talked to us shortly after the President's death.

Mr. SPECTER. Do you recall who talked to you on that occasion?

Dr. CARRICO. No; I don't recall his name.

Mr. SPECTER. What was the content of that interview?

Dr. CARRICO. We spoke to him in Dr. Shires' office in the medical school concerning the President's death, mostly my part was just a statement that the written statement that I had submitted was true.

Mr. SPECTER. I now call your attention, Doctor, to a document heretofore identified as Commission Exhibit No. 392, to a 2-page summary which purports to bear your signature, and dated November 22, 1963, 1626 hours, and ask you first of all if that is a photostatic copy of a report which you submitted?

Dr. CARRICO. Yes; it is.

Mr. SPECTER. And, is that your signature at the end?

Dr. CARRICO. Yes.

Mr. SPECTER. And are the facts set forth in there true and correct?

Dr. CARRICO. They are.

Mr. SPECTER. With respect to this notation of a ragged wound of the trachea, which is contained in your report, could you describe that in more specific detail?

Dr. CARRICO. In inserting the endotracheal tube, a larynzo scope was inserted and it was noted that there was some discoloration at the lateral edge of the larynx and there appeared to be some swelling and hematoma and in looking through the chords which were partially open, a ragged tissue and some blood was seen within the trachea itself. This was the extent of what I saw.

Mr. SPECTER. Would that specific portion of the wound give any indication as to direction of the bullet?

Dr. CARRICO. No; it wouldn't.

Mr. SPECTER. Was there any characteristic within the neck area to give any indication of the direction of the bullet?

Dr. CARRICO. No, sir.

Mr. SPECTER. Did the Secret Service man whom you just described ask you any questions beyond whether the contents of your report were true?

Dr. CARRICO. I can't recall any specific questions. He did ask some others and they did concern the wounds, and what we felt the wounds were from, the direction, and so forth.

Mr. SPECTER. And what response did you make to those inquiries?

Dr. CARRICO. Essentially the same as I have here. I said I don't remember specifically.

Mr. SPECTER. Have you talked to any other representative of the Federal Government prior to today?

Dr. CARRICO. Not in connection with this.

Mr. SPECTER. Well, have you talked to someone in connection with something else?

Dr. CARRICO. Just some Government employment—Civil Service.

Mr. SPECTER. But the only time you talked to anyone about your treatment of President Kennedy and your observations relating to that treatment was on this one occasion with the Secret service?

Dr. CARRICO. Yes; except I just recalled since that time, another Secret Service Agent—I did speak to him briefly. He asked me if I had any other information and I said "no".

Mr. SPECTER. Is that the total contents of that conversation?

Dr. CARRICO. Yes.

Mr. SPECTER. Prior to the time we went on the record here before you were sworn in, did you and I have a brief conversation about the purpose of this disposition, and the general nature of the questions which I would ask you?

Dr. CARRICO. Yes, sir.

Mr. SPECTER. And was the information which you gave me at that time the same as that to which you have testified here on the record?

Dr. CARRICO. Yes; it was.

Mr. SPECTER. Have you ever changed any of your opinions regarding your treatment and observations of President Kennedy?

Dr. CARRICO. Not as I recall.

Mr. SPECTER. By the way, Dr. Carrico, how old are you at the present time?

Dr. CARRICO. Twenty-eight.

Mr. SPECTER. Was any bullet found in the President's body.

Dr. CARRICO. Not by us.

Mr. SPECTER. Do you have any other notes or written record of any sort concerning your treatment of President Kennedy?

Dr. CARRICO. Not concerning the treatment. I have a note I wrote to my children for them to read some day, but it doesn't concern the treatment.

Mr. SPECTER. What does that concern?

Dr. CARRICO. It just concerns the day and how I felt about it and why it happened—maybe.

Mr. SPECTER. Personal observations on your part?

Dr. CARRICO. Yes.

Mr. SPECTER. Did you participate in any of the press conferences?

Dr. CARRICO. No.

Mr. SPECTER. Do you have anything to add which you think might be of assistance in any way to the President's Commission?

Dr. CARRICO. No, sir; I don't believe I do.

Mr. SPECTER. Dr. Carrico, have I made available to you a letter requesting your appearance on Monday, March 30, before the Commission, and do you acknowledge receipt of that?

Dr. CARRICO. I do.

Mr. SPECTER. And would it be possible for you to attend and testify at that time?

Dr. CARRICO. I certainly can.

Mr. SPECTER. Washington, D.C.

Dr. CARRICO. Yes.

Mr. SPECTER. Thank you very much, Dr. Carrico.

Dr. CARRICO. Yes, sir.

TESTIMONY OF DR. MALCOLM OLIVER PERRY

The testimony of Dr. Malcolm Oliver Perry was taken at 3:25 p.m., on March 25, 1964, at Parkland Memorial Hospital, Dallas, Tex., by Mr. Arlen Specter, assistant counsel of the President's Commission.

Mr. SPECTER. May the record show that Dr. Malcolm O. Perry is present in response to a letter request that he appear here to have his deposition taken in connection with the proceedings of the President's Commission on the Assassination of President Kennedy, which is now

13

inquiring into all facets of the shooting, including the medical attention received by President Kennedy at Parkland Hospital, in which Dr. Perry participated.

With that preliminary statement of purpose, would you please stand up, Dr. Perry, and raise your right hand?

Do you solemnly swear that the testimony you give before the President's Commission in these deposition proceedings will be the truth, the whole truth, and nothing but the truth, so help you God?

Dr. PERRY. I do.

Mr. SPECTER. All right. Would you state your full name for the record, please?

Dr. PERRY. Malcolm Oliver Perry.

Mr. SPECTER. What is your profession, sir?

Dr. PERRY. Physician and surgeon.

Mr. SPECTER. And how old are you?

Dr. PERRY. Thirty-four.

Mr. SPECTER. Are you duly licensed to practice medicine in the State of Texas?

Dr. PERRY. Yes.

Mr. SPECTER. Would you outline briefly your educational background, please?

Dr. PERRY. Starting with high school?

Mr. SPECTER. That will be fine.

Dr. PERRY. I attended high school at Allen High School and at Plano High School, graduating from the latter in 1947. I entered the University of Texas from whence I duly graduated with a degree of Bachelor of Arts in 1951. I went to Southwestern Medical School of the University of Texas for the subsequent 4 years, graduating in 1955 with a degree of Doctor of Medicine. I interned at Letterman's Army Hospital in San Francisco, and returned to a residency in surgery at Parkland Hospital in July 1958. I finished that residency in June 1962, and then returned to San Francisco and spent 1 year as additional specialization in vascular surgery. I then returned in September 1963, to Southwestern Medical School of the University of Texas as an assistant professor of surgery.

Mr. SPECTER. What were your duties on November 22, 1963?

Dr. PERRY. Well, as is accustomed, I was at that time on two services, both a general surgery service and a vascular surgery service as a consultant and attending surgeon.

Mr. SPECTER. And, what were you doing specifically shortly after noontime on November 22?

Dr. PERRY. Well, at the time of the incident in question, I was having lunch in the main dining room with the chief resident, Dr. Ronald Jones, in preparation for the usual Friday rounds at 1 o'clock with the residents.

Mr. SPECTER. And what occurred during the course of that luncheon?

Dr. PERRY. Dr. Jones, as I say, and I were having lunch when an emergency call came over the speaker system for Dr. Tom Shires, who is the chief of surgery. I knew that Dr. Shires was in Galveston giving a paper and was not in the hospital, so Dr. Jones picked up the page to see if he or I could be of assistance. We were informed by the hospital operator that Mr. Kennedy had been shot and was being brought to Parkland Hospital for care.

Mr. SPECTER. And what action did you take as a result of learning those factors?

Dr. PERRY. The dining room was located one floor up from the emergency room, so Dr. Jones and I went immediately to the emergency room to render what assistance we could.

At the time of our arrival in the emergency room, the President was already there, and as I entered trauma room No. 1, Dr. James Carrico, the surgical resident on duty, had just placed an endotracheal tube to assist respiration.

Mr. SPECTER. Who was present in addition to Dr. Carrico, if you recall, at that time?

Dr. PERRY. I cannot with accuracy relate all the people that were there—Dr. Carrico, I saw and spoke to briefly. There were several other people in the room. There were several nurses there—I don't know at this time who they were. Mrs. Kennedy was in the room and there was a gentleman with her and there were several other gentlemen both in the door and right outside the door to the room. Some of them, I assume, part of the legal force.

Mr. SPECTER. Did you observe any other doctors in the room at that time?

Dr. PERRY. No, sir; I did not. There was somebody else in the room, but I don't know who it was. I remember only Dr. Carrico—I had the impression that one of the interns was in the room, but this may be an impression gathered after the fact.

Mr. SPECTER. What did you observe as to the President's condition at the time you first saw him?

14

Dr. PERRY. He was lying supine on the emergency cart directly in the center of the room under the overhead lamp. His shirt had been removed, and intravenous infusion was being begun in the right leg, I believe. Dr. Carrico was at the head of the table attaching the oxygen apparatus to assist in respiration.

I noted there was a large wound of the right posterior parietal area in the head exposing lacerated brain. There was blood and brain tissue on the cart. The President's eyes were deviated and dilated and he was unresponsive. There was a small wound in the lower anterior third in the midline of the neck, from which blood was exuding very slowly.

Mr. SPECTER. Will you describe that wound as precisely as you can, please?

Dr. PERRY. The wound was roughly spherical to oval in shape, not a punched-out wound, actually, nor was it particularly ragged. It was rather clean cut, but the blood obscured any detail about the edges of the wound exactly.

Mr. SPECTER. What was the condition of the edges of the wound, if you can recollect?

Dr. PERRY. I couldn't state with certainty, due to the fact that they were covered by blood and I did not make a minute examination. I determined only the fact that there was a wound there, roughly 5 mm. in size or so.

Mr. SPECTER. Have you now described it as precisely as you can; that wound?

Dr. PERRY. I think so.

Mr. SPECTER. What else, if anything, did you observe as to the condition of the President?

Dr. PERRY. Spasmodic respiratory efforts were obvious, but I did not detect a pulse nor a heart beat on a very rapid examination. It was apparent that respirations were ineffective, even with the use of the endotracheal tube and oxygen. At that point I asked Dr. Carrico if this was a wound in his neck or had he begun the tracheotomy, and he said it was a wound and I, at that point, asked someone to get me a tracheotomy tray, and put on some gloves and initiated the procedure.

Mr. SPECTER. Now, have you described everything that you can recollect about your observations of the President before you started to work on him?

Dr. PERRY. There was no evidence to that cursory examination of any other wound. I did not move the President. I did not turn him over.

Mr. SPECTER. Why did you not turn him over?

Dr. PERRY. At that point it was necessary to attend to the emergent procedure and a satisfactory effective airway is uppermost in such a condition. If you are unable to obtain an effective airway, then the other procedures are to be of no avail.

Mr. SPECTER. Well, on the subject of turning him over, did you ever turn him over?

Dr. PERRY. I did not.

Mr. SPECTER. Why didn't you turn him over after you had taken the initial action on him?

Dr. PERRY. After the tracheotomy tube was in place and we were breathing for him, Dr. Clark and I had begun external cardiac massage, since we had been unable to detect a heart beat, blood pressure, or pulse. I continued with the cardiac massage while Dr. Clark examined the head wound, and he and Dr. Jenkins conferred in regard to the electrocardiogram. It was determined that none of the resuscitative measures were effective and the procedures were then abandoned.

I had no further business in the room at that point, and I left the room momentarily. I returned within a minute or so, because I had left my coat   where I dropped it and asked one of the nurses to hand me my coat, and I left the room and went to the operating suite from there.

Mr. SPECTER. And did that conclude your participation in the treatment of President Kennedy?

Dr. PERRY. It did.

Mr. SPECTER. What is your best estimate as to the time you arrived in the Emergency Room?

Dr. PERRY. I really don't know the time. It was about 12:30 or so when I was eating and the call must have come thereabouts, and I didn't look at my watch at that time, nor did I have an opportunity to look at it again until after I had left the room.

Mr. SPECTER. What is your best estimate as to the time which elapsed from the point that you knew it was 12:30, until the time you arrived at the emergency room?

Dr. PERRY. It must have been within the next few minutes. I really don't know. As I say, we were sitting there eating and I had no occasion to look at my watch again. At that time I was much too busy to consult it further.

Mr. SPECTER. What is your best estimate as to the time you left the emergency room after finishing your treatment and work on the President?

Dr. PERRY. After I left trauma room No. 1, I went outside and washed my hands and then I retrieved my coat and I sat down for a few minutes in a chair there in the emergency room for probably 10 or 15 minutes, I suppose, and then I went from there to the operating suite to assist in the care of the Governor, so I must have left the emergency room probably somewhere around 1:15 or 1:20, I would gather.

Mr. SPECTER. At approximately what time was the President pronounced to be dead?

Dr. PERRY. I don't know this for a fact, other than what was related to me by Dr. Clark, and he tells me that this was at 1 o'clock. Once again, I did not verify the time.

Mr. SPECTER. Have you described all of the efforts which were made to revive the President?

Dr. PERRY. There were other procedures done that I did not do during this period. I did not describe in detail the performance of the tracheotomy. It seems that that is really not necessary at this time, unless you want it.

Mr. SPECTER. Will you describe it in detail, the procedures which were followed in the efforts to save the President's life?

Dr. PERRY. All right. Well, to regress, then, at the time I began the tracheotomy, I made an incision right through the wound which was present in the neck in order to gain complete control of any injury in the underlying trachea.

I made a transverse incision right through this wound and carried it down to the superficial fascia, to expose the strap muscles overlying the thyroid and the trachea. There was an injury to the right lateral aspect of the trachea at the level of the external wound. The trachea was deviated slightly to the left and it was necessary to divide the strap muscles on the left side in order to gain access to the trachea. At this point, I recall, Dr. Jones right on my left was placing a catheter into a vein in the left arm because he handed me a necessary instrument which I needed in the performance of the procedure.

The wound in the trachea was then enlarged to admit a cuffed tracheotomy tube to support respiration. I noted that there was free air and blood in the superior right mediastinum.

Although I saw no injury to the lung or to the pleural space, the presence of this free blood and air in this area could be indicative of a wound of the right hemithorax, and I asked that someone put a right chest tube in for seal drainage. At the time I did not know who did this, but I have been informed that Dr. Baxter and Dr. Paul Peters inserted the chest tube and connected it to underwater drainage.

Blood transfusions and fluid transfusions were being given at this time, and through the previous venesections that had been done by Dr. Jones and Dr. Carrico.

Also, the President had received 300 mg. of Solucortef in order to support his adrenal glands, since it was common medical knowledge that he suffered from adrenal insufficiency.

Of course, oxygen and pressure breathing were being effected under the guidance of Dr. Jenkins and Dr. Giesecke, who were handling the anesthesia machine at the head of the table.

Dr. Bashour and Dr. Seldin, in addition to Dr. Clark, had arrived and also assisted in monitoring cardiac actions, as indicated by the oscilloscope and the cardiotachioscope.

Mr. SPECTER. Have you now described all of the operative procedures performed on the President?

Dr. PERRY. Yes, all that I am familiar with.

Mr. SPECTER. Are there any doctors who participated other than those whom you have already identified in the course of your description?

Dr. PERRY. Yes, sir; immediately on arriving there, and as I say, Dr. Jones and I, and I saw Dr. Carrico, and I have the impression there was another physician there, but I don't know who it was. I asked that an emergency call be placed for Dr. Kemp Clark, chief of neurosurgery, for Dr. Robert McClelland, and Dr. Charles Baxter, assistant professors of surgery. They responded immediately. I don't know how long it took them to get there, but they were probably there within the next few minutes. My first recollection of Dr. McClelland and Dr. Baxter being there was when I was doing the tracheotomy, they suddenly were there assisting me. I don't know when they came in the room, nor do I know when Dr. Clark or the other gentlemen arrived, and must have been 10 or 12 doctors all told by then.

Mr. SPECTER. Are there any others whom you could identify?

Dr. PERRY. Dr. Peters—I previously mentioned, Dr. Paul Peters, assistant professor of urology, Dr. Fouad Bashour, associate professor of medicine, and chief of cardiology, and Dr. Don Seldin, chief of medicine.

I mentioned Dr. M. T. Jenkins, chief of anesthesia, and Dr. Giesecke, his assistant professor of anesthesiology—that's the only people that I saw directly.

Mr. SPECTER. Could the first doctor whom you saw have been Dr. Don Curtis?

Dr. PERRY. That's entirely possible—I don't recall.

Mr. SPECTER. Was Dr. Dulany there?

Dr. PERRY. I have initially had the impression that Dr. Dulany was in the room when I came in there, but as I understand it, he actually was just going into the room across the hall, but

16

he was there by the door when I came in, but I had the impression he was leaving that room, but I understand he was not, that actually he was going—just going in the room across the hall with the Governor, although I initially thought Dr. Dulany was there.

Mr. SPECTER. What did you observe, if anything with respect to bruising in the interior portion of the President's neck?

Dr. PERRY. There was considerable hematoma in the right lateral portion of the neck and the right superior mediastinum, as I noted. As for bruising, per se, it would be difficult to describe that, since by definition, hematoma would be a collection of blood, and there was so much blood that the tissues were discolored. I did not attempt to ascertain trajectory or path of the bullet at the time, but directed myself to obtaining an adequate airway and carried my examination no further down than it was necessary to assure myself that the trachea was controlled and that there was no large vessel injury at that level.

Mr. SPECTER. Were there sufficient facts available to you for you to reach a conclusion as to the cause of the wound on the front side of the President's neck?

Dr. PERRY. No, sir, there was not. I could not determine whether or how this was inflicted, per se, since it would require tracing the trajectory.

Mr. SPECTER. What did you observe as to the President's head, specifically?

Dr. PERRY. I saw no injuries other than the one which I noted to you, which was a large avulsive injury of the right occipitoparietal area, but I did not do a minute examination of his head.

Mr. SPECTER. Did you notice a bullet hole below the large avulsed area?

Dr. PERRY. No; I did not.

Mr. SPECTER. Dr. Perry, earlier I asked you whether you turned over the President at any time during the course of your treatment or examination of him, and you indicated that you had not, and I then asked you why, and you proceeded to tell me of the things that you did in sequence, as being priority items to try to save his life. Why did you not turn him over at the conclusion of those operative procedures?

Dr. PERRY. Well, actually, I didn't have a specific reason, other than it had been determined that he had expired. There was nothing further that I could do and it was not my particular prerogative to make a minute examination to determine any other cause. I felt that that was a little bit out of my domain.

Mr. SPECTER. Did you have any occasion to examine the President's clothing to ascertain direction of the missile?

Dr. PERRY. No; I did not. The only aspect of clothing that I know about—I happen to recall pushing up the brace which he had on in an attempt to feel a femoral pulse when I arrived, and I could not, but the shirt had been removed by the personnel there in the emergency room, I assume.

Mr. SPECTER. What did you observe as to the description of that brace?

Dr. PERRY. I couldn't give you a description. I just saw and felt the lower edge of one, and I reached to feel the left femoral pulse.

Mr. SPECTER. Did you see whether the President was wearing any sort of an Ace bandage on the midsection of his body when his trousers were taken down?

Dr. PERRY. There was evidence of an Ace bandage—I saw it sticking out from the edge on the right side, as I recall. I don't believe it was on the midsection, although it may have been. I believe it was on his right leg—his right thigh.

Mr. SPECTER. Do you know whether it was on the left leg and thigh as well?

Dr. PERRY. No, I don't. I just saw that briefly when I was reaching for that pulse and I didn't do any examination at all of the lower trunk or lower extremities.

Mr. SPECTER. Did you personally make any examination by feeling, or in any other way, of the President's back?

Dr. PERRY. I did not.

Mr. SPECTER. Did you participate in a press conference or press conferences following the death of the President?

Dr. PERRY. Yes.

Mr. SPECTER. And when was the first of such press conferences?

Dr. PERRY. I don't know the exact time, Mr. Specter. It must have been within the hour, I would say; I don't know exactly.

Mr. SPECTER. And who was present at that press conference by way of identifying, if you can, the members of the news media?

Dr. PERRY. I have no idea. The press conference was held in classrooms 1 and 2 combined here at Parkland. The room was quite full of people. I remember noting some surprise how quickly they had put in a couple of telephones at the back. There were numerous cameras and lights, and flashbulbs, and I went there with one of the administrators, Mr. Landregan, and Dr. Kemp Clark and Mr. Hawkes, who was identified to me as being with the White House Press. I don't know—there were numerous people of the press.

Mr. SPECTER. What doctors appeared and spoke at that press conference?

Dr. PERRY. Dr. Clark, myself, and Dr. Baxter was also there. He arrived a little bit late. I called him just before I went down and asked him and Dr. McClelland to come. I could not find Dr. McClelland. He apparently was busy with a patient at the time. I recall Dr. Baxter came in after the press conference had begun, but I don't believe he said anything. Dr. Clark and I answered the majority of the questions.

Mr. SPECTER. Well, what questions were asked of you and what responses did you give at that press conference?

Dr. PERRY. Well, there were numerous questions asked, all the questions I cannot remember, of course. Specifically, the thing that seemed to be of most interest at that point was actually trying to get me to speculate as to direction of the bullets, the number of bullets, and the exact cause of death.

The first two questions I could not answer, and my reply to them was that I did not know, if there were one or two bullets, and I could not categorically state about the nature of the neck wound, whether it was an entrance or an ☐ exit wound, not having examined the President further—I could not comment on any other injuries.

As regards the cause of death, Dr. Clark and I concurred that massive brain trauma with attendant severe hemorrhage was the underlying cause of death, and then there were questions asked in regard to what we did, and I described as I have for you, although not in such detail—essentially the resuscitative measures that were taken at that time; namely, the reinfusion of a balanced salt solution of blood, Solucortef, assisting of respiration with oxygen and pressure apparatus, the tracheotomy, and the chest tubes and the monitoring with the cardiotachioscope.

Mr. SPECTER. Did you express a view as to what might have happened with respect to the number of bullets?

Dr. PERRY. I was asked by several of the people of the press, initially, if there were one or two or more bullets, and to that, Dr. Clark and I both replied that we could not say. I was then asked if it was conceivable that it could have been caused by one bullet, and I replied in the affirmative, that I did not know, but it was conceivable.

Mr. SPECTER. Did you elaborate on how it could have been caused by one bullet?

Dr. PERRY. I was asked if this were one bullet, how would it occur, and I said, "It is conceivable or possible that a bullet could enter and strike the spinal column and be deviated superiorly to exit from the head."

Mr. SPECTER. And where would that point of entry have been?

Dr. PERRY. The surmise was made that if the point of entry were in the neck, how would it have happened, and that is the way I would have reconstructed it. Again, this was speculation.

Mr. SPECTER. Did you denominate it clearly as speculation?

Dr. PERRY. I did.

Mr. SPECTER. Or, what could have been as opposed to what your opinion was?

Dr. PERRY. I did. I said this was conceivable—this was possible, but again, Dr. Clark and I emphasized again that we did not know whether there was one or two bullets.

Mr. SPECTER. Did you express any view as to whether it might have been one bullet or two bullets or either, or what?

Dr. PERRY. I said I did not know.

Mr. SPECTER. And were you asked any other questions at that press conference that you can recollect as being important at this time?

Dr. PERRY. Someone did ask us about Mrs. Kennedy, and I recall that I mentioned that I did not speak to her, but that she was very composed and very quiet.

Mr. SPECTER. Now, were you a part of any other press conferences?

Dr. PERRY. Yes; I was.

Mr. SPECTER. And when did the next one occur?

Dr. PERRY. There were several organized press conferences that occurred in the administration suite in the hospital, Mr. Specter, and I don't know the exact times of these. There were several later that afternoon. There were some the following day, on Saturday, also held in the administrator's office, and then there were subsequent conferences in relation to the other incident that occurred on Sunday with Mr. Oswald. I don't know how many there were.

Mr. SPECTER. Were all these conferences set up by the administration of the hospital?

Dr. PERRY. They were all conducted here. They weren't necessarily—I wouldn't say—set up by the administration. They were done here at the hospital, with one exception, of which you are aware, that I spoke with you about the gentleman that came to me when I was out of town.

18

Mr. SPECTER. Will you elaborate upon what occurred on that occasion, please?

Dr. PERRY. I had taken the course of complying with the press insofar as was possible about what I could speak that was common knowledge and which had already been covered at the initial press conference. I had done that in the administrative suite or in the hospital or in the medical school under an organized situation as opposed to doing it, say, at home.

I left town Monday following the incident on Sunday with Oswald, in order to secure a little bit of rest for myself and my family, and approximately 36 hours later, members of the press had located me and requested an interview, which I granted, denying any photographs and the interview consisted of essentially the same thing that I had given to the previous press conference at the hospital.

Mr. SPECTER. Where was that interview conducted?

Dr. PERRY. That was in McAllen, Tex.

Mr. SPECTER. In the course of all of these press conferences did you say anything other than that which you have already related you said during the course of the first press conference?

Dr. PERRY. That would require a little bit of thought. I don't think in essence I said anything different. Of course, the wording certainly would have been different. I subsequently had a little bit more knowledge about the initial episode attendant of course upon my discussions with the other doctors and the writing out of our statements, knowledge which I did not have initially, which may have made subsequent statements perhaps more accurate as regards to time and people, but in essence, things that I did and things that I said that I did are essentially the same in all of these.

Mr. SPECTER. Dr. Perry, I now show you a group of papers heretofore identified as Commission Exhibit No. 392, and I turn to two sheets which are dated November 22, 1963, which have the name "Perry" beside the doctor and purport to bear your signature, and the time—1630 hours, 22 November 1963, and I ask you if this is a photostatic copy of the handwritten report which you submitted concerning the attention you gave to the President on the day of the assassination?

Dr. PERRY. Yes; it is.

Mr. SPECTER. Is this your signature appearing on the second sheet?

Dr. PERRY. That is my signature.

Mr. SPECTER. And are the facts set forth herein true and correct?

Dr. PERRY. They are, to the best of my knowledge, correct.

Mr. SPECTER. Dr. Perry, have contents of the autopsy report conducted at Bethesda Naval Hospital been made available to you?

Dr. PERRY. They have.

Mr. SPECTER. And are the findings in the autopsy report consistent with your observations and conclusions concerning the source and nature of the President's wounds?

Dr. PERRY. Yes; they are. I think there are no discrepancies at all. I did not have that information initially, and as a result was somewhat confused about the nature of the wounds, as I noted—I could not tell whether there was one or two bullets, or from whence they came, but the findings of the autopsy report are quite compatible with those findings which I noted at the time that I saw the President.

Mr. SPECTER. And have you noted in the autopsy report the reference to the presence of a wound on the upper right posterior thorax just above the upper border of the scapula, being 7 by 4 mm. in oval dimension and being located 14 cm. from the tip of the right acromion process and 14 cm. below the tip of the right mastoid process?

Dr. PERRY. Yes; I saw that.

Mr. SPECTER. Assuming that was a point of entry of a missile, which parenthetically was the opinion of the three autopsy surgeons, and assuming still further that the missile which struck the President at that spot was a 6.5-mm. jacketed bullet shot from a rifle at a distance of 166 to 250 feet, having a muzzle velocity of approximately 2,000 feet per second, and that upon entering the President's body, the bullet traveled between two strap muscles, through a fascia channel, without violating the pleural cavity, striking the trachea, causing the damage which you testified about being on the interior of the President's throat, and exited from the President's throat in the wound which you have described in the midline of his neck, would your findings and observations as to the nature of the wound on the throat be consistent with the set of facts I just presented to you?

Dr. PERRY. It would be entirely compatible.

Mr. SPECTER. And what is the basis for your conclusion that the situation that I presented to you would be entirely compatible with your observations and findings?

19

Dr. PERRY. The wound in the throat, although as I noted, I did not examine it minutely, was fairly small in nature, and an undeformed, unexpanded missile exiting at rather high speed would leave very little injury behind, since the majority of its energy was expended after it had left the tissues.

Mr. SPECTER. And would the hole that you observed on the President's throat then be consistent with such an exit wound?

Dr. PERRY. It would. There is no way to determine from my examination as to exactly how accurately I could depict an entrance wound from an exit wound, without ascertaining the entire trajectory. Such a wound could be produced by such a missile.

Mr. SPECTER. Were any facts on trajectory available to you at the time of the press conferences that you described?

Dr. PERRY. They were not.

Mr. SPECTER. In response to an earlier question which I asked you, I believe you testified that you did not have sufficient facts available initially to form an opinion as to the source or direction of the cause of the wound, did you not?

Dr. PERRY. That's correct, although several leading questions were directed toward me at the various conferences.

Mr. SPECTER. And to those leading questions you have said here today that you responded that a number of possibilities were present as to what might have happened?

Dr. PERRY. That's correct. I had no way of ascertaining, as I said, the true trajectory. Often questions were directed as to—in such a manner as this: "Doctor, is it possible that if he were in such and such a position and the bullet entered here, could it have done that?" And my reply, "Of course, if it were possible, yes, that is possible, but similarly, it did not have to be so, necessarily."

Mr. SPECTER. So that, from the physical characteristics which you observed in and of themselves, you could not come to any conclusive opinion?

Dr. PERRY. No, sir; I could not, although I have been quoted, I think, as saying, and I might add parenthetically, out of context, without the preceding question which had been directed, as saying that such was the case, when actually, I only admitted that the possibility existed.

Mr. SPECTER. And in the hypothetical of the rather extended nature that I just gave you that your statement that that is consistent with what you found, is that also predicated upon the veracity of the factors, which I have asked you to assume?

Dr. PERRY. That is correct, sir. I have no way to authenticate either by my own knowledge.

Mr. SPECTER. Has your recollection of the nature of the President's neck wound changed at any time from November 22 to the present time?

Dr. PERRY. No, sir. I recall describing it initially as being between 3 and 5 cm. in size and roughly spherical in shape, not unlike a rather large puncture wound, I believe is the word I used initially.

Mr. SPECTER. Have you ever changed your opinion on the possible alternatives as to what could have caused the President's wounds?

Dr. PERRY. No, sir; I have no knowledge even now of my own as to the cause of the wounds. All I can report on is what I saw, and the wound is that as I have described it. It could have been caused conceivably by any number of objects.

Mr. SPECTER. So, that the wound that you saw on the President's neck would be consistent with an exit wound under the factors that I described to you?

Dr. PERRY. Yes.

Mr. SPECTER. Or, it might be consistent with an entry wound under a different set of factors?

Dr. PERRY. That's correct, sir. I, myself, have no knowledge of that. I do not think that it is consistent, for example, with an exit wound of a large expanded bullet—voluntarily I would add that.

Mr. SPECTER. Well, would a jacketed 6.5-mm. bullet fit the description of a large expanded bullet?

Dr. PERRY. No, sir; it would not.

Mr. SPECTER. Based on the information in the autopsy report about a 6- by 15-mm. hole in the lower part of the President's skull on the right side in conjunction with the large part of the skull of the President which you observed to be missing, would you have an opinion as to the source of the missile which inflicted those wounds?

20

Dr. PERRY. Since I did not see the initial wound which you mentioned, the smaller one, and only saw the large avulsive wound of the head and the scalp, there is no way for me to determine from whence it came.

Mr. SPECTER. Well, if you assume the presence of the first small wound, taking as a fact that there was such a wound, now, would that present sufficient information for you to formulate an opinion as to source or trajectory?

Dr. PERRY. Well, I couldn't testify as to exact source, but if the wound, the smaller wound that you noted were present, it could certainly result in the large avulsive wound as it exited from the skull. As to the ultimate source, there would still be no way for me to tell.

Mr. SPECTER. Well, could you tell sufficient to comment on whether it came from the front or back of the President?

Dr. PERRY. In the absence of other wounds of the head, the presence of the small wound which you described, in addition to the large avulsive wound of the skull and the scalp which I observed would certainly indicate that the two were related and would indicate both an entrance and an exit wound, if there were no other wounds.

Mr. SPECTER. And which would be the wound of entrance, then?

Dr. PERRY. The smaller wound—the smaller wound.

Mr. SPECTER. Now, did you have occasion to talk via the telephone with Dr. James J. Humes of the Bethesda Naval Hospital?

Dr. PERRY. I did.

Mr. SPECTER. And will you relate the circumstances of the calls indicating first the time when they occurred.

Dr. PERRY. Dr. Humes called me twice on Friday afternoon, separated by about 30-minute intervals, as I recall. The first one, I, somehow think I recall the first one must have been around 1500 hours, but I'm not real sure about that; I'm not positive of that at all, actually.

Mr. SPECTER. Could it have been Saturday morning?

Dr. PERRY. Saturday morning—was it? It's possible. I remember talking with him twice. I was thinking it was shortly thereafter.

Mr. SPECTER. Well, the record will show.

Dr. PERRY. Oh, sure, it was Saturday morning—yes.

Mr. SPECTER. What made you change your view of that?

Dr. PERRY. You mean Friday?

Mr. SPECTER. Did some specific recollection occur to you which changed your view from Friday to Saturday?

Dr. PERRY. No, I was trying to place where I was at that time—Friday afternoon, and at that particular time, when I paused to think about it, I was actually up in the operating suite at that time, when I thought that he called initially. I seem to remember it being Friday, for some reason.

Mr. SPECTER. Where were you when you received those calls?

Dr. PERRY. I was in the Administrator's office here when he called.

Mr. SPECTER. And what did he ask you, if anything?

Dr. PERRY. He inquired about, initially, about the reasons for my doing a tracheotomy, and I replied, as I have to you, during this procedure, that there was a wound in the lower anterior third of the neck, which was exuding blood and was indicative of a possible tracheal injury underlying, and I did the tracheotomy through a transverse incision made through that wound, and I described to him the right lateral injury to the trachea and the completion of the operation.

He subsequently called back—at that time he told me, of course, that he could not talk to me about any of it and asked that I keep it in confidence, which I did, and he subsequently called back and inquired about the chest tubes, and why they were placed and I replied in part as I have here. It was somewhat more detailed. After having talked to Drs. Baxter and Peters and I identified them as having placed it in the second interspace, anteriorly, in the midclavicular line, in the right hemithorax, he asked me at that time if we had made any wounds in the back. I told him that I had not examined the back nor had I knowledge of any wounds of the back.

Mr. SPECTER. Would you relate the circumstances surrounding an article which appeared about you in the Saturday Evening Post, Dr. Perry?

Dr. PERRY. The Saturday Evening Post contacted the department of surgery here, and talked with Dr. Tom Shires, chief of surgical services, in regard to a possible article on the treatment of the President. This was declined by us, and we requested that no such article be printed, and Dr. Shires informed me shortly thereafter about this conversation. Subsequently, an article was printed, which apparently was a copyrighted item. It first appeared in the New York Herald Tribune. It contained my picture and a picture of trauma room No. 1, and described the incidents surrounding the treatment of the President. Some of that information was obtained by personal interview of myself and Dr. Shires on Saturday morning, and I assume that the rest of it was obtained from various people here.

Mr. SPECTER. Was the content of that story accurate?

Dr. PERRY. There were certain inaccuracies—the overall content was fairly consistent—there were inaccuracies in identification of participants and there were some inaccuracies in regards to conversations purported to have been held, and I do not, however, have knowledge about some of the other references made in the article, since they were apparently based on interviews with people other than myself.

Mr. SPECTER. Dr. Perry, have you talked to any representatives of the Federal Government about this matter prior to today?

Dr. PERRY. Yes, I have.

Mr. SPECTER. Would you relate whom you have talked to and on what occasions? As best you can recollect it.

Dr. PERRY. Well, I talked to several people, and I regret that I did not keep a record of it, and I find at this time that a lot of these things such as Dr. Humes' call, I suppose I should have kept a little better record, since everything was so kaleidoscopic that I have a very difficult time putting the proper sequence on it. I talked to several people who identified themselves both by name and with credentials as being affiliated with the Secret Service.

Mr. SPECTER. On how many occasions have you talked with Secret Service personnel?

Dr. PERRY. At least three times, sir. Now, I can't give you the exact dates of these, and unfortunately the last two gentlemen, I can't even remember their names now.

Mr. SPECTER. How about the first gentleman?

Dr. PERRY. No, his either. I was trying to think of the last two. I indicated that they both had the same last name, but at the present time it escapes me.

Mr. SPECTER. What did you tell them in essence?

Dr. PERRY. Essentially what I have told you in regard to my impressions and my care of the President.

Mr. SPECTER. Has there ever been any variation in the information which you have given the Federal investigators?

Dr. PERRY. No, sir; not in essence. There may have been a variation in wording or sequence of my presentation, but the treatment as I outlined it to you and as I outlined it to them, to the best of my knowledge, has been essentially consistent.

Mr. SPECTER. Have you talked to any other representatives of the Federal Government besides the Secret Service men?

Dr. PERRY. I talked to two gentlemen initially within—who identified themselves as being with the Federal Bureau of Investigation. I do not recall their names either.

Mr. SPECTER. What did they ask you about?

Dr. PERRY. Essentially the same questions in regard to what I might speculate as to the origin of the missiles and their trajectory, and I replied to them as I have to you that I could not ascertain this of my own knowledge, and described the wounds to the extent I saw them.

Mr. SPECTER. Have you set forth here today the same information which you gave to the FBI?

Dr. PERRY. Yes, I think this is considerably in more detail, being essentially the same thing.

Mr. SPECTER. Have you now told me about all of the talks you have had with representatives of the Federal Government prior to today?

Dr. PERRY. I think I have.

Mr. SPECTER. And did you and I sit down and talk about the purpose of this deposition and the questions which I would be asking you on the record, before this deposition started?

Dr. PERRY. Yes; we did.

Mr. SPECTER. And did you give me the same information which you provided on the record here today?

Dr. PERRY. I have.

Mr. SPECTER. Do you have anything to add which you think might be helpful in any way to the President's Commission?

Dr. PERRY. No, sir.

Mr. SPECTER. Dr. Perry, we appreciate your coming for your deposition today, and I have given you a letter requesting your presence in Washington on Monday morning at 9 o'clock and I would ask you, for the record, to acknowledge receipt of letter, if you will, please.

Dr. PERRY. Yes; I have the letter here and I will be there.

Mr. SPECTER. Thank you, very much, sir. Let me ask you one more question, Dr. Perry, for the record, before we terminate this deposition. What experience have you had, if any, with gunshot wounds?

Dr. PERRY. I think in the course of my training here at Parkland, which is a city-county hospital and handles the great majority of the trauma cases that occur in Dallas County, that I have seen a fairly considerable number of traumatic wounds caused by knives, automobile accidents, gunshot wounds of various types.

Mr. SPECTER. Have you had any experience with gunshot wounds, in addition to that obtained here at Parkland?

Dr. PERRY. You mean, in the service?

Mr. SPECTER. Yes, sir.

Dr. PERRY. No, I had occasion to see only one gunshot wound while I was in the service.

Mr. SPECTER. Can you estimate how many gunshot wounds you have seen while you have been at Parkland?

Dr. PERRY. Probably it would be numbered in the hundreds.

Mr. SPECTER. Have you had any formal training in ballistics?

Dr. PERRY. No, other than the fact that I do some hunting and amateur hand loader.

Mr. SPECTER. Amateur what?

Dr. PERRY. Amateur hand loader—hand load ammunition.

Mr. SPECTER. Thank you very much.

Dr. PERRY. All right. Thank you.

TESTIMONY OF DR. WILLIAM KEMP CLARK

The testimony of Dr. William Kemp Clark was taken at 11:50 a.m., on March 21, 1964, at Parkland Memorial Hospital, Dallas, Tex., by Mr. Arlen Specter, assistant counsel of the President's Commission.

Mr. SPECTER. Would you stand up please, Dr. Clark, and raise your right hand?

Do you solemnly swear that the testimony you will give before the President's Commission on the Assassination of President Kennedy in this deposition proceeding will be the truth, the whole truth, and nothing but the truth, so help you God?

Dr. CLARK. I do.

Mr. SPECTER. You may be seated.

Dr. CLARK. Thank you.

Mr. SPECTER. The President's Commission is investigating all facts related to the Assassination of President Kennedy, and you have been asked to testify in this deposition proceeding relating to the medical treatment received by President Kennedy at Parkland Memorial Hospital and all facts incident thereto.

Dr. Clark, have you received a letter from the President's Commission enclosing a copy of the Executive Order establishing the Commission and a copy of a Senate and House Joint Resolution about the Commission, and a letter relating to the taking of testimony by the Commission?

Dr. CLARK. I have.

Mr. SPECTER. And are you willing to proceed with this deposition today, even though 3 days have not elapsed between the time you received the letter and this morning?

Dr. CLARK. Yes.

Mr. SPECTER. Would you state your full name for the record, please?

Dr. CLARK. William Kemp Clark.

Mr. SPECTER. Will you outline in a general way your educational background, please?

Dr. CLARK. Yes. I graduated from the University of Texas in Austin, 1944. I graduated from the University of Texas Medical Branch at Galveston in 1948. I interned at Indiana University Medical Center and was a resident in surgery there from 1948 to 1950. I spent 2 years in the Air Force and then took my residency in neurological surgery at Columbia Presbyterian Hospital in New York City. This was from 1953 to 1956, at which time I came to the University of Texas, Southwestern Medical School, as chairman of the division of neurological surgery.

Would you like the professional qualifications?

Mr. SPECTER. Yes; may I have the professional qualifications in summary form, if you will, please.

Dr. CLARK. I am board certified by the American Board of Neurological Surgery. I am a Fellow with the American College of Surgeons. I am a member of the Harvey Cushing Society.

Mr. SPECTER. What is the Harvey Cushing Society, by the way?

Dr. CLARK. It is the largest society of neurological surgeons in the world.

Mr. SPECTER. And what do your duties consist of with respect to the Southwestern Medical School of the University of Texas?

Dr. CLARK. I am in charge of the division of neurological surgery and carry the responsibility of administering this department or this division, to arrange the instruction of medical students in neurological surgery and to conduct research in this field.

Mr. SPECTER. What were your duties back on November 22, 1963?

Dr. CLARK. Essentially these. I also, as chairman of the division, have the responsibility as director of neurological surgery at Parkland Memorial Hospital which is the major teaching hospital of the medical school.

Mr. SPECTER. Did you receive notification on November 22, 1963, that the President had been wounded and was en route to this hospital?

Dr. CLARK. Yes, sir; I did.

Mr. SPECTER. Do you know at approximately what time you got that notification?

Dr. CLARK. Approximately 12:20 or 12:30.

Mr. SPECTER. And what action, if any, did you take as a result of receiving that notification?

Dr. CLARK. I went immediately to the emergency room at Parkland Hospital. I was in the laboratory at Southwestern Medical School when this word reached me by phone from the hospital.

Mr. SPECTER. And at approximately what time did you then arrive at the emergency room?

Dr. CLARK. I would estimate it took a minute and a half to two minutes, so I would guess that I arrived approximately 12:30.

Mr. SPECTER. And who was present, if anyone, upon your arrival, attending to the President?

Dr. CLARK. Dr. Jenkins, that is M. T. Jenkins, I suppose I ought to say, Dr. Ronald Jones, Dr. Malcolm Perry, Dr. James Carrico; arriving either with me or immediately thereafter were Dr. Robert McClelland, Dr. Paul Peters, and Dr. Charles Baxter.

Mr. SPECTER. What did you observe the President's condition to be on your arrival there?

Dr. CLARK. The President was lying on his back on the emergency cart. Dr. Perry was performing a tracheotomy. There were chest tubes being inserted. Dr. Jenkins was assisting the President's respirations through a tube in his trachea. Dr. Jones and Dr. Carrico were administering fluids and blood intravenously. The President was making a few spasmodic respiratory efforts. I assisted in withdrawing the endotracheal tube from the throat as Dr. Perry was then ready to insert the tracheotomy tube. I then examined the President briefly.

My findings showed his pupils were widely dilated, did not react to light, and his eyes were deviated outward with a slight skew deviation.

I then examined the wound in the back of the President's head. This was a large, gaping wound in the right posterior part, with cerebral and cerebellar tissue being damaged and exposed. There was considerable blood loss evident on the carriage, the floor, and the clothing of some of the people present. I would estimate 1,500 cc. of blood being present.

As I was examining the President's wound, I felt for a carotid pulse and felt none. Therefore, I began external cardiac massage and asked that a cardiotachioscope be connected. Because of my position it was difficult to administer cardiac massage. However, Dr. Jones stated that he felt a femoral pulse.

Mr. SPECTER. What is a femoral pulse?

Dr. CLARK. A femoral artery is the main artery going to the legs, and at the junction of the leg and the trunk you can feel the arterial pulsation in this artery. Because of my position, cardiac massage was taken over by Dr. Malcolm Perry, who was more advantageously situated.

Mr. SPECTER. What did the cardiotachioscope show at that time?

Dr. CLARK. By this time the cardiotachioscope, we just call it a cardiac monitor for a better word——

Mr. SPECTER. That's a good word.

Dr. CLARK. The cardiotachioscope had been attached and Dr. Fouad Bashour had arrived. There was transient electrical activity of the President's heart of an undefined type. Approximately, at this time the external cardiac massage became ineffectual and no pulsations could be felt. At this time it was decided to pronounce the President dead.

Mr. SPECTER. At what time was this fixed?

Dr. CLARK. Death was fixed at 1 p.m.

Mr. SPECTER. Was that a precise time or an approximate time, or in what way did you fix the time of death at 1 o'clock?

Dr. CLARK. This was an approximation as it is, first, extremely difficult to state precisely when death occurs. Secondly, no one was monitoring the clock, so an approximation of 1 o'clock was chosen.

Mr. SPECTER. Who was it who actually fixed the time of death?

Dr. CLARK. I did.

Mr. SPECTER. And did you have any part in the filling out of the death certificate?

Dr. CLARK. Yes.

Mr. SPECTER. And what did you do with respect to that?

Dr. CLARK. I filled out the death certificate at the request of Dr. George Burkley, the President's physician at the White House, signed the death certificate as a registered physician in the State of Texas, and gave this to him to accompany the body to Washington.

Mr. SPECTER. Did you advise anyone else in the Presidential party of the death of the President?

Dr. CLARK. Yes; I told Mrs. Kennedy, the President's wife, of his death.

Mr. SPECTER. And what, if anything, did she respond to you?

Dr. CLARK. She told me that she knew it and thanked me for our efforts.

Mr. SPECTER. Were any bullets or parts of bullets found in the President's body?

Dr. CLARK. Not by me, nor did I see any such missiles recovered at Parkland Hospital.

Mr. SPECTER. Were you a part of any press conference which followed on the day of the assassination?

Dr. CLARK. Yes, sir; I was.

Mr. SPECTER. And who made the arrangements for the press conference?

Dr. CLARK. Mr. Malcolm Kilduff, the Presidential press secretary.

Mr. SPECTER. At what time did the press conference occur?

Dr. CLARK. Approximately 2:30.

Mr. SPECTER. Where was it held?

Dr. CLARK. It was held in room 101–102, Parkland Hospital.

Mr. SPECTER. What mechanical instruments were used, if any, by the press at the conference?

Dr. CLARK. Tape recorders and television cameras, as well as the usual note pads and pencils, and so forth.

Mr. SPECTER. And who was interviewed during the course of the press conference and photographed?

Dr. CLARK. Dr. Malcolm Perry and myself.

Mr. SPECTER. No one else?

Dr. CLARK. No.

Mr. SPECTER. What, if anything, did you say then in the course of that press conference?

Dr. CLARK. I described the President's wound in his head in very much the same way as I have described it here. I was asked if this wound was an entrance wound, an exit wound, or what, and I said it could be an exit wound, but I felt it was a tangential wound.

Mr. SPECTER. Which wound did you refer to at this time?

Dr. CLARK. The wound in the head.

Mr. SPECTER. Did you describe at that time what you meant by "tangential"?

Dr. CLARK. Yes, sir; I did.

Mr. SPECTER. What definition of "tangential" did you make at that time?

Dr. CLARK. As I remember, I defined the word "tangential" as being—striking an object obliquely, not squarely or head on.

Mr. SPECTER. Will you describe at this time in somewhat greater detail the consequences of a tangential wound as contrasted with another type of a striking?

Dr. CLARK. Let me begin by saying that the damage suffered by an organ when struck by a bullet or other missile——

Mr. SPECTER. May the record show that I interrupted the deposition for about 2 minutes to ascertain what our afternoon schedule would be here because the regular administration office ordinarily closes at 12 o'clock, which was just about 15 minutes ago, and then we resumed the deposition of Dr. Clark as he was discussing the concept of tangential and other types of striking.

Go ahead, Doctor.

Dr. CLARK. The effects of any missile striking an organ or a function of the energy which is shed by the missile in passing through this organ when a bullet strikes the head, if it is able to pass through rapidly without shedding any energy into the brain, little damage results, other than that part of the brain which is directly penetrated by the missile. However, if it strikes the skull at an angle, it must then penetrate much more bone than normal, therefore, is likely to shed more energy, striking the brain a more powerful blow.

25

Secondly, in striking the bone in this manner, it may cause pieces of the bone to be blown into the brain and thus act as secondary missiles. Finally, the bullet itself may be deformed and deflected so that it would go through or penetrate parts of the brain, not in the usual direct line it was proceeding.

Mr. SPECTER. Now, referring back to the press conference, did you define a tangential wound at that time?

Dr. CLARK. Yes.

Mr. SPECTER. And what else did you state at the press conference at 2:30 on November 22?

Dr. CLARK. I stated that the President had lost considerable blood, that one of the contributing causes of death was this massive blood loss, that I was unable to state how many wounds the President had sustained or from what angle they could have come.

I finally remember stating that the President's wound was obviously a massive one and was insurvivable.

Mr. SPECTER. What did Dr. Perry say at that time, during the course of that press conference, when the cameras were operating?

Dr. CLARK. As I recall, Dr. Perry stated that there was a small wound in the President's throat, that he made the incision for the tracheotomy through this wound. He discovered that the trachea was deviated so he felt that the missile had entered the President's chest. He asked for chest tubes then to be placed in the pleural cavities. He was asked if this wound in the throat was an entrance wound or an exit wound. He said it was small and clean so it could have been an entrance wound.

Mr. SPECTER. Did he say anything else that you can recollect now in response to the question of whether it was a wound of entrance or exit?

Dr. CLARK. No, sir; I cannot recall.

Mr. SPECTER. Were you a part of a second press conference, Dr. Clark?

Dr. CLARK. Yes, sir.

Mr. SPECTER. And when did that second press conference occur?

Dr. CLARK. On Saturday, the 23d.

Mr. SPECTER. At about what time?

Dr. CLARK. Sometime in the morning, as I recall.

Mr. SPECTER. Going back to the first press conference for just a minute, which television networks were involved on that?

Dr. CLARK. Without sounding facetious, everyone, including some I had never heard of.

Mr. SPECTER. Can you recollect any besides the three major networks—ABC, CBS, and NBC?

Dr. CLARK. This is all I remember. I remember seeing in the room two reporters from Dallas newspapers whom I know and the radio and television stations were also present.

Mr. SPECTER. Now, going back to the second conference which I had started asking you about, had you had an opportunity to tell me what time of day that was?

Dr. CLARK. It was in the morning, as I recall.

Mr. SPECTER. And what television stations or networks were involved in that conference?

Dr. CLARK. Again, all three major networks, and I believe through our local affiliates. It does not seem as though this one was as jammed and as full as the first one.

Mr. SPECTER. And who arranged that press conference?

Dr. CLARK. That press conference was arranged by Mr. Steve Landregan, assistant administrator and public relations officer for the hospital. This is his office.

Mr. SPECTER. And who spoke at that press conference while the television cameras were grinding?

Dr. CLARK. Dr. Perry and myself.

Mr. SPECTER. And what did you say at that time?

Dr. CLARK. Essentially the same thing as I had on the first press conference, again defining tangential, and again describing the President's wound as being massive and unsurvivable.

Mr. SPECTER. And what did Dr. Perry, at that time, say?

Dr. CLARK. Dr. Perry said very little. He described the President's condition as he first saw him, when he was first called, and he described the manner in which he was called to the emergency room.

Mr. SPECTER. Did he say anything about whether the neck wound was a point of entry or exit?

Dr. CLARK. I do not remember—I specifically discussed this—may I add something to what I said in the first press conference?

Mr. SPECTER. Yes; please do, if you find something that comes to mind, please feel free to add that.

Dr. CLARK. All right. Let me check what I remember Dr. Perry said at the first press conference. He was asked if the neck wound could be a wound of entrance or appeared to be a wound of exit, and Dr. Perry said something like "possibly or conceivably," or something of this sort.

Mr. SPECTER. And, did he elaborate as to how that projectory would have been possible in that press conference?

Dr. CLARK. He did not elaborate on this. One of the reporters with gestures indicated the direction that such a bullet would have to take, and Dr. Perry quite obviously had to agree that this is the way it had to go to get from there to the top of his head.

Mr. SPECTER. But that was a possible trajectory under the circumstances?

Dr. CLARK. Yes.

Mr. SPECTER. How would that have been postulated in terms of striking specific parts of the body?

Dr. CLARK. Well, on a speculation, this would mean that the missile would have had to have been fired from below—upward or that the President was hanging upside down.

Me. SPECTER. Did Dr. Perry discuss anything with you prior to that second conference about a telephone call from Washington, D.C.?

Dr. CLARK. Yes; he did.

Mr. SPECTER. Would you relate briefly what Dr. Perry told you about that subject?

Dr. CLARK. Yes; Dr. Perry stated that he had talked to the Bethesda Naval Hospital on two occasions that morning and that he knew what the autopsy findings had shown and that he did not wish to be questioned by the press, as he had been asked by Bethesda to confine his remarks to that which he knew from having examined the President, and suggested that the major part of this press conference be conducted by me.

Mr. SPECTER. Was anyone else present when he expressed those thoughts to you?

Dr. CLARK. I believe that Mr. Price and Dr. Shires were present. I could be wrong on that.

Mr. SPECTER. Now, were you a part of a third press conference?

Dr. CLARK. Yes, sir.

Mr. SPECTER. And when did that occur?

Dr. CLARK. During the following week—I have forgotten exactly the day.

Mr. SPECTER. And what networks were involved at that time?

Dr. CLARK. It was CBS.

Mr. SPECTER. Was that a television conference?

Dr. CLARK. Yes; this was filmed.

Mr. SPECTER. And who arranged that conference?

Dr. CLARK. Again, Mr. Landregan.

Mr. SPECTER. And who spoke at that conference?

Dr. CLARK. Dr. Shaw, Dr. Shires, Dr. Baxter, Dr. McClelland, Dr. Jenkins, Dr. Gieseke, and myself.

Mr. SPECTER. Was Dr. Perry there at that time?

Dr. CLARK. Yes; Dr. Perry was there.

Mr. SPECTER. Would you outline briefly what you said at that time, if it differed in any way from what you said before?

Dr. CLARK. No, sir; it did not.

Mr. SPECTER. What did Dr. Perry say at that time?

Dr. CLARK. Essentially the same thing that he had said before, describing the wound in the throat, describing the condition of the President, how he was called and so forth.

Mr. SPECTER. Did he comment at that time as to whether it was an entrance wound or an exit wound or what?

Dr. CLARK. I don't remember.

Mr. SPECTER. And what did Dr. Shaw say at that time?

Dr. CLARK. Dr. Shaw described Governor Connally's chest wound. He described what was done for him, the operation in some detail. He described the fact that Governor Connally was conscious up until the time he was anesthetized in the operating room.

Mr. SPECTER. And what did Dr. Shires say at that time?

Dr. CLARK. Dr. Shires described the wounds suffered by Oswald and what was done in an attempt to save him.

Mr. SPECTER. And how about Dr. Gieseke, what did he say?

Dr. CLARK. Dr. Gieseke corroborated Dr. Shaw's statements regarding Governor Connally's condition and his remaining conscious until he was anesthetized by Dr. Gieseke.

Mr. SPECTER. What did Dr. Baxter say at that conference?

Dr. CLARK. Dr. Baxter described President Kennedy's condition as he saw it, stated that he had assisted in the placing in the chest tubes on President Kennedy, and that he had been present at Oswald's operation.

Mr. SPECTER. Did Dr. Baxter describe the neck wound that President Kennedy suffered with specific respect as to whether it was point of entry or exit?

Dr. CLARK. I don't remember—I don't believe he did.

Mr. SPECTER. Now, have we covered all the doctors who spoke at that press conference?

Dr. CLARK. Except Dr. Jenkins.

Mr. SPECTER. And what did Dr. Jenkins say at that time?

Dr. CLARK. Dr. Jenkins described being called to attend President Kennedy, how he got there with his anesthesia machine, that he found an endotracheal tube had already been inserted. He hooked up and he described the activities in the emergency room, operating room No. 1, and he described the stopping of the President's heart and the decision to pronounce him dead. He went ahead to describe the operation on Mr. Oswald and the extent of blood loss, etc., which he had sustained.

Mr. SPECTER. Now, were you involved in still a subsequent press conference?

Dr. CLARK. Yes, sir; I was.

Mr. SPECTER. And with whom was that press conference?

Dr. CLARK. This was with NBC and was approximately 2 weeks after the assassination.

Mr. SPECTER. And who arranged that press conference?

Dr. CLARK. Mr. Landregan.

Mr. SPECTER. And was that filmed?

Dr. CLARK. Yes, that was also filmed.

Mr. SPECTER. And who spoke at that time?

Dr. CLARK. I spoke alone as a representative of the department and so stated in the conference.

Mr. SPECTER. And what did you say at that time?

Dr. CLARK. Essentially the same thing as had been stated before.

Mr. SPECTER. Now, were you a part of still another press conference?

Dr. CLARK. Yes.

Mr. SPECTER. When was that?

Dr. CLARK. The week after the assassination.

Mr. SPECTER. And with whom was that press conference?

Dr. CLARK. With BBC.

Mr. SPECTER. Who arranged that?

Dr. CLARK. Mr. Landregan, again.

Mr. SPECTER. And did anyone else participate in that press conference with you?

Dr. CLARK. No.

Mr. SPECTER. And was that televised, filmed, or simply recorded?

Dr. CLARK. It was simply recorded.

Mr. SPECTER. And what did you say at that time?

Dr. CLARK. Exactly the same thing as I have said at the previous conferences, describing the President's condition, his wound, and what transpired after I arrived.

Mr. SPECTER. At any of the press conferences were you asked about a hole on the left side of the President's head?

Dr. CLARK. Yes.

Mr. SPECTER. At which conference or conferences?

Dr. CLARK. I was asked about this at the CBS conference and I stated that I personally saw no such wound.

Mr. SPECTER. And who asked you about it at that time, if you recall?

Dr. CLARK. The man who was conducting the conference. This was brought up by one of the physicians, I think Dr. McClelland, that there was some discussion of such a wound.

Mr. SPECTER. Did Dr. McClelland say that he had seen such a wound?

Dr. CLARK. No.

Mr. SPECTER. What was the origin, if you know, as to the inquiry on the wound, that is, who suggested that there might have been a wound on the left side?

Dr. CLARK. I don't recall—I don't recall.

Mr. SPECTER. Had there been some comment that the priests made a comment that there was a wound on the left side of the head?

Dr. CLARK. I heard this subsequently from one of the reporters who attended the press conference with NBC.

Mr. SPECTER. Were priests actually in trauma room 1?

Dr. CLARK. Yes, sir.

Mr. SPECTER. Where were they in relation to the President at that time?

Dr. CLARK. They were on the right side of the President's body.

Mr. SPECTER. Now, you described the massive wound at the top of the President's head, with the brain protruding; did you observe any other hole or wound on the President's head?

Dr. CLARK. No, sir; I did not.

Mr. SPECTER. Did you observe, to make my question very specific, a bullet hole or what appeared to be a bullet hole in the posterior scalp, approximately 2.5 cm. laterally to the right, slightly above the external occipital protuberant, measuring 15 by 6 mm.

Dr. CLARK. No, sir; I did not. This could have easily been hidden in the blood and hair.

Mr. SPECTER. Did you observe any bullet wounds or any other wound on the back side of the President?

Dr. CLARK. No, sir; I did not.

Mr. SPECTER. Was the President ever turned over while he was in the emergency room?

Dr. CLARK. Not in my presence; no, sir.

Mr. SPECTER. And did you leave before, with, or after all the other doctors who were in attendance?

Dr. CLARK. I left after all the other doctors who were in attendance, because I stayed with Dr. Burkley until we had the death certificate signed and the arrangements had been made to transport the President's body out of Parkland Hospital.

Mr. SPECTER. You say Dr. Burkley or Buckley?

Dr. CLARK. Dr. Burkley.

Mr. SPECTER. That's the President's private physician?

Dr. CLARK. Yes.

Mr. SPECTER. Dr. Clark, would your observations be consistent with some other alleged facts in this matter, such as the presence of a lateral wound measuring 15 by 6 mm. on the posterior scalp approximately 2.5 cm. laterally to the right and slightly above the external occipital proturberant—that is to say, could such a hole have been present without your observing it?

Dr. CLARK. Yes, in the presence of this much destruction of skull and scalp above such a wound and lateral to it and the brief period of time available for examination—yes, such a wound could be present.

Mr. SPECTER. The physicians, surgeons who examined the President at the autopsy specifically, Commander James J. Humes, H-u-m-e-s (spelling); Commander J. Thornton Boswell, B-o-s-w-e-l-l (spelling), and Lt. Col. Pierre A. Finck, F-i-n-c-k (spelling), expressed the joint opinion that the wound which   I have just described as being 15 by 6 mm. and 2.5 cm. to the right and slightly above the external occipital protuberant was a point of entrance of a bullet in the President's head at a time when the President's head was moved slightly forward with his chin dropping into his chest, when he was riding in an open car at a slightly downhill position. With those facts being supplied to them in a hypothetical fashion, they concluded that the bullet would have taken a more or less straight course, exiting from the center of the President's skull at a point indicated by an opening from three portions of the skull reconstructed, which had been brought to them—would those findings and those conclusions be consistent with your observations if you assumed the additional facts which I have brought to your attention, in addition to those which you have personally observed?

Dr. CLARK. Yes, sir.

Mr. SPECTER. Dr. Clark, in the line of your specialty, could you comment as to the status of the President with respect to competency, had he been able to survive the head injuries which you have described and the total wound which he had?

Dr. CLARK. This, of course, is a question of tremendous importance. Just let me state that the loss of cerebrellar tissue would probably have been of minimal consequence in the performance of his duties. The loss of the right occipital and probably part of the right parietal lobes would have been of specific importance. This would have led to a visual field deficit, which would have interfered in a major way with his ability to read, not the interpretation of reading matter per se, but the acquisition of information from the printed page. He would have had specific difficulty with finding the next line in a book or paper. This would have proven to be a specific handicap in getting information on which, as the President of the United States, he would have to act.

How much damage he would have had to his motor system, that is, the ability to control or coordinate his left extremities, I would not know. This conceivably could have been a problem

29

in enabling him to move about, to appear in public, et cetera. Finally, and probably most important, since the brain, as far as at its higher levels, largely as a unit, the loss of this much brain tissue likely would have impaired his ability in abstract reasoning, imagination; whereas, the part of the President's brain struck is not that part specifically concerned with these matters. The effect of loss of considerable brain tissue does affect the total performance of the organ in these matters. There would be grave doubts in my mind as to our ability as physicians to give a clear answer regarding his ability to function as President of the United States.

Our ability to judge this is sometimes sorely tried when dealing with people with considerably less intellectual and moral demands made upon them.

Mr. SPECTER. Doctor, did you prepare certain written reports based on your participation in the treatment of President Kennedy?

Dr. CLARK. Yes, sir; I did.

Mr. SPECTER. And I now show you a document which has been supplied to the President's Commission, which we have marked as Commission Exhibit No. 392, and I now show you the second and third sheets, which purport to be the summary made by you and ask if that was prepared by you?

Dr. CLARK. Yes, sir; it was.

Mr. SPECTER. And, are the facts set forth in those two sheets true and correct?

Dr. CLARK. Yes, sir.

Mr. SPECTER. And I now show you a 2¾-page summary which purports to bear your signature, being dated November 22, 1963, and I ask you if that, in fact, is your signature?

Dr. CLARK. Yes; it is.

Mr. SPECTER. And, was, in fact, this report made in your own hand concerning the treatment which you rendered to the President?

Dr. CLARK. Yes, sir.

Mr. SPECTER. And are the facts set forth therein true and correct?

Dr. CLARK. Yes, sir.

Mr. SPECTER. Have you made any other written report or other writings of any sort concerning this matter?

Dr. CLARK. No; I have not.

Mr. SPECTER. Have you been interviewed or discussed this matter with any Federal representative prior to today?

Dr. CLARK. Yes, sir; I have.

Mr. SPECTER. And whom did you talk to?

Dr. CLARK. I talked to an FBI agent a few days after the assassination, in Mr. Jack Price's office.

Mr. SPECTER. And who is Mr. Price, for the record at this point?

Dr. CLARK. He is the administrator of Parkland Memorial Hospital. This agent asked me if I had recovered any missiles or fragments of missiles from the President's body. I said I did not, and he asked me if I knew of anyone in Parkland Hospital who had recovered such evidence and I assured him I did not.

Mr. SPECTER. Did he ask you anything further?

Dr. CLARK. No, sir.

Mr. SPECTER. Did you tell him anything further?

Dr. CLARK. No, sir. I offered to answer any questions he might have asked and he said that was all he wished to know.

Mr. SPECTER. And did you talk to any other representative of the Federal Government at any time before today?

Dr. CLARK. Yes; I talked to a member of the Secret Service approximately a month after the assassination. I talked to him on two occasions, once by phone, and he asked me if I had a copy of the written report submitted by Dr. Ronald Jones, and I told him I did not.

I subsequently talked to him in person. He showed me the summary that I prepared and sent to Dr. Burkley, the same document I just identified here, and my own handwritten report of the events of the afternoon of the 22d of November. He asked me if I prepared these and I told him I had. He asked me if I had any other written records. I told him I did not. He said, "Do you have any additional information than you have written?" I said I did not. He thanked me very much for coming.

Mr. SPECTER. Have you now summarized all of the conversations you have had with any representative of the Federal Government prior to today?

Dr. CLARK. Yes, sir.

Mr. SPECTER. And have you had any conversations with any representative of the State government prior to today?

Dr. CLARK. No, sir.

Mr. SPECTER. Before you were sworn in to have your deposition taken, did you and I have a discussion about this matter?

Dr. CLARK. Yes, sir; a pleasant discussion of what the function of this Commission is.

Mr. SPECTER. And, also, all of what I would be asking once the record was open and we started taking your deposition?

Dr. CLARK. Yes, sir.

Mr. SPECTER. And have we covered on the record with the court reporter transcribing all the subjects which you and I discussed informally and prior to the start of the more formal session here?

Dr. CLARK. Yes, sir.

Mr. SPECTER. Do you have anything which you would care to add, which you think might possibly be helpful to the Commission in any way, Dr. Clark?

Dr. CLARK. No, sir; I'm afraid I don't.

Mr. SPECTER. Thank you very much for coming. We surely appreciate it, Dr. Clark. Thank you, Dr. Clark.

Dr. CLARK. Thank you.

TESTIMONY OF DR. KEMP CLARK RESUMED

The testimony of Dr. Kemp Clark was taken at 12:05 p.m., on March 25, 1964, at Parkland Memorial Hospital, Dallas, Tex., by Mr. Arlen Specter, assistant counsel of the President's Commission.

Mr. SPECTER. May the record show that Dr. Kemp Clark has returned to have a few additional questions asked of him following the deposition which was taken on March 21.

Dr. Clark, the purpose of this additional deposition is the same as the first one, except that I am going to ask you a few additional questions based upon a translation of an article which appeared in "L' Express", which has been provided to me since the deposition of last Saturday.

Would you please stand up again and raise your right hand?

Do you solemnly swear that the testimony you will give before the President's Commission in this deposition proceeding will be the truth, the whole truth, and nothing but the truth, so help you God?

Dr. CLARK. I do.

Mr. SPECTER. Dr. Clark, I have made available to you, have I not, what purports to be a translation from French of the "L' Express" issue of February 20, 1964?

Dr. CLARK. Yes, sir.

Mr. SPECTER. And let me read for the record and for you this excerpt.

"On his part according to the New York Times of November 27, 'Dr. Kemp Clark, who signed the Kennedy death certificate, declared that a bullet hit him right where the knot of his necktie was.' He added," apparently referring to you, "'this bullet penetrated into his chest and did not come out'. The surgeon went on to say that the second wound of the President was 'tangential' and that it had been caused by a bullet which hit 'the right side of his head'".

Dr. Clark, my first question is—what, if anything, did you say to a New York Times representative or anyone, for that matter, with respect to whether a bullet hit the President where the knot of his necktie was.

Dr. CLARK. I remember using the phrase to describe the location of a wound in the President's throat as being at the point of his knot of his necktie. I do not recall ever specifically stating that this was an entrance wound, as has been said before. I was not present when the President arrived and did not see this wound. If any statement regarding its entrance or exit was made by me, it was indicating that there was a small wound described there by the physicians who first saw the President.

A specific quotation regarding entrance or exit, I feel, is a partial quotation or incompletely quoted from me. The part pertaining to the bullet entering the President's chest rests on the reasons for the placing of the chest tubes which were being inserted when I arrived. It was the assumption, based on the previously described deviation of the trachea and the presence of blood in the strap muscles of the neck that a wound or missile wound might have entered the President's chest.

Mr. SPECTER. Well, what was there, Dr. Clark, in the deviation of the trachea and the presence of blood in the strap muscles of the neck which so indicated?

Dr. CLARK. Assuming that a missile had entered the pleural space, if there had been bleeding into the pleural space, the trachea would have been deviated or had there been leakage of air into the pleural space, the trachea would have been deviated, as it is the main conduit of air to the two lungs. Collapse of a lung would have produced, or will produce deviation of the trachea. There being a wound in the throat, there being blood in the strap muscles and there being deviation of the trachea in the presence of a grievously wounded patient without opportunity for X-ray or other diagnostic measures, Dr. Perry assumed that the findings in the neck were due to penetration of the missile into the chest. For this reason, he requested chest tubes to be placed.

Mr. SPECTER. Well, is the deviation of the trachea and the presence of bleeding on the strap muscles of the neck and the other factors which you have recited equally consistent with a wound of exit on the neck?

Dr. CLARK. Yes, sir. Furthermore, let me say that the presence of the deviation of the trachea, with blood in the strap muscles, are by no means diagnostic of penetration of the chest, and the placing of the chest tubes was prophylactic had such an eventuality occurred.

Mr. SPECTER. Was there any external indication that there was a missile in the chest?

Dr. CLARK. No, sir.

Mr. SPECTER. Was it the preliminary thought that the missile might have been in the chest by virtue of the fact that this wound was noted on the neck?

Dr. CLARK. Yes; with the other factors I have enumerated.

Mr. SPECTER. And at that time, not knowing what the angle might have been or any of the surrounding circumstances, then you proceeded to take precautionary measures as if there might have been a missile in the chest at some point?

Dr. CLARK. That is correct. Measures were taken, assuming the worst had happened.

Mr. SPECTER. As the quotation appears in the issue of "L' Express," "This bullet penetrated into his chest and did not come out," would that then be an accurate quotation of something that you said, Dr. Clark?

Dr. CLARK. No, sir.

Mr. SPECTER. Dr. Clark, while you are here again, I would like to ask you a few additional questions.

Let the record show that since I have taken your deposition, I have taken the depositions of many additional witnesses and none has been transcribed, so I am not in a position to refer to a record to see what I asked you before or to frankly recollect precisely what I asked you before, so, to some extent these questions may be overlapping.

Did you observe the President's back at that time when he was in the emergency room?

Dr. CLARK. No, sir.

Mr. SPECTER. What was the reason for your not looking at his back?

Dr. CLARK. First, the duration of time that the President was alive in the emergency room was a brief duration. All efforts were bent toward saving his life rather than inspection for precise location of wounds. After his death it was not our position to try to evaluate all of the conceivable organs or areas of the body, knowing that an autopsy would be performed and that this would be far more meaningful than a cursory external examination here.

Mr. SPECTER. Was there any bleeding wound in the President's back?

Dr. CLARK. In the back of his head.

Mr. SPECTER. But how about on the back of his body, was there any bleeding wound noted?

Dr. CLARK. Since we did not turn the President over, I cannot answer that specifically. We saw none, as I previously stated.

Mr. SPECTER. Did you undertake any action to ascertain whether there had been a violation to a major extent of the back part of his body?

Dr. CLARK. No, sir.

Mr. SPECTER. That is, none was taken by you personally?

Dr. CLARK. That's correct.

Mr. SPECTER. Dr. Carrico testified earlier today, being the first doctor to reach him, that he felt the President's back to determine whether there was any major violation of that area.

Would that be a customary action to take to ascertain whether there was any major wound, by the doctor who first examined the patient?

Dr. CLARK. Yes, sir.

Mr. SPECTER. Assuming that the President had a bullet wound of entry on the upper right posterior thorax, just above the upper border of the scapula, 14 cms. from the right acromion process, 14 cm. below the tip of the right mastoid process, would there have been a bloody type wound?

Dr. CLARK. I'm sorry—your question?

Mr. SPECTER. Would such a wound of entry by a missile traveling approximately 2,000 feet per second, approximately 6.5 mm. in diameter, cause a bloody type of a wound?

Dr. CLARK. No, sir. Such a wound could have easily been overlooked in the presence of the much larger wound in the right occipital region of the President's skull, from which considerable blood loss had occurred which stained the back of his head, neck and upper shoulders.

Mr. SPECTER. Dr. Clark, I want to ask you a question as it is raised here in "L' Express".

"How did the practitioner who signed the death certificate of the President fail to take the trouble to turn him over?"

Of course, that refers to you and will you give me your answer to that question, as the news media has posed it?

Dr. CLARK. Quite simply, as I previously stated, the duration of time the President was alive was occupied by attempts to save his life. When these failed, further examination of the patient's body was not done, as it was felt that little could be gained or learned·that would be helpful in deciding the course of events leading up to his assassination, that is, examination by me, as I knew an autopsy would be performed which would be far more meaningful and revealing than any cursory external examination conducted in the emergency room by me.

Mr. SPECTER. Now, was the action taken by you in signing the death certificate based upon the examination which you made in accordance with what you believed to be good medical practice?

Dr. CLARK. Yes, sir.

Mr. SPECTER. So that the characterization here of "L' Express" that the failure to turn the President over would not constitute gross negligence in your professional judgment, as they have characterized it here.

Dr. CLARK. No, sir. One other point, if I may here?

Mr. SPECTER. Yes.

Dr. CLARK. In order to move the President's body to Bethesda where the autopsy was to be performed, a death certificate had to be filled out in conformance with Texas State law to allow the body to be transported. This is the second part of the signing of the death certificate.

Mr. SPECTER. Do you have anything to add, Dr. Clark, which you think might be helpful at all in the inquiry being made by the President's Commission?

Dr. CLARK. No; I don't think so.

Mr. SPECTER. And did you and I chat for just a moment or two about the questions I would ask you on this supplemental deposition before it went on the record?

Dr. CLARK. Yes, sir.

Mr. SPECTER. And have you talked to any representative of the Federal Government between the time I took your deposition last Saturday and this Wednesday morning?

Dr. CLARK. No, sir.

Mr. SPECTER. Thank you very much, Dr. Clark.

Dr. CLARK. All right.

TESTIMONY OF DR. ROBERT NELSON McCLELLAND

The testimony of Dr. Robert Nelson McClelland was taken on March 21, 1964, at Parkland Memorial Hospital, Dallas, Tex., by Mr. Arlen Specter, assistant counsel of the President's Commission.

Mr. SPECTER. Will you raise your right hand?

Dr. MCCLELLAND. Yes.

Mr. SPECTER. Do you solemnly swear that the testimony you give in these proceedings will be the truth, the whole truth, and nothing but the truth, so help you God?

Dr. MCCLELLAND. I do.

Mr. SPECTER. Dr. McClelland, the purpose of this proceeding is to take your deposition in connection with an investigation which is being conducted by the President's Commission on the Assassination of President Kennedy, and the specific purpose of our requesting you to answer questions relates to the topic of the medical care which President Kennedy received at Parkland Memorial Hospital.

Dr. McClelland, will you tell us your full name for the record, please?

Dr. MCCLELLAND. Robert Nelson McClelland.

Mr. SPECTER. Have you received a letter from the Commission which enclosed a copy of the Executive order creating the Commission, and a copy of the Congressional Resolution pertaining to the Commission, and a copy of the procedures for taking testimony under the Commission?

Dr. MCCLELLAND. Yes.

Mr. SPECTER. And is it satisfactory with you to answer these questions for us today, even though you haven't had the 3 days between the time of the receipt of the letter and today?

Dr. MCCLELLAND. Yes.

Mr. SPECTER. What is your profession, Doctor?

Dr. MCCLELLAND. I am a doctor of medicine.

Mr. SPECTER. Would you outline briefly your educational background, starting with your graduation from college, please?

Dr. MCCLELLAND. Since graduation from college I attended medical school at the University of Texas, medical branch in Galveston, Tex., and received the M.D. degree from that school in 1954. I then went to Kansas City, Kans., where I did a rotating internship at the University of Kansas Medical Center from June 1954 to June 1955. Following that period I was a general medical officer in the Air Force for 2 years in Germany, and subsequent to my release from active duty, I became a general surgery resident at Parkland Memorial Hospital in Dallas in August of 1957. I remained at Parkland from that date to August 1959, at which time I entered private practice for ten months, and then reentered my general surgery training program at Parkland in June 1960. I completed my 4 years of general surgical training in June 1962. Following that time I became a full-time instructor of surgery on the staff of the University of Texas, Southwestern Medical School, and I am at the present time an associate professor of surgery at that school.

Mr. SPECTER. Dr. McClelland, in connection with your duties at Parkland Hospital, or before, have you had any experience with gunshot wounds?

Dr. MCCLELLAND. Yes.

Mr. SPECTER. Where in your background did you acquire that experience?

Dr. MCCLELLAND. Largely during residency training and subsequent to that in my capacity here on the staff.

Mr. SPECTER. And what has provided the opportunity for your experience here at Parkland in residency training and on the staff with respect to acquiring knowledge of gunshot wounds?

Dr. MCCLELLAND. Largely this has been related to the type of hospital which Parkland is; namely, City-County Hospital which receives all of the indigent patients of this county, many of whom are involved frequently in shooting altercations, so that we do see a large number of that type patient almost daily.

Mr. SPECTER. Could you approximate for me the total number of gunshot wounds which you have had an opportunity to observe?

Dr. MCCLELLAND. I would estimate that it would be in excess of 200.

Mr. SPECTER. What was your duty assignment back on November 22, 1963?

Dr. MCCLELLAND. At that time I was showing a film on surgical techniques to a group of students and residents on the second floor of Parkland Hospital in the surgical suite, where I was notified of the fact that President Kennedy was being brought to the Parkland emergency room after having been shot.

Mr. SPECTER. And what action, if any, did you take following that notification?

Dr. MCCLELLAND. Immediately upon hearing that, I accompanied the Resident, Dr. Crenshaw, who brought this news to me, to the emergency room, and down to the trauma room 1 where President Kennedy had been taken immediately upon arrival.

Mr. SPECTER. And approximately what time did you arrive in Emergency Room 1?

Dr. MCCLELLAND. This is a mere approximation, but I would approximate or estimate, rather, about 12:40.

Mr. SPECTER. And who was present, if anyone, at the time of your arrival?

Dr. MCCLELLAND. At the time I arrived, Dr. Perry—would you like the full names of all these?

Mr. SPECTER. That would be fine, I would appreciate that.

Dr. MCCLELLAND. Dr. Malcolm Perry, Dr. Charles Baxter, Dr. Charles Crenshaw, Dr. James Carrico, Dr. Paul Peters.

Mr. SPECTER. Were they all present at the time you arrived?

Dr. MCCLELLAND. They were not present when I arrived.

Mr. SPECTER. Will you start with the ones who were present?

Dr. MCCLELLAND. Starting with the ones who were present, I'm sorry, the ones who were present when I arrived were Drs. Carrico, Perry and Baxter. The others I mentioned arrived subsequently or about the same time that I did.

Mr. SPECTER. Then, what other doctors, if any, arrived after you did, in addition to those whom you have already mentioned?

Dr. MCCLELLAND. In addition, the ones that arrived afterwards, were Dr. Kenneth Salyer.

Mr. SPECTER. S-a-l-y-e-r?

Dr. MCCLELLAND. S-a-l-y-e-r, Dr. Fouad, F-o-u-a-d Bashour, Dr. Donald Seldin----

Mr. SPECTER. S-e-l-d-i-n?

Dr. MCCLELLAND. S-e-l-d-i-n—I believe that's all.

Mr. SPECTER. What did you observe as to President Kennedy's condition at that time?

Dr. MCCLELLAND. Well, on initially coming into the room and inspecting him from a distance of only 2 or 3 feet as I put on a pair of surgical gloves, it was obvious that he had sustained a probably mortal head injury, and that his face was extremely swollen and suffused with blood appeared cyanotic——

Mr. SPECTER. "Cyanotic"—may I interrupt—just what do you mean by that in lay terms?

Dr. MCCLELLAND. This mean bluish discoloration, bluish-black discoloration of the tissue. The eyes were somewhat protuberant, which is usually seen after massive head injuries denoting increased intracranial pressure, and it seemed that he perhaps was not making, at the time at least, spontaneous respiratory movements, but was receiving artificial respiration from a machine, an anesthesia machine.

Mr. SPECTER. Who was operating that machine?

Dr. MCCLELLAND. The machine—there was a changeover, just as I came in, one of the doctors in the room, I don't recall which one, had been operating what we call an intermittent positive pressure breathing machine.

Mr. SPECTER. Had that machine been utilized prior to your arrival?

Dr. MCCLELLAND. It was in use as I arrived, yes, and about the same time I arrived—this would be one other doctor who came in the room that I forgot about—Dr. Jenkins, M. T. Jenkins, professor of anesthesiology, came into the room with a larger anesthesia machine, which is a better type machine with which to maintain control of respiration, and this was then attached to the tube in the President's tracheotom; anyway, respiratory movements were being made for him with these two machines, which were in the process of being changed when I came in.

Then, as I took my post to help with the tracheotomy, I was standing at the end of the stretcher on which the President was lying, immediately at his head, for purposes of holding a tracheotom, or a retractory in the neck line.

Mr. SPECTER. What did you observe, if anything, as to the status of the neck wound when you first arrived?

Dr. MCCLELLAND. The neck wound, when I first arrived, was at this time converted into a tracheotomy incision. The skin incision had been made by Dr. Perry, and he told me—although I did not see that—that he had made the incision through a very small, perhaps less than one quarter inch in diameter wound in the neck.

Mr. SPECTER. Do you recall whether he described it any more precisely than that?

Dr. MCCLELLAND. He did not at that time.

Mr. SPECTER. Has he ever described it any more precisely for you?

Dr. MCCLELLAND. He has since that time.

Mr. SPECTER. And what description has he given of it since that time?

Dr. MCCLELLAND. As well as I can recall, the description that he gave was essentially as I have just described, that it was a very small injury, with clear   cut, although somewhat irregular margins of less than a quarter inch in diameter, with minimal tissue damage surrounding it on the skin.

Mr. SPECTER. Now, was there anything left for you to observe of that bullet wound, or had the incision obliterated it?

Dr. MCCLELLAND. The incision had obliterated it, essentially, the skin portion, that is.

Mr. SPECTER. Before proceeding to describe what you did in connection with the tracheostomy, will you more fully describe your observation with respect to the head wound?

Dr. MCCLELLAND. As I took the position at the head of the table that I have already described, to help out with the tracheotomy, I was in such a position that I could very closely examine the head wound, and I noted that the right posterior portion of the skull had been extremely blasted. It had been shattered, apparently, by the force of the shot so that the parietal bone was protruded up through the scalp and seemed to be fractured almost along its right posterior half, as well as some of the occipital bone being fractured in its lateral half, and this sprung open the bones that I mentioned in such a way that you could actually look down into the skull cavity itself and see that probably a third or so, at least, of the brain tissue, posterior cerebral tissue and some of the cerebellar tissue had been blasted out. There was a large amount of bleeding which was occurring mainly from the large venous channels in the skull which had been blasted open.

Mr. SPECTER. Was he alive at the time you first saw him?

35

Dr. MCCLELLAND. I really couldn't say, because as I mentioned in the hectic activity—I really couldn't say what his blood pressure was or what his pulse was or anything of that sort. The only thing I could say that would perhaps give evidence—this is not vital activity—at most, is that maybe he made one or two spontaneous respiratory movements but it would be difficult to say, since the machine was being used on him, whether these were true spontaneous respirations or not.

Mr. SPECTER. Would you now describe the activity and part that you performed in the treatment which followed your arrival?

Dr. MCCLELLAND. Yes; as I say, all I did was simply assist Dr. Perry and Dr. Baxter in doing the tracheotomy. All three of us worked together in making an incision in the neck, tracting the neck muscles out of the way, and making a small opening into the trachea near the spot where the trachea had already been blasted or torn open by the fragment of the bullet, and inserting a large metal tracheotomy tube into this hole, and after this the breathing apparatus was attached to this instead of the previous tube which had been placed here.

Mr. SPECTER. In conducting that operation, did you observe any interior damage to the President?

Dr. MCCLELLAND. Yes.

Mr. SPECTER. Will you describe that for me, please?

Dr. MCCLELLAND. That damage consisted mainly of a large amount of contusion and hematoma formation in the tissue lateral to the right side of the trachea and the swelling and bleeding around this site was to such extent that the trachea was somewhat deviated to the left side, not a great deal, but to a degree at least that it required partial cutting of some of the neck muscles in order to get good enough exposure to put in the tracheotomy tube, but there was a good deal of soft tissue damage and damage to the trachea itself where apparently the missile had gone between the trachea on the right side and the strap muscles which were applied closely to it.

Mr. SPECTER. What other treatment was given to President Kennedy at the time you were performing the procedures you have just described?

Dr. MCCLELLAND. To the best of my knowledge, the other treatment had consisted of the placement of cutdown sites in his extremities, namely, the making of incisions over large veins in the arms and, I believe, in the leg; however, I'm not sure about that, since I was not paying too much attention to that part of the activity, and large plastic tubes were placed into these veins for the giving of blood and fluids, and as I recall, he received a certain amount of blood, but I don't know exactly how much, since I was not actually giving the blood.

In addition to that, of course, while we were working on the tracheotomy incision, the other physicians that I have mentioned were attaching the President rapidly to a cardiac monitor, that is to say, an electrocardiogram, for checking the presence of cardiac activity, and in addition, chest tubes were being placed in the right and left chest—both, as I recall.

Mr. SPECTER. Do you recall who was placing those tubes?

Dr. MCCLELLAND. One of the tubes, I believe, was placed by Dr. Peters. The other one, I'm not right certain, I don't really recall—I perhaps better not say.

Mr. SPECTER. Do you know about how long that took in placing those chest tubes?

Dr. MCCLELLAND. As well as I am aware, the tubes were both placed in. What this involves is simply putting a trocar, a large hollow tube, and that is put into the small incision, into the anterior chest wall and slipping the tube into the chest between a group of ribs for purposes of relieving any collection of air or fluid which is present in the lungs. The reason this was done was because it was felt that there was probably quite possibly a mediastinal injury with perhaps suffusion of blood and air into one or both pleural cavities.

Mr. SPECTER. What effect did this medical treatment have on President Kennedy?

Dr. MCCLELLAND. As near as we could tell, unfortunately, none. We felt that from the time we saw him, most of us agreed, all of us agreed rather, that this was a mortal wound, but that in spite of this feeling that all attempts possible should be made to revive him, as far as establishing the airway breathing for him, and replacing blood and what not, but unfortunately the loss of blood and the loss of cerebral and cerebellar tissues were so great that the efforts were of no avail.

Mr. SPECTER. Was he conscious at that time that you saw him?

Dr. MCCLELLAND. No.

Mr. SPECTER. And, at what time did he expire?

Dr. MCCLELLAND. He was pronounced dead at 1 p.m. on November 22.

Mr. SPECTER. What was the cause of death in your opinion?

Dr. MCCLELLAND. The cause of death, I would say, would be massive head injuries with loss of large amounts of cerebral and cerebellar tissues and massive blood loss.

36

Mr. SPECTER. Did you observe anything in the nature of a wound on his body other than that which you have already described for me?

Dr. MCCLELLAND. No.

Mr. SPECTER. In what position was President Kennedy maintained from the time you saw him until the pronouncement of death?

Dr. MCCLELLAND. On his back on the cart.

Mr. SPECTER. On his what?

Dr. MCCLELLAND. On his back on the stretcher.

Mr. SPECTER. Was he on the stretcher at all times?

Dr. MCCLELLAND. Yes.

Mr. SPECTER. In the trauma room No. 1 you described, is there any table onto which he could be placed from the stretcher?

Dr. MCCLELLAND. No; generally we do not move patients from the stretcher until they are ready to go into the operating room and then they are moved onto the operating table.

Mr. SPECTER. Well, in fact, was he left on the stretcher all during the course of these procedures until he was pronounced dead?

Dr. MCCLELLAND. That's right.

Mr. SPECTER. Then, at any time was he positioned in a way where you could have seen the back of his body?

Dr. MCCLELLAND. No.

Mr. SPECTER. Did you observe any gunshot wound on his back?

Dr. MCCLELLAND. No.

Mr. SPECTER. Have you had discussions with the other doctors who attended President Kennedy as to the possible nature of the wound which was inflicted on him?

Dr. MCCLELLAND. Yes.

Mr. SPECTER. And what facts did you have available either to you or to the other doctors whom you talked this over with, with respect to the nature of the wound, source of the wounds, and that sort of thing?

Dr. MCCLELLAND. Immediately we had essentially no facts. We knew nothing of the number of bullets that had supposedly been fired. We knew nothing of the site from which the bullet had been fired, essentially none of the circumstances in the first few minutes, say, 20 or 30 minutes after the President was brought in, so that our initial impressions were based upon extremely incomplete information.

Mr. SPECTER. What were your initial impressions?

Dr. MCCLELLAND. The initial impression that we had was that perhaps the wound in the neck, the anterior part of the neck, was an entrance wound and that it had perhaps taken a trajectory off the anterior vertebral body and again into the skull itself, exiting out the back, to produce the massive injury in the head. However, this required some straining of the imagination to imagine that this would happen, and it was much easier to explain the apparent trajectory by means of two bullets, which we later found out apparently had been fired, than by just one then, on which basis we were originally taking to explain it.

Mr. SPECTER. Through the use of the pronoun "we" in your last answer, to whom do you mean by "we"?

Dr. MCCLELLAND. Essentially all of the doctors that have previously been mentioned here.

Mr. SPECTER. Did you observe the condition of the back of the President's head?

Dr. MCCLELLAND. Well, partially; not, of course, as I say, we did not lift his head up since it was so greatly damaged. We attempted to avoid moving him any more than it was absolutely necessary, but I could see, of course, all the extent of the wound.

Mr. SPECTER. You saw a large opening which you have already described?

Dr. MCCLELLAND. I saw the large opening which I have described.

Mr. SPECTER. Did you observe any other wound on the back of the head?

Dr. MCCLELLAND. No.

Mr. SPECTER. Did you observe a small gunshot wound below the large opening on the back of the head?

Dr. MCCLELLAND. No.

Mr. SPECTER. Based on the experience that you have described for us with gunshot wounds and your general medical experience, would you characterize the description of the wound that Dr. Perry gave you as being a wound of entrance or a wound of exit, or was the description which you got from Dr. Perry and Dr. Baxter and Dr. Carrico who were there before, equally consistent with whether or not it was a wound of entrance or a wound of exit, or how would you characterize it in your words?

37

Dr. MCCLELLAND. I would say it would be equally consistent with either type wound, either an entrance or an exit type wound. It would be quite difficult to say—impossible.

Mr. SPECTER. Dr. McClelland, I show you now a statement or a report which has been furnished to the Commission by Parkland Hospital and has been identified in a previous Commission hearing as Commission Exhibit No. 392, and I direct your attention specifically to a page, "Third Report", which was made by you, and I would ask you first of all if this is your signature which appears at the bottom of Page 2, and next, whether in fact you did make this report and submit it to the authorities at Parkland Hospital?

Dr. MCCLELLAND. Yes.

Mr. SPECTER. And are all the facts set forth true and correct to the best of your knowledge, information and belief?

Dr. MCCLELLAND. To the best of my knowledge, yes.

Mr. SPECTER. Dr. McClelland, did you and I sit down together for just a few minutes before I started to take your deposition today?

Dr. MCCLELLAND. Yes, sir.

Mr. SPECTER. And I discussed this matter with you?

Dr. MCCLELLAND. Yes.

Mr. SPECTER. And, during the course of our conversations at that time, did we cover the same material in question form here and to which you have responded in answer form with the court reporter here today?

Dr. MCCLELLAND. Yes.

Mr. SPECTER. And has the information which you have given me on the record been the same as that which you gave me off of the record in advance?

Dr. MCCLELLAND. Yes.

Mr. SPECTER. Do you have any interest, Dr. McClelland in reading your testimony over or signing it at the end, or would you be willing to waive any such signature of the testimony?

Dr. MCCLELLAND. I would be willing to waive my signature.

Mr. SPECTER. Thank you so much for coming and giving us your deposition today.

Dr. MCCLELLAND. All right, thank you.

TESTIMONY OF DR. ROBERT M. McCLELLAND RESUMED

The testimony of Dr. Robert M. McClelland was taken at 3:25 p.m., on March 25, 1964, at Parkland Memorial Hospital, Dallas, Tex., by Mr. Arlen Specter, assistant counsel of the President's Commission.

Mr. SPECTER. May the record show that Dr. Robert M. McClelland has returned to have a brief additional deposition concerning a translation of "L' Express" which has been called to my attention in the intervening time which has elapsed between March 21, when I took Dr. McClelland's deposition on the first occasion, and today.

Dr. McClelland, will you raise your right hand? Do you solemnly swear that the testimony you will give to the President's Commission in this deposition proceeding will be the truth, the whole truth and nothing but the truth, so help you God?

Dr. MCCLELLAND. I do.

Mr. SPECTER. Dr. McClelland, I show you a translation from the French, of the magazine, "L' Express" issue of February 20, 1964, and ask you if you would read this item, with particular emphasis on a reference to a quotation or statement made by you to a reporter from the St. Louis Post Dispatch.

Dr. MCCLELLAND. (Examined instrument referred to.)

Mr. SPECTER. Now, have you had an opportunity to read over that excerpt?

Dr. MCCLELLAND. Yes.

Mr. SPECTER. Did you talk to a reporter from the St. Louis Post Dispatch about this matter?

Dr. MCCLELLAND. Yes.

Mr. SPECTER. And what was his name?

Dr. MCCLELLAND. Richard Dudman.

Mr. SPECTER. And when did you have that conversation with Mr. Dudman?

Dr. MCCLELLAND. As well as I recall, it was the day after the assassination, as nearly as I can recall, but I'm not certain about that.

Mr. SPECTER. Will you tell me as closely as you remember what he said to you and you said to him, please?

Dr. MCCLELLAND. The main point he seemed to be making was to attempt to define something about the wound, the nature of the wound, and as near as I can recall, I indicated to him that the wound was a small undamaged—appearing punctate area in the skin of the neck, the anterior part of the neck, which had the appearance of the usual entrance wound of a bullet, but that this certainly could not be—you couldn't make a statement to that effect with any complete degree of certainty, though we were, as I told him, experienced in seeing wounds of this nature, and usually felt that we could tell the difference between an entrance and an exit wound, and this was, I think, in essence what I told him about the nature of the wound.

Mr. SPECTER. Now, had you actually observed the wound prior to the time the tracheotomy was performed on that neck wound?

Dr. MCCLELLAND. No; my knowledge of the entrance wound, as I stated, in my former deposition, was merely from what Dr. Perry told me when I entered the room and began putting on a pair of surgical gloves to assist with the tracheotomy.

Dr. Perry looked up briefly and said that they had made an incision and were in the process of making an incision in the neck, which extended through the middle of the wound in question in the front of the neck.

Mr. SPECTER. Now, you have just characterized it in that last answer as an entrance wound.

Dr. MCCLELLAND. Well, perhaps I shouldn't say the wound anyway, not the entrance wound—that might be a slip of the tongue.

Mr. SPECTER. Do you have a firm opinion at this time as to whether it is an entrance wound or exit wound or whatever?

Dr. MCCLELLAND. Of course, my opinion now would be colored by everything that I've heard about it and seen since, but I'll say this, if I were simply looking at the wound again and had seen the wound in its unchanged state, and which I did not, and, of course, as I say, it had already been opened up by the tracheotomy incision when I saw the wound—but if I saw the wound in its state in which Dr. Perry described it to me, I would probably initially think this were an entrance wound, knowing nothing about the circumstances as I did at the time, but I really couldn't say—that's the whole point. This would merely be a calculated guess, and that's all, not knowing anything more than just seeing the wound itself.

Mr. SPECTER. But did you, in fact, see the wound prior to the time the incision was made?

Dr. MCCLELLAND. No.

Mr. SPECTER. So that any preliminary thought you had even, would be based upon what you had been told by Dr. Perry?

Dr. MCCLELLAND. That's right.

Mr. SPECTER. Now, did you tell Mr. Dudman of the St. Louis Post Dispatch that you did not in fact see the wound in the neck, but your only information of it came from what Dr. Perry had told you?

Dr. MCCLELLAND. I don't recall whether I told him that or not. I really don't remember whether I said I had seen the wound myself or whether I was merely referring to our sort of collective opinion of it, or whether I told him I had not seen the wound and was merely going by Dr. Perry's report of it to me. I don't recall now, this far away in time exactly what I said to him.

Mr. SPECTER. Dr. McClelland, I want to ask you a few additional questions, and some of these questions may duplicate questions which I asked you last Saturday, and the reason for that is, we have not yet had a chance to transcribe the deposition of last Saturday, so I do not have before me the questions I asked you at that time and the answers you gave, and since last Saturday I have taken the depositions of many, many doctors on the same topics, so it is not possible for me to be absolutely certain of the specific questions which I asked you at that time, but permit me to ask you one or several more questions on the subject.

First, how many bullets do you think were involved in inflicting the wounds on President Kennedy which you observed?

Dr. MCCLELLAND. At the present time, you mean, or at the immediate moment?

Mr. SPECTER. Well, take the immediate moment and then the present time.

Dr. MCCLELLAND. At the moment, of course, it was our impression before we had any other information from any other source at all, when we were just confronted with the acute emergency, the brief thoughts that ran through our minds were that this was one bullet, that perhaps entered through the front of the neck and then in some peculiar fashion which we really had, as I mentioned the other day, to strain to explain to ourselves, had coursed up the front of the vertebra and into the base of the skull and out the rear of the skull.

This would have been a very circuitous route for the bullet to have made, so that when we did find later on what the circumstances were surrounding the   assassination, this was much more readily explainable to ourselves that the two wounds were made by two separate bullets.

Mr. SPECTER. And what is your view or opinion today as to how many bullets inflicted the injuries of President Kennedy?

Dr. MCCLELLAND. Two.

Mr. SPECTER. Now, what would be the reason for your changing your opinion in that respect?

Dr. MCCLELLAND. Oh, just simply the later reports that we heard from all sources, of all the circumstances surrounding the assassination. Certainly no further first-hand information came to me and made me change my mind in that regard.

Mr. SPECTER. Dr. McClelland, let me ask you to assume a few additional facts, and based on a hypothetical situation which I will put to you and I'll ask you for an opinion.

Assume, if you will, that President Kennedy was shot on the upper right posterior thorax just above the upper border of the scapula at a point 14 cm. from the tip of the right acromion process and 14 cm. below a tip of the right mastoid process, assume further that that wound of entry was caused by a 6.5-mm. missile shot out of a rifle having a muzzle velocity of approximately 2,000 feet per second, being located 160 to 250 feet away from President Kennedy, that the bullet entered on the point that I described on the President's back, passed between two strap muscles on the posterior aspect of the President's body and moved through the fascial channel without violating the pleura cavity, and exited in the midline lower third anterior portion of the President's neck, would the hole which Dr. Perry described to you on the front side of the President's neck be consistent with the hole which such a bullet might make in such a trajectory through the President's body?

Dr. MCCLELLAND. Yes; I think so.

Mr. SPECTER. And what would your reasoning be for thinking that that would be a possible hole of exit on those factors as I have outlined them to you?

Dr. MCCLELLAND. Well, I think my reasoning would be basically that the missile was traveling mainly through soft tissue, rather than exploding from a bony chamber and that by the time it reached the neck that it had already lost, because of the distance from which it was fired, even though the muzzle velocity was as you stated—would have already lost a good deal of its initial velocity and kinetic strength and therefore would have perhaps made, particularly, if it were a fragment of the bullet as bullets do sometimes fragment, could have made a small hole like this in exiting. It certainly could have done that.

Mr. SPECTER. What would have happened then to the other portion of the bullet if it had fragmented?

Dr. MCCLELLAND. It might have been left along, or portions of it along the missile track—sometimes will be left scattered up and down this. Other fragments will maybe scatter in the wound and sometimes there will be multiple fragments and sometimes maybe only a small fragment out of the main bullet, sometimes a bullet will split in half—this is extremely difficult for me to say just what would happen in a case like that.

Mr. SPECTER. Well, assuming this situation—that the bullet did not fragment, because the autopsy report shows no fragmentation, that is, it cannot show the absence of fragmentation, but we do know that there were no bullets left in the body at any point, so that no fragment is left in.

Dr. MCCLELLAND. I think even then you could make the statement that this wound could have resulted from this type bullet fired through this particular mass of soft tissue, losing that much velocity before it exited from the body. Where you would expect to see this really great hole that is left behind would be, for instance, from a very high velocity missile fired at close range with a heavy caliber bullet, such as a .45 pistol fired at close range, which would make a small entrance hole, relatively, and particularly if it entered some portion of the anatomy such as the head, where there was a sudden change in density from the brain to the skull cavity, as it entered. As it left the body, it would still have a great deal of force behind it and would blow up a large segment of tissue as it exited. But I don't think the bullet of this nature fired from that distance and going through this large area of homogenous soft tissue would necessarily make the usual kind of exit wound like I just described, with a close range high velocity heavy caliber bullet.

This is why it would be difficult to say with certainty as has been implied in some newspaper articles that quoted me, that you could tell for sure that this was an entrance or an exit wound. I think this was blown up a good deal.

Mr. SPECTER. Dr. McClelland, why wasn't the President's body turned over?

Dr. MCCLELLAND. The President's body was not turned over because the initial things that were done as in all such cases of extreme emergency are to first establish an airway and second, to stop hemorrhage and replace blood, so that these were the initial things that were carried out immediately without taking time to do a very thorough physical examination, which of course would have required that these other emergency measures not be done immediately.

Mr. SPECTER. Did you make any examination of the President's back at all?

Dr. MCCLELLAND. No.

40

Mr. SPECTER. Was any examination of the President's back made to your knowledge?

Dr. MCCLELLAND. Not here—no.

Mr. SPECTER. Do you have anything to add which you think might be helpful in any way to the Commission?

Dr. MCCLELLAND. No; I think not except again to emphasize perhaps that some of our statements to the press about the nature of the wound may have been misleading, possibly—probably because of our fault in telling it in such a way that they misinterpreted our certainty of being able to tell entrance from exit wounds, which as we say, we generally can make an educated guess about these things but cannot be certain about them. I think they attributed too much certainty to us about that.

Mr. SPECTER. Now, have you talked to anyone from the Federal Government about this matter since I took your deposition last Saturday?

Dr. MCCLELLAND. No.

Mr. SPECTER. And did you and I chat for a moment or two with my showing you this translation of "L' Express" prior to the time we went on the record here?

Dr. MCCLELLAND. Yes.

Mr. SPECTER. And is the information which you gave to me in response to my questions the same that we put on the record here?

Dr. MCCLELLAND. To the best of my knowledge—yes.

Mr. SPECTER. Thank you very much, Dr. McClelland.

Dr. MCCLELLAND. All right. Thank you.

TESTIMONY OF DR. CHARLES RUFUS BAXTER

The testimony of Dr. Charles Rufus Baxter was taken at 11:15 a.m., on March 24, 1964, at Parkland Memorial Hospital, Dallas, Tex., by Mr. Arlen Specter, assistant counsel of the President's Commission.

Mr. SPECTER. May the record show that Dr. Charles Baxter is present in response to a letter requesting him to appear and give his deposition. For the record I shall state that the President's Commission on the Assassination of President Kennedy is investigating all facets of the shooting, including the medical treatment performed on President Kennedy.

Dr. Baxter has been asked to give a deposition on his participation in connection with the care and medical treatment of President Kennedy, and with that statement of purpose, would you please stand up, Dr. Baxter, and raise your right hand.

Do you solemnly swear the testimony you give before the President's Commission in the course of this deposition proceeding will be the truth, the whole truth and nothing but the truth, so help you God?

Dr. BAXTER. I do.

Mr. SPECTER. Would you state your full name, please?

Dr. BAXTER. Charles Rufus Baxter.

Mr. SPECTER. What is your profession, sir?

Dr. BAXTER. I am a medical doctor of surgery, general surgeon.

Mr. SPECTER. Will you outline briefly your educational background?

Dr. BAXTER. University of Texas—1948 through 1950. Southwestern Medical School, 1950 through 1954, 1955 straight medicine internship, 1956 medicine residency—internal medicine residency. 1956 through 1958, surgical research at Brooke Army Medical Center, 1958 through 1964—surgical residency, and 1964 through the present—this is 1964, I got out of the Army—in 1958, 1958 through 1962—surgery residency, and 1962 until now, assistant professor of surgery.

Mr. SPECTER. And are you board certified, Doctor?

Dr. BAXTER. Yes.

Mr. SPECTER. And what boards have you passed?

Dr. BAXTER. The American Board of Surgeons.

Mr. SPECTER. And what year were you so certified?

Dr. BAXTER. 1963.

Mr. SPECTER. And what is your specific title at the medical school?

Dr. BAXTER. Assistant professor of surgery.

Mr. SPECTER. Did you have occasion to aid in the treatment of President Kennedy at Parkland Hospital?

Dr. BAXTER. Yes.

Mr. SPECTER. And will you outline briefly the circumstances surrounding your being called to render such assistance?

Dr. BAXTER. I was conducting the student health service in the hours of 12 to 1 and was contacted there by the supervisor of the emergency room, who told me that the President was on the way to the emergency room, having been shot.

I went on a dead run to the emergency room as fast as I could and it took me about 3 or 4 minutes to get there.

Mr. SPECTER. Approximately what time did you arrive at the emergency room?

Dr. BAXTER. I think it was 12:40—thereabouts.

Mr. SPECTER. And who was present at that time?

Dr. BAXTER. Dr. Carrico and Dr. Jones and Dr. Jenkins—several nurses.

Mr. SPECTER. Can you identify the nurses?

Dr. BAXTER. Yes; Mrs. Nelson—and who else? There were two or three others whose names—Miss Henchliffe was there.

Mr. SPECTER. Miss Bowron?

Dr. BAXTER. Who?

Mr. SPECTER. Was Miss Bowron there?

Dr. BAXTER. Yes; I believe so.

Mr. SPECTER. Were any other nurses there?

Dr. BAXTER. One or two more, but I'm not sure of their names.

Mr. SPECTER. Can you identify any other doctors who were there at that time?

Dr. BAXTER. Oh, let's see—I'm not sure whether the others came before or after I did. There was Crenshaw, Peters, and Kemp Clark, Dr. Bashour finally came. I believe Jackie Hunt—yes—she was, I believe she was the anesthesiologist who came.

Mr. SPECTER. Was Dr. Don Curtis there?

Dr. BAXTER. I'm not sure—I just don't remember.

Mr. SPECTER. When you arrived, what did you observe as to the condition of the President?

Dr. BAXTER. He was very obviously in extremis. There was a large gaping wound in the skull which was covered at that time with blood, and its extent was not immediately determined. His eyes were bulging, the pupils were fixed and dilated and deviated outward, both pupils were deviated laterally. At that time his breathing was being assisted so that whether he was breathing on his own or not, I couldn't determine.

Mr. SPECTER. In what way was his breathing being assisted?

Dr. BAXTER. With an anesthesia machine.

Mr. SPECTER. Would you continue to describe what you observed as to his condition?

Dr. BAXTER. There were no pulses that I could feel present. The anesthesiologist told me that he did still have a heartbeat.

Mr. SPECTER. Who is that who said that to you?

Dr. BAXTER. Well, I believe this was Carrico who said that his heart was still beating. There was present at the time two intravenous catheters in place with fluids running. We were informed at that time—well, having looked over the rest of the body, the only other wound was in his neck, that we saw.

Dr. Carrico said that he had observed a tracheal laceration. At that moment Dr. Jones, I believe, was placing in a left anterior chest tube because of this information. We proceeded at that time with a tracheotomy.

Mr. SPECTER. Who performed the tracheotomy?

Dr. BAXTER. Dr. Perry and myself, with the assistance of Dr. McClelland, and I believe that's all—there may have been one more person that held the retractor.

Mr. SPECTER. What else, if anything, did you do for President Kennedy at that time?

Dr. BAXTER. During the tracheotomy, I helped with the insertion of a right anterior chest tube, and then helped Dr. Perry complete the tracheotomy. At that point none of us could hear a heartbeat present. Apparently this had ceased during the tracheotomy and the chest tube placement.

We then gave him or Dr. Perry and Dr. Clark alternated giving him closed chest cardiac massage only until we could get a cardioscope hooked up to tell us if there were any detectible heartbeat electrically present, at least, and there was none, and we discussed at that moment whether we should open the chest to attempt to revive him, while the closed chest massage was going on, and we had an opportunity to look at his head wound then and saw that the damage was beyond hope, that is, in a word—literally the right side of his head had been blown off. With this and the observation that the cerebellum was present—a large quantity of brain was present on the cart, well—we felt that such an additional heroic attempt was not warranted, and we did not pronounce him dead but ceased our efforts, and awaited the priest and last rites before we pronounced him dead.

Mr. SPECTER. Did the priest then arrive to perform the last rites?

Dr. BAXTER. Yes.

Mr. SPECTER. At what time was he pronounced dead?

Dr. BAXTER. As I recall, it was 1:08, I'm not sure, it may have been that that was Oswald.

Mr. SPECTER. But it was approximately 1 o'clock? Then, could the time of death be fixed with any precision?

Dr. BAXTER. I don't think so—the time elapsing in all of this resuscitation and the time the heart actually ceased, I don't think one could be very sure of it. It was sometime between a quarter to 1 and 1 o'clock.

Mr. SPECTER. Have you now described all of the efforts which were made to save the life of the President?

Dr. BAXTER. Only with the exception, I think, of the fluids that were administered. He was given hydrocortisone because of his previous medical condition. He was given no negative blood because the blood loss was rather fierce and, I believe that's all.

Mr. SPECTER. What other doctors arrived during the course of the treatment, in addition to those whom you have already mentioned?

Dr. BAXTER. I don't recall—I know that there were more doctors present in the room, but their names, I'm not sure of. The reason I'm not sure is because we had some of the same crew and a different crew on the Governor and on Oswald, and I'm afraid that I've gotten them mixed up.

Mr. SPECTER. Now, will you describe in as much particularity as you can the nature of the head wound?

Dr. BAXTER. The only wound that I actually saw—Dr. Clark examined this above the manubrium of the sternum, the sternal notch. This wound was in temporal parietal plate of bone laid outward to the side and there was a large area, oh, I would say 6 by 8 or 10 cm. of lacerated brain oozing from this wound, part of which was on the table and made a rather massive blood loss mixed with it and around it.

Mr. SPECTER. Did you notice any bullet hole below that large opening at the top of the head?

Dr. BAXTER. No; I personally did not.

Mr. SPECTER. Will you describe with as much particularity as you can the wound which you noticed on the President's neck?

Dr. BAXTER. The wound on the neck was approximately an inch and a half above the manubrium of the sternum, the sternal notch. This wound was in my estimation, 4 to 5 mm. in widest diameter and was a spherical wound. The edges of it—the size of the wound is measured by the hole plus the damaged skin around the area, so that it was a very small wound. And, it was directly in the midline. Now, this wound was excised in the performance of the tracheotomy and on the entry into the deeper tissues of the neck, there was considerable contusion of the muscles of the anterior neck and a moderate amount of bleeding around the trachea. The trachea was deviated slightly, I believe, to the left.

Our tracheotomy incision was made in the second tracheal ring which was immediately above the area of damage—where we thought the damaged area of the trachea was, which we did not dissect out, but once the endrotracheal tube was placed, the tracheotomy tube was placed into the trachea, it was below this tear in the trachea, and gave us good control or perfect control of respiration.

Mr. SPECTER. Were the characteristics of the wound on the neck sufficient to enable you to form an opinion with reasonable medical certainty as to what was the cause of the hole?

Dr. BAXTER. Well, the wound was, I think, compatible with a gunshot wound. It did not appear to be a jagged wound such as one would expect with a very high velocity rifle bullet. We could not determine, or did not determine at that time whether this represented an entry or an exit wound. Judging from the caliber of the rifle that we later found or become acquainted with, this would more resemble a wound of entry. However, due to the density of the tissues of the neck and depending upon what a bullet of such caliber would pass through, the tissues that it would pass through on the way to the neck, I think that the wound could well represent either exit or entry wound.

Mr. SPECTER. Assuming some factors in addition to those which you personally observed, Dr. Baxter, what would your opinion be if these additional facts were present: First, the President had a bullet wound of entry on the right posterior thorax just above the upper border of the scapula with the wound measuring 7 by 4 mm. in oval shape, being 14 cm. from the tip of the right acromion process and 14 cm. below the tip of the right mastoid process—assume this is the set of facts, that the wound just described was caused by a 6.5 mm. bullet shot from approximately 160 to 250 feet away from the President, from a weapon having a muzzle velocity

43

of approximately 2,000 feet per second, assuming as a third factor that the bullet passed through the President's body, going in between the strap muscles of the shoulder without violating the pleura space and exited at a point in the midline of the neck, would the hole which you saw on the President's throat be consistent with an exit point, assuming the factors which I have just given to you?

Dr. BAXTER. Although it would be unusual for a high velocity missile of this type to cause a wound as you have described, the passage through tissue planes of this density could have well resulted in the sequence which you outline; namely, that the anterior wound does represent a wound of exit.

Mr. SPECTER. What would be the considerations which, in your mind, would make it, as you characterized it, unlikely?

Dr. BAXTER. It would be unlikely because the damage that the bullet would create would be—first its speed would create a shock wave which would damage a larger number of tissues, as in its path, it would tend to strike, or usually would strike, tissues of greater density than this particular missile did and would then begin to tumble and would create larger jagged—the further it went, the more jagged would be the damage that it created; so that ordinarily there would have been a rather large wound of exit.

Mr. SPECTER. But relating the situation as I hypothesized it for you?

Dr. BAXTER. Then it is perfectly understandable that this wound of exit was not of any greater magnitude than it was.

Mr. SPECTER. Dr. Baxter, is there a channel through which the bullet could have passed in the general direction which I have described to you where there would be very few tissues and virtually no tissues of great density?

Dr. BAXTER. Yes; passing through the fascial plane which you have described, it could well not have these things happen to it, so that it would pass directly through—almost as if passing through a sheet of paper and the wound of exit would be no larger than the wound we saw.

Mr. SPECTER. What would the situation there be as to the shock wave which you have heretofore described?

Dr. BAXTER. There would be a large amount of tissue damage which is not ordinarily seen immediately after a bullet has passed through. This is damage that is recognized several days later.

Mr. SPECTER. What causes the shock waves there, Doctor?

Dr. BAXTER. This is just the velocity imparting pressure to surrounding tissues which damages them. It does not show, however, in the early course after a missile has passed through.

Mr. SPECTER. Well, would the shock waves have any effect upon the size, and nature of the hole of exit?

Dr. BAXTER. No.

Mr. SPECTER. And if the bullet passed through the fascial plane without striking tissues of great density, would it have a tendency to tumble at all?

Dr. BAXTER. No, it would not.

Mr. SPECTER. What has your experience been, if any, Doctor, with gunshot wounds?

Dr. BAXTER. For the past 6 years—we admit and treat, I would estimate, around 500 gunshot wounds per year—thereabouts.

Mr. SPECTER. Have you ever had any formal training in gunshot wounds?

Dr. BAXTER. Only that I received in the Army, with demonstration of various velocities and that type missile wounds.

Mr. SPECTER. Where was President Kennedy lying when you first saw him, Dr. Baxter?

Dr. BAXTER. On the cart, on the emergency cart in trauma room 1.

Mr. SPECTER. Was he ever taken off of that cart from the time you first saw him until the time he was pronounced dead?

Dr. BAXTER. No.

Mr. SPECTER. Was he ever turned over?

Dr. BAXTER. No.

Mr. SPECTER. Would your examination have been conducted in any different way had this particular victim not been the President of the United States?

Dr. BAXTER. I think—yes—in that we would have, particularly, postmortem examined the body much more carefully than we did. We would certainly have undressed him completely and determined all of the direction of the wounds at the time. This did not seem feasible under the circumstances.

Mr. SPECTER. Why was it not feasible under the circumstances?

Dr. BAXTER. Mrs. Kennedy was in the room, there was a large number of people in the room by that time—Secret Service Agents, the priests and so on. As soon as the President was

44

pronounced dead, the Secret Service more or less—well, requested that we clear the room and leave them with the President's body, which was done. Everything that the Secret Service wished was carried out.

Mr. SPECTER. What was that?

Dr. BAXTER. Everything that the Secret Service asked us to do, we did, as rapidly as possible and this was one of their requests.

In addition, I must say that the emotional condition of all of us at that time was such that probably we would not—we didn't feel that we should do any more, since we were certain that autopsy would take care of all that we were going to miss.

Mr. SPECTER. Did the emotional situation have any effect in your professional opinion on the quality of the medical care which was rendered to the President?

Dr. BAXTER. No; none at all. We, I think, everyone present in the room was certainly emotionally involved in the care of the President, but in no instance did I see less than the most meticulous and best judgment used in the care of the President.

Mr. SPECTER. And what, in your opinion, was the cause of death, Dr. Baxter?

Dr. BAXTER. Gunshot wound to the head.

Mr. SPECTER. Would you have an opinion as to whether or not President Kennedy would have survived the gunshot wound which you observed in the neck?

Dr. BAXTER. We saw no evidence that it had struck anything in the neck that would not be well taken care of by simply—by the tracheotomy and chest tubes.

Mr. SPECTER. Did you find any bullets in the President's body?

Dr. BAXTER. No, we did not.

Mr. SPECTER. Any fragments of bullets in the President's body?

Mr. BAXTER. No, sir.

Mr. SPECTER. Dr. Baxter, I now show you Commission Exhibit 392, which has been heretofore identified in Commission Proceedings as the report from Parkland Memorial Hospital, and I now call your attention to a page which purports to bear your signature, and a written report which you rendered under date of November 22, 1963. I ask you, first of all, if that is your signature?

Dr. BAXTER. Yes.

Mr. SPECTER. And, if this is the report which you submitted?

Dr. BAXTER. Yes.

Mr. SPECTER. Do you have any other writings or notes of any sort concerning your care of President Kennedy?

Dr. BAXTER. No.

Mr. SPECTER. Will you read into the record, Dr. Baxter, the contents of your report, because it is a little hard to read in spots?

Dr. BAXTER. "I was contacted at approximately 12:40 that the President was on the way to the Emergency Room, having been shot. On arrival there, I found an endotracheal tube in place with assisted respirations, a left chest tube being inserted, and cutdowns going in one leg and in the left arm.

The President had a wound in the midline of the neck. On first observation of the remaining wounds, the temporal and parietal bones were missing and the brain was lying on the table with extensive lacerations and contusions. The pupils were fixed and deviated laterally and dilated. No pulse was detectable, respirations were (as noted) being supplemented. A tracheotomy was performed by Dr. Perry and I and a chest tube inserted into the right chest (second interspace anteriorly). Meanwhile, 2 pints of O negative blood was administered by pump without response. When all of these measures were complete, no heartbeat could be detected, closed chest massage was performed until a cardioscope could be attached, which revealed no cardiac activity was obtained.

Due to the extensive and irreparable brain damage which was detected, no further attempt to resuscitate the heart was made."

Mr. SPECTER. And that bears your signature?

Dr. BAXTER. Charles R. Baxter, M.D., assistant professor of surgery, Southwestern Medical School, University of Texas.

Mr. SPECTER. Dr. Baxter, has any representative of the Federal Government ever talked to you about this matter prior to today?

Dr. BAXTER. The only person was a Secret Service Agent about—approximately three weeks ago who asked me if I had any additional written comments anywhere or had made any writings on the medical treatment of the President, and the answer was "No."

45

Mr. SPECTER. Now, prior to the time that the court reporter started to transcribe my questions and your answers, did you and I briefly discuss this deposition proceeding, its purpose and the questions which I would ask you?

Dr. BAXTER. Yes.

Mr. SPECTER. And are the answers given on the record here the same as you gave me in our brief conversation before the transcription was started?

Dr. BAXTER. Yes.

Mr. SPECTER. Do you have anything to add which you think might be helpful in any way to the work of the Commission?

Dr. BAXTER. No.

Mr. SPECTER. Thank you very much for coming, Dr. Baxter.

Dr. BAXTER. Thank you.

TESTIMONY OF DR. MARION THOMAS JENKINS

The testimony of Dr. Marion Thomas Jenkins was taken at 5:30 p.m., on March 25, 1964, at Parkland Memorial Hospital, Dallas, Tex., by Mr. Arlen Specter, assistant counsel of the President's Commission.

Mr. SPECTER. May the record show that Dr. M. T. Jenkins has appeared in response to a letter request in connection with the inquiry of the President's Commission on the Assassination of President Kennedy, to testify concerning his observations and medical treatment performed by him on President Kennedy, and with this preliminary statement of purpose, would you stand up, please, Dr. Jenkins, and raise your right hand.

Do you solemnly swear the testimony you give before the President's Commission in this deposition proceeding, will be the truth, the whole truth, and nothing but the truth, so help you God?

Dr. JENKINS. I do.

Mr. SPECTER. Would you state your full name for the record, please?

Dr. JENKINS. Marion Thomas Jenkins.

Mr. SPECTER. What is your profession, please?

Dr. JENKINS. I'm a physician.

Mr. SPECTER. Are you licensed by the State of Texas to practice medicine?

Dr. JENKINS. Yes.

Mr. SPECTER. And what is your specialty, Dr. Jenkins?

Dr. JENKINS. Anesthesiology.

Mr. SPECTER. Will you outline your educational background for me, please?

Dr. JENKINS. I am a graduate of the University of Texas in 1937. I have a B.A. degree and an M.D. degree from the University of Texas Medical Branch at Galveston in 1940, rotating internship at the University of Kansas Hospital, Kansas City, Kans., 1940–41; Assistant Residency in Internal Medicine, John Sealy Hospital in Galveston, Tex., 1941–42; active duty in the U.S. Navy as a Medical Officer, 1942 to 1946; Resident in Surgery—Parkland Hospital, Dallas, 1946–47; Resident in anesthesiology in the Massachusetts General Hospital, Boston, 1947–48; and Director of the Department of Anesthesiology, Parkland Hospital and Parkland Memorial Hospital, 1948 to the present; Professor and Chairman of the Department of Anesthesiology, University of Texas, Southwestern Medical School—since 1951. Diplomate—other certification, do you want this?

Mr. SPECTER. Yes, what Boards are you certified?

Dr. JENKINS. I am a Diplomate of the American Board of Anesthesiology and also fellow of the American College of Anesthesiologists.

Mr. SPECTER. And what year were you certified by the American Board?

Dr. JENKINS. 1952.

Mr. SPECTER. Did you have occasion to assist in the treatment of President Kennedy on November 22, 1963?

Dr. JENKINS. Yes.

Mr. SPECTER. And will you relate briefly the circumstances surrounding your being called into that case?

Dr. JENKINS. Well, I was in the dining room with other members of the hospital staff when we heard the Chief of Surgery, Dr. Tom Shires, being paged "Stat." This is a rather unusual call, for the Chief of any service to be called "Stat" as this is the emergency call.

Mr. SPECTER. What does that mean, "Stat"?

Dr. JENKINS. "Stat" means emergency, that's just a code word that has been used for years in medical terms. He was paged twice this way, and one of the surgical residents, Dr. Ronald

Jones, answered the phone, thinking something bad must be up and that he would call the Chief of Surgery. I was sitting near the telephone and Dr. Jones immediately came back by with a very anguished look and the color was drained from his face—I'm sure I had that impression, and he said, "The President has been shot and is on his way to the hospital." At the same time we heard the sirens of the ambulance as they turned into the driveway from Harry Hines into the hospital drive, and it was obvious that this was the car coming in because the ambulance sirens usually stop in the street, but these came on clear to the building.

Mr. SPECTER. That's Harry Hines Boulevard right in front of the hospital?

Dr. JENKINS. Yes; I ran up the stairs to the Anesthesia Department, that's on the second floor—one floor above the dining room, where I was, and notified two members of the Department, the first two I saw, my Chief Associate, Dr. A. H. Giesecke, Jr., and Dr. Jackie Hunt, that the President had been shot and was being brought to the emergency room and for them to bring all the resuscitative equipment we have including an anesthesia machine. The emergency room is set up well, but we are used to working with our own equipment and I asked them to bring it down and I ran down the back stairs, two flights down, and I arrived in the emergency room just after or right behind him being wheeled in, I guess.

Mr. SPECTER. At about what time did you arrive at the emergency room?

Dr. JENKINS. Oh, this was around 12:30–12:35 to 12:40. I shouldn't be indefinite about this—in our own specialty practice, we watch the clock closely, and there are many things we have to keep up with, but I didn't get that time exactly, I'll admit.

Mr. SPECTER. Who was present at the time of your arrival in the emergency room, if anyone?

Dr. JENKINS. The hallway was loaded with people.

Mr. SPECTER. What medical personnel were in attendance?

Dr. JENKINS. Including Mrs. Kennedy, I recognized, and Secret Service men, I didn't know whether to block the way or get out of it, as it turned out. Dr. James Carrico and Dr. Dulany—Dick Dulany, I guess you have his name, and several nurses were in the room.

Mr. SPECTER. Could you identify the nurses?

Dr. JENKINS. Well, not really. I could identify them only having later looked around and identified from my own record that I have, the names of all who were there later. Now, whether they are the same ones when I first went there, I don't know. I have all the names in my report, it seemed to me.

Mr. SPECTER. Could you now identify all of the nurses from your later observations of them?

Dr. JENKINS. Well, I can identify who was in there at the close of the procedure, that is, the doctors, as well as those who were helping.

Mr. SPECTER. Fine, would you do that for us, please?

Dr. JENKINS. These included a Mrs. or Miss Patricia Hutton and Miss Diana Bowron, B-o-w-r-o-n (spelling), and a Miss Henchliffe—I don't know her first name, but I do know it is Henchliffe.

Mr. SPECTER. Margaret?

Dr. JENKINS. Margaret—certainly. Those three—there were probably some student nurses too, whom I didn't recognize. Shall I continue?

Mr. SPECTER. Yes, please. Have you now covered all the people you recollect as being in the room?

Dr. JENKINS. Well, as I came into the room, I saw only the—actually—you know, in the haste of the coming of the President, two doctors whom I recognized, and there were other people and I have identified all I remember.

Mr. SPECTER. What did you observe as to the President's condition when you arrived in the emergency room?

Dr. JENKINS. Well, I was aware of what he was in an agonal state. This is not a too unfamiliar state that we see in the Service, as much trauma as we see, that is, he had the agonal respiratory gasp made up of jerking movements of the mylohyoid group of muscles. These are referred to sometimes as chin jerk, tracheal tug or agonal muscles of respiration. He had this characteristic of respiration. His eyes were opened and somewhat exophthalmic and color was greatly suffused, cyanotic—a purplish cyanosis.

Still, we have patients in the state, as far as cyanosis and agonal type respiration, who are resuscitatable. Of course, you don't stop at this time and think, "Well, this is a hopeless circumstance,"—because one in this state can often be resuscitated—this represents the activities prior to one's demise sometimes, and if it can be stopped, such as the patient is oxygenated again and circulation reinstituted, he can be saved.

47

Dr. Carrico had just introduced an endotracheal tube, I'm very proud of him for this because it's not as easy as it sounds. At times and under the circumstances—it was harder—he had just completed a 3-month rotation on the anesthesiology service, and I thought this represented good background training for a smart individual, and he told me he had a cuff on the endotracheal tube and he introduced it below the wound.

The reason I said this, of course, this is a reflex—there is a tube, the endotracheal tube, if it is pushed down a little too far it can go into the right main stem of the bronchus impairing respiration from both lungs, or both chests.

There was in the room an intermittent positive pressure breathing apparatus, which can be used to respire for a patient. As I connected this up, however, Dr. Carrico and I connected it up to give oxygen by artificial respiration, Dr. Giesecke and Dr. Hunt arrived on the scene with the anesthesia machine and I connected it up instead with something I am more familiar with—not for anesthesia, I must insist on that—it was for the oxygenation, the ability to control ventilation with 100 percent oxygen.

As I came in there, other people came in also. This is my recollection. Now, by this time I was in familiar surroundings, despite the anguish of the circumstance.

Despite the unusual circumstance, in terms of the distinguished personage who was the patient, I think the people who had gathered or who had congregated were so accustomed to doing resuscitative procedures of this nature that they knew where to fit into the resuscitation team without having a preconceived or predirected plan, because, as obviously—some people were doing things not necessarily in their specialty, but there was the opening and there was the necessity for this being done.

There were three others who came in as I did who recognized at once the neck wound, in fact, where the wound was, would indicate that we would have serious pulmonary problems unless a tracheotomy tube was put in. This is one way of avoiding pushing air out through a fractured trachea and down into each chest cavity, which would cause a pneumothorax or a collapse of the lungs. These were doctors Malcolm Perry, Charley Baxter, and Robert McClelland, who with Dr. Carrico's help, I believe, started the tracheotomy.

About this time Drs. Kemp Clark and Paul Peters came in, and Dr. Peters because of the appearance of the right chest, the obvious physical characteristics of a pneumothorax, put in a closed chest drainage—chest tube. Because I felt no peripheral pulse and was not aware of any pulse, I reported this to Dr. Clark and he started closed chest cardiac massage.

There were other people—one which started an I.V. in a cutdown in the right leg and one a cutdown in the left arm. Two of my department connected up the cardioscope, in which we had electrical silence on the cardioscope as Dr. Clark started closed chest massage. That's the sequence of events as I reconstructed them that day and dictated them on my report, which you have here, I think.

Mr. SPECTER. Speaking of your report, Dr. Jenkins, permit me to show you a group of papers heretofore identified as Commission Exhibit No. 392 which has also been identified by Mr. Price, the hospital Administrator, as being photostatic copies of original reports in his possession and controlled as Custodian of Records, and I show you what purports to be a report from you to Mr. Price, dated November 22, 1963, and ask you if in fact this 2-page report was submitted by you to Mr. Price?

Dr. JENKINS. Yes; it was.

Mr. SPECTER. Now, going back to the wound which you observed in the neck, did you see that wound before the tracheotomy was performed?

Dr. JENKINS. Yes; I did, because I was just connecting up the endotracheal tube to the machine at the time and that's when Dr. Carrico said there was a wound in the neck and I looked at it.

Mr. SPECTER. Would you describe that wound as specifically as you can?

Dr. JENKINS. Well, I'm afraid my description of it would not be as accurate, of course, as that of the surgeons who were doing the tracheotomy, because my look was a quick look before connecting up the endotracheal tube to the apparatus to help in ventilation and respiration for the patient, and I was aware later in the day, as I should have put it in the report, that I thought this was a wound of exit because it was not a clean wound, and by "clean" clearly demarcated, round, punctate wound which is the usual wound of an entrance wound, made by a missile and at some speed. Of course, entrance wounds with a lobbing type missile, can make a jagged wound also, but I was of the impression and I recognized I had the impression it was an exit wound. However, my mental appreciation for a wound—for the wound in the neck, I believe, was sort of—was overshadowed by recognition of the wound in the scalp and skull plate.

Mr. SPECTER. Have you now described the wound in the neck as specifically as you can at this moment?

Dr. JENKINS. I believe so.

Mr. SPECTER. Now, will you now describe the wound which you observed in the head?

Dr. JENKINS. Almost by the time I was—had the time to pay more attention to the wound in the head, all of these other activities were under way. I was busy connecting up an apparatus to respire for the patient, exerting manual pressure on the breathing bag or anesthesia apparatus, trying to feel for a pulse in the neck, and then reaching up and feeling for one in the temporal area, seeing about connecting the cardioscope or directing its being connected, and then turned attention to the wound in the head.

Now, Dr. Clark had begun closed chest cardiac massage at this time and I was aware of the magnitude of the wound, because with each compression of the chest, there was a great rush of blood from the skull wound. Part of the brain was herniated; I really think part of the cerebellum, as I recognized it, was herniated from the wound; there was part of the brain tissue, broken fragments of the brain tissue on the drapes of the cart on which the President lay.

Mr. SPECTER. Did you observe any wounds immediately below the massive loss of skull which you have described?

Dr. JENKINS. On the right side?

Mr. SPECTER. Yes, sir.

Dr. JENKINS. No—I don't know whether this is right or not, but I thought there was a wound on the left temporal area, right in the hairline and right above the zygomatic process.

Mr. SPECTER. The autopsy report discloses no such development, Dr. Jenkins.

Dr. JENKINS. Well, I was feeling for—I was palpating here for a pulse to see whether the closed chest cardiac massage was effective or not and this probably was some blood that had come from the other point and so I thought there was a wound there also.

Mr. SPECTER. At approximately what time was President Kennedy pronounced dead?

Dr. JENKINS. Well, this was pronounced, we know the exact time as 1300, according to my watch, at least, at the time.

Mr. SPECTER. And what, in your opinion, was the cause of death?

Dr. JENKINS. Cerebral injury—brain injury.

Mr. SPECTER. Was President Kennedy ever turned over during the course of this treatment at Parkland?

Dr. JENKINS. No.

Mr. SPECTER. Why was he not turned over, Dr. Jenkins?

Dr. JENKINS. Oh, I think this was beyond our prerogative completely. I think as we pronounced the President dead, those in attendance who were there just sort of melted away, well, I guess "melted" is the wrong word, but we felt like we were intruders and left. I'm sure that this was considerably beyond our prerogative, and the facts were we knew he had a fatal wound, and I think my own personal feeling was that this was—would have been meddlesome on anybody's part after death to have done any further search.

Mr. SPECTER. Was any examination of his back made before death, to your knowledge?

Dr. JENKINS. No, no; I'm sure there wasn't.

Mr. SPECTER. Did he remain on the stretcher cart at all times while he was being cared for?

Dr. JENKINS. Yes, sir.

Can I say something that isn't in the report here, or not?

Mr. SPECTER. Yes; let's go off the record a minute.

(Discussion off the record between Counsel Specter and the witness, Dr. Jenkins.)

Mr. SPECTER. May the record show that we are back on the record and Dr. Jenkins has made an interesting observation about the time of the declaration of death, and I will ask you, Dr. Jenkins, for you to repeat for the record what you have just said off the record.

Dr. JENKINS. As the resuscitative maneuvers were begun, such as "chest cardiac massage," there was with each compression of the sternum, a gush of blood from the skull wound, which indicated there was massive vascular damage in the skull and the brain, as well as brain tissue damage, and we recognized by this time that the patient was beyond the point of resuscitation, that he was in fact dead, and this was substantiated by getting a silent electrical pattern on the electrocardiogram, the cardioscope that was connected up.

However, for a period of minutes, but I can't now define exactly, since I didn't put this in a report, after we knew he was dead, we continued attempted resuscitative maneuvers.

When we saw the two priests who arrived in the corridor outside the emergency room where this was taking place, I went to the door and asked one of those—after turning over my ventilation, my respiration job to another one of my department—and asked him what is the proper time to declare one dead. That is, I am not a Catholic and I was not sure of the time for the last rites. As I remember now, he said, "The time that the soul leaves the body—is not at

49

exactly the time that medical testimony might say that death was declared." There would be a period of time and so if we wished to declare him dead at that time they would still have the final rites.

Mr. SPECTER. Did they then have the final rites after the time he was declared dead medically?

Dr. JENKINS. Well, just a minute now—I suspect that was hazy to me that day—I'm not sure, it's still hazy. This was a very personal—on the part of the very anguished occasion, and Mrs. Kennedy had come back into the room and most of the people were beginning to leave because they felt like this was such a grief stricken and private affair that they should not be there. It was real intrusion even after they put forth such efforts at resuscitation and I'm not sure now whether the priests came in while I was still doing the resuscitative procedure, respiration at least, and while Dr. Clark was still doing the other. My memory is that we had stopped. I was still present, however, and that's the reason I'm not clear, because I hadn't left the room and I was still there as the rites were performed and a prayer was said.

Mr. SPECTER. Dr. Jenkins, would your observation of the wound and your characterization of it as an exit hole be consistent with a set of facts which I will ask you to assume for purposes of giving me your view or opinion.

Assume, first of all, if you will, that President Kennedy had a wound on the upper right posterior thorax just above the upper border of the scapula, measuring 14 cm. from the tip of the right acromion process and 14 cm. below the tip of the right mastoid process, and that the missile was a 6.5 mm. jacketed bullet fired from a weapon having a muzzle velocity of approximately 2,000 feet per second and approximately 160 to 250 feet from the President, and that after entering the President's body at the point indicated, the missile traveled between two strap muscles and through a fascia plane without violating the pleura cavity, and then struck the right side of the trachea and exited through the throat, would the throat wound which you observed be consistent with such a wound inflicted in the manner I have just described?

Dr. JENKINS. As far as I know, it wouldn't be inconsistent with it, Mr. Specter.

Mr. SPECTER. What has your experience been with gunshot wounds, that is, to what extent have you had experience with such wounds?

Dr. JENKINS. Well, having been Chief of the Anesthesia Service here for this 16 years, we have a rather large trauma emergency service, and so I see gunshot wounds many times a week. I'm afraid I couldn't hazard a guess at the moment as to how many we see a year, and I'm afraid probably if I knew, I would not like to admit to this number, but I do go further in saying that my main interest is not in the tracks of the wounds. My main interest is what physiological changes that they have caused to the patient that I am to anesthetize or a member of the department is to anesthetize, what has happened to the cardiovascular system, respiratory, and neurological, and so I am aware of the wounds of entrance and exit only by a peripheral part of my knowledge and activities during the time.

Mr. SPECTER. Have you ever had any formal training in ballistics or in exit wounds or entrance wounds—bullet wounds?

Dr. JENKINS. No, I have not.

Mr. SPECTER. Have you talked to any representative of the Federal Government at any time prior to today?

Dr. JENKINS. Oh, there was a man whose name I don't remember now, who showed what looked like the proper credentials from the FBI, who came to ask only whether the report I had submitted to Mr. Price for the hospital record or for Mr. Price's record constituted all the reports I had. That's the only time, and that was the extent of our conversation, I think.

Mr. SPECTER. And is that the only written record you have of your participation in the treatment of the President?

Dr. JENKINS. Oh, I submitted one to the Dean of the Medical School, essentially the same, and a very little more. I don't think you have that. I don't know whether you want it or not.

Mr. SPECTER. Yes, I would like to see it.

Dr. JENKINS. It is essentially the same report—however—can I ask you something off of the record here?

Mr. SPECTER. Sure.

(Discussion between Counsel Specter and the witness, Dr. Jenkins, off the record.)

Mr. SPECTER. The record will show that we have been off the record on a couple of matters which I am going to now put on the record, but I will ask the court reporter to identify this as Dr. Jenkins' Exhibit No. 36.

(Instrument referred to marked by the Reporter as Dr. Jenkins' Exhibit No. 36, for identification.)

Mr. SPECTER. I will ask you, Dr. Jenkins, for the record to identify this as a report which you submitted to Dean Gill.

Dr. JENKINS. Yes, it is.

Mr. SPECTER. And is this in conjunction with the report you submitted to Mr. Price—do these reports constitute all the writings you have on your participation in the treatment of President Kennedy?

Dr. JENKINS. Yes; that's right.

Mr. SPECTER. One of the comments we were just discussing off the record—I would like to put on the record, Dr. Jenkins, is the question as to whether or not the wound in the neck would have been fatal in your opinion, absent the head wound. What would your view of that be?

Dr. JENKINS. Well, from my knowledge of the wound in the neck, this would not have been fatal, except for one thing, and that is—you have not told me whether the wound with its point of entrance and point of exit had contacted the vertebral column in its course?

Mr. SPECTER. It did not.

Dr. JENKINS. In that case I would not expect this wound to have been fatal.

Mr. SPECTER. What is your view, Dr. Jenkins, as to whether the wounds which you observed were caused by one or two bullets?

Dr. JENKINS. I felt quite sure at the time that there must have been two bullets—two missiles.

Mr. SPECTER. And, Dr. Jenkins, what was your reason for that?

Dr. JENKINS. Because the wound with the exploded area of the scalp, as I interpreted it being exploded, I would interpret it being a wound of exit, and the appearance of the wound in the neck, and I also thought it was a wound of exit.

Mr. SPECTER. Have you ever changed any of your original opinions in connection with the wounds received by President Kennedy?

Dr. JENKINS. I guess so. The first day I had thought because of his pneumothorax, that his wound must have gone—that the one bullet must have traversed his pleura, must have gotten into his lung cavity, his chest cavity, I mean, and from what you say now, I know it did not go that way. I thought it did.

Mr. SPECTER. Aside from that opinion, now, have any of your other opinions about the nature of his wounds or the sources of the wounds been changed in any way?

Dr. JENKINS. No; one other. I asked you a little bit ago if there was a wound in the left temporal area, right above the zygomatic bone in the hairline, because there was blood there and I thought there might have been a wound there (indicating).

Mr. SPECTER. Indicating the left temporal area?

Dr. JENKINS. Yes; the left temporal, which could have been a point of entrance and exit here (indicating), but you have answered that for me. This was my only other question about it.

Mr. SPECTER. So, that those two points are the only ones on which your opinions have been changed since the views you originally formulated?

Dr. JENKINS. Yes, I think so.

Mr. SPECTER. On the President's injuries?

Dr. JENKINS. Yes, I think so.

Mr. SPECTER. Is the conversation you had with that Secret Service Agent the only time you were interviewed by anyone from the Federal Government prior to today about this subject?

Dr. JENKINS. As far as I remember—I don't believe so.

Mr. SPECTER. Now, you say that was the only time you were interviewed?

Dr. JENKINS. Yes, as far as I remember—I have had no formal interviews. I have been asked—there have been some people calling on the phone. As you know, there were many calls from various sources all over the country after that, wanting to know whether we had done this method of treatment or some other method and what principles we followed.

Mr. SPECTER. But the only one you can identify as being from the Federal Government is the one you have already related from the Secret Service?

Dr. JENKINS. Yes.

Mr. SPECTER. And did you and I have a very brief conversation before the deposition started today, when you gave me some of your views which you expounded and expanded upon during the course of the deposition on the record?

Dr. JENKINS. Yes.

Mr. SPECTER. And is there anything which you think of to add that you believe would be of some assistance or any assistance to the President's Commission in its inquiry?

Dr. JENKINS. I believe not, Mr. Specter.

Mr. SPECTER. Well, thank you very much, Dr. Jenkins.

Dr. JENKINS. All right.

TESTIMONY OF DR. RONALD COY JONES

The testimony of Dr. Ronald Coy Jones was taken at 10:20 a.m., on March 24, 1964, at Parkland Memorial Hospital, Dallas, Tex., by Mr. Arlen Specter, assistant counsel of the President's Commission.

Mr. SPECTER. May the record show at this point that Dr. Ronald Jones has arrived in response to a letter of request to give his deposition for the President's Commission on the assassination of President Kennedy.

Dr. Jones, the purpose of the President's Commission is to investigate all the facts relating to the shooting and subsequent medical treatment of President Kennedy and we have asked you to appear to testify concerning your knowledge of that treatment.

With that statement of purpose, will you stand up and raise your right hand. Do you solemnly swear the testimony you give before the President's Commission during the course of this deposition proceeding will be the truth, the whole truth, and nothing but the truth, so help you God?

Dr. JONES. I do.

Mr. SPECTER. Would you state your full name for the record, please?

Dr. JONES. Ronald Coy Jones.

Mr. SPECTER. What is your profession, sir?

Dr. JONES. General Surgery—resident physician.

Mr. SPECTER. Are you duly licensed by the State of Texas to practice medicine?

Dr. JONES. Yes.

Mr. SPECTER. Will you outline briefly your educational background?

Dr. JONES. I graduated—I went to undergraduate school at the University of Arkansas from 1950 to 1953, in pre-med. From 1953 through 1957, I went to medical school and graduated from the University of Tennessee in Memphis, and in 1957 through 1958 I took an internship in Los Angeles County General Hospital.

From there I went to the University of Oklahoma and took a 2-year general practice residency, 1 year, the first year, entailing a year of internal medicine and its subspecialties, and a second year of surgery and its subspecialties, which was approved by the American Board of Surgeons for 1 year of surgical training, and from 1960 until the present time I have taken an additional 4 years of general surgery at Parkland, and have served as Chief Resident of Surgery.

Mr. SPECTER. Did you have occasion to aid in the medical treatment of President Kennedy on November 22, 1963?

Dr. JONES. Yes, sir.

Mr. SPECTER. Would you relate briefly the circumstances surrounding your being called into the case?

Dr. JONES. I was eating lunch with Dr. Perry and I heard the operator page Dr. Tom Shires of the staff on two occasions, and the second time I answered the phone and the operator told me that the President had been shot and was being brought to the emergency room.

I turned around and immediately notified Miss Audrey Bell, who is the operating room supervisor so that any arrangements could be made for immediate surgery, and Dr. M. T. Jenkins, who is the Chief of the Anesthesiology Department. From there I went across the room and notified Dr. Perry of the shooting and we both went together to the emergency room, and it was at that time we arrived shortly after the President had been brought in.

Mr. SPECTER. What is your best estimate as to the time you arrived at the emergency room?

Dr. JONES. It was, I would say, around 23 or 25 minutes until 1.

Mr. SPECTER. And who was present, if anyone, at the time you arrived?

Dr. JONES. Dr. James Carrico, and possibly Dr. Richard Dulany, and I'm not sure that he was there or was there for just a few minutes after we arrived. I do recall seeing him there as one of the first ones.

Mr. SPECTER. Was any nurse present at that time?

Dr. JONES. The head nurse in the emergency room was presentand——

Mr. SPECTER. Do you know her name?

Dr. JONES. It's left my mind right now—I know her.

Mr. SPECTER. Could that be Miss Henchliffe?

Dr. JONES. She was there, I believe.

Mr. SPECTER. Mrs. Bowron?

Dr. JONES. No—just the—

Mr. SPECTER. Mrs. Nelson?

Dr. JONES. Nelson.

Mr. SPECTER. Was anyone else present then, other than those whom you have already mentioned at the time you arrived?

Dr. JONES. There were three nurses there—Mrs. Nelson, Miss Henchliffe and Miss Bowron.

Mr. SPECTER. And were any other doctors present when you arrived?

Dr. JONES. Dr. Carrico was the only doctor other than possibly Dr. Dulany, and I do know Dr. Carrico was there when I arrived.

Mr. SPECTER. Was Dr. Don Curtis there when you arrived?

Dr. JONES. I didn't see him.

Mr. SPECTER. And who arrived with you, if you recall?

Dr. JONES. Dr. Perry.

Mr. SPECTER. And what did you observe the President's condition to be upon your arrival?

Dr. JONES. He appeared to be terminal, if not already expired, and Dr. Carrico said that he had seen some attempted respirations, agonal respirations, and with that history, we went ahead with emergency measures to try to restore the airway.

Mr. SPECTER. When you say "attempted agonal respiration," do you mean an effort by the President?

Dr. JONES. Yes.

Mr. SPECTER. Or, an effort by someone else to induce respiration?

Dr. JONES. No, these apparently were as Dr. Carrico saw the President was attempting to respire on his own, however, I did not personally see this in the brief seconds that I stood there before I went ahead and started work.

Mr. SPECTER. What is the lay definition for agonal respiration?

Dr. JONES. These are the respirations that are somewhat of a strain, that is, seen in a patient who is expiring—just very short, irregular type respirations.

Mr. SPECTER. Would you continue now to describe what you observed to be the President's condition?

Dr. JONES. We felt that he was in extreme shock, merely by the fact that there was no motion, that he was somewhat cyanotic, his eyes were—appeared to be fixed; there was no evidence of motion of the eyes; and we noticed that he did not have a satisfactory airway or was not breathing on his own in a satisfactory way to sustain life so that we felt that either an endotracheal tube had to be instituted immediately, which was done by Dr. Carrico. We felt that this was not adequate and since tracheotomy equipment was in the room, we felt that he would profit more by tracheotomy and that we could be certain that he was getting adequate oxygen.

Mr. SPECTER. What was done with respect to applying oxygen to the President then?

Dr. JONES. Well, a tracheotomy was done, and then an adapter was fitted to this tube, and we had an anesthesia machine there by this time with Dr. Jenkins available so that he could give him straight oxygen from the machine.

Mr. SPECTER. Did you observe anything else with respect to the President's condition at that time?

Dr. JONES. You mean as far as wounds—that he had?

Mr. SPECTER. Did you observe any wounds?

Dr. JONES. As we saw him the first time, we noticed that he had a small wound at the midline of the neck, just above the suprasternal notch, and this was probably no greater than a quarter of an inch in greatest diameter, and that he had a large wound in the right posterior side of the head.

Mr. SPECTER. When you say "we noticed," whom do you mean by that?

Dr. JONES. Well, Dr. Perry and I were the two that were there at this time observing.

Mr. SPECTER. Did Dr. Perry make any comment about the nature of the wound at that time? Either wound?

Dr. JONES. Not that I recall.

Mr. SPECTER. Will you describe as precisely as you can the nature of the head wound?

Dr. JONES. There was large defect in the back side of the head as the President lay on the cart with what appeared to be some brain hanging out of this wound with multiple pieces of skull noted next with the brain and with a tremendous amount of clot and blood.

Mr. SPECTER. Will you describe as precisely as you can the wound that you observed in the throat?

Dr. JONES. The wound in the throat was probably no larger than a quarter of an inch in diameter. There appeared to be no powder burn present, although this could have been masked

53

by the amount of blood that was on the head and neck, although there was no obvious amount of powder present. There appeared to be a very minimal amount of disruption of interruption of the surrounding skin. There appeared to be relatively smooth edges around the wound, and if this occurred as a result of a missile, you would have probably thought it was a missile of very low velocity and probably could have been compatible with a bone fragment of either—probably exiting from the neck, but it was a very small, smooth wound.

Mr. SPECTER. Did you notice any lump in the throat area?

Dr. JONES. No; I didn't.

Mr. SPECTER. Was there any blood on the throat area in the vicinity of the wound which you have described of the throat?

Dr. JONES. Not a great deal of blood, as if in relation to the amount that was around the head—not too much.

Mr. SPECTER. What further action was taken by the medical team in addition to that which you have described on the tracheotomy?

Dr. JONES. Well, as Dr. Perry started the tracheotomy, I started the cut down in the left arm to insert a large polyethylene catheter, to give an I.V. so that we could give I.V. solutions as well as blood, and at the same time another doctor or two were doing some cutdowns in the lower extremities around the ankle. We made the cutdown in the left arm in the cephalic vein very rapidly and I.V. fluids were started immediately and as I was doing this, Dr. Perry was performing the tracheotomy, and it was about this time that Dr. Baxter came in and went ahead to assist Dr. Perry with the tracheotomy, and as they made a deeper incision in the neck to isolate the trachea, they thought they saw some gush of air and the possibility of a pneumothorax on one side or the other was entertained, and since I was to the left of the President, I went ahead and put in the anterior chest tube in the second intercostal space.

Mr. SPECTER. Was that tube fully inserted, Doctor?

Dr. JONES. I felt that the tube was fully inserted, and this was immediately connected to underwater drainage.

Mr. SPECTER. What do you mean by "connected to underwater drainage", Dr. Jones?

Dr. JONES. The tube is connected to a bottle whereby it aerates in the chest from a pneumothorax and as the patient breathes, the air is forced out under the water and produces somewhat of a suction so that the lung will reexpand and will not stay collapsed and this will give adequate aeration to the body, and we decided to go ahead and put in a chest tube on the opposite side; since I could not reach the opposite side due to the number of people that were working on the President. Dr. Baxter was over there helping Dr. Perry on that side, as well as Dr. Paul Peters, the assistant head of urology here, and the three of us then inserted the chest tube on the right side, primarily done by Dr. Baxter and Dr. Peters on the right side.

Mr. SPECTER. Then what other treatment, if any, was afforded President Kennedy?

Dr. JONES. After the tracheotomy was done, the intravenous fluid, blood was started—I believe that the President was also administered some hydrocortisone because of his history of adrenal insufficiency, and at this time an electrocardiogram had been connected and it showed no evidence of a heartbeat. Closed cardiac massage was then first begun by Dr. Perry and then I believe that after about 5 minutes no significant or no myocardial activity was present and he was pronounced dead.

Mr. SPECTER. What history did you refer to of President Kennedy's adrenal insufficiency?

Dr. JONES. As I recall, there had been in news that the President had several years ago been on some type of steroid therapy and that he possibly had Addison's disease. We had no documented evidence that he did or did not, but caution was taken nonetheless in case his insufficiency was of severe enough nature, because at the time of severe trauma a patient with adrenal insufficiency often goes into a rapid degree of adrenal insufficiency and can expire from lack of steroids being produced from the adrenal gland in such a stressed situation.

Mr. SPECTER. Did you obtain that history from Mrs. Kennedy, or any other person on the scene?

Dr. JONES. No.

Mr. SPECTER. You just relied upon what had been occurring in the news?

Dr. JONES. Yes.

Mr. SPECTER. What would that reaction cause, if anything, if the President had no adrenal insufficiency?

Dr. JONES. This would not cause severe effects on any organ at all if the adrenal gland were producing enough steroids.

Mr. SPECTER. Did any other doctors arrive during the time this treatment was going on, other than those whom you have already mentioned?

54

Dr. JONES. Several doctors did subsequently appear in the room—Dr. McClelland appeared shortly after Dr. Baxter, within a matter of just a very few minutes, as well as Dr. Kemp Clark, who is head of neurosurgery here.

Mr. SPECTER. Any other doctors?

Dr. JONES. Dr. Jenkins was there and I think these are primarily the ones that actually had any part, as far as taking care of the President, although there were some other doctors in the room.

Mr. SPECTER. Dr. Jones, I now hand you a report which purports to bear your signature, labeled "Summary of treatment of the President," dated November 23, 1963, which I shall now ask the Court Reporter to mark as Dr. Jones' Exhibit No. 1.

(Instrument mentioned marked by the Reporter as Dr. Jones' Exhibit No. 1, for identification.)

Mr. SPECTER. I ask you if this in fact is your signature?

Dr. JONES. Yes.

Mr. SPECTER. And I ask you if this was the report which you submitted concerning your participation of the treatment of President Kennedy?

Dr. JONES. Yes; it was.

Mr. SPECTER. In this report, Dr. Jones, you state the following, "Previously described severe skull and brain injury was noted as well as a small hole in anterior midline of the neck thought to be a bullet entrance wound." What led you to the thought that it was a bullet entrance wound, sir?

Dr. JONES. The hole was very small and relatively clean cut, as you would see in a bullet that is entering rather than exiting from a patient. If this were an exit wound, you would think that it exited at a very low velocity to produce no more damage than this had done, and if this were a missile of high velocity, you would expect more of an explosive type of exit wound, with more tissue destruction than this appeared to have on superficial examination.

Mr. SPECTER. Would it be consistent, then, with an exit wound, but of low velocity, as you put it?

Dr. JONES. Yes; of very low velocity to the point that you might think that this bullet barely made it through the soft tissues and just enough to drop out of the skin on the opposite side.

Mr. SPECTER. What is your experience, Doctor, if any, in the treatment of bullet wounds?

Dr. JONES. During our residency here we have approximately 1 complete year out of the 4 years on the trauma service here, and this is in addition to the 2 months that we spend every other day and every other night in the emergency room during our first year, so that we see a tremendous number of bullet wounds here in that length of time, sometimes as many as four and five a night.

Mr. SPECTER. Have you ever had any formal training in bullet wounds?

Dr. JONES. No.

Mr. SPECTER. Have you ever had occasion to observe a bullet wound which was inflicted by a missile at approximate size of a 6.5 mm. bullet which passed   through the body of a person and exited from a neck without striking anything but soft tissue from the back through the neck, where the missile came from a weapon of the muzzle velocity of 2,000 feet per second, and the victim was in the vicinity of 160 to 250 feet from the weapon?

Dr. JONES. No; I have not seen a missile of this velocity exit in the anterior portion of the neck. I have seen it in other places of the body, but not in the neck.

Mr. SPECTER. What other places in the body have you seen it, Dr. Jones?

Dr. JONES. I have seen it in the extremity and here it produces a massive amount of soft tissue destruction.

Mr. SPECTER. Is that in the situation of struck bone or not struck bone or what?

Dr. JONES. Probably where it has struck bone.

Mr. SPECTER. In a situation where it strikes bone, however, the bone becomes so to speak a secondary missile, does it not, in accentuating the soft tissue damage?

Dr. JONES. Yes.

Mr. SPECTER. Dr. Jones, did you have any speculative thought as to accounting for the point of wounds which you observed on the President, as you thought about it when you were treating the President that day, or shortly thereafter?

Dr. JONES. With no history as to the number of times that the President had been shot or knowing the direction from which he had been shot, and seeing the wound in the midline of the neck, and what appeared to be an exit wound in the posterior portion of the skull, the only speculation that I could have as far as to how this could occur with a single wound would be that it would enter the anterior neck and possibly strike a vertebral body and then change its course and exit in the region of the posterior portion of the head. However, this was—there was some doubt that a missile that appeared to be of this high velocity would suddenly change its course by striking, but at the present—at that time, if I accounted for it on the basis of one shot, that would have been the way I accounted for it.

Mr. SPECTER. And would that account take into consideration the extensive damage done to the top of the President's head?

Dr. JONES. If this were the course of the missile, it probably—possibly could have accounted for it, although I would possibly expect it to do a tremendous amount of damage to the vertebral column that it hit and if this were a high velocity missile would also think that the entrance wound would probably be larger than the one that was present at the time we saw it.

Mr. SPECTER. Did you observe whether or not there was any damage to the vertebral column?

Dr. JONES. No, we could not see this.

Mr. SPECTER. Did you discuss this theory with any other doctor or doctors?

Dr. JONES. Yes; this was discussed after the assassination.

Mr. SPECTER. With whom?

Dr. JONES. With Dr. Perry—is the only one that I recall specifically, and that was merely as to how many times the President was shot, because even immediately after death, within a matter of 30 minutes, the possibility of a second gunshot wound was entertained and that possibly he had been shot more than once.

Mr. SPECTER. Did you observe any wound on the President's back?

Dr. JONES. No.

Mr. SPECTER. Was the President ever turned over?

Dr. JONES. Not while I was in the room.

Mr. SPECTER. What was he on when you first saw him?

Dr. JONES. He was on an emergency room cart, which is on wheels and can be changed to varying heights and also varying positions, as far as elevating the head or elevating the feet, lowering the head and so forth.

Mr. SPECTER. Was he ever taken off that cart from the time he was brought into the emergency room to the time he was pronounced to be dead?

Dr. JONES. No.

Mr. SPECTER. Doctor, are you working toward board certification at this time?

Dr. JONES. Yes.

Mr. SPECTER. And what is your status on your progress with that, generally?

Dr. JONES. I will finish my formal training in surgery in July of this year, which will complete 5 years of general surgery residency.

Mr. SPECTER. How old are you at the present time, Dr. Jones?

Dr. JONES. Thirty-one.

Mr. SPECTER. Have you discussed this matter with any representatives of the Federal Government prior to today?

Dr. JONES. Yes, I believe the Secret Service has been here on at least two occasions.

Mr. SPECTER. And what did they ask you on those occasions?

Dr. JONES. I think, primarily, to verify that what I had written was true and that I had been one of the first doctors to be in the room with the President.

Mr. SPECTER. Did they ask you anything else other than that?

Dr. JONES. On one occasion they asked if there were any other pieces of paper that had been written on as to the care that had been administered to the President that I had not turned in, and I told them "No."

Mr. SPECTER. And did you and I sit down and talk for a few minutes before we went on the record in this deposition, with me indicating to you the general purpose and the line of questioning, and you setting forth the same information which we have put on the record here today?

Dr. JONES. Yes, sir.

Mr. SPECTER. Do you have anything to add which you think might be helpful to the Commission in any way?

Dr. JONES. No, sir.

Mr. SPECTER. That concludes the deposition. Thank you very much, Dr. Jones.

Dr. JONES. All right.

TESTIMONY OF DR. DON TEEL CURTIS

The testimony of Dr. Don Teel Curtis was taken at 9:25 a.m., on March 24, 1964, at Parkland Memorial Hospital, Dallas, Tex., by Mr. Arlen Specter, assistant counsel of the President's Commission.

Mr. SPECTER. Let the record show that present are Dr. Don Curtis and the court reporter, in connection with the deposition proceeding being conducted by the President's Commission on the Assassination of President Kennedy, which is inquiring into all facets of the assassination, including the medical treatment performed for President Kennedy.

Dr. Don Curtis is appearing here this morning in response to a letter requesting him to testify concerning his knowledge of that medical treatment of President Kennedy. With that preliminary statement of the general objective of the Commission and the specific objective of this deposition proceeding, Dr. Curtis, will you rise and raise your right hand, please?

Do you solemnly swear the testimony you give before this Presidential Commission in this deposition proceeding will be the truth, the whole truth, and nothing but the truth, so help you God?

Dr. CURTIS. I do.

Mr. SPECTER. Would you state your full name for the record, please?

Dr. CURTIS. Dr. Don Teel, T-e-e-l (spelling) Curtis.

Mr. SPECTER. And what is your occupation or profession?

Dr. CURTIS. Oral surgeon.

Mr. SPECTER. Would you outline briefly your educational background?

Dr. CURTIS. I attended my freshman year at Boulder, Colo., Colorado University, 2 subsequent years of undergraduate work at Texas University, 4 years at Baylor Dental College, and I have been interning here for a year and a half.

Mr. SPECTER. What year did you graduate from Baylor Dental College?

Dr. CURTIS. 1962.

Mr. SPECTER. What is your age at the present time?

Dr. CURTIS. Twenty-six.

Mr. SPECTER. And what has your work consisted of here at Parkland Hospital?

Dr. CURTIS. I have functioned as an intern in oral surgery and also now am a resident this year in oral surgery.

Mr. SPECTER. Are you a licensed dentist?

Dr. CURTIS. Yes.

Mr. SPECTER. And when did you obtain that status in the State of Texas?

Dr. CURTIS. I think in August of 1962.

Mr. SPECTER. Did you have occasion to assist in the medical treatment of President John F. Kennedy on November 22, 1963?

Dr. CURTIS. Yes.

Mr. SPECTER. Would you outline briefly the circumstances surrounding your call or your joining in the participation in that medical effort?

Dr. CURTIS. I was—do you want me to tell from the time that I got to the emergency room?

Mr. SPECTER. Yes—how did you happen to get to the emergency room?

Dr. CURTIS. I was in our out-patient clinic and saw the President's car, or I saw that it had arrived at the emergency room entrance, and I went over there as a matter of curiosity and was directed into the emergency room and there was directed by a policeman into the room where President Kennedy was.

Mr. SPECTER. About what time was that?

Dr. CURTIS. I don't know—it was shortly after he arrived.

Mr. SPECTER. Approximately how long after he arrived?

Dr. CURTIS. I would say it was within—I would say within a minute after he arrived at the trauma room, although there's no way for me to know that.

Mr. SPECTER. Who was present in the trauma room at that time?

Dr. CURTIS. Dr. Carrico and a nurse, I believe.

Mr. SPECTER. Do you know the identity of the nurse?

Dr. CURTIS. No.

Mr. SPECTER. What did you observe, if anything, as to the condition of President Kennedy at that time?

Dr. CURTIS. I observed that he was in a supine position, with his head extended, and I couldn't see on my arrival—I couldn't see the nature of the wounds, however, Dr. Carrico was standing at the patient's head. Dr. Carrico had just placed an endotracheal tube and I participated in applying the Bird machine respirator into the endotracheal tube for artificial respiration.

Mr. SPECTER. How does it happen that you would participate to that effect in view of the fact that you are an oral surgeon?

Dr. CURTIS. We participate in the emergency room on traumatic injuries of both the face and the entire patient, because the face is hooked onto a patient. We have a tour through anesthesia. We spend time on general anesthesia where we learn management of the patient's airway which makes us, I would say, qualified, for airway management. In our training here at the hospital we many, many times have patients on intravenous infusion and so we are well acquainted with the procedures attendant with the management of I.V. fluids.

Mr. SPECTER. Is there always someone from oral surgery available at the trauma area?

Dr. CURTIS. One of the oral surgeons is on call at the emergency room at all times and we try to stay within a very short distance from the emergency room. We see many patients in the emergency room area.

Mr. SPECTER. Is that for the purpose of rendering aid for someone who would be injured in a way which would call for an oral surgeon?

Dr. CURTIS. Yes—maxillofacial injuries.

Mr. SPECTER. And in addition, you help out in a general way when there is an emergency situation?

Dr. CURTIS. Yes.

Mr. SPECTER. Now, was there anything in President Kennedy's condition which called for the application of your specific specialty?

Dr. CURTIS. No; there wasn't.

Mr. SPECTER. So, you aided in a general way in the treatment of him as an emergency case?

Dr. CURTIS. Yes.

Mr. SPECTER. Now, would you continue to tell me what you have observed with respect to his condition when you first saw him, including what you noted, if anything, with respect to his respiration.

Dr. CURTIS. It is very difficult to say whether or not the President was making a respiratory effort, but I'm not sure that he wasn't making a respiratory effort.

Mr. SPECTER. Do you think that he was making a respiratory effort?

Dr. CURTIS. He could have been, and that's as far as I can go on it.

Mr. SPECTER. Did you observe movements of the chest?

Dr. CURTIS. I thought I did.

Mr. SPECTER. What was his coloring?

Dr. CURTIS. He was pink—he wasn't cyanotic when I saw him.

Mr. SPECTER. And will you explain in lay terms what cyanotic means for the record at this point?

Dr. CURTIS. When the hemoglobin of the blood is reduced, it turns a blue color and the patient becomes blue, when a certain percentage of the hemoglobin is reduced. That's not a lay term either, but when the patient is in oxygen need or oxygen want, cyanosis would be apparent.

Mr. SPECTER. And how does that manifest itself in the patient?

Dr. CURTIS. The patient will be a blue, gray, ashen color.

Mr. SPECTER. What action was Dr. Carrico taking upon your arrival?

Dr. CURTIS. He had placed an endotracheal tube in the President's trachea for artificial respiration.

Mr. SPECTER. Was he doing anything else?

Dr. CURTIS. Yes; he was applying the Bird machine.

Mr. SPECTER. Will you describe what other steps he was taking, if any?

Dr. CURTIS. He directed that a tracheotomy setup be brought to the emergency room, and I think it was Dr. Carrico directed me to start the I.V. fluids.

Mr. SPECTER. And what, if anything, did you do in response to his direction?

Dr. CURTIS. I assisted him in fitting the tube from the Bird machine to the endotracheal tube and I assisted in removing some of the President's clothes and did the cutdown on his leg.

Mr. SPECTER. And what, specifically, did you do pursuant to the cutdown on his leg?

Dr. CURTIS. A small incision was made on the ankle and a vein is bluntly dissected free, small holes placed in the vein and a venous catheter is placed in this vein and a purse string ligature is then tied around the catheter at one end, and then the wound was closed with sutures.

Mr. SPECTER. Now, did you do anything else to the President following that operative procedure?

Dr. CURTIS. Then, the initial cutdown that I started was ineffective and infiltrated into the tissues. I think possibly I cut the knot too close of the purse string ligature, so I was getting ready to do another one and it was decided since fluids were going in the other leg, it wouldn't be necessary.

Mr. SPECTER. What other action did you take, if any, in the treatment of the President?

Dr. CURTIS. That's all.

Mr. SPECTER. Did you remain in the trauma room No. 1?

Dr. CURTIS. I did until he was pronounced dead.

Mr. SPECTER. What action was taken by anyone else in the trauma room while you were there?

Dr. CURTIS. My attention was focused on what I was doing, so I wasn't aware—I knew that a cutdown was being performed and that is about all I could see. I mean, I knew that a tracheotomy was being performed.

Mr. SPECTER. What other doctors were present there at that time?

Dr. CURTIS. I know that Dr. Perry was there and I know Dr. Baxter was there, and then I recall Dr. Jenkins from the Anesthesia Department, and Dr. Seldin, Dr. Crenshaw, and that's about all the doctors—I could think of others probably, but I can't remember now.

Mr. SPECTER. Can you identify any other nurses who were there?

Dr. CURTIS. No; I can't—I wasn't paying attention to the nurses.

Mr. SPECTER. During the course of your presence near President Kennedy, did you have any opportunity to observe any wounds on his body?

Dr. CURTIS. After I had completed the cutdown, I went around to the right side of the patient and saw the head wound.

Mr. SPECTER. And what did you observe there?

Dr. CURTIS. Oh—fragments of bone and a gross injury to the cranial contents, with copious amounts of hemorrhage.

Mr. SPECTER. Did you observe any other wound on the President?

Dr. CURTIS. No; I didn't. As I said before, I noticed the mass in the pre-tracheal area.

Mr. SPECTER. And when you say "as you said before," you mean in our previous discussions prior to going on the record here?

Dr. CURTIS. Yes.

Mr. SPECTER. And will you state now for the record what you did notice with respect to the tracheal area?

Dr. CURTIS. The President's head was extended or hyperextended and I noticed that in the suprasternal notch there was a mass that looked like a hematoma to me, or a blood clot in the tissues.

Mr. SPECTER. How big was that hematoma?

Dr. CURTIS. Oh, I think it was 5 cm. in size.

Mr. SPECTER. What color was it?

Dr. CURTIS. It had no color—there was just skin overlying it.

Mr. SPECTER. What did it appear to be?

Dr. CURTIS. Probably a hematoma.

Mr. SPECTER. Did you observe any perforation or hole in the President's throat?

Dr. CURTIS. No; I didn't. But that doesn't mean it wasn't there.

Mr. SPECTER. Did you have an opportunity to look closely for it?

Dr. CURTIS. I focused my attention on his neck for an instant, and that's all.

Mr. SPECTER. Did you hear any discussion among any of the doctors about an opening on his neck?

Dr. CURTIS. No; I didn't.

Mr. SPECTER. Did you make any written report concerning your activity on the President?

Dr. CURTIS. No; I didn't.

Mr. SPECTER. Have you any notes or writings of any sort concerning your work with the President?

Dr. CURTIS. No.

Mr. SPECTER. Have you talked to any representatives of the Federal Government about your participation in treating President Kennedy before today?

Dr. CURTIS. No; I haven't.

Mr. SPECTER. Prior to the time that we went on the record here with the court reporter, did you and I have a very brief conversation concerning the purpose of the deposition and the general questions which I would ask you on the record?

Dr. CURTIS. Yes.

Mr. SPECTER. And is the information which you have provided on the record the same as that which you gave me before the court reporter started taking notes?

Dr. CURTIS. Yes.

Mr. SPECTER. Do you have anything to add which you think would be helpful to the Commission in its work?

Dr. CURTIS. No; I don't think so.

Mr. SPECTER. Thank you very much, Dr. Curtis, for coming here today.

Dr. CURTIS. All right.

TESTIMONY OF DR. FOUAD A. BASHOUR

The testimony of Dr. Fouad A. Bashour was taken at 1:15 p.m., on March 25, 1964, at Parkland Memorial Hospital, Dallas, Tex., by Mr. Arlen Specter, assistant counsel of the President's Commission.

Mr. SPECTER. May the record show that Dr. Fouad Bashour has appeared pursuant to a letter of request from the President's Commission on the Assassination of President Kennedy, in connection with the Commission's inquiry into all of the factors surrounding the assassination of the President, including medical treatment received at Parkland Hospital, and Dr. Bashour's knowledge, if any, as related to the treatment in the emergency room.

With that preliminary statement of purpose, Dr. Bashour, would you mind rising and then raise your right hand?

Do you solemnly swear that the testimony you give before the President's Commission in this deposition proceeding will be the truth, the whole truth, and nothing but the truth, so help you God?

Dr. BASHOUR. I do.

Mr. SPECTER. Would you state your full name for the record, please?

Dr. BASHOUR. F-o-u-a-d (spelling), Fouad A. Bashour.

Mr. SPECTER. What is your profession, sir?

Mr. BASHOUR. I am an internist with a specialization in cardiology. I am associate professor of medicine.

Mr. SPECTER. Are you duly licensed by the State of Texas to practice medicine here?

Dr. BASHOUR. Yes.

Mr. SPECTER. And are you board certified at the present time?

Dr. BASHOUR. No, sir; I don't have my board because I am not yet a citizen. I will be taking my citizenship this year, I hope, and then I will be able to sit for the board.

Mr. SPECTER. Did you have occasion to assist in the treatment of President Kennedy back on November 22, 1963?

Dr. BASHOUR. Yes; we were called from the dining room, the doctors' dining room, and we went directly to the President Kennedy room.

Mr. SPECTER. When you say "we" whom do you mean by that?

Dr. BASHOUR. Dr. Seldin and myself—we left the dining room and went right straight down to the President's room.

Mr. SPECTER. And what is Dr. Seldin's first name?

Dr. BASHOUR. Donald.

Mr. SPECTER. And what is his specialty, if any?

Dr. BASHOUR. He's chairman of the department of medicine and professor of medicine. He is a specialist and a recognized famous specialist in renal diseases.

Mr. SPECTER. And what, in lay language, does that facet of medicine involve?

Dr. BASHOUR. Kidney diseases.

Mr. SPECTER. Did Dr. Seldin accompany you into the emergency room where President Kennedy was located?

Dr. BASHOUR. We went to the room together and then I was left alone because this is a problem—a heart problem.

Mr. SPECTER. Did Dr. Seldin remain in the room with you?

Dr. BASHOUR. Well, he came and stayed for—he just left the room after we came in.

Mr. SPECTER. How long did he stay in the room?

Dr. BASHOUR. A few seconds.

Mr. SPECTER. Who was present in the room when you arrived?

Dr. BASHOUR. When I arrived, Dr. Kemp Clark was doing the cardiac massage on the President, Dr. Jenkins was in charge of controlling artificial respiration of the President, and the probably there were some three or four—I don't remember.

Mr. SPECTER. And what did you observe the President's condition to be at the time you arrived?

Dr. BASHOUR. The President was lying on the stretcher, the head wound was massive, the blood was dripping from the head, and at that time the President had an endotracheal tube, and his pupils were dilated, his eyes were staring, and they were not reactive, there was no pulsations, his heart sounds were not present, and his extremities were cold.

Then, we attached the scope—the cardioscope and there was a flip, this was probably artificial. Upon stopping the cardiac machine, there was no cardiac activity. That means the heart was standing still. We continued cardiac massage and still there was no cardiac activities, so the President was declared dead shortly thereafter.

Mr. SPECTER. At approximately what time was he declared dead?

Dr. BASHOUR. Well, according to my notes, we said here, "Declared dead about 12:55," or so.

Mr. SPECTER. Was that a precise time fixed or was that just a general approximation?

Dr. BASHOUR. No, sir; approximation.

Mr. SPECTER. When you refer to the "flip" what do you mean by that, Dr. Bashour?

Dr. BASHOUR. On the scope—some change in the baseline of the scope.

Mr. SPECTER. Did that indicate some activity in the President's heart?

Dr. BASHOUR. No, sir; not necessarily.

Mr. SPECTER. What else could have accounted for the flip besides that?

Dr. BASHOUR. Anything extraneous could have accounted for that.

Mr. SPECTER. So, you require a number of flips before you inquire if there is heart activity?

Dr. BASHOUR. Well, it depends on the configuration of the flip—if the flip resembles an electrocardiogram activity—it shows cardiac activity.

Mr. SPECTER. Was that configuration of the flip like heart activity or not?

Dr. BASHOUR. It wasn't, as far as I know.

Mr. SPECTER. That is your field, is it not, you read those flips?

Dr. BASHOUR. Well, it's my field to see the electrocardiograms; yes.

Mr. SPECTER. And, in your professional opinion, the flip which you saw was not a conclusive indicator of heart activity?

Dr. BASHOUR. As a matter of fact, when he removed his hand, there was nothing.

Mr. SPECTER. And who is "he"?

Dr. BASHOUR. Dr. Clark, who was doing the cardiac massage.

Mr. SPECTER. What else was done to the President, if anything, in addition to those things you have already mentioned after you arrived on the scene?

Dr. BASHOUR. Really, as far as I know, it was the end of the scene—nothing was done afterward.

Mr. SPECTER. Did you observe any wound besides the head wound which you have just described?

Dr. BASHOUR. No; I did not observe any wounds.

Mr. SPECTER. What was the condition of the front part of the President's neck upon your arrival?

Dr. BASHOUR. The only thing—it was covered with the endotracheal tube—I did not really pay attention to it.

Mr. SPECTER. Did you have an opportunity to see the neck wound before the tracheotomy was performed?

Dr. BASHOUR. No; I came after everything was done to him.

Mr. SPECTER. Doctor, I show you a group of papers heretofore marked as "Commission Exhibit No. 392," and I call your attention to the photostatic copy of a sheet which purports to be a report made by you on November 22, 1963, at 4:45 p.m., is that your report?

Dr. BASHOUR. Yes.

Mr. SPECTER. And is that in fact your signature?

Dr. BASHOUR. Yes.

Mr. SPECTER. And are the facts set forth therein the essence of what you observed and what you know about this matter?

Dr. BASHOUR. Yes.

Mr. SPECTER. Have you talked to anyone from the Federal Government prior to today about your treatment of President Kennedy?

Dr. BASHOUR. There was a security officer or something called me on the phone one day and said did I write any note besides this note on the chart, and I said "No." I don't know his name even.

Mr. SPECTER. What note was he referring to?

61

Dr. BASHOUR. This note here.

Mr. SPECTER. He asked you if you wrote what?

Dr. BASHOUR. Other notes than this.

Mr. SPECTER. If you had any other notes?

Dr. BASHOUR. Yes.

Mr. SPECTER. And do you have any other notes other than the one I have just shown you?

Dr. BASHOUR. No.

Mr. SPECTER. Did the Secret Service agent ask you anything else other than that?

Dr. BASHOUR. No.

Mr. SPECTER. And did you talk to any other representative of the Federal Government on any occasion prior to today?

Dr. BASHOUR. No, sir.

Mr. SPECTER. And, did you and I talk for a few minutes about the type of questions I would be asking you during this deposition?

Dr. BASHOUR. Yes.

Mr. SPECTER. And is the information which you have given me on the record here and written down by the court reporter the same as you told me before she arrived?

Dr. BASHOUR. Yes.

Mr. SPECTER. And, will you give me just an outline of your educational background, Doctor?

Dr. BASHOUR. I got my baccalaureate from French Government in 1941—first part. I got my second part, baccalaureate in mathematics and science in 1942, I got my B.A. degree in 1944 from the American University of Beirut, my M.D. degree in 1949, and my Ph. D. in 1957 from the University of Minnesota. I came back to this country in 1959 from the American University of Beirut, as an instructor, and from 1959 to 1963 I jumped from instructor to assistant professor to associate professor in February 1963.

Mr. SPECTER. Do you have anything to add which you think will be helpful in any way to the President's Commission?

Dr. BASHOUR. No, sir.

Mr. SPECTER. Thank you very much for coming, Dr. Bashour.

Dr. BASHOUR. Thank you very much.

TESTIMONY OF DR. GENE COLEMAN AKIN

The testimony of Dr. Gene Coleman Akin was taken at 11:30 a.m., on March 25, 1964, at Parkland Memorial Hospital, Dallas, Tex., by Mr. Arlen Specter, assistant counsel of the President's Commission.

Mr. SPECTER. May the record show that Dr. Gene Akin is present in response to a letter request that he appear to have his deposition taken in connection with an inquiry being conducted by the President's Commission on the Assassination of President Kennedy. Dr. Akin is being asked to appear here today to testify concerning his knowledge, if any, about the condition of President Kennedy on arrival in Parkland Hospital and his treatment here.

With that preliminary statement of purpose, Dr. Akin, will you rise and raise your right hand, please?

Do you solemnly swear the testimony you shall give before the President's Commission in this deposition proceeding will be the truth, the whole truth and nothing but the truth, so help you God?

Dr. AKIN. I do.

Mr. SPECTER. Will you state your full name, please?

Dr. AKIN. Gene Coleman Akin.

Mr. SPECTER. What is your profession?

Dr. AKIN. Medicine.

Mr. SPECTER. Are you duly licensed to practice in Texas, to practice medicine?

Dr. AKIN. Yes.

Mr. SPECTER. Do you have any specialty?

Dr. AKIN. Anesthesiology.

Mr. SPECTER. And are you board-certified?

Dr. AKIN. No.

Mr. SPECTER. Are you working toward board-certification?

Dr. AKIN. Yes.

Mr. SPECTER. Would you outline briefly your educational background?

Dr. AKIN. Premedical school at University of Texas in Austin, medical school, Southwestern Medical School Branch of the University of Texas, internship, Dallas Methodist Hospital, and anesthesiology residence at Parkland Memorial Hospital, starting in July 1962.

Mr. SPECTER. And, in what year did you graduate from medical school?

Dr. AKIN. 1961.

Mr. SPECTER. And how old are you at the present time, Doctor?

Dr. AKIN. Thirty-four.

Mr. SPECTER. Did you have occasion to render assistance to President John F. Kennedy on November 22, 1963?

Dr. AKIN. Briefly.

Mr. SPECTER. Would you state how you came to be called into the case?

Dr. AKIN. I was notified while I was on duty in the operating suite of the hospital that anesthesia assistance was needed in the emergency room. President Kennedy supposedly had been shot and had been brought to the emergency room, and I immediately went down the back elevator to the emergency room to see if I could be of assistance, and when I walked in, a tracheotomy was being performed. President Kennedy still had an endotracheal tube, an oro-tracheal tube in place, and the connector from this to the Bird respirator was removed. The anesthesia machine had been simultaneously rolled into the room and Dr. Jenkins connected the anesthesia machine to the oro-tracheal tube and it stayed there for a brief period, until the tracheotomy tube was placed in the tracheotomy, at which time I connected the breathing tubes from the anesthesia machine to the tracheotomy and held this in place while Dr. Jenkins controlled the ventilation with 100-percent oxygen from the anesthesia machine.

Mr. SPECTER. Did you assist Dr. Jenkins then in his work?

Dr. AKIN. Only insofar as I held the endotracheal connector in place into the tracheotomy tube.

Mr. SPECTER. What doctors in addition to Dr. Jenkins then were present, if any, at the time of your arrival?

Dr. AKIN. You mean everybody in the room? I don't know that I can name all of them.

Mr. SPECTER. Name as many as you can, if you will, please?

Dr. AKIN. There was Dr. Jenkins, there was myself for a brief period, there was Dr. Giesecke, Dr. Jackie Hunt—they left shortly after arriving. I heard later that they had gone across the hall to Governor Connally's room to assist him; Dr. Malcolm Perry, Dr. Charles Baxter, Dr. Kemp Clark, Dr. Bob McClelland, Dr. James Carrico, Dr. Ron Jones, was there. I think, shortly after I arrived, and Dr. Fouad Bashour came in from cardiology; Dr. Don Seldin walked in briefly, I can't remember the team that worked on the cutdowns on the legs—I can't remember that. This is sort of hazy, because it was a couple of days later we went through the same business over again and I am liable to say that there was somebody there that worked on Kennedy that actually had worked on Oswald, because I was on the Oswald mess too. This is all that I remember were positively there. I remember their being there, but there were others that I am not sure of.

Mr. SPECTER. What did you observe as to the President's condition?

Dr. AKIN. He looked moribund in my medical judgment.

Mr. SPECTER. Did you observe any wounds on him at the time you first saw him?

Dr. AKIN. There was a midline neck wound below the level of the cricoid cartilage, about 1 to 1.5 cm. in diameter, the lower part of this had been cut across when I saw the wound, it had been cut across with a knife in the performance of the tracheotomy. The back of the right occipitalparietal portion of his head was shattered, with brain substance extruding.

Mr. SPECTER. Returning to the wound which you first described, can you state in any more detail the appearance of it at the time you first saw it?

Dr. AKIN. I don't think I could—this is about all I noticed. I noticed this wound very briefly and it was a matter of academics as to how he sustained the wound. My attention, because of my standing on the right side of the patient who was lying supine, my attention was very soon directed to the head wound, and this was my major concern.

Mr. SPECTER. And as to the neck wound, did you have occasion to observe whether there was a smooth, jagged, or what was the nature of the portion of the neck wound, which had not been cut by the tracheotomy?

Dr. AKIN. It was slightly ragged around the edges.

Mr. SPECTER. And when you said that——

Dr. AKIN. No powder burns; I didn't notice any powder burns.

Mr. SPECTER. What was the dimension of the punctate wound, without regards to the tracheotomy which was being started?

Dr. AKIN. It looked—it was as you said, it was a punctate wound. It was roughly circular, about, I would judge, 1.5 cm. in diameter.

Mr. SPECTER. What did you mean when you just made your reference to the academic aspect with the wound, Dr. Akin?

Dr. AKIN. Well, naturally, the thought flashed through my mind that this might have been an entrance wound. I immediately thought it could also have been an exit wound, depending upon the nature of the missile that made the wound.

Mr. SPECTER. What would be the circumstances on which it might be one or the other?

Dr. AKIN. Well, if the President had been shot with a low velocity missile, such as fire from a pistol, it was more likely to have been an entrance wound, is that what you mean?

Mr. SPECTER. Yes.

Dr. AKIN. If, however, he had been shot with a high velocity military type of rifle, for example, it could be either an entrance wound or an exit wound.

Mr. SPECTER. Why do you say it could be either an entrance wound or an exit wound with respect to the rifle?

Dr. AKIN. Well, because a high velocity missile coming from a military rifle, especially if the missile were a jacketed missile, a copper- or steel-jacketed missile, itself, the missile itself is not distorted when it passes through soft tissue, and the wound made when the bullet leaves the body, is a small wound, much like the wound of entrance, but like I said, I didn't devote much time to conjecture about this.

Mr. SPECTER. How much experience have you had, if any, on gunshot wounds, doctor?

Dr. AKIN. I can't really give you, say, how many cases a week I see of this. Most of my experience with this is in an anesthetic situation with patients coming into the hospital, having sustained gunshot injuries, most of them are injured with low velocity missiles, smaller caliber— .22 caliber to .38 caliber, and most of them are not injured in a through and through fashion. In other words, I don't see too many exit wounds, the bullets are slow moving, and they enter the body and don't leave it. They usually stay in it, so consequently I could not be considered an expert in exit wounds.

Mr. SPECTER. Is that the general line of bullet wounds which come into Parkland Hospital, would you say?

Dr. AKIN. What I have just described, you mean?

Mr. SPECTER. Yes.

Dr. AKIN. Yes; I think so. Most of the people seem to be shot with cheap ammunition fired out of inferior weapons.

Mr. SPECTER. Would your experience with the type of bullet wounds you have just described be about the same as the other doctors have here at Parkland, or would there be some difference between what you have seen on bullet wounds and what the other doctors have seen?

Dr. AKIN. I think so, except there is one difference—I am not ordinarily on duty in the emergency room, so I am not very often the first doctor to see one of these people injured in this fashion. When I see them they are people who have sustained a gunshot injury, but who lived to make it to the operating room. We, I'm sure, have a lot of people who are shot and who are dead on arrival at the emergency room, and they are examined by the emergency room physicians, and I never see them, so there would be a lot of people down there that I never have seen. They might be injured with a hunting rifle or a good quality ammunition, and I would not have seen them.

Mr. SPECTER. Dr. Akin, permit me, if you will, to give you a set of facts which I will ask you to assume for the purpose of giving me an opinion, if you are able to formulate one. Assume that the President was struck by a 6.5 mm. missile which had a muzzle velocity of approximately 2,000 feet per second at a time when the President was approximately 160 to 250 feet away from the weapon. Assume further that the bullet entered the President's body in the upper right posterior thorax just above the upper border of the scapula at a point 14 cm. from the tip of the right acromion process and 14 cm. below the tip of the right mastoid process. Assume further that the missile traveled through or in between, rather, the strap muscles without penetrating either muscle but going in between the two in the area of his back and traveled through the fascial channel without violating the pleura cavity, and that the bullet struck the side of the trachea and exited from the throat in the position of the punctate wound which you have described you saw, would the wound you saw be consistent with a wound of exit under the factors that I have just outlined to you?

Dr. AKIN. As far as I know, it is perfectly compatible from what you have described, except when you say it passed through without injuring the strap muscles, are you talking about the anterior strap muscles of the neck or are you talking about the posterior muscles of the neck?

Mr. SPECTER. The anterior strap muscles of the neck.

64

Dr. AKIN. It's a matter of clarification because there are no strap muscles posterior, by my terminology. Yes, this is perfectly consistent with what I know about, or what I have been told by military experts, concerning high velocity missile injuries.

Mr. SPECTER. And what is the basis of your information from the military experts you just referred to?

Dr. AKIN. Military rifle demonstrations when I was a senior student at Brooks Air Force Base in San Antonio. We took a brief two day tour there with demonstrations of high velocity missile injury.

Mr. SPECTER. With respect to the head wound, Dr. Akin, did you observe below the gaping wound which you have described any other bullet wound in the back of the head?

Dr. AKIN. No; I didn't. I could not see the back of the President's head as such, and the right posterior neck was obscured by blood and skull fragments and I didn't make any attempt to examine the neck.

Mr. SPECTER. Did you have any opportunity to observe the President's clothes?

Dr. AKIN. I noticed them.

Mr. SPECTER. With respect to examining the shirt, for example, to see what light that would shed, if any, on the trajectory of the bullet?

Dr. AKIN. No; I didn't. The front of the chest was uncovered, the pants had been loosened and lowered below the iliac crest, and the only article of clothing I noticed in particular was his back corset.

Mr. SPECTER. What did you observe with respect to the back corset which you just mentioned?

Dr. AKIN. It had been loosened and was just lying loose.

Mr. SPECTER. Can you describe the corset, indicating how wide it was?

Dr. AKIN. The only portion I saw was the front portion of the corset and   it was about, I'd say, 5 or 6 inches in width, and made out of some white heavy fabric with the usual straps and buckles.

Mr. SPECTER. Did you notice any Ace bandage strapping the President's buttocks area?

Dr. AKIN. No.

Mr. SPECTER. Was that area of his anatomy visible to you?

Dr. AKIN. Not his buttocks, he was lying supine.

Mr. SPECTER. Was President Kennedy ever turned over, to your knowledge?

Dr. AKIN. Not while I was there.

Mr. SPECTER. And how long were you there altogether, Dr. Akin?

Dr. AKIN. Oh, probably 15, maybe 20—perhaps 20 minutes.

Mr. SPECTER. Were you present when he was pronounced to be dead?

Dr. AKIN. Yes—I didn't leave until Dr. Clark and Dr. Jenkins had mutually agreed that nothing else could be done.

Mr. SPECTER. What time was he pronounced dead?

Dr. AKIN. 1300 hours.

Mr. SPECTER. And what, in your opinion, was the cause of death?

Dr. AKIN. Massive gunshot injury to the brain—primary cause.

Mr. SPECTER. You have already described some of the treatment which was performed on the President; could you supplement that by describing what else was done for the President?

Dr. AKIN. Other than the placement of chest tubes, artificial respiration, brief external cardiac massage—I don't know. Anything else I said would be hearsay, and I understand that he did receive some cortisone. He received so much Ringer's lactate, but this is not of my own personal knowledge.

Mr. SPECTER. How many bullets were involved in the wounds inflicted on the President, Dr. Akin?

Dr. AKIN. Probably two.

Mr. SPECTER. Have you ever changed any of your original opinions in connection with your observations of the President or any opinions you formed in connection with what you saw?

Dr. AKIN. You mean as to how he was injured?

Mr. SPECTER. Yes, as to how he was injured.

Dr. AKIN. Well, no; not really because I didn't have any opinions, necessarily. Any speculation that I might have done about how he was injured was just that, it was just speculation. I didn't form an opinion until it was revealed where he was when he was injured and where the alleged assassin was when he fired the shots, so I didn't have any opinions. It was my immediate assumption that when I saw the extent of the head wound, I assumed at that point that he had probably been hit in the head with a high velocity missile because of the damage that had been done. The same thing happened to his head and would happen to a sealed can of sauerkraut that you hit with a high velocity missile.

Mr. SPECTER. Did you have any opinion as to the direction that the bullet hit his head?

Dr. AKIN. I assume that the right occipitalparietal region was the exit, so to speak, that he had probably been hit on the other side of the head, or at least tangentially in the back of the head, but I didn't have any hard and fast opinions about that either.

Mr. SPECTER. Have you been interviewed by any representative of the Federal Government prior to today?

Dr. AKIN. You mean concerning this matter?

Mr. SPECTER. Concerning this matter.

Dr. AKIN. I think I was probably interviewed by a member of the Secret Service some weeks ago.

Mr. SPECTER. What did you say to him?

Dr. AKIN. Virtually the same thing, as I recall—I didn't make as long a statement, he just wanted to know where I was and what I did and I told him briefly and that seemed to satisfy him.

Mr. SPECTER. And is that the only time you have been interviewed by any representative of the Federal Government concerning this matter prior to today?

Dr. AKIN. Yes; as far as I can remember.

Mr. SPECTER. And before I started to take your deposition, did you and I have a very brief discussion about the nature of the deposition and the questions I would ask you?

Dr. AKIN. Yes.

Mr. SPECTER. And did you give me about the same information, exactly the same information you have put on the record here this morning?

Dr. AKIN. To my knowledge; yes.

Mr. SPECTER. Do you have anything to add which you think might be of assistance to the President's Commission in their inquiry?

Dr. AKIN. No; I don't think so. I don't know exactly if there is any disagreement or discrepancy in the testimony from the various people who have testified, so I don't know. This is all I saw.

Mr. SPECTER. That's fine. Thank you very much, Dr. Akin.

Dr. AKIN. That's all right, thank you.

TESTIMONY OF DR. PAUL CONRAD PETERS

The testimony of Dr. Paul Conrad Peters was taken at 4 p.m., on March 24, 1964, at Parkland Memorial Hospital, Dallas, Tex., by Mr. Arlen Specter, assistant counsel of the President's Commission.

Mr. SPECTER. May the record show that Dr. Paul Peters is present, having responded to a request to have his deposition taken in connection with the investigation of the President's Commission on the Assassination of President Kennedy, which is investigating all aspects of the assassination, including the medical treatment of President Kennedy at Parkland Memorial Hospital, and for the latter sequence of events we have asked Dr. Peters to appear and testify what he knows, if anything, concerning that medical attention.

With that statement of purpose in calling you, Dr. Peters, may I ask you to rise and raise your right hand?

Do you solemnly swear that the testimony you give before the President's Commission in this deposition proceeding will be the truth, the whole truth and nothing but the truth, so help you God?

Dr. PETERS. I do.

Mr. SPECTER. Now, will you state your full name for the record, please?

Dr. PETERS. Paul Conrad Peters.

Mr. SPECTER. And what is your profession, sir?

Dr. PETERS. Doctor of medicine.

Mr. SPECTER. And will you outline for me briefly your educational background?

Dr. PETERS. I went to college at Indiana University in Bloomington, Ind., and received an A.B. degree from Indiana University in 1950, and received an M.D. degree from Indiana University in 1953. I took my internship at the Philadelphia General Hospital, 1953 and 1954. I took my residency in Urological Surgery at Indiana University from 1954 to 1957, and from 1957 to 1963 I was chief of Urology at U.S.A.F. Hospital, Carswell, which is the largest hospital in SAC, and I was regional consultant to the surgeon general in Urological surgery. Since July 1963, I have been assistant professor of Urology at Southwestern Medical School.

Mr. SPECTER. And are you board certified, Dr. Peters?

Dr. PETERS. I am certified by the American Board of Urology—1960.

66

Mr. SPECTER. Did you have occasion to render medical services to President John Kennedy on November 22, 1963?

Dr. PETERS. Yes.

Mr. SPECTER. And would you outline briefly the circumstances relating to your arriving on the scene where he was?

Dr. PETERS. As I just gave you a while ago?

Mr. SPECTER. Yes.

Dr. PETERS. I was in the adjacent portion of the hospital preparing material for a lecture to the medical students and residents later in the day, when I heard over the radio that the President had been shot and there was a great deal of confusion at the time and the extent of his injuries was not immediately broadcast over the radio, and I thought, because of the description of the location of the tragedy he would probably be brought to Parkland for care, and so I went to the emergency room to see if I could render assistance.

Mr. SPECTER. And at about what time did you arrive at the emergency room?

Dr. PETERS. Well, could I ask a question or two?

Mr. SPECTER. Sure.

Dr. PETERS. As I recall, he was shot about 12:35 our time; is that correct?

Mr. SPECTER. I believe that's been fixed most precisely at 12:30, Dr. Peters.

Dr. PETERS. So, I would estimate it was probably about 12:50 when I got there, I really don't know for certain.

Mr. SPECTER. Whom did you find present, if anyone, when you arrived?

Dr. PETERS. When I arrived the following people I noted were present in the room: Drs. Perry, Baxter, Ron Jones, and McClelland. The first thing I noticed, of course, was that President Kennedy was on the stretcher and that his feet were slightly elevated. He appeared to be placed in a position in which we usually treat a patient who is in shock, and I noticed that Dr. Perry and Dr. Baxter were present and that they were working on his throat. I also noticed that Dr. Ron Jones was present in the room. I took off my coat and asked what I could do to help, and then saw it was President Kennedy. I really didn't know it was President Kennedy until that time. Dr. Perry was there and he and Dr. Baxter were doing the tracheotomy and we asked for a set of tracheotomy tubes to try and get one of the appropriate size. I then helped Dr. Baxter assemble the tracheotomy tube which he inserted into the tracheotomy wound that he and Dr. Perry had created.

Mr. SPECTER. Were there any others present at that time, before you go on as to what aid you rendered?

Dr. PETERS. I believe Dr. Carrico——

Mr. SPECTER. Any other doctors present?

Dr. PETERS. And Dr. Jenkins was present.

Mr. SPECTER. Have you now covered all of those who were present at that time?

Dr. PETERS. And Dr. Shaw walked into the room and left—for a moment—but he didn't stay. He just sort of glanced at the President and went across the hall. Mrs. Kennedy was in the corner with someone who identified himself as the personal physician of the President—I don't remember his name.

Mr. SPECTER. Dr. Burkley?

Dr. PETERS. I don't know his name. That's just who he said he was, because he was asking that the President be given some steroids, which was done.

Mr. SPECTER. He requested that.

Dr. PETERS. That's right, he said he should have some steroids because he was an Addisonian.

Mr. SPECTER. What do you mean by that in lay language?

Dr. PETERS. Well, Addison's disease is a disease of the adrenal cortex which is characterized by a deficiency in the elaboration of certain hormones that allow an individual to respond to stress and these hormones are necessary for life, and if they cannot be replaced, the individual may succumb.

Mr. SPECTER. And Dr. Burkley, or whoever was the President's personal physician, made a request that you treat him as an Addisonian?

Dr. PETERS. That's right—he recommended that he be given steroids because he was an Addisonian—that's what he said.

Mr. SPECTER. Were there any nurses present at that time?

Dr. PETERS. I don't remember a nurse being in the room all the time, but they were coming in and out.

Mr. SPECTER. Have you identified all the people who were present to the best of your recollection?

67

Dr. PETERS. Did I mention Dr. Robert McClelland, he was also there.

Mr. SPECTER. Was Dr. Dulany there?

Dr. PETERS. I don't remember him, he may have been.

Mr. SPECTER. Who else was there, if anyone, that you can recall, or have you now given me everyone you can recall?

Dr. PETERS. Well, I am giving you my impression of the situation as I walked in and those are the ones I remember right now. Dr. Kemp Clark also came in during the maneuvering.

Mr. SPECTER. Well, who else came in during the course of the operative procedures?

Dr. PETERS. The anesthesiologists, Drs. Jenkins and Gene Akin, I believe, came in.

Mr. SPECTER. Did anyone else come in?

Dr. PETERS. I am not certain of anyone else.

Mr. SPECTER. Now, tell us what aid was rendered to President Kennedy.

Dr. PETERS. Dr. Perry and Dr. Baxter were doing the tracheotomy and a set of tracheotomy tubes was obtained and the appropriate size was determined and I gave it to Baxter, who helped Perry put it into the wound, and Perry noted also that there appeared to be a bubbling sensation in the chest and recommended that chest tubes be put in. Dr. Ron Jones put a chest tube in on the left side and Dr. Baxter and I put it in on the right side—I made the incision in the President's chest, and I noted that there was no bleeding from the wound.

Mr. SPECTER. Did you put that chest tube all the way in on the right side?

Dr. PETERS. That's our presumption—yes.

Mr. SPECTER. And what else was done for the President?

Dr. PETERS. About the same time—there was a question of whether he really had an adequate pulse, and so Dr. Ronald Jones and I pulled his pants down and noticed that he was wearing his brace which had received a lot of publicity in the lay press, and also that he had an elastic bandage wrapped around his pelvis at—in a sort of a figure eight fashion, so as to encompass both thighs and the lower trunk.

Mr. SPECTER. What was the purpose of that bandage?

Dr. PETERS. I presume that it was—my thoughts at the time were that he probably had been having pelvic pain and had put this on as an additional support to stabilize his lower pelvis. It seemed quite interesting to me that the President of the United States had on an ordinary $3 Ace bandage probably in an effort to stabilize his pelvis. I suppose he had been having some back pain and that was my thought at the time, but we removed this bandage in an effort to feel a femoral pulse. We were never certain that we got a good pulse.

Mr. SPECTER. Would you describe in as much detail as you can the type of brace he was wearing?

Dr. PETERS. Well, it appeared similar to a corset.

Mr. SPECTER. How thick was it?

Dr. PETERS. I would estimate it was one-eighth of an inch.

Mr. SPECTER. An eighth of an inch thick?

Dr. PETERS. Yes.

Mr. SPECTER. And how high was it?

Dr. PETERS. Well, it completely encompassed his midsection.

Mr. SPECTER. It encompassed his midsection?

Dr. PETERS. His circumference—yes—and it was probably, I would guess about 8 to 11 inches.

Mr. SPECTER. In width?

Dr. PETERS. Yes.

Mr. SPECTER. Running in his waist area at the top of his hips up to the lower part of his chest?

Dr. PETERS. I would estimate that it went from the lower part of his chest to the pelvic girdle. About this time it was noted also that he had no effective heart action, and Dr. Perry asked whether he should open the chest and massage the heart. In the meantime, of course, the tracheotomy had been done and completed and had been hooked on to apparatus for assisting his respiration.

Mr. SPECTER. And what action, if any, was taken on the open-heart massage?

Dr. PETERS. It was pointed out that an examination of the brain had been done. Dr. Jenkins had observed the brain and Dr. Clark had observed the brain and it was pointed out to Dr. Perry that it appeared to be a mortal wound, and involving the brain, and that open-heart massage would probably not add anything to what had already been done, and that external cardiac massage is known to be as efficient as direct massage of the heart itself.

Mr. SPECTER. Was there any further treatment rendered to the President?

Dr. PETERS. Yes, Dr. Perry began immediate external compression of the chest in an effort to massage the heart, even before he asked the question as to whether the thoracotomy should be done. As soon as there was a question as to whether there was a pulse or not, he immediately began external chest compression.

Mr. SPECTER. What other action was taken to aid the President, if any?

Dr. PETERS. Well, cut downs were done on the extremities, and tubes were inserted in the veins, and I know on the right ankle anteriorly, and I believe in the left arm and also in the left leg, in order to administer fluid and blood which he did receive.

Mr. SPECTER. Have you now described all of the medical attention given the President?

Dr. PETERS. Well, I believe I have.

Mr. SPECTER. And was the President subsequently pronounced dead?

Dr. PETERS. That's correct.

Mr. SPECTER. And about what time was that pronouncement made?

Dr. PETERS. I could not give you the time within 5 or 10 minutes—I can tell you this much, though, I know what actually did happen.

Mr. SPECTER. Tell me that.

Dr. PETERS. I was—we pronounced him dead and I was in the room, present while the priest gave him the last rites, during which time there was Dr. Jenkins and Dr. Baxter and Dr. McClelland, Mrs. Kennedy, the priest, and myself. Dr. Perry had left, as had most of the others by that time.

Mr. SPECTER. Why did you remain?

Dr. PETERS. Well, I just hadn't gotten out of the door when the priest first came in and Dr. Jenkins asked everyone to leave except those people I have just named.

Mr. SPECTER. Why did he exclude those from the group which were to leave?

Dr. PETERS. Well, I think they were nurses, and several other people he thought just best not remain and I'm sure that there was no intention to personally exclude anyone behind his request. He just sort of looked around and saw who appeared to be there and asked the others to leave.

Mr. SPECTER. What did you observe as to the nature of the President's wound?

Dr. PETERS. Well, as I mentioned, the neck wound had already been interfered with by the tracheotomy at the time I got there, but I noticed the head wound, and as I remember—I noticed that there was a large defect in the occiput.

Mr. SPECTER. What did you notice in the occiput?

Dr. PETERS. It seemed to me that in the right occipitalparietal area that there was a large defect. There appeared to be bone loss and brain loss in the area.

Mr. SPECTER. Did you notice any holes below the occiput, say, in this area below here?

Dr. PETERS. No, I did not and at the time and the moments immediately following the injury, we speculated as to whether he had been shot once or twice because we saw the wound of entry in the throat and noted the large occipital wound, and it is a known fact that high velocity missiles often have a small wound of entrance and a large wound of exit, and I'm just giving you my honest impressions at the time.

Mr. SPECTER. What were they?

Dr. PETERS. Well, I wondered whether or not he had been shot once or twice—that was my question at the time.

Mr. SPECTER. When you say "we speculate," whom do you mean by that?

Dr. PETERS. Well, the doctors in attendance there.

Mr. SPECTER. Any doctor specifically?

Dr. PETERS. I wouldn't mention anyone specifically, we all discussed it. I did not know whether or not he had been shot once or twice.

Mr. SPECTER. Did you have an opportunity to observe the wound on his neck prior to the time the tracheotomy was performed?

Dr. PETERS. No, I did not. The tracheotomy was already being done by Dr. Baxter and Dr. Perry when I got in the room. I did not see the wound on his neck.

Mr. SPECTER. Did you make any written reports on the treatment of President Kennedy?

Dr. PETERS. No, I did not; no one asked me to.

Mr. SPECTER. Did you prepare any notes of any sort, or do you have any notes of any sort?

Dr. PETERS. No; I do not.

Mr. SPECTER. What was the cause of death in your opinion?

Dr. PETERS. I would assume that it was irreversible damage to the centers in the brain which control the heart and respiration.

69

Mr. SPECTER. Have you talked to any representatives of the Federal Government about this matter prior to today?

Dr. PETERS. No; I have not.

Mr. SPECTER. And prior to the time the court reporter came in, did you and I have a brief discussion as to the nature of this deposition and the questions that I would ask you?

Dr. PETERS. No; I was not informed as to any specific questions. I knew the general nature of the testimony which I would give.

Mr. SPECTER. From the discussion?

Dr. PETERS. From the letter I had received from the counsel signed by Mr. Rankin.

Mr. SPECTER. And did you and I have a brief conversation here in this room today before the court reporter came in?

Dr. PETERS. Yes; we did.

Mr. SPECTER. Do you have anything to add which you think might be of assistance to the President's Commission in its investigation?

Dr. PETERS. I do not—regarding the immediate condition of the President.

Mr. SPECTER. Thank you very much for coming, Dr. Peters, we are very much obliged to you.

Dr. PETERS. Thank you.

TESTIMONY OF DR. ADOLPH HARTUNG GIESECKE, JR.

The testimony of Dr. Adolph Hartung Giesecke, Jr., was taken at 1:40 p.m., on March 25, 1964, at Parkland Memorial Hospital, Dallas, Tex., by Mr. Arlen Specter, assistant counsel of the Presidents Commission.

Mr. SPECTER. May the record show that Dr. A. H. Giesecke, Jr., is present in response to a letter request from the Commission to appear at this deposition proceeding in connection with the President's Commission to Investigate the Assassination of President Kennedy, including his medical treatment at Parkland Hospital.

Dr. Giesecke has been asked to appear to testify about his knowledge of the treatment that President Kennedy and Governor Connally received at Parkland Hospital on November 22, and with that preliminary statement of purpose and objective, would you please stand up, Dr. Giesecke, and raise your right hand?

Do you solemnly swear that the testimony you give before this President's Commission in these deposition proceedings will be the truth, the whole truth and nothing but the truth, so help you God?

Dr. GIESECKE. Yes; I do.

Mr. SPECTER. Will you state your full name, please, for the record?

Dr. GIESECKE. Adolph Hartung Giesecke, Jr. H-a-r-t-u-n-g (spelling).

Mr. SPECTER. What is your profession?

Dr. GIESECKE. I am a physician and anesthesiologist.

Mr. SPECTER. Are you duly licensed to practice medicine in the State of Texas?

Dr. GIESECKE. Yes.

Mr. SPECTER. Are you board-certified?

Dr. GIESECKE. No, sir.

Mr. SPECTER. Are you working for board-certification?

Dr. GIESECKE. Yes.

Mr. SPECTER. Will you outline briefly your educational background, please?

Dr. GIESECKE. I graduated—how far back do you want me to go?

Mr. SPECTER. Start with college, graduation from college, if you would, please.

Dr. GIESECKE. I was on an accelerated plan through the University of Texas but have no college degree. I matriculated to medical school in 1953, September 1953, graduated May 30, 1957, from the University of Texas Medical Branch at Galveston, Tex. I did my internship at William Beaumont Army Hospital at El Paso, following which I served 24 months on active duty in the Army as an aviation medical officer. I was stationed primarily at the Presidio at San Francisco, Calif. Upon discharge from the Army, I came to Parkland Hospital, completed a 3-year residency in anesthesiology in July 1963. Since that time I have been an assistant professor on the anesthesiology staff at Southwestern Medical School.

Mr. SPECTER. Did you have occasion to render medical attention to President Kennedy on November 22, 1963?

Dr. GIESECKE. Yes.

Mr. SPECTER. Will you outline the circumstances under which you were called into that matter?

Dr. GIESECKE. I was eating lunch in the cafeteria when Dr. Jenkins approached the table and told me that the President had been shot and asked me to bring some resuscitative equipment from the operating room to the emergency room, which I did.

Mr. SPECTER. And at what time did you arrive at the emergency room, approximately?

Dr. GIESECKE. Can I look and see when I induced the Governor?

Mr. SPECTER. Yes. May the record show that Dr. Giesecke is now referring to a letter from A. H. Giesecke, Jr., M.D., to Mr. C. J. Price, administrator, dated November 25, 1963, which I will ask the reporter to mark as "Dr. Giesecke's Exhibit No. 1."

(Instrument referred to marked by the reporter as "Dr. Giesecke Exhibit No. 1," for identification.)

Mr. SPECTER. Let me ask you a question or two, first about this, Dr. Giesecke, to qualify—is this a copy of the report which you submitted to Mr. Price?

Dr. GIESECKE. Yes, that is a real copy.

Mr. SPECTER. And all the facts contained in this report are true and correct?

Dr. GIESECKE. Yes.

Mr. SPECTER. And do they concern the treatment which was rendered by you to President Kennedy and Governor Connally?

Dr. GIESECKE. That's correct.

Mr. SPECTER. Now, refer to that if you wish, if it will help you answer the last question.

Dr. GIESECKE. I arrived in the emergency room at 12:40 p.m., between 12:40 and 12:45.

Mr. SPECTER. And who was present at the time you arrived?

Dr. GIESECKE. Dr. Jenkins was present, Dr. Carrico, Dr. Dulany, Dr. Baxter, Dr. Perry, Dr. McClelland, and Drs. Akin and Hunt arrived at the same time that I did.

Mr. SPECTER. Were there any other people present, such as nurses?

Dr. GIESECKE. Mrs. Kennedy was in the room—I could not say—I can't say who else was there. There may have been a nurse there, I just don't remember. It seemed to me there was a Secret Service man there too, with Mrs. Kennedy.

Mr. SPECTER. Are you sure Dr. Dulany was there, as distinguished from being with Governor Connally?

Dr. GIESECKE. Perhaps—perhaps—I'm shaky on that.

Mr. SPECTER. The reason I asked you about that specifically is because Dr. Carriro testified this morning that he and Dr. Dulany were on duty and Dr. Dulany went immediately with Governor Connally and Dr. Carrico went to President Kennedy.

Dr. GIESECKE. That may well be.

Mr. SPECTER. What was the condition of the President when you arrived?

Dr. GIESECKE. There was a great deal of blood loss which was apparent when he came in the room—the cart was covered with blood and there was a great deal of blood on the floor. There was—I could see no spontaneous motion on the part of the President. In other words, he made no movement during the time that I was in the room. As I moved around towards the head of the emergency cart with the anesthesia machine and the resuscitative equipment and helped Dr. Jenkins to hook the anesthesia machine up to the President to give him oxygen, I noticed that he had a very large cranial wound, with loss of brain substance, and it seemed that most of the bleeding was coming from the cranial wound.

Mr. SPECTER. What did you observe specifically as to the nature of the cranial wound?

Dr. GIESECKE. It seemed that from the vertex to the left ear, and from the browline to the occiput on the left-hand side of the head the cranium was entirely missing.

Mr. SPECTER. Was that the left-hand side of the head, or the right-hand side of the head?

Dr. GIESECKE. I would say the left, but this is just my memory of it.

Mr. SPECTER. That's your recollection?

Dr. GIESECKE. Right, like I say, I was there a very short time—really.

Mr. SPECTER. Did you observe any other wound or bullet hole below the large area of missing skull?

Dr. GIESECKE. No; when I arrived the tracheotomy was in progress at that time and so I observed no other wound except the one on the cranium.

Mr. SPECTER. On the cranium itself, did you observe another bullet hole below the portion of missing skull?

Dr. GIESECKE. No, sir; this was found later by Dr. Clark—I didn't see this.

Mr. SPECTER. What makes you say that that hole was found later by Dr. Clark?

Dr. GIESECKE. Well, this is hearsay—I wasn't there when they found it and I didn't notice it.

Mr. SPECTER. Well, Dr. Clark didn't observe that hole.

Dr. GIESECKE. Oh, he didn't—I'm sorry.

71

Mr. SPECTER. From whom did you hear that the hole had been observed, if you recollect?

Dr. GIESECKE. Oh—I must be confused. We talked to so many people about these things—I don't remember.

Mr. SPECTER. Now, with respect to the condition of the President's neck, what was its status at the time you first observed it?

Dr. GIESECKE. Well, like I say, they were performing the tracheotomy, and I personally saw no wound in the neck other than the tracheotomy wound. As soon as the tracheotomy was completed, we removed the endotracheal tube and hooked the anesthesia machine to the tracheotomy tube and efforts were made then to put in a chest tube, an anterior chest tube.

Mr. SPECTER. How long were you with President Kennedy altogether?

Dr. GIESECKE. Approximately 5 minutes.

Mr. SPECTER. Have you now described everything which was done during the time you were there?

Dr. GIESECKE. No—after having assisted Dr. Jenkins in establishing a ventilation, I then hooked up a cardiotachioscope or an electronic electrocardiographic monitor to the President by putting needles in the skin and plugging the thing in the wall, plugging the monitor in the wall. Before the machine had sufficient time to warm up to see if there were any electrical activity, then I was called out of the room.

Mr. SPECTER. And did you have any occasion to return to the room where the President was?

Dr. GIESECKE. No.

Mr. SPECTER. And where were you called to?

Dr. GIESECKE. I was called across the hall where Governor Connally was being moved out of the emergency treatment room and toward the operating room.

Mr. SPECTER. And what action did you take at that time, if any?

Dr. GIESECKE. I had my equipment with me—I had taken my equipment with me from the room where the President was, having ascertained that Dr. Jenkins didn't need anything that I had, and so I proceeded to the elevator. We moved the equipment and the Governor—the Governor went on the first elevator and I caught the second one.

Mr. SPECTER. And where did you go on the second elevator?

Dr. GIESECKE. To the second floor where the operating suite is, moved off of the elevator and down to operating room 5, which was being set up for the Governor. The Governor had arrived and I obtained from the anesthesia orderly an anesthesia machine, checked it for safe operation, and discussed the Governor's condition a little bit with him, and determined that he was conscious and that he could respond to questions and that he hadn't eaten in the previous several hours, and proceeded to induce an anesthesia.

Mr. SPECTER. Now, are all the details of your activity in connection with Governor Connally's operation contained in the report marked "Dr. Giesecke's Exhibit No. 1"?

Dr. GIESECKE. Yes.

Mr. SPECTER. Now, you mentioned a few minutes ago that you talked about this matter with a number of people—whom have you talked to, Dr. Giesecke?

Dr. GIESECKE. Well, of course, we discussed it with Dr. Jenkins and various members of the anesthesia staff. We have discussed it with—I've forgotten that gentleman's name, but he was from the American Medical Association, as a historian. We discussed it with Dr. Mike Bush, who then reported it in the Anesthesiology Newsletter, which is a publication of the American Society of Anesthesiologists, and then discussed it with the Secretary of—may I retract that. That's about it—that's the extent of the discussion, except with other members of the surgical staff and the anesthesia staff and these people.

Mr. SPECTER. Have you ever discussed this matter with any representative of the Federal Government prior to today?

Dr. GIESECKE. Yes; there was a well documented Secret Service man here who said he was from the Warren Commission about a month ago, I imagine.

Mr. SPECTER. What do you mean by "well documented"?

Dr. GIESECKE. Well, I mean he had a badge and a card and he seemed to be legitimate.

Mr. SPECTER. And what did you tell him, if anything?

Dr. GIESECKE. He was asking rather specifically if we had made other notes than the reports that we had already submitted, so in essence it was just a matter of telling him, "No, I didn't have any other information written down except what I had already given."

Mr. SPECTER. And what had you already given—that letter report?

Dr. GIESECKE. Yes, sir.

Mr. SPECTER. That is marked "Giesecke Exhibit No. 1"?

Dr. GIESECKE. Yes.

Mr. SPECTER. Has any other representative talked to you from the Federal Government about this matter?

Dr. GIESECKE. No.

Mr. SPECTER. This afternoon prior to the time we went on the record, did I ask you a few questions and discuss the nature of this deposition proceeding, and did you give me information just as you have on the record here after the court reporter started to take everything down?

Dr. GIESECKE. Yes; that's correct. She was out of the room for a few minutes before we started.

Mr. SPECTER. Do you have anything to add which you think might be helpful to the Warren Commission in its investigation?

Dr. GIESECKE. No, I think that pretty well covers what I did.

Mr. SPECTER. May I thank you very much, Dr. Giesecke? That's fine.

Dr. GIESECKE. Thank you.

TESTIMONY OF DR. JACKIE HANSEN HUNT

The testimony of Dr. Jackie Hansen Hunt was taken at 1:12 p.m., on March 24, 1964, at Parkland Memorial Hospital, Dallas, Tex., by Mr. Arlen Specter, assistant counsel of the President's Commission.

Mr. SPECTER. May the record show that Dr. Jackie H. Hunt is present, and may I show for the record that the President's Commission on the Assassination of President Kennedy is conducting an inquiry into all the facts surrounding the assassination of the President, and the medical care performed on President Kennedy at Parkland Memorial Hospital.

Dr. Hunt appears here today in response to a letter requesting that her deposition be taken, and may the record reflect the additional fact that Dr. Hunt is a lady doctor.

Would you at this time, Dr. Hunt, stand up and raise your right hand?

Do you solemnly swear that the testimony you give before the President's Commission in this deposition proceeding will be the truth, the whole truth, and nothing but the truth, so help you God?

Dr. HUNT. I do, sir.

Mr. SPECTER. Will you state your full name, please?

Dr. HUNT. Jackie Hansen Hunt, H-a-n-s-e-n (spelling).

Mr. SPECTER. And what is your profession?

Dr. HUNT. Medical doctor.

Mr. SPECTER. And, are you duly licensed to practice medicine by the State of Texas?

Dr. HUNT. I am.

Mr. SPECTER. And in what year were you so licensed?

Dr. HUNT. 1950.

Mr. SPECTER. Will you outline briefly your educational background, please?

Dr. HUNT. I graduated from medical school at Tulane College of Medicine in 1949. I had a year of rotating internship followed by a year of pediatric residency. In 1961 I started a residency in anesthesiology, which I completed in 1963, and I am now a fellow in anesthesiology.

Mr. SPECTER. Are you board certified, then, Dr. Hunt, at this time?

Dr. HUNT. No.

Mr. SPECTER. Are you working toward board certification?

Dr. HUNT. Yes, I am. I am eligible and will take the first part in June.

Mr. SPECTER. Did you have occasion on November 22 to render medical aid to the late President Kennedy?

Dr. HUNT. Yes.

Mr. SPECTER. Will you relate briefly the circumstances surrounding your being called into the case?

Dr. HUNT. I was in Parkland Hospital on duty with the anesthesiology department and was notified by our chief of staff, Dr. M. T. Jenkins, that the President had been shot. Together with Dr. Giesecke and Dr. Akin, I got an anesthesia machine and put it on an elevator and checked it out and set it up on the way to the emergency room and took it into the emergency room where the President was and he had been intubated, and I helped Dr. Jenkins connect the anesthesia machine to the endotracheal tube which at that time was being run, I believe, by a Bird machine, and after making certain that the connections were properly done, I placed the equipment in Dr. Jenkins' hands.

Mr. SPECTER. What doctors were present when you arrived there, Dr. Hunt?

Dr. HUNT. Dr. Jenkins, Dr. Male Perry—quite a number of others—I just can't remember who was there today.

Mr. SPECTER. Were any nurses present?

Dr. HUNT. Yes—I don't know the names of any of them.

Mr. SPECTER. What, if anything, did you observe as to the condition of President Kennedy?

Dr. HUNT. The first good look I took at him I noticed that his eyes were opened and that the pupils were widely dilated and fixed and so I assumed that he was in essence dead.

Mr. SPECTER. At approximately what time did you arrive in the emergency room?

Dr. HUNT. I don't know—it would have been—I would think near 12:45, but I have really never even thought about it and I frankly don't remember.

Mr. SPECTER. And how long after you arrived did you have an opportunity to observe the President in the way which you have just described?

Dr. HUNT. How long was it from the time I came in until I looked at him?

Mr. SPECTER. Yes, ma'am.

Dr. HUNT. A minute—2 minutes.

Mr. SPECTER. Did you have any other observations at that time?

Dr. HUNT. No—other than that everyone was working on him. They were doing cardiac massage, closed chest massage, I.V.'s were running, and others were being started.

Mr. SPECTER. I.V.'s?

Dr. HUNT. Intravenous fluids and, of course, our department was breathing for him.

Mr. SPECTER. And when you say "breathing for him," what do you mean by that?

Dr. HUNT. Ventilating him—an endotracheal tube down into the trachea attached to an anesthesia machine with 100 percent oxygen going, and by manual compression of the bag, ventilating him.

Mr. SPECTER. Did you observe any wounds on the President?

Dr. HUNT. I actually did not see the wounds.

Mr. SPECTER. Did you at any time see a wound to the head?

Dr. HUNT. No; I didn't see it.

Mr. SPECTER. And was there something obscuring your view from seeing the head wound?

Dr. HUNT. Yes; I could see his face and I could also see that a great deal of blood was running off of the table from his right side and I was on his left side.

Mr. SPECTER. Were you near his head or foot or the middle of the body?

Dr. HUNT. I was about midbody actually, well, no—more at his shoulder, when I leaned over to look at him.

Mr. SPECTER. Did you ever observe any wound in the neck?

Dr. HUNT. I did not actually see the wound in the neck. I say that because I assumed there was a wound—someone's hand was there and there was blood present, but there was blood on nearly everyone.

Mr. SPECTER. What was the condition of his throat when you first observed him, if you did observe it at all?

Dr. HUNT. I couldn't—I don't know—I can't say. You mean, as far as inside or outside?

Mr. SPECTER. Outside.

Dr. HUNT. I don't actually remember seeing anything except someone's hands were using a sponge or something was present in the area.

Mr. SPECTER. What medical operation, if any, was performed on his throat?

Dr. HUNT. I don't know.

Mr. SPECTER. Did you observe a tracheotomy being performed on his throat?

Dr. HUNT. No—that's not to say that they were not doing one.

Mr. SPECTER. What else was done for the President other than that which you have already described?

Dr. HUNT. Well, let's see, I don't—as far as actual observation, I didn't—other things were done—I left at this time and went to Governor Connally.

Mr. SPECTER. At about what time did you leave President Kennedy?

Dr. HUNT. I was probably in the room no more than 4 minutes at the most.

Mr. SPECTER. Had he been pronounced dead by the time you left?

Dr. HUNT. No; he had not.

Mr. SPECTER. And where did you go when you left the President's room?

Dr. HUNT. Straight across to operating room 2.

Mr. SPECTER. And what did you find in operating room 2 when you arrived there?

Dr. HUNT. Governor Connally was present there and——

Mr. SPECTER. What doctors, if any, were present when you arrived?

74

Dr. HUNT. Red Duke—I'm sorry, I just don't remember who the others were. There were three or four.

Mr. SPECTER. What action was being taken with respect to Governor Connally upon your arrival there?

Dr. HUNT. They were placing chest tubes, as a matter of fact, they had one in and were putting the other one in, and were—they had an I.V. going, I believe someone had done a cutdown, and they were checking other wounds. He had a wound on his arm and another wound down on his leg, I think, and that was about it—preparing to take him promptly up to surgery.

Mr. SPECTER. And what did you do on that occasion?

Dr. HUNT. I walked in and Dr. Duke looked up and the first thing I did was to look at the Governor—I took his pulse and he spoke to me and said something, and noted his color.

Mr. SPECTER. What did the Governor say to you?

Dr. HUNT. He said something like, "It hurts," not anything real specific, but he did at least speak, and it was a conscious thought type of thing, so that he was more or less alert, responding, so then I stepped back into the hall and signaled a fellow, a medical student who has been in our department, that is rotating through anesthesia, and I happened to see him just outside the door, and I asked him to please go upstairs and bring me another unit of equipment and then came back in and told Dr. Duke I had sent for equipment, although I didn't believe the Governor was going to need it, and he said that he was very glad that I had and he, too, didn't think he would need it, but he should have it as a standby, and then they brought me a machine and my table down and I stayed with the Governor until he was ready to go upstairs, but he did not require any respiratory aid because he was not that critical.

Mr. SPECTER. Did you participate any further with the treatment of Governor Connally?

Dr. HUNT. When we were ready to go upstairs, I went back to the room where the President was and Dr. Giesecke, who is a staff member from our department, appeared relatively free and I asked him if he would come and go upstairs with the Governor and I came on upstairs in a different route. I didn't go in the elevator with the Governor—Dr. Giesecke went with him, and helped Dr. Giesecke get under way with the surgery.

Mr. SPECTER. How did you go upstairs, by what route?

Dr. HUNT. I don't know—I don't remember.

Mr. SPECTER. Is there any other elevator going up to the operating rooms?

Dr. HUNT. Yes; there are four elevators.

Mr. SPECTER. But do those lead from the emergency rooms?

Dr. HUNT. No; you come down this long hallway up to those of the ground floor.

Mr. SPECTER. Is there more than one elevator for the stretcher to go through from the emergency room up to the second floor operating rooms?

Dr. HUNT. Yes; they can—they come up to these.

Mr. SPECTER. What route would they have to take to do this?

Dr. HUNT. They would have to come directly out of the emergency room and down this main hallway to this front bank of elevators.

Mr. SPECTER. That would be a pretty long route, would it not?

Dr. HUNT. Actually, it isn't very long. I don't know in yards or paces even, but there are three elevators there.

Mr. SPECTER. What route did Governor Connally use?

Dr. HUNT. I think they took him by the back elevator, the one that comes down into the emergency room.

Mr. SPECTER. Is that the one they customarily use to take people from the emergency area into the operating room?

Dr. HUNT. Yes; if there is an emergency it goes straight up—they usually use that one.

Mr. SPECTER. You say you went back to President Kennedy's room?

Dr. HUNT. Yes.

Mr. SPECTER. And what did you observe there at that time?

Dr. HUNT. At that time I did notice, and possibly this was there earlier, I noticed that they had gotten more monitoring equipment in and connected the electronic equipment for monitoring the electrocardiogram.

Mr. SPECTER. At what time did you return to President Kennedy's room?

Dr. HUNT. I don't know—it would probably have been maybe 3 or 4 or 5 minutes from the time I stepped out, because I went across the hall—I didn't know the Governor was there, and someone told me and I went in and just took a brief look at him to sort of size up his condition, and stepped out and sent for my equipment and went back in and stayed until they brought my equipment. It would have been a little longer than 4 or 5 minutes because they had to bring the equipment down the elevator and it had arrived and been there a few minutes—3 or 4 minutes before we were ready to take him upstairs.

Mr. SPECTER. And what was going on in the President's room when you returned there?

Dr. HUNT. Well, there were still a goodly number of people, oh, at least 10 people, possibly there were more—I'm not real sure, but there were still—at that time there were, I know, at least three anesthesiologists in there—Dr. Jenkins, Dr. Akin, and Dr. Giesecke, and I believe Dr. Baxter was in there, and Dr. Perry was still there.

Mr. SPECTER. Were they still working on the President at that time?

Dr. HUNT. Yes, sir; I don't know what they were doing.

Mr. SPECTER. How long did you stay on that occasion?

Dr. HUNT. Just, oh, a minute—just long enough to catch Dr. Giesecke's eye and let him know I was there and going out.

Mr. SPECTER. And did you ever return to the President's room?

Dr. HUNT. No; I don't believe I did—no; I'm sure I didn't, because I came on upstairs with Governor Connally.

Mr. SPECTER. And did you participate then with Governor Connally's operation?

Dr. HUNT. I helped Dr. Giesecke during the induction of anesthesia.

Mr. SPECTER. Have you talked to any representative of the Federal Government prior to today?

Dr. HUNT. No; I haven't.

Mr. SPECTER. Did you make any written report of your participation in the care of Governor Connally and President Kennedy?

Dr. HUNT. Not directly. Dr. Giesecke called me one day and said that, I think it was the A.M.A. was here and just wanted to verify my movements for the day, which I told him and he in turn told them that—I did not appear before them.

Mr. SPECTER. Did you make any written reports yourself?

Dr. HUNT. No.

Mr. SPECTER. Do you have any notes of any sort concerning your participation?

Dr. HUNT. None whatsoever.

Mr. SPECTER. Prior to the time the court reporter started to take down the transcript of my questions and your answers, did you and I have a brief discussion about the purpose of this deposition?

Dr. HUNT. Yes.

Mr. SPECTER. And the questions I would ask you?

Dr. HUNT. Yes.

Mr. SPECTER. And is the information which you have provided on the record the same as you told me before the written deposition started?

Dr. HUNT. Elaborated somewhat.

Mr. SPECTER. Do you have anything to add which you think might be of aid to the Commission in its investigation?

Dr. HUNT. No, sir; I don't.

Mr. SPECTER. Thank you very much for appearing, Dr. Hunt.

Dr. HUNT. Thank you.

TESTIMONY OF DR. KENNETH EVERETT SALYER

The testimony of Dr. Kenneth Everett Salyer was taken at 6:15 p.m., on March 25, 1964, at Parkland Memorial Hospital, Dallas, Tex., by Mr. Arlen Specter, assistant counsel of the President's Commission.

Mr. SPECTER. May the record show that Dr. Kenneth Salyer is present in response to an inquiry that he appear to have his deposition taken in connection with the inquiries being conducted by the President's Commission on the Assassination of President Kennedy, which is looking into all facts of the shooting, including the wounds of the President and the care he received at Parkland Hospital.

With that preliminary statement of purpose, Dr. Salyer, will you stand up and raise your right hand?

Do you solemnly swear that the testimony you will give before the President's Commission in the course of this deposition will be the truth, the whole truth, and nothing but the truth, so help you God?

Dr. SALYER. I do.

Mr. SPECTER. Have you had an opportunity to examine the document or the Executive order creating the President's Commission and Rules for the taking of testimony?

Dr. SALYER. Yes; I have.

Mr. SPECTER. And are you willing to have your deposition taken today without having the formal three days of written notice, which you have a right to, if you wish?

Dr. SALYER. Yes.

Mr. SPECTER. You are willing to waive that right, is that right?

Dr. SALYER. Yes.

Mr. SPECTER. Would you state your full name for the record, please?

Dr. SALYER. Kenneth Everett Salyer.

Mr. SPECTER. What is your profession?

Dr. SALYER. Physician.

Mr. SPECTER. Are you duly licensed to practice medicine by the State of Texas?

Dr. SALYER. Yes; I am.

Mr. SPECTER. And would you outline briefly your educational background, please?

Dr. SALYER. A B.S. degree at the University of Kansas, an M.D. degree at the University of Kansas, and internship at Parkland, and now a first year resident in surgery at Parkland Hospital.

Mr. SPECTER. In what year did you graduate from the University of Kansas Medical School?

Dr. SALYER. 1962.

Mr. SPECTER. And how old are you, Dr. Salyer?

Dr. SALYER. I am 27.

Mr. SPECTER. Will you relate briefly the circumstances surrounding your being called in to assist in the treatment of President Kennedy?

Dr. SALYER. Well, for the month of November, as part of our rotation on surgery, I spent that month on neurosurgery, and being on call that day for any emergencies which come in to our emergency room related to neurosurgical problems, we would be called down to the emergency room to see these, and I was upstairs viewing a movie when I heard that the President had arrived and so I thought I should go down to the emergency room and see what the situation was.

Mr. SPECTER. And, upon your arrival at the emergency room, who was present?

Dr. SALYER. Oh, I don't recall—I know that there were a room full of doctors—I could list specific ones that I remember if you would like.

Mr. SPECTER. Would you please?

Dr. SALYER. I don't really think I could give you every one, but I remember Dr. Jenkins and Dr. Perry and Dr. Baxter, and also Dr. Bob McClelland and Dr. Carrico and Dr. Crenshaw, and I think a Dr. Gene Akin was there also—at that time, when I first came in.

Mr. SPECTER. Can you think of any others?

Dr. SALYER. No; I don't recall any others—there could have been some, there were a lot of people sort of moving in and out. There certainly were a lot of nurses in there at that time.

Mr. SPECTER. Can you identify any of the nurses who were there?

Dr. SALYER. No; I can't.

Mr. SPECTER. What was the President's condition at the time you arrived?

Dr. SALYER. It was critical.

Mr. SPECTER. What did you observe about him with respect to any wounds he may have sustained?

Dr. SALYER. Well, I observed that he did have some sucking wound of some type on his neck, and that he also had a wound of his right temporal region—these were the two main wounds.

Mr. SPECTER. Did you have an opportunity to observe his throat?

Dr. SALYER. No; I really did not. I think there were a lot of people—a lot of doctors more closely around him. I might mention also, I think just right after I came in the room Dr. Clark and Dr. Grossman also arrived.

Mr. SPECTER. Doctor who?

Dr. SALYER. Dr. Grossman, just briefly. He's a neurosurgeon also.

Mr. SPECTER. What is his name?

Dr. SALYER. Dr. Grossman—Bob Grossman. He was just there, I think, briefly.

Mr. SPECTER. How long was he there?

Dr. SALYER. I couldn't say—I'm not sure he came in the room. I know they were together—I cannot say that for sure.

Mr. SPECTER. To what extent did Dr. Crenshaw participate?

Dr. SALYER. Dr. Crenshaw participated about the extent that I did. We were occupied in making sure an I.V. was going and hanging up a bottle of blood.

Mr. SPECTER. Is the—is Dr. Crenshaw a resident?

Dr. SALYER. Yes, he is third-year resident. That's the reason I remember him specifically because we were sort of working there together on that.

Mr. SPECTER. I had asked you a moment ago whether you had an opportunity to observe the condition of the President's throat.

Dr. SALYER. Right.

Mr. SPECTER. What was your answer to that question?

Dr. SALYER. The answer was—there were a lot of doctors standing around, and I didn't really get to observe the nature of the wound in the throat.

Mr. SPECTER. At approximately what time did you arrive at the emergency room where the President was situated?

Dr. SALYER. I really don't know.

Mr. SPECTER. What was done for the President by way of treatment that you observed?

Dr. SALYER. Well, an adequate airway eventually, of course, some external cardiac massage—he had I.V.'s—intravenous fluids going in a number of sites, and all of the acute measures we administered him.

Mr. SPECTER. I didn't hear you at the end of your answer.

Dr. SALYER. I said—all of the many other measures that we administered—I don't recall specifically some of the other details as far as medications and so forth.

Mr. SPECTER. What did you observe with respect to the head wound?

Dr. SALYER. I came in on the left side of him and noticed that his major wound seemed to be in his right temporal area, at least from the point of view that I could see him, and other than that—nothing other than he did have a gaping scalp wound—cranial wound.

Mr. SPECTER. Has anyone from the Federal Government talked to you about your observations of this matter?

Dr. SALYER. No one has.

Mr. SPECTER. Do you have anything to add which you think may be of aid to the President's Commission in its inquiry?

Dr. SALYER. No, I believe not.

Dr. SPECTER. Thank you very much, Dr. Salyer.

Dr. SALYER. Thank you.

TESTIMONY OF DR. MARTIN G. WHITE

The testimony of Dr. Martin G. White was taken at 6:35 p.m., on March 25, 1964, at Parkland Memorial Hospital, Dallas, Tex., by Mr. Arlen Specter, assistant counsel of the President's Commission.

Mr. SPECTER. May the record show that Dr. Martin White is present in response to a request that he appear to have his deposition taken because he has been identified in prior depositions as being one of the doctors in attendance on President Kennedy.

Dr. White, have you had an opportunity to examine the Executive order creating the Presidential Commission?

Dr. WHITE. Yes.

Mr. SPECTER. And have you had an opportunity to examine the resolution setting forth the rules for taking depositions?

Dr. WHITE. Yes.

Mr. SPECTER. Are you willing to have your deposition taken without the 3-day notice to which you have a right under the rules, if you wish to receive formal written notice? And have three days after mailing before you appear to have your deposition taken?

Dr. WHITE. No, I want to have it taken now.

Mr. SPECTER. You are willing to waive that requirement?

Dr. WHITE. Yes.

Mr. SPECTER. Will you stand up, then, and raise your right hand?

Do you solemnly swear that the testimony you give before the President's Commission in this deposition proceeding will be the truth, the whole truth, and nothing but the truth, so help you God?

Dr. WHITE. I do.

Mr. SPECTER. Would you state your full name for the record, please?

Dr. WHITE. Martin G. White.

Mr. SPECTER. What is your profession, sir?

Dr. WHITE. M.D.—physician.

Mr. SPECTER. Are you duly licensed in the State of Texas to practice medicine?

Dr. WHITE. In this institution.

Mr. SPECTER. What is your educational background, please?

Dr. WHITE. I have a bachelor of medicine degree from Northwestern University and a master of science degree from Northwestern University and a doctor of medicine degree from Northwestern University.

Mr. SPECTER. How old are you, Doctor?

Dr. WHITE. Twenty-five.

Mr. SPECTER. Were you in attendance when President Kennedy was being treated on November 22, 1963?

Dr. WHITE. I was.

Mr. SPECTER. And what were the circumstances of your being called into the case?

Dr. WHITE. I was the intern assigned to the surgery section of the emergency room on that day and was there when the President's body was brought into the emergency room.

Mr. SPECTER. And what did you do in connection with the President's treatment?

Dr. WHITE. I put an intervenous cutdown in the President's right foot.

Mr. SPECTER. Did you have an opportunity to observe any of his wounds?

Dr. WHITE. I saw the wound in his head as he was brought into the trauma room where he was treated.

Mr. SPECTER. Did you observe any other wounds?

Dr. WHITE. No, I did not see any other.

Mr. SPECTER. Did you observe specifically a wound in the neck?

Dr. WHITE. I did not look and did not observe any.

Mr. SPECTER. How long were you present while the President was being treated?

Dr. WHITE. I would estimate about 10 to 15 minutes.

Mr. SPECTER. And did you leave prior to the time he was pronounced to be dead?

Dr. WHITE. Yes; I did.

Mr. SPECTER. Why did you leave?

Dr. WHITE. My duties had been completed and there was work elsewhere, with the Governor, to be done.

Mr. SPECTER. Who was present at the time you were there, Dr. White?

Dr. WHITE. As best I can recall, Dr. Carrico and I were the physicians immediately present when the President's body was brought in, plus a number of individuals who accompanied the cart on which his body was lying, and the only individual who I knew in that group was his wife, Mrs. Kennedy.

Mr. SPECTER. And what doctors were present at the time you left the room?

Dr. WHITE. Well, it would be impossible for me to tell you all the people that were there, but I knew Dr. Carrico, Dr. Baxter, Dr. Perry and Dr. Zedelitz, Z-e-d-e-l-i-t-z (spelling)—I know they were there.

Mr. SPECTER. Doctor who—what is his first name?

Dr. WHITE. William Zedelitz.

Mr. SPECTER. To what extent did he participate?

Dr. WHITE. I don't believe that he had any—I don't know what he did other than the fact that when I was doing the cutdown he assisted me by just placing some tape over the catheters we used to do this with.

Mr. SPECTER. Is he an intern as you are?

Dr. WHITE. He is a surgical resident here at this hospital.

Mr. SPECTER. Who else was present?

Dr. WHITE. I can't be sure that I saw anyone else, although, as I say—many people were there whose faces I can't recall.

Mr. SPECTER. Can you identify any of the nurses who were present?

Dr. WHITE. Yes; one of the nurses—there were two there, Jeanette, and her last name—I don't know at the present time, and she is chief nurse in the emergency room.

Mr. SPECTER. Doris Nelson?

Dr. WHITE. Yes.

Mr. SPECTER. Jeanette Standridge?

Dr. WHITE. Yes; Jeanette Standridge was the other nurse.

Mr. SPECTER. Do you have anything to add which you think might be of help to the Commission?

Dr. WHITE. No; I don't.

Mr. SPECTER. Thank you very much, Dr. White for coming.

Dr. WHITE. All right, thank you.

TESTIMONY OF DR. ROBERT SHAW

The testimony of Dr. Robert Shaw was taken at 6 p.m., on March 23, 1964, at Parkland Memorial Hospital, Dallas, Tex., by Mr. Arlen Specter, assistant counsel of the President's Commission.

Mr. SPECTER. May the record show that Dr. Robert Shaw is present, having responded to a request to have his deposition taken in connection with the President's Commission on the Assassination of President Kennedy, which is investigating all facts relating to the medical care of President Kennedy and Governor Connally, and Dr. Shaw has been requested to appear and testify concerning the treatment on Governor Connally.

Dr. Shaw, will you rise and raise your right hand, please.

Do you solemnly swear that the testimony you give before the President's Commission in the course of this deposition proceeding will be the truth, the whole truth, and nothing but the truth, so help you God?

Dr. SHAW. I do.

Mr. SPECTER. Will you state your full name for the record, please?

Dr. SHAW. Robert Roeder Shaw.

Mr. SPECTER. And what is your profession, sir?

Dr. SHAW. Physician and surgeon.

Mr. SPECTER. Will you outline briefly your educational background, please?

Dr. SHAW. I received my B.A. degree from the University of Michigan in 1927 and M.D. degree in 1933. My surgical training was obtained at Roosevelt Hospital in New York City, July 1934 to July 1936, and my training in thoracic surgery at the University Hospital, Ann Arbor, Mich., July 1936 to July 1938. Do you want me to say what happened subsequent to then?

Mr. SPECTER. Yes; will you outline your medical career in brief form subsequent to that date, please?

Dr. SHAW. I entered private practice, limited to thoracic surgery, August 1, 1938. I have continuously practiced this specialty in Dallas, with the exception of the period from June 1942 to December 1945, when I was a member of the Medical Corps of the Army of the United States, serving almost all of this period in the European theatre of operations. I was again absent from Dallas from December 1961 until June 1963, when I headed the medico team and performed surgery at the Avicenna Hospital at Kabul, Afghanistan.

Mr. SPECTER. Are you Board certified, Dr. Shaw?

Dr. SHAW. Yes. I am certified by the Board of Thoracic Surgery, date of certification— 1948. At the present time I am professor of thoracic surgery and chairman of the division of thoracic surgery at the University of Texas, Southwestern Medical School.

Mr. SPECTER. Did you have occasion to perform any medical care for President Kennedy on November 22, 1963?

Dr. SHAW. No.

Mr. SPECTER. Did you have occasion to care for Governor Connally?

Dr. SHAW. Yes.

Mr. SPECTER. Would you relate the circumstances of your being called in to care for the Governor, please?

Dr. SHAW. I was returning to Parkland Hospital and the medical school from a conference I had attended at Woodlawn Hospital, which is approximately a mile away, when I saw an open limousine going past the intersection of Industrial Boulevard and Harry Hines Boulevard under police escort. As soon as traffic had cleared, I proceeded on to the medical school. On the car radio I heard that the President had been shot at while riding in the motorcade. Upon entering the medical school, a medical student came in and joined three other medical students. He stated that President Kennedy had been brought in dead on arrival to the emergency room of Parkland Hospital and that Governor Connally had been shot through the chest. Upon hearing this, I proceeded immediately to the emergency room of the hospital and arrived at the emergency room approximately 5 minutes after the President and Governor Connally had arrived.

Mr. SPECTER. Where did you find Governor Connally at that time, Dr. Shaw?

Dr. SHAW. I found Governor Connally lying on a stretcher in emergency room No. 2. In attendance were several men, Dr. James Duke, Dr. David Mebane, Dr. Giesecke, an anesthesiologist. As emergency measures, the open wound on the Governor's right chest had been covered with a heavy dressing and manual pressure was being applied. A drainage tube had been inserted into the second interspace in the anterior portion of the right chest and connected to a water-sealed bottle to bring about partial reexpansion of the collapsed right lung. An intravenous needle had been inserted into a vein in the left arm and intravenous fluid was running.

I was informed by Dr. Duke that blood had already been drawn and sent to the laboratory to be crossmatched with 4 pints of blood, to be available at surgery. He also stated that the operating room had been alerted and that they were merely waiting for my arrival to take the Governor to surgery, since it was obvious that the wound would have to be debrided and closed.

Mr. SPECTER. At what time did the operation actually start, Dr. Shaw?

Dr. SHAW. That, I would have to refresh my memory on that—now, this, of course—the point he began the anesthesia—that would be about right—but I have to refresh my memory.

Mr. SPECTER. Permit me to make available on the record for you the operative record which has been heretofore marked as Commission Exhibit No. 392, with the exhibit consisting of the records of Parkland Hospital on President Kennedy as well as Governor Connally and I call your attention to a 2-page report which bears your name as the surgeon, under date of November 22, 1963, of thoracic surgery for Governor Connally, and, first, I ask you if in fact this report was prepared by you?

Dr. SHAW. It was.

Mr. SPECTER. Now, with that report, is your recollection refreshed as to the starting time of the operation on Governor Connally's chest?

Dr. SHAW. Yes; the anesthesia was begun at 1300 hours.

Mr. SPECTER. Which would be 1 p.m.?

Dr. SHAW. 1 p.m., and the actual incision was made at 1335 or 1:35 p.m.

Mr. SPECTER. And what time did that operation conclude?

Dr. SHAW. My operation was completed at 1520 hours, or 3:20.

Mr. SPECTER. Will you describe Governor Connally's condition, Dr. Shaw, directing your attention first to the wound on his back?

Dr. SHAW. When Governor Connally was examined, it was found that there was a small wound of entrance, roughly elliptical in shape, and approximately a cm. and a half in its longest diameter, in the right posterior shoulder, which is medial to the fold of the axilla.

Mr. SPECTER. What is the axilla, in lay language, Dr. Shaw?

Dr. SHAW. The arm pit.

Mr. SPECTER. Dr. Shaw, will you describe next the wound of exit?

Dr. SHAW. Yes; the wound of exit was below and slightly medial to the nipple on the anterior right chest. It was a round, ragged wound, approximately 5 cm. in diameter. This wound had obviously torn the pleura, since it was a sucking wound, allowing air to pass to and fro between the pleura cavity and the outside of the body.

Mr. SPECTER. Define the pleura, please, Doctor, in lay language.

Dr. SHAW. The pleura is the lining of the chest cavity with one layer of pleura, the parietal pleura lining the inside of the chest wall, diaphragm and the mediastinum, which is the compartment of the body containing the heart, its pericardial sac, and great vessels.

Mr. SPECTER. What were the characteristics of these two bullet wounds which led you to believe that one was a wound of entry and one was a wound of exit, Dr. Shaw?

Dr. SHAW. The wound of entrance is almost invariably the smaller wound, since it perforates the skin and makes a wound approximately or slightly larger than the missile. The wound of exit, especially if it has shattered any bony material in the body, will be the larger of the wounds.

Mr. SPECTER. What experience, Doctor, have you had, if any, in evaluating gunshot wounds?

Dr. SHAW. I have had considerable experience with gunshot wounds and wounds due to missiles because of my war experience. This experience was not only during the almost 2 years in England, but during the time that I was head of the Thoracic Center in Paris, France, for a period of approximately a year.

Mr. SPECTER. Would you be able to give an approximation of the total number of bullet wounds you have had occasion to observe and treat?

Dr. SHAW. Considering the war experience and the addition of wounds seen in civilian practice, it probably would number well over a thousand, since we had over 900 admissions to the hospital in Paris.

Mr. SPECTER. What was the line of trajectory, Dr. Shaw, between the point in the back of the Governor and the point in the front of the Governor, where the bullet wounds were observed?

Dr. SHAW. Considering the wound of entrance and the wound of exit, the trajectory of the bullet was obliquely downward, considering the fact that the Governor was in a sitting position at the time of wounding.

Mr. SPECTER. As an illustrative guide here, Dr. Shaw——

Dr. SHAW. May I add one sentence there?

81

Mr. SPECTER. Please do.

Dr. SHAW. The bullet, in passing through the Governor's chest wall struck the fifth rib at its midpoint and roughly followed the slanting direction of the fifth rib, shattering approximately 10 cm. of the rib. The intercostal muscle bundle above the fifth rib and below the fifth rib were surprisingly spared from injury by the shattering of the rib, which again establishes the trajectory of the bullet.

Mr. SPECTER. Would the shattering of the rib have had any effect in deflecting the path of the bullet from a straight line?

Dr. SHAW. It could have, except that in the case of this injury, the rib was obviously struck so that not too dense cancellus portion of the rib in this position was carried away by the bullet and probably there was very little in the way of deflection.

Mr. SPECTER. At this time, Dr. Shaw, I would like to call your attention to an exhibit which we have already had marked as Dr. Gregory's Exhibit No. 1, because we have used this in the course of his deposition earlier today and this is a body diagram, and I ask you, first of all, looking at Diagram No. 1, to comment as to whether the point of entry marked on the right shoulder of Governor Connally is accurate?

Dr. SHAW. Yes. The point of entry as marked on this exhibit I consider to be quite accurate.

Mr. SPECTER. Is the size and dimension of the hole accurate on scale, or would you care to make any adjustment or modification in that characterization by picture?

Dr. SHAW. As the wound entry is marked on this figure, I would say that the scale is larger than the actual wound or the actual depicting of the wound should be. As I described it, it was approximately a centimeter and a half in length.

Mr. SPECTER. Would you draw, Dr. Shaw, right above the shoulder as best you can recollect, what that wound of entry appeared at the time you first observed it? Would you put your initials right beside that?

(The witness, Dr. Shaw, complied with the request of Counsel Specter.)

Mr. SPECTER. Now, directing your attention to the figure right beside, showing the front view, does the point of exit on the lower chest of the figure there correspond with the point of exit on the body of Governor Connally?

Dr. SHAW. Yes; I would say that it conforms in every way except that it was a little nearer to the right nipple than depicted here.

Off the record, just a minute.

(Discussion between Counsel Specter and the witness, Dr. Shaw, off the record.)

Mr. SPECTER. Dr. Shaw, in our off-the-record conversation, you called my attention to your thought that the nipple line is incorrectly depicted on that figure, would you, therefore, in ink mark on there the nipple line which would be more accurate proportionately to that body?

Dr. SHAW. Yes; I feel the nipple line as shown on this figure is a little high and should be placed at a lower point on the body, which would bring the wound of exit, which I feel is in the proper position, more in line with the actual position of the nipple.

Mr. SPECTER. Now, with the wound of exit as it is shown there, does that correspond in position with the actual situation on Governor Connally's body as you have redrawn the proportion to the nipple line?

Dr. SHAW. It does.

Mr. SPECTER. Would you put an "X" through the old nipple line so we have obscured that and put your initials beside those two marks, if you would, please?

Dr. SHAW. By the "X-1"?

Mr. SPECTER. Yes, please.

(The witness, Dr. Shaw, complied with request of Counsel Specter in drawing on the figure heretofore mentioned.)

Mr. SPECTER. Now, as to the proportion of the hole depicting the point of exit, is that correct with respect to characterizing the situation on Governor Connally?

Dr. SHAW. It is, and corresponds with the relative size of the two wounds as I have shown on the other figure.

Mr. SPECTER. Would you at this time, right above the right shoulder there, draw the appearances of the point of exit as nearly as you can recollect it on Governor Connally?

Dr. SHAW. This is right.

Mr. SPECTER. You say the hole which appears on Governor Connally is just about the size that it would have been on his body?

Dr. SHAW. Yes; it is drawn in good scale.

Mr. SPECTER. In good scale to the body?

82

Dr. SHAW. Yes.

Mr. SPECTER. Would you draw it on another portion of the paper here in terms of its absolute size?

Dr. SHAW. Five cm. it would be—about like that—do you want me to mark that?

Mr. SPECTER. Put your initials right in the center of that circle.

Dr. SHAW. I'll just put "wound of exit."

Mr. SPECTER. Fine—just put "wound of exit—actual size" and put your initials under it.

(The witness, Dr. Shaw, complied with request of Counsel Specter.)

Mr. SPECTER. Let the record show that Dr. Shaw has marked "wound of exit—actual size" with his initials R.R.S. on the diagram 1.

Now, looking at diagram 2, Dr. Shaw, does the angle of declination on the figure correspond with the angle that the bullet passed through Governor Connally's chest?

Dr. SHAW. It does.

Mr. SPECTER. Is there any feature of diagram 3 which is useful in further elaborating that which you have commented about on diagram 1?

Dr. SHAW. No. Again off the record?

Mr. SPECTER. All right, off the record.

(Discussion between Counsel Specter and the witness, Dr. Shaw, off the record.)

Mr. SPECTER. You have just commented off the record, Dr. Shaw, that the wound of entry is too large proportionately to the wound of exit, but aside from that, is there anything else on diagram 3 which will be helpful to us?

Dr. SHAW. No.

Mr. SPECTER. Is there anything else on diagram 4 which would be helpful by way of elaborating that which appeared on diagram 2?

Dr. SHAW. No.

Mr. SPECTER. Now as to the treatment or operative procedure which you performed on Governor Connally, would you now describe what you did for him?

Dr. SHAW. As soon as anesthesia had been established and an endotracheal tube was in place so that respiration could be controlled with positive pressure, the large occlusive dressing which had been applied in the emergency room was removed. This permitted better inspection of the wound of exit, air passed to and fro through the damaged chest wall, there was obvious softening of the bony framework of the chest wall as evidenced by exaggerated motion underneath the skin along the line of the trajectory of the missile.

The skin of the chest wall axilla and back were thoroughly cleaned and aseptic solution was applied for further cleaning of the skin, the whole area was draped so as to permit access to both the wound of exit and the entrance wound. Temporarily, the wound of entrance was covered with a sterile towel.

First an elliptical incision was made to remove the ragged edges of the wound of exit. This incision was then extended laterally and upward in a curved direction so as to not have the incision through the skin and subcutaneous tissue directly over the line of the trajectory of the bullet where the chest had been softened.

It was found that approximately 10 cm. of the fifth rib had been shattered and the rib fragments acting as secondary missiles had been the major contributing factor to the damage to the anterior chest wall and to the underlying lung.

Mr. SPECTER. What do you mean, Doctor, by the words "fragments acting as secondary missiles"?

Dr. SHAW. When bone is struck by a high velocity missile it fragments and acts much like bowling pins when they are struck by a bowling ball—they fly in all directions.

Mr. SPECTER. Will you continue now and further describe the treatment which you performed?

Dr. SHAW. The bony fragments were removed along with all obviously damaged muscle. It was found that the fourth and fifth intercoastal muscle bundles were almost completely intact where the rib had been stripped out. There was damage to the latissimus dorsi muscle, but this was more in the way of laceration, so that the damage could be repaired by suture. The portion of parietal pleura which had not been torn by the injury was opened along the length of the resected portion of the fifth rib. The jagged ends of the fifth rib were cleaned with a rongeur; approximately 200 cc. of clot and liquid blood was removed from the pleura cavity; inspection of the lung revealed that the middle lobe had a long tear which separated the lobe into approximately two equal segments. This tear extended up into the hilum of the lobe, but had not torn a major bronchus or a major blood vessel. The middle lobe was repaired with a running No. 3 O chromic gut approximating the tissue of the depths of the lobe, with two sutures, and then

83

approximating the visceral pleura on both the medial and lateral surface with a running suture of the same material—same gut.

Upon repair of the lobe it expanded well upon pressure on the anesthetic bag with very little in the way of peripheral leak.

Attention was next turned to the lower lobe. There was a large hematoma in the anterior basal segment of the right lower lobe extending on into the median basal segment. At one point there was a laceration in the surface of the lobe approximating a centimeter in length, undoubtedly caused by one of the penetrating rib fragments. A single mattress suture No. 3 O chromic gut on an atromitac needle was used to close this laceration from which blood was oozing.

Next, the diaphragm and all parts of the right mediastinum was examined but no injury was found.

The portion of the drainage tube which had already been placed in the second interspace in the anterior axillary line which protruded into the chest was cut away, since it was deemed to be longer than necessary. A second drainage tube was placed through a stab wound in the eighth interspace in the posterior axillary line and both of these tubes were connected to a water sealed bottle. The fourth and fifth intercoastal muscle bundles were then approximated with interrupted sutures of No. O chromic gut.

The remaining portion of the serratus anterior muscle was then approximated across the closure of the intercostal muscles. The laceration at the latissimus dorsi muscle was then approximated with No. O chromic guts suture. Before closing the skin and subcutaneous tissue a stab wound approximately 2 cm. in length was made near the lower tip of the right scapula and a latex rubber drain was drawn up through this stab wound to drain subscapular space. This drain was marked with a safety pin. The subcutaneous tissue was then closed with interrupted sutures of No. O chromic gut, inverting the knots. The skin was closed with interrupted vertical mattress sutures of black silk.

Attention was next turned to the wound of entrance. The skin surrounding the wound was removed in an elliptical fashion, enlarging the incision to approximately 3 cm. Examination of the depths of this wound reveal that the latissimus dorsi muscle alone was injured, and the latex rubber drain could be felt immediately below the laceration in the muscle. A single mattress suture was used to close the laceration in the muscle. The skin was then closed with interrupted vertical mattress sutures of black silk. The drainage tubes going into the pleura cavity were then secured with safety pins and adhesive tape and a dressing applied to the entire incision. This concluded the operation for the wound of the chest, and at this point Dr. Gregory and Dr. Shires entered the operating room to care for the wounds of the right wrist and left thigh.

Mr. SPECTER. What did you observe, Dr. Shaw, as to the wound of the right wrist?

Dr. SHAW. Well, I would have to say that my observations are probably not accurate. I knew that the wound of the wrist had fractured the lower end of the right radius and I saw one large wound on the—I guess you would call it the volar surface of the right arm and a small wound on the dorsum of the right wrist.

Mr. SPECTER. Which appeared to you to be the point of entrance, Dr. Shaw?

Dr. SHAW. To me, I felt that the wound of entrance was the wound on the volar surface or the anterior surface with the hand held in the upright or the supine position, with the wound of exit being the small wound on the dorsum.

Mr. SPECTER. What were the characteristics of those wounds which led you to that conclusion?

Dr. SHAW. Although the wound of entrance, I mean, although the wound that I felt was a wound of entrance was the larger of the two, it was my feeling that considering the large wound of exit from the chest, that this was consistent with the wound that I saw on the wrist. May we go off the record?

Mr. SPECTER. Sure.

(Discussion between Counsel Specter and the witness Dr. Shaw off the record.)

Mr. SPECTER. Now, let's go back on the record.

Dr. SHAW. I'll start by saying that my examination of the wrist was a cursory one because I realized that Dr. Gregory was going to have the responsibility of doing what was necessary surgically for this wrist.

Mr. SPECTER. Had you conferred with him preliminarily to starting your operation on the chest so that you knew he would be standing by, I believe as you testified earlier, to perform the wrist operation?

Dr. SHAW. Yes—Dr. Gregory was in the hallway of the operating room before I went in to operate on Governor Connally and while I was scrubbing preparatory to the operation, I told him that there was a compound comminuted fracture of the radius of the Governor's right hand that would need his attention.

Mr. SPECTER. Let the record show that while we were off the record here a moment ago, Dr. Shaw, you and I were discussing the possible angles at which the Governor might have been sitting in relation to a trajectory of a bullet consistent with the observations which you recollect and consistent with what seems to have been a natural position for the Governor to have maintained, in the light of your view of the situation. And with that in mind, let me resume the questioning and put on the record very much of the comments and observations you were making as you and I were discussing off the record as this deposition has proceeded.

Now, you have described a larger wound on the volar or palm side of the wrist than was present on the dorsal or back side of the wrist, and you have expressed the opinion that it was the point of entry on the volar side of the wrist as opposed to a point of exit on the back side of the wrist, even though as you earlier said, ordinarily the point of entry is smaller and the point of exit is larger.

Now, will you repeat for the record, Dr. Shaw, the thinking—your thinking which might explain a larger point of entry and a smaller point of exit on the wrist.

Dr. SHAW. Yes. As a matter of fact, when I first examined Governor Connally's wrist, I did not notice the small wound on the dorsum of the wrist and only saw the much larger wound on the radial side of the volar surface of the wrist. I didn't know about the second small wound until I came in when Dr. Gregory was concluding his operation on the wrist. He informed me that there was another small wound through the skin through which a missile had obviously passed.

Mr. SPECTER. Now, which wound was that, Dr. Shaw?

Dr. SHAW. This was the wound on the dorsum or the dorsal surface of the wrist.

Mr. SPECTER. Did you then observe that wound?

Dr. SHAW. Yes; I saw this wound.

Mr. SPECTER. And where was that wound located to the best of your recollection?

Dr. SHAW. This wound was slightly more distal on the arm than the larger wound and located almost in the midportion of the dorsum of the wrist.

Mr. SPECTER. Would that correspond with this location which I read from Dr. Gregory's report on the dorsal aspect of the right wrist over the junction of the distal fourth of the radius and shaft approximately 2 cm. in length.

Dr. SHAW. The wound was approximately 2 cm. in length?

Mr. SPECTER. Yes; would that correspond with the wound which you observed?

Dr. SHAW. Yes; I saw it at the time that he was closing it and that would correspond with the wound I observed.

Mr. SPECTER. He has described that as what he concluded to be the wound of entry on the dorsal aspect of the right wrist, but your thought was that perhaps that was the wound of exit?

Dr. SHAW. Yes; in trying to reconstruct the position of Governor Connally's body, sitting in the jump seat of the limousine, and the attitude that he would assume in turning to the right— this motion would naturally bring the volar surface of the right wrist in contact with the anterior portion of the right chest.

Mr. SPECTER. Well, is your principal reason for thinking that the wound on the dorsal aspect is a wound of exit rather than a wound of entry because of what you consider to be the awkward position in having the dorsal aspect of the wrist either pointing upward or toward the chest?

Dr. SHAW. Yes, I think I am influenced a great deal by the fact that in trying to assume this position, I can't comfortably turn my arm into a position that would explain the wound of the dorsal surface of the wrist as a wound of entrance, knowing where the missile came out of the chest and assuming that one missile caused both the chest wound and the arm wound.

Mr. SPECTER. Might not then that conclusion be affected if you discard the assumption that one missile caused all the wounds?

Dr. SHAW. Yes, if two missiles struck the Governor, then it would not be necessary to assume that the larger wound is the wound of entrance.

Mr. SPECTER. Now, would not another explanation for the presence of a wound on the dorsal aspect of the wrist be if the Governor were sitting in an upright position on the jump seat with his arm resting either on an arm rest inside the car or on a window of the car with the elbow protruding outward, and as he turned around, turning in a rotary motion, his wrist somewhat toward his body so that it was present in an angle of approximately 45 degrees to his body, being slightly moving toward his body.

Dr. SHAW. Well, I myself, am not able to get my arm into that position. If the wound, as I assume to be in the midportion of the forearm here and the wound of exit would be here (illustrating) I can't get my arm into that position as to correspond to what we know about the trajectory of the bullet into the chest.

Mr. SPECTER. Assuming that the bullet through the chest then also went through the wrist?

Dr. SHAW. Yes.

Mr. SPECTER. Now, aside from the trajectory and the explanation of one bullet causing all the damage and focusing just on the nature of the wound on the wrist, what conclusion would you reach as to which was the point of entrance and which was the point of exit?

Dr. SHAW. I would feel that the wound on the volar surface of the wrist was the wound of entrance and that perhaps the bullet being partially spent by its passage through the chest wall, struck the radius, fragmenting it, but didn't pass through the wrist, and perhaps tumbled out into the clothing of Governor Connally with only a small fragment of this bullet passing on through the wrist to go out into the left thigh.

Mr. SPECTER. Now, would that be consistent with a fragment passing through the wrist which was so small that virtually the entire missile, or 158 grains of it, would remain in the central missile?

Dr. SHAW. Yes. The wound on the volar surface, I'm sorry, on the dorsum of the wrist and the wound in the thigh which was obviously a wound of entrance, since the fragment is still within the thigh, were not too dissimilar in size.

Mr. SPECTER. Was the wound in the thigh itself, that is, aside from the size of the fragment which remains in the leg, as small as the hole on the dorsal aspect of the wrist?

Dr. SHAW. My memory is that the wound in the thigh through the skin was about the same as the mound on the skin of the dorsum of the wrist, but I didn't make an accurate observation at the time.

Mr. SPECTER. Would your thinking on that be affected any if I informed you that Dr. Shires was of the view and had the recollection that the wound on the thigh was much larger than a hole accounted for by the size of fragments which remained in the femur.

Dr. SHAW. Of course, Dr. Shires actually treated and closed this wound, but since this wound was made through the skin in a tangentialmanner——

Mr. SPECTER. Now, you are referring to the wound of the thigh?

Dr. SHAW. I am referring to the wound of the thigh—was made in a tangential manner, it did not go in at a direct right angle, the slit in the skin in the thigh could be considerably longer than the actual size of the missile itself, because this is a sharp fragment that would make a cutting—it would cause a laceration rather than a puncture wound.

Mr. SPECTER. So, the hole in the thigh would be consistent with a very small fragment in the femur?

Dr. SHAW. Yes.

Mr. SPECTER. Now, a moment ago I asked you what would be your opinion as to the point of entry and the point of exit based solely on the appearances of the holes on the dorsal and volar aspects of the wrist, and you responded that you still thought, or that you did think that the volar aspect was the point of entry with the additional thought that the missile might not have gone through the wrist, but only a fraction having gone through the wrist—now, my question is in giving that answer, did you consider at that time the hypothesis that the wound on the wrist was caused by the same missile which went through the Governor's chest, or was that answer solely in response to the characteristics of the wound on the wrist alone?

Dr. SHAW. I have always felt that the wounds of Governor Connally could be explained by the passage of one missile through his chest, striking his wrist and a fragment of it going on into his left thigh. I had never entertained the idea that he had been struck by a second missile.

Mr. SPECTER. Well, focusing for just a minute on the limited question of the physical characteristics of the wounds on the wrist, if you had that and nothing more in this case to go on, what would your opinion be as to which point was entry and which point was exit?

Dr. SHAW. Ordinarily, we usually find the wound of entrance is smaller than the wound of exit. In the Governor's wound on the wrist, however, if the wound on the dorsum of the wrist is the wound of entrance, and this large missile passed directly through his radius, I'm not clear as to why there was not a larger wound of exit than there was.

Mr. SPECTER. You mean on the volar aspect?

Dr. SHAW. Yes; if a whole bullet hit here——

Mr. SPECTER. Indicating the dorsal aspect?

Dr. SHAW. Yes; and came out through here, why it didn't carry more bone out through the wrist than it did, and the bone was left in the wrist—the bone did not come out. In other words, when it struck the fifth rib it made a hole this big around (indicating) in the chest in carrying bone fragments out through the chest wall.

Mr. SPECTER. Wouldn't that same question arise if it went through the volar aspect and exited through the dorsal aspect?

Dr. SHAW. It wouldn't if you postulated that the bullet did not pass through the wrist, but struck the wrist.

Mr. SPECTER. That would be present in either event, though, if you postulated if the bullet struck the dorsal aspect of the wrist, and did not pass through, but only a missile passed through the volar aspect.

Dr. SHAW. Yes; in that case, however, considering the wound of exit from the chest, and if that same bullet went on through the wrist, I would still expect a pretty good wound of entrance.

Mr. SPECTER. You see, I am trying now, Dr. Shaw, to disassociate the thought that this is the same missile, so that I'm trying to look at it just from the physical characteristics of the appearance of the wounds on the two sides of the wrist.

Dr. SHAW. May we go off the record just a minute?

Mr. SPECTER. Sure—off the record.

(Discussion between Counsel Specter and the witness, Dr. Shaw, off the record.)

Mr. SPECTER. Let us go back on the record and let the record reflect that we have been discussing another aspect concerning Dr. Shaw's thought that if the main missile had gone through the entire radius, that there would have been more damage, presumably, to the arteries and tendons on the underside of the wrist, and I then called Dr. Shaw's attention to one additional factor in Dr. Gregory's testimony which is reflected in his report that "on the radial side of the arm, small fine bits of cloth consistent with fine bits of mohair were found," which was one of the reasons for Dr. Gregory's thinking that the path was from the dorsal aspect to the volar aspect.

Dr. SHAW. Yes.

Mr. SPECTER. And Dr. Shaw's reply, if this is correct, Doctor, that you would know of no readily available explanation for that factor in the situation?

Dr. SHAW. Except that it might have been carried by the small fragment which obviously passed through the wrist and attached to that.

Mr. SPECTER. But could the fragment have carried it from the radial side on it if it had been traveling from the volar side to the radial side?

Dr. SHAW. Yes; it could have carried it through and deposited it on the way through.

Mr. SPECTER. I see, so it might have started on the volar aspect and could have gone on through.

Dr. SHAW. You know, if we could get that suit of his, it would help a lot.

Mr. SPECTER. Well, we are going to examine clothing if at all possible.

Dr. SHAW. Because, I think it would have been almost impossible—I think if you examine the clothing and if you had a hole here in his coat and no hole on this side——

Mr. SPECTER. Indicating a hole on the femur side——

Dr. SHAW. That would almost clear that thing up.

Mr. SPECTER. Yes; it would be very informational in our analysis of the situation.

Dr. SHAW. I doubt if there is a hole in both sides of the sleeve—the sleeve wouldn't be quite that long, I don't think.

Mr. SPECTER. Dr. Shaw, my next question involves whether you have ever had a conversation with Governor Connally about the sequence of events of the day he was shot?

Dr. SHAW. Yes, we have talked on more than one occasion about this. The Governor admits that certain aspects of the whole incident are a bit hazy. He remembers hearing a shot. He recognized it as a rifle shot and turned to the right to see whether President Kennedy had been injured. He recognized that the President had been injured, but almost immediately, he stated, that he felt a severe shock to his right chest. He immediately experienced some difficulty in breathing, and as he stated to me, he thought that he had received a mortal wound.

Mr. SPECTER. Did he tell you why he thought the wound was mortal?

Dr. SHAW. He just knew that he was badly hit, as he expressed it.

Mr. SPECTER. Did he comment on whether or not he heard a second shot before he felt this wound in his chest?

Dr. SHAW. He says that he did not hear a second shot, but did hear—no, wait a minute, I shouldn't say that. He heard only two shots so that he doesn't know which shot other than the first one he did not hear. He only remembers hearing two shots, his wife says distinctly she heard three.

Mr. SPECTER. Mrs. Connally said she heard three?

Dr. SHAW. Mrs. Connally distinctly remembered three shots.

Mr. SPECTER. And, Governor Connally said he heard two shots?

Dr. SHAW. Two shots.

Mr. SPECTER. Would that not be consistent with a situation where he was hit by the second shot and lost consciousness?

Dr. SHAW. Yes; the shock of the wounding might have prevented him from hearing the rifle report.

Mr. SPECTER. Would you have expected him to hear a third shot after he was wounded by a second shot?

Dr. SHAW. He didn't lose consciousness at that time, although he said he did lose consciousness during a part of the trip from the point of wounding to the hospital.

Mr. SPECTER. Did Governor Connally tell you whether or not he heard President Kennedy say anything?

Dr. SHAW. He said that all he heard was the President say, "Oh," that's the only thing he told me.

Mr. SPECTER. Did Mrs. Connally state whether or not she heard the President say anything?

Dr. SHAW. My memory isn't good for that. I don't remember what Mrs. Connally told me on that.

Mr. SPECTER. Are you continuing to treat Governor Connally at the present time?

Dr. SHAW. Yes, although the treatment of the chest is practically at an end, because the chest has reached a satisfactory state of healing.

Mr. SPECTER. Did you continue to treat the Governor all during his stay at Parkland Hospital?

Dr. SHAW. Yes, I attended him several times daily.

Mr. SPECTER. Dr. Shaw, would you think it consistent with the facts that you know as to Governor Connally's wounds that he could have been struck by the same bullet which passed through President Kennedy, assuming that a missile with the muzzle velocity of 2,000 feet per second, a 6.5-millimeter bullet, passed through President Kennedy at a distance of 160 to 250 feet from the rifle, passing through President Kennedy's body, entering on his back and striking only soft tissue and exiting on his neck; could that missile have also gone through Governor Connally's chest in your opinion?

Dr. SHAW. Yes, taking your description of the first wound sustained by the President, which I, myself, did not observe, and considering the position of the two men in the limousine, I think it would be perfectly possible for the first bullet to have passed through the soft tissues of the neck of President Kennedy and produced the wounds that we found on Governor Connally.

Mr. SPECTER. Could that bullet then have produced all the wounds that you found on Governor Connally?

Dr. SHAW. Yes, I would still be postulating that Governor Connally was struck by one missile.

Mr. SPECTER. Now, as you sit here at the moment on your postulation that Governor Connally was struck by one missile, is that in a way which is depicted by diagram No. 5 on the exhibit heretofore marked as "Dr. Gregory's Exhibit No. 1?"

Dr. SHAW. Yes; I feel that the line of trajectory as marked on this diagram is accurate as it could be placed from my memory of this wound.

Mr. SPECTER. And, on that trajectory, how do you postulate the bullet then passed through the wrist from dorsal to volar or from volar to dorsal?

Dr. SHAW. My postulation would be from volar to dorsal.

Mr. SPECTER. Now, then, going back to diagram No. 1, Dr. Shaw, there is one factor that we did not call your attention to or have you testify about, and that is—the marking that the exit is on the volar side and the entry is on the dorsal side as it was remarked by Dr. Gregory, that would then be inconsistent of your view of the situation, would it not?

Dr. SHAW. Yes, it would be.

Mr. SPECTER. And similarly on diagram No. 3, where the exit is marked on the volar, and the entry is marked on the dorsal, that would also be inconsistent with your view of the situation?

Dr. SHAW. Yes—he has the wound on the back being quite a bit larger than the wound on the front here, doesn't he?

Mr. SPECTER. Yes, the wound as it appears here on the diagram is larger.

Dr. SHAW. That wasn't my memory.

Mr. SPECTER. But I don't think that that is necessarily as to scale in this situation. Would it be possible from your knowledge of the facts here, Dr. Shaw, that President Kennedy might have been struck by the bullet passing through him, hitting nothing but soft tissues, and that bullet could have passed through Governor Connally's chest and a second bullet might have struck Governor Connally's wrist?

Dr. SHAW. Yes; this is a perfectly tenable theory.

Mr. SPECTER. And, then, the damage to Governor Connally's thigh might have come from either of the bullets which passed through the chest or a second bullet which struck the wrist?

Dr. SHAW. That is true—as far as the wounds are concerned, this theory, I feel, is tenable. It doesn't conform to the description of the sequence of the events as described by Mrs. Connally.

Mr. SPECTER. In what respect Dr. Shaw?

Dr. SHAW. Well she feels that the Governor was only struck by one bullet.

Mr. SPECTER. Why does she feel that way; do you know, sir?

Dr. SHAW. As soon as he was struck she pushed him to the bottom of the car and got on top of him and it would mean that there would be a period of—well if there were 5½ seconds between the three shots, there would be a couple seconds there that would have given her time to get him down into the car, and as she describes the sequence, it is hard to see how he could have been struck by a second bullet.

Mr. SPECTER. If she pushed him down immediately after he was shot on the first occasion?

Dr. SHAW. Yes.

Mr. SPECTER. But if her reaction was not that fast so that he was struck twice, of course then there would be a different situation, depending entirely on how fast she reacted.

Dr. SHAW. I think if he had been struck first in the wrist and not struck in the chest, he would have known that. He only remembers the hard blow to the back of his chest and doesn't remember being struck in the wrist at all.

Mr. SPECTER. Might he not have been struck in the chest first and struck by a subsequent shot in the wrist?

Dr. SHAW. Yes; but that's hard to postulate if he was down in the bottom of the car.

Mr. SPECTER. Dr. Shaw, have you been interviewed by any representatives of the Federal Government prior to today?

Dr. SHAW. Yes.

Mr. SPECTER. And who talked to you about this case?

Dr. SHAW. I don't have his name. I perhaps could find it. It was a member of the Secret Service.

Mr. SPECTER. On how many occasions were you talked to by a Secret Service man?

Dr. SHAW. Once.

Mr. SPECTER. And what did you tell him?

Dr. SHAW. I told him approximately the same that has been told in this transcript.

Mr. SPECTER. And prior to the time we started to go on the record with the court reporter taking this down verbatim, did you and I have a discussion about the purpose of the deposition and the questions that I would ask you?

Dr. SHAW. Yes.

Mr. SPECTER. And were the answers which you provided me at that time the same as those which you have testified to on the record here this afternoon?

Dr. SHAW. Yes.

Mr. SPECTER. Do you have any other written record of the operation on Governor Connally other than that which has been identified here in Commission Exhibit No. 392?

Dr. SHAW. No; this is a copy of the operative record that went on to the chart of Governor Connally which is in the possession of the record room of Parkland Hospital.

Mr. SPECTER. Do you have anything else which you could tell us which you think might be helpful to the Commission in any way, Dr. Shaw?

Dr. SHAW. No; I believe that we have covered all of the points that are germane to this incident. Anything else that I would have would actually be hearsay.

Mr. SPECTER. Thank you very much, sir, for appearing.

Dr. SHAW. All right, you are welcome.

Mr. SPECTER. Off the record.

(Discussion between Counsel Specter and the witness, Dr. Shaw, off the record.)

Mr. SPECTER. Dr. Shaw, permit me to ask you one or two more questions. Did you find any bullets in Governor Connally's body?

Dr. SHAW. No.

Mr. SPECTER. Did you find any fragments of bullets in his chest?

Dr. SHAW. No; only fragments of shattered rib.

Mr. SPECTER. And did you find, or do you know whether any fragment was found in his wrist or the quantity of fragments in his wrist?

Dr. SHAW. It is my understanding that only foreign material from the suit of Governor Connally was found in the wrist, although in the X-ray of the wrist there appeared to be some minute metallic fragments in the wrist.

Mr. SPECTER. As to the wound on the back of Governor Connally, was there any indication that the bullet was tumbling prior to the time it struck him?

Dr. SHAW. I would only have to say that I'm not a ballistics expert, but the wound on his chest was not a single puncture wound, it was long enough so that there might have been some tumbling.

Mr. SPECTER. You mean the wound on his back?

Dr. SHAW. The wound on his back—yes, it was long enough so that there might have been some tumbling. In other words, it was not a spherical puncture wound.

Mr. SPECTER. So it might have had some tumbling involved, or it might not have?

Dr. SHAW. Yes; I don't know whether the clothes would have occasioned this or not.

Mr. SPECTER. My question would be that perhaps some tumbling might have been involved as a result of decrease in velocity as the bullet passed through President Kennedy, whether there was any indication from the surface of the wound which would indicate tumbling.

Dr. SHAW. The wound entrance was an elliptical wound. In other words, it had a long diameter and a short diameter. It didn't have the appearance of a wound caused by a high velocity bullet that had not struck anything else; in other words, a puncture wound.

Now, you have to also take into consideration, however, whether the bullet enters at a right angle or at a tangent. If it enters at a tangent there will be some length to the wound of entrance.

Mr. SPECTER. So, would you say in net that there could have been some tumbling occasioned by having it pass through another body or perhaps the oblique character of entry might have been occasioned by the angle of entry.

Dr. SHAW. Yes; either would have explained a wound of entry.

Mr. SPECTER. Fine, thank you very much, Doctor.

Dr. SHAW. Thank you.

TESTIMONY OF DR. CHARLES FRANCIS GREGORY

The testimony of Dr. Charles Francis Gregory was taken at 2:30 p.m., on March 23, 1964, at Parkland Memorial Hospital, Dallas, Tex., by Mr. Arlen Specter, assistant counsel of the President's Commission.

Mr. SPECTER. May the record show that at the start of this session that I have here at the moment Dr. Charles Gregory, who has appeared here in response to a letter of request from the President's Commission on the Assassination of President Kennedy.

May I say to you, Dr. Gregory, that the purpose of the Commission is to investigate all facets relating to the assassination, including the wounding of President Kennedy, and the wounding of Governor Connally, and we have asked you to appear here for the purpose of testifying concerning your treatment of Governor Connally. Our rules specify that we make a brief statement of the purpose of the Commission, and the purpose of our calling on you.

Now, will you stand up and raise your right hand?

Do you solemnly swear the testimony you will give before the President's Commission in this deposition proceeding will be the truth, the whole truth, and nothing but the truth, so help you God?

Dr. GREGORY. I do.

Mr. SPECTER. Will you state your full name for the record, please?

Dr. GREGORY. Dr. Charles Francis Gregory.

Mr. SPECTER. And what is your profession, sir?

Dr. GREGORY. I am a physician and surgeon.

Mr. SPECTER. Will you outline your educational background, please?

Dr. GREGORY. Yes; I received a bachelor of science degree from Indiana University in 1941, and a doctor of medicine in 1944. I have completed 5 years of post-graduate training in orthopedic surgery at the Indiana University Medical Center in 1951. I remained there excepting for an interlude with the U.S. Navy in 1953 and 1954, until 1956. In 1956 I assumed my present position, which is that of professor of orthopedic surgery and chairman of the division of orthopedic surgery at the Southwestern Medical School, University of Texas.

Mr. SPECTER. Dr. Gregory, are you certified by the American Board?

Dr. GREGORY. I am certified by the American Board of Orthopedic Surgery; yes, sir.

Mr. SPECTER. And what year were you so certified?

Dr. GREGORY. In 1953. I am now a member of the American Board of Orthopedic Surgery, as a matter of fact.

Mr. SPECTER. Dr. Gregory, what experience, if any, have you had in the treatment of gunshot wounds?

Dr. GREGORY. My experience with the treatment of gunshot wounds began with my training in orthopedic surgery, but its greatest impetus occurred in 1953 and 1954 in the Korean theatre of operations with the U.S. Navy. Since that time here at the Parkland Hospital in Dallas our service has attended a considerable number of such injuries, plus my experience is continuing.

Mr. SPECTER. Could you approximate the total number of gunshot wounds you have had experience with?

Dr. GREGORY. I have had personal experience with, I suppose, in approximately 500 such missile wounds.

Mr. SPECTER. Dr. Gregory, back on November 22, 1963, did you have occasion to treat Governor Connally?

Dr. GREGORY. I did.

Mr. SPECTER. Will you relate briefly the circumstances surrounding your call to treat the Governor?

Dr. GREGORY. I had been seeing patients in the health service at the medical school building on the morning of November 22 and was there when word was received that the President had been shot. I did not then know that the Governor had also been injured. I came to the emergency room of Parkland Hospital and upon gaining entrance to it, inquired as to whether or not Mr. Kennedy's wounds were of a nature that would require my assistance.

I was advised that they were not. I then took a number of persons from the emergency room area with me away from it in order to reduce the confusion, and I went to the orthopedic ward on the fifth floor west of Parkland Hospital. After attending some of the patients on that ward, I was preparing to leave the hospital and went by the operating room area to see whether or not I could be of any other assistance, and was apprised then that a page was out for me. At that time Dr. Shaw advised me that Governor Connally had been wounded and that among his wounds were those to the right forearm and the left thigh. He had asked that I stay and attend those wounds after he had completed care of the Governor's chest wound.

Mr. SPECTER. At approximately what time did you have that conversation with Dr. Shaw?

Dr. GREGORY. To the best of my knowledge, that conversation must have been about between 1 and 1:15 in the afternoon of November 22.

Mr. SPECTER. And that conversation was with Dr. Shaw?

Dr. GREGORY. Dr. Robert Shaw.

Mr. SPECTER. Now, what part did Dr. Robert Shaw have in the treatment of Governor Connally in a general way?

Dr. GREGORY. Well, Dr. Robert Shaw attended the most serious wound that the Governor sustained, which was one to his right chest, and it was his operation which took precedence over all others.

Mr. SPECTER. And, was that operation completed before your operation commenced?

Dr. GREGORY. Yes; Dr. Shaw's operation had been completed before we even arranged the Governor's right arm and left thigh for definitive care.

Mr. SPECTER. At approximately what time did your operation of Governor Connally begin?

Dr. GREGORY. My operation on Governor Connally began about 4 o'clock p.m. on Friday, November 22.

Mr. SPECTER. And approximately how long did it last?

Dr. GREGORY. The better part of an hour—I should judge—45 to 50 minutes.

Mr. SPECTER. Who, if anyone, assisted you in that operation?

Dr. GREGORY. I was assisted by the junior orthopedic resident, Dr. William Osborne, and the orthopedic intern, Dr. John Parker.

Mr. SPECTER. What was Governor Connally's condition when you first saw him with respect to his chest wounds, first, if you will, please tell us?

Dr. GREGORY. I did not see Governor Connally myself until he had been taken into the operating room and had had an endotracheal tube placed in his larynx and had been anesthetized. Having accomplished this, the very precarious mechanics of respiration had been corrected and his general status at that time was quite satisfactory.

Mr. SPECTER. What observations did you have with respect to his wound in the chest?

91

Dr. GREGORY. I had none, really, for the business of prepping and draping was underway at that time, and I did not intrude other than to observe very casually, and I don't remember any details of it.

Now, I did see in the course of the operation the wound in his chest, the wound of entry, and its posterior surface and the wound of exit on the anterior surface.

Mr. SPECTER. What did the wound of entry look like, Doctor?

Dr. GREGORY. It appeared to me that the wound of entry was sort of a linear wound, perhaps three-quarters of an inch in length with a rounded central portion. Whereas, the wound of exit was rather larger than this, perhaps an inch and a half across.

Mr. SPECTER. And at approximately what part of the body was the wound that you described as the wound of entry?

Dr. GREGORY. In view of the drapes that were on the Governor at the time, I will have to speculate, but as I recall best, it was in an area probably 2 inches below and medial to the right nipple.

Mr. SPECTER. Is that the wound of entry or exit?

Dr. GREGORY. That's the wound of exit.

Mr. SPECTER. How about the wound of entry?

Dr. GREGORY. The wound of entry was too obscure for me to identify, since it was just in general over the posterior aspect of his chest.

Mr. SPECTER. What did you observe with respect to the wound of his wrist?

Dr. GREGORY. I didn't see the wound of his wrist until after the chest operation had been completed, because his arm was covered by the operation drapes, the surgical drapes for the chest procedure.

Mr. SPECTER. And when you did have an opportunity to observe the wound of the wrist, what did you then see?

Dr. GREGORY. I observed the wound on the dorsal aspect of his wrist, which was about 2 cm. in length, ragged, somewhat irregular, and lay about an inch and a half or 2 inches above the wrist joint. It was a little to the radial side of the wrist area.

There was a second wound in the wrist on the volar surface, about a centimeter and a half proximal to the distal flexion crease and this wound was a transverse laceration no more than a centimeter in length and did not gape.

Mr. SPECTER. When you say on the dorsal aspect, what is that?

Dr. GREGORY. In lay terms, that's equivalent to the back of the hand.

Mr. SPECTER. And the volar is equivalent to what?

Dr. GREGORY. The palm surface of the hand.

Mr. SPECTER. What conclusion, if any, did you reach as to which was the wound of entry and exit on the wrist?

Dr. GREGORY. Based on certain findings in the wound at the time the debridement was carried out——

Mr. SPECTER. Will you define debridement before you proceed with that?

Dr. GREGORY. Yes; debridement is a surgical term used to designate that procedure in attending a wound which removes by sharp excision all nonvital tissue in the area together with any identifiable foreign objects.

In attending this wound, it was evident early that clot had been carried into the wound from the dorsal surface to the bone and into the fracture. This would imply that an irregular missile had passed through the wrist from the dorsal to the volar aspect.

Mr. SPECTER. Now, were there any characteristics in the volar aspect which would indicate that it was a wound of exit?

Dr. GREGORY. No; there were none, really. It was my assumption that the missile had expended much of its remaining energy in passing through the radius bone, which it did before it could emerge through the soft tissues.

Mr. SPECTER. Did you observe any foreign objects identifiable as bits of fragments or portions of a bullet missile?

Dr. GREGORY. A preliminary X-ray had indicated that there were metallic fragments or at least metallic fragments which cast metallic shadows in the soft tissues around the wounded forearm. Two or three of these were identified and were recovered and were observed to be metallic in consistency. These were turned over to appropriate authorities for further disposition.

Mr. SPECTER. Approximately how large were those fragments, Dr. Gregory?

Dr. GREGORY. I would judge that they were first—flat, rather thin, and that their greatest dimension would probably not exceed one-eighth of an inch. They were very small.

Mr. SPECTER. Would you have sufficient experience with gunshot wounds to comment as to whether a 6.5-mm. bullet could have passed through the Governor's wrist in the way you have described, leaving the fragments which you have described and still have virtually all the bullet missile intact, or having 158 grains of a bullet at that time?

Dr. GREGORY. Well, I am not an expert on ballistics, but one cannot escape certain ballistic implications in this business.

I would say, first of all, that how much of the missile remains intact as a mass depends to some extent on how hard the metal is. Obviously, if it is very soft, as lead, it may lose more fragments and therefore more weight and volume than it might if it is made of a harder material or is jacketed in some way.

Now, the energy in the missile is a product, not so much of its mass as it is of its velocity, for by doubling the velocity, you can increase the kinetic energy in the force it transmits, fourfold, since the formula for determining energy in these cases is a matter of mass times velocity squared, rather than just linear functional velocity. So, some knowledge of how much of the cartridge force might have been behind the missile would be useful here too.

Mr. SPECTER. For the purpose of this consideration, I am interested to know the the metal which you found in the wrist was of sufficient size so that the bullet which passed through the wrist could not have emerged virtually completely intact or with 158 grains intact, or whether the portions of the metallic fragments were so small that that would be consistent with having virtually the entire 6.5-mm. bullet emerge.

Dr. GREGORY. Well, considering the small volume of metal as seen by X-ray, and the very small dimensions of the metal which was recovered, I think several   such fragments could have been flaked off of a total missile mass without reducing its volume greatly.

Now, just how much, depends of course upon what the original missile weighed. In other words, on the basis of the metal left behind in Governor Connally's body, as far as I could tell, the missile that struck it could be virtually intact, insofar as mass was concerned, but probably was distorted.

Mr. SPECTER. Would you have any idea at all as to what the fragments which you observed in the Governor's wrist might weigh, Doctor?

Dr. GREGORY. No, not really, but it would have been very small—very small.

Mr. SPECTER. What treatment or action did you take with respect to treating the Governor's wrist for him, Dr. Gregory?

Dr. GREGORY. Upon completing the debridement, we were then faced with a decision as to whether we should suture his wound in the conventional manner or not, and we chose not to, leaving the wound open in deference to potential infection that might be produced by retained fragments of clothing. Having decided upon that course of action, the fractured radius bone was then manipulated into a reduced position and the entire limb was encased in a plaster-paris cast.

Mr. SPECTER. Did that complete your operative procedure?

Dr. GREGORY. That completed my operative procedure for that day for Governor Connally—yes.

Mr. SPECTER. What other wounds, if any, did you notice on the Governor at that time?

Dr. GREGORY. In addition to the chest wound and the wound just described in his right forearm there was a wound in the medical aspect of his left thigh. This was almost round and did not seem to have disturbed the tissues badly, but did definitely penetrate and pass through the skin and to the fascia beneath. I could not tell from the superficial inspection whether it had passed through the fascia. An X-ray was made of his thigh at that time and there was not present in his thigh any missile of sufficient magnitude, in my opinion, to have produced the wound observed on his medial aspect. Repeat X-rays failed to reveal any such missile and an additional examination failed to reveal any wound of exit.

Mr. SPECTER. What did the X-rays reveal with respect to the presence of a missile?

Dr. GREGORY. In the thigh there was a very small shadow, perhaps 1 mm. by 2 mm. in dimension, lying close to the medial aspect of the femur, that is, the thigh bone, but was in my opinion much too small to have accounted for the dimensions of the wound on the medial aspect of his thigh or a wound of that character.

Mr. SPECTER. What were the dimensions of the wound on the medial aspect of his thigh?

Dr. GREGORY. I would say that that wound was about a centimeter in diameter, much larger than the identifiable fragment of metal in the thigh. I might add that this prompted some speculation on our part, my part, which was voiced to someone that some search ought to be made in the Governor's clothing or perhaps in the auto or some place, wherever he may have been, for the missile which had produced this much damage but which was not resident in him.

Mr. SPECTER. Approximately what type of a missile would it have taken to produce a wound which you have described on his thigh?

Dr. GREGORY. Well, it would take a fragment of metal of approximately the same diameter—a centimeter, and in general—round.

93

Mr. SPECTER. Would that correspond with the measurement of a 6.5-mm. missile?

Dr. GREGORY. I will have to guess—I don't know what dimension—of a 6.5-mm.—yes, a 6.5-mm. would be .65 cm., approximately, yes, that could have very well have occurred from such a missile, yes, sir.

Mr. SPECTER. Dr. Gregory. I now show you two typewritten pages which are a portion of a document identified as Commission Exhibit No. 392, which in its total aspect constitutes all of the medical records from Parkland Hospital on President Kennedy and Governor Connally and the two pages to which I direct your attention relate an operation on Governor Connally, where you are listed as the surgeon, and I ask you if you will take a minute and look those over and tell us whether or not that is your report on the operation which you have just been describing.

Dr. GREGORY. (Examining instrument referred to.) Yes, this appears to be the essence of the report which I dictated at the conclusion of my operation on Governor Connally.

Mr. SPECTER. And are the facts contained in this report the same as those to which you have testified here today?

Dr. GREGORY. I think they are—I hope so.

Mr. SPECTER. Now, will you describe in a general way what treatment you have given Governor Connally following the time when you completed this report on November 22, 1963?

Dr. GREGORY. The Governor remained in Parkland Hospital for some 2 weeks after his admission. On the 5th day after the operation, in the Governor's hospital room, the wound on the dorsal surface of his wrist was closed by wire sutures and this was carried out in the room. On the 10th day, I believe it was, the 10th day from injury, the Governor was taken back to the operating room and there under a light general anesthesia, his wounds were dressed and inspected, and a new plaster of paris cast was applied at that time.

The Governor was then permitted up and about with his arm in a sling, and shortly thereafter returned to the Governor's Mansion in Austin. I visited Governor Connally in the Governor's Mansion in Austin about 1 week after his discharge from the hospital, simply for check-up examination and I found things to be in a satisfactory state.

I saw the Governor again about 1 month after his discharge, in the office of Dr. Robert A. Dennison in Austin, Tex., and another examination this time, including an X-ray, was made, and again the condition of his right forearm and of the fractured bone were considered to be satisfactory.

Now, I've got to think of the next date—off of the record or on as you wish—

Mr. SPECTER. All right, we will go off of the record, Doctor, while you are thinking that through.

Dr. GREGORY. All right.

(Discussion between Counsel Specter and the Witness Gregory off the record.)

Mr. SPECTER. All right, Dr. Gregory.

Dr. GREGORY. I'll say on or about February 14, the Governor came to Dallas and on that occasion we removed his cast, obtained an X-ray, found his fracture to be healing satisfactorily, and so we applied a new cast. The Governor wore that cast until 1 week ago, when he again came to Dallas. The cast was removed, and X-ray revealed satisfactory healing of his fracture, and the cast, as a continuous form of treatment, was discontinued.

At the present time the Governor is on a regiment of exercises, and he wears a demountable splint, whenever it looks as though the electorate may be over enthusiastic by shaking his hand.

Mr. SPECTER. Do you anticipate any future cast for Governor Connally?

Dr. GREGORY. I anticipate probably an uneventful, though slow, recovery of normal function in his right arm and wrist and hand.

I think he will have some permanent impairment, but I think he will have a very minimal amount of disability, and I do not at this time anticipate any need for any further surgical intervention. That will have to become manifest by the appearance of some other as yet unanticipated symptom.

I would like to add that on each of the examination interviews here in Dallas, the Governor was also checked over by Dr. Robert Shaw, from the point of view of recovery from his chest wound.

Mr. SPECTER. Dr. Gregory, I now show you a series of diagrams which are a part of reports bearing Commission No. 326 and may the record show these differ from Commission Exhibit numbers, reflecting the number assigned to reports.

I am going to ask the Court Reporter to mark this particular copy as Dr. Gregory's Exhibit No. 1.

(Instrument marked by the Reporter as Dr. Gregory's Exhibit No. 1, for identification.)

Mr. SPECTER. I am going to ask you, pointing first to Diagram No. 1, whether or not this accurately depicts the wounds of Governor Connally?

Dr. GREGORY. This one does not.

Mr. SPECTER. In what respect?

Dr. GREGORY. In the respect that the wound of entry is shown to exist on the volar surface of the forearm, whereas, it was on the dorsal surface of the forearm in my view—in my opinion—and the reverse holds for the wound of exit.

Mr. SPECTER. Will you take my pen and correct those as they should be, Doctor Gregory?

Dr. GREGORY. (Complied with request of Counsel Specter.)

Mr. SPECTER. Now, turning to Exhibit, Diagram No. 2 on this exhibit, and calling your attention specifically to the point of entry and the point of exit on the diagram of a man standing, does that correspond with the angle of declination on Governor Connally's wound?

Dr. GREGORY. To the best of my knowledge, this would fairly accurately depict that angle. If I were to have any reservation at all, it would be with reference to the height or the position of the wounds of entry, as being marked a little high, but this is recalling from memory, and it may not be correct.

Mr. SPECTER. I now call your attention to Diagram No. 3 on this sequence and ask if this accurately depicts the condition of the Governor's wounds?

Dr. GREGORY. I think that this one comes more closely into line with their actual location, especially with reference to the wound of entry in the posterior aspect of the chest. It is a little lower here, as I recall it to be. Those of the wrist, I think are accurately depicted, and that of the thigh are believed to be accurately depicted.

Mr. SPECTER. And on these wrist wounds, do they show the point of entry to be on the dorsal aspect and the point of exit to be on the volar aspect?

Dr. GREGORY. According to the anatomical position, I believe that they do; yes.

Mr. SPECTER. Now, looking at Diagram No. 4, does this again correspond with your recollection of the angle of decline on Governor Connally?

Dr. GREGORY. Again, if I have a reservation it would be to the wound of entry and the posterior aspect as being shown a little higher than it actually existed.

Mr. SPECTER. Now, Dr. Gregory, I turn to Diagram No. 5, which depicts a seated man and what does Diagram No. 5 depict to your eye with respect to what action is described on the seated man?

Dr. GREGORY. Well, I should say that this composite has alined the several parts of the body demonstrated in such a way that a single missile following a constant trajectory could have accounted for all of the wounds which are shown.

Moreover, this is consistent with the point of entry which is depicted on the side views showing the angle of declination. I submit that the angle of declination in passing through the chest could be very simply altered by having an individual lean forward a few degrees, and similarly could be made much deeper by having him lean backward, without really changing the basic relationship between the parts, nor in any way affecting the likelihood that all parts could have come into this same trajectory.

Mr. SPECTER. Would you consider it possible, in your professional opinion, for the same bullet to have inflicted all of the wounds which you have described on Governor Connally?

Dr. GREGORY. Yes; I believe it very possible, for a number of reasons. One of these—is the apparent loss of energy manifested at each of the various body surfaces, which I transected, the greatest energy being at the point of entry on the posterior aspect of the chest and of the fifth rib, where considerable destruction was done and the least destruction having been done in the medial aspect of the thigh where the bullet apparently expended itself.

Mr. SPECTER. What destruction was done on the fifth rib, Dr. Gregory?

Dr. GREGORY. It is my understanding from conversations with Dr. Shaw, and I believe his medical reports bear this out, that the fifth rib was literally shattered by the missile.

We know that high velocity bullets striking bone have a strong tendency to shatter bones and the degree to which the fifth rib was shattered was considerably in excess of the amount of shattering which occurred in the radius—the forearm.

Mr. SPECTER. And what conclusion, if any, did you draw as to the velocity of the missile, as to the time it struck each of those bony portions?

Dr. GREGORY. I think that the missile was continually losing velocity with each set of tissues which it encountered and transected, and the amount of damage done is progressively less from first entrance in the thorax to the last entrance in the thigh.

Mr. SPECTER. Do you think it possible that Governor Connally was shot by two bullets, with one hitting in the posterior part of his body and the second one striking the back side of his wrist?

Dr. GREGORY. The possibility exists, but I would discount it for these reasons—ordinarily, a missile in flight—I'll qualify that—a high velocity missile in flight does not tend to carry organic material into the wound which it creates.

I believe if you will inspect the record which was prepared by Dr. Shaw, there is no indication that any clothing or other organic material was found in the chest wound.

An irregular missile can carry debris into a wound and such debris was carried into the wound of the wrist.

I would have expected that an undistorted high velocity missile striking the wrist would not have carried material into it.

Mr. SPECTER. Was there any other characteristic which led and leads you to conclude that the wrist was not the initial point of impact of a single high velocity bullet?

Dr. GREGORY. Yes. Based on our experience with high velocity missile wounds of the forearm produced by rifles of the deer hunting calibre, there is tremendous soft tissue destruction as well as bone fragmentation which not infrequently culminates in amputation of the part.

I do not believe that the missile wound in Governor Connally's right forearm was produced by a missile of such magnitude at the time it struck him. It either had to be one of lower initial energy or a missile which had been partially expended elsewhere before it struck his wrist.

Mr. SPECTER. Would that opinion apply if you assumed that the missile had initial velocity when leaving the muzzle of the weapon of 200 feet per second?

Dr. GREGORY. That's not a very high velocity missile.

Mr. SPECTER. Pardon me—2,000 feet per second.

Dr. GREGORY. I should say that a missile at 2,000 feet per second that strikes the forearm is likely to blow it very nearly off, if it is a missile of any mass as well.

Mr. SPECTER. Well, assume that you have a muzzle velocity of 2,000 feet per second and assume the mass is 6.5 mm., and assume further that the distance between the muzzle and the wrist is approximately 160 to 250 feet away, what would you expect, based on your experience, that the consequences would be on that wrist?

Dr. GREGORY. I will have to say that most of the high velocity rifle wounds that I have seen of the forearm have, in fact, been at a closer range than that which you have stipulated, but I doubt that a range of 155 or 200 feet would seriously reduce the energy, and I would expect a similar wound, under the circumstances which you have described.

Mr. SPECTER. Let me add another possibility in this sequence, Dr. Gregory, and ask you your opinion with respect to an additional intervening victim in the path of the same bullet to this effect—assume that President Kennedy was riding in an open automobile directly behind Governor Connally, and that at a distance of approximately 175 feet President Kennedy was struck by a bullet from a weapon with a muzzle velocity of 2,000 feet per second, carrying a 6.5 mm. missile and that the missile entered in the upper right of the President's back very near the neckline and passed through his body, striking no bony material, and emerged from the throat of the President. Is it possible that missile could have then entered the back of the Governor and inflicted the chest wound which you have described?

Dr. GREGORY. I would have to concede that that would be possible—yes.

Mr. SPECTER. What would your professional opinion be, if you can formulate one, as to whether or not that actually did happen in this situation?

Dr. GREGORY. I really couldn't formulate an objective opinion about it. Only, for this reason, that it would then become a question simply of trajectories, and lining the two bodies up in such a way that this sequence of events could have occurred. I would hazard one guess, that is, that had the missile that struck Governor Connally passed through President Kennedy first, that though the missile would not have been distorted necessarily, it would very probably have begun to tumble. Now, if you like, I will define that for you.

Mr. SPECTER. Would you please?

Dr. GREGORY. A tumbling is a second—it actually is a third component of motion that a missile may go through in its trajectory. First, there is a linear motion from muzzle to target on point of impact. In order to keep a missile on its path, there is imparted to it a rotary motion so that it is spinning. Now, both of these are commensurate with the constant trajectory. A third component, which is tumbling, and is literally the end over end motion, which may be imparted to a missile should it strike something in flight that deflects but does not stop it—in this circumstance the wound of entry created by such a missile usually is quite large and the destruction it creates is increased, as a matter of fact, by such tumbling, and I would have

96

therefore expected to see perhaps some organic material carried into a large wound of entry in Governor Connally's back.

These are only theoretical observations, but these are some of the reasons why I would believe that the missile in the Governor behaved as though it had never struck anything except him.

Mr. SPECTER. Did you observe the nature of the wound in the Governor's back?

Dr. GREGORY. Only so far as I saw it as Dr. Shaw was preparing to operate on it, but I was unable to see the nature of the wound as he carried out his operation. I did, however, specifically question him about this matter of containing foreign material, clothing, etc.

Mr. SPECTER. What did he say about that?

Dr. GREGORY. Well, as I recall it, he said none was found, and I would not have expected any to be found as I explained to you, if this was the initial impact of that missile.

Mr. SPECTER. Well, wouldn't you think it possible, bearing in mind that my last question only went as to whether the same bullet could have gone through President Kennedy and inflicted the wound on Governor Connolly's chest, would you think it possible that the same missile could have gone through President Kennedy in the way I described and have inflicted all three of the wounds, that is, the entry and exit on the chest, the entry and exit on the wrist, and the entry into the thigh which you described.

Dr. GREGORY. I suspect it's possible, but I would say it would have to be a remarkably powerful missile to have done so.

Mr. SPECTER. Dr. Gregory, have you been interviewed about this matter prior to today by any representative of the Federal Government?

Dr. GREGORY. Yes; on two or three occasions I have talked to a properly identified member of the Secret Service, Mr. Warren, I believe it was.

Mr. SPECTER. And what was the nature of the information which you gave to Mr. Warren on those occasions?

Dr. GREGORY. Essentially the same thing as I have told you here, but in much less detail.

Mr. SPECTER. And have you ever talked to anyone besides Mr. Warren and me about these matters, from the Federal Government?

Dr. GREGORY. No; not that I know of. I was on a day or so after the assassination spoken to in these offices by a member of the Federal Bureau of Investigation, but it was a very brief interview.

Mr. SPECTER. What was that about?

Dr. GREGORY. And I think it was the question of whether or not I had been able to recover any metal from Governor Connally which they might use for ballistic analysis.

I regret to say I don't know the gentleman's name, but he too was properly identified.

Mr. SPECTER. And prior to the time when the Court Reporter started to transcribe the deposition which you have been kind enough to provide us with, had you and I been talking about the same subjects which you have answered questions on all during the course of this deposition?

Dr. GREGORY. Yes.

Mr. SPECTER. And during the time that you first were interviewed by the Secret Service down through the present moment, have you had the same general opinion concerning the matters which you have testified about here today?

Dr. GREGORY. Yes.

Mr. SPECTER. Do you have anything to add which you think would be helpful in any way to the work of the Commission?

Dr. GREGORY. No; not really. This is the only articulation I have had with this whole episode concerning Governor Connally's wound and his subsequent recovery and none other.

Mr. SPECTER. Thank you very much, Dr. Gregory, for coming.

Dr. GREGORY. Very well.

TESTIMONY OF DR. GEORGE T. SHIRES

The testimony of Dr. George T. Shires was taken at 4:35 p.m., on March 23, 1964, at Parkland Memorial Hospital, Dallas, Tex., by Mr. Arlen Specter, assistant counsel of the President's Commission.

Mr. SPECTER. Let the record show that as we are reconvening this session and about to commence the deposition of Dr. George T. Shires, that the preliminary statement is being made that this is pursuant to the investigation being conducted by the President's Commission on the Assassination of President Kennedy to determine all the facts relating to the shooting, including the treatment rendered to Governor Connally as well as President Kennedy, and that Dr. Shires has appeared here today in response to a letter of request from the President's Commission to

97

testify concerning his knowledge of the treatment which he and other medical personnel at Parkland Hospital performed on Governor Connally.

Will you rise, please, Dr. Shires and raise your right hand. Do you solemnly swear that the testimony you will give before the President's Commission in this deposition proceeding will be the truth, the whole truth, and nothing but the truth, so help you God?

Dr. SHIRES. I do.

Mr. SPECTER. Would you state your full name, please, for the record?

Dr. SHIRES. George Thomas Shires.

Mr. SPECTER. And what is your profession, sir?

Dr. SHIRES. Professor of Surgery and Chairman of the Department of Surgery, University of Texas, Southwestern Medical School.

Mr. SPECTER. And you are a medical doctor by profession, I assume?

Dr. SHIRES. Yes; M.D.

Mr. SPECTER. Would you outline briefly your educational background?

Dr. SHIRES. Undergraduate education at the University of Texas in Austin, Tex.; graduate medical education at the University of Texas, Southwestern Medical School in Dallas; internship, Massachusetts Memorial Hospital in Boston, Mass.; surgical residency—Parkland Memorial Hospital in Dallas, Tex.; two tours of active duty in the United States Navy, first as research investigator at the Naval Medical Research Institute, National Naval Medical Center, Bethesda, Md.; second as Associate Surgeon, United States Naval Hospital Ship *Haven*—do you want staff positions?

Mr. SPECTER. Please, give me those, as well.

Dr. SHIRES. Subsequently, Clinical Instructor in Surgery, University of Texas, Southwestern Medical School, progressing through Assistant Professor of Surgery, Associate Professor of Surgery, Professor of Surgery, and Chairman of the Department of Surgery.

Mr. SPECTER. What was your year of graduation from college, Dr. Shires?

Dr. SHIRES. This was premedical, and at that time the war was on, so it was a premedical 3 years—it was 1944.

Mr. SPECTER. And what year did you receive your medical degree?

Dr. SHIRES. 1948.

Mr. SPECTER. Are you Board certified at the present time?

Dr. SHIRES. Yes.

Mr. SPECTER. And, in what year were you so certified?

Dr. SHIRES. I was certified by the American Board of Surgery in 1956.

Mr. SPECTER. Did you have occasion to render any medical treatment for President Kennedy back on November 22, 1963?

Dr. SHIRES. No; I was not in town at the time the shooting occurred. I was in Galveston, Tex., at the meeting of the Western Surgical Association.

Mr. SPECTER. Did you have occasion to render medical attention and services to Governor Connally, Dr. Shires?

Dr. SHIRES. Yes.

Mr. SPECTER. Will you state briefly the circumstances under which you were called into this case?

Dr. SHIRES. After the President and the Governor were brought to Parkland Hospital, it was determined—well—all aid was given to the President that was available, and it was determined that Governor Connally's injuries were multiple, the primary injury to Governor Connally was to the chest.

Dr. Shaw, who is the professor of surgery—I don't need to tell their titles—you will have all that?

Mr. SPECTER. Yes—correct.

Dr. SHIRES. Dr. Shaw ascertained the condition of Governor Connally, instituted therapy, and had the hospital notify me in Galveston of the status of the President and also the Governor.

Mr. SPECTER. Were you able to return then to Dallas in time to assist in the operative procedures on Governor Connally?

Dr. SHIRES. Yes.

Mr. SPECTER. And at approximately what time did you return to Dallas?

Dr. SHIRES. Approximately 3 p.m.

Mr. SPECTER. And what participation did you have in the operative procedures on Governor Connally?

Dr. SHIRES. At the time I returned, the chest procedure was in progress. The orthopedic procedure on the arm and the leg debridement were ready to be started. I scrubbed and performed the leg procedure.

Mr. SPECTER. What did you observe, if anything, as to the condition of Governor Connally's chest wound?

Dr. SHIRES. At the time I arrived, the chest wound had been debrided and was being closed. His general condition at that point was very good. He was receiving blood and the arm and leg wounds were being prepared for surgery.

Mr. SPECTER. Did you have any opportunity to observe the wound on his back?

Dr. SHIRES. Not at that time.

Mr. SPECTER. Did you have any opportunity to observe a wound on his chest?

Dr. SHIRES. Once again, not at that time—later, but not at that time.

Mr. SPECTER. Well, what did you observe at a later time concerning the wound on his back and on his chest?

Dr. SHIRES. Well, in part of his postoperative care, which was a large part of the treatment, we were concerned, of course, with all the wounds, and he had several chest wounds. These, at the time I saw them, had been debrided and were the site of draining, so that their initial appearance was completely altered by having had surgical debridement, so they were clean postsurgical wounds with drainage, at the time I first saw them.

Mr. SPECTER. Would their alteration and condition preclude you from giving an opinion as to whether they were points of entry or points of exit?

Dr. SHIRES. They would—really.

Mr. SPECTER. What did you observe at the time you arrived at the hospital as to the condition of his wrist, if anything?

Dr. SHIRES. At that point his wrist was being prepared for surgery, and although I did not examine this in detail, since I was concerned with the thigh wound, there appeared to be a through and through wound of the wrist which looked like a missile wound.

Mr. SPECTER. Were you able to formulate any opinion as to the point of entry or the point of exit?

Dr. SHIRES. No; since I didn't examine it in detail; no, not really.

Mr. SPECTER. And what did you observe as to the wound on the thigh?

Dr. SHIRES. The wound on the thigh was a peculiar one. There was a 1 cm. puncate missile wound over the junction of the middle and lower third of the leg and the medial aspect of the thigh. The peculiarity came in that the X-rays of the left leg showed only a very small 1 mm. bullet fragment imbedded in the femur of the left leg. Upon exploration of this wound, the other peculiarity was that there was very little soft tissue damage, less than one would expect from an entrance wound of a centimeter in diameter, which was seen on the skin. So, it appeared, therefore, that the skin wound was either a tangential wound or that a larger fragment had penetrated or stopped in the skin and had subsequently fallen out of the entrance wound.

Mr. SPECTER. What size fragment was there in the Governor's leg at that time?

Dr. SHIRES. We recovered none. The small one that was seen was on X-ray and it was still in the femur and being that small, with no tissue damage after the debridement, it was thought inadvisable to remove this small fragment.

Mr. SPECTER. Is that fragment in the bone itself at the present time?

Dr. SHIRES. Yes.

Mr. SPECTER. What would your best estimate be as to the size of that fragment?

Dr. SHIRES. One millimeter in diameter—one to two.

Mr. SPECTER. Would you have any estimate as to how much that might weigh in grains?

Dr. SHIRES. In grains—a fraction of a grain, maybe, a tenth of a grain—very small.

Mr. SPECTER. A tenth of one grain?

Dr. SHIRES. Yes.

Mr. SPECTER. What size bullet would it take to create the punctate hole which you described in the thigh?

Dr. SHIRES. This would depend entirely on the angle and the speed and weight of the bullet. For example, a small missile on a tangent may create a surprisingly large defect. A large bullet with fast or a relatively slow velocity will create the same defect.

Mr. SPECTER. What operative procedures did you employ?

Dr. SHIRES. Progressive debridement from skin, fat, fascia, muscle, irrigation, and through and through enclosure with stainless steel alloy wire and removable sutures.

Mr. SPECTER. Does that complete a general description of what you did to Governor Connally?

Dr. SHIRES. In the operating room, yes.

Mr. SPECTER. Approximately what time did that operation start?

Dr. SHIRES. Approximately 1 o'clock.

Mr. SPECTER. The operation that you were concerned with?

Dr. SHIRES. Oh, the operation that I was concerned with must have started at 3:30 or 4 o'clock, I guess it was.

Mr. SPECTER. And about what time did it end?

Dr. SHIRES. My portion of it—about 20 minutes later.

Mr. SPECTER. And who, if anyone, assisted you in that portion of the operation?

Dr. SHIRES. Doctors Robert McClelland, Charles Baxter, and Ralph Don Patman.

Mr. SPECTER. Dr. Shires, I am showing you a document identified heretofore as Commission Exhibit No. 392, which is the report of Parkland Hospital on the treatment of President Kennedy and Governor Connally, and I show you a Parkland Memorial Hospital operative record, dated November 22, 1963, which lists you as the surgeon, and ask you whether or not this represents the report made by you on the operative procedures on Governor Connally?

Dr. SHIRES. Yes; it does.

Mr. SPECTER. And, are those the same as the matters which you have heretofore described during the course of this deposition as to what you did?

Dr. SHIRES. Yes.

Mr. SPECTER. Now, what treatment, if any, have you performed on Governor Connally subsequent to November 22?

Dr. SHIRES. A tremendous amount—postoperative care was of the essence here in that he had multiple injuries, massive blood and fluid replacement, so that to describe the care is really a detail of postoperative—I don't know how much of this you want—in other words, he had clotting defects—I don't know whether you want to take this down—I just want to ask you how much detail you would like?

Mr. SPECTER. Start off with a general description—perhaps, I will direct your attention to some specific areas to abbreviate it.

First of all, how frequently did you see him after November 22, 1963?

Dr. SHIRES. For the first several days I saw him approximately every 2 to 4 hours for an hour or so each visit, and many times for 6 and 8 hours at a stretch.

Mr. SPECTER. And after that time how frequently did you see him?

Dr. SHIRES. Decreasing frequency over the next 3 weeks—never less than three or four times a day, even after he was convalescing.

Mr. SPECTER. How long was he in the hospital?

Dr. SHIRES. I don't really know the number of days he was in the hospital.

Mr. SPECTER. After he left the hospital, have you seen him?

Dr. SHIRES. Yes; I saw him again approximately 2 weeks, I guess it was, after he left the hospital, in Austin. He developed a superficial saphenous thrombophlebitis in the right leg, not the one that the injury occurred in. This was undoubtedly incident to a catheter cutdown having been placed in this leg for administration of blood and fluids while he was in the hospital. He unequivocally had a clot in the saphenous vein and at this time was placed on bed rest, antibiotics, anticoagulants and responded very satisfactorily.

Mr. SPECTER. Do you anticipate seeing him in the future?

Dr. SHIRES. Do I?

Mr. SPECTER. Yes.

Dr. SHIRES. Not for his wounds. No—the only followup care that he really requires at the moment is the bone—the orthopedic followup, which incidentally is also completely healed.

Mr. SPECTER. Doctor, look, if you will, at a document which we have marked Dr. Gregory X-1, used in the course of the deposition of Dr. Gregory, which immediately preceded yours and directing your attention first to Diagram Number 1, would the entry and exit holes on Governor Connally's back and chest, being entry and exit, respectively, and the exit and entry on the wrist with the entry being on the back side of the wrist and the exit on the front side of the wrist, correspond with your observations of Governor Connally?

Dr. SHIRES. Yes; they would.

Mr. SPECTER. Now, going to Diagram 2, which depicts a man standing, would that correspond to the angle of the entry and exit wounds?

Dr. SHIRES. Yes.

Mr. SPECTER. Now, going to Diagram No. 3, would that diagram correspond with the wounds on Governor Connally as you recollect them to be?

Dr. SHIRES. Yes.

Mr. SPECTER. Going now to Diagram 4, would that again correspond with the wounds on Governor Connally?

Dr. SHIRES. Yes.

Mr. SPECTER. And as to Diagram No. 5, what does that represent?

Dr. SHIRES. This, at the time of the discussion of Governor Connally's injuries with his wife, before he really regained consciousness from surgery, was the apparent position that he was in in the car, which would explain one missile producing all three wounds.

Mr. SPECTER. Did you have a discussion with Mrs. Connally?

Dr. SHIRES. Yes; with Mrs. Connally.

Mr. SPECTER. And when was that discussion?

Dr. SHIRES. Right after the surgery—this was the 22d, late in the afternoon.

Mr. SPECTER. And what, if anything, did she tell you as to the Governor's position?

Dr. SHIRES. She had thought, and I think correctly so, that he had turned to his right after he heard the first shot, apparently, to see what had happened to the President, and he then later confirmed this, that he heard the first shot, turned to his right, and then was hit.

I forgot about that a moment ago, incidentally. He definitely remembers turning after hearing the first shot, before he was struck with a bullet. I forgot about that.

Mr. SPECTER. When did Governor Connally tell you that?

Dr. SHIRES. Oh, several days later.

Mr. SPECTER. While he was in the hospital?

Dr. SHIRES. Oh, yes—4 or 5 days later and we were constructing the events.

Mr. SPECTER. What was the occasion for your conversation with him?

Dr. SHIRES. In part of his routine care one morning, as he was reconstructing his memory of events, because his memory was quite hazy, since he had a sucking wound of the chest and came in here relatively in anoxia, he had some cyanosis, as you know.

Mr. SPECTER. What is cyanosis?

Dr. SHIRES. Not enough oxygen of the tissues and this means they turn blue.

Mr. SPECTER. Would that affect his memory?

Dr. SHIRES. Yes; sure would and did, and he remembers very little after he fell over in the car—he is very hazy, until, oh, probably the second day post-operatively.

Mr. SPECTER. Would that affect his memory as to what happened before the wound?

Dr. SHIRES. No.

Mr. SPECTER. Or, would that affect only his memory while he was suffering from lack of oxygen?

Dr. SHIRES. Probably just while he was suffering from lack of oxygen. He didn't have that much hypoxia. Hypoxia or anoxia or lack of oxygen could affect his memory. Had this been severe, this could have affected his memory for preceding events, but his hypoxia fortunately did not last that long, and he never showed real evidence of brain damage from the anoxia, so that I think his memory for events up until the time he recalls falling over in the car is probably accurate.

Mr. SPECTER. Would you relate just as exactly as you can for us what he said to you, and the nature of the conversation, with your replies, and how it went as closely as you can recount it now?

Dr. SHIRES. He recounted, and as I remember this particular occasion, Mrs. Connally was in the room too, and reconstructing events, she related the story of her last conversation with the President, relating to him, that the reception had been warm and that she was glad he couldn't say that people of Texas and in Dallas didn't like him and admire him, and she was very pleased with the way things had gone the whole visit. Then, the next event that occurred was that she remembers hearing a shot, he remembered hearing a shot—he remembers turning to the right, he remembered being struck by a bullet, and his next thought as he fell over toward his wife was "They're going to kill all of us," and that's the last really clear memory that he expressed to me until he remembers vaguely being in the emergency room, but very little of that, and then he remembers waking up in the recovery room several hours later.

Mr. SPECTER. Did he say anything to you about who he meant by "they"?

Dr. SHIRES. He didn't say—he didn't comment on it at all.

Mr. SPECTER. Did he describe the nature of the sound which he heard?

Dr. SHIRES. I don't believe he did—no.

Mr. SPECTER. Did anybody describe the nature of the sound?

Dr. SHIRES. I think Mrs. Connally did. I think she thought it was, if I'm not wrong, she thought it was a loud retort, either a gun or a firecracker. I think she thought it was a bullet and I think he did too—thought it was a gun—I believe he did too.

Mr. SPECTER. Now, did Governor Connally say anything about hearing President Kennedy say anything?

Dr. SHIRES. No—no, he didn't.

Mr. SPECTER. Did Mrs. Connally say anything about whether President Kennedy said anything?

Dr. SHIRES. No, she didn't. She remembered Mrs. Kennedy saying some things, but she didn't remember anything about the President having uttered a word.

Mr. SPECTER. What did Mrs. Kennedy say, according to Mrs. Connally?

Dr. SHIRES. Oh, it's vague, even in my memory, but things to the effect that her husband had been shot and—well, that was really the essence of it. It wasn't phrased that way.

Mr. SPECTER. Focusing on the time sequence—what did Governor Connally say as to the timing, number one, the time he was hit, and number two, the time he had heard a sound, and number three, the time he turned—those three factors? In what sequence did he relate them?

Dr. SHIRES. As he recalled it, he heard a shot, he turned to the right and felt himself receiving a shot—in that order—in a matter of a few seconds.

Mr. SPECTER. Where did he feel himself receive a shot?

Dr. SHIRES. In the right chest.

Mr. SPECTER. Did he make any comment about feeling anything in his wrist?

Dr. SHIRES. No; I don't believe he did.

Mr. SPECTER. How about feeling anything in his thigh?

Dr. SHIRES. I don't believe he ever commented on that to me.

Mr. SPECTER. Did he say anything else to you at that time about his recollections on the day of the assassination?

Dr. SHIRES. No; other than this striking feeling he had after he was hit, that someone was trying to kill all of them—apparently he remembers that quite clearly, right after he was hit, but that's all.

Mr. SPECTER. Did you discuss his recollection of the events of the assassination day with Governor Connally on any other occasion?

Dr. SHIRES. Oh, yes; sporadically, during his convalescence.

Mr. SPECTER. What else did he say to you at any other time?

Dr. SHIRES. He was just simply asking questions about things that happened to him in the Emergency Room, in the Operating Room, and he was a little surprised that he didn't recall them better, but this was after he was wounded in here, but that was really the main thing—he was surprised that he didn't remember some of the things—like the cutdowns for blood and that sort of thing that were done to him, and, of course, this is obviously because he was so anoxic at the time.

Mr. SPECTER. Did he ever describe anything in more detail in his recollection of the things on the day of the assassination?

Dr. SHIRES. No.

Mr. SPECTER. Now, going back to the first conversation you had with Mrs. Connally on November 22d, did she say anything more to you other than that which you have already testified about?

Dr. SHIRES. No—those were mainly the remarks that she made. I don't remember any others, except—well, no—most of the others were—we were discussing the Governor's condition and outlook and chances for recovery and that sort of thing.

Mr. SPECTER. Now, looking again at Diagram No. 5, what is your professional opinion, if you have one, as to whether Governor Connally's chest injury, wrist injury, and thigh injury were caused by the same bullet?

Dr. SHIRES. Well we all thought, me included, that this was probably one missile, one bullet.

Mr. SPECTER. When you say "we all thought," whom do you mean by that?

Dr. SHIRES. Dr. Shaw, Dr. Gregory—as we were reconstructing the events in the operating room in an attempt to plot out trajectory as best we could, this appeared to be our opinion.

Mr. SPECTER. Did any of your assistants consult with you in those calculations?

Dr. SHIRES. I guess nearly all of them we have listed.

Mr. SPECTER. Dr. McClelland, Dr. Baxter and Dr. Patman?

Dr. SHIRES. Yes.

Mr. SPECTER. How about Dr. Osborne and Dr. Parker?

Dr. SHIRES. They were working with Dr. Gregory. If they discussed it, I'm sure they did—it was before I got there.

Mr. SPECTER. How about Dr. Boland and Dr. Duke who worked with Dr. Shaw?

Dr. SHIRES. Now, again, I talked to them and they were discussing it as they did the chest procedure, and again thought the same thing. Everyone was under the impression this was one missile—through and through the chest, through and through the arm and the thigh.

Mr. SPECTER. Was there any one of the doctors on either of these three teams who had a different point of view?

Dr. SHIRES. Not that I remember.

Mr. SPECTER. Do you think it is possible that Governor Connally could have been struck by two bullets, one entering his back and emerging from his chest and the second going into his wrist?

Dr. SHIRES. I'm sure it is possible, because missile sites are so variable, depending upon the size of the bullet, the speed at which it travels, whether it was tumbling or not. We have seen all kinds of combinations of entrance and exit wounds and it's just impossible to state with any certainty, looking at a given wound, what the nature of the missile was, so I am sure it is possible.

Mr. SPECTER. Do you think it is possible that, assuming a missile being a bullet 6.5 mm. with a velocity of over 2,000 feet per second, and the distance between the weapon and the victim being approximately 160 to 250 feet, that the same bullet might have passed through President Kennedy, entering his back near the midline and emerging from his neck, and then entering Governor Connally in the back and emerging from his chest, into his wrist, through his wrist and into the thigh?

Dr. SHIRES. I assume that it would be possible. The main thing that would make me think that this was not the case in that he remembers so distinctly hearing a shot and having turned prior to the time he was hit, and in the position he must have been, particularly here in Figure 5, I think it's obvious that he did turn rather sharply to the right and this would make me think that it was a second shot, but this is purely conjecture, of course.

Mr. SPECTER. Well, is there anything, aside from what he told you, that is, anything in the characteristics of the wounds on President Kennedy and the wounds on Governor Connally which would lead you to conclude that it was not the same bullet?

Dr. SHIRES. No—there is nothing. It could have been—purely from the standpoint of the wounds, it is possible.

Mr. SPECTER. You referred just a minute ago to his turning position?

Dr. SHIRES. Yes.

Mr. SPECTER. Is the postulation of a turning by Governor Connally necessary to explain the point of entry in the back, exit in the chest, entry in the wrist, and exit in the wrist, and entry into the thigh, in order to have that line—to state it differently, is it necessary to postulate turning by the Governor?

Dr. SHIRES. Depending upon the angle of the trajectory—I suppose not. I don't know what the angle of the trajectory was from where the bullet was fired.

Mr. SPECTER. Assuming an angle of declination of approximately 45 degrees?

Dr. SHIRES. This, I don't know without drawing it out, but as long as his right arm is drawn in front of him next to the exit wound on the chest, he is in a sitting position, if the angle of declination was right, then I think he could have received this facing straight forward.

Mr. SPECTER. Now, on the wrist, would that be palm of the wrist, back of the wrist, or how?

Dr. SHIRES. I don't understand.

Mr. SPECTER. In what position would the wrist have had to be in, in order to have the same bullet make all three wounds?

Dr. SHIRES. The main point was that his arm be up here. In other words, in some fashion, however his hand happened to be turned, but he had to have his right arm raised up, next to his chest.

Mr. SPECTER. His wrist would have to be up with the palm down, would it not?

Dr. SHIRES. As depicted here.

Mr. SPECTER. In order for the point of entry to be on the dorsal side?

Dr. SHIRES. That's right, again, which makes it a little more likely he was turning, since ordinarily you pronate your wrist as you turn, whereas, this would have been a little strange for him to have been sitting like this, but again, depending on what he had in his hand. It's just a question of which side is up.

Mr. SPECTER. But it would be more natural, you say, for the palm to be down in the turning, which was as contrasted with a relaxed sitting position where it would be more likely his palm would be facing in towards his chest area?

Dr. SHIRES. Right.

Mr. SPECTER. Do you have any knowledge as to the damage which was done to the rib?

Dr. SHIRES. Only from hearsay from Dr. Shaw, that's all.

Mr. SPECTER. Do you have any knowledge as to what fragments there were in the chest, bullet fragments, if any?

Dr. SHIRES. No, again except from postoperative X-rays, there is a small fragment remaining, but the initial fragments I think Dr. Shaw saw before I arrived.

Mr. SPECTER. How about the fragments in the wrist, do you have any knowledge of that?

Dr. SHIRES. Again, there were small fragments which I saw during the procedure on the wrist, but I was not directly involved in that procedure.

Mr. SPECTER. What opinion do you have, if any, Dr. Shires, as to whether the wound in the thigh might have been inflicted from a missile that did not pass through any other part of the Governor's body, assuming that it was a 6.5-mm. bullet with a muzzle velocity of 2,000 feet per second, traveling approximately 160 to 250 feet between the end of the weapon and the point of impact on the thigh?

Dr. SHIRES. Well, again, in that wound—it was strange in that the hole in the skin was too large for the amount of damage inflicted on the underlying tissues, so that had this been the case, this would have had to have been a tangential wound. Had it been a tangential wound, then it's possible that small fragments could have gone into bone as it did and that the damage to the soft tissues was done only by that small fragment, so that the major portion of the bullet simply hit the skin in a tangent and went on in its course elsewhere.

Mr. SPECTER. Well, is it possible that the bullet could have hit Governor Connally with the thigh being the initial point of impact and do the damage which was done there with the high velocity missile that I have just described for you?

Dr. SHIRES. Is it possible to get a wound like that?

Dr. SPECTER. Yes, sir.

Dr. SHIRES. Yes; as long as it's on a tangent.

Mr. SPECTER. Is it likely to receive a wound like that from a high velocity weapon of 2,000 feet per second and at about 160 to 250 feet?

Dr. SHIRES. If it's a tangential wound, tangential wounds can be very strange. A large bullet can cause a small hole if its on a tangent or a small bullet can rip out a fairly large hole on a tangent. It just depends on the time of contact and the angle of contact with the skin. That's why it's awfully hard to predict.

Mr. SPECTER. So that wound could have either been the first striking of the Governor from the bullet, or it could have been from a missile whose velocity was spent after going through President Kennedy and through the Governor's body and wrist and then caused that wound in the thigh?

Dr. SHIRES. That's right, if it was a tangential bullet.

Mr. SPECTER. Dr. Shires, have you ever been contacted by any representative of the Federal Government prior to today?

Dr. SHIRES. Yes.

Mr. SPECTER. And who was it who contacted you?

Dr. SHIRES. I don't recall the name—it was two individuals from the Secret Service. They presented their credentials at the time to the administration and then subsequently to me and they were given copies of our operative reports, statements made by people concerned with the President and Governor at the time, and then subsequently one of those same two men from Secret Service returned and charted the entrance and exit wounds which you have described previously, or we have looked at previously in these five diagrams.

Mr. SPECTER. Have you ever been interviewed by any other representative of the Federal Government before today?

Dr. SHIRES. No; not in person. I discussed over the phone with the FBI—well, that was with regard to Oswald. I discussed over the phone what happened to the bullet that was taken from Oswald, but not with regard to the President or the Governor—no.

Mr. SPECTER. On your prior interviews by the Secret Service, sir, did they cover the same subjects which you and I have gone over today, or were other subjects covered?

Dr. SHIRES. No; essentially the same subjects.

Mr. SPECTER. And was any different information given to you by the Secret Service at that time of either of those two occasions?

Dr. SHIRES. No; the same as we have discussed here.

Mr. SPECTER. Now, prior to the time when you were sworn in and the court reporter started to take the deposition in shorthand form, did you and I have a brief discussion about the purpose of the deposition and the subject matters of interest to the Commission?

Dr. SHIRES. Yes.

Mr. SPECTER. And was the same information given by you to me during the course of that informal discussion as you have testified to on the record here this afternoon?

Dr. SHIRES. Yes; in less detail.

Mr. SPECTER. And do you have anything which you would care to add which you think might be helpful to the Commission in its work?

Dr. SHIRES. No.

Mr. SPECTER. Well, fine, that concludes the deposition, thank you very much, Dr. Shires.

Dr. SHIRES. Are you interested in Oswald—that's my only other question?

Mr. SPECTER. Well, let's talk about it a little off the record.

(Discussion between Counsel Specter and witness Dr. Shires off the record at this point.)

Mr. SPECTER. Let's go back on the record. Dr. Shires, before concluding the deposition, permit me to ask you just a few additional questions about care for Lee Harvey Oswald.

First of all, I again show you Commission exhibit No. 392, the last two pages which purport to be an operative record of Parkland Memorial Hospital on November 24, 1963, concerning treatment of Mr. Oswald, with you listed as the surgeon, and I'll ask you to take a look at these two sheets and tell us whether or not that is a report which you prepared on treatment of Mr. Oswald?

Dr. SHIRES. Yes, it is.

Mr. SPECTER. Will you outline in a very general way what his condition was when you first saw him?

Dr. SHIRES. When he was first seen in the emergency room, he was unconscious, without blood pressure or pulse, but with an audible heart beat, and attempts, feeble though they were, attempts in respiration. There was an entrance wound over the left lower chest and the bullet could be felt subcutaneously over the lower chest lateral projecting this trajectory through the body and looking   at his general condition, it was fairly obvious that the bullet had transgressed virtually every major organ and vessel in the abdominal cavity, which later proved to be the case.

Mr. SPECTER. What did you do for him?

Dr. SHIRES. He was given resuscitation, including an endotracheal tube, intravenous fluids, blood, moved to the operating room, prepared, draped, an abdominal incision, laparotomy made, just as is described in the record. The injuries were in fact mortal and involved both major vessels in the abdomen, the aorta, the inferior vena cava, and there had been massive exanguinating hemorrhage into the abdomen—in and around the abdomen.

After securing control of all the many, many bleeding points and the bleeding organs, he never had regained consciousness. Approximately 15, 16—whatever it is, approximately, pints of blood had been given, and he had suffered irreparable anoxia from the initial massive blood loss incident to the gunshot wound. When his heart did stop, even though we felt this was a terminal cessation of heartbeat, efforts were made at resuscitation by open heart massage and all that went with it, but never once was an effective heartbeat obtained, so that our initial impression was that it was correct in that this was simply cardiac death and not cardiac arrest.

Mr. SPECTER. Did you come close to saving him, in the vernacular—in lay terms?

Dr. SHIRES. There has never been recorded in medical literature recovery from a wound like this. There was too much blood lost too fast. Had the injury occurred right outside the operating room, it might have been possible to reduce the period of anoxia that comes from overwhelming blood loss like this, sufficiently to have corrected it. We did control all the bleeding points with a lot of difficulty, finally all bleeding points were controlled and this was a mortal wound—there was no question about that.

Mr. SPECTER. Are the details of your observations, examination, and treatment of Mr. Oswald set forth in the two pages of this report which I have just shown you in Commission No. 392?

Dr. SHIRES. Yes, the operative reports that are contained there.

Mr. SPECTER. Thank you very much, Dr. Shires.

Dr. SHIRES. Thank you.

TESTIMONY OF DR. RICHARD BROOKS DULANY

The testimony of Dr. Richard Brooks Dulany was taken at 6:20 p.m., on March 25, 1964, at Parkland Memorial Hospital, Dallas, Tex., by Mr. Arlen Specter, assistant counsel of the President's Commission.

Mr. SPECTER. May the record show that Dr. Richard Dulany is present in response to the request that he appear to have his deposition taken and he has been requested to appear here because he has been identified in prior depositions as perhaps being one of the first doctors to see President Kennedy.

Dr. Dulany, have you had an opportunity to examine the Executive Order creating the President's Commission?

Dr. DULANY. Yes, sir.

105

Mr. SPECTER. And the rules and regulations relating to the taking of testimony?

Dr. DULANY. Yes, sir.

Mr. SPECTER. Are you willing to have your deposition taken here today, even though you haven't had the 3 days' notice which you have a right to, if you want it?

Dr. DULANY. Yes, sir.

Mr. SPECTER. You are willing to waive that requirement?

Dr. DULANY. Yes.

Mr. SPECTER. Will you stand up now and raise your right hand?

Do you solemnly swear that the testimony you give before the President's Commission in this deposition proceeding will be the truth, the whole truth, and nothing but the truth, so help you God?

Dr. DULANY. I do.

Mr. SPECTER. Would you state your full name for the record?

Dr. DULANY. Richard Brooks Dulany.

Mr. SPECTER. What is your profession?

Dr. DULANY. M.D.—Medical Doctor.

Mr. SPECTER. Are you licensed to practice medicine in the State of Texas?

Dr. DULANY. Yes, sir.

Mr. SPECTER. And would you outline your educational background, please, starting with college—graduation from college?

Dr. DULANY. From college I went to the University Medical School of Oklahoma and then took my internship here at Parkland Hospital and was in the service for 2 years in the Navy, and I just got back from the service in November, and started a residency here in surgery.

Mr. SPECTER. Did you have occasion to participate in the care of President Kennedy on November 22, 1963?

Dr. DULANY. Is this all recorded now?

Mr. SPECTER. Yes.

Dr. DULANY. Well, as I stated, I principally cared for the Governor and then after his emergency treatment had been cared for, I went into the room where President Kennedy was being cared for.

Mr. SPECTER. Were you present from the start of the Governor's treatment?

Dr. DULANY. Yes, sir.

Mr. SPECTER. And about what time did you go into the room where the President was being treated?

Dr. DULANY. Well, I believe the Governor was supposed to have been in the surgery suite upstairs within 12 minutes after he came in, and so I'm sure I must have been in the room where the President was, about 7 minutes or so afterwards.

Mr. SPECTER. What time was that, about, as best you can place it?

Dr. DULANY. I don't really recollect the specific times.

Mr. SPECTER. What did you observe as to the condition of the President when you entered?

Dr. DULANY. Well, at this time his pupils were fixed and dilated and he had a large head wound—that was the first thing I noticed.

There was already a tracheotomy tube in the neck wound or what was later described as a wound, and had a cutdown running and several other doctors were putting chest tubes in.

Mr. SPECTER. What doctors were present at that time?

Dr. DULANY. I really can't be accurate on that. I remember Dr. Clark and Dr. Jenkins and Dr. Giesecke, Dr. Carrico, Dr. Martin White, and of course, the doctor that was probably down first of the staff members, Dr. Malcolm Perry, and I remember Dr. McClelland, and Dr. Peters were in there.

Mr. SPECTER. Are those all the doctors you remember as being down there?

Dr. DULANY. I believe those are all.

Mr. SPECTER. Can you identify any of the nurses who were there?

Dr. DULANY. No, I don't believe so. I can't remember them.

Mr. SPECTER. Is there anything that you think that you know would be helpful to the President's Commission in its inquiry into this matter?

Dr. DULANY. I don't believe I could add anything any more than you probably already know.

Mr. SPECTER. Did you observe any neck wound on the President?

Dr. DULANY. No, sir; I didn't.

Mr. SPECTER. The tracheotomy had already been performed?

Dr. DULANY. It had been placed in.

106

Mr. SPECTER. Had the incision already been made when you first saw the President's neck?

Dr. DULANY. I really didn't examine it close enough to make any statement along that line.

Mr. SPECTER. Then, did you observe any wound in the President's neck at all?

Dr. DULANY. No, I just know that the tracheotomy was in and later I was told that this was a wound when it was first seen—you know, that's the best I can tell you.

Mr. SPECTER. That's fine, Dr. Dulany, thank you very much for appearing here today.

Dr. DULANY. Yes; thank you.

TESTIMONY OF RUTH JEANETTE STANDRIDGE

The testimony of Ruth Jeanette Standridge was taken at 1:35 p.m., on March 21, 1964, at Parkland Memorial Hospital, Dallas, Tex., by Mr. Arlen Specter, assistant counsel of the President's Commission.

Mr. SPECTER. Miss Standridge, would you stand up and raise your right hand, please?

Do you solemnly swear the testimony you give before the President's Commission on the Assassination of President Kennedy in these deposition proceedings will be the truth, the whole truth, and nothing but the truth, so help you God?

Miss STANDRIDGE. I do.

Mr. SPECTER. All right, you may be seated.

Miss Standridge, the President's Commission is investigating the assassination of President Kennedy and all the facts relating thereto, and we have asked you to appear to have your deposition taken in connection with the treatment which was given to Governor Connally in Parkland Memorial Hospital and to President Kennedy in Parkland Memorial Hospital, and all facts relating to that.

Have you received a letter from the President's Commission requesting that you appear?

Miss STANDRIDGE. Well, there was a letter came and I was out of town and they opened it, the supervisor opened it and she had the letter, but I haven't seen it yet.

Mr. SPECTER. You haven't seen it yet?

Miss STANDRIDGE. No.

Mr. SPECTER. Well, let me show you the enclosures which were in the letter so that you may be familiar with them. Here is a copy of the White House Executive order establishing the Commission, and here is a resolution establishing the rules for taking testimony. Permit me to explain to you that the rules require that we give you 3 days' notice, so that if you would request it now, we could delay taking your deposition until sometime next week, if you would prefer, or if you are agreeable to have us take your deposition, we can go right ahead and take it now.

Miss STANDRIDGE (reading instruments referred to). Thank you, you can just go ahead if you want to—it's all right with me.

Mr. SPECTER. It doesn't make any difference to you whether it is today or next week?

Miss STANDRIDGE. No; it does not.

Mr. SPECTER. Would you state your full name, please?

Miss STANDRIDGE. Ruth Jeanette Standridge.

Mr. SPECTER. What is your occupation or profession?

Miss STANDRIDGE. Head nurse of the emergency rooms.

Mr. SPECTER. At what hospital?

Miss STANDRIDGE. Parkland Memorial Hospital.

Mr. SPECTER. What were your duties on November 22, 1963?

Miss STANDRIDGE. I was working as charge nurse in the major surgery area in Parkland Memorial Hospital.

Mr. SPECTER. And did you receive notification that the President of the United States was en route to Parkland Hospital?

Miss STANDRIDGE. Yes; by my supervisor, Doris Nelson.

Mr. SPECTER. And at about what time did you receive that notification?

Miss STANDRIDGE. About 12:30, I guess.

Mr. SPECTER. And what action, if any, did you take as a result of getting that notice?

Miss STANDRIDGE. Immediately went to trauma room 2 and I was in trauma room 2 and began to set up Renger liquid and check the suction machine.

Mr. SPECTER. And was trauma room 1 set up?

Miss STANDRIDGE. Mrs. Nelson was setting trauma room 1 up at the same time.

Mr. SPECTER. Were you present when one or more of the victims arrived?

Miss STANDRIDGE. Yes.

Mr. SPECTER. And who was it arrived?

Miss STANDRIDGE. Governor Connally was brought into trauma room 2 first.

Mr. SPECTER. Did you observe President Kennedy arrive?

Miss STANDRIDGE. No; I was busy with the Governor.

Mr. SPECTER. And what did you do when the Governor arrived?

Miss STANDRIDGE. Well, we began to take his clothing off and the orderlies continued that and the doctors and I started handing the syringe and medicine and things necessary to start the IV.

Mr. SPECTER. And, what do you mean by "IV"?

Miss STANDRIDGE. Intravenous fluids.

Mr. SPECTER. And did you assist in the taking off of Governor Connally's clothes?

Miss STANDRIDGE. Yes.

Mr. SPECTER. What, if anything, did you notice with respect to the Governor's shirt?

Miss STANDRIDGE. There was blood on the front of it.

Mr. SPECTER. Was there any bullet hole on the front of the shirt?

Miss STANDRIDGE. Not that I can say for sure.

Mr. SPECTER. There could have been or could not have been, but you just don't know?

Miss STANDRIDGE. There could have been, but mostly it was just blood that we noticed.

Mr. SPECTER. Did you notice anything on the coat?

Miss STANDRIDGE. There was blood on the coat.

Mr. SPECTER. Was he wearing his suit coat?

Miss STANDRIDGE. Yes.

Mr. SPECTER. Did you notice whether or not there was any bullet hole in the coat?

Miss STANDRIDGE. I didn't see one.

Mr. SPECTER. What was Governor Connally's position when you first saw him?

Miss STANDRIDGE. He was laying on his back on the cart.

Mr. SPECTER. And what kind of cart was he lying on?

Miss STANDRIDGE. The emergency cart on rollers.

Mr. SPECTER. What is that emergency cart constructed of?

Miss STANDRIDGE. Well, it's just a thin fixture with rubber padding on the top, and it is used to transfer the patients to the wards, and to X-ray and to surgery.

Mr. SPECTER. Is it made of metal?

Miss STANDRIDGE. Of metal with four big tires on it.

Mr. SPECTER. With four roller tires on it?

Miss STANDRIDGE. Yes.

Mr. SPECTER. And what was on the cart underneath the Governor?

Miss STANDRIDGE. Well, there was just a sheet was all we had on there.

Mr. SPECTER. Was there anything on top of the Governor?

Miss STANDRIDGE. Well, we put a sheet, when we unclothed him.

Mr. SPECTER. Was he completely undressed?

Miss STANDRIDGE. Yes.

Mr. SPECTER. And was he lying on top of that cart while he was being undressed?

Miss STANDRIDGE. Yes.

Mr. SPECTER. And who assisted you in the process of undressing him?

Miss STANDRIDGE. Well, David Sanders was helping, he was my orderly that was in the room, and also an aid, Rosa Majors, and she took the money out of his pants, and Dr. Fueishier.

Mr. SPECTER. How do you spell that?

Miss STANDRIDGE. F-u-e-i-s-h-i-e-r (spelling), and Dr. Duke, and there was a couple of other doctors—I don't remember who they were, but they were up at the head, Dr. Fueishier and Dr. Duke, and Dr. Shaw came in before they got the Governor's clothes off.

Mr. SPECTER. Did you notice any object in Governor Connally's clothing?

Miss STANDRIDGE. Not unusual.

Mr. SPECTER. Did you notice a bullet, specifically?

Miss STANDRIDGE. No.

Mr. SPECTER. Did you hear the sound of anything fall?

Miss STANDRIDGE. I didn't.

Mr. SPECTER. Were there other noises going on in the room at that time?

Miss STANDRIDGE. Yes, there were.

Mr. SPECTER. Was Governor Connally completely undressed in the emergency room?

Miss STANDRIDGE. I believe so, to the best of my knowledge he was, I think everything was taken off.

Mr. SPECTER. And what was done with Governor Connally following the completion of his being undressed?

Miss STANDRIDGE. He was immediately carried to the elevator—emergency elevator.

Mr. SPECTER. And in what way was he carried to the emergency elevator?

Miss STANDRIDGE. On the emergency cart that he came into emergency room on.

Mr. SPECTER. Is that also describable as a stretcher?

Miss STANDRIDGE. Yes.

Mr. SPECTER. You say "Yes"?

Miss STANDRIDGE. Yes.

Mr. SPECTER. Did you assist in pushing him into the elevator?

Miss STANDRIDGE. I started and then there was enough doctors pushing him and I went back to get his clothing and by the time I came back up again—I went just as quickly as I could walk back to trauma room 2 and got the clothing, I ran back up to catch him, and the elevator was closing with him on it.

Mr. SPECTER. Did you actually see Governor Connally being wheeled into the elevator?

Miss STANDRIDGE. No, the door was closing as I got back around. I started with him down the hall and then before I got back, they had put him into the elevator.

Mr. SPECTER. Who assisted in pushing him out of the emergency room and down the hall—is it a little ways?

Miss STANDRIDGE. Well, it's through the OB and GYN section.

Mr. SPECTER. Is that "Obstetrics and Gynecology" section?

Miss STANDRIDGE. Yes; you go through that section to get to this elevator from the major surgery section.

Mr. SPECTER. How far did you help push him from the major surgery section?

Miss STANDRIDGE. About from the door that went into OBGN.

Mr. SPECTER. About how far is that?

Miss STANDRIDGE. Oh, about 20 feet, I guess, and they had about another 20 feet to go before they turned to the left to get to the elevator, which is about 6 or 8 feet.

Mr. SPECTER. So, you left him and went back to the emergency room to get his clothes, and when you came back, did you see any part of the stretcher?

Miss STANDRIDGE. Well, I could just see—I could see the stretcher—yes; and the doors and everybody in the elevator and the door was closed in.

Mr. SPECTER. Could you see Governor Connally on the stretcher?

Miss STANDRIDGE. No, not—I think his feet were at the end—I could just see feet—I believe the feet were there at that door, you know.

Mr. SPECTER. And, you saw the same doctors around the stretcher who were pushing him when you last saw him?

Miss STANDRIDGE. Yes.

Mr. SPECTER. Are you sure that was Governor Connally?

Miss STANDRIDGE. No, that's what I said—I just saw his feet, which I assumed it was—it was the same doctors.

Mr. SPECTER. About how long elapsed from the time you stopped pushing the stretcher until the time you got there to look and see just his feet?

Miss STANDRIDGE. Just a second, I mean, just a few seconds.

Mr. SPECTER. You went back and got his clothes?

Miss STANDRIDGE. Yes.

Mr. SPECTER. What did you do with those clothes?

Miss STANDRIDGE. I asked the administrator who should I give them to, and they told me to give them to Governor Connally's party and they were in the minor medicine section and I went out there and there were two gentlemen out there and I asked them who I wanted to see—I wanted to see somebody in Governor Connally's party, and they opened the door and they asked for somebody, and he said he was—he identified himself as Cliff Carter.

Mr. SPECTER. Did you give him the clothing?

Miss STANDRIDGE. Yes.

Mr. SPECTER. Do you know what he did with it?

Miss STANDRIDGE. No.

Mr. SPECTER. Have you heard what he did with it?

Miss STANDRIDGE. I've heard that it got lost and they found it in Representative Gonzales' office in a closet.

Mr. SPECTER. And is he a Texas Representative?

Miss STANDRIDGE. I believe so.

Mr. SPECTER. In his office closet where?

Miss STANDRIDGE. In Washington, D.C.

Mr. SPECTER. Are you limited in anyway from entering into the operating room area?

Miss STANDRIDGE. We are limited, but there is a place where the spots are painted on the floor that is is legal for us to go through into the hallway into the nurses' station.

Mr. SPECTER. You can go around in part of the operating room area?

Miss STANDRIDGE. Isn't into the premises—it's just in the hallway into the nurses' station.

Mr. SPECTER. And what is the reason for limiting you from going beyond that into the operating room area?

Miss STANDRIDGE. Well, we are not considered—we would be contaminating.

Mr. SPECTER. Well, is there some problem about flammable gases up there?

Miss STANDRIDGE. Anesthesia equipment, that's right, and these spots are painted there, and if you don't have the proper shoes on, they will be a conductor, you know, and these spots are there for that area.

Mr. SPECTER. Was Governor Connally removed from the stretcher at anytime while he was in the emergency room?

Miss STANDRIDGE. No; he wasn't. He never went to X-ray or he wasn't taken off at all.

Mr. SPECTER. Does the elevator that the stretcher was pushed into go only to the operating room?

Miss STANDRIDGE. No; it stops on first floor and also goes up to delivery—up to the delivery room on third floor.

Mr. SPECTER. What is on first floor?

Miss STANDRIDGE. No patients—only classrooms and administrative offices—business offices.

Mr. SPECTER. What is on third floor?

Miss STANDRIDGE. The delivery room—it opens up into the delivery room and then the post mortem wards.

Mr. SPECTER. Do you have anything you would like to add which you think might be helpful to us in any way?

Miss STANDRIDGE. Well, not that I can think of other than that I have already stated.

Mr. SPECTER. Did you see President Kennedy's stretcher at any time?

Miss STANDRIDGE. Yes; I was in the room—I took the mop in. The orderlies mopped the floor and we cleaned the wall, the blood off of the walls and so forth, to get it presentable before Mrs. Kennedy came back in.

Mr. SPECTER. And was President Kennedy in the room at that time?

Miss STANDRIDGE. Yes.

Mr. SPECTER. Did you see him there?

Miss STANDRIDGE. Yes.

Mr. SPECTER. And you identified him from what you knew he looked like?

Miss STANDRIDGE. Yes.

Mr. SPECTER. And how was he clothed at that time?

Miss STANDRIDGE. Well, as far as from his waist up—was all that was uncovered and they were trying to protect his head with a sheet—it was wrapped around his head.

Mr. SPECTER. What clothing did he have on from the waist down?

Miss STANDRIDGE. It was just a sheet cover—I don't know of anything under the cover, whether there was or not. I assumed he was all unclothed, which we do routinely.

Mr. SPECTER. He was all unclothed?

Miss STANDRIDGE. I said I assumed he was—I don't know.

Mr. SPECTER. What did he have from the waist up?

Miss STANDRIDGE. Nothing.

Mr. SPECTER. What was he on at that time?

Miss STANDRIDGE. A stretcher cart.

Mr. SPECTER. Did you see what happened to that stretcher afterward?

Miss STANDRIDGE. I didn't notice. They moved it from the room.

Mr. SPECTER. Do you know what happened to the sheets that were on the President's stretcher?

Miss STANDRIDGE. No; I don't.

Mr. SPECTER. Did you and I meet previously before I started to take the deposition here today and talk about the procedures for the investigation by the Warren Commission?

Miss STANDRIDGE. Yes.

Mr. SPECTER. And have you and I been discussing here, with me asking questions and you making answers all the things which we talked about before the court reporter came in?

Miss STANDRIDGE. I believe so.

110

Mr. SPECTER. Have you ever talked to any other representative of the Federal Government?

Miss STANDRIDGE. The Secret Service—yes, sir.

Mr. SPECTER. And did you talk with them once or more than once?

Miss STANDRIDGE. Well, I talked with them one time in Mr. Wright's office and another time just briefly—he came to see the layout of the emergency room.

Mr. SPECTER. Whose office—Mr. Wright?

Miss STANDRIDGE. Personnel manager here.

Mr. SPECTER. What did the Secret Service men ask you about on those occasions?

Miss STANDRIDGE. Well, just the same thing we have gone over today.

Mr. SPECTER. And you talked with the Secret Service man in another part of the hospital on another day, you say?

Miss STANDRIDGE. I think he came back up into the emergency room at that time.

Mr. SPECTER. What did you talk about in the emergency room at that time?

Miss STANDRIDGE. Well, Mrs. Nelson, she showed him the different areas.

Mr. SPECTER. And you identified some of the things?

Miss STANDRIDGE. No, sir.

Mr. SPECTER. Have you ever talked with any other representative of the Federal Government?

Miss STANDRIDGE. No.

Mr. SPECTER. Any representative of the State government?

Miss STANDRIDGE. No.

Mr. SPECTER. Thank you very much. Those are all—those are the only questions I have.

Miss STANDRIDGE. Thank you for that.

TESTIMONY OF JANE CAROLYN WESTER

The testimony of Jane Carolyn Wester was taken on March 20, 1964, at Parkland Memorial Hospital, Dallas. Tex., by Mr. Arlen Specter, assistant counsel of the President's Commission.

Mr. SPECTER. Miss Wester, this is Miss Oliver the court reporter and she will take down your testimony here and will you raise your right hand and take the oath?

Do you solemnly swear that the testimony you will give in this proceeding will be the truth, the whole truth, and nothing but the truth, so help you God?

Miss WESTER. I do.

Mr. SPECTER. May the record preliminarily show that the purpose of this proceeding is in connection with the President's Commission on the Assassination of President Kennedy to ascertain facts relating to the assassination and all medical treatment obtained by President Kennedy and Governor Connally following their being shot.

The witness at the moment is Miss Jane Wester who has been asked to testify concerning any facts of which she has knowledge concerning treatment of President Kennedy or Governor Connally and the disposition of Governor Connally's clothing and sheet in which he was wrapped at the time the Governor was brought into the operating room at Parkland Memorial Hospital.

Mr. SPECTER. Will you state your full name, for the record, please?

Miss WESTER. Jane Carolyn Wester.

Mr. SPECTER. And what is your residence address, Miss Wester?

Miss WESTER. 1107 Brockbank, Dallas.

Mr. SPECTER. Have you received a letter of notification from the President's Commission on the Assassination of President Kennedy advising you that I would contact you for the purpose of taking testimony from you in connection with this proceeding, Miss Wester?

Miss WESTER. Yes; I have.

Mr. SPECTER. And at that time did you receive the copies of the Executive order creating the Commission and the rules and regulations relating to the taking of testimony?

Miss WESTER. Yes, sir; I did.

Mr. SPECTER. And are you satisfied to appear here today and answer some questions relating to your participation in the treatment of Governor Connally?

Miss WESTER. Yes, sir; I am.

Mr. SPECTER. And President Kennedy?

Miss WESTER. Yes, sir.

Mr. SPECTER. What is your occupation or profession, please?

Miss WESTER. I am a registered nurse.

Mr. SPECTER. And at what institution are you employed?

Miss WESTER. Parkland Memorial Hospital, Dallas.

Mr. SPECTER. And how long have you been so employed at Parkland Memorial Hospital?

Miss WESTER. Nine years—or 9 1/2.

Mr. SPECTER. Will you outline your duties in a general way as they were back on November 22, 1963?

Miss WESTER. I am assistant supervisor in the operating room, and I assign personnel duties, direct them in their activities.

Mr. SPECTER. Did you receive notice on that date that President Kennedy and Governor Connally were en route to Parkland Memorial Hospital to receive treatment?

Miss WESTER. I was not aware that they were in the hospital.

Mr. SPECTER. When was it first brought to your attention, if at all?

Miss WESTER. At noon, around noon—noontime—I'm not sure as to the exact time it was. I was relieving the secretary for lunch and the phone rang. Someone in the pathology department asked if the President were in the operating room and I answered them, "No," and they said that a Secret Service agent was down there and as soon as the President did arrive in the operating room, would I please call them.

Mr. SPECTER. What was your next connection, if any, with respect to the treatment of either President Kennedy or Governor Connally at Parkland?

Miss WESTER. I received a phone call from the emergency room asking us to set up for a craniotomy.

Mr. SPECTER. And what is a craniotomy in lay language?

Miss WESTER. That's an exploration of the head.

Mr. SPECTER. Was there any other request made at that time?

Miss WESTER. Yes—well—immediately following, following that I received a call to set up for a thoracotomy, which is an exploration of the chest.

Mr. SPECTER. And were those two set ups made in accordance with the requests you received?

Miss WESTER. Yes; I immediately assigned personnel to set up these two rooms for these two cases.

Mr. SPECTER. And what room was used for the craniotomy?

Miss WESTER. The craniotomy was set up in room 7.

Mr. SPECTER. And what room was used for the thoracotomy?

Miss WESTER. The thoracotomy was set up in room 5.

Mr. SPECTER. And on what floor were the two rooms?

Miss WESTER. Well, on the south wing of the second floor.

Mr. SPECTER. What happened next in connection with this matter?

Miss WESTER. I assigned personnel to take care of the doorways to keep traffic out of the operating room and keep people back—keep the halls clear. Shortly thereafter, Governor Connally arrived in the operating room with several doctors—arrived by stretcher.

Mr. SPECTER. Now, in what way did a stretcher arrive from the first floor, or by what means of locomotion?

Miss WESTER. The stretcher arrived by an elevator which is in the operating room—it comes directly from emergency room and which—there were several doctors with him that brought the stretchers up.

Mr. SPECTER. And what happened to the stretcher after it left the elevator on the second floor of the operating room area?

Miss WESTER. The doctors brought this and were proceeding down the hall, and I met them in the center of the operating room suite itself.

Mr. SPECTER. About how far is that from the elevator door?

Miss WESTER. Approximately 50 feet.

Mr. SPECTER. What was done then with Governor Connally on the stretcher, following the point where you met them?

Miss WESTER. We proceeded to room 5 and outside of room 5 we transferred Governor Connally from the stretcher onto an operating table and removed his clothes from the bottom of the stretcher and placed them in the hallway by the operating table.

Mr. SPECTER. In what way was Governor Connally dressed or robed when you first saw him on the stretcher?

Miss WESTER. As far as I know, the only thing he had was a sheet on him. He had no hospital gown or anything else that I know of on.

Mr. SPECTER. Had his clothes then been removed by that time?

Miss WESTER. Yes; he arrived without his clothes. They were on the bottom of the cart in a paper sack.

Mr. SPECTER. And you said he was transferred from the stretcher onto an operating table?

Miss WESTER. Yes.

Mr. SPECTER. Now, was that inside the operating room? Or outside the operating room?

Miss WESTER. No; it's in the hallway right outside room 5—we transferred him onto the operating table, and then moved the table into the operating room.

Mr. SPECTER. And did he have any clothing on at the time you transferred him from the stretcher onto the operating table?

Miss WESTER. I don't recall any clothes that he had on.

Mr. SPECTER. What was then done with Governor Connally on the operating table?

Miss WESTER. The operating table was moved into the operating room and at that time they proceeded to start anesthetics on him and put him to sleep.

Mr. SPECTER. What doctors were in attendance of Governor Connally at that time?

Miss WESTER. Dr.—there were many—Dr. Giesecke, G-i-e-s-e-c-k-e (spelling)—there were so many. Dr. Ray, I believe, was there, and there were many others—right offhand, I can't remember.

Mr. SPECTER. Did you go into the operating room at that time?

Miss WESTER. I went as far as the doorway with him.

Mr. SPECTER. Now, what was done with the stretcher on which he came to that point?

Miss WESTER. I took the stretcher and rolled it to the center area of the operating room suite—rolled the sheets up on the stretcher into a small bundle.

Mr. SPECTER. Was there one sheet or more than one sheet?

Miss WESTER. I believe there were two sheets and I rolled one inside the other up into a small bundle.

Mr. SPECTER. What is the next normal procedure with respect to the number of sheets on such a stretcher in like circumstances?

Miss WESTER. The cart—the mattress on the cart is covered with one sheet, the patient is usually covered with another. When they arrive in the operating room the sheet covering the patient is removed and a grey cotton blanket is placed over the patient and the sheets are rolled up and usually returned to the emergency room with the cart.

Mr. SPECTER. What else, if anything, was on that stretcher?

Miss WESTER. There were several glassine packets, small packets of hypodermic needles—well, packed in and sterilized in. There were several others-some alcohol sponges and a roll of 1-inch tape. Those things, I definitely know, were on the cart, and the sheets, of course.

Mr. SPECTER. Were there any other objects on the cart, on the stretcher cart?

Miss WESTER. Right off, I can't remember——

Mr. SPECTER. Do you recollect whether there were any gloves on the cart?

Miss WESTER. There could have been—I don't recall right off—I can't remember that.

Mr. SPECTER. Do you recall whether there were any tools on one end of the stretcher?

Miss WESTER. I know I set something down on the cart, I think it was a curved hemostat—I couldn't say for sure—I'm not sure.

Mr. SPECTER. Now, you have testified that you met Governor Connally on the stretcher when he was 50 feet from the elevator door. Is there any object at about that spot that is a landmark, so to speak, of that particular spot?

Miss WESTER. Where I met Governor Connally in the operating room?

Mr. SPECTER. Yes.

Miss WESTER. There is a clock.

Mr. SPECTER. About how far from the clock is the door to the operating room, room 5, where Governor Connally was taken?

Miss WESTER. I would say approximately 75 feet.

Mr. SPECTER. Now, what did you do with the stretcher after Governor Connally was taken off of it?

Miss WESTER. I moved the stretcher back to the center area, fairly close to the clock, it wasn't right under it, but fairly close, and an orderly, R. J. Jimison, walked up——

Mr. SPECTER. His initials are R. J.?

Miss WESTER. And he stood at the cart while I rolled the sheets up and removed the items from the cart, and from there he took the cart and proceeded to the elevator with it and the last time I saw him he was standing at the elevator with the cart waiting for him to be picked up.

Mr. SPECTER. Did you see that stretcher any more that day?

Miss WESTER. Not that I know of.

Mr. SPECTER. Will you describe in a general way what that stretcher looked like?

Miss WESTER. Well, it has four wheels and a lower shelf, a thin mattress on [ ] it, and side rails on it, on each side of the cart. It has a rubber rim at the edge of it, sort of a bumper type to the upper shelf of the cart.

Mr. SPECTER. And what is it constructed of?

Miss WESTER. Well, it's a metal—steel.

Mr. SPECTER. What was done with the mattress?

Miss WESTER. It remained on the cart. It was not moved then, only the sheets were left and rolled into a bundle. And, when the sheets were rolled into a bundle, I didn't actually lift them up.

Mr. SPECTER. Did you see Miss Jeanette Standridge at any time in connection with this particular movement of the stretcher?

Miss WESTER. No.

Mr. SPECTER. Did you see Mrs. Henrietta Ross at any time in connection with this particular movement of the stretcher?

Miss WESTER. No; I believe she walked up on my right as I was rolling the sheets up.

Mr. SPECTER. Did you see Darrell C. Tomlinson at any time in connection with this particular movement of the stretcher?

Miss WESTER. No.

Mr. SPECTER. Were you interviewed by the Secret Service about these events at some time in the past?

Miss WESTER. Yes; I was.

Mr. SPECTER. Were you interviewed by anyone else?

Miss WESTER. No.

Mr. SPECTER. And did the Secret Service interview on one occasion or more than one occasion?

Miss WESTER. Only one occasion.

Mr. SPECTER. And immediately prior to your being sworn in and starting to take this deposition, did I have a very brief conversation with you about the purpose of this proceeding?

Miss WESTER. Yes; you did.

Mr. SPECTER. And about the facts to which you have testified since this formal deposition started?

Miss WESTER. Yes.

Mr. SPECTER. And at that did you tell me all the facts previously testified to here to this effect?

Miss WESTER. Yes.

Mr. SPECTER. Did the sheet on which the Governor was lying have anything on it?

Miss WESTER. It had some blood.

Mr. SPECTER. Have you made any notes or any written record of that sort concerning the matters about which you have testified here today?

Miss WESTER. No; I haven't.

Mr. SPECTER. That concludes the deposition, and I thank you very much for appearing here.

Miss WESTER. Fine.

TESTIMONY OF MRS. HENRIETTA M. ROSS

The testimony of Mrs. Henrietta M. Ross was taken at 6:50 p.m., on March 25, 1964, at Parkland Memorial Hospital, Dallas, Tex., by Mr. Arlen Specter, assistant counsel of the President's Commission.

Mr. SPECTER. May the record show that the oath has been administered to Mrs. Henrietta Ross who is appearing here in response to a letter request to testify as part of the inquiry of the President's Commission on the Assassination of President Kennedy, which involves the treatment of President Kennedy and Governor Connally at Parkland Hospital.

Mrs. Ross has been asked to appear and testify concerning her knowledge about the stretcher cart on which Governor Connally was transported while in the hospital.

Mr. SPECTER. With that preliminary statement, I'll ask you, Mrs. Ross, to state your full name?

Mrs. ROSS. Mrs. Henrietta Magnolia Ross.

Mr. SPECTER. And where are you employed?

Mrs. ROSS. Parkland Hospital.

Mr. SPECTER. In what capacity?

Mrs. ROSS. Operating room technician.

Mr. SPECTER. And what were your duties on November 22, 1963?

Mrs. ROSS. Stand in the hall and guard the hall and not let anyone pass by I did not know.

Mr. SPECTER. Did you have occasion to see Governor Connally?

Mrs. ROSS. Yes; as he came down the hall on the cart.

Mr. SPECTER. Did you see him as he left the elevator?

Mrs. ROSS. Yes.

Mr. SPECTER. About what time was that?

Mrs. ROSS. About—it should have been after 1 o'clock because I was supposed to go to a class that day and I couldn't go.

Mr. SPECTER. Who was with him at the time, if anyone?

Mrs. ROSS. There were doctors all around in the corridor and I don't know exactly who—I only remember one person and that was Dr. Gustafason, because he gave me his coat to hang up as he was passing.

Mr. SPECTER. Was Miss Jane Wester there?

Mrs. ROSS. She was up there; yes, sir.

Mr. SPECTER. And what did you see them do with the Governor, if anything?

Mrs. ROSS. They pushed him down in front of room 5 and onto the operating table and put him on it.

Mr. SPECTER. What were they pushing him on?

Mrs. ROSS. On a stretcher from the emergency room.

Mr. SPECTER. Will you describe the stretcher for me, please, starting with what was it made of?

Mrs. ROSS. It has four legs, four wheels and has a little rubber sheet on it. I mean, a rubber mattress, and the length of the normal body is the length of the cart.

Mr. SPECTER. Is it made of metal?

Mrs. ROSS. Yes, sir.

Mr. SPECTER. And what was done with the stretcher cart after they rolled Governor Connally off of it?

Mrs. ROSS. It was pushed back up toward room 3.

Mr. SPECTER. Is that toward the elevator?

Mrs. ROSS. Yes, sir.

Mr. SPECTER. And by whom was it pushed?

Mrs. ROSS. Jimison.

Mr. SPECTER. R. J. Jimison?

Mrs. ROSS. I don't know Jimison's initials, sir.

Mr. SPECTER. He's one of the orderlies there?

Mrs. ROSS. Yes, sir.

Mr. SPECTER. And where did you last see the stretcher?

Mrs. ROSS. In front of room 3.

Mr. SPECTER. Did Jimison have it in his control at that time?

Mrs. ROSS. The last time I looked he was pushing it; yes, sir.

Mr. SPECTER. Have you talked to the Secret Service about this?

Mrs. ROSS. Yes, sir.

Mr. SPECTER. On how many occasions?

Mrs. ROSS. One time.

Mr. SPECTER. Did you talk to anyone else from the Federal Government about this matter?

Mrs. ROSS. No, sir.

Mr. SPECTER. Do you have anything to add which you think might be helpful to the Commission?

Mrs. ROSS. No, sir.

Mr. SPECTER. Thank you very much for appearing.

Mrs. ROSS. Thank you.

TESTIMONY OF R. J. JIMISON

The testimony of R. J. Jimison was taken at 2:35 p.m., on March 21, 1964, at Parkland Memorial Hospital, Dallas. Tex., by Mr. Arlen Specter, assistant counsel of the President's Commission.

Mr. SPECTER. Would you stand up, please, Mr. Jimison, and raise your right hand.

Do you solemnly swear the testimony you shall give before this Commission in the deposition proceedings will be the truth, the whole truth, and nothing but the truth, so help you God?

Mr. JIMISON. I do.

Mr. SPECTER. Mr. Jimison, have you received a letter of notification from the President's Commission advising you that you would be contacted to have your deposition taken?

Mr. JIMISON. Yes, sir.

Mr. SPECTER. And did that letter contain in it a copy of the Executive order creating the Commission, a copy of the joint congressional resolution about the Commission, and the procedures for taking depositions by the Commission?

Mr. JIMISON. I believe it did.

Mr. SPECTER. Are you willing to have your deposition taken today, sir; do you have any objection to my asking you some questions and having them reported by the court reporter here?

Mr. JIMISON. No; I do not.

Mr. SPECTER. By whom are you employed, Mr. Jimison?

Mr. JIMISON. I would just say the hospital—County Hospital.

Mr. SPECTER. Parkland Memorial Hospital?

Mr. JIMISON. Yes; Parkland Memorial Hospital.

Mr. SPECTER. What kind of work do you do here?

Mr. JIMISON. Orderly.

Mr. SPECTER. Let the record show that you have a badge on which says, "R. J. Jimison".

Mr. JIMISON. Right.

Mr. SPECTER. "Orderly." And is that your full name?

Mr. JIMISON. Yes, sir.

Mr. SPECTER. And what does the "R" stand for?

Mr. JIMISON. That's just an initial name.

Mr. SPECTER. And how about the "J"?

Mr. JIMISON. Same.

Mr. SPECTER. So, people call you "R. J."?

Mr. JIMISON. Right.

Mr. SPECTER. What were your duties back on November 22, 1963, Mr. Jimison?

Mr. JIMISON. My duties was the same as usual; that is, to transport patients to and fro, reclean rooms, betwixt each case.

Mr. SPECTER. Did you have occasion to see President Kennedy on that day?

Mr. JIMISON. I did not.

Mr. SPECTER. Did you have occasion to see Governor Connally on that day?

Mr. JIMISON. I did.

Mr. SPECTER. What were the circumstances under which you saw Governor Connally?

Mr. JIMISON. Well, I would say it wasn't such a pleasant circumstance, but he was lying on a carriage, a hospital carriage, and I was—I assisted in helping move him from the carriage to the operating table.

Mr. SPECTER. Where was he when you first saw him?

Mr. JIMISON. He was on the second floor in the operating room suite, near room 4, where his operation was performed.

Mr. SPECTER. Was he taken to room 4 or room 5?

Mr. JIMISON. He was taken in room—I thought it was room 4, but maybe it could have been room 5, but I taken it to be room 4, because like I told you, I helped lift him off of the table, but usually we help put them in the room—at that time there was so many doctors that I didn't.

Mr. SPECTER. Did you see Governor Connally from the time he came off of the elevator?

Mr. JIMISON. No.

Mr. SPECTER. What floor were you on when you first saw him?

Mr. JIMISON. I was on two.

Mr. SPECTER. How far was he from the elevator when you first saw him?

Mr. JIMISON. I guess he must have been about 20 feet.

Mr. SPECTER. And how far was it from the elevator to the place where you were?

Mr. JIMISON. About how many feet? About 20 or 30 feet.

Mr. SPECTER. Was he near the big clock when you first saw him, the clock that is overhead in the center there?

Mr. JIMISON. Yes.

Mr. SPECTER. And were there doctors around him at that time?

116

Mr. JIMISON. Yes.

Mr. SPECTER. And did you help push the stretcher from that point to——

Mr. JIMISON. (interrupting) No; I followed behind him to room 4 and I helped them take him off.

Mr. SPECTER. You helped them take Governor Connally and put him on the operating table?

Mr. JIMISON. I did.

Mr. SPECTER. And what then was done with the stretcher that he was on?

Mr. JIMISON. Well, the stretcher at that time was moved back from the table, of course, because they had to make room for the doctors to get up close to the table, which was back just a'ways and when I got free—whether it was Miss Wester or Mrs. Ross there—they pushed it back a little further, but they didn't get quite to the elevator with it; I came along and pushed it onto the elevator myself and loaded it on and pushed the door closed.

Mr. SPECTER. What was on the stretcher at that time?

Mr. JIMISON. I noticed nothing more than a little flat mattress and two sheets as usual.

Mr. SPECTER. And what was the position of the sheets?

Mr. JIMISON. Of course, them sheets was, of course, as usual, flat out on the bed.

Mr. SPECTER. Had they been rolled up?

Mr. JIMISON. More or less, not rolled, which, yes, usually they is, the mattress and sheets are all just throwed, one of them about halfway, it would be just throwed about halfway.

Mr. SPECTER. Were the sheets flat or just turned over?

Mr. JIMISON. Well, just turned over.

Mr. SPECTER. Were they crumpled up in any way?

Mr. JIMISON. Well, there was a possibility it was strictly—a tragic day.

Mr. SPECTER. It was what?

Mr. JIMISON. It was a tragic day.

Mr. SPECTER. Right, and everybody was a little shook up on account of it?

Mr. JIMISON. We didn't look too close.

Mr. SPECTER. Was there anything else on the stretcher?

Mr. JIMISON. I never noticed anything else at all.

Mr. SPECTER. Could there have been some empty packets of hypodermic needles or an alcohol sponge?

Mr. JIMISON. There could have been.

Mr. SPECTER. Or a 1-inch roll of tape?

Mr. JIMISON. There could have been something—small stuff, but nothing large like bundles or anything like that.

Mr. SPECTER. What did you do with the stretcher then, you said?

Mr. JIMISON. Pushed it on the rear elevator, which goes downstairs.

Mr. SPECTER. Is there any other elevator which goes downstairs to the emergency area?

Mr. JIMISON. Not close in the emergency area—that's the only one.

Mr. SPECTER. What was the purpose for your putting it on that elevator?

Mr. JIMISON. It goes back to emergency because it can be cleaned up there and remade and put in use again.

Mr. SPECTER. Is it customarily your job to put it back on the elevator?

Mr. JIMISON. Yes; it is.

Mr. SPECTER. Did you ever take it down and put it in order yourself?

Mr. JIMISON. No, sir; we never carry it down ourselves. The fact is—the purpose is—we have enough to do up there, and we have men up there to take care of that.

Mr. SPECTER. Somebody else is supposed to take the elevator up there? Is that right?

Mr. JIMISON. One of them—we put it on the elevator, then it becomes the responsibility of the emergency room.

Mr. SPECTER. Was there any other stretcher placed on that elevator later that day?

Mr. JIMISON. Not during my shift.

Mr. SPECTER. Are you the only man who would put the stretcher on the elevator if there were one?

Mr. JIMISON. No, I is not, but might near—I could might near see of anybody—from where the elevator sits from where the halls were—I could might near see all of the stretchers put on there.

Mr. SPECTER. If a stretcher was put on there it would have to be in your presence?

Mr. JIMISON. I would have had to be hid where I wouldn't be able to see it.

Mr. SPECTER. What time did you put the stretcher from Governor Connally on the elevator?

117

Mr. JIMISON. I'm not too sure I know of the time. I really don't know exactly the time.

Mr. SPECTER. Well, about how long after he was taken into the operating room, did you?

Mr. JIMISON. It was lesser than 10 minutes before or after.

Mr. SPECTER. What time did you get off that day?

Mr. JIMISON. 3:30.

Mr. SPECTER. And you say there was no other stretcher placed on that elevator from the time you put Governor Connally's stretcher on until the end of the day?

Mr. JIMISON. Until the end of my shift. You see, that's the emergency—from the emergency that we had from that time that he was brought up until I was relieved from duty that afternoon.

Mr. SPECTER. Did you notice any bullets on the stretcher?

Mr. JIMISON. I never noticed any at all.

Mr. SPECTER. Did I sit down and talk with you for a few minutes before the court reporter came in to take this all down here today?

Mr. JIMISON. Yes.

Mr. SPECTER. And have I asked you questions and have you given me answers just like in our short discussion before this deposition started?

Mr. JIMISON. (No response.)

Mr. SPECTER. Did you and I talk about the same things we have been talking about since the court reporter came in?

Mr. JIMISON. Yes.

Mr. SPECTER. Have you ever been talked to by any other person from the Federal Government?

Mr. JIMISON. Yes, I have.

Mr. SPECTER. And who was that?

Mr. JIMISON. I don't remember his name, but shortly after that happened—I don't know, as I say, it was the Federal Government.

Mr. SPECTER. What branch was he from?

Mr. JIMISON. I thought he was from the Secret Service.

Mr. SPECTER. How many times did you talk to somebody from the Secret Service?

Mr. JIMISON. Well, I talked to him once; he just talked to me once.

Mr. SPECTER. And what about?

Mr. JIMISON. The same thing.

Mr. SPECTER. And did you ever talk to anybody else about this fact?

Mr. JIMISON. No.

Mr. SPECTER. Do you have anything to add, that you think might be helpful to us?

Mr. JIMISON. Well, no, because the fact is—because that's pretty well covered—just, I actually want to give facts about something I know something about, and during the time I know something about, and what actually happened from the time I got off—I couldn't tell you, but I do know there wasn't no carriage from the time that carriage was picked up until I got off from duty.

This ain't actually—not in it, but due to this—this is—what I'm fixing to say is off of the book—I couldn't see after President Kennedy because I didn't—I never did get up to the floor—so I didn't see him. I am glad if was any kind of help, Mr. Specter.

Mr. SPECTER. You have been, Mr. Jimison, and we appreciate your coming in and helping us a lot.

Mr. JIMISON. Same back to you.

Mr. SPECTER. Thank you.

TESTIMONY OF DARRELL C. TOMLINSON

The testimony of Darrell C. Tomlinson was taken on March 20, 1964, at Parkland Memorial Hospital, Dallas, Tex., by Mr. Arlen Specter, assistant counsel of the President's Commission.

Mr. SPECTER. Mr. Tomlinson, this is Miss Oliver, and she is the court reporter. Will you stand up and hold up your right hand and take the oath, please?

Do you solemnly swear that in the taking of your deposition in these proceedings, you will tell the truth, the whole truth, and nothing but the truth, so help you God?

Mr. TOMLINSON. I do.

Mr. SPECTER. Would you state your full name, for the record?

Mr. TOMLINSON. Darrell Carlisle Tomlinson.

Mr. SPECTER. Mr. Tomlinson, the purpose of this deposition proceeding is to take your deposition in connection with an inquiry made by the President's Commission in connection with the Assassination of President Kennedy to determine from you all the facts, if any, which you know concerning the events surrounding the assassination of President Kennedy and any treatment which was given at Parkland Memorial Hospital to either President Kennedy or Governor Connally, or anything that happened to any physical objects connected with either one of those men.

First of all, did you receive a letter advising you that the Commission was interested in having one of its staff lawyers take your deposition concerning this matter?

Mr. TOMLINSON. Yes.

Mr. SPECTER. And did that letter include in it a copy of the Executive order creating the Commission?

Mr. TOMLINSON. Yes.

Mr. SPECTER. And a copy of the congressional resolution concerning the creation of the President's Commission?

Mr. TOMLINSON. Yes.

Mr. SPECTER. And a copy of the resolution governing questioning of witnesses by members of the Commission's staff?

Mr. TOMLINSON. Yes.

Mr. SPECTER. And are you willing today for me to ask you some questions about what you observed or know about this matter?

Mr. TOMLINSON. Yes, sir.

Mr. SPECTER. And it is satisfactory with you to proceed today rather than to have 3 days from the time you got the letter, which was yesterday?

Mr. TOMLINSON. It's immaterial.

Mr. SPECTER. It's immaterial to you?

Mr. TOMLINSON. It's immaterial—it's at your convenience.

Mr. SPECTER. That's fine. We appreciate that, Mr. Tomlinson.

The reason is, that you have the right to a 3-day notice, but if it doesn't matter to you, then we would like to go ahead and take your information today.

Mr. TOMLINSON. Yes.

Mr. SPECTER. We call that a waiver under the law, if it is all right with you for us to talk with you today, then I want to go ahead and do that; is that all right?

Mr. TOMLINSON. Yes.

Mr. SPECTER. Well, where are you employed, Mr. Tomlinson?

Mr. TOMLINSON. Parkland Hospital.

Mr. SPECTER. And what is your capacity?

Mr. TOMLINSON. I am classed as the senior engineer.

Mr. SPECTER. And what duties are involved in general?

Mr. TOMLINSON. I'm in charge of the powerplant here at the hospital, which takes care of the heating and air-conditioning services for the building.

Mr. SPECTER. Will you describe the general physical layout relating to the emergency area and how you get from the emergency area, say, to the second floor emergency operating rooms of Parkland Memorial Hospital?

Mr. TOMLINSON. You mean just the general lay?

Mr. SPECTER. Yes, sir; please.

Mr. TOMLINSON. Well, we have one elevator that goes from the basement to the third floor, that's what we call the emergency elevator. It's in the south section of the hospital and that would be your most direct route to go from the ground floor, which emergency is on, to the operating rooms on two.

Mr. SPECTER. Now, did you have anything to do with that elevator on November 22, sometime around the noon hour?

Mr. TOMLINSON. Yes.

Mr. SPECTER. And what did you have to do with that elevator?

Mr. TOMLINSON. Well, we received a call in the engineer's office, the chief engineer's office, and he requested someone to operate the elevator.

Mr. SPECTER. Was there any problem with the elevator with respect to a mechanical difficulty of any sort?

Mr. TOMLINSON. No, sir; it was an ordinary type elevator, and if it isn't keyed off it will stop every time somebody pushes a button, and they preferred it to go only to the second floor and to the ground floor unless otherwise instructed by the administrator.

Mr. SPECTER. So, what were you to do with this elevator?

Mr. TOMLINSON. Key it off the ground, between ground and second floor.

Mr. SPECTER. So that you would operate it in that way?

119

Mr. TOMLINSON. Yes; make a manual operation out of it.

Mr. SPECTER. When you came upon that elevator, what time was it, to the best of your recollection?

Mr. TOMLINSON. It was around 1 o'clock.

Mr. SPECTER. Was there anything on the elevator at that time?

Mr. TOMLINSON. There was one stretcher.

Mr. SPECTER. And describe the appearance of that stretcher, if you will, please.

Mr. TOMLINSON. I believe that stretcher had sheets on it and had a white covering on the pad.

Mr. SPECTER. What did you say about the covering on the pad, excuse me?

Mr. TOMLINSON. I believe it was a white sheet that was on the pad.

Mr. SPECTER. And was there anything else on that?

Mr. TOMLINSON. I don't believe there was on that one, I'm not sure, but I don't believe there was.

Mr. SPECTER. What, if anything, did you do with that stretcher?

Mr. TOMLINSON. I took it off of the elevator and put it over against the south wall.

Mr. SPECTER. On what floor?

Mr. TOMLINSON. The ground floor.

Mr. SPECTER. Was there any other stretcher in that area at that time?

Mr. TOMLINSON. There was a stretcher about 2 feet from the wall already there.

(Indicating on drawing to which the witness referred.)

Mr. SPECTER. Now, you have just pointed to a drawing which you have made of this situation, have you not, while we were talking a few minutes before the court reporter started to take down your testimony?

Mr. TOMLINSON. Yes, sir.

Mr. SPECTER. Now, would you mark in ink with my pen the stretcher which you pushed off of the elevator?

Mr. TOMLINSON. I think that it was this one right here (indicating).

Mr. SPECTER. Will you draw the outline of it in ink and mark an "A" right in the center of that?

(Witness complied with request of Counsel Specter.)

Mr. SPECTER. Now, would you mark in ink the position of the stretcher which was already on the first floor?

Mr. TOMLINSON. This was the ground floor.

Mr. SPECTER. Pardon me, on the ground floor? Is there a different designation for the first floor?

Mr. TOMLINSON. Yes.

Mr. SPECTER. Where is the first floor?

Mr. TOMLINSON. One above the ground. We have basement, ground, first, second, and third on that elevator.

Mr. SPECTER. What floor was Governor Connally taken to, if you know?

Mr. TOMLINSON. He was on two, he was in the operating rooms up on two. That's our surgical suites up there.

Mr. SPECTER. And what level is the emergency entrance of the hospital on?

Mr. TOMLINSON. Well, it's the ground floor—it's there at the back of the hospital, you see, it's built on the incline there.

Mr. SPECTER. And the elevator which you found in this area was on the ground floor?

Mr. TOMLINSON. The elevator?

Mr. SPECTER. The stretcher.

Mr. TOMLINSON. Yes.

Mr. SPECTER. Will you mark with a "B" the stretcher which was present at the time you pushed stretcher "A" off of the elevator?

Mr. TOMLINSON. (Witness complied with the request of Counsel Specter.) I believe that's it.

Mr. SPECTER. Now, what, if anything, did you later observe as to stretcher "B"?

Mr. TOMLINSON. Well, sir; I don't recall how long it had been exactly, but an intern or doctor, I didn't know which, came to use the men's room there in the elevator lobby.

Mr. SPECTER. Where is the men's room located on this diagram?

Mr. TOMLINSON. It would be right there (indicating) beside the "B" stretcher.

Mr. SPECTER. Would you draw in ink there the outline of that room in a general way?

Mr. TOMLINSON. Well, I really don't know.

Mr. SPECTER. And would you mark that with the letter "C"?

(Witness complied with request of Counsel Specter.)

Mr. SPECTER. That's fine. What happened when that gentleman came to use the men's room?

Mr. TOMLINSON. Well, he pushed the stretcher out from the wall to get in, and then when he came out he just walked off and didn't push the stretcher back up against the wall, so I pushed it out of the way where we would have clear area in front of the elevator.

Mr. SPECTER. And where did you push it to?

Mr. TOMLINSON. I pushed it back up against the wall.

Mr. SPECTER. What, if anything, happened then?

Mr. TOMLINSON. I bumped the wall and a spent cartridge or bullet rolled out that apparently had been lodged under the edge of the mat.

Mr. SPECTER. And that was from which stretcher?

Mr. TOMLINSON. I believe that it was "B".

Mr. SPECTER. And what was on "B", if you recall; if anything?

Mr. TOMLINSON. Well, at one end they had one or two sheets rolled up; I didn't examine them. They were bloody. They were rolled up on the east end of it and there were a few surgical instruments on the opposite end and a sterile pack or so.

Mr. SPECTER. A sterile what?

Mr. TOMLINSON. A sterile pack.

Mr. SPECTER. What do you mean by that?

Mr. TOMLINSON. Like gauze or something like that.

Mr. SPECTER. Was there an alcohol sponge?

Mr. TOMLINSON. There could have been.

Mr. SPECTER. Was there a roll of 1-inch tape?

Mr. TOMLINSON. No; I don't think so.

Mr. SPECTER. Were there any empty packets from hypodermic needles?

Mr. TOMLINSON. Well, now, it had some paper there but I don't know what they came from.

Mr. SPECTER. Now, Mr. Tomlinson, are you sure that it was stretcher "A" that you took out of the elevator and not stretcher "B"?

Mr. TOMLINSON. Well, really, I can't be positive, just to be perfectly honest about it, I can't be positive, because I really didn't pay that much attention to it. The stretcher was on the elevator and I pushed it off of there and I believe we made one or two calls up before I straightened out the stretcher up against the wall.

Mr. SPECTER. When you say "one or two calls," what do you mean by that?

Mr. TOMLINSON. Went to pick up the technician from the second floor to bring him down to the ground floor to get blood.

Mr. SPECTER. And when you say before you straightened the stretcher up, what do you mean by that?

Mr. TOMLINSON. Well, we just rolled them out of the way where we had some room on the elevator—that's a small elevator.

Mr. SPECTER. So, when you rolled them out of the elevator, when you rolled the stretcher out of the elevator, did you place it against the wall at that time?

Mr. TOMLINSON. No.

Mr. SPECTER. Were both of these stretchers constructed in the same way?

Mr. TOMLINSON. Similar—yes.

Mr. SPECTER. Will you describe the appearance of the stretcher with reference to what it was made of and how many shelves it had, and that sort of thing?

Mr. TOMLINSON. Well, it's made of tubed steel with a flat iron frame on the top where you lay the patient and it has one shelf down between the four wheels.

Mr. SPECTER. Does it have any bumpers on it?

Mr. TOMLINSON. Yes, and it has rubber bumpers.

Mr. SPECTER. Does it have any rail to keep the patient on?

Mr. TOMLINSON. Yes; they have the rails on the side made of tubed steel. The majority of them have those.

Mr. SPECTER. Now, just before we started this deposition, before I placed you under oath and before the court reporter started to take down my questions and your answers, you and I had a brief talk, did we not?

Mr. TOMLINSON. Yes.

Mr. SPECTER. And we discussed in a general way the information which you have testified about, did we not?

Mr. TOMLINSON. Yes, sir.

Mr. SPECTER. And at the time we started our discussion, it was your recollection at that point that the bullet came off of stretcher A, was it not?

Mr. TOMLINSON. B.

Mr. SPECTER. Pardon me, stretcher B, but it was stretcher A that you took off of the elevator.

Mr. TOMLINSON. I believe that's right.

Mr. SPECTER. But there is no question but that at the time we started our discussion a few minutes before the court reporter started to take it down,   that your best recollection was that it was stretcher A which came off of the elevator?

Mr. TOMLINSON. Yes, I believe that was it—yes.

Mr. SPECTER. Have you been interviewed about this matter by any other Federal representative?

Mr. TOMLINSON. Yes.

Mr. SPECTER. Who interviewed you about it?

Mr. TOMLINSON. I don't remember the name of either one of them, but one was the FBI man and one was the Secret Service man.

Mr. SPECTER. How many times did the FBI interview you?

Mr. TOMLINSON. Once.

Mr. SPECTER. How many times did the Secret Service interview you?

Mr. TOMLINSON. Once.

Mr. SPECTER. When did the FBI interview you?

Mr. TOMLINSON. I believe they were the first to do it.

Mr. SPECTER. Approximately when was that?

Mr. TOMLINSON. I think that was the latter part of November.

Mr. SPECTER. And when did the Secret Service interview you?

Mr. TOMLINSON. Approximately a week later, the first part of December.

Mr. SPECTER. Now, do you recollect what the FBI man asked you about?

Mr. TOMLINSON. Just about where I found the bullet.

Mr. SPECTER. Did he ask you about these stretchers?

Mr. TOMLINSON. Well, he asked me about the stretchers, yes, just about the same thing we've gone over here.

Mr. SPECTER. What did the Secret Service man ask you about?

Mr. TOMLINSON. Approximately the same thing, only, we've gone into more detail here.

Mr. SPECTER. What did you tell the Secret Service man about which stretcher you took off of the elevator?

Mr. TOMLINSON. I told him that I was not sure, and I am not—I'm not sure of it, but as I said, I would be going against the oath which I took a while ago, because I am definitely not sure.

Mr. SPECTER. Do you remember if you told the Secret Service man which stretcher you thought you took off of the elevator?

Mr. TOMLINSON. Well, we talked about taking a stretcher off of the elevator, but then when it comes down on an oath, I wouldn't say for sure, I really don't remember.

Mr. SPECTER. And do you recollect whether or not you told the Secret Service man which stretcher you took off of the elevator?

Mr. TOMLINSON. What do you mean?

Mr. SPECTER. You say you can't really take an oath today to be sure whether it was stretcher A or stretcher B that you took off the elevator?

Mr. TOMLINSON. Well, today or any other day, I'm just not sure of it, whether it was A or B that I took off.

Mr. SPECTER. Well, has your recollection always been the same about the situation, that is, today, and when you talked to the Secret Service man and when you talked to the FBI man?

Mr. TOMLINSON. Yes; I told him that I wasn't sure.

Mr. SPECTER. So, what you told the Secret Service man was just about the same thing as you have told me today?

Mr. TOMLINSON. Yes, sir.

Mr. SPECTER. When I first started to ask you about this, Mr. Tomlinson, you initially identified stretcher A as the one which came off of the elevator car?

Mr. TOMLINSON. Yes; I think it's just like that.

Mr. SPECTER. And, then, when——

Mr. TOMLINSON (interrupting). Here's the deal—I rolled that thing off, we got a call, and went to second floor, picked the man up and brought him down. He went on over across, to clear out of the emergency area, but across from it, and picked up two pints of, I believe it was, blood. He told me to hold for him, he had to get right back to the operating room, so I held, and the minute he hit there, we took off for the second floor and I came back to the ground. Now, I don't know how many people went through that—I don't know how many people hit them—I don't know anything about what could have happened to them in between the time I was gone, and I made several trips before I discovered the bullet on the end of it there.

Mr. SPECTER. You think, then, that this could have been either, you took out of the elevator as you sit here at the moment, or you just can't be sure?

Mr. TOMLINSON. It could be, but I can't be positive or positively sure—I think it was A, but I'm not sure.

Mr. SPECTER. That you took off of the elevator?

Mr. TOMLINSON. Yes.

Mr. SPECTER. Now, before I started to ask you questions under oath, which have been taken down here, I told you, did I not, that the Secret Service man wrote a report where he said that the bullet was found on the stretcher which you took off of the elevator—I called that to your attention, didn't I?

Mr. TOMLINSON. Yes; you told me that.

Mr. SPECTER. Now, after I tell you that, does that have any effect on refreshing your recollection of what you told the Secret Service man?

Mr. TOMLINSON. No; it really doesn't—it really doesn't.

Mr. SPECTER. So, would it be a fair summary to say that when I first started to talk to you about it, your first view was that the stretcher you took off of the elevator was stretcher A, and then I told you that the Secret Service man said it was—that you had said the stretcher you took off of the elevator was the one that you found the bullet off, and when we talked about the whole matter and talked over the entire situation, you really can't be completely sure about which stretcher you took off of the elevator, because you didn't push the stretcher that you took off of the elevator right against the wall at first?

Mr. TOMLINSON. That's right.

Mr. SPECTER. And, there was a lot of confusion that day, which is what you told me before?

Mr. TOMLINSON. Absolutely. And now, honestly, I don't remember telling him definitely—I know we talked about it, and I told him that it could have been. Now, he might have drawed his own conclusion on that.

Mr. SPECTER. You told the Secret Service agent that you didn't knowwhere——

Mr. TOMLINSON (interrupting). He asked me if it could have been brought down from the second floor.

Mr. SPECTER. You got the stretcher from where the bullet came from, whether it was brought down from the second floor?

Mr. TOMLINSON. It could have been—I'm not sure whether it was A I took off.

Mr. SPECTER. But did you tell the Secret Service man which one you thought it was you took off of the elevator?

Mr. TOMLINSON. I'm not clear on that—whether I absolutely made a positive statement to that effect.

Mr. SPECTER. You told him that it could have been B you took off of the elevator?

Mr. TOMLINSON. That's right.

Mr. SPECTER. But, you don't remember whether you told him it was A you took off of the elevator?

Mr. TOMLINSON. I think it was A—I'm not really sure.

Mr. SPECTER. Which did you tell the Secret Service agent—that you thought it was A that you took off of the elevator?

Mr. TOMLINSON. Really, I couldn't be real truthful in saying I told him this or that.

Mr. SPECTER. You just don't remember for sure whether you told him you thought it was A or not?

Mr. TOMLINSON. No, sir; I really don't remember. I'm not accustomed to being questioned by the Secret Service and the FBI and by you and they are writing down everything, I mean.

Mr. SPECTER. That's all right. I understand exactly what you are saying and I appreciate it and I really just want to get your best recollection.

We understand it isn't easy to remember all that went on, on a day like November 22d, and that a man's recollection is not perfect like every other part of a man, but I want you to tell me just what you remember, and that's the best you can do today, and I appreciate that, and so does the President's Commission, and that's all we can ask a man.

123

Mr. TOMLINSON. Yes, I'm going to tell you all I can, and I'm not going to tell you something I can't lay down and sleep at night with either.

Mr. SPECTER. Do you know where the stretcher came from that you found on the elevator?

Mr. TOMLINSON. No, sir; I do not. It could have come from two, it could have come from three, it could have come from some other place.

Mr. SPECTER. You didn't see anybody put it there?

Mr. TOMLINSON. No, sir—it was on the elevator when I got there. There wasn't anyone on the elevator at the time when I keyed it off.

Mr. SPECTER. And when you say "keyed it off," you mean?

Mr. TOMLINSON. Put it in manual operation.

Mr. SPECTER. Mr. Tomlinson, does it make any difference to you whether you sign this deposition at the end or not?

Mr. TOMLINSON. No.

Mr. SPECTER. We very much appreciate your coming, Mr. Tomlinson. Thank you very much. Those are all the questions I have.

Mr. TOMLINSON. All right. Thank you.

Mr. SPECTER. Off the record.

(Discussion between counsel and the witness Tomlinson regarding a proposed exhibit.)

Mr. SPECTER. On the record.

Now that the deposition of Mr. Tomlinson has been concluded, I am having the paper marked as Tomlinson Exhibit No. 2.

(Instrument marked by the reporter as Tomlinson Exhibit No. 2, for identification.)

Mr. SPECTER. May the record show that Mr. Tomlinson is present, and will you identify this paper marked Tomlinson Exhibit No. 2 as the one which contains the diagram of the emergency room and the letters A and B of the stretchers we have been discussing?

Mr. TOMLINSON. That's just the elevator lobby in emergency.

Mr. SPECTER. And this is the diagram which you drew for us?

Mr. TOMLINSON. Yes.

Mr. SPECTER. That's all, and thank you very much.

TESTIMONY OF DIANA HAMILTON BOWRON

The testimony of Diana Hamilton Bowron was taken at 2:05 p.m., on March 24, 1964, at Parkland Memorial Hospital, Dallas, Tex., by Mr. Arlen Specter, assistant counsel of the President's Commission.

Mr. SPECTER. May the record show that Diana Bowron is present following a verbal request that she appear here to have her deposition taken. During the course of deposition proceedings on March 20 and March 21, it came to my attention that Miss Bowron would have information of value to the Commission, and authorization was provided through the General Counsel, J. Lee Rankin, for her deposition to be taken.

Miss Bowron, the President's Commission is investigating the assassination of President Kennedy and is interested in certain facts relating to his treatment and presence at Parkland Memorial Hospital, and we have asked you to appear here to testify concerning your knowledge of his presence here.

Now, I have shown you, have I not, the Executive order appointing the Presidential Commission and the resolution authorizing the taking of testimony at depositions by Commission staff members, have I not?

Miss BOWRON. Yes.

Mr. SPECTER. And are you willing to have your deposition taken today without 3 days' written notice, as we ordinarily provide?

Miss BOWRON. Yes.

Mr. SPECTER. So, are you willing to waive that technical requirement?

Miss BOWRON. Yes, I am.

Mr. SPECTER. All right. Will you stand up and raise your right hand?

Do you solemnly swear the testimony you will give before the President's Commission in these deposition proceedings will be the truth, the whole truth, and nothing but the truth, so help you God?

Miss BOWRON. I do.

Mr. SPECTER. What is your permanent residence address, Miss Bowron?

Miss BOWRON. 1107 Brockbank, Dallas 29, Tex.

Mr. SPECTER. Will you spell that street name and speak up more loudly?

Miss BOWRON. B-r-o-c-k-b-a-n-k [spelling].

Mr. SPECTER. Thank you. Are you a native of Dallas, or of some other area?

Miss BOWRON. I am a native of England.

Mr. SPECTER. And how long have you been in Dallas?

Miss BOWRON. Since August 4, 1963.

Mr. SPECTER. And what are the circumstances surrounding your employment here at Parkland Memorial Hospital?

Miss BOWRON. I answered an advertisement in August and came over on a year's contract and to work in the emergency room.

Mr. SPECTER. Are you a registered nurse?

Miss BOWRON. Yes.

Mr. SPECTER. And what is your educational background?

Miss BOWRON. I went to private boarding school and to secondary school, and then I went through nurses training for 3 years and 3 months in England. I finished in February of last year.

Mr. SPECTER. And how old are you at the present time?

Miss BOWRON. Twenty two.

Mr. SPECTER. Did you have occasion to render assistance to President Kennedy back on November 22, 1963?

Miss BOWRON. I did; yes, sir.

Mr. SPECTER. Will you relate briefly the circumstances surrounding your being called in to assist in that case?

Miss BOWRON. I was assigned to work in the minor medicine and surgery area, and I was passing through major surgery, and I heard over the intercom that they needed carts out at the emergency room entrance, so the orderly from the triage desk, which was passing through and he and I took one cart from major surgery and ran down the hall and by the cashier's desk there were some men I assume were Secret Service men.

Mr. SPECTER. Did you know at that time whom you were going to aid?

Miss BOWRON. No, sir.

Mr. SPECTER. You later assumed they were Secret Service men?

Miss BOWRON. Yes, sir, and they encouraged us to run down to the door.

Mr. SPECTER. And did you have a stretcher with you at that time?

Miss BOWRON. Yes, sir.

Mr. SPECTER. And was one stretcher or more than one stretcher being brought forward at that time?

Miss BOWRON. There was another stretcher being brought forward from the OB—GYN section.

Mr. SPECTER. That's the obstetrics and gynecology section?

Miss BOWRON. Yes.

Mr. SPECTER. And were you wheeling one stretcher by yourself or was some one helping?

Miss BOWRON. No, the orderly from the triage desk was helping us.

Mr. SPECTER. Was helping you?

Miss BOWRON. Yes.

Mr. SPECTER. Who was that?

Miss BOWRON. Joe—I've forgotten what his last name is. I'm sorry. I know his first name is Joe and he's on duty today.

Mr. SPECTER. And who was bringing the other stretcher?

Miss BOWRON. I don't know, sir. I heard afterwards, that Dr. Midgett took one stretcher. I don't know who was assisting him.

Mr. SPECTER. And what is Dr. Midgett's first name?

Miss BOWRON. Bill.

Mr. SPECTER. And, where did you take your stretcher?

Miss BOWRON. To the left-hand side of the car as you are facing it, and we had to move Governor Connally out first because he was in the front. We couldn't get to the back seat. While all the Secret Service men were moving Governor Connally I went around to the other side of the car to try to help with the President and then we got him onto the second cart and then took him straight over to trauma room 1.

Mr. SPECTER. Trauma room No. 1?

Miss BOWRON. Yes.

Mr. SPECTER. And describe in a general way Governor Connally's condition when you first saw him?

125

Miss BOWRON. He was very pale, he was leaning forward and onto Mrs. Connally but apparently—I didn't notice very much—I was more concerned with the person in the back of the car—the President.

Mr. SPECTER. And what, in a general way, did you observe with respect to President Kennedy's condition?

Miss BOWRON. He was moribund—he was lying across Mrs. Kennedy's knee and there seemed to be blood everywhere. When I went around to the other side of the car I saw the condition of his head.

Mr. SPECTER. You saw the condition of his what?

Miss BOWRON. The back of his head.

Mr. SPECTER. And what was that condition?

Miss BOWRON. Well, it was very bad—you know.

Mr. SPECTER. How many holes did you see?

Miss BOWRON. I just saw one large hole.

Mr. SPECTER. Did you see a small bullet hole beneath that one large hole?

Miss BOWRON. No, sir.

Mr. SPECTER. Did you notice any other wound on the President's body?

Miss BOWRON. No, sir.

Mr. SPECTER. And what action did you take at that time, if any?

Miss BOWRON. I helped to lift his head and Mrs. Kennedy pushed me away and lifted his head herself onto the cart and so I went around back to the cart and walked off with it. We ran on with it to the trauma room and she ran beside us.

Mr. SPECTER. And who was in the trauma room when you arrived there?

Miss BOWRON. Dr. Carrico.

Mr. SPECTER. Where did Dr. Carrico join you?

Miss BOWRON. At the—I couldn't really tell you exactly, but it was inside major surgery. Miss Henchliffe, the other nurse who is assigned to major surgery, was in the trauma room already setting the I.V.'s—the intravenous bottles up.

Mr. SPECTER. And were there any other nurses present at that time when the President arrived in the trauma area?

Miss BOWRON. I don't think so, sir.

Mr. SPECTER. Were there any doctors present besides Dr. Carrico?

Miss BOWRON. I didn't notice anybody—there may have been.

Mr. SPECTER. What action did you observe Dr. Carrico take, if any?

Miss BOWRON. We tried to start an I.V. cutdown and I don't know whether it was his left or his right leg, and Miss Henchliffe and I cut off his clothing and then after that everybody just arrived at once and it was more or less everybody sort of helping everybody else. We opened the chest tube trays and the venesectron trays.

Mr. SPECTER. How long were you present in the emergency room No. 1?

Miss BOWRON. I was in there until they needed some blood, which was the second lot of blood. I went—ran out across to the blood bank and came back and went into the trauma room. By that time they had decided that he was dead, they said.

And then, we stayed in there with him and cleaned him up, removed all of his clothing and put them all together and Miss Henchliffe gave them to ███ one of the Secret Service men, and we stayed with the body until the coffin came, and helped put him in there, and then we——

Mr. SPECTER. When you say "we", whom do you mean by "we"?

Miss BOWRON. Miss Henchliffe and myself.

Mr. SPECTER. Anybody besides the two of you?

Miss BOWRON. Yes; there was an orderly called David Sanders who helped us to clean the floor, because there were leaves and sheets and everything was rather a mess on the floor and he came to clean the floor for us so that it wouldn't look so bad when Mrs. Kennedy went in. And then Mrs. Kennedy wanted to be alone with him after the priests left, so we all came out and sat there outside and she was alone with him in the trauma room, and we didn't go in any more after that.

Mr. SPECTER. Did you see him at any time after that?

Miss BOWRON. No, sir—only when they were wheeling him out in the coffin.

Mr. SPECTER. What doctors were present during the time he was being treated?

Miss BOWRON. Dr. Carrico and—who else was there—there were so many.

Mr. SPECTER. Do you recall any of the names?

Miss BOWRON. I don't.

Mr. SPECTER. Was there any other nurses present other than those you have already mentioned?

126

Miss BOWRON. Miss Standridge, Jeanette Standridge came in, Mrs. Nelson—the supervisor.

Mr. SPECTER. Any other nurses present there?

Miss BOWRON. Not that I could say, sir—I don't know the name of any.

Mr. SPECTER. While the doctors were working on President Kennedy, did you ever have any opportunity to observe his neck?

Miss BOWRON. No; I didn't, until afterwards.

Mr. SPECTER. Until after what?

Miss BOWRON. Until after they had pronounced him dead and we cleaned up and removed the trach tube, and indeed we were really too shocked to really take much notice.

Mr. SPECTER. Did you ever see his neck prior to the time you removed the trach tube?

Miss BOWRON. No, sir.

Mr. SPECTER. Now, did you personally participate in removing President Kennedy's body from the stretcher?

Miss BOWRON. No, sir—I didn't touch him. We held him with the sheet.

Mr. SPECTER. Were you present when his body was removed from the stretcher?

Miss BOWRON. Yes; I was.

Mr. SPECTER. And did you observe the stretcher from which his body was removed to be the same stretcher that he had been brought into trauma room No. 1 on?

Miss BOWRON. Yes.

Mr. SPECTER. That's the stretcher you took out there for him?

Miss BOWRON. Yes.

Mr. SPECTER. And what sheets were present on the stretcher or in the adjacent area used in the care of President Kennedy?

Miss BOWRON. The sheets that had already been on the stretcher when we took it out with the President on. When we came back after all the work had been done on him—so that Mrs. Kennedy could have a look before he was, you know, really moved into the coffin. We wrapped some extra sheets around his head so it wouldn't look so bad and there were some sheets on the floor so that nobody would step in the blood. Those were put down during all the work that was going on so the doctors wouldn't slip.

Mr. SPECTER. What was done with all of the sheets on the stretcher and on floor area there?

Miss BOWRON. They were all gathered up and put into a linen scape.

Mr. SPECTER. Did you gather them up yourself?

Miss BOWRON. Yes.

Mr. SPECTER. All of them?

Miss BOWRON. Yes; with the help of Miss Henchliffe.

Mr. SPECTER. And did the two of you put them in the linen hamper?

Miss BOWRON. Yes; I put them in the linen hamper myself.

Mr. SPECTER. What was done with the stretcher then?

Miss BOWRON. The stretcher was then wheeled across into trauma room No. 2, which was empty.

Mr. SPECTER. Was there anything on the stretcher at all when it was wheeled into trauma room No. 2?

Miss BOWRON. Not that we noticed, except the rubber mattress that was left on it.

Mr. SPECTER. Would you have noticed anything had anything been on that stretcher?

Miss BOWRON. Yes; I think so.

Mr. SPECTER. And where was the stretcher when you last saw it?

Miss BOWRON. Being wheeled across into trauma room 2.

Mr. SPECTER. Now, I am going to show you three photostatic copies of newspaper stories which I will ask the Court Reporter to mark Bowron Exhibit Nos. 2, 3 and 4.

(Instruments referred to marked by the Reporter as Bowron Exhibit Nos. 2, 3, and 4, for identification.)

Mr. SPECTER. Will you look at those and tell me whether or not those are photostatic copies of newspaper accounts of your story of this assassination day?

Miss BOWRON. They are photostatic copies of the articles that appeared in the newspapers, but they are not all my story.

Mr. SPECTER. What newspapers did they appear in?

Miss BOWRON. I believe this is the "Observer".

Mr. SPECTER. You are referring to BX Number 2 and what city is that published in?

Miss BOWRON. London.

Mr. SPECTER. And BX Number 3 came from where?

Miss BOWRON. I think that this was "The Mail—The Daily Mail".

Mr. SPECTER. Appearing in what city?

Miss BOWRON. It appears in all cities. It is a national newspaper.

Mr. SPECTER. In England?

Miss BOWRON. Yes; it is prepared in England.

Mr. SPECTER. And how about BX-4?

Miss BOWRON. Well, this I think was "The Mirror" I think.

Mr. SPECTER. What city is The Mirror published in?

Miss BOWRON. That is a national newspaper.

Mr. SPECTER. Appearing in England?

Miss BOWRON. Yes.

Mr. SPECTER. Were there any stories in any other newspapers about you and your participation in the events of the day at Parkland?

Miss BOWRON. I believe there was one—I think it was an Australian paper and Mrs. Nelson received a letter from there with an article and which was the same as I think—as this one.

Mr. SPECTER. BX-4?

Miss BOWRON. Yes.

Mr. SPECTER. And does that constitute all the stories which appeared about your participation in this event?

Miss BOWRON. Yes.

Mr. SPECTER. Now, will you state briefly the circumstances under which this information was obtained, if you know?

Miss BOWRON. Mrs. Nelson spoke to me and told me that there had been two English reporters in Dallas who had been asking about me, and she told them where to get in touch with me, and the next day they came to the emergency room and wanted to speak to me and I said I couldn't tell them anything other than I was from England, gave them my home address, and the fact that I had been present and I was the one who went out to the car and brought the President in and being with him until they finished, and that was all that I told them.

Mr. SPECTER. Did you give them any information beyond that?

Miss BOWRON. No, sir; and they told me that there would probably be some English reporters calling on my parents at home, and I am the only child and my mother worries, so I called home the next—that night and told my parents that I had been on duty and that there would probably be some reporters calling on them, and they weren't to worry about it but they weren't to say anything that—except that I had been on duty and that was all.

Mr. SPECTER. Have you been interviewed by any representative of the Federal Government prior to today?

Miss BOWRON. Yes, sir.

Mr. SPECTER. By whom?

Miss BOWRON. I don't really know—he was an FBI agent.

Mr. SPECTER. And when was that?

Miss BOWRON. It was a week or two, I think, after the assassination.

Mr. SPECTER. And what did he ask you and what did you tell him?

Miss BOWRON. He asked us more or less the same questions you have asked us.

Mr. SPECTER. What did you tell him?

Miss BOWRON. The same as I told you.

Mr. SPECTER. When you say "us," whom do you mean by "us"?

Miss BOWRON. Mrs. Nelson was there and Miss Henchliffe and myself.

Mr. SPECTER. Have you talked to any other representatives of the Federal Government prior to today?

Miss BOWRON. No, sir.

Mr. SPECTER. And did I discuss with you the purpose of the deposition and the nature of the questions that I would ask you immediately before we went on the record with this being taken down by the Court Reporter?

Miss BOWRON. Yes.

Mr. SPECTER. And did you give me the same information which you have put on the record here today?

Miss BOWRON. Yes.

Mr. SPECTER. Do you have anything to add that you think might be helpful in any way to the Commission?

Miss BOWRON. Yes. When we were doing a cutdown on the President's left arm, his gold watch was in the way and they broke it—you know, undid it and it was slipping down and I just dropped it off of his hand and put it in my pocket and forgot completely about it until his body was being taken out of the emergency room and then I realized, and ran out to give it to one of the Secret Service men or anybody I could find and found this Mr. Wright.

Mr. SPECTER. Was that the same day?

Miss BOWRON. Yes—he had only just gone through O.B.—I was just a few feet behind him.

Mr. SPECTER. Do you think of anything else that might be of assistance to the Commission?

Miss BOWRON. No, sir.

Mr. SPECTER. Thank you very much for coming, Miss Bowron.

Miss BOWRON. Thank you.

Mr. SPECTER. Thank you a lot.

Miss BOWRON. All right, thank you.

TESTIMONY OF MARGARET M. HENCHLIFFE

The testimony of Margaret M. Henchliffe was taken at 2 p.m., on March 21, 1964, at Parkland Memorial Hospital, Dallas, Tex., by Mr. Arlen Specter, assistant counsel of the President's Commission.

Mr. SPECTER. Miss Henchliffe, the purpose of our asking you to come in today is in connection with the investigation being conducted by the President's Commission on the Assassination of President Kennedy. The Commission has not written to you because, we have learned from Mrs. Doris Nelson in the deposition taken yesterday that you have some information of value to provide to us so that the regular procedure has not been followed of sending you a copy of the Executive order or of the resolution concerning the procedures of the taking of testimony.

Permit me to make those documents available to you.

(Handed instruments to the Witness Henchliffe.)

Let me say that since yesterday I have contacted Mr. J. Lee Rankin, General Counsel, in Washington and he has authorized the taking of this deposition by letter, which I received today, so that it has been authorized, and the real question I have with you is whether it is all right with you to provide us with the information you have today, as opposed to sometime next week after you have had the 3 days' notice which you are entitled to if you want it?

Miss HENCHLIFFE. It is all right with me.

Mr. SPECTER. Is it all right with you to proceed and have your deposition taken today?

Miss HENCHLIFFE. Yes, sir.

Mr. SPECTER. Do you solemnly swear that the testimony you shall give before this Commission as it is holding deposition proceedings now will be the truth, the whole truth, and nothing but the truth, so help you God?

Miss HENCHLIFFE. Yes.

Mr. SPECTER. Will you state your full name, please?

Miss HENCHLIFFE. Margaret M. Henchliffe.

Mr. SPECTER. What is your occupation or profession?

Miss HENCHLIFFE. I am a nurse, registered nurse.

Mr. SPECTER. And where are you employed?

Miss HENCHLIFFE. Parkland Memorial Hospital.

Mr. SPECTER. And where were you employed on November 22, 1963?

Miss HENCHLIFFE. Parkland Memorial Hospital.

Mr. SPECTER. And were you notified on that date that the President was on his way to the hospital?

Miss HENCHLIFFE. No, sir; I didn't know it at the time until later.

Mr. SPECTER. When did you first learn about it, if at all?

Miss HENCHLIFFE. I found out who it was when I went out to get blood.

Mr. SPECTER. About what time of day was that?

Miss HENCHLIFFE. Well. I guess it was about 2 minutes after he came in.

Mr. SPECTER. Did you observe him at some place in the hospital?

Miss HENCHLIFFE. I was working with him in the emergency room.

Mr. SPECTER. Had he arrived in the emergency room when you first arrived at the site of the emergency room?

Miss HENCHLIFFE. Do what?

Mr. SPECTER. Were you in the area of the emergency room before he came there?

Miss HENCHLIFFE. Yes.

Mr. SPECTER. Did you see him actually wheeled into the emergency room?

Miss HENCHLIFFE. Yes; in fact, I helped wheel him on into trauma room 1.

Mr. SPECTER. And, where was he when you first saw him?

Miss HENCHLIFFE. He was between trauma rooms 1 and 2.

Mr. SPECTER. Did you see him when he was brought into the hospital itself?

Miss HENCHLIFFE. At the emergency entrance—no. It was after he came into the emergency room.

Mr. SPECTER. He came into the emergency area?

Miss HENCHLIFFE. Yes.

Mr. SPECTER. And then you saw him and helped wheel him, you say, into the emergency room No. 1?

Miss HENCHLIFFE. Yes.

Mr. SPECTER. And who else was present at the time you first saw him when he had just come into the emergency area?

Miss HENCHLIFFE. Let me see, I think Dr. Carrico was there—he was there very shortly after—afterwards.

Mr. SPECTER. He was there when you arrived? Or arrived shortly after you did?

Miss HENCHLIFFE. Well, actually I went in ahead of the cart with him and I was the first one in with him, and just in a minute, or seconds, Dr. Carrico came in.

Mr. SPECTER. And what other doctors arrived, if any?

Miss HENCHLIFFE. Oh, gee. Let's see—there was Dr. Baxter, Dr. Perry, and you want all of them that were in the room?

Mr. SPECTER. If you can remember them.

Miss HENCHLIFFE. Dr. Kemp Clark, Dr. Jenkins, Dr. Peters, Dr. Crenshaw, and there was some woman anesthetist that I don't know which—who it was.

Mr. SPECTER. What did you observe to be the President's condition when you first saw him?

Miss HENCHLIFFE. I saw him breathe a couple of times and that was all.

Mr. SPECTER. Did you see any wound anywhere on his body?

Miss HENCHLIFFE. Yes, he was very bloody; his head was very bloody when I saw him at the time.

Mr. SPECTER. Did you ever see any wound in any other part of his body?

Miss HENCHLIFFE. When I first saw him—except his head.

Mr. SPECTER. Did you see any wound on any other part of his body?

Miss HENCHLIFFE. Yes; in the neck.

Mr. SPECTER. Will you describe it, please?

Miss HENCHLIFFE. It was just a little hole in the middle of his neck.

Mr. SPECTER. About how big a hole was it?

Miss HENCHLIFFE. About as big around as the end of my little finger.

Mr. SPECTER. Have you ever had any experience with bullet holes?

Miss HENCHLIFFE. Yes.

Mr. SPECTER. And what did that appear to you to be?

Miss HENCHLIFFE. An entrance bullet hole—it looked to me like.

Mr. SPECTER. Could it have been an exit bullet hole?

Miss HENCHLIFFE. I have never seen an exit bullet hole—I don't remember seeing one that looked like that.

Mr. SPECTER. What were the characteristics of the hole?

Miss HENCHLIFFE. It was just a little round—just a little round hole, just a little round jagged-looking—jagged a little bit.

Mr. SPECTER. What experience have you had in observing bullet holes, Miss Henchliffe?

Miss HENCHLIFFE. Well, we take care of a lot of bullet wounds down there—I don't know how many a year.

Mr. SPECTER. Have you ever had any formal studies of bullet holes?

Miss HENCHLIFFE. Oh, no; nothing except my experience in the emergency room.

Mr. SPECTER. In what?

Miss HENCHLIFFE. In the emergency room is all.

Mr. SPECTER. What was done to the President after he arrived at the emergency room?

Miss HENCHLIFFE. Well the first thing, his endotracheal tube was inserted.

Mr. SPECTER. Were you present all the time he was in the emergency room?

Miss HENCHLIFFE. Except when I left out to get blood.

Mr. SPECTER. And how long were you gone?

Miss HENCHLIFFE. Oh, about 3 minutes or so—3 or 4 minutes.

Mr. SPECTER. And were you present when he was pronounced dead?

Miss HENCHLIFFE. Yes, sir.

Mr. SPECTER. What was done with the President's body after he was pronounced to be dead?

Miss HENCHLIFFE. Well, after the last rites were said, we then undressed him and cleaned him up and wrapped him up in sheets until the coffin was brought.

Mr. SPECTER. And after the coffin arrived, what was done with his body?

Miss HENCHLIFFE. He was placed in the coffin.

Mr. SPECTER. What had he been on up until that time?

Miss HENCHLIFFE. An emergency room cart.

Mr. SPECTER. And is that also described as a stretcher?

Miss HENCHLIFFE. A stretcher—yes.

Mr. SPECTER. Would you describe what this stretcher looked like?

Miss HENCHLIFFE. Well, how do you describe a stretcher—it's just along——

Mr. SPECTER. Made of metal?

Miss HENCHLIFFE. Yes; it's made of metal.

Mr. SPECTER. On roller wheels?

Miss HENCHLIFFE. Roller wheels with a rubber mattress on it, rubber covered mattress on it.

Mr. SPECTER. And after he was taken off of the stretcher, what was left on the stretcher at that time?

Miss HENCHLIFFE. Just some sheets and I guess there were some dirty syringes and needles laying on it that we picked up.

Mr. SPECTER. That you picked up—where were they placed?

Miss HENCHLIFFE. We placed them on a tray and took them all out to the utility room.

Mr. SPECTER. How many sheets were there on the stretcher?

Miss HENCHLIFFE. Well, I am really not sure—there was probably about two or three.

Mr. SPECTER. And in what position were they all on the stretcher after President Kennedy's body was removed?

Miss HENCHLIFFE. Well, one was covering the whole mattress and there was one or two that we had left just under his head, that had been placed under his head.

Mr. SPECTER. And what was done with those sheets?

Miss HENCHLIFFE. They were all rolled up and taken to the dirty linen hamper.

Mr. SPECTER. Do you know who took those to the dirty linen hamper?

Miss HENCHLIFFE. To the best of my knowledge, the orderly.

Mr. SPECTER. And who was he?

Miss HENCHLIFFE. David Sanders—is that his name?

Mr. SPECTER. And what was done with the stretcher?

Miss HENCHLIFFE. It was rolled into the room across the hall.

Mr. SPECTER. Did you actually see the stretcher that President Kennedy was on rolled into the room across the hall?

Miss HENCHLIFFE. Yes.

Mr. SPECTER. And into which room was it rolled?

Miss HENCHLIFFE. Room 2.

Mr. SPECTER. What was that?

Miss HENCHLIFFE. Room 2.

Mr. SPECTER. Emergency room No. 2?

Miss HENCHLIFFE. Yes, sir.

Mr. SPECTER. And, when it was rolled into emergency room 2, were the sheets still all on, or were they off at that time?

Miss HENCHLIFFE. I believe they were off.

Mr. SPECTER. Is it possible that the stretcher that Mr. Kennedy was on was rolled with the sheets on it down into the area near the elevator?

Miss HENCHLIFFE. No, sir.

Mr. SPECTER. Are you sure of that?

Miss HENCHLIFFE. I am positive of that.

Mr. SPECTER. Have you anything to add that you think might be helpful to the Commission?

Miss HENCHLIFFE. No, sir; I don't think of anything.

Mr. SPECTER. Did I talk to you about the purpose of the Commission and the same questions that I have been asking and the answers that you have been giving for a few minutes before the Court reporter came in to take this down in shorthand?

Miss HENCHLIFFE. Yes.

Mr. SPECTER. And did you give me the same information at that time?

Miss HENCHLIFFE. To the best of my ability.

Mr. SPECTER. Thank you very much for coming.

Miss HENCHLIFFE. Okay.

(At this point the witness, Henchliffe, was thereupon excused from the deposing room.)

(In approximately 3 minutes thereafter the witness returned to the deposing room and the deposition continued as follows:)

Mr. SPECTER. Let me ask you a couple of questions more, Miss Henchliffe, one other question, or two, before you go.

Was the wound on the front of the neck surrounded by any blood?

Miss HENCHLIFFE. No, sir.

Mr. SPECTER. Was there any blood at all in that area?

Miss HENCHLIFFE. No, sir.

Mr. SPECTER. What was there about the wound, if you recall anything special, which gave you the impression it was an entrance wound?

Miss HENCHLIFFE. Well, it was just a small wound and wasn't jagged like most of the exit bullet wounds that I have seen.

Mr. SPECTER. If there was a high-powered rifle, or a high-powered rifle was going at a fast speed, as fast as 2,000 feet per second, which encountered only soft tissue in the body, would you have sufficient knowledge to know whether or not the appearance of that hole would be consistent with an exit wound?

Miss HENCHLIFFE. Well, from some information I received in talking to someone about guns later on, they said that this is possible. But you have a small exit wound—you could have a small exit wound.

Mr. SPECTER. Under what circumstances?

Miss HENCHLIFFE. As you described—a very fast bullet that didn't hit anything but soft tissue going through.

Mr. SPECTER. And do you have any other source of information or basis for having an opinion whether it was an entrance wound or an exit wound other than that source of information you just described, plus your general experience here at Parkland as a nurse?

Miss HENCHLIFFE. No, sir.

Mr. SPECTER. How long have you been at Parkland as a nurse?

Miss HENCHLIFFE. Well, I have had emergency room experience for about 5 years here and a couple of years at Baylor Hospital.

Mr. SPECTER. And is that the total sum of your experience?

Miss HENCHLIFFE. In the emergency room.

Mr. SPECTER. And what other experience have you had besides emergency room experience?

Miss HENCHLIFFE. Well, in the operating room here.

Mr. SPECTER. How long have you had operating room experience here?

Miss HENCHLIFFE. 3 years.

Mr. SPECTER. And how long have you been a registered nurse altogether?

Miss HENCHLIFFE. 12 years—almost 12 years.

Mr. SPECTER. And what is the source of information about the appearance of an exit wound from a high-powered gun which you have just described?

Miss HENCHLIFFE. I don't remember who I was talking to now. I was just talking to someone one day about gunshots and after this report came out that said that any high-powered gun that this could happen.

Mr. SPECTER. That it could be an exit wound which looked very much like an entrance wound with the missile striking nothing but soft tissue?

Miss HENCHLIFFE. Yes, sir.

Mr. SPECTER. Do you have anything else to add?

Miss HENCHLIFFE. No.

Mr. SPECTER. Thank you very much.

Miss HENCHLIFFE. All right.

TESTIMONY OF DORIS MAE NELSON

The testimony of Doris Mae Nelson was taken on March 20, 1964, at Parkland Memorial Hospital, Dallas, Tex., by Mr. Arlen Specter, assistant counsel of the President's Commission.

Mr. SPECTER. Mrs. Nelson, this is Miss Oliver, the court reporter, and will you raise your right hand and take the oath?

132

Do you solemnly swear that the testimony you give in this proceeding will be the truth, the whole truth, and nothing but the truth, so help you God?

Mrs. NELSON. I do.

Mr. SPECTER. May the record show that Mrs. Doris Nelson is appearing to testify in this deposition proceeding conducted by the President's Commission on the Assassination of President Kennedy to provide whatever facts, if any, she may know concerning the treatment received by President Kennedy and Governor Connally at Parkland Memorial Hospital on November 22, 1963.

Mr. SPECTER. Will you state your full name for the record, please?

Mrs. NELSON. Doris Mae Nelson. Do you want my maiden name?

Mr. SPECTER. Fine, yes; what is your maiden name?

Mrs. NELSON. Morris, M-o-r-r-i-s [spelling].

Mr. SPECTER. Mrs. Nelson, have you had an opportunity to view the joint resolution of the 88th Congress and the Executive order which established the President's Commission?

Mrs. NELSON. Yes; I read it yesterday.

Mr. SPECTER. And have you had an opportunity to view the resolution of the President's Commission covering questioning of witnesses by members of the Commission staff?

Mrs. NELSON. Yes.

Mr. SPECTER. And are you willing to be questioned today concerning this matter, even though you have not had 3 days' notice?

Mrs. NELSON. Yes.

Mr. SPECTER. Therefore waiving the right which you have, a 3 days' notice under the resolution?

Mrs. NELSON. Yes.

Mr. SPECTER. What is your occupation or profession?

Mrs. NELSON. I am a registered nurse, supervisor of the emergency room at Parkland Memorial Hospital.

Mr. SPECTER. And how long have you been so occupied?

Mrs. NELSON. A year and 6 months as supervisor of the emergency room.

Mr. SPECTER. What were your duties in a general way on November 22, 1963?

Mrs. NELSON. I was primarily responsible for assigning personnel in the treatment of the injured patients and carrying out security measures with the Secret Service.

Mr. SPECTER. What notification, if any, did you receive on that date concerning injuries to President Kennedy?

Mrs. NELSON. I received a phone call approximately 3 to 5 minutes prior to their arrival, from the telephone operator, stating that the President had been shot and was being brought to the emergency room.

Mr. SPECTER. What action after that did you take in preparing for the President's arrival?

Mrs. NELSON. I immediately took the surgical resident into trauma room No. 1, notified him of the incident, and asked the—also told the head nurse that the President had been shot and was being brought to the emergency room.

Then, I went into trauma room 2, after the head nurse had told me that trauma room 1 was set up for any emergency, and proceeded to open a bottle of intravenous fluid and set it up for an emergency situation.

Mr. SPECTER. Did you know at that time that anyone else had been injured?

Mrs. NELSON. No; we were not notified as to anyone else being injured.

Mr. SPECTER. What occurred with respect to the arrival of any injured party at Parkland Memorial Hospital thereafter?

Mrs. NELSON. As I walked out of trauma room No. 2 I heard someone calling for stretchers and an orderly ran back into the area and got a stretcher and ran out of the door, and a few seconds later Governor Connally, who at that time I did not know who it was but recognized him as not being the President, arrived and I directed them into trauma room 2.

Mr. SPECTER. Did the orderly take out one stretcher, or was more than one stretcher taken out?

Mrs. NELSON. I do not know exactly how many stretchers were taken out at the time because I was not out at that area.

Mr. SPECTER. Did another stretcher come into the area?

Mrs. NELSON. Yes; immediately behind the Governor another stretcher was brought back into the emergency room and on this stretcher was President Kennedy.

Mr. SPECTER. How were you able to identify President Kennedy?

Mrs. NELSON. Well, I could look and see him and tell that it was him.

133

Mr. SPECTER. What part did you see?

Mrs. NELSON. The—mainly his head.

Mr. SPECTER. Was there any coat covering his face?

Mrs. NELSON. There was a coat thrown across the top of him, not completely covering his face, and Mrs. Kennedy—do you want me to tell about Mrs. Kennedy and the flowers?

Mr. SPECTER. Yes; continue. Yes; in answering the questions, Mrs. Nelson, feel perfectly free to make as full an answer to the question—I hesitate to have you stop, so that the record we make will appear continuous and everything may be recorded fully for our record purposes.

Mrs. NELSON. Mrs. Kennedy was walking beside the stretcher and the roses that she had been given at the airport were lying on top of the President and her hat was also lying on top of the President as he was brought into the emergency room.

Mr. SPECTER. Where was he then taken?

Mrs. NELSON. He was immediately taken into trauma room 1.

Mr. SPECTER. And who, if anyone, was present at that time to attend him in a medical way?

Mrs. NELSON. Dr. Carrico, a surgical resident was there at the time that he was brought in, and Dr. Perry, an associate professor of surgery arrived shortly thereafter, and several doctors arrived, Dr. Baxter, associate professor of surgery, Dr. Kemp Clark, professor of neurosurgery and chairman of the department; Dr. Bashour—

Mr. SPECTER. Spell, please.

Mrs. NELSON. B-a-s-h-o-u-r (spelling), chairman of the Department of Cardiology, and several other doctors who I cannot recall all the names at the present time.

Mr. SPECTER. Were you present inside of the emergency room where President Kennedy was taken?

Mrs. NELSON. When what?

Mr. SPECTER. Were you in there at the time they were treating him, caring for him at any time?

Mrs. NELSON. On one occasion I went into the room and this was mainly to ask Mrs. Kennedy if she had rather wait out in the hallway rather than in the room where they were treating the President, and I was told by the Secret Service agent that she may stay in there if she wished.

Mr. SPECTER. Is there any table, or was there any table in the emergency room to which President Kennedy was taken that he could be placed on from the stretcher?

Mrs. NELSON. No.

Mr. SPECTER. Is it the normal situation to have no table present in the emergency room?

Mrs. NELSON. The only one there is in case an ambulance should bring a patient in, but if a patient comes in the emergency room on a stretcher, then the stretcher that is in there is removed. Then the patient remains on the same stretcher that he comes into the emergency room on.

Mr. SPECTER. And was there a stretcher in the emergency room at the time President Kennedy was taken in on a second stretcher?

Mrs. NELSON. It was taken out when they wheeled it in.

Mr. SPECTER. Were there any sheets on the stretcher that President Kennedy was on?

Mrs. NELSON. Yes.

Mr. SPECTER. After President Kennedy was taken off of the stretcher, did you have occasion to observe that stretcher?

Mrs. NELSON. Yes; the stretcher was stripped by the nursing personnel working in the room and the stretcher was moved across from trauma room 1 to trauma room 2 in order to get the stretcher out of the room.

Mr. SPECTER. What personnel stripped the stretcher?

Mrs. NELSON. Margaret Henchliffe, H-e-n-c-h-l-i-f-f-e [spelling], and Diana Bowron, D-i-a-n-a B-o-w-r-o-n [spelling].

Mr. SPECTER. Did you actually observe Diana Bowron or Margaret Henchliffe strip the stretcher?

Mrs. NELSON. No; I did not. This was the report that I received afterwards.

Mr. SPECTER. From whom did you receive that report?

Mrs. NELSON. From these two nurses.

Mr. SPECTER. Did you see the stretcher after it was stripped in the emergency room to which President Kennedy was taken?

Mrs. NELSON. No, I saw it after it was wheeled from trauma room 1 to trauma room 2, because I was standing there at the doorway between the two rooms with the Secret Service Police.

Mr. SPECTER. But it was actually in trauma room 1?

Mrs. NELSON. Yes.

Mr. SPECTER. As it was being wheeled out to trauma room 2 and at the time it was being wheeled out, was there any sheet on it at all——

Mrs. NELSON. No.

Mr. SPECTER. Rolled up on it in any way at all?

Mrs. NELSON. No.

Mr. SPECTER. Did you see where the stretcher was then placed?

Mrs. NELSON. Yes, it was put into trauma room 2.

Mr. SPECTER. Where was President Kennedy's body at that time?

Mrs. NELSON. It was in—it had been placed in a casket in trauma room 1.

Mr. SPECTER. And was the casket on any sort of an object or was it on the floor or what?

Mrs. NELSON. It was on a form of roller-type table.

Mr. SPECTER. And did—do you know what President Kennedy's body was in, if anything, at that time?

Mrs. NELSON. Yes, one of the nurses, Miss Hutton, came out and said that the President was having extensive bleeding from the head and they had wrapped four sheets around it but it was still oozing through, so I sent her to the second floor to obtain a mattress cover, a plastic mattress cover, to put in the casket prior to putting his body in the casket, so the mattress cover was placed in the casket and I did not see this happen, but this is how it was explained to me by the nurse, and the plastic was placed on the mattress cover and the cover was around the mattress.

Mr. SPECTER. Which nurse explained that to you?

Mrs. NELSON. Miss Bowron and Miss Henchliffe.

Mr. SPECTER. And what was done with the sheets which had been used to absorb the blood from the President's body?

Mrs. NELSON. Well, there were approximately four sheets wrapped around him and the remaining sheets that were on the stretcher were pulled up and thrown in the linen hamper, according to Miss Bowron and Miss Henchliffe.

Mr. SPECTER. And where is that linen hamper located?

Mrs. NELSON. That linen hamper is located in the utility room area of the emergency room, which is just outside of the trauma room area.

Mr. SPECTER. And what floor is that on?

Mrs. NELSON. On the ground floor of the hospital.

Mr. SPECTER. What was done with Governor Connally?

Mrs. NELSON. Governor Connally was in the emergency room for a very short period, approximately 15 to 20 minutes, at which time he had chest tubes inserted, intravenous fluid started, anesthesia or oxygen given to him, and he was taken immediately from the emergency room to the operating room accompanied by several doctors.

Mr. SPECTER. Did you see him inside trauma room No. 2?

Mrs. NELSON. Yes; I did.

Mr. SPECTER. And did you observe him when he was taken out of trauma room No. 2?

Mrs. NELSON. Yes, I saw him when he went upstairs to the operating room.

Mr. SPECTER. And how did he get upstairs to the operating room?

Mrs. NELSON. On a stretcher carried by several of the doctors. Miss Standridge went in front, and opened doorways and went to the elevator. I could not see her at the elevator but this is what she told me.

Mr. SPECTER. How far could you see her?

Mrs. NELSON. Oh, approximately 30 feet.

Mr. SPECTER. And who is Miss Standridge?

Mrs. NELSON. Head nurse in the emergency room.

Mr. SPECTER. What is her first name?

Mrs. NELSON. Jeanette.

Mr. SPECTER. You say the stretcher was carried?

Mrs. NELSON. Well, it was wheeled.

Mr. SPECTER. And what does the stretcher look like that Governor Connally was on?

Mrs. NELSON. Well, there are no specific details, it's an average type of movable four-wheel stretcher, made out of metal, with a plastic mattress on the stretcher. It has an elevation between—on the sides, so that the—I don't know how to explain exactly.

Mr. SPECTER. A bumper-type effect?

Mrs. NELSON. It has a bumper on the side.

135

Mr. SPECTER. Is there a tray underneath the place where the body was resting?

Mrs. NELSON. Yes.

Mr. SPECTER. And is that the same general description of a stretcher that President Kennedy was brought in on?

Mrs. NELSON. Yes; they were the same type.

Mr. SPECTER. Mrs. Nelson, I'm going to show you a four-page statement which is marked "Activities of Doris Nelson, R.N., beginning 12 noon, Friday, November 22, 1963," after I ask that it be marked as an exhibit in connection with this deposition.

(Reporter marked the instrument referred to as Nelson Exhibit No. 1.)

Mr. SPECTER. Is this a photostatic copy of the statement which you gave to Mr. Jack Price, the administrator of the hospital, concerning your activities on November 22, 1963, as they pertain to this matter?

Mrs. NELSON. Yes; it is.

Mr. SPECTER. And are the facts set forth herein true and correct to the best of your knowledge, information and belief?

Mrs. NELSON. Yes; they are.

Mr. SPECTER. Did I meet with you for a few moments before we started this deposition and explain the purpose of the proceeding?

Mrs. NELSON. Yes; you did.

Mr. SPECTER. Did I ask you the same questions which we have discussed here during the course of my questioning before the court reporter?

Mrs. NELSON. Yes.

Mr. SPECTER. Thank you very much for providing this deposition to us.

Mrs. NELSON. You are quite welcome.

Mr. SPECTER. Off the record.

(Discussion off the record between Mr. Specter and the witness, Mrs. Doris Nelson.)

Mr. SPECTER. Back on the record, just a minute.

Mrs. Nelson, I will ask you if you would sign the end of this statement here, that it is your statement?

Mrs. NELSON. (Signed statement referred to.)

Mr. SPECTER. And are you willing to waive a requirement, if it is any formal requirement, as to the signing of this deposition?

Mrs. NELSON. Yes; I am.

Mr. SPECTER. Thank you very much.

TESTIMONY OF CHARLES JACK PRICE

The testimony of Charles Jack Price was taken at 4:50 p.m., on March 25, 1964, at Parkland Memorial Hospital, Dallas, Tex., by Mr. Arlen Specter, assistant counsel of the President's Commission.

Mr. SPECTER. May the record show that C. Jack Price is present to have his deposition taken in connection with the inquiry of the President's Commission on the Assassination of President Kennedy, which is concerned with the medical care rendered at Parkland Memorial Hospital to President John F. Kennedy and to Governor John B. Connally.

Authorization has been obtained to take the deposition of Mr. Price and he has had access to the copy of the Executive order creating the President's Commission——

Mr. PRICE. Yes.

Mr. SPECTER. And the rules relating to the taking of depositions of witnesses. Is it satisfactory with you to have your deposition taken without having the 3-day waiting period between the request and the taking of the deposition?

Mr. PRICE. Yes.

Mr. SPECTER. Would you stand up, Mr. Price, and raise your right hand?

Do you solemnly swear that the testimony you give before the President's Commission and in this deposition proceeding will be the truth, the whole truth, and nothing but the truth, so help you God?

Mr. PRICE. I do.

Mr. SPECTER. Would you state your full name for the record, please?

Mr. PRICE. Charles Jack Price.

Mr. SPECTER. And what is your official title here?

Mr. PRICE. Administrator, Dallas County Hospital district, comprised of Parkland Memorial Hospital and Woodlawn Hospital.

Mr. SPECTER. Mr. Price, in connection with your duties at Parkland Memorial Hospital, did you request that all of the individuals who participated in the care and treatment of President Kennedy and Governor Connally, or at least those who were principally concerned with that treatment, prepare and submit reports to you concerning that treatment?

Mr. PRICE. Yes; through Dr. Kemp Clark, who is chairman of our medical records committee.

Mr. SPECTER. And where have those records been kept after submission through Dr. Kemp Clark?

Mr. PRICE. The records were brought directly to my office. In fact, some of the records were written in my office and since that time have been kept in my custody, specifically under lock and key in my desk drawer.

Mr. SPECTER. I show you a document which has heretofore been marked as "Commission Exhibit No. 392," and I ask you if this constitutes all of the records of the doctors who examined and treated President Kennedy and Governor Connally which are in your possession, that is all the records which were made by the examining doctors?

Mr. PRICE. (Examining instrument referred to.) Do you want my comments as I go through this or do you want me to look through it and say "Yes," or "No"?

Mr. SPECTER. Yes; I would like to just be sure for the record that those are all of the records. You and I went through them the other day informally and at that time you supplemented my records to some extent, which I will put on the deposition record here.

Mr. PRICE. Yes.

Mr. SPECTER. Perhaps, before going to Commission Exhibit No. 392, permit me to have this photostatic copy marked Mr. Price's Exhibit No. 2.

(Instrument referred to marked by the reporter as Price Exhibit No. 2, for identification.)

Mr. SPECTER. And I ask you if this is a photostatic copy of a letter which was sent by Dr. Kemp Clark to Dr. Burkley, the President's private physician?

Mr. PRICE. It is.

Mr. SPECTER. And with that, the summary of all the treatments performed at Parkland, which was prepared by Dr. Kemp Clark?

Mr. PRICE. That's right.

Mr. SPECTER. And below that, another summary sheet which bears the corrected notation, with your signature over it, that the President arrived at the emergency room at exactly 12:38 p.m., with 12:43 scratched out?

Mr. PRICE. That's correct.

Mr. SPECTER. Now, as you move through your file, permit me to also ask the reporter to mark as Mr. Price's Exhibit No. 3, an affidavit of Ulah McCoy, and I'll ask you if that is a copy of an original in your file?

(Instrument referred to marked by the reporter as Price Exhibit No. 3, for identification.)

Mr. PRICE. Yes; it is.

Mr. SPECTER. And I will ask her to mark as Mr. Price Exhibit No. 4 an affidavit of Doris Nelson and I'll ask you if that is a copy of a report in your possession?

(Instrument referred to marked by the reporter as Price Exhibit No. 4, for identification.)

Mr. PRICE. Yes.

Mr. SPECTER. Your next report is one from Dr. M. T. Jenkins?

Mr. PRICE. Professor and chairman of the department of anesthesiology.

Mr. SPECTER. And is that a copy of the document which you are looking at here?

Mr. PRICE. It is.

Mr. SPECTER. As part of Exhibit 392?

Mr. PRICE. That's right, and my next one is the statement of Dr. W. Kemp Clark.

Mr. SPECTER. And is that the original of a copy of which appears in this group of papers as Exhibit No. 392?

Mr. PRICE. Yes; it is. The next one that I have is the statement of Dr. Perry.

Mr. SPECTER. And is that the original of a copy of a statement which appears in Exhibit 392?

Mr. PRICE. Yes; the statement of Dr. Charles W. Baxter.

Mr. SPECTER. Is that the original of a copy which appears in Exhibit 392?

Mr. PRICE. Yes; it is; that's the statement of Dr. Carrico.

Mr. SPECTER. And is this the copy of the original of Dr. Carrico's statement?

Mr. PRICE. Yes; it is; and this is Dr. McClelland's statement.

Mr. SPECTER. I now show you a photostatic copy of what purports to be Dr. McClelland's statement, and is that a copy of the original in your file?

Mr. PRICE. Yes; it is.

137

Mr. SPECTER. What is your next report?

Mr. PRICE. My next report is Dr. Bashour's report.

Mr. SPECTER. And I show you a sheet in the group of papers marked Exhibit 392, and ask you if that is a photostatic copy of the original in your file?

Mr. PRICE. Yes; it is.

Mr. SPECTER. And what is next?

Mr. PRICE. My next one is the summary of Dr. Ronald C. Jones.

Mr. SPECTER. Now, I'll ask you if this is a photostatic copy of the original of the statement by Dr. Ronald Jones which is in your file?

Mr. PRICE. May I see it, please?

Mr. SPECTER. Yes.

(Handed instrument referred to to the witness.)

Mr. PRICE. Yes; it is.

Mr. SPECTER. Now, does that constitute all of the original records concerning the treatment of President John F. Kennedy in your file?

Mr. PRICE. With one exception—there is in the file that I have of Governor Connally the original of the transcript of "Registration of patients," which I furnished you a photostat of, our number being 01811.

Mr. SPECTER. And is this a photostatic copy of that registration of patients?

Mr. PRICE. It is; and I think I reviewed it with you at the time I gave this to you—the transverse of patients No. 2 and No. 5.

Mr. SPECTER. No. 5 is marked John Connally and No. 2 is John F. Kennedy, and how should that have been marked?

Mr. PRICE. The first patient in the hospital was Governor Connally.

Mr. SPECTER. So, he should have been No. 2?

Mr. PRICE. So, he should have been No. 2 as shown on the transcript.

Mr. SPECTER. And the President should have been noted as No. 5?

Mr. PRICE. The President should have been noted as No. 5.

(Instrument referred to marked by the reporter as Price Exhibit No. 5, for identification.)

Mr. PRICE. The simultaneous arrival at the ambulance dock would not affect the time as shown in the corrected copy that I gave you of the arrival there.

Mr. SPECTER. Now, turn if you will, to the records on Governor Connally and I will ask you if as part of Commission Exhibit 392, we have photostatic copies of the operative records starting, first with the operation performed by Dr. Shaw.

Mr. PRICE. I have the original of that but this is the complete medical charts that I have here.

Mr. SPECTER. As to this report alone, do you have the original in that record?

Mr. PRICE. Here it is.

Mr. SPECTER. And is this an exact photocopy of the original report prepared by Dr. Robert Shaw, the original of which appears in your record on Governor Connally?

Mr. PRICE. It is.

Mr. SPECTER. Is this an exact photostatic copy of the report of Dr. Charles Gregory?

Mr. PRICE. There has been since this photostat was made and forwarded to you—Dr. Gregory, prior to signing the official copy, did make some pencil corrections, and I will be glad to have the original photostated or Xeroxed now and give you a corrected copy if you would like?

Mr. SPECTER. That would be fine, and perhaps it would be faster just to read those changes into our record here. However, let's pursue the line of getting a Xerox copy.

Now, turning to the report of Dr. Shires, is this a true and correct photostatic copy of Dr. Shires' report?

Mr. PRICE. It is; it is a correct copy.

Mr. SPECTER. Now, I show you a large group of papers which I am going to ask the reporter to mark Mr. Price Exhibits Nos. 6, 7, 8, and 9.

(Instruments referred to marked by the reporter as Price Exhibits Nos. 6, 7, 8, and 9, for identification.)

Mr. SPECTER. I now show you a group of papers, and as they are being marked, if you would take a look at them. Price Exhibit No. 6—I'll ask you if these are photostatic copies of reports which you have made available to me of originals which you have in your file made by various members of your staff, concerning the events of November 22, and November 24.

Mr. PRICE. Do you want these individually or as a group?

Mr. SPECTER. If you would identify the contents of the statement by the exhibit number which we have put on it, starting with the first numerical designation, would probably be the simplest. Exhibit 6 is what?

Mr. PRICE. Exhibit No. 6 is a Xerox copy of the floor plan of the emergency area. This is correct.

The Exhibit No. 7, the statement is unsigned, but this is the Xerox copy of the summary submitted to me by my assistant, Mr. Steve Landregan.

Mr. SPECTER. And what is his position with the hospital?

Mr. PRICE. He is assistant administrator.

Mr. SPECTER. In charge of press relations among other things?

Mr. PRICE. In charge of press relations among other things.

Mr. SPECTER. And what is Exhibit No. 8?

Mr. PRICE. Exhibit No. 8 is a Xerox copy of Peter Geilich's statement to me. Mr. Geilich is administrative assistant, with primary assignment over at the Woodlawn unit, and is also the acting director of our outpatient clinic.

Mr. SPECTER. And what is Exhibit No. 9?

Mr. PRICE. Exhibit No. 9 is a summary of the activities of Robert Dutton, Bob Dutton, who is administrative assistant and is currently our evening administrator.

(Instruments marked as Price Exhibits Nos. 10 through 32 at this time, for identification.)

Mr. SPECTER. Exhibit 10 is what?

Mr. PRICE. Exhibit 10 is a summary of activities of Mrs. Carol Reddick, who is administrative aide.

Exhibit No. 11 is a summary of activities of Mrs. Elizabeth L. Wright, our director of nursing service.

Mr. SPECTER. What is Exhibit No. 12?

Mr. PRICE. Exhibit No. 12 is a summary of the activities of Diana Bowron, who is an emergency room nurse.

Mr. SPECTER. Exhibit No. 13?

Mr. PRICE. Exhibit No. 13 is a summary of the activities of Sallie Lennon.

Mr. SPECTER. What is her position?

Mr. PRICE. She is a nurse.

Mr. SPECTER. I hand you Price Exhibit No. 14.

Mr. PRICE. This is a statement of the activities of C. Watkins, who is an R.N. in the emergency room.

Mr. SPECTER. And I hand you Price Exhibit No. 15

Mr. PRICE. Exhibit No. 15 is a report of the activities of Faye Dean Shelby, and she is a nurse in the emergency room.

Mr. SPECTER. Price Exhibit No. 16?

Mr. PRICE. This is the activities of Era Lumpkin, an aide in the emergency area.

Mr. SPECTER. Price Exhibit No. 17?

Mr. PRICE. Exhibit No. 17 is a report on the activities of Jean Tarrant, who is an aide in the major medicine emergency room.

Mr. SPECTER. I now hand you Price Exhibit No. 18.

Mr. PRICE. Exhibit 18 is the activities of Frances Scott, who is assigned to the emergency room.

Mr. SPECTER. Exhibit No. 19?

Mr. PRICE. Exhibit No. 19 is the activities of Willie Haywood, who is an orderly in the emergency room.

Mr. SPECTER. I now hand you Price Exhibit No. 20.

Mr. PRICE. This is a summary of the activities of Bertha L. Lozano, who is a registered nurse in the emergency room.

Mr. SPECTER. Price Exhibit No. 21?

Mr. PRICE. Exhibit No. 21 is a summary of the activities of Pat Hutton, who is an aide in the emergency room.

Mr. SPECTER. I'll hand you Price Exhibit No. 22.

Mr. PRICE. I'm sorry, I said Hutton was an aide. She's an R.N.—in registration—a nurse.

Mr. SPECTER. And what is Exhibit No. 22?

Mr. PRICE. It is a summary of the activities of Shirley Randall, an aide in the emergency room.

Mr. SPECTER. And what is Price Exhibit No. 23?

Mr. PRICE. A summary of the activities of Rosa M. Majors, an aide in the emergency room.

Mr. SPECTER. And what is Price Exhibit 24?

Mr. PRICE. Price Exhibit 24 is a summary of the activities of Jill Pomeroy, who is a ward clerk in the emergency room.

Mr. SPECTER. And what is Price Exhibit No. 25?

Mr. PRICE. A summary of the activities of David Sanders, who is an orderly in the emergency room.

Mr. SPECTER. And what is Price Exhibit No. 26?

Mr. PRICE. Exhibit 26 is a summary of the activities of Tommy Dunn, who is an orderly in the emergency room.

Mr. SPECTER. And what is Price Exhibit No. 27?

Mr. PRICE. A summary of the activities of Joe Richards, an orderly in the emergency room.

Mr. SPECTER. And what is Price Exhibit No. 28?

Mr. PRICE. Exhibit No. 28 is a statement of the activities of Jeanette Standridge, an R.N. in the emergency room.

Mr. SPECTER. And what is Price Exhibit 29?

Mr. PRICE. A summary of the activities of O. P. Wright, who is the personnel director and a director of hospital security, and reports from the individual guards under his supervision.

Mr. SPECTER. And what is Price Exhibit No. 30?

Mr. PRICE. A summary of the activities of Margaret Henchliffe, who is assigned to the emergency room.

Mr. SPECTER. What is Price Exhibit No. 31?

Mr. PRICE. A summary of the activities of Doris Nelson, who is the emergency room supervisor.

Mr. SPECTER. And what is Price Exhibit No. 32?

Mr. PRICE. A summary of the activities of Robert G. Holcomb, who is assistant administrator in charge of correlating the professional services of the hospital.

Mr. SPECTER. What is Price Exhibit No. 33?

Mr. PRICE. This is a summary of my personal impressions of the events that transpired on November 24.

Mr. SPECTER. And what is Price Exhibit 34?

Mr. PRICE. This is a summary of my activities at the office Saturday and Sunday, the 23d and 24th.

Mr. SPECTER. Are those all of the summaries of those who made reports to you?

Mr. PRICE. Yes; they are. These are primarily the summaries of individuals who were involved in the care of our late President, in the care of Governor Connally, and in the care of Oswald, who were requested to make these summaries to my office as their activities would not normally be stated on patients' charts or in other records of the hospital.

Mr. SPECTER. I now hand you Price Exhibit No. 35 and ask you if that is a photostatic copy of the report of Dr. Charles Gregory, after it was altered in a few minor respects as shown on the face of the record?

Mr. PRICE. Well, if I may change this terminology?

Mr. SPECTER. Sure.

Mr. PRICE. This is a copy of Dr. Charles Gregory's records as it appears in Governor Connally's charts, which he corrected prior to signing the transcript. What I was trying to say, or wanted to make clear, was that frequently in transcribing, the medical secretaries who transcribe operative records, they make mistakes, and I wanted to be sure that there was no suggestion that the record was altered, when what Dr. Gregory has done was to write in corrections that were noticed at the time he read it and signed it.

Mr. SPECTER. I understand it was transcribed, and when he reviewed it before signing it he noticed inaccuracies in the transcription.

Mr. PRICE. That's right. This is correct. Your phraseology is much better than mine.

Mr. SPECTER. Thank you very much, Mr. Price.

Mr. PRICE. Thank you, sir.

Mr. SPECTER. That's all. I wanted to put all of these in the record, Jack, to show that they are duly authenticated by the appropriate custodian of the records.

Mr. PRICE. Well, I wanted to be sure that there was no hint that the record had been altered here.

Mr. SPECTER. Yes; I understand that. I think you are absolutely right on that. Thank you.

Mr. PRICE. All right. Thank you.

TESTIMONY OF MALCOLM O. COUCH

The testimony of Malcolm O. Couch was taken at 9:43 a.m., on April 1, 1964, in the office of the U.S. attorney, 301 Post Office Building, Bryan and Ervay Streets, Dallas, Tex., by Mr. David W. Belin, assistant counsel of the President's Commission.

Mr. BELIN. Will you please rise and raise your right hand and be sworn, sir?

Do you solemnly swear that the testimony you're about to give will be the truth, the whole truth and nothing but the truth, so help you God?

Mr. COUCH. I do.

Mr. BELIN. Be seated, please.

Mr. BELIN. You are Malcolm O. Couch?

Mr. COUCH. That's right.

Mr. BELIN. Mr. Couch, we are taking your deposition here in Dallas to record your testimony for the President's Commission on the Assassination of President Kennedy—is that correct?

Mr. COUCH. That's right, sir.

Mr. BELIN. Do you request that an attorney be present here to represent you?

Mr. COUCH. No.

Mr. BELIN. We have written you about the taking of this deposition and I assume that you have waived notice of the taking of the deposition—is that correct?

Mr. COUCH. That's right.

Mr. BELIN. Mr. Couch, you have the right to look at the deposition and sign it, or you can follow the general custom and rely on the court reporter and waive the signing of the deposition—whatever you would like to do. If you would like to sign it, you can; if you want to waive signing it, you can also. Whatever you want to do.

Mr. COUCH. All right. I'll sign it.

Mr. BELIN. You want to sign it?

Mr. COUCH. Yes, sir.

Mr. BELIN. All right.

Mr. Couch, where do you live?

Mr. COUCH. 4215 Live Oak in Dallas.

Mr. BELIN. And how old are you?

Mr. COUCH. Twenty-five.

Mr. BELIN. And were you born in Texas?

Mr. COUCH. Yes; born in Dallas and raised in Dallas.

Mr. BELIN. And what is your educational background? Did you go through high school?

Mr. COUCH. I went to Woodrow Wilson High School here in Dallas, I have a Bachelor of Arts degree from John Brown University; and I will receive a Master of Theology degree this May from Dallas Seminary.

Mr. BELIN. You then plan, when you receive your Master of Theology degree, to become a minister?

Mr. COUCH. I will be ordained. I don't know if I will have a church or not, but I will be ordained.

Mr. BELIN. Are you married, Mr. Couch?

Mr. COUCH. Yes.

Mr. BELIN. Any family at all?

Mr. COUCH. Yes; one boy—since last Friday.

Mr. BELIN. Since last Friday? Well, congratulations to you. I assume your wife and baby are doing well?

Mr. COUCH. Yes, sir.

Mr. BELIN. What did you major in at college?

Mr. COUCH. Social science.

Mr. BELIN. What is your present occupation, Mr. Couch?

Mr. COUCH. Part-time television news cameraman with WFAA-TV in Dallas.

Mr. BELIN. When you say "part time," do you mean you're going to school part time——

Mr. COUCH. Right.

Mr. BELIN. And spending part time with WFAA-TV?

Mr. COUCH. Right.

Mr. BELIN. How long have you been employed by WFAA-TV?

Mr. COUCH. Uh—for 2 years straight. But I worked with them full and part time, I believe, back in—starting in 1955 to 1957.

Mr. BELIN. And then what happened in 1957?

141

Mr. COUCH. I went to college.

Mr. BELIN. You went to college full time?

Mr. COUCH. Right.

Mr. BELIN. And then you got out in 1961?

Mr. COUCH. I got out in January 1960.

Mr. BELIN. January 1960?

Mr. COUCH. Yes—and came back to Dallas and went into graduate school here.

Mr. BELIN. And when you came back to Dallas, you went to work with WFAA-TV?

Mr. COUCH. No; no. I began going to Dallas Seminary, but—uh—I worked for Keitz & Herndon Film Studios—[spelling] K-e-i-t-z and H-e-r-n-d-o-n.

Mr. BELIN. Have you had any other jobs since you've gotten out of college other than those?

Mr. COUCH. I worked a year for Camp Elhar, as executive director of the camp. It's a Christian camp here in Dallas.

Mr. BELIN. Is this for youngsters?

Mr. COUCH. Right.

Mr. BELIN. Boys and girls?

Mr. COUCH. Right.

Mr. BELIN. And when did that employment take place?

Mr. COUCH. Uh—I believe it was September 1961—and ended in September 1962. I started working for WFAA in March of 1962. And I've been there 2 years.

Mr. BELIN. In other words, part of the time while you were working with this camp, you were also part time with WFAA-TV?

Mr. COUCH. Right.

Mr. BELIN. And then when you started to work on your Masters in Theology, you stopped working?

Mr. COUCH. No. I started work on my Masters when I came back from college——

Mr. BELIN. Oh, I see.

Mr. COUCH. In January of 1960. It's a 4-year course.

Mr. BELIN. I see.

Mr. Couch, I want to take you back to November 22, 1963, and ask you whether or not you were employed by WFAA-TV at that time?

Mr. COUCH. Yes; I was.

Mr. BELIN. In connection with your employment, what is the fact as to whether or not you had anything to do with the coverage of the visit of President Kennedy to Dallas?

Mr. COUCH. Yes; I did.

Mr. BELIN. Could you just state what your duties were and what you did that day?

Mr. COUCH. I was assigned to cover the arrival of the President at the airport and to ride in the motorcade through town and, then, to ride with the motorcade of the President back to the airport when he left.

Mr. BELIN. Now, when you were assigned, were you assigned as a reporter, as a photographer, or in what capacity?

Mr. COUCH. As a photographer.

Mr. BELIN. Would this be moving picture film or still shots, or both?

Mr. COUCH. Moving only.

Mr. BELIN. Moving picture film only?

Mr. COUCH. Yes.

Mr. BELIN. Were you at Love Field in Dallas when the President arrived?

Mr. COUCH. That's right; uh-huh.

Mr. BELIN. Did you take moving pictures of him there?

Mr. COUCH. That's right.

Mr. BELIN. Then you got in the motorcade?

Mr. COUCH. Right; uh-huh.

Mr. BELIN. And the motorcade proceeded, first, from Love Field toward downtown Dallas—is that correct?

Mr. COUCH. That's right.

Mr. BELIN. Do you remember the route you took through downtown Dallas?

Mr. COUCH. Uh—roughly. It was out through the airport parkway to Mockingbird Lane to Lemmon, down Lemmon to Turtle Creek, down Turtle Creek to—uh—I'm not sure of those streets. I think McKinney or Cedar Springs. I'm not sure.

Mr. BELIN. Well, if you aren't particularly sure—okay. What about when you got downtown to the center of Dallas? Do you remember what streets you went on?

Mr. COUCH. Yes. Well, we came in on Harwood and then turned right on Main at the City Hall.

Mr. BELIN. And then you took Main to where?

Mr. COUCH. Main down to—uh—Houston.

Mr. BELIN. All right. You were heading, now, west on Main down to Houston?

Mr. COUCH. Right.

Mr. BELIN. About where in the motorcade was your car? Do you remember offhand?

Mr. COUCH. Uh-uh—roughly—and I'm not sure—the fifth or sixth car back from the lead car. I'm not sure which one.

Mr. BELIN. Now, do you remember, as you approached Houston Street on Main about how fast the motorcade was going?

Mr. COUCH. I would estimate—uh—20 miles an hour. The speed had picked up some. Everyone gave a sigh a relief that—uh—it was over; and one of the cameramen, I remember, his camera broke and another one was out of film. Everyone was relaxed. And—uh—of course, then we turned north on Houston, and it was there that we heard the first gunshot.

Mr. BELIN. All right. Before we get to the first gunshot—do you remember who was riding in the car with you?

Mr. COUCH. Uh—an best I can, it was Jimmy Darnell—Channel 5: uh—Bob Jackson—Times Herald; Jim Underwood—KRLD-TV; and the fellow—uh—Mr. Dillard—Tom Dillard—Dallas Morning News. And the driver of the car; I don't know his name.

Mr. BELIN. Were you sitting in the front or the back seat?

Mr. COUCH. Sitting in the back.

Mr. BELIN. Do you remember anything about your position as to the way you were sitting in the back?

Mr. COUCH. Yes; I was almost in the middle and sitting on the—it was a convertible—and sitting on the back of the back seat, with my feet on the seat.

Mr. BELIN. Your feet were on the seat—and you would be sitting on the top of the back seat?

Mr. COUCH. That's right.

Mr. BELIN. There were three of you in the back?

Mr. COUCH. Yes; three in the back.

Mr. BELIN. And were you in the middle or to the right or to the left?

Mr. COUCH. I was about in the middle.

Mr. BELIN. All right. Now, as you turned north on Houston, do you remember about how fast you were going?

Mr. COUCH. Well, I'd say still that—of course, allowing for the turn—that the pace of the motorcade was about the same. We were clipping along and, as I said, I do have films after we had turned the other corner, and you could still see that the motorcade was moving fairly fast.

Mr. BELIN. Were there any motorcycle policemen riding alongside the motorcade, that you remember?

Mr. COUCH. Yes; there were.

Mr. BELIN. Do you remember the names of any of those people?

Mr. COUCH. No; I don't.

Mr. BELIN. Were they two-wheel or three-wheel motorcycles?

Mr. COUCH. Two-wheel.

Mr. BELIN. Was there one riding alongside of your car?

Mr. COUCH. Uh—he was. I remember distinctly one was on my right going down Main. They would jockey from time to time in different positions. As I recall, on Houston, I don't remember any beside us on Houston. As I say, they would fade back and forth. Sometimes they would be; sometimes they wouldn't.

Mr. BELIN. All right.

Now, as you turned onto Houston, you said that you heard what you described as a——

Mr. COUCH. It sounded like a motorcycle backfire at first—the first time we heard it—the first shot.

Mr. BELIN. Do you remember about where your car was at the time you heard the first noise?

Mr. COUCH. I would say—uh—15 or 20 feet from the turn—from off of Main onto Houston.

Mr. BELIN. Fifteen or 20 feet from the turn?

Mr. COUCH. We had already completed the turn.

Mr. BELIN. After you had completed the turn, then 15 or 20 feet further on you heard the first shot—the first noise?

143

Mr. COUCH. Because, I remember I was talking and we were laughing and I was looking back to a fellow on my—that would be on my right—I don't know who it was—we were joking. We had just made the turn. And I heard the first shot.

Mr. BELIN. What happened—or what did anyone say?

Mr. COUCH. As I recall, nothing—there was no particular reaction; uh—nothing unusual. Maybe everybody sort of looked around a little, but didn't think much of it. And—uh—then, in a few seconds, I guess from 4–5 seconds later, or even less, we heard the second shot. And then we began to look—uh, not out of thinking necessarily it was a gunshot, but we began to look in front of us—in the motorcade in front of us. And, as I recall, I didn't have any particular fears or feelings at the second shot. By the third shot, I felt that it was a rifle. Almost sure it was. And, as I said, the shots or the noises were fairly close together they were fairly even in sound—and—uh, by then, one could recognize, or if he had heard a high-powered rifle, he would feel that it was a high-powered rifle. You would get that impression.

Mr. BELIN. Do you remember where your vehicle was by the time you heard the third shot?

Mr. COUCH. I'd say we were about 50 feet from making—or maybe 60 feet—from making the left-hand turn onto Elm.

Mr. BELIN. Did you hear more than three shots?

Mr. COUCH. No.

Mr. BELIN. Had you heard any noises, what you'd describe like a motorcycle backfiring or firecrackers, prior to the time that you made your turn north onto Houston?

Mr. COUCH. Well, way uptown on Main Street, a motorcycle did backfire right beside us—and we all jumped and had a good laugh over it. And the three shots sounded, at first—the first impression was that this was another motorcycle backfiring.

Mr. BELIN. Now, between the first and the second shots, is there anything else you remember doing or you remember hearing or seeing that you haven't related here at this time?

Mr. COUCH. Nothing unusual between the shots. Uh—as I say, the first shot, I had no particular impression; but the second shot, I remember turning—several of us turning—and looking ahead of us. It was unusual for a motorcycle to backfire that close together, it seemed like. And after the third shot, Bob ▮ Jackson, who was, as I recall, on my right, yelled something like, "Look up in the window! There's the rifle!"

And I remember glancing up to a window on the far right, which at the time impressed me as the sixth or seventh floor, and seeing about a foot of a rifle being—the barrel brought into the window.

I saw no one in that window—just a quick 1-second glance at the barrel.

Mr. BELIN. In what building was that?

Mr. COUCH. This was the Texas Book Depository Building.

Mr. BELIN. At the corner of Houston and Elm in Dallas?

Mr. COUCH. That's right.

Mr. BELIN. You said it was the sixth or the seventh floor. Do you know how many floors there are in that building—or did you know at that time?

Mr. COUCH. No; I didn't know at that time.

Mr. BELIN. Did it look like to you he was on the top floor or next to the top floor or the second to the top floor—or——

Mr. COUCH. It looked like it was the top. And when you first glance at the building, you're thrown off a little as to the floors because there's a ridge—uh, it almost looks like a structure added onto the top of the building, about one story above. So, you have to recount.

Of course, at the time, I wasn't counting, but——

Mr. BELIN. You just remember, to the best of your recollection, that it was either the sixth or seventh floor?

Mr. COUCH. That's right.

Mr. BELIN. And when you say, "the far right"——

Mr. COUCH. That would be the far east.

Mr. BELIN. The far east of what side of the building?

Mr. COUCH. The south side of the building.

Mr. BELIN. Do you remember whether or not that window at which you saw the rifle, you say, being withdrawn—first of all, could you tell it was a rifle?

Mr. COUCH. Yes, I'd say you could. Uh—if a person was just standing on the—as much as I saw, if the factors that did happen, did not happen, you might not say that it was a rifle. In other words, if you just saw an object being pulled back into a window, you wouldn't think anything of it. But with the excitement intense right after that third shot and what Bob yelled, my impression was that it was a rifle.

144

Mr. BELIN. Did you see anything more than a steel barrel of a rifle?

Mr. COUCH. No.

Mr. BELIN. Could you tell whether or not the rifle had any telescopic sight on it?

Mr. COUCH. No.

Mr. BELIN. Did you see any of the stock of the rifle?

Mr. COUCH. No.

Mr. BELIN. Did you see any person pulling the rifle?

Mr. COUCH. No.

Mr. BELIN. Do you remember whether or not, if you can remember, the window was open or halfway open or what?

Mr. COUCH. It was open. To say that it was half or three-quarters open, I wouldn't say. My impression was that it was all the way open—but that was an impression.

Mr. BELIN. Did you see anything else in the window that you remember—any boxes or anything like that?

Mr. COUCH. No; I didn't.

Mr. BELIN. You didn't notice whether there was or was not—or do you definitely remember that you did not notice any?

Mr. COUCH. No; I didn't notice anything.

Mr. BELIN. Did you see any other people in any other windows in the building?

Mr. COUCH. Yes; I recall seeing—uh—some people standing in some of the other windows—about, roughly, third or fourth floor in the middle of the south side. I recall one—it looked like a Negro boy with a white T-shirt leaning out one of those windows looking up—up to the windows up above him.

Mr. BELIN. Uh-huh. Is there anything else you can remember about the building?

Mr. COUCH. No; that's just about the only impression I had at the moment.

Mr. BELIN. Now, you related what you heard Bob Jackson say. Did anyone else say anything in the car?

Mr. COUCH. No one else said anything, that I recall, about a rifle, or anything.

Mr. BELIN. Where was the car when you saw this rifle being withdrawn?

Mr. COUCH. I'd say about 25 feet before we made the turn onto Elm. Our car was facing the south side of the building.

Mr. BELIN. All right. Then what happened after Bob Jackson made his exclamation and you saw what you just related?

Mr. COUCH. Well, I picked up my camera. As I recall, I had it in my hand, but it was down leaning against my legs. And I picked it up and made a quick glance at a setting and raised it to my eye. And—uh—you can see from my film that we're just turning the corner. We start the turn and we turn the corner, and you can see people running. As I recall, there's a quick glance at the front entrance of the Texas Depository Book Building. You can see people running and you can see about the first three cars, maybe four, in front of me as we complete the turn.

And then I took pictures of—uh—a few people on my left and a group, or a sweeping, of the crowd on my right standing on the corner.

Mr. BELIN. Did you take any pictures of the School Book Depository Building itself?

Mr. COUCH. Not of the south side at that moment.

After we went, say, 50 to 75 feet on down Elm, uh—we began to hang on because the driver picked up speed. We got down under the—I think there's three trestles there, three crossings underneath the—uh—at the very bottom of Elm Street——

Mr. BELIN. Is that what they call the triple-underpass?

Mr. COUCH. Right.

And—uh—I think, as I recall, right after we'd made the turn on Elm, one or two of the fellows jumped out. But after we got all the way down underneath the three trestles we finally persuaded the driver—who wasn't too anxious to stop—to stop and—uh—we all jumped out.

And I ran, I guess it was about 75 yards or a little more back up to the School Depository Building and took some sweeping pictures of the crowd standing around. I didn't stay there long.

Mr. BELIN. Did you take any pictures of the Depository Building entrance?

Mr. COUCH. No—uh——

Mr. BELIN. When you came back up there?

Mr. COUCH. Not with determination. I cannot recall at this moment whether some of my pictures I took when I ran back might have a sweeping shot of the entrance through a wide angle lens. But not with determination. I didn't plan to take pictures of it.

Mr. BELIN. Would these shots—these wide angle lens shots, if anyone were standing in front of the building or leaving the building at that time, would you be able to identify them, or would they be too far away?

145

Mr. COUCH. They would be too far away. Possibly if the frames were blown up, one might determine if someone was standing there—identify someone.

Mr. BELIN. About how many minutes after the last shot would you say you came back to take these pictures?

Mr. COUCH. Well, I'd say it took me—uh—maybe a minute and a half to get back to there after this third shot—because we weren't but seconds getting down underneath that underpass after we made the turn.

Mr. BELIN. Uh-huh.

Mr. COUCH. And—uh—I jumped out and ran back. So, I'd say not over a minute and a half.

Mr. BELIN. And then you started taking general sweeping shots of the area?

Mr. COUCH. Right.

Mr. BELIN. Were most of the shots directed at people along the side there as to what their reactions were, or were most of the shots directed at the School Book Depository Building?

Mr. COUCH. Mostly of the people standing around, the policemen and shots such as this.

Mr. BELIN. In what direction, generally, would the camera have been pointed, and where would you have been standing when you took these pictures?

Mr. COUCH. Some of the pictures, I remember, the camera was pointing south—because I was standing on the little knoll which is just at the foot and west of the Depository Building, where the little park area begins. There's a sidewalk that runs between the Book Depository property, I would assume and the park. And I was standing on that little sidewalk.

Mr. BELIN. And your camera was pointing south?

Mr. COUCH. Pointing south. That's right. Now, after I had taken I don't know how many feet of film of people standing around, I—uh—we—I think there was one or two other fellows with me and who they were, now, I can't remember; they were photographers—we stopped a car that was going by with a boy in it—a young boy of about high school age—and asked him to take us out to Parkland. And as the car started off, I started my camera and I have a sweeping shot moving west from about—uh—maybe the middle of the Book Depository Building from ground level on past the park area—a sweeping shot with the car moving.

Mr. BELIN. And that's about it insofar as the School Book Depository Building is concerned?

Mr. COUCH. Well, no. After we got out to Stemmons—they'd set up a roadblock just as you entered Stemmons Expressway.

Mr. BELIN. Uh-huh.

Mr. COUCH. We jumped out of the car and I took, I believe it was, a 2-inch lens shot of the Book Depository Building of the west wall.

Mr. BELIN. Of the west wall?

Mr. COUCH. Yes.

Mr. BELIN. Not of the front entrance?

Mr. COUCH. No.

Mr. BELIN. Is there any particular reason, Mr. Couch, why you didn't take your first pictures of the School Book Depository Building itself when you say you saw a rifle being withdrawn?

Mr. COUCH. Well, uh—as best I can recall, the excitement on the ground of people running and policemen "revving" up their motorcycles—and I have a real nice shot of a policeman running toward me with his pistol drawn—the activity on the ground kept my attention. The reason I did not stay and take pictures of the Depository Building—which I had originally intended to do when I got out of the motorcade—was that—uh—another cameraman from our station, A. J. L'Hoste—[spelling] L-'-H-o-s-t-e—he came running up and—uh—when he ran up, why I said, "You stay here and get shots of the building and go inside—and I'm going to go back—I'm going to follow the President."

Mr. BELIN. All right. Was he also a moving picture cameraman?

Mr. COUCH. Yes; right.

Mr. BELIN. Where was he at the time you made this statement?

Mr. COUCH. Uh—he was standing on that little sidewalk that runs between the—I met him on the little sidewalk between the Book Depository property and the beginning of the parkway.

Mr. BELIN. That would be the west side of the Depository Building?

Mr. COUCH. That's right; that's right. It's there that I saw the blood on the sidewalk.

Mr. BELIN. All right. Now, you say you saw blood on the sidewalk, Mr. Couch?

Mr. COUCH. That's right.

Mr. BELIN. Where was that?

Mr. COUCH. This was the little walkway—steps and walkway that leads up to the corner, the west corner, the southwest corner of the Book Depository Building. Another little sidewalk, as I recall, turns west and forms that little parkway and archway right next to the Book Depository Building.

Mr. BELIN. Did this appear to be freshly created blood?

Mr. COUCH. Yes; right.

Mr. BELIN. About how large was this spot of blood that you saw?

Mr. COUCH. Uh—from 8 to 10 inches in diameter.

Mr. BELIN. Did people around there say how it happened to get there, or not?

Mr. COUCH. No; no one knew. People were watching it—that is, watching it carefully and walking around it and pointing to it.

Uh—just as I ran up, policemen ran around the west corner and ran—uh—northward on the side of the building. And my first impression was that—uh—that they had chased someone out of the building around that corner, or possibly they had wounded someone. All the policemen had their pistols pulled. And people were pointing back around those shrubs around that west corner and—uh—you would think that there was a chase going on in that direction.

Again, the reason that I didn't follow was because A. J. had come up, and my first concern was to get back with the President.

Mr. BELIN. This pool of blood—about how far would it have been north of the curbline of Elm Street as Elm Street goes to the expressway?

Mr. COUCH. I'd say—uh—well, from Elm Street, you mean, itself?

Mr. BELIN. Yes. This is from that part of Elm Street that goes into the expressway?

Mr. COUCH. I'd say—uh—50 to 60 feet, and about 15 feet or 10 to 15 feet from the corner of the Texas Depository Building.

Mr. BELIN. It would have been somewhere along that park area there?

Mr. COUCH. Right.

Mr. BELIN. Was there anything else you noticed by this pool of blood?

Mr. COUCH. No. There were no objects on the ground. We looked for something. We thought there would be something else, but——

Mr. BELIN. There was nothing?

Mr. COUCH. Huh-uh.

Mr. BELIN. Now, this A. J.——?

Mr. COUCH. L'Hoste. That's "L" apostrophe.

Mr. BELIN. Yes; I have that. I have made a note of the spelling, along with the phonetic sound.

Do you know if he got any pictures of the south side of the School Book Depository?

Mr. COUCH. No; I don't recall what he got—as I recall—now, I may be wrong, this is a guess—that he did not take any pictures.

Mr. BELIN. He did not take any?

Mr. COUCH. No.

Mr. BELIN. Do you know of anyone that took any pictures of the south side of the School Book Depository Building, particularly the front entrance of the building, shortly after the assassination?

Dr. COUCH. No; only what I have seen in Time magazine.

Mr. BELIN. Only what you've seen in Time magazine?

Mr. COUCH. Right.

Mr. BELIN. Now, did you ever know or hear of Lee Harvey Oswald before any of this?

Mr. COUCH. No.

Mr. BELIN. Have you ever met Jack Ruby?

Mr. COUCH. No.

Mr. BELIN. There is an FBI report that states that you had heard hearsay statements that someone had seen Jack Ruby emerge from the rear of the Texas School Book Depository Building around that time. Did anyone ever tell you that?

Mr. COUCH. Yes. Uh—where I first heard it, I could not now recall; but—uh—the story went that—uh—Wes Wise, who works for KRLD——

Mr. BELIN. TV?

Mr. COUCH. Yes—saw him moments after the shooting—how many moments, I don't know—5 minutes, 10 minutes—coming around the side of the building, coming around the east side going south, I presume.

Mr. BELIN. Did you ever talk to Wes Wise as to whether or not he actually saw this, or is this just hearsay?

Mr. COUCH. No; I didn't. This is just hearsay.

Mr. BELIN. Let me ask you this: Is there any observation, other than hearsay, that you have about this entire sequence of events that you have not related here?

Mr. COUCH. No; I can't think of anything. No.

Mr. BELIN. In this same FBI report of an interview with you, it states that—and by the way, I did not show this to you when you first chatted about this—is that correct?

Mr. COUCH. Uh-huh; that's right.

Mr. BELIN. There is a statement as to the time sequence—that you heard, first, two loud noises about 10 seconds apart. And you related here that it would have been 5 seconds apart or less. Do you remember whether or not at the time you gave your first statement to the FBI you said 10 seconds or would you have said about 10 seconds or would you have said less than 10 seconds—or could this be inaccurate, as sometimes happens?

Mr. COUCH. I don't recall now. Ten seconds is not a reasonable time; even if I said "about 10 seconds." I know a little bit more about timing than that. We have to time our stories pretty close—and that's a long time.

Mr. BELIN. And what's your best recollection now as to the amount of time between shots?

Mr. COUCH. Well, I would say the longest time would be 5 seconds, but it could be from 3 to 5.

Mr. BELIN. And would this be true between the first and the second shots as well as between the second and third—or would there have been a difference?

Mr. COUCH. As I recall, the time sequence between the three were relatively the same.

Mr. BELIN. Now, Mr. Couch, shortly before we commenced taking this deposition, you and I met for the first time. Is that correct?

Mr. COUCH. That's correct.

Mr. BELIN. And then we came to this room and we chatted for a few minutes before we started taking a formal deposition. Is that correct?

Mr. COUCH. That's correct.

Mr. BELIN. Now, is there anything that we talked about pertaining to the assassination that in any way differs or conflicts with the testimony that you have just given?

Mr. COUCH. No; no.

Mr. BELIN. What is the fact as to whether or not I questioned you in great detail about each question or whether or not I just asked you to relate the story to me?

Mr. COUCH. You asked me to give general highlight impressions before we began.

Mr. BELIN. And then, after you gave those to me, we started taking the deposition—is that correct?

Mr. COUCH. That's correct.

Mr. BELIN. And then you repeated on the deposition what we had talked about—is that right?

Mr. COUCH. That's right—in more detail.

Mr. BELIN. Is there anything else that you can think of at this time which, in any way, would affect the investigation of the assassination of President Kennedy?

Mr. COUCH. No; I cannot think of anything.

Mr. BELIN. Well, we want to thank you very much for taking your time to come down here. We know that you're a busy man. We also would like you to convey our thanks to station WFAA-TV for allowing you to come down here. We appreciate it very much.

Mr. COUCH. Thank you, sir.

Mr. BELIN. Mr. Couch, we're going back on the record again. You're still under oath—and I'm not quite sure whether I asked this question, but I had better ask it again.

When you saw this rifle being withdrawn. About how much of it could you see at first?

Mr. COUCH. I'd say just about a foot of it.

Mr. BELIN. And in what direction was the barrel pointing at the time you saw it being withdrawn?

Mr. COUCH. Approximately a 45° angle westward—which would be pointing down Elm Street.

Mr. BELIN. Down Elm Street as it goes into the expressway there?

Mr. COUCH. That's right.

Mr. BELIN. And when you say "45° angle" would that be up or down, or are you referring to the angle of incline, or the angle of west and south?

Mr. COUCH. The angle of incline—from a horizontal position.

Mr. BELIN. All right. So, you would estimate about a 45° angle downward pointing in what would be a southwesterly direction?

Mr. COUCH. Uh—westerly direction. From looking straight on at the building, one could not tell the—uh—angle, whether it was more southward or not. In other words, something sticking out the building, I couldn't tell. It was not—it did not appear to me that it was sticking straight out the window, so to speak.

Mr. BELIN. Yes. Is there anything else that you noticed about the gun?

Mr. COUCH. No.

Mr. BELIN. All right. Thank you. I just wanted to make sure I got that on the record.

TESTIMONY OF TOM C. DILLARD

The testimony of Tom C. Dillard was taken at 9:15 a.m., on April 1, 1964, in the office of the U.S. attorney, 301 Post Office Building, Bryan and Ervay Streets, Dallas, Tex., by Mr. Joseph A. Ball, assistant counsel of the President's Commission.

Mr. BALL. State your name.

Mr. DILLARD. Tom C. Dillard.

Mr. BALL. Will you stand and raise your right hand, please?

Mr. DILLARD (Complying).

Mr. BALL. Do you solemnly swear the testimony given before this Commission will be the truth, the whole truth, and nothing but the truth, so help you God?

Mr. DILLARD. I do.

Mr. BALL. My name is Joseph A. Ball. I am staff counsel for the President's Commission on the Assassination of President Kennedy. You have already been requested to be present have you not——

Mr. DILLARD. By letter; yes.

Mr. BALL. By letter which you received last week?

Mr. DILLARD. Yes, sir.

Mr. BALL. What is your occupation?

Mr. DILLARD. I am a photographer.

Mr. BALL. I might state the purpose of questioning you is to ask you questions as to any knowledge you might have as to the facts concerning the assassination of President Kennedy on November 22, 1963, at Dallas, Tex.

Mr. DILLARD. I understand. My occupation is journalist; I am chief photographer of the Dallas Morning News, do some aviation writing but my primary job is head of the photographic department and, of course, I do outside work for the paper on photographic work.

Mr. BALL. How old are you?

Mr. DILLARD. I'm 49.

Mr. BALL. What has been your general education?

Mr. DILLARD. High school, very few college courses.

Mr. BALL. What?

Mr. DILLARD. High school and very few college courses.

Mr. BALL. Where did you go to school?

Mr. DILLARD. I didn't go to school. I graduated Fort Worth, from the old Central High School, went to the Officer Candidate School in the Military and Air University.

Mr. BALL. How long have you been with the paper?

Mr. DILLARD. The Dallas News since 1947 and I was with the Star Telegram, went to work in 1929.

Mr. BALL. Have you been a photographer for the papers all these years?

Mr. DILLARD. Well, yes; of course, the first years, when I was started at the age of 15, I was a copy boy and did various reporting and whatever we could do on the paper. I was 15 when I started.

Mr. BALL. On November 22, you were in the motorcade who followed President Kennedy, weren't you?

Mr. DILLARD. That is correct. I understand our car was about number six in the line.

Mr. BALL. Did you meet the President at Love Field?

Mr. DILLARD. That's right.

Mr. BALL. And then you rode in the motorcade from Love Field into Dallas?

Mr. DILLARD. Right.

Mr. BALL. Who was in your car?

Mr. DILLARD. I remember Jim Underwood, he's an announcer for KRLD-TV and cameraman, acting as a cameraman that day; and Bob Jackson of the Times-Herald, cameraman; and Couch with our TV station, Channel 8, and did you have information his name is Couch?

Mr. BALL. That's right; and the man that drove——

149

Mr. DILLARD. Channel 5—Darnell, I think his name is, and the driver of the car which I don't believe I remember his name. It was a Chevrolet convertible.

Mr. BALL. Your car was about sixth, was it?

Mr. DILLARD. I believe.

Mr. BALL. From the President's car?

Mr. DILLARD. From the President's car. We lost our position out at the airport. I understood we were supposed to have been quite a bit closer. We were assigned as the prime photographic car which, as you probably know, normally a truck precedes the President on these things and certain representatives of the photographic press ride with the truck. In this case, as you know, we didn't have any and this car that I was in was to take any photographs which was of spot-news nature.

Mr. BALL. As you turned from Main Street onto Houston, was the President's car in sight at that time?

Mr. DILLARD. No; and the whole parade, the whole trip to town, I could only distinguish the President's car on very few occasions in high rises in the ground, when we got on hills. It was difficult because the people in the cars ahead of me were sitting on the backs of cars which pretty well covered the President's car for me. We had a very, very poor view of the President's car at any time from the time the parade started.

Mr. BALL. Can you tell me whether or not the President's car had made the turn off Houston Street when your car turned north on Houston?

Mr. DILLARD. It had.

Mr. BALL. It had?

Mr. DILLARD. No; I won't say it had. I think it had because, like I say, I could never see the car very well. I believe it had.

Mr. BALL. Where were you sitting in the car?

Mr. DILLARD. I was sitting in the right front.

Mr. BALL. Who was in the front seat with you?

Mr. DILLARD. Oh, I don't remember; I think Jackson was sitting beside me—no; I believe Jackson was sitting in the back. I don't remember what our locations were.

Mr. BALL. But you know you were in the right front?

Mr. DILLARD. Yeah.

Mr. BALL. Did you hear something unusual as you were driving north on Houston?

Mr. DILLARD. Yes; I heard an explosion which I made the comment that I believe, in my memory, I believe I said, "My God, they've thrown a torpedo" and why I said "torpedo", I don't know. If you wish, I'll goahead——

Mr. BALL. Go ahead with your story.

Mr. DILLARD. Well, then I later estimated, immediately later, estimated, oh, 4, about 3 or 4 seconds, another explosion and my comment was, "No, It's heavy rifle fire," and I remember very distinctly I said, "It's very heavy rifle fire."

Mr. BALL. How many explosions did you hear?

Mr. DILLARD. I heard three—the three approximately equally spaced.

Mr. BALL. What is the best estimate of the position of your car with reference to the turn at Main and Houston when you heard the first explosion?

Mr. DILLARD. Perhaps, oh, just a few feet around the corner and it seems we had slowed a great deal. It seems that our car had slowed down so that we were moving rather slowly and perhaps just passed the turn when I heard the first explosion.

Mr. BALL. Did you hear anyone in your car say anything?

Mr. DILLARD. Well, after the third shot I know my comment was, "They killed him." I don't know why I said that but Jackson—there was some running comment about what can we do or where is it coming from and we were all looking. We had an absolutely perfect view of the School Depository from our position in the open car, and Bob Jackson said, "There's a rifle barrel up there." I said, "Where?" I had my camera ready. He said, "It's in that open window." Of course, there were several open windows and I scanned the building.

Mr. BALL. Which building?

Mr. DILLARD. The School Depository. And at the same time I brought my camera up and I was looking for the window. Now, this was after the third shot and Jackson said, "There's the rifle barrel up there," and then he said it was the second from the top in the right-hand side, and I swung to it and there was two figures below, and I just shot with one camera, 100-mm. lens on a 35-mm. camera which is approximately a two times daily photo twice normal lens and a wide angle on a 35-mm. which took in a considerable portion of the building and I shot those pictures in rapid sequence with the two cameras.

Mr. BALL. You shot how many pictures?

150

Mr. DILLARD. Two pictures.

Mr. BALL. With one camera or two different cameras?

Mr. DILLARD. Two different cameras—one daily photo, not extreme daily photo, but twice the normal lens.

Mr. BALL. You say your cameras were ready? How were they ready?

Mr. DILLARD. Hung around my neck and held in my hand.

Mr. BALL. You brought them up and focused and shot?

Mr. DILLARD. Well, on the whole ride, I had been watching the tops of buildings and watching for any signs or anything unusual which, of course, is a newsman's chore on a parade like that. We were badly—in a very bad position from our viewpoint to cover anything on the parade, so we were all, as any news photographer is, rather tense when he is covering a Presidential or an affair of that sort and he is trying to get whatever pictures possible and watching for every possibility, and so we all tried for a number of things. Incidentally, the only unusual thing in the parade that I noticed was the President—I understand the President stopped his car at Lemmon and Loma Alta, which is out in the near suburbs of Dallas, as I understand, at the request of a sign that said, "Mr. President, stop and shake hands with us." I jumped out of the car—it was a convertible with the top down—and tried to run to get pictures of it but by that time the parade started and I was unable to get up that far.

Mr. BALL. When you shot these two pictures of the Texas School Book Depository Building, how far were you from the building, would you say?

Mr. DILLARD. From the window or from the——

Mr. BALL. From the building. That would be, I suppose, a measurement along the street.

Mr. DILLARD. I would say it was just before we reached the corner of Elm and Houston Streets.

Mr. BALL. You were south of Elm and Houston, were you?

Mr. DILLARD. Yes.

Mr. BALL. About how far? Well, perhaps as a photographer, you can give me a more accurate estimate this way; tell me how far you think your camera was from the upper windows when you shot that picture?

Mr. DILLARD. Oh, it wasn't over 50, 60 yards.

Mr. BALL. Did you see anything in the windows?

Mr. DILLARD. No.

Mr. BALL. You didn't see a rifle barrel?

Mr. DILLARD. No.

Mr. BALL. But you did see some figures or forms in the window?

Mr. DILLARD. Only in the windows which was the windows below.

Mr. BALL. How many forms did you see in the windows below?

Mr. DILLARD. I saw two men in the windows, at least the arched windows. I saw them in my picture. I was making the picture my eyes were covering.

Mr. BALL. You saw them as you were taking the picture?

Mr. DILLARD. I may have; I don't know.

Mr. BALL. Do you remember if you saw two or three figures?

Mr. DILLARD. I don't remember.

Mr. BALL. But you did see some figures and you cannot be accurate?

Mr. DILLARD. Right.

Mr. BALL. Your car stopped where?

Mr. DILLARD. I remember, we were stopping and starting down Houston Street or moving very slowly while this shooting was going on, and I know we came around the corner of Houston and Elm and saw people lying on the ground down the hill on the sides of the lawns there in the plaza, and I jumped out of my car. The car stopped then and I got out and I don't know what happened.

Mr. BALL. What did you do after you go out?

Mr. DILLARD. Well, I made a picture of cars moving into the sun under the underpass, somebody chasing the car and I looked at the situation in that area and saw absolutely nothing of the Presidential car or anything that appeared worth photographing to me at the time.

Mr. BALL. How long did you stay around there?

Mr. DILLARD. Perhaps 2 minutes.

Mr. BALL. Then where did you go?

Mr. DILLARD. Another car, Chevrolet convertible, of the party came by with, I assume, dignitaries in it and I jumped on the back of it and we started—I told them, of course, who I was and we started out Stemmons Expressway toward the Trade Mart and I explained to them what I

151

knew and tried to hold onto the back of that car at rather high speed. I never saw the Presidential car.

Mr. BALL. Do you have any idea or any impression as to the source of the explosions—what direction it was coming from?

Mr. DILLARD. Yes, I felt that, at the time, I felt like it was coming from a north area and quite close, and I might qualify I have had a great deal of experience. I am a gun nut and have a great number of high-powered rifles at home, so I know a little bit about guns.

Mr. BALL. You have had experience with rifles?

Mr. DILLARD. Yes, I have shot a great deal, so I am familiar with the noise that they made in that area. We were getting a sort of reverberation which made it difficult to pinpoint the actual direction but my feeling was that it was coming into my face and, in that I was facing north toward the School Depository—I might add that I very definitely smelled gun powder when the car moved up at the corner.

Mr. BALL. You did?

Mr. DILLARD. I very definitely smelled it.

Mr. BALL. By that you mean when you moved up to the corner of Elm and Houston?

Mr. DILLARD. Yes; now, there developed a very brisk north wind.

Mr. BALL. That was in front of the Texas School Book Depository?

Mr. DILLARD. Yes, it's rather close—the corner is rather close. I mentioned it, I believe, that it was rather surprising to me.

Mr. BALL. Who did you mention it to?

Mr. DILLARD. Bob, I'm sure.

Mr. BALL. Bob Jackson?

Mr. DILLARD. Yeah, Bob and I were talking about it.

Mr. BALL. You developed your pictures, didn't you?

Mr. DILLARD. I don't remember.

Mr. BALL. Or did you turn them over?

Mr. DILLARD. I printed them.

Mr. BALL. You printed them?

Mr. DILLARD. Yes, I don't remember whether I developed that roll or not. I may have.

Mr. BALL. Did you do that the same day?

Mr. DILLARD. Yes, immediately thereafter, shortly after I came back from the hospital.

Mr. BALL. Then you examined the pictures that you had taken—those two pictures you had taken?

Mr. DILLARD. Yes.

Mr. BALL. I have——

Mr. DILLARD. There was never any question in my mind that there was more than or less than three explosions which were all heavy rifle fire, in my opinion, of the same rifle. The same rifle fired three shots.

Mr. BALL. Do you still have the two negatives?

Mr. DILLARD. Yes; of these [indicating]?

Mr. BALL. Yes.

Mr. DILLARD. Yes.

Mr. BALL. You have them in your possession?

Mr. DILLARD. At the Dallas News; they're in a box kept locked in the managing editor's office.

Mr. BALL. Suppose we could do this. I have pictures here which you can identify but perhaps it might be a little closer to the source if we do this. Could you make me up two prints for your deposition from those negatives?

Mr. DILLARD. Well, I guess so.

Mr. BALL. Off the record.

(Off-record discussion.)

Mr. BALL. You will endorse your signature on each copy as being a print made from your negatives, is that satisfactory?

Mr. DILLARD. Suits me; I could get it notarized.

Mr. BALL. You don't need to do that because we can attach it as a copy to this deposition.

Mr. DILLARD. I could sign these; of course, you want that other.

Mr. BALL. We have two here. First of all, you made one picture with a wide lens?

Mr. DILLARD. Yes.

Mr. BALL. And you made a picture with a short lens?

Mr. DILLARD. Long lens—short and wide are the same.

Mr. BALL. A short, wide lens and one long lens. Now, I show you two pictures and I mark one "A" and mark one "B." Look them over and tell me whether or not those are prints from the picture that you made that day.

Mr. DILLARD. These are prints from one of the negatives I made on November 22.

Mr. BALL. And then you will furnish us two prints, one from each negative which we will mark as "C" and "D" and you will initial them, is that correct?

Mr. DILLARD. That is correct.

Mr. BALL. Do you mind initialing the "A" and "B" and we will make it part of this deposition—just on the back?

Mr. DILLARD. One of them will be the same picture as these two. These two are prints from one of my negatives.

Mr. BALL. That will be all right.

Mr. DILLARD. I have another negative.

Mr. BALL. Which you will make a print of?

Mr. DILLARD. If you wish.

Mr. BALL. Make up a print from each negative. Now, you made a statement to Agent Keutzer of the Federal Bureau of Investigation on the 25th of November 1963, didn't you, or thereabouts?

Mr. DILLARD. Yes.

Mr. BALL. And at that time, you told him that you first heard a noise which sounded like a torpedo, didn't you?

Mr. DILLARD. Yes, I said——

Mr. BALL. Off the record.

(Off-record discussion.)

Mr. BALL. Did you tell him that hearing another sound similar to that, you realized it was gunfire?

Mr. DILLARD. Yes.

Mr. BALL. And you heard the third shot. Now, the statement says that upon hearing the third shot, the car in which he was riding was stopped almost in front of the Texas School Book Depository Building.

Mr. DILLARD. My car?

Mr. BALL. Yes.

Mr. DILLARD. Yes.

Mr. BALL. Did you hear Bob Jackson of the Dallas Times-Herald exclaim "I see a rifle; it's up in the open window".

Mr. DILLARD. Yes.

Mr. BALL. And Jackson pointed to the Texas School Book Depository located at Elm and Houston Streets?

Mr. DILLARD. That's right.

Mr. BALL. And you looked up at the building and you did not see a rifle protruding from any window?

Mr. DILLARD. I did not see a rifle.

Mr. BALL. But you did take two photographs?

Mr. DILLARD. Correct.

Mr. BALL. And you still have those negatives?

Mr. DILLARD. That's true.

Mr. BALL. Were you ever in a position where you could see anyone leave the Texas School Book Depository Building?

Mr. DILLARD. Briefly, only in the very short time, perhaps a period of 3 or 4 minutes, that I was in the general area. After the third shot, I was probably not there over 3 or 4 minutes.

Mr. BALL. Did you see anybody leave the building?

Mr. DILLARD. To my knowledge; no.

Mr. BALL. I think that's everything. Will you waive signature on this?

Mr. DILLARD. Sure.

Mr. BALL. Thank you, sir.

Mr. DILLARD. That's all right, glad to help.

TESTIMONY OF JAMES ROBERT UNDERWOOD

The testimony of James Robert Underwood was taken at 11:25 a.m., on April 1, 1964, in the office of the U.S. attorney, 301 Post Office Building, Bryan and Ervay Streets, Dallas, Tex., by Mr. Joseph A. Ball, assistant counsel of the President's Commission.

Mr. BALL. Mr. Underwood, will you stand up and be sworn?

153

(Complying.)

Mr. BALL. Do you solemnly swear the testimony you are about to give before this Commission shall be the truth, the whole truth, and nothing but the truth, so help you God?

Mr. UNDERWOOD. I do.

Mr. BALL. Will you state your name, please?

Mr. UNDERWOOD. My name is James Robert Underwood.

Mr. BALL. Your occupation?

Mr. UNDERWOOD. I am the assistant news director of KRLD-TV and radio in Dallas.

Mr. BALL. On November 22, 1963, you were in the motorcade, the Presidential motorcade?

Mr. UNDERWOOD. Yes, sir; I was three cars behind the President.

Mr. BALL. Who was in the car with you?

Mr. UNDERWOOD. There was a photographer from channel 5, WBAP-TV, whose name is James Darnell, and a photographer from the Dallas Morning News—I know his name but I can't think of it right now——

Mr. BALL. Tom Dillard?

Mr. UNDERWOOD. Yes; Tom Dillard, and a photographer from the Dallas Times-Herald whose name is Bob Jackson, also a photographer from WFAA-TV and I do not know his name. I heard it but I don't remember it.

Mr. BALL. There was a driver, also?

Mr. UNDERWOOD. Yes; the driver I later found out was a member of the department of public safety.

Mr. BALL. You are a photographer, also?

Mr. UNDERWOOD. Yes, sir; I wear many hats in my business but one of which is news photographer.

Mr. BALL. Did you have your camera with you that day?

Mr. UNDERWOOD. Yes, sir; I did.

Mr. BALL. What is your experience; where were you born; where did you go to school; how did you get to get the experience that fit you for your present job? Just in your own words, tell me something about yourself.

Mr. UNDERWOOD. I was born in Oklahoma City, Okla., in 1922; I served in the Marine Corps from 1940 until 1943, almost 4 years, and after that I attended the University of Tulsa and after that I worked—I began working in radio as an announcer while I was going to college. When I got out of college, I went to Corpus Christi, Tex. That was about 1947 and I became program director and news director of a radio station in Corpus Christi and I stayed there until 1950 when I went to a station in Jacksonville, Fla., where I was also program director and news director, and in 1953, I came to Dallas, and I worked for a year and a half for WFAA-TV as an announcer, then I freelanced in television and radio from September of 1954 until November— and I have to count for a minute—6 years this November that would be until November 1958 when I went to work for KRLD-TV and Radio News and shortly thereafter I became assistant news director but I earned part of my living, I still freelance in television which is all freelance in television and I have a regular job which entails every type of reporting, including photography which I enjoy doing.

Mr. BALL. On the day of the assassination, you were in the motorcade with these men you mentioned and you think your car was third behind the Presidential car?

Mr. UNDERWOOD. Yes; and I thought it was six or seven. I shot sound on film of the President's arrival and Vice President's arrival at Dallas Love Field the morning he came in on the 22d and then I took off the rather cumbersome sound on film equipment and took my hand camera because I had an assigned place in the motorcade and I could not tell out there because of the many people I could not tell what position we were in. I could not see that far ahead to determine exactly where we were in the motorcade, although I knew we were in the front of it. The motorcade stopped once on the way downtown, this was briefly, and I jumped over this side—we were in a convertible—and ran toward the President's car and I was aware of the crowd and the motorcade immediately started and I ran back to the convertible, not wanting to be left, and looking afterward at the films that I took there, I could then count the cars there. I realized we were three behind him, according to my movies we took. When we turned onto Main Street downtown and headed west toward the scene of where the assassination took place, either the regulator or the mainspring in my camera broke and I was without a camera. I knew that we had two men, at least two men on the parade route who were on the street and would be filming the motorcade as we came by and I hoped to exchange my broken camera for one of theirs because I knew I could make more use of the one that would operate. The only problem was we went down Main Street so rapidly it would have been impossible to get anything from someone standing on the street and at Main and Record one of our men was stationed and I tried to holler at him my camera was broken and I wanted to switch and I started to and there was no point in it because we passed there that rapidly. I thought it was the fastest motorcade that passed through a crowd; this was really moving, as far as I was concerned. Then, we came to the scene where the shots were fired. Do you want me to go on?

Mr. BALL. From the time you turned, tell me what you observed after you made the turn at Main and Houston to drive north on Houston.

Mr. UNDERWOOD. After we turned onto Houston Street, the car I was in was about, as far as I can remember, about in the middle of the block or a little bit north of the center of the block, which is a short block, when I heard the first shot.

Mr. BALL. Between Main and Elm?

Mr. UNDERWOOD. Yes; between Main and Elm, closer to the Elm intersection, Elm and Houston intersection, when I heard the first shot fired. I thought it was an explosion. I have heard many rifles fired but it did not sound like a rifle to me. Evidently must have been a reverberation from the buildings or something. I believe I said to one of the other fellows it sounds like a giant firecracker and the car I was in was about in the intersection of Elm and Houston when I heard a second shot fired and moments later a third shot fired and I realized that they were by that time, the last two shots, I realized they were coming from overhead.

Mr. BALL. You realized they were coming from overhead and that would be from what source?

Mr. UNDERWOOD. That would be from the Texas School Book Depository Building.

Mr. BALL. It sounded like they were coming from that direction?

Mr. UNDERWOOD. Yes, sir; the last two. Now, the first was just a loud explosion but it sounded like a giant firecracker or something had gone off. By the time the third shot was fired, the car I was in stopped almost through the intersection in front of the Texas School Book Depository Building and I leaped out of the car before the car stopped. Bob Jackson from the Herald said he thought he saw a rifle in the window and I looked where he pointed and I saw nothing. Below the window he was pointing at, I saw two colored men leaning out there with their heads turned toward the top of the building, trying, I suppose, to determine where the shots were coming from.

Mr. BALL. What words did you hear Bob Jackson say?

Mr. UNDERWOOD. I don't know that I can remember exactly except I did hear him say words to the effect that "I saw a rifle" and I looked at that instant and I saw nothing myself. If he saw a rifle, I did not.

Mr. BALL. At that point when you looked, where was your car?

Mr. UNDERWOOD. Our car was in the intersection, in the intersection of Elm and Houston Street.

Mr. BALL. Had it made the turn yet?

Mr. UNDERWOOD. It had partially made the turn or had just begun to make the turn. Frankly, I was looking up and around and I saw at the same time people falling on the ground down the street toward the underpass and my first impression was some of these people falling to the ground had been shot.

Mr. BALL. Did your car stop?

Mr. UNDERWOOD. Our car stopped and the minute it stopped I leaped out of the car.

Mr. BALL. Where was your car when it stopped?

Mr. UNDERWOOD. Right in the intersection, perhaps just past the intersection, turned onto Elm.

Mr. BALL. Did you get out before the car parked along the curb?

Mr. UNDERWOOD. Yes, sir; the minute it stopped, I leaped over the side.

Mr. BALL. What did you do?

Mr. UNDERWOOD. I left my camera in the car, the camera that was broken, and ran as fast as I could back toward the man we had at Record and Main in order to get a camera. There I was without a camera; the only thought I had was to get a camera.

Mr. BALL. Did you get one?

Mr. UNDERWOOD. Yes; I ran the full block back to Main Street and our man there, name of Sanderson, was running down Main toward Houston. He was running to meet me, although he didn't know what was happening and that my camera was broke. Suddenly, motorcycles and sirens had been turned on police cars and were all headed toward Main. I met him just around the corner on Main past Houston and grabbed his camera and said, "Someone had been shooting at the President." I didn't know this but I assumed it happened. I   took his camera and got back to the scene. When I got back to the scene, most of the people in the area were running up the grassy slope toward the railway yards just behind the Texas School Book Depository Building. Actually, I assumed, which is the only thing I could do, I assumed perhaps who had fired the shots had run in that direction. I recognized at least a dozen deputy sheriffs running also in that area—it seems to me that many, and I ran up there and took some films and they were running through the railroad yard and they very quickly found nothing and I was having, frankly, a hard time breathing because I had done more running in those few minutes than I am used to doing. I gasped out to a couple people—I don't know who they are—that I thought the shots came from that building and one of the fellows in the car with me said they had seen a rifle barrel in the building.

Mr. BALL. This group of men were deputy sheriffs?

Mr. UNDERWOOD. For the most part, yes; I don't think I could recall—Lemmy Lewis I see in my mind, but I am not sure Lemmy was there. This was a kaleidoscope of things happening. In my business, you need to make a quick appraisal of what is happening if you are going to shoot pictures of it. I was confused and out of breath and unbelieving of what happened.

Mr. BALL. Where did you go from the grassy slopes?

Mr. UNDERWOOD. I went from the railroad yards—actually, I was back in the track area—I went immediately with these men at a run to the Texas School Depository.

Mr. BALL. Which entrance?

Mr. UNDERWOOD. The front entrance.

Mr. BALL. On Elm?

Mr. UNDERWOOD. Yes; and I ran down there and I think I took some pictures of some men—yes, I know I did, going in and out of the building. By that time there was one police officer there and he was a three-wheeled motorcycle officer and a little colored boy whose last name I remember as Eunice.

Mr. BALL. Euins?

Mr. UNDERWOOD. It may have been Euins. It was difficult to understand when he said his name. He was telling the motorcycle officer he had seen a colored man lean out of the window upstairs and he had a rifle. He was telling this to the officer and the officer took him over and put him in a squad car. By that time, motorcycle officers were arriving, homicide officers were arriving and I went over and asked this boy if he had seen someone with a rifle and he said "Yes, sir." I said, "Were they white or black?" He said, "It was a colored man." I said, "Are you sure it was a colored man?" He said, "Yes sir" and I asked him his name and the only thing I could understand was what I thought his name was Eunice.

Mr. BALL. Was he about 15?

Mr. UNDERWOOD. I couldn't tell his age; looked to me to be younger. I would have expected him to be about 10 or 11 years old.

Mr. BALL. Then what did you do?

Mr. UNDERWOOD. I stayed in front of the building; actually, I stayed in the intersection of Elm and Houston and took movies of police arriving and fire—and I think some fire equipment arrived on the scene, one firetruck or two firetrucks, I'm not sure, and I just shot some general film on the area. I have since searched that film to see if I could see any face in it that would have been important to this.

Mr. BALL. Leaving the building?

Mr. UNDERWOOD. Yes; but I haven't found any except that of officers arriving and just people generally in the area; none of it, though, that you could—I spent several days at this, I guess during January when things had calmed down. I was on the side street of the building, around the front of the building and in the intersection for the next 10 minutes, then I went across the street to the courthouse and phoned several news reports to C.B.S. in New York and described what was taking place in the building at that time. There were firemen with ladders in front of the building and officers running in and out and they cordoned off the building and kept the spectators out of the building, but there was quite a time lapse between the time the shots were fired and the time anyone checked the building. The main effort was to run to the railroad yards instead of the School Book Depository.

Mr. BALL. I think that's all. Mr. Underwood, this will be typed up and you can waive signature if you wish or you can sign it if you wish.

Mr. UNDERWOOD. I don't have to sign it. I will waive signature.

TESTIMONY OF JAMES N. CRAWFORD

The testimony of James N. Crawford was taken at 11:15 a.m., on April 1, 1964, in the office of the U.S. attorney, 301 Post Office Building, Bryan and Ervay Streets, Dallas, Tex., by Mr. Joseph A. Ball, assistant counsel of the President's Commission.

156

Mr. BALL. Mr. Crawford, I'm Joe Ball and this is Lillian Johnson.

Mr. CRAWFORD. Glad to know you. I know Lillian Johnson. How is Irving, by the way?

Mr. BALL. Will you stand up, please, and hold up your right hand?

Mr. CRAWFORD (complying).

Mr. BALL. Do you solemnly swear the testimony you will give before this Commission shall be the truth, the whole truth and nothing but the truth, so help you God?

Mr. CRAWFORD. I swear.

Mr. BALL. My name is Joe Ball. I'm staff counsel with the President's Commission on the Assassination of President Kennedy and I have been authorized to question you and ask you to give us such information as you have as to the facts of the assassination and those things that you observed on November 22, 1963. Will you state your name for the court reporter?

Mr. CRAWFORD. My name is James N. Crawford.

Mr. BALL. What is your occupation?

Mr. CRAWFORD. I am deputy district clerk.

Mr. BALL. You received a request from the Commission in writing, did you not, requesting you to give this testimony?

Mr. CRAWFORD. I did.

Mr. BALL. You received it some time last week?

Mr. CRAWFORD. Actually, it came to the office Saturday. I did not receive it until Monday.

Mr. BALL. That will be Monday, March 30?

Mr. CRAWFORD. Yes.

Mr. BALL. Where were you born?

Mr. CRAWFORD. I was born in Greenville, Texas.

Mr. BALL. What was your general education?

Mr. CRAWFORD. High school in Greenville, Texas, and college at Texas A. & M.

Mr. BALL. What did you do after that, just a general sketch of some of your occupations?

Mr. CRAWFORD. I worked for the Texas Company in New Orleans and have been in and out of the furniture business and in the oil business here in Dallas until I went with the county.

Mr. BALL. How long have you been with the county of Dallas?

Mr. CRAWFORD. About 10 years.

Mr. BALL. You are a deputy county clerk there?

Mr. CRAWFORD. District clerk.

Mr. BALL. On November 22, 1963, about around 12 o'clock or so, where were you?

Mr. CRAWFORD. I was in the office of the district clerk.

Mr. BALL. Did you later leave and go out into the street?

Mr. CRAWFORD. About 12:25, we left the office and went out to the corner of Houston and Elm.

Mr. BALL. You went with whom?

Mr. CRAWFORD. Mary Ann Mitchell.

Mr. BALL. She works in the office with you?

Mr. CRAWFORD. She is in the office with me.

Mr. BALL. What is her occupation in the office?

Mr. CRAWFORD. Assistant to the district clerk.

(At this point, Mr. James Underwood enters the hearing.)

Mr. BALL. Where is your office located in Dallas?

Mr. CRAWFORD. It's located on the ground floor of the Records Building.

Mr. BALL. What street?

Mr. CRAWFORD. That's Record and Elm—that's Commerce, isn't it, Jim?

Mr. UNDERWOOD. What's that?

Mr. CRAWFORD. What is the street just north of the courthouse—that's Elm.

Mr. UNDERWOOD. It's bordered by Elm, Main, Record, and Houston.

Mr. BALL. You are located on the corner of——

Mr. CRAWFORD. Elm.

Mr. BALL. Elm and——

Mr. CRAWFORD. And Record.

Mr. BALL. And Record, and then you walked which direction?

Mr. CRAWFORD. Well, actually, the courthouse is—I suppose our office would be considered on Elm and Houston.

Mr. BALL. When you left your office, you walked on what street?

Mr. CRAWFORD. Walked on Elm to Houston, rather than Record.

Mr. BALL. In other words, you walked west on Elm towards Houston?

Mr. CRAWFORD. Right.

Mr. BALL. To what corner of Elm and Houston?

Mr. CRAWFORD. That would be the corner of the courthouse. Do you want the direction of the intersection?

Mr. BALL. Yes, where was it? Southeast, northwest corner of Elm?

Mr. CRAWFORD. It's the northwest corner of the courthouse.

Mr. BALL. The northwest corner of the courthouse—it's the southeast corner of the intersection?

Mr. CRAWFORD. Southeast corner of the intersection.

Mr. BALL. Where were you when you watched the President pass?

Mr. CRAWFORD. I was at that location.

Mr. BALL. Which corner of the intersection?

Mr. CRAWFORD. The southeast corner of the intersection.

Mr. BALL. Where was the Texas School Book Depository Building from where you were standing?

Mr. CRAWFORD. It would be on the northwest corner of the intersection.

Mr. BALL. Directly across?

Mr. CRAWFORD. Yes; right.

Mr. BALL. Did you have a good view at that point of the south exposure of the Texas School Book Depository?

Mr. CRAWFORD. I had a very good angle.

Mr. BALL. Did you see the President's car pass?

Mr. CRAWFORD. I did.

Mr. BALL. And just tell me in your own words what you observed after that?

Mr. CRAWFORD. As I observed the parade, I believe there was a car leading the President's car, followed by the President's car and followed, I suppose, by the Vice President's car and, in turn, by the Secret Service in a yellow closed sedan. The doors of the sedan were open. It was after the Secret Service sedan had gone around the corner that I heard the first report and at that time I thought it was a backfire of a car but, in analyzing the situation, it could not have been a backfire of a car because it would have had to have been the President's car or some car in the cavalcade there. The second shot followed some seconds, a little time elapsed after the first one, and followed very quickly by the third one. I could not see the President's car——

Mr. BALL. At that time?

Mr. CRAWFORD. That's right; I couldn't even see the Secret Service car, at least I wasn't looking for it. As the report from the third shot sounded, I looked up. I had previously looked around to see if there was somebody shooting firecrackers   to see if I could see a puff of smoke, and after I decided it wasn't a backfire from an automobile and as the third report was sounded, I looked up and from the far east corner of the sixth floor I saw a movement in the only window that was open on that floor. It was an indistinct movement. It was just barely a glimpse.

Mr. BALL. Which window?

Mr. CRAWFORD. That would be the far east window——

Mr. BALL. On the——

Mr. CRAWFORD. On the sixth floor of the Texas School Book Depository. I turned to Miss Mitchell and made the statement that if those were shots they came from that window. That was based mainly on the fact of the quick movement observed in the window right at the conclusion of the report.

Mr. BALL. Could you give me any better description than just a movement? Could you use any other words to describe what you saw by way of color or size of what you saw moving?

Mr. CRAWFORD. If I were asked to describe it, I would say that it was a profile, somewhat from the waist up, but it was a very quick movement and rather indistinct and it was very light colored. It was either light colored or it was reflection from the sun. When the gun was found, or when a gun was found, I asked the question if it was white, simply because if it was a gun I saw, then it was either white or it was reflecting the sun so it would appear white or light colored.

Mr. BALL. Did you see any boxes in that window?

Mr. CRAWFORD. Yes, directly behind the window, oh possibly three feet or less, there were boxes stacked up behind the window and I believe it was the only place in the building that I observed where boxes were stacked just like that.

Mr. BALL. Did you see any boxes in the window?

Mr. CRAWFORD. No, I didn't see any. There wasn't any boxes in the window.

Mr. BALL. Did you stay there at that point very long, the southeast corner?

Mr. CRAWFORD. No; as I said. I couldn't observe the President's car and I had no actual knowledge that he had been shot, so realizing that we should get the information almost immediately from the radio which had been covering the motorcade—we had been listening to it prior to going on the street—I thought our best information would come from that, so we went, Miss Mitchell and I, went back into the office. I have no way of knowing the time. I would say it was a minute or—I would say a minute.

Mr. BALL. After you heard the shots, did you return to the office?

Mr. CRAWFORD. Yes.

Mr. BALL. The movement that you saw that you describe as something light and perhaps a profile from the waist up, you mean it looked like a profile of a person?

Mr. CRAWFORD. That was—I had a hard time describing that. When I saw it, I automatically in my mind came to the conclusion that it was a person having moved out of the window. Now, to say that it was a brown haired, light skinned individual, I could not do that.

Mr. BALL. Could you tell whether it was a man or woman?

Mr. CRAWFORD. I could not.

Mr. BALL. You made a report to the Federal Bureau of Investigation on the 10th of January?

Mr. CRAWFORD. Yes.

Mr. BALL. Before I ask you about your report, did you have any impression as to the source of the sound, from what direction the sound came, the sound of the explosions?

Mr. CRAWFORD. Yes; I do. As I mentioned before, the sound, I thought it was a backfire in the cavalcade from down the hill, down the hill toward the underpass.

Mr. BALL. You mean west on Elm?

Mr. CRAWFORD. Yes, and that was a little confusing and in analyzing it later, evidently the report that I heard, and probably a lot of other people, the   officers or the FBI, it evidently was a sound that was reflected by the underpass and therefore came back. It did not sound to me, ever, as I remember, the high-powered rifle sounding. It was not the sharp crack.

Mr. BALL. What caused you to look up at the Texas School Book Depository Building?

Mr. CRAWFORD. The sound had to be coming from somewhere; the noise was being made at some place, so I didn't see anyone shooting firecrackers or anything else and I thought "this idiot surely shouldn't do such a thing," but if they were, where were they, and if they were shots, where were they coming from, and that caused me to search the whole area on Houston Street and in front of the Texas Depository on Elm Street and then up and that's how I happened to be looking up at the time, rather than observing things in the street, probably.

Mr. BALL. Did you ever see any smoke?

Mr. CRAWFORD. No, sir; I did not.

Mr. BALL. In your remark to Mary Ann Mitchell, did you say "if those were shots, they came from that window"?

Mr. CRAWFORD. Yes.

Mr. BALL. That is what you reported to the FBI agent, also?

Mr. CRAWFORD. Yes, I suppose; at that time, I was still not absolutely sure that they were shots and that's why I said if they were shots. I was basing that, I am sure I was basing that mainly on the fact of this quick movement that I observed. In other words, if I were firing the shots, I would have jumped back immediately at the conclusion of them.

Mr. BALL. Later on, did you go back in the street and talk to someone?

Mr. CRAWFORD. Yes.

Mr. BALL. Did you talk to a deputy sheriff?

Mr. CRAWFORD. Allen Swett.

Mr. BALL. What did you tell him?

Mr. CRAWFORD. I told him to have the men search the boxes directly behind this window that was open on the sixth floor—the window in the far east corner.

Mr. BALL. Did you tell him anything of what you had seen?

Mr. CRAWFORD. I don't think so. I think I was so amazed that I could walk across the street and walk up to this building that was supposedly under surveillance and the man had not been—I say "the man"—there had not been anyone apprehended.

Mr. BALL. How long was it after you heard the shots that you walked up to Allen Swett and talked to him?

Mr. CRAWFORD. My guess is it could have been anywhere from 10–20 minutes. My guess would be around 15–20 minutes.

Mr. BALL. In the statement you made to the FBI agent, he reports you said you walked to the Texas School Book Depository where you contacted Deputy Sheriff Allen Swett and advised him of the movement you had seen in the sixth floor window?

Mr. CRAWFORD. I must have said something about the movement. I did tell him to search those windows, I think.

Mr. BALL. Could you in your own words give us your memory of what you told Allen Swett?

Mr. CRAWFORD. I would probably have said, as I remember it, that to have the men search—have someone search the boxes directly behind that window. I had seen some movement directly after the shots. That was, I think, all I said. I did not—there was no conversation and at the conclusion of my statement, he directed several men up there.

Mr. BALL. Did you ever go in the building yourself?

Mr. CRAWFORD. I did not and I still have not been in there.

Mr. BALL. I think that's all, Mr. Crawford. Thanks very much.

Mr. CRAWFORD. Thank you, Mr. Ball.

Mr. BALL. Incidentally, will you waive signature on this?

Mr. CRAWFORD. Yes; I will.

TESTIMONY OF MARY ANN MITCHELL

The testimony of Mary Ann Mitchell was taken at 2:30 p.m., on April 1, 1964, in the office of the U.S. attorney, 301 Post Office Building, Bryan and Ervay Streets, Dallas, Tex., by Mr. Joseph A. Ball, assistant counsel of the President's Commission.

Mr. BALL. Miss Mitchell, will you stand up, please, and be sworn; hold up your right hand. (Complying.)

Mr. BALL. Do you solemnly swear the testimony you will be giving before this Commission will be the truth, the whole truth, and nothing but the truth, so help you God?

Miss MITCHELL. Yes; I do.

Mr. BALL. Will you state your name, please?

Miss MITCHELL. Mary Ann Mitchell.

Mr. BALL. What is your occupation?

Miss MITCHELL. I am a deputy district clerk.

Mr. BALL. For Dallas County?

Miss MITCHELL. For the county of Dallas.

Mr. BALL. What kind of work is that; do you work in the court?

Miss MITCHELL. No; I work in the main office of the clerk of the district courts.

Mr. BALL. Tell me something about your background—where were you born, where were you raised, what schools did you go to?

Miss MITCHELL. I was born in Roanoke, Tex., which is in Denton County, about 30 miles north of here; graduated from high school in Denton in 1942. I went to college for 2 years at Arlington and moved to Dallas and came to work here in June of 1944. I have held several secretarial and stenographic type jobs before I went to work for the county of Dallas and that was in 1950 and I have been there since then.

Mr. BALL. Since 1950, you have been with the county with the Clerk of the District Court of Dallas County?

Miss MITCHELL. Yes, sir.

Mr. BALL. On the 22d of November 1963, about noontime, where were you?

Miss MITCHELL. About noontime?

Mr. BALL. Yes.

Miss MITCHELL. I was in the office about noon.

Mr. BALL. Working?

Miss MITCHELL. Working, which is in the basement of the Records Building.

Mr. BALL. Did you leave there some time, leave the office to see the parade that morning?

Miss MITCHELL. Yes, as a matter of fact, I went up to see the parade since we are in the basement.

Mr. BALL. What time did you leave the building?

Miss MITCHELL. At possibly 12:25 or 12:27, something like that.

Mr. BALL. Whom were you with?

Miss MITCHELL. I left the office with Jim Crawford.

Mr. BALL. Where did you go?

Miss MITCHELL. I went out onto the street and down to the corner of the building.

Mr. BALL. That means you would be on what corner of what streets?

Miss MITCHELL. I went out the Elm Street entrance of the building and I was on the corner of Elm and Record—I'm sorry, Elm and Houston.

Mr. BALL. Which corner?

Miss MITCHELL. I knew you were going to ask that and I decided it's probably the northwest corner. I am not good at directions.

Mr. BALL. Let's put it this way——

Miss MITCHELL. It's the corner diagonally across the intersection from the Texas School Book Depository.

Mr. BALL. The Texas School Book Depository is on the northwest corner; that would put you on the southeast corner.

Miss MITCHELL. Yes, sir; I was thinking about which corner of the building.

Mr. BALL. The northwest corner of the building and the southeast corner of the intersection, is that right?

Miss MITCHELL. Yes, sir.

Mr. BALL. Were you near the curb when you were standing?

Miss MITCHELL. Yes; I was on the curb.

Mr. BALL. Did you see the President's car pass?

Miss MITCHELL. Yes; I did.

Mr. BALL. Tell me in your own words what you noticed and what you heard after the President's car passed; what did you see and what did you hear?

Miss MITCHELL. Well, the President's car passed and, of course, I watched it as long as I could see it but, as I remember, immediately behind it was a car full of men with the top down and quite a few of them were standing and I assumed they were Secret Service men, so after the car turned the corner and started down the hill, I couldn't see over the heads of the standing men for very long, so then I turned back to watch the other people in the caravan, whatever you call it, and probably about the time the car in which Senator Yarborough was riding had just passed, I heard some reports. The first one—there were three—the second and third being closer together than the first and second and probably on the first one my thought was that it was a firecracker and I think on the second one I thought that some police officer was after somebody that wasn't doing right and by the third report Jim Crawford had said the shots came from the building and as I looked up there then we realized that if the shots were coming from that building there was bound to have been somebody shooting at the people in the cars.

Mr. BALL. You heard Jim Crawford say something about if they were shots—what were his words exactly?

Miss MITCHELL. Well, I'm not sure that he said—I think he just said, "Those shots came from that building," just assuming that everybody could have figured out by then that they were shots.

Mr. BALL. Did you look at the building?

Miss MITCHELL. Yes; I did.

Mr. BALL. Did you see anybody in any of the windows?

Miss MITCHELL. I don't remember. I understand there were some porters that were leaning out of the fifth floor windows but I don't remember whether I saw them or not. I know where I thought he was pointing and where I was looking I couldn't see anybody so I never was sure which window he thought he was pointing to.

Mr. BALL. Was he pointing?

Miss MITCHELL. I am almost sure that he was because I was trying to figure out exactly where he was.

Mr. BALL. What did you do after that, if anything?

Miss MITCHELL. Well, looked back around at the crowd, I'm sure, because I expected to see the Secret Service men and police escorts just start pouring everywhere when we decided what the shots were and then looking at the people that were falling on the ground and started milling around and then I went back in the office.

Mr. BALL. And you did not come out again?

Miss MITCHELL. No; I did not come out again.

Mr. BALL. Did you, at any time, say anything like "oh, no, no" in reply to what Mr. Crawford said?

Miss MITCHELL. Well, yes, I'm sure I did.

Mr. BALL. In reply to what remark of his?

Miss MITCHELL. Oh, I don't know. I don't know possibly it was when he was talking about the shots coming from the building but I don't remember if he said anything else.

Mr. BALL. Well, if you excuse me just a minute, let me look in my notes here. These are the notes from which I refresh my memory here.

Miss MITCHELL. I can remember what I was saying and doing better than I can what other people were.

Mr. BALL. Is there anything else that you remember that you said?

161

Miss MITCHELL. Besides when I said something about "oh, no, no" or "oh, my goodness" or "oh, my God" or whatever I said?

Mr. BALL. Yes; that's right.

Miss MITCHELL. Yes; I said, "This is no place for us, let's get out of here." I thought if we would get out of their way, the police officers could work better.

Mr. BALL. That's when you left?

Miss MITCHELL. That's when I left and he came with me. I had locked the office and I had the key to the office still in my hand so I could get back in very fast.

Mr. BALL. I think that's all. Do you want to look this over and read it and sign it or do you want to waive signature?

Miss MITCHELL. Either way. We were out of the office such a short time because we had spotters in the building so we would know when the parade was coming and we could run out. We had so many people in the building who worked there upstairs and they called us when it was coming so we could go outside.

Mr. BALL. If you wish, we can waive your signature; the young lady will write it up and send it back to Washington, is that all right with you?

Miss MITCHELL. Yes; that's fine.

Mr. BALL. I think that's all. Thank you very much for coming up today.

TESTIMONY OF MRS. BARBARA ROWLAND

The testimony of Mrs. Barbara Rowland was taken at 4 p.m., on April 7, 1964, in the office of the U.S. attorney, 301 Post Office Building, Bryan and Ervay Streets, Dallas, Tex., by Mr. David W. Belin, assistant counsel of the President's Commission.

Mr. BELIN. Mrs. Rowland, will you stand and be sworn. Do you solemnly swear that the testimony you are about to give before this President's Commission on the Assassination of President Kennedy is the truth, the whole truth, and nothing but the truth, so help you God?

Mrs. ROWLAND. Yes, sir.

Mr. BELIN. Would you please state your name.

Mrs. ROWLAND. Barbara Rowland.

Mr. BELIN. Is it Miss or Mrs.?

Mrs. ROWLAND. Mrs.

Mr. BELIN. To whom are you married?

Mrs. ROWLAND. Arnold Lewis Rowland.

Mr. BELIN. Your husband has already gone to Washington to testify before the Commission in Washington, is that correct?

Mrs. ROWLAND. Yes, sir.

Mr. BELIN. What is your occupation right now? What are you doing?

Mrs. ROWLAND. I am a housewife.

Mr. BELIN. Are you a high school graduate?

Mrs. ROWLAND. No, sir.

Mr. BELIN. Are you still attending high school?

Mrs. ROWLAND. No; but I plan to go back later.

Mr. BELIN. In the fall?

Mrs. ROWLAND. Yes, sir.

Mr. BELIN. Where is your husband working?

Mrs. ROWLAND. He's got a new job. He is working for Life Circulation Co., or corporation, I don't know which.

Mr. BELIN. What does he do?

Mrs. ROWLAND. He is a telephone solicitor.

Mr. BELIN. For magazine subscriptions?

Mrs. ROWLAND. Yes, sir.

Mr. BELIN. Is your husband a high school graduate or not?

Mrs. ROWLAND. No.

Mr. BELIN. Did you meet while you were going to high school?

Mrs. ROWLAND. Yes, sir.

Mr. BELIN. How old is your husband, by the way?

Mrs. ROWLAND. He is 18.

Mr. BELIN. When were you married?

Mrs. ROWLAND. We were married May 16, 1963.

Mr. BELIN. So you will be having your anniversary in another few weeks?

Mrs. ROWLAND. Yes.

Mr. BELIN. Do you know if I got on the record your residence?

Mrs. ROWLAND. 1131A Phinney.

Mr. BELIN. Is that in Dallas?

Mrs. ROWLAND. Yes.

Mr. BELIN. Are you originally from Dallas?

Mrs. ROWLAND. Yes, sir.

Mr. BELIN. You lived here all your life?

Mrs. ROWLAND. Except the summer we lived in Oregon.

Mr. BELIN. Is your husband originally from Dallas?

Mrs. ROWLAND. He is from Corpus Christi.

Mr. BELIN. Has he lived in Texas all of his life, do you know, or not?

Mrs. ROWLAND. No. He has lived in Texas and Kansas and Oregon and Arizona, and I don't know where else.

Mr. BELIN. When did he live in Kansas?

Mrs. ROWLAND. About 2 years ago, I think.

Mr. BELIN. Do you know what he was doing when he was in Kansas?

Mrs. ROWLAND. He was going to school and working, I don't know what as. I think he worked in a cafe.

Mr. BELIN. Do you know how far your husband got through school?

Mrs. ROWLAND. Well, his credits are all mixed up. I think he lacks one or two semesters.

Mr. BELIN. Of completing high school?

Mrs. ROLAND. Yes.

Mr. BELIN. You said you were going back to school. Does he plan to keep working, or does he plan to go back to school?

Mrs. ROWLAND. He plans to go back to school sometime. I'm not sure when.

Mr. BELIN. To finish high school?

Mrs. ROWLAND. And college. Go to college, I think.

Mr. BELIN. Well, has he ever made any application for college yet, that you know of?

Mrs. ROWLAND. I don't know for certain.

Mr. BELIN. Do you know, or has he ever said to you that he has?

Mrs. ROWLAND. He told me he was going to make an application at Oregon State, and— but I don't know if he ever made any applications anywhere.

Mr. BELIN. Would you categorize yourself insofar as your grades that you got in high school, would they have been C's, B's, or A's, or what?

Mrs. ROWLAND. A's and a few B's.

Mr. BELIN. What was your major?

Mrs. ROWLAND. English.

Mr. BELIN. If you had one?

Mrs. ROWLAND. I was going to major in English, Math, and Spanish.

Mr. BELIN. All three?

Mrs. ROWLAND. In high school.

Mr. BELIN. What about your husband? Did you know what he was majoring in?

Mrs. ROWLAND. Math, I think.

Mr. BELIN. Do you know about what his grades were?

Mrs. ROWLAND. Varied.

Mr. BELIN. What do you mean by that?

Mrs. ROWLAND. He made A's and B's in some subjects, and he made C's and D's, I think, in other subjects.

Mr. BELIN. Was this before you were married?

Mrs. ROWLAND. Yes. He says he has an A average, but I don't believe him.

Mr. BELIN. Why? Did he tell you that?

Mrs. ROWLAND. Yes. He told me that, because I saw a few of his report cards.

Mr. BELIN. Pardon?

Mrs. ROWLAND. I saw a few of his report cards and they weren't all A's.

Mr. BELIN. For what years would that have been?

Mrs. ROWLAND. I don't remember. I just saw them.

Mr. BELIN. Mrs. Rowland, I want to get just a little bit more background information. After you were married, were you employed at all or not?

Mrs. ROWLAND. I worked for Sanger Harris during the Christmas season this year, this past year.

Mr. BELIN. Other than that?

Mrs. ROWLAND. Well, I worked for about 3 days for a friend of mine at a dry goods store.

163

Mr. BELIN. What about your husband? What jobs has he held since you were married?

Mrs. ROWLAND. Let's see, he worked at West Foods in Salem,——

Mr. BELIN. Was this after you were married?

Mrs. ROWLAND. Yes.

Mr. BELIN. Did you go to Oregon after you were married?

Mrs. ROWLAND. Yes. We were married May 16, and we went to Oregon about, we left the next day, and we got there about the 21st or something like that. He worked at West Foods in Salem; Exchange Lumber in Salem; Myron Frank in Salem, and after we moved back down here and——

Mr. BELIN. When did you move back down to Texas?

Mrs. ROWLAND. In September.

Mr. BELIN. Were these jobs that he held of the same type, or did he work first at one place and then——

Mrs. ROWLAND. One place and then another.

Mr. BELIN. Any particular reason why he changed jobs, that you know of?

Mrs. ROWLAND. Well, the first job was dirty and difficult and he didn't like it.

Mr. BELIN. What was he doing then?

Mrs. ROWLAND. He was working in a mushroom plant.

Mr. BELIN. As what?

Mrs. ROWLAND. I think he was carrying them out, I don't know exactly what he was doing with them. Then he worked at Myron Frank which was a department store.

Mr. BELIN. What did he do there?

Mrs. ROWLAND. He worked as a cook.

Mr. BELIN. Is he a good cook?

Mrs. ROWLAND. Pretty good cook.

Mr. BELIN. Are you better than he is?

Mrs. ROWLAND. I am not a very good cook.

Mr. BELIN. All right.

Mrs. ROWLAND. Anyway, he worked there. It was a temporary job when he got it, and when the time, when the period was up, he got another job as a, what do you call it, a shipping clerk at the Exchange Lumber Co., and he worked there until a few days before we left.

Mr. BELIN. Then you went back to Dallas sometime in September?

Mrs. ROWLAND. Yes.

Mr. BELIN. Then what did your husband do?

Mrs. ROWLAND. I don't remember the first job. He worked for Pizza Inn as a cook and he worked for Civic Reading Club as a telephone solicitation job, and he worked for P. F. Collier Co., as a salesman, and then he worked, now he is working for Life Circulation Co. as a telephone solicitor.

Mr. BELIN. How long did he have these jobs? The first one, how long did he work there, approximately?

Mrs. ROWLAND. I don't know. I think he worked at Pizza Inn for about two and a half months, maybe. And he worked for P. F. Collier for about 4 weeks, I think, but he didn't do anything there. I mean he wasn't very successful. And he worked for Civic Reading Club about 2 months, I guess.

Mr. BELIN. And now he is working for?

Mrs. ROWLAND. Life Circulation Co.

Mr. BELIN. Were you working at all during the fall, or what were you doing?

Mrs. ROWLAND. He worked for Sanger Harris during the Christmas season, too.

Mr. BELIN. Were you?

Mrs. ROWLAND. Yes. That is the only job. That is all I have worked.

Mr. BELIN. Were you going to school at all in the fall, or not?

Mrs. ROWLAND. Yes; at the beginning of the fall we were both going to school. But we couldn't quite afford to stay, and so because his job was only part-time——

Mr. BELIN. So did either one of you quit or both?

Mrs. ROWLAND. Both.

Mr. BELIN. About when did you both quit?

Mrs. ROLAND. In November, I believe it was.

Mr. BELIN. Would this have been before or after the shooting of President Kennedy?

Mrs. ROLAND. Well, we stopped going before the assassination, but we officially dropped afterwards.

Mr. BELIN. Well, let me ask you this. On the morning of the assassination, where were you?

Mrs. ROLAND. We were on Houston Street near the drive-in entrance of the records building between Elm and Main Streets.

Mr. BELIN. Before that, where had you been that morning?

Mrs. ROWLAND. At my mother's home.

Mr. BELIN. You had been at your mother's home that morning from about when to when?

Mrs. ROWLAND. Well, we were living with my mother, and so from that morning when we got up, and we walked part way——

Mr. BELIN. When did you leave your mother's home, about?

Mrs. ROWLAND. I think it was about 10 or 10:30, and we caught the bus. We walked a few blocks toward town, because we thought we would be too late to come see him, and we caught the bus, I don't know exactly what time it was when we got to town, but I think it was about 11:30, and about 15 minutes before the motorcade came by is when he told me about the man up in the window.

Mr. BELIN. All right, now, you caught a bus near your mother's place?

Mrs. ROWLAND. Yes.

Mr. BELIN. About what time?

Mrs. ROWLAND. The Ledbetter bus.

Mr. BELIN. About what time do you think you caught the bus?

Mrs. ROLAND. I don't know, about 10:30, I guess.

Mr. BELIN. When did that get you downtown?

Mrs. ROWLAND. About 11. I don't know exactly. I don't remember times very well.

Mr. BELIN. Well, let me ask you this. After you got downtown, what did you do?

Mrs. ROWLAND. We just stood there waiting for the motorcade.

Mr. BELIN. Well. I will kind of work backwards. How long did you stand waiting for the motorcade before the motorcade came by, if you remember?

Mrs. ROWLAND. About 25 minutes, I think.

Mr. BELIN. How long did it take you to get from the bus stop?

Mrs. ROWLAND. The bus stop was right there.

Mr. BELIN. Do you figure if the motorcade came by at around 12:30, you figure you got down to the spot at 12 or 12:05?

Mrs. ROWLAND. Yes.

Mr. BELIN. If you got down to that spot at 12 or 12:05, how many minutes prior to that time do you think you got on the bus?

Mrs. ROWLAND. About 45.

Mr. BELIN. You figure it might have been a 45-minute bus ride?

Mrs. ROWLAND. Yes.

Mr. BELIN. That would have meant that you would have got on the bus around 11:15 or so?

Mrs. ROWLAND. Yes.

Mr. BELIN. Do you remember how long you waited for the bus before you got it?

Mrs. ROWLAND. We were walking while waiting for the bus, and it was about, I guess, 20 minutes.

Mr. BELIN. So you figured you walked around about 20 minutes?

Mrs. ROWLAND. Yes.

Mr. BELIN. So you figured you would have left your mother's home shortly before 11?

Mrs. ROWLAND. Yes.

Mr. BELIN. You are nodding your head yes?

Mrs. ROWLAND. Yes.

Mr. BELIN. All right, did you notice anything while you were watching, waiting for the motorcade?

Mrs. ROWLAND. We saw an airplane. Now, while we were waiting for the motorcade, well, there was a man across the street who fainted in the park.

Mr. BELIN. You were standing now on what street?

Mrs. ROWLAND. On Houston Street.

Mr. BELIN. That would be on the east or the west side of Houston?

Mrs. ROWLAND. West side—east side.

Mr. BELIN. East side. In front of what building?

Mrs. ROWLAND. In front of the records, at the side of the records building.

Mr. BELIN. Do you know any particular spot that you were standing?

Mrs. ROWLAND. We were standing near the drive-in entrance. There is an elevator there, too.

Mr. BELIN. Near the elevator that comes out of the ground?

Mrs. ROWLAND. Yes.

Mr. BELIN. All right, you said you noticed a man across the street fainted. Anything else that you and your husband noticed?

Mrs. ROWLAND. Well, my husband and I were talking about Mr. Stevenson's visit and the way the people had acted, and we were talking about security measures, and he said he saw a man on the sixth floor of the School Book Depository Building, and when I looked up there I didn't see the man, because I didn't know exactly what window he was talking about at first.

And when I found out which window it was, the man had apparently stepped back, because I didn't see him.

Mr. BELIN. Which window was it?

Mrs. ROWLAND. It was the far left-hand window.

Mr. BELIN. As you face the building?

Mrs. ROWLAND. Yes.

Mr. BELIN. It would be the window to the south side of the building?

Mrs. ROWLAND. Yes.

Mr. BELIN. Would it be on the eastern part of the south side or the western part of the south side?

Mrs. ROWLAND. West.

Mr. BELIN. Would it be the farthermost west window?

Mrs. ROWLAND. Yes; the farthermost west pair of windows.

Mr. BELIN. The farthermost west pair of windows. What did your husband say to you?

Mrs. ROWLAND. Well, we assumed that it was a Secret Service man.

Mr. BELIN. But what did he say, if you remember?

Mrs. ROWLAND. He told me that he saw a man there who looked like he was holding a rifle, and that it must be a security man guarding the motorcade.

Mr. BELIN. Is there anything else that you can remember that he told you?

Mrs. ROWLAND. No.

Mr. BELIN. What did you do when he told you that?

Mrs. ROWLAND. Nothing. I just generally agreed with him.

Mr. BELIN. What do you mean "generally agree"? Did you see the man?

Mrs. ROWLAND. No; I didn't see the man, but I said I guess that was what it was.

Mr. BELIN. You mean you agreed that he must have been a security officer?

Mrs. ROWLAND. Yes.

Mr. BELIN. I notice you are not wearing glasses now. Do you wear glasses?

Mrs. BOWLAND. Yes; sometimes.

Mr. BELIN. Are you near-sighted or far-sighted?

Mrs. BOWLAND. Near-sighted.

Mr. BELIN. Did you have any trouble looking at this window?

Mrs. BOWLAND. No; I saw the window plainly, and I saw some people hanging, looking out of some other windows, but he said that the man was standing in the background.

Mr. BELIN. Did he say about how far back?

Mrs. BOWLAND. I think he said about 12 feet, I don't know exactly.

Mr. BELIN. Did he say how much of the man he could see?

Mrs. BOWLAND. Apparently he could see at least from the waist up, because he said that the man was wearing a light shirt, and that he was holding the rifle at a port arms position.

Mr. BELIN. Did he say whether the man was white or colored?

Mrs. BOWLAND. He said he thought he was white.

Mr. BELIN. Did he say whether the man was an old man or a young man?

Mrs. BOWLAND. He said a young man.

Mr. BELIN. Did he say whether the man was fat or thin?

Mrs. BOWLAND. He said he was either tall or thin. I mean, if he was tall, he could have been well built, but if he was not very tall, then he was thin.

Mr. BELIN. Did he say whether or not the man had on a hat?

Mrs. BOWLAND. I don't think he said whether he did or not. But if he had seen a hat, I think he would have said so.

Mr. BELIN. Did he say what color hair the man had?

Mrs. BOWLAND. I am not positive.

Mr. BELIN. About how many minutes was this before the motorcade came by that he saw this?

Mrs. BOWLAND. About 15 minutes.

Mr. BELIN. Did he say anything else about the man?

Mrs. BOWLAND. Not that I remember, except that he was wearing a light colored shirt or jacket.

Mr. BELIN. Did he say anything about any other people in any other windows?

Mrs. BOWLAND. No; I don't think so.

Mr. BELIN. Now, did you notice any other people standing in any other windows or leaning out?

Mrs. BOWLAND. I am not sure if I did at that moment.

Mr. BELIN. Later on?

Mrs. BOWLAND. I saw some people either earlier or later looking out the windows.

Mr. BELIN. Do you remember anything about any of the people you saw?

Mrs. BOWLAND. Some of them were colored men. I don't think I saw any women.

Mr. BELIN. Did you see any white men?

Mrs. BOWLAND. I am not positive.

Mr. BELIN. Do you remember where you saw any of these Negro men?

Mrs. BOWLAND. On a lower floor, about the fourth floor, I think, and nearer the center window. The windows nearer the center.

Mr. BELIN. On some floor lower than the sixth floor, which you think was the fourth floor?

Mrs. BOWLAND. About the fourth floor.

Mr. BELIN. Did you and your husband comment about these other men?

Mrs. BOWLAND. We may have said something about there being other people watching, I am not sure.

Mr. BELIN. Did you particularly watch the sixth floor because of the fact that you had seen or your husband had seen a person on the sixth floor?

Mrs. BOWLAND. We looked at it for a few minutes, but we didn't look back, and when we heard the shots, we didn't look back up there. I grabbed his hand and started running toward the car.

Mr. BELIN. Let me ask you this now. From the time that you saw or your husband said he saw a man on the southwest part of the sixth floor, which   you say was about 15 minutes before the motorcade came by, how much longer did you look back up at the building?

Mrs. ROWLAND. Just about 2 or 3 minutes.

Mr. BELIN. After that?

Mrs. ROWLAND. About 2 minutes.

Mr. BELIN. You mean about 2 minutes after that time?

Mrs. ROWLAND. Yes.

Mr. BELIN. So that would be up to a time of about 13 minutes before the motorcade came by?

Mrs. ROWLAND. Yes.

Mr. BELIN. Did you ever look back at the building after that period of time?

Mrs. ROWLAND. I may have glanced at it, but I don't remember looking back for the purpose of seeing the man.

Mr. BELIN. All right, or any man there?

Mrs. ROWLAND. Any man there.

Mr. BELIN. What were you doing from the 13 minutes on before the motorcade came until the time it came?

Mrs. ROWLAND. Just talking and looking.

Mr. BELIN. Where were you looking?

Mrs. ROWLAND. At the street and the other people, and we talked about some men who were carrying cameras.

Mr. BELIN. Now when you were standing watching the motorcade or standing watching the street scene, do you remember if your husband was to your right or to your left? Was he closer towards the School Book Depository Building?

Mrs. ROWLAND. No; he was to my left most of the time, I think.

Mr. BELIN. What was he doing?

Mrs. ROWLAND. Just standing there talking.

Mr. BELIN. Talking to you?

Mrs. ROWLAND. Yes.

Mr. BELIN. Do you know whether or not if he ever looked back at the building?

Mrs. ROWLAND. I wouldn't know for certain.

Mr. BELIN. Did he ever tell you he was looking back at the building?

Mrs. ROWLAND. No.

Mr. BELIN. Did you ever notice him looking back at the building?

167

Mrs. ROWLAND. Not that I remember.

Mr. BELIN. Was he generally looking at you when he was talking with you?

Mrs. ROWLAND. Not necessarily. He might have been looking around at the street or at the building.

Mr. BELIN. Or at anything?

Mrs. ROWLAND. Yes.

Mr. BELIN. Anything else at that place then that you specifically remember before the motorcade came by? Did your husband say anything about seeing anyone in the building, or did you talk any more about the man with the rifle?

Mrs. ROWLAND. I really don't remember very much about what happened afterward. I mean it was just——

Mr. BELIN. I mean between, in the 15 minutes preceding the motorcade?

Mrs. ROWLAND. I remember hearing on the radio that the President was passing Ervay Street. It wasn't on our radio, somebody else's radio, and that is about all.

Mr. BELIN. Anything else you can think of?

Mrs. ROWLAND. No.

Mr. BELIN. By the way, what color dress were you wearing that day?

Mrs. ROWLAND. Oh, my, I am fairly certain I was either wearing a green suit or red and gray suit, but I am not positive.

Mr. BELIN. What kind of coat, if you were wearing a coat?

Mrs. ROWLAND. I was wearing a brown coat, brown suede coat.

Mr. BELIN. Do you remember what your husband was wearing?

Mrs. ROWLAND. He was wearing a plaid sports jacket, probably. I am not sure which sports jacket, but I think he was wearing a plaid sports jacket that was blue and had some black and grey in it.

Mr. BELIN. Was he wearing any overcoat over the sports jacket?

Mrs. ROWLAND. Oh, no; I wasn't wearing that brown coat, I don't think. I think I was wearing an olive coat. He probably had his overcoat, but it is more of a raincoat.

Mr. BELIN. Were you wearing gloves?

Mrs. ROWLAND. Yes.

Mr. BELIN. Was he wearing gloves?

Mrs. ROWLAND. Yes.

Mr. BELIN. Were you wearing a hat?

Mrs. ROWLAND. No; a scarf.

Mr. BELIN. Was he wearing a hat, do you remember?

Mrs. ROWLAND. He might have been. He wears one sometimes. Sometimes he doesn't.

Mr. BELIN. Is there anything else you remember about what happened prior to the time the motorcade came by?

Mrs. ROWLAND. No.

Mr. BELIN. All right, now, will you please tell us what happened as the motorcade went by?

Mrs. ROWLAND. Well, Mrs. Kennedy was wearing a blue—I mean a pink or maybe a rose—it was either pink or rose dress or suit, I couldn't say, because she was sitting. She had a pink hat or rose, the same shade as her dress.

And I remember noticing that the President's hair was sort of red, that is all. They were facing mainly toward the other side of the street and waving, and as they turned the corner we heard a shot, and I didn't recognize it as being a shot. I just heard a sound, and I thought it might be a firecracker.

And the people started laughing at first, and then we heard two more shots, and they were closer than the first and second, and that is all.

Mr. BELIN. How many shots did you hear all told?

Mrs. ROWLAND. Three.

Mr. BELIN. When you said you heard two more shots that were closer than the first and second, what did you mean?

Mrs. ROWLAND. I meant the second and third were closer than the first and second.

Mr. BELIN. Mrs. Rowland, did you have any idea where the shots came from or the sound?

Mrs. ROWLAND. Well, the people generally ran towards the railroad tracks behind the School Book Depository Building, and so I naturally assumed they came from there, because that is where all the policemen and everyone was going, and I couldn't tell where the sounds came from.

Mr. BELIN. So you just started over after them?

168

Mrs. ROWLAND. Yes.

Mr. BELIN. Did your husband go with you?

Mrs. ROWLAND. Yes; I grabbed his hand and he couldn't go anyplace else.

Mr. BELIN. Were you running or walking over there?

Mrs. ROWLAND. It wasn't a very fast run, but it wasn't a walk.

Mr. BELIN. Did you talk about anything, about the man that you had seen in the window?

Mrs. ROWLAND. No. But he was reluctant to start running, and he might have been looking up there, I don't know. But we didn't say anything about the man.

Mr. BELIN. What did you do when you got over there? Where did you run to?

Mrs. ROWLAND. To the colonnade over on the north side of Elm Street.

Mr. BELIN. As Elm Street goes down to the freeway?

Mrs. ROWLAND. Yes.

Mr. BELIN. Then where did you go?

Mrs. ROWLAND. We walked towards the railroad tracks, but the policeman wouldn't let anybody go further.

Mr. BELIN. Then what did you do?

Mrs. ROWLAND. We just stood there and he was speculating on what had happened, and he was looking around at everything, and the policeman inspected a Coke drink bottle that was there, and my husband found a pen, very cheap ballpoint pen that you get as an advertisement, and he gave it to   the policeman, and then he mentioned the man he had seen in the School Book Depository Building, and then the man took us to the records building.

Mr. BELIN. Who did your husband mention this to? Was this some police officer?

Mrs. ROWLAND. I am not certain. The first man he mentioned it to was wearing plain clothes, and we didn't see him again, I don't think. And then there were some other men who took us to the building. I don't know who they were.

Mr. BELIN. Then what did you do when you got to the building? Did you stay with your husband?

Mrs. ROWLAND. Yes.

Mr. BELIN. He was questioned in the building?

Mrs. ROWLAND. Yes.

Mr. BELIN. Did you hear what your husband said?

Mrs. ROWLAND. Yes.

Mr. BELIN. Could you describe what went on in the building?

Mrs. ROWLAND. When we first came in, we went into an office that had glass windows around it. There was a man sitting there with a child. I think it was a boy and he said that he had seen the President shot and he said that—he didn't say there were three shots, I think he said there was one, or maybe he said there were more than three, but he didn't say there were three shots.

Then we went out into an open area in the building, a fairly open area, and there were some reporters in there, and they started asking us questions which we didn't answer, because mainly we didn't have time.

Then we were taken into a very small office and a lady took his written statement and my statement, and there were three other people who came in, three other witnesses who came in.

There were two young men together, and one young lady who came in.

Mr. BELIN. All right, now, when you gave your statement to the police and your husband gave his statement to the police, or to whoever the people were taking the statement, do you remember what your husband said?

Mrs. ROWLAND. Yes. Do I have to tell you again?

Mr. BELIN. Well, did he say substantially what you said?

Mrs. ROWLAND. Yes; I think so.

Mr. BELIN. Anything else that he said that you haven't related here?

Mrs. ROWLAND. I believe he may have said that the man had dark hair. Either he said that the man had dark hair, or he didn't see what color the man's hair was. And he said just about the same thing I said here, I think.

Mr. BELIN. All right, anything else that was said there by your husband?

Mrs. ROWLAND. I don't remember anything else.

Mr. BELIN. Did your husband at that time say whether or not he had kept any watch on the window of the School Book Depository Building after he saw this man with the gun?

Mrs. ROWLAND. No.

Mr. BELIN. You mean he——

Mrs. ROWLAND. He didn't say.

Mr. BELIN. Did he say whether or not he had seen any other people in the windows of the School Book Depository Building?

Mrs. ROWLAND. Yes; I am fairly certain that he said there were other people looking out the windows.

Mr. BELIN. Did he say whether or not there were any other people on that same floor looking out the windows?

Mrs. ROWLAND. I am not certain whether he said or not. But I know there weren't any other people on that floor looking out the windows that could be seen from the outside.

Mr. BELIN. How do you know that?

Mrs. ROWLAND. I mean I know they couldn't be seen from the outside, because I couldn't see them. I am nearsighted.

Mr. BELIN. Were you keeping any watch on the building after the time you saw the man with the rifle?

Mrs. ROWLAND. Well——

Mr. BELIN. Did you look up at that building from time to time?

Mrs. ROWLAND. Well, I didn't pay any special attention to the building, but I am sure I glanced at the building more than once afterwards, because I can't just stand and stare in one direction.

Mr. BELIN. Do you mean you were just glancing at that building as you were glancing at other places?

Mrs. ROWLAND. Yes, sir.

Mr. BELIN. When you were glancing at that building, do you remember whether you glanced at it, say, within 10 minutes prior to the motorcade?

Mrs. ROWLAND. I don't remember. But most of the windows on that floor were closed, and the people who were looking out usually were looking out at an open window.

Mr. BELIN. Did you see any people look out of any open windows?

Mrs. ROWLAND. Yes.

Mr. BELIN. About how many did you see all told, if you can remember?

Mrs. ROLAND. Two or three, I think.

Mr. BELIN. Any more than two or three looking out of windows?

Mrs. ROWLAND. Not that I remember.

Mr. BELIN. Do you remember whether or not any of those that you saw looking out of windows were looking out of the sixth floor?

Mrs. ROWLAND. They weren't.

Mr. BELIN. They were not? Were they on any floor higher than the sixth floor?

Mrs. ROWLAND. No.

Mr. BELIN. Were they all on floors lower than the sixth floor?

Mrs. ROWLAND. Yes.

Mr. BELIN. Did your husband state in the presence of you at any time while he was giving any of these statements on the afternoon of November 22, whether or not he saw any people looking out of the building?

Mrs. ROWLAND. Yes.

Mr. BELIN. Where did he say he saw them?

Mrs. ROWLAND. He didn't say exactly where he saw them, but the windows on the floor above the sixth floor were all closed, and I think they were never open.

Mr. BELIN. All right. So they wouldn't have been on the seventh floor?

Mrs. ROWLAND. No.

Mr. BELIN. Did he say whether or not he saw any people looking out of any other windows on the sixth floor?

Mrs. ROWLAND. He didn't say, I don't believe.

Mr. BELIN. Did he say what floor? He didn't say whether he did or did not, is that your testimony, or did he say that he did not?

Mrs. ROWLAND. I don't believe he said whether or not he saw any other people on the sixth floor.

Mr. BELIN. What did he say about what he saw? Do you remember about how many people he said he saw looking out of the windows?

Mrs. ROWLAND. I don't believe he said any certain number of people.

Mr. BELIN. Do you remember anything that he said about that?

Mrs. ROWLAND. He just said that there were some other people looking out of some windows in the same building.

Mr. BELIN. Did he specifically locate them in any way?

Mrs. ROWLAND. No.

Mr. BELIN. All right, is there any other thing that your husband said in your presence that afternoon pertaining to this School Book Depository Building?

Mrs. ROWLAND. No; I don't believe so.

Mr. BELIN. How long did you stay over there?

Mrs. ROWLAND. We were there until about 2:00 or 3:00, I think.

Mr. BELIN. Then what did you do?

Mrs. ROWLAND. Then we left and walked around town and tried to get a newspaper, and before we left, we knew that the President was dead.

From that—for a while, we were in a room alone with a lady who came in to testify, and said that she had seen a blond man carrying a rifle in a rifle bag, and he said that probably it couldn't have been the man he saw because the man he saw was dark-haired.

Mr. BELIN. Did this woman say where she was—where she saw the blond-haired man?

Mrs. ROWLAND. I believe she said in front of some sporting goods store. I am not certain.

Mr. BELIN. Did she say where the sporting goods store was?

Mrs. ROWLAND. Some place downtown, but I don't remember exactly.

Mr. BELIN. Was it in the immediate vicinity of the School Book Depository Building?

Mrs. ROWLAND. Meaning?

Mr. BELIN. Within a block of it?

Mrs. ROWLAND. No.

Mr. BELIN. Did she say when she saw a blond-haired man carrying a rifle?

Mrs. ROWLAND. I am not positive exactly what time she said, but it was before, she said, she heard about the President being shot, and she came back there to tell them she had seen a man earlier carrying a gun in a rifle case.

Mr. BELIN. She had seen some man, that had blond hair, downtown carrying a gun in a rifle case?

Mrs. ROWLAND. Yes.

Mr. BELIN. That is all she knew?

Mrs. ROWLAND. Yes, sir.

Mr. BELIN. Anything else?

Mrs. ROWLAND. Well, I believe that is all she knew.

Mr. BELIN. Is there anything else that you can add?

Mrs. ROWLAND. Well, there were two young men who came in too, and they said something about seeing a man carrying a rifle downtown. I believe they also said he was a blond man.

Mr. BELIN. Anything else?

Mrs. ROWLAND. That he was over 6 feet, and he was well built, from what they said, and that is all I know.

Mr. BELIN. What did your husband say about that?

Mrs. ROWLAND. He didn't comment, I don't think.

Mr. BELIN. Was there anything else that took place while you and your husband were over giving your statements, that you can think of right now? Anything else that your husband said?

Mrs. ROWLAND. Not that I remember.

Mr. BELIN. All right, then, where did you go?

Mrs. ROWLAND. We left and we walked in an easterly direction and we went to a coin shop and looked around for a while, and then I went home and he went to work.

Mr. BELIN. Where was he working?

Mrs. ROWLAND. At the Pizza Inn on West Davis. He caught a bus and went to work, and I caught a bus and went home.

Mr. BELIN. Then what happened? When did you see him next?

Mrs. ROWLAND. No, wait a minute, I didn't go home very soon. The bus—there was poor bus service, and I didn't go home until quite, until about 9:00, I think, and I saw him the next morning.

Mr. BELIN. Had he been contacted at the Pizza Inn later that night, do you know, or not?

Mrs. ROWLAND. I don't think so.

Mr. BELIN. All right, now, were either you or he contacted at any time during that day by any law enforcement agency?

Mrs. ROWLAND. I don't think we were contacted the next day.

Mr. BELIN. That would have been Saturday?

Mrs. ROWLAND. Saturday, I know we weren't. I am not positive.

Mr. BELIN. When were you next contacted, either on that Saturday or that Sunday?

Mrs. ROWLAND. I think so. I am not positive.

Mr. BELIN. Let me ask you how many times after November 22 were you contacted by some law enforcement agency?

Mrs. ROWLAND. Me personally?

Mr. BELIN. You personally.

Mrs. ROWLAND. I spoke to law enforcement officers about three or four times, I think.

Mr. BELIN. About how many times in November? Once on the 22d?

Mrs. ROWLAND. Yes. And we were contacted once Sunday morning at the Pizza Inn during November. I think it was the next Sunday.

Mr. BELIN. The 24th?

Mrs. ROWLAND. Yes. And we were contacted one morning, I am not positive, I think it might have been that Saturday, the following Saturday, the 23d—the Saturday following the assassination, at my mother's home, and I am not positive how many times.

Mr. BELIN. Were you present at any of these times that your husband was contacted?

Mrs. ROWLAND. Yes.

Mr. BELIN. Were you present, for instance, on the Sunday morning, November 24th?

Mrs. ROWLAND. Yes.

Mr. BELIN. Do you remember what your husband said at that time?

Mrs. ROWLAND. He repeated the statement he had made in the—well, the police officers brought a written statement and asked him if that was in general what he had to say, and he said, "Yes," and they asked him specific questions about it and he answered them.

Mr. BELIN. Was there anything else that was said?

Mrs. ROWLAND. I don't believe so.

Mr. BELIN. Was there anything that your husband said that was not on that written statement?

Mrs. ROWLAND. I am not positive.

Mr. BELIN. Do you remember him saying anything—do you remember him telling the police officer that the statement was correct, or do you remember him telling them anything?

Mrs. ROWLAND. Yes; he signed. There might have been a change or two in the statement and then he signed it and said that he verified that it was correct, to the best of his knowledge.

Mr. BELIN. Did he tell the police officer anything that was not on that statement that should be?

Mrs. ROWLAND. I don't believe so.

Mr. BELIN. Was he asked whether or not he saw any other people in any other windows?

Mrs. ROWLAND. I don't believe he was specifically asked that question.

Mr. BELIN. Did he tell any of the police officers that he saw any people in any other windows?

Mrs. ROWLAND. I am not certain.

Mr. BELIN. Do you know whether or not he told them, the police officers, that there was any other person on the sixth floor that he saw?

Mrs. ROWLAND. He never said that there was another person on the sixth floor, in my presence, that I can remember.

Mr. BELIN. Were you present when he was with the police officers?

Mrs. ROWLAND. At times.

Mr. BELIN. On Sunday morning, November 24th?

Mrs. ROWLAND. Yes.

Mr. BELIN. Were you personally with him throughout the time that he was with the police officers?

Mrs. ROWLAND. Yes.

Mr. BELIN. And he, in your presence, never said that he saw anyone on the sixth floor other than the man with the rifle?

Mrs. ROWLAND. No. He never said in my presence that there was another man other than the man with the rifle on the sixth floor.

Mr. BELIN. It is a little bit like there has been asked a negative question and you don't know whether to answer yes or no to the question, is that right, Mrs. Rowland?

Mrs. ROWLAND. Yes, sir.

Mr. BELIN. Now were you present at any subsequent interviews that your husband had with any law enforcement agency?

Mrs. ROWLAND. I was present when Mr. Howlett came to ask, to tell him that he should go to Washington, that he wanted him to go to Washington.

Mr. BELIN. What did your husband say to that?

172

Mrs. ROWLAND. He said, "Okay."

Mr. BELIN. Did he talk to you, by the way, about his testimony when he got back from Washington? Did he talk to you about his testimony in front of the Commission?

Mrs. ROWLAND. No.

Mr. BELIN. Has he ever talked to you about his testimony? Before you came down here, for instance, has he talked to you about what he said in front of the Commission?

Mrs. ROWLAND. Not that I remember.

Mr. BELIN. Going back to his interview with the police, do you know how many interviews he had after the one on Sunday, November 24?

Mrs. ROWLAND. I think he had about six or eight interviews in all. I mean all inclusive.

Mr. BELIN. Would that include the one with Mr. Howlett telling him to go to Washington?

Mrs. ROWLAND. Yes. I am not positive of the number.

Mr. BELIN. Let me ask you this. From November 24 to November 30, that week, do you know how many interviews he had?

Mrs. ROWLAND. No; I don't know.

Mr. BELIN. Now, has he ever told you that he had seen anyone else on the sixth floor other than this man with the gun that you described in the southwest corner window?

Mrs. ROWLAND. No, sir.

Mr. BELIN. Has he ever told you that he told anyone else that he saw anyone else on the sixth floor?

Mrs. ROWLAND. No, sir.

Mr. BELIN. Did your husband ever complain to you that he was being questioned too much by any law enforcement agency?

Mrs. ROWLAND. I don't think so, not that I remember.

Mr. BELIN. Did he ever complain to you that any statement that he gave was not taken down?

Mrs. ROWLAND. Not that I remember.

Mr. BELIN. Was there any complaint that he ever made to you about law enforcement agencies?

Mrs. ROWLAND. Not about the law enforcement agencies, but in the Dallas Morning News on February 11, 14—11th or 14th, they had an article in there, and they had some things in the article that he didn't say.

Mr. BELIN. Like what?

Mrs. ROWLAND. Like that the man was good looking. I mean, because he said he couldn't recognize the man. That is what he told me.

Mr. BELIN. Apart from what the Dallas Morning News said, then, did he have any complaints about his contacts with either the FBI or Secret Service or the sheriffs office or the city police of Dallas?

Mrs. ROWLAND. None that I remember.

Mr. BELIN. Mrs. Rowland, you made a statement toward the beginning part of this deposition that your husband said that he had all A's, but that you knew different, because you had seen the report card.

Mrs. ROWLAND. He said he had an A average.

Mr. BELIN. But that you knew different?

Mrs. ROWLAND. Well, he may have had an A average overall A average, but some of his cards didn't have A's altogether.

Mr. BELIN. Well, you mentioned that he had A's and B's and some C's and some D's?

Mrs. ROWLAND. The one I saw.

Mr. BELIN. Do you remember what years those would have been for?

Mrs. ROWLAND. No, sir.

Mr. BELIN. Sometimes some people are prone to exaggerate more than others, and without in any way meaning to take away from the testimony of your   husband as to what he saw in the building at the time, just from your general experience, do you feel you can rely on everything that your husband says?

Mrs. ROWLAND. I don't feel that I can rely on everything anybody says.

Mr. BELIN. Well, this is really an unfair question for me to ask any wife about her husband, and I am not asking it very correctly, but——

Mrs. ROWLAND. At times my husband is prone to exaggerate. Does that answer it?

Mr. BELIN. I think it does.

Is there anything else you want to add to that, or not?

173

Mrs. ROWLAND. Usually his exaggerations are not concerned with anything other than himself. They are usually to boast his ego. They usually say that he is really smarter than he is, or he is a better salesman than he is, something like that.

Mr. BELIN. Anything else you care to add?

Mrs. ROWLAND. No, sir.

Mr. BELIN. Again, I apologize for any—for in any way trying to embarrass you or anything, but your husband did see a man on the sixth floor and it is important for us to try and find out everything we can to test his accuracy as to what he saw, and so this is why I have been asking these questions.

You and I have never met before?

Mrs. ROWLAND. Not that I ever remember.

Mr. BELIN. When we did meet, I immediately brought you in here and we started taking your deposition under oath, isn't that true?

Mrs. ROWLAND. Yes, sir.

Mr. BELIN. We didn't chat about anything before we started taking your deposition, did we?

Mrs. ROWLAND. No.

Mr. BELIN. Now you mentioned the fact that the newspaper misquoted your husband?

Mrs. ROWLAND. Yes, sir.

Mr. BELIN. Is there any other time when you know that he complained about being misquoted insofar as the facts of the assassination are concerned?

Mrs. ROWLAND. When we had our first written statement, the police officer, I believe he was an FBI agent, restated everything we said, and it was typed in the—in that form. But he also asked if it was, if that was the general meaning of what we had said, so he didn't complain. But anyway, it wasn't in his exact words, I mean.

Mr. BELIN. Was there anything inaccurate about the statement?

Mrs. ROWLAND. No; I don't think so.

Mr. BELIN. Did your husband ever make any complaints to you about anything inaccurate in any statements that he had given?

Mrs. ROWLAND. If he did, I don't remember it.

Mr. BELIN. Is there anything else that you can think of that might in any way be relevant to this whole area of inquiry?

Mrs. ROWLAND. No, sir.

Mr. BELIN. Let me ask you this. Did you or your husband rather, ever see a picture of Lee Harvey Oswald on television?

Mrs. ROWLAND. I saw either the actual shooting on television of Mr. Oswald or either a rerun, and I saw his picture in the newspaper, but I don't know if my husband ever saw it or not.

But he did—we heard on the radio the afternoon of the assassination that Lee Harvey Oswald had been accused of the shooting.

Mr. BELIN. Did you or your husband know anyone by the name of Lee Harvey Oswald?

Mr. ROWLAND. No, sir.

Mr. BELIN. Did you or your husband know Jack Ruby?

Mrs. ROWLAND. Not to my knowledge, I never have known him, and I don't think he has. If he has, he never told me.

Mr. BELIN. Anything else you can think of?

Mrs. ROWLAND. No, sir.

Mr. BELIN. Well, we certainly appreciate your coming down here. You have been most helpful, Mrs. Rowland.

One final thing. You have an opportunity to either come back and read what the court reporter has, the transcript after it is typed, and sign it, or else you can waive coming down and taking the time to read it and sign it, and have it go directly to Washington.

Do you care to come down to read it?

Mrs. ROWLAND. Yes, sir.

Mr. BELIN. If you like to, you have every right to do so.

Mrs. ROWLAND. Yes; I would.

Mr. BELIN. You will be contacted then, and you can come down and read it and make any corrections, if you like.

Mrs. ROWLAND. Yes; could I, other than making corrections have it rewritten in better English?

Mr. BELIN. No, I'm afraid my English at times isn't very good, Mrs. Rowland, and we have to let it go the way it is right now. By corrections, I mean anything where you feel the court reporter might not have accurately transcribed the words that you and I said here.

Mrs. ROWLAND. Yes, sir.

Mr. BELIN. If either one used bad grammar, the English teachers will have to look down their noses at us.

Thank you.

Mrs. ROWLAND. Thank you.

TESTIMONY OF RONALD B. FISCHER

The testimony of Ronald B. Fischer was taken at 11:20 a.m., on April 1, 1964, in the office of the U.S. attorney, 301 Post Office Building, Bryan and Ervay Streets, Dallas, Tex., by Mr. David W. Belin, assistant counsel of the President's Commission.

Mr. BELIN. Mr. Fischer, will you rise to be sworn, please, and raise your right hand?

Do you solemnly swear that the testimony you are about to give is the truth, the whole truth, and nothing but the truth, so help you God?

Mr. FISCHER. I do.

Mr. BELIN. Will you please state your name?

Mr. FISCHER. Ronald B. Fischer.

Mr. BELIN. And where do you live, Mr. Fischer?

Mr. FISCHER. 4007 Flamingo Way, Mesquite, Tex.

Mr. BELIN. Is this a suburb of Dallas?

Mr. FISCHER. Yes.

Mr. BELIN. What is your occupation?

Mr. FISCHER. I'm an auditor.

Mr. BELIN. For whom?

Mr. FISCHER. Dallas County auditor.

Mr. BELIN. And where do you work?

Mr. FISCHER. I work at 407 records building.

Mr. BELIN. And where is the records building?

Mr. FISCHER. That's in Dallas.

Mr. BELIN. Where in Dallas?

Mr. FISCHER. It covers one square block area bounded by Main, Record, Elm, and Houston.

Mr. BELIN. How old are you, Mr. Fischer?

Mr. FISCHER. Twenty-five.

Mr. BELIN. Married?

Mr. FISCHER. Yes.

Mr. BELIN. Children?

Mr. FISCHER. Two.

Mr. BELIN. Did you go to school here in Dallas?

Mr. FISCHER. Yes—high school, yes.

Mr. BELIN. What high school did you go to?

Mr. FISCHER. W. W. Samuell.

Mr. BELIN. Did you complete high school or not?

Mr. FISCHER. Yes.

Mr. BELIN. Have you participated in any postgraduate work since you graduated from high school?

Mr. FISCHER. Yes.

Mr. BELIN. What is that?

Mr. FISCHER. I've taken courses toward an accounting degree at Arlington State College, Arlington, Tex.

Mr. BELIN. Are these correspondence courses or have you actually attended the school?

Mr. FISCHER. No; I've attended the school.

Mr. BELIN. How long did you attend that school?

Mr. FISCHER. I attended 1 year, full time and I attended 1 year, night school.

Mr. BELIN. And what have you done since after you left Arlington?

Mr. FISCHER. All of the time since I've left Arlington, I've been working for the Dallas County auditor—with the exception of a correspondence course that I'm taking at the present time.

Mr. BELIN. Well, by that, you mean you're still working full time but you are taking the correspondence course also?

Mr. FISCHER. Yes.

Mr. BELIN. You have been working for 4 or 5 years for the auditor's office?

Mr. FISCHER. Five years.

Mr. BELIN. Now, Mr. Fischer, I want to take you back to November 22, 1963, and ask you if you remember watching or getting ready to watch, the Presidential motorcade on that day? Do you remember that?

Mr. FISCHER. Yes.

Mr. BELIN. And were you with anyone else, or not?

Mr. FISCHER. Bob Edwards—he works in the same office that I do.

Mr. BELIN. Does he work there now?

Mr. FISCHER. No; he doesn't. At the present time, he's attending a college in Oklahoma but I don't remember the name. It's in Tahlequah, I believe. I don't know the name of the college.

Mr. BELIN. Could that be—I think it's [spelling] T-a-h-l-e-q-u-a-h?

Mr. FISCHER. I think that's it.

Mr. BELIN. Now, when did you and Mr. Edwards leave your place of employment on that day to watch the motorcade?

Mr. FISCHER. Oh, about—well, let's see. We got off for lunch at a quarter of twelve and Mr. Lynn, our boss, said that we could take—go ahead and go on down the street after we got through with lunch, in other words, don't come back to the office after lunch. Just go on down the street and watch the parade. Everybody was due back after the parade was over.

Mr. BELIN. Uh-huh.

Mr. FISCHER. So, I went to lunch at a quarter of twelve, and ate until about 12 o'clock, and then Bob and I went down to the street—oh, 5 or 10 after 12—and we stood, at first, on Main Street right outside the records building. And then about 12:15 or 12:20, we were trying to find a place where we could see better, so we walked down to Houston and then one block down Houston to Elm and stood there until the parade came by.

Mr. BELIN. Now, do you know when you got to corner of Houston and Elm—approximately?

Mr. FISCHER. About 12:20.

Mr. BELIN. 12:20?

Mr. FISCHER. Yes, sir.

Mr. BELIN. And where were you standing on the corner of Houston and Elm?

Mr. FISCHER. We were standing right on the curb—uh—on the southwest corner of Elm and Houston.

Mr. BELIN. Where were you with relation to that lagoon that's there?

Mr. FISCHER. Well, that lagoon is rather long. We were standing in front of it, across the sidewalk. I believe it's the curb and the sidewalk and this   little bit of grass, and then the lagoon. And we were standing right on the curb there.

Mr. BELIN. You were standing on the curb at about the point where the actual curve of the curb is at the intersection—or not?

Mr. FISCHER. I'd say where the curb starts to curve. Because, when the shots were fired, we looked around at the motorcade and couldn't see it—because—uh—of the people that were standing along the curb there. We just couldn't see it. Had we been on further around, we could have just looked down the street and seen it.

Mr. BELIN. So, you would have been really standing on the curb which would be the west curb of Houston Street, just where it starts to make the curve to go onto Elm there. Is that correct?

Mr. FISCHER. That's correct.

Mr. BELIN. Now, would you describe what you saw as you were standing on that curb?

Mr. FISCHER. About 10 or 15 seconds before the parade—first car of the parade came around the corner.

Mr. BELIN. Now what corner is that?

Mr. FISCHER. Of Houston and Main.

Mr. BELIN. Uh-huh.

Mr. FISCHER. Which would have been the first time we could have seen any of the cars because of the building—about 10 or 15 seconds before the first car came around that corner, Bob punched me and said, "Look at that guy there in that window." And he made some remark—said, "He looks like he's uncomfortable"—or something.

And I looked up and I watched the man for, oh, I'd say, 10 or 15 seconds. It was until the first car came around the corner of Houston and Main. And, then, when that car did come around the corner, I took my attention off of the man in the window and started watching the parade. The man held my attention for 10 or 15 seconds, because he appeared uncomfortable for one, and, secondly, he wasn't watching—uh—he didn't look like he was watching for the parade. He looked like he was looking down toward the Trinity River and the triple underpass down at the end—toward the end of Elm Street. And—uh—all the time I watched him, he never moved his head, he never—he never moved anything. Just was there transfixed.

Mr. BELIN. In what window did you see the man?

Mr. FISCHER. It was the corner window on Houston Street facing Elm, in the fifth or sixth floor.

Mr. BELIN. On what side of the—first of all, what building was this you saw him in?

Mr. FISCHER. The Texas School Book Depository Building.

Mr. BELIN. And what side of the building would the window have been in?

Mr. FISCHER. It would have been—well, as you're looking toward the front of the building, it would have been to your right.

Mr. BELIN. Well, the building itself has four sides—a north, east, south, and a west side—the entire sides of the building. Would this have been the north, south, east, or west side of the building?

Mr. FISCHER. It would have been the south side—the entrance.

Mr. BELIN. All right. Now, on that south side of the building—now, was it the center part of the south side, the east part of the south side, or the west part of the south side?

Mr. FISCHER. The east part of the south side.

Mr. BELIN. All right.

Now, with reference to the east corner of the south side there—would it have been the first window next to that corner, the second, the third, or the fourth—or what?

Mr. FISCHER. First window.

Mr. BELIN. From the east corner of the south side?

Mr. FISCHER. Yes.

Mr. BELIN. Do you remember anything about the man? Could you describe his appearance at all? First of all, how much of him could you see?

Mr. FISCHER. I could see from about the middle of his chest past the top of his head.

Mr. BELIN. All right.

Mr. FISCHER. He was in the—as you're looking toward that window, he was in the lower right portion of the window. He seemed to be sitting a little forward.

And he had—he had on an open-neck shirt, but it—uh—could have been a sport shirt or a T-shirt. It was light in color; probably white, I couldn't tell whether it had long sleeves or whether it was a short-sleeved shirt, but it was open-neck and light in color.

Uh—he had a slender face and neck—uh—and he had a light complexion—he was a white man. And he looked to be 22 or 24 years old.

Mr. BELIN. Do you remember anything about the color of his hair?

Mr. FISCHER. His hair seemed to be—uh—neither light nor dark; possibly a light—well, possibly a—well, it was a brown was what it was; but as to whether it was light or dark, I can't say.

Mr. BELIN. Did he have a thick head of hair or did he have a receding hair-line—or couldn't you tell?

Mr. FISCHER. I couldn't tell. He couldn't have had very long hair, because his hair didn't seem to take up much space—of what I could see of his head. His hair must have been short and not long.

Mr. BELIN. Well, did you see a full view of his face or more of a profile of it, or what was it?

Mr. FISCHER. I saw it at an angle but, at the same time, I could see—I believe I could see the tip of his right cheek as he looked to my left.

Mr. BELIN. Now, could you be anything more definite as to what direction he was looking at?

Mr. FISCHER. He looked to me like he was looking straight at the triple underpass.

Mr. BELIN. Down what street?

Mr. FISCHER. Elm Street.

Mr. BELIN. Down Elm?

Mr. FISCHER. Toward the end of Elm Street.

Mr. BELIN. As it angles there and goes under the triple underpass there?

Mr. FISCHER. Yes, sir.

Mr. BELIN. Could you see his hands?

Mr. FISCHER. No.

Mr. BELIN. Could you see whether or not he was holding anything?

Mr. FISCHER. No; I couldn't see.

Mr. BELIN. Could you see any other objects in the window?

Mr. FISCHER. There were boxes and cases stacked all the way from the bottom to the top and from the left to the right behind him. It looked—uh—it's possible that there weren't cases directly behind him because I couldn't see because of him. But—uh—all the rest of the window—a portion behind the window—there were boxes. It looked like there was space for a man to walk through there between the window and the boxes. But there were boxes in the window, or close to the window there.

Mr. BELIN. Could you see any other people in any other windows there that you remember?

Mr. FISCHER. I couldn't see any other people in the windows. I don't remember seeing any others.

Mr. BELIN. By this, do you mean that you are sure there were none, or that you just do not remember seeing any?

Mr. FISCHER. I don't remember seeing any.

Mr. BELIN. Now, after you saw the man, then the motorcade turned onto Houston from Main—is that correct?

Mr. FISCHER. Yes.

Mr. BELIN. Did you ever see the man again in the window?

Mr. FISCHER. No.

Mr. BELIN. Did you ever look back at the window?

Mr. FISCHER. I never looked back at the window.

Mr. BELIN. Well, could you describe what happened as you watched the motorcade turn? First, about how fast did the motorcade appear to be going?

Mr. FISCHER. When the motorcade passed me, it was—uh—the driver was in process of making the wide turn there from Houston to Elm, and he was going very slow. I'd say, uh—10–15 miles an hour.

Mr. BELIN. All right.

Then what happened?

Mr. FISCHER. Well, the motorcade—the limousine made the wide turn and—uh—they went out of our view just as they began to straighten up onto Elm Street because there were people standing along the curb all the way around—and that's when the limousine went out of my view and I started watching the other cars behind the Presidential limousine.

Mr. BELIN. And then what happened?

Mr. FISCHER. Well, as I looked around to watch these other cars, I heard a shot. At first I thought it was a firecracker. And—uh—everybody got quiet. There was no yelling or shouting or anything. Everything seemed to get real still. And—uh—the second shot rang out, and then everybody—from where I was standing—everybody started to scatter. And—uh—then the third shot.

At first, I thought there were four, but as I think about it more, there must have been just three.

Mr. BELIN. At first, you thought there were four shots?

Mr. FISCHER. Yes.

Mr. BELIN. Now, you said the first one you thought was a firecracker?

Mr. FISCHER. Yes.

Mr. BELIN. What about the second one? Did you think that was a firecracker, too?

Mr. FISCHER. No. When the second shot rang out. It was too much like the first to be a firecracker. I have heard high-powered rifles fire before. The—uh—first shot fooled me, I think, because of the sound bouncing off the buildings. But the second shot was too much like the first and it was too loud—both shots were too loud to be a firecracker. And I knew it was a shot.

Mr. BELIN. Have you had any experience with high-powered rifles before?

Mr. FISCHER. Very little; but I have shot several.

Mr. BELIN. What about the third shot? Did you think that was a firecracker or what?

Mr. FISCHER. No; I knew it was a shot, too. I knew someone was shooting at something. Uh—it didn't—it still didn't dawn on me that anyone would try to shoot at the President, but I knew that somebody was shooting at something. I didn't know whether it was a real pistol or a real rifle—but I knew somebody was shooting a firearm.

Mr. BELIN. Where did the shots appear to be coming from?

Mr. FISCHER. They appeared to be coming from just west of the School Book Depository Building. There were some railroad tracks and there were some railroad cars back in there.

Mr. BELIN. And they appeared to be coming from those railroad cars?

Mr. FISCHER. Well, that area somewhere. From where I was standing, I couldn't see the cars themselves until I had run across the street and up the hill.

Mr. BELIN. The shots seemed to be how far apart?

Mr. FISCHER. That's hard to say. I've been thinking about that. And-uh—I'd guess—3 to 4 seconds.

Mr. BELIN. Was that between the first and the second or between the second and the third?

Mr. FISCHER. Between both. As far as I can remember, the shots were evenly spaced.

Mr. BELIN. Is there anything else about the shots that you remember?

Mr. FISCHER. No—only that they were very loud.

Mr. BELIN. Anything else about the man in the window that you remember?

Mr. FISCHER. (Pausing before reply.) No.

Mr. BELIN. All right. What did you do or see or hear after you hear the shots?

Mr. FISCHER. After the second shot we, Bob and I both, started running down the sidewalk on Elm Street, on the south side of Elm, and there were still people that were milling around and shuffling around. When the second shot broke, like I say, a lot of people started running, some people still stood but a lot of people started running. Uh—and then when the third shot went off, we just almost reached the curb and then just as the limousine went under the triple underpass, we got to the street—Elm Street—where we could actually see—uh—well—where the shots had gone, and—uh—we ran across the street where there were a man, his wife and two children laying on the ground. Now, that was on the north side of Elm Street about halfway between Houston and the triple underpass and we ran down there where this man and his wife and two boys were. Someone was helping them up off the ground, and the man said at that time that the President had been shot.

And, after that, we stood there for 10 or 15 seconds and then we ran up to the top of the hill there where all the Secret Service men had run, thinking that that's where the bullets had come from since they seemed to be searching that area over there. They jumped off—out of cars and ran up the side of the hill there and onto the tracks where these passenger—freight cars were.

Mr. BELIN. Anything else that you remember?

Mr. FISCHER. (Pausing before reply.) No.

Mr. BELIN. What did you do after that, then?

Mr. FISCHER. After that, we went back up to the building where we work—the records building—and went on upstairs to the office. And that's where Bob and I separated and—he had some things to do—I think he had some stuff that had to go down to another office and he left. After we got up there, he got some paper and then left. I stayed there for a little while and——

Mr. BELIN. Well, first of all, about when did you get back to the records building do you feel?

Mr. FISCHER. Uh—it must have been 5—5 minutes after the first shot was fired. Something like that.

Mr. BELIN. All right. When you went back there, did you walk by the front of the Texas School Book Depository Building?

Mr. FISCHER. No; when we went back, we came—we went back the same way we came. We went straight across Elm and then up to Houston on the south side of Elm, and then crossed.

Mr. BELIN. Did you notice whether or not people were going in or coming out of the School Book Depository Building?

Mr. FISCHER. There seemed to be a lot of people around—uh—the front; but, of course, there were a lot of people all over the street.

Mr. BELIN. All right. You got back up to the building—the records building—and then what did you do?

Mr. FISCHER. Well, as I said, we went up to the fourth floor to our office. Uh—I stayed there for 5 or 10 minutes. Bob had left. And then I went next door in the purchasing department where they've got a radio. I was trying to—I didn't—I don't guess I really believed yet that it had happened—that the President had been shot. And—uh—I was trying to find out on the radio just exactly what did happen.

And I stayed in the purchasing department 5 minutes or so—well, 5 or 10 minutes, and then I went back down the hall where some people had a radio standing out in the hall. They had another station on, and still nobody knew anything.

Then, I went back to the office about—oh, maybe 5 or 10 minutes till 1, and-uh—we heard a bunch of sirens, police cars, and leaned out the window, and police cars were all surrounding the Texas School Book Depository Building. And when I saw all that and saw the detectives in the window, the officers, I knew that—I realized that the shots—that they must have the assassin in there or the man who did the shooting—or something was wrong with the building.

179

So, I realized then that it possibly was the man I saw since he was the only one I remember in a window and that it had something to do with the building—that it's possible that the man I saw had something to do with it.

About that time a deputy from the sheriff's office came up and asked me if I was Ronald Fischer, and I said, "Yes;" and he said that Sheriff Decker wanted to see me in his office right now.

Mr. BELIN. About what time was this now?

Mr. FISCHER. This was at—oh—1 o'clock on or about 1 o'clock.

Mr. BELIN. You then went to Sheriff Decker's office?

Mr. FISCHER. I went to Decker's office and—uh—Bob Edwards was in there. He looked up—and he had given them my name and told them—at least, this is what he told me—that he told them that we had both been standing there together and had seen this man in the window of the School Book Depository Building. So, that's why they came to get me—because he had told them.

There were a lot of other people in the office—12 or 15 other people. They all seemed to be connected with it in some way or another. And I noticed, too, in Sheriff Decker's office was this man and woman and two boys that we had talked to down the street there on Elm that had hit the ground when the shots started.

Mr. BELIN. Now, this man that you saw in the window—did he appear to be standing or sitting—or couldn't you tell?

Mr. FISCHER. He must not have been standing because I don't think the floor was that far away. He could have been standing—I'll take that back. He would have had to have been crouched over. He didn't look like he was crouched over or bent over. He must have been—I'm guessing—but I'm thinking he must have been on his knees or maybe sitting, on a box maybe. But he—I don't think that it's possible that he was standing.

Mr. BELIN. Was he sitting or crouching, or whatever he was doing, in a straight-up position?

Mr. FISCHER. No; he was leaning forward slightly.

Mr. BELIN. About how far forward was he leaning—or couldn't you tell?

Mr. FISCHER. Oh, it was slightly—enough to where I could tell, but—oh—his head wasn't out of the window and his head wasn't past the window sill. If he had been much further back in, it would have been hard for me to see him at all.

Mr. BELIN. Now, sometime afterwards, you signed a written statement at the sheriff's office—is that it?

Mr. FISCHER. Yes.

Mr. BELIN. And, later, did some policemen bring out a picture of an individual and ask you to try and identify him?

Mr. FISCHER. Yes.

Mr. BELIN. Did they tell you whose picture it was?

Mr. FISCHER. Yes.

Mr. BELIN. Whose picture did they say it was?

Mr. FISCHER. Well, they actually showed me two pictures—one of Lee Harvey Oswald, and one of Jack Ruby.

Mr. BELIN. All right. And what did you say?

Mr. FISCHER. I told them that that could have been the man.

Mr. BELIN. Now, which one did you say could have been the man?

Mr. FISCHER. Lee Harvey Oswald. That that could have been the man that I saw in the window of the School Book Depository Building, but that I was not sure. It's possible that a man fit the general description that I gave—but I can't say for sure.

Mr. BELIN. Was there anything different—do you remember the picture?—between the picture you saw and the man you saw in the window?

Mr. FISCHER. Yes; one thing—and that is in the picture he looked like he hadn't shaved in several days at least. And—uh—I don't know whether at that distance, looking at him from the street in the School Book Depository Building—if I could have been able to—if I could have seen that. I think, if he had been unshaven in the window, it would have made his complexion appear—well—rather dark; but I remember his complexion was light; that is, unless he had just a light beard.

Mr. BELIN. Was the sun shining on his face when you saw him in the window or not—or don't you remember?

Mr. FISCHER. No; uh—no the sun wasn't shining on his face. He was back in the shadow of the window.

Mr. BELIN. When did the policeman come out with this picture—on the same day or on the next day?

Mr. FISCHER. No; it was—uh—no, it was several days after. I can't remember whether it was a week or 2 weeks or—it was at least a week. I don't remember exactly when it was but it was a week, at least.

Mr. BELIN. Let me ask you this: Was there anything else different between the man you saw in the picture and the man you saw in the window?

Mr. FISCHER. (Pausing before reply.) No.

Mr. BELIN. What about the color of his hair? Do you remember what the color of the hair was of the man in the picture?

Mr. FISCHER. Yes; it was brown. It was a darker shade of brown but it was definitely brown.

Mr. BELIN. What do you mean, "a darker shade of brown?"

Mr. FISCHER. Well, it wasn't—it wasn't—uh—well, I guess there are a lot of shades of brown. But it wasn't—uh—it wasn't a light brown. It was a—in the picture it showed up as definitely a darker brown. I can't think of anything to compare it to.

Mr. BELIN. Well, when you saw the man in the window, did he appear to have light brown hair, dark brown, medium brown—or what kind of hair did he have?

Mr. FISCHER. Well, it wasn't dark and it wasn't light. Uh—he didn't have black hair and he didn't have blonde hair. It—uh—must have been a brown but, like I say, there are a lot of different shades of brown and I'm not—I can't—it's hard for me to say just exactly what shade of brown I saw that he had. I know what shade he had in the picture but——

Mr. BELIN. Well, I hand you a copy of a statement which I believe—at least has the signature on it—and ask you to see if this looks like it's your signature?

Mr. FISCHER. [After perusing paper.] Yes.

Mr. BELIN. All right. I'm going to call this "Fischer Deposition Exhibit No. 1," and ask you to read this statement, which appears to be dated November 22, 1963, and ask you to state if there's anything in that statement that does not appear to be accurate.

(Thereupon, the statement of Mr. Fischer dated Nov. 22, 1963, is identified as "Fischer Deposition Exhibit No. 1.)

Mr. FISCHER. You want me to read this now?

Mr. BELIN. You can just read it to yourself and then you can tell me when you get through whether or not there is anything in that statement that doesn't appear to be accurate.

Mr. FISCHER. [After reading Exhibit No. 1.] That is correct.

Mr. BELIN. Is this what you told these people there?

Mr. FISCHER. Yes.

Mr. BELIN. Now, in this statement it says that the man appeared to be in his twenties—is that what you told them?

Mr. FISCHER. Yes.

Mr. BELIN. It says that all you could see was his head, now you've told me here today that you could see his chest?

Mr. FISCHER. Yes; from the middle of his chest up. I could see his shoulders. Uh—the man taking that particular piece of paper was a court reporter in the records building, and he didn't—he didn't relate—he had about 12 of these things to take—well, yeah, 12 or 15—however many people there were in the sheriff's office at that time. And he was, like I say, he was in a hurry to get it down and I said I could see his head—and, so, he put that down. And that is right. I could see his head.

Mr. BELIN. The statement here says that he was light-headed and that he had on an open-neck shirt. Did he have an open-neck shirt on?

Mr. FISCHER. Yes.

Mr. BELIN. Now, what about being light-headed?

Mr. FISCHER. By "light-headed," I meant that he didn't have black hair. He didn't have dark—he didn't have—well, when I say "dark," I mean black. He didn't have black hair. He didn't have blonde hair. When I said, "light-headed," I didn't mean blonde—or I would have said that, but—uh.

Mr. BELIN. What color of hair did you mean? Did you say "light-headed"?

Mr. FISCHER. I believe I did say "light-headed"—because I didn't—like I say—I didn't want it to appear that he was dark.

Mr. BELIN. By "dark," what color do you mean?

Mr. FISCHER. Black.

181

Mr. BELIN. Well, once again, I'll ask you, to the best of your recollection, what color hair did he have?

Mr. FISCHER. Uh—like I say, it's too hard for me to—uh—to tell one way or the other. At the distance I was, uh—it's just—it's just too hard for me to—I'm not going to say it because I don't know for sure, just exactly what shade of hair he did have. It wasn't blonde and it wasn't black. Somewhere in between. And it was a shade of brown that as to whether it was a dark brown, a light brown, a medium brown, or whatever you call it—I don't know.

Mr. BELIN. All right.

The statement says that you saw him in the window there. Do you remember how far the window was open?

Mr. FISCHER. The window was open almost all the way open if not, all the way open.

Mr. BELIN. By that "all the way"—when you have a window all the way open of that kind, of course, you just have a half of the window case that is open. Is that correct?

Mr. FISCHER. That's right, You still have half an area of the opening covered by glass.

Mr. BELIN. Was it the bottom area that was open or the top area?

Mr. FISCHER. The bottom area. The window looked to be—uh—a window that raised from the bottom up.

Mr. BELIN. And it appeared to be almost as fully open as you could, or fully open?

Mr. FISCHER. Or fully open. Yes—Or I wouldn't have been able to see the cases and see past the top of his head had it not been—and his shoulders.

Mr. BELIN. Now, on this written statement it says that you remember a tall girl walking into the School Book Depository Building there at about the time you saw the man?

Mr. FISCHER. Yes.

Mr. BELIN. Did you see such a girl walk in the building?

Mr. FISCHER. I can't remember. It must have been before. It must have been just before—uh—I saw the man in the window. I can't remember very well. It's been too long. I believe it was before I saw the man in the window that I saw her walk into the building. Like I say, I made a mental note of it but I didn't pay too much attention at the time.

Mr. BELIN. Now, sometime later, after November 22, you were interviewed by the FBI. Do you remember that?

Mr. FISCHER. Yes; in the records building.

Mr. BELIN. And did the FBI man have any pictures with him at all, or not?

Mr. FISCHER. I don't remember whether he had pictures or not. It seems like he did.

Mr. BELIN. Could you identify the man you saw in the window from any of the pictures?

Mr. FISCHER. Uh—not—in fact, I believe they asked me—I believe they did have pictures of him. It seems like I recall them asking me if it could have been the picture that they identified as Lee Harvey Oswald, or if it could have been the picture of Jack Ruby.

Mr. BELIN. Now what did you say about the Jack Ruby picture?

Mr. FISCHER. I told them that I didn't think it could be him because—uh—he didn't—he didn't have near enough hair, it didn't look like to me.

Mr. BELIN. What about his build?

Mr. FISCHER. And that, too. His face was just a little—uh—fat; whereas-uh—Oswald's picture was rather a slender face and neck.

Mr. BELIN. Did the man you saw in the window have a high forehead or a low forehead—or do you remember?

Mr. FISCHER. I can't—I can't remember seeing that—uh—that well. I don't know if I could have—if I saw it now, whether I could tell you whether he had a large forehead or not.

Mr. BELIN. Do you have any estimate of how far you were from that window when you saw him?

Mr. FISCHER. Uh—from the point where I was standing when I saw him in the window to him, it must have been, I would say, at least a hundred feet.

Mr. BELIN. All right. Now, did you ever tell anyone, or might you have told them, that you saw this person a minute or two before you saw the motorcade, rather than as you told us here today, 15 or 20 seconds before you first saw the motorcade?

Mr. FISCHER. Yes.

Mr. BELIN. Did you ever tell anyone it was a minute or two before you saw the motorcade?

Mr. FISCHER. Well, I might have said "a minute or two" in just terms. I don't remember saying that but.

Mr. BELIN. But what is the——

Mr. FISCHER. Shortly before.

Mr. BELIN. Shortly?

182

Mr. FISCHER. Shortly before.

Mr. BELIN. Do you definitely remember that it was this 15 or 20 seconds or so before you saw the motorcade, or might it have been a minute or two before you saw the motorcade?

Mr. FISCHER. I don't think it was over a minute. It could—it was less than a minute—because, as I recall, that's what—that's the reason I turned my attention from him and I looked back down the street.

Mr. BELIN. All right. Is there anything else you can think of that bears on the assassination, or anything you saw or did or heard that you haven't related here?

Mr. FISCHER. (Pausing before reply.) No.

Mr. BELIN. Did you say "No"?

Mr. FISCHER. No—I can't think of anything.

Mr. BELIN. Shortly before this interview began, you and I met for the first time—is that correct?

Mr. FISCHER. Yes.

Mr. BELIN. And we first chatted a few minutes about what you saw before we started taking your testimony on the record?

Mr. FISCHER. Yes.

Mr. BELIN. What is the fact as to whether or not I asked you to tell me your story or whether or not, instead, I asked you questions and tried to, in any way, lead you—or so forth?

Mr. FISCHER. I answered the questions as I think that I saw the events happen—as I saw the events happen. I was not quizzed on what to say or anything of that nature. I've merely related what I think that I saw.

Mr. BELIN. Is there anything that you told me of before we started taking the deposition that has not been included in this deposition—that you can think of?

Mr. FISCHER. [Pausing before reply.] No; not that I can think of.

Mr. BELIN. All right.

I believe that ends the deposition.

I want to thank you for your courtesy in coming here, Mr. Fischer. We appreciate your taking the time to do it. And we would also appreciate your conveying our appreciation to the Dallas County Auditor for letting you take this time off. Will you do that, please?

Mr. FISCHER. Yes; and thank you.

TESTIMONY OF ROBERT EDWIN EDWARDS

The testimony of Robert Edwin Edwards was taken at 11 a.m., on April 9, 1964, in the office of the U.S. attorney, 301 Post Office Building, Bryan and Ervay Streets, Dallas, Tex., by Mr. David W. Belin, assistant counsel of the President's Commission.

Mr. BELIN. Would you stand and raise your right hand and be sworn, please.

Do you solemnly swear that the testimony you are about to give will be the truth, the whole truth, and nothing but the truth, so help you God?

Mr. EDWARDS. I do.

Mr. BELIN. Your name, please?

Mr. EDWARDS. Robert Edwin Edwards.

Mr. BELIN. Where do you live, Mr. Edwards?

Mr. EDWARDS. Tahlequah, Okla.

Mr. BELIN. What do you do up there?

Mr. EDWARDS. I am going to school, college, Northeastern State College.

Mr. BELIN. What year of school are you in? Are you a freshman?

Mr. EDWARDS. No; I am a senior.

Mr. BELIN. You are a senior.

Mr. EDWARDS. Right.

Mr. BELIN. You have been going up to school there for several years?

Mr. EDWARDS. Two years I went there. I laid out last year and worked here in Dallas.

Mr. BELIN. Are you originally from Dallas?

Mr. EDWARDS. No; Graham, Tex.

Mr. BELIN. Where did you go to school?

Mr. EDWARDS. Graham High School in Graham, Tex.

Mr. BELIN. What did you do when you got out of school?

Mr. EDWARDS. I attended Abilene College.

Mr. BELIN. For a year?

Mr. EDWARDS. One year.

Mr. BELIN. Then what?

Mr. EDWARDS. Decatur Baptist College, which is a junior college.

Mr. BELIN. Then what did you do?

Mr. EDWARDS. Northeastern State College in Tahlequah, Okla.

Mr. BELIN. Laid out last year?

Mr. EDWARDS. Yes; I am finishing up this semester.

Mr. BELIN. What did you do last fall?

Mr. EDWARDS. I worked at the courthouse there.

Mr. BELIN. Is that the Dallas County Courthouse?

Mr. EDWARDS. Right.

Mr. BELIN. Where is that located?

Mr. EDWARDS. Let's say down on Main. I guess that would be sufficient.

Mr. BELIN. Main Street?

Mr. EDWARDS. Right.

Mr. BELIN. What street crosses there, do you remember?

Mr. EDWARDS. Well, you mean—give me a multiple choice and I will tell you.

Mr. BELIN. Harwood?

Mr. EDWARDS. No.

Mr. BELIN. Record?

Mr. EDWARDS. Right.

Mr. BELIN. What about Elm? Houston Street?

Mr. EDWARDS. It runs right behind it, if I am not mistaken.

Mr. BELIN. Were you working on the day the President came to Dallas?

Mr. EDWARDS. That's correct.

Mr. BELIN. That was November 22, 1963, I believe on a Friday, is that correct?

Mr. EDWARDS. That's correct.

Mr. BELIN. Did you have lunch before the motorcade came by or not?

Mr. EDWARDS. Yes; I did.

Mr. BELIN. Were you with anyone?

Mr. EDWARDS. Ronald Fischer.

Mr. BELIN. Ronald Fischer. Did he work with you in that office?

Mr. EDWARDS. Yes; he did.

Mr. BELIN. What were you doing there? By the way, what was your job?

Mr. EDWARDS. Just a utility clerk.

Mr. BELIN. What did you do after lunch?

Mr. EDWARDS. Came back and worked. I don't know exactly what time. For a little while until it was time for the President to come by, and then we left.

Mr. BELIN. Where did you go?

Mr. EDWARDS. Sir?

Mr. BELIN. Where did you go? You say you left. Where did you go?

Mr. EDWARDS. You mean left the office?

Mr. BELIN. Yes.

Mr. EDWARDS. Down on—I get the streets mixed up. Let's see, it would be Houston.

Mr. BELIN. Houston?

Mr. EDWARDS. Yes; I guess it would be Houston across the street in the little park right across from the courthouse, straight across from, facing the Depository.

Mr. BELIN. Well, let me ask you this now.

Mr. EDWARDS. That is Elm, I guess that is what it is. I guess that is Elm Street.

Mr. BELIN. When you used the word "Depository," what building do you mean?

Mr. EDWARDS. Texas School Book Depository.

Mr. BELIN. Texas School Book Depository Building?

Mr. EDWARDS. That building is at the corner of Elm and Houston, isn't it? Houston comes this way?

Mr. BELIN. Well, Houston, I believe, runs in a north-south direction. Elm runs in a east-west direction. Would a map help you at all?

Mr. EDWARDS. Yes.

Mr. BELIN. Let me see if I can get one for you here.

I am handing you a portion of a map. You see Houston Street here on this map?

Mr. EDWARDS. Yes.

Mr. BELIN. And you see Elm Street running this way, and the arrow pointing north, so Houston runs north and south.

Mr. EDWARDS. Where do you put the courthouse?

Mr. BELIN. The courthouse would be off this strip of map, but that is Elm and here is Houston. This little black square would be the Texas School Book Depository Building.

Mr. EDWARDS. It would have to be Houston and Elm.

Mr. BELIN. Here is Elm going in the parkway here. Do you see that right there?

Mr. EDWARDS. Yes.

Mr. BELIN. All right, Main Street would be running toward the bottom of the map?

Mr. EDWARDS. Yes; it was here.

Mr. BELIN. You are putting your finger at the point which would be to the west of Houston Street and to the south of Elm as it goes into the parkway, is that right?

You see the arrow pointing northwest would be to your left on the map, and you are going to be west of Houston Street and south of Elm going in the parkway, is that correct?

Mr. EDWARDS. Yes; I would be over here, right over here.

Mr. BELIN. Here is the parkway. Can you see it upside down here? Let's see if I can show you a picture.

Mr. EDWARDS. I am sorry. I don't have a picture.

Mr. BELIN. Here is a map and on the map north is shown with an arrow. You see it right here?

Mr. EDWARDS. Yes.

Mr. BELIN. Mr. Edwards, have you now located yourself on this map?

Mr. EDWARDS. Yes; I have.

Mr. BELIN. All right, where were you located?

Mr. EDWARDS. I guess I would plant myself right there.

Mr. BELIN. You are planting yourself now at a spot which would be on the west side of Houston Street near that entrance of Elm Street into the parkway   there, and you would be facing in a northerly direction toward the School Book Depository Building, is that correct?

Mr. EDWARDS. That's correct.

Mr. BELIN. Who were you standing with?

Mr. EDWARDS. Ronald Fischer.

Mr. BELIN. What time did you get there?

Mr. EDWARDS. I don't know.

Mr. BELIN. How long before the motorcade came by, if you know?

Mr. EDWARDS. Where is that little paper and I will tell you.

Mr. BELIN. Can you remember without looking at any paper right now?

Mr. EDWARDS. No; not really. I can guess.

Mr. BELIN. What is your best guess? We will understand that it is just a guess.

Mr. EDWARDS. Maybe I'd better not guess.

Mr. BELIN. All right, if you don't care to guess, that is fine. We would prefer that you not make any statement unless you feel fairly sure about it.

What did you do when you got to this point?

Mr. EDWARDS. Stood there and waited for the motorcade to come.

Mr. BELIN. Did you look around at all?

Mr. EDWARDS. Certainly.

Mr. BELIN. Did you ever take a look at the south side of the Texas School Book Depository Building? That would be facing—you would be looking at the south side of the building?

Mr. EDWARDS. Yes.

Mr. BELIN. Did you ever look at that at all?

Mr. EDWARDS. Yes.

Mr. BELIN. Before the motorcade came by?

Mr. EDWARDS. Yes.

Mr. BELIN. What did you see?

Mr. EDWARDS. Nothing of importance except maybe one individual who was up there in the corner room of the sixth floor which was crowded in among boxes.

Mr. BELIN. You say on the sixth floor?

Mr. EDWARDS. Yes.

Mr. BELIN. What portion of the sixth floor as you looked at the building to your right or to your left?

Mr. EDWARDS. To my right.

Mr. BELIN. How near the corner?

Mr. EDWARDS. The corner window.

Mr. BELIN. The corner window there?

Mr. EDWARDS. Right.

Mr. BELIN. Could you describe this individual at all? Was he a white man or a Negro?

Mr. EDWARDS. White man.

Mr. BELIN. Tall or short, if you know?

Mr. EDWARDS. I couldn't say.

Mr. BELIN. Did he have anything in his hand at all that you could see?

Mr. EDWARDS. No.

Mr. BELIN. Could you see his hands?

Mr. EDWARDS. I don't remember.

Mr. BELIN. What kind of clothes did he have on?

Mr. EDWARDS. Light colored shirt, short sleeve and open neck.

Mr. BELIN. How much of him could you see? Shoulder up, waist up, knees up, or what?

Mr. EDWARDS. From the waist on. From the abdomen or stomach up.

Mr. BELIN. Was the man fat, thin, or average in size?

Mr. EDWARDS. Oh, about average. Possibly thin.

Mr. BELIN. Could you tell whether he was light skinned or medium skin or what, if you could tell?

Mr. EDWARDS. No.

Mr. BELIN. Was the sun shining in or not, if you know?

Mr. EDWARDS. Don't know.

Mr. BELIN. Was the sun out that day?

Mr. EDWARDS. Yes.

Mr. BELIN. What color hair did the man have?

Mr. EDWARDS. Light brown.

Mr. BELIN. Light brown hair?

Mr. EDWARDS. That is what I would say; yes, sir.

Mr. BELIN. Did you see any other people on the sixth floor?

Mr. EDWARDS. No.

Mr. BELIN. Did you notice whether or not there were any, or just did you look and see any?

Mr. EDWARDS. I notice that there—I just didn't see any.

Mr. BELIN. What about the next floor above? Did you see any people on the floor above?

Mr. EDWARDS. No.

Mr. BELIN. What about on any floors below? See any people on the fifth floor?

Mr. EDWARDS. No.

Mr. BELIN. Fourth floor?

Mr. EDWARDS. No.

Mr. BELIN. Third floor?

Mr. EDWARDS. Possibly.

Mr. BELIN. Second floor?

Mr. EDWARDS. I believe so.

Mr. BELIN. First floor?

Mr. EDWARDS. I don't know.

Mr. BELIN. All right, now, you signed an affidavit for the sheriff's department where you stated that you saw a man at the window on the fifth floor, and the window was wide open all the way, and there was a stack of books around him, I could see. And you just told me you didn't see a man on the fifth floor. Was that affidavit correct or not?

Mr. EDWARDS. That is incorrect. That has been straightened out since.

Mr. BELIN. What do you mean it has been straightened out?

Mr. EDWARDS. Well, they discussed it with me later and I took that back. That was the FBI. It was the sixth floor, though.

Mr. BELIN. How do you know it was the sixth floor? Sixth floor rather than the fifth floor?

Mr. EDWARDS. I went with them and I showed them the window, and I didn't count the bottom floor.

Mr. BELIN. You mean the first time when you made the affidavit you didn't count the bottom floor?

Mr. EDWARDS. That's right.

Mr. BELIN. When you went out with the FBI, they asked you to point out the window?

Mr. EDWARDS. Right.

Mr. BELIN. And you pointed out the same window you saw on November 22?

Mr. EDWARDS. Yes, sir.

Mr. BELIN. Then you weren't counting the bottom floor?

186

Mr. EDWARDS. They did.

Mr. BELIN. Did you watch them count?

Mr. EDWARDS. Yes.

Mr. BELIN. Do you remember how many floors from the top it was?

Mr. EDWARDS. I think seven in all, seven floors. It is next to the top.

Mr. BELIN. Do you know whether or not the hair of the man was short, average, or long on the man that you saw in the window that day?

Mr. EDWARDS. Don't know.

Mr. BELIN. Now what conversation did you and Ronald Fischer have about this man, if anything? Do you remember what he said?

Mr. EDWARDS. I made a statement to Ronny that I wondered who he was hiding from since he was up there crowded in among the boxes, in a joking manner.

Mr. BELIN. You mean you said it in a joking manner?

Mr. EDWARDS. Yes.

Mr. BELIN. What did Fischer say to you?

Mr. EDWARDS. I don't recall what he said, but I know that we said a few things. It wasn't of any importance at the time. And we looked up at him, both of us.

Mr. BELIN. How long did you look at him?

Mr. EDWARDS. Just a few seconds.

Mr. BELIN. Then what took your attention away, if any, or did you just start looking somewhere else?

Mr. EDWARDS. Started looking somewhere else.

Mr. BELIN. How long after that did the motorcade come by?

Mr. EDWARDS. Thirty seconds or a minute.

Mr. BELIN. Anything else that you can remember that you or Ronald Fischer said?

Mr. EDWARDS. No.

Mr. BELIN. Anything else you can think of that might be relevant at all?

Mr. EDWARDS. No.

Mr. BELIN. How many shots did you hear, if you remember?

Mr. EDWARDS. Well, I heard one more then than was fired, I believe.

Mr. BELIN. You mean you said on the affidavit you heard four shots?

Mr. EDWARDS. I still right now don't know how many was fired. If I said four, then I thought I heard four.

Mr. BELIN. If you said four, you mean the affidavit—maybe we'd better introduce it into the record as Edward's Deposition Exhibit A. Where do you think the shots came from?

Mr. EDWARDS. I have no idea.

Mr. BELIN. In the affidavit you stated that the shots seemed to come from the building there. Did you really say that or not?

Mr. EDWARDS. No; I didn't say that.

Mr. BELIN. All right, anything else you can think of?

Mr. EDWARDS. No.

Mr. BELIN. I want to thank you for coming down here. You have an opportunity, if you want, to come back and read this deposition and sign it, or else you can waive the signing and reading of it and it will be sent directly to Washington by the court reporter. It makes no difference to us. You can read and sign or can waive reading and signing.

Mr. EDWARDS. I don't want to make an extra trip.

Mr. BELIN. Do you want to waive it then?

Mr. EDWARDS. Yes.

Mr. BELIN. Thank you, sir.

TESTIMONY OF MRS. JEAN LOLLIS HILL

The testimony of Mrs. Jean Lollis Hill was taken at 2:30 p.m., on March 24, 1964, in the office of the U.S. attorney, 301 Post Office Building, Bryan and Ervay Streets, Dallas, Tex., by Mr. Arlen Specter, assistant counsel of the President's Commission.

Mr. SPECTER. May the record show that Mrs. Jean Lollis Hill is present at this moment in response to a letter request that she appear and give a deposition to the President's Commission investigating the assassination of President Kennedy.

May I say for the record, Mrs. Hill, that the Commission is investigating all of the facts relating to the shooting and, and we have asked you to appear here today to tell us what you know, if anything, relating to the actual assassination, because we understand you were on the scene or nearby at that time.

May the record further reflect that Mrs. Hill was sent a letter under date of March 18, 1964. With that preliminary statement, I will ask you, Mrs. Hill, to stand and raise your right hand, if you will please.

Do you solemnly swear that the testimony you shall give before the President's Commission in this deposition proceeding will be the truth, the whole truth, and nothing but the truth, so help you God?

Mrs. HILL. I do.

Mr. SPECTER. Will you be seated, please, Mrs. Hill? And would you state your full name for the record?

Mrs. HILL. Jean Lollis Hill.

Mr. SPECTER. Mrs. Hill, have you received a letter request?

Mrs. HILL. Yes, sir; I have.

Mr. SPECTER. Under date of March 18, 1964?

Mrs. HILL. I have it here.

Mr. SPECTER. Well, when did you see that letter request?

Mrs. HILL. Well, I guess I got it 2 or 3 days afterward—March 18—so I must have gotten it Monday—no; I couldn't have gotten it yesterday—I got it Saturday.

Mr. SPECTER. That would have been March 21?

Mrs. HILL. That's right.

Mr. SPECTER. All right. May the record show that a court reporter is present and is taking verbatim transcript of the deposition of Mrs. Hill, with the court reporter, Mrs. Hill, and myself being present, and that all of the report is being transcribed and has been transcribed from the time Mrs. Hill arrived, is that correct, Mrs. Hill?

Mrs. HILL. That is correct.

Mr. SPECTER. Where were you on the day of November 22, 1963, at about noontime?

Mrs. HILL. I was standing directly across from the Texas School Depository Building on a grassy slope and the triangle toward the underpass.

Mr. SPECTER. And that would have been Dealey Plaza?

Mrs. HILL. If that's what the name of it is.

Mr. SPECTER. Now, would that be on the——

Mrs. HILL. It was to the left of the motorcade.

Mr. SPECTER. To the left of the motorcade as the motorcade proceeded forward?

Mrs. HILL. That's right.

Mr. SPECTER. So, you would have been on the south side of Elm Street?

Mrs. HILL. That's right.

Mr. SPECTER. Now, what had you done immediately before noontime, Mrs. Hill?

Mrs. HILL. We had been there for about an hour and a half and had been walking up and down and back and forth.

Mr. SPECTER. When you say "we" whom do you mean by that?

Mrs. HILL. My friend, Mary Moorman, that took the picture.

Mr. SPECTER. She had a camera with her?

Mrs. HILL. Yes; a Polaroid. We had been taking pictures all morning.

Mr. SPECTER. And did you have a camera with you?

Mrs. HILL. No.

Mr. SPECTER. And tell me what you observed as the President's motorcade passed by?

Mrs. HILL. You mean——

Mr. SPECTER. Start any place that you find most convenient and just tell me in your own way what happened.

Mrs. HILL. Well, as they came toward us, we had been taking pictures with this Polaroid camera and since it was a Polaroid we knew we had only one chance to get a picture, and at the time she had taken a picture just a few minutes before and I had grabbed it out of the camera and wrapped it and put it in my pocket. Just about that time he drew even with us.

Mr. SPECTER. And when you say "he" you mean?

Mrs. HILL. The President's car. We were standing on the curb and I jumped to the edge of the street and yelled, "Hey, we want to take your picture," to him and he was looking down in the seat—he and Mrs. Kennedy and their heads were turned toward the middle of the car looking down at something in the seat, which later turned out to be the roses, and I was so afraid he was going to look the other way because there were a lot of people across the street and we were, as far as I know, we were the only people down there in that area, and just as I yelled, "Hey," to him, he started to bring his head up to look at me and just as he did the shot rang out. Mary took the picture and fell on the ground and of course there were more shots.

188

Mr. SPECTER. How many shots were there altogether?

Mrs. HILL. I have always said there were some four to six shots. There were three shots—one right after the other, and a distinct pause, or just a moment's pause, and then I heard more.

Mr. SPECTER. How long a time elapsed from the first to the third of what you described as the first three shots?

Mrs. HILL. They were rapidly—they were rather rapidly fired.

Mr. SPECTER. Could you give me an estimate on the timespan on those three shots?

Mrs. HILL. No; I don't think I can.

Mr. SPECTER. Now, how many shots followed what you described as the first three shots?

Mrs. HILL. I think there were at least four or five shots and perhaps six, but I know there were more than three.

Mr. SPECTER. Now, much time elapsed from the very first shot until the very last shot, will you estimate?

Mrs. HILL. I don't think I could, properly, but my girl friend fell on the ground after about—during the shooting—right, I would say, just immediately after she had taken the picture—probably about the third shot. She fell on the ground and grabbed my slacks and said, "Get down, they're shooting." And, I knew they were but I was too stunned to move, so I didn't get down. I just stood there and gawked around.

Mr. SPECTER. Can't you give me any better idea on the sequence of the shots other than to say that there were three shots right in a row and then a moment's pause and an additional shot or shots.

Mrs. HILL. In what way?

Mr. SPECTER. Is there any way you could be more specific by way of time lapses among any of the shots, from the first to the second shot, the second to the third, or in that manner?

Mrs. HILL. The three were fired as though one person were firing; I mean, to me. They were fired just like you could reload and fire again or whatever you do with a gun.

Mr. SPECTER. With what sort of an action?

Mrs. HILL. I think that the firing that was done could have been done with the type gun that they say the assassinator used.

Mr. SPECTER. And what type gun was that, according to your understanding?

Mrs. HILL. A bolt action.

Mr. SPECTER. And how about the shots that followed the three shots, then, what would the sequence of timing have been on those?

Mrs. HILL. I thought they were different—I thought the sequence was different.

Mr. SPECTER. How will you describe the sequence?

Mrs. HILL. Quicker—more automatic.

Mr. SPECTER. Were there as few as four, as you recollected?

Mrs. HILL. I won't say positively, I think I can still seemingly hear it, and I would still say there were more, you know, I'm saying 4 to 6. I know there were at least 4, and I just almost swear that I heard 5 or 6.

Mr. SPECTER. Could there have been more than 6 that you heard?

Mrs. HILL. I couldn't say that I heard more than that.

Mr. SPECTER. Could you say for certain that you did not hear more than that?

Mrs. HILL. Yes; I didn't hear any more than that.

Mr. SPECTER. What was the position of the President, as best you recollect it, at the time the first shot was heard by you?

Mrs. HILL. He was slightly turned, he was sitting back in the seat, like turned toward Mrs. Kennedy and his head was down, and his hands were like this (indicating).

Mr. SPECTER. His hands were in his lap?

Mrs. HILL. No—not really.

Mr. SPECTER. How would you describe the position of his hands?

Mrs. HILL. He was sitting here [indicating] and Mrs. Kennedy—he was like this [indicating].

Mr. SPECTER. You are indicating the right hand on the left knee?

Mrs. HILL. Yes.

Mr. SPECTER. With the body turned slightly toward the person on his left?

Mrs. HILL. Yes.

Mr. SPECTER. Who would have been Mrs. Kennedy?

Mrs. HILL. Yes.

Mr. SPECTER. And were you watching him at this time?

Mrs. HILL. Yes, I was looking right at his face.

Mr. SPECTER. And what reaction, if any, did he have at the time of the first shot?

189

Mrs. HILL. As I said, I had yelled at him and he had started to raise his head up and I saw his head start to come up and all at once a bullet rang out and he slumped forward like this [indicating].

Mr. SPECTER. Lurched or slumped, as you say, to the left?

Mrs. HILL. Yes.

Mr. SPECTER. Did his head drop down?

Mrs. HILL. Yes; he was just, you know, slumping down like this.

Mr. SPECTER. Did you have a chance to see anything of Governor Connally at that exact second?

Mrs. HILL. There was a scrambling around in the front seat. I didn't know who was riding with him, I hadn't paid any attention to who was riding with him in the car, but I never did see Mrs. Connally. I guess my story is probably colored by what I have heard.

Mr. SPECTER. Tell me what you have heard that you think maybe that colored your story?

Mrs. HILL. About what the Connallys say about the shots, which shots hit where and everything.

Mr. SPECTER. What is that that you have heard?

Mrs. HILL. Well, I have heard that 1 shot hit Kennedy and also hit Connally, that the same shot that hit Kennedy hit Connally.

Mr. SPECTER. Where did you hear that, Mrs. Hill?

Mrs. HILL. I don't know.

Mr. SPECTER. What else have you heard?

Mrs. HILL. And also that Mrs. Connally jumped up and covered Mr. Connally with her body and pushed him to the floor, but I never did see Mrs. Connally.

Mr. SPECTER. Did you ever see Governor Connally?

Mrs. HILL. Yes; I did see him; I didn't know who he was, but I did see him and I knew that someone had been hit.

Mr. SPECTER. Where was he pushed in the car?

Mrs. HILL. Well, I just vaguely know that he was toward the front.

Mr. SPECTER. Well, was he in the front seat of the ear or was he between President Kennedy and the front seat of the car, or where was he?

Mrs. HILL. Between President Kennedy?

Mr. SPECTER. You know that there were jump seats in the car so that there would have been people sitting three positions forward, one in the back seat—President Kennedy and Mrs. Kennedy, on the right in the jump seat—Governor Connally and Mrs. Connally and in the front seat, two Secret Service agents—people sitting three positions forward?

Mrs. HILL. I saw the Secret Service agents.

Mr. SPECTER. Had you been, prior to the time I told you just now, familiar with that arrangement of the personnel in the car?

Mrs. HILL. Yes; I knew that, and as I said, I didn't know who the people were in the car because I am new here—I don't know the Connallys, I just knew that people were in the car.

Mr. SPECTER. Did you notice the person sitting in the jump seat on the right-hand side, that would be the person immediately in front of President Kennedy?

Mrs. HILL. Well, I would say it was Mr. Connally.

Mr. SPECTER. Did you observe him at any specific time?

Mrs. HILL. I saw a man fall to the floor.

Mr. SPECTER. And when, in point of time, did you see him fall?

Mrs. HILL. After the President was shot, but I wouldn't—it wasn't with the first shot. To me he wasn't hit when the first shot hit.

Mr. SPECTER. And what is the basis for your saying that, Mrs. Hill?

Mrs.. HILL. Well, I just think that he was hit after Kennedy was hit because, well, just the way that it looked, I would say that he was hit later.

Mr. SPECTER. Now, do you associate the time that Governor Connally appeared to have been hit with any specific shot that you heard?

Mrs. HILL. The second.

Mr. SPECTER. And what specifically did you observe at the time of the second shot?

Mrs. HILL. Well, that's what I thought had happened—that they had hit someone in the front part of the car.

Mr. SPECTER. And what did you observe at the time of the third shot?

Mrs. HILL. President Kennedy was hit again and he had further buffeted his body and I didn't realize at the time what it was—I remarked to my friends in the police station that day— did she notice his hair standing up, because it did. It just rippled up like this.

Mr. SPECTER. And at what time was that?

Mrs. HILL. On the third shot.

Mr. SPECTER. Did you notice Governor Connally at the time of the third shot?

Mrs. HILL. I never saw him again.

Mr. SPECTER. What occurred at the time of the fourth shot which you believe you heard?

Mrs. HILL. Well, at that time, of course, there was a pause and I took the other shots—about that time Mary grabbed me and was yelling and I had looked away from what was going on here and I thought, because I guess from the TV and movies, that it was Secret Service agents shooting back. To me, if somebody shoots at somebody they always shoot back and so I just thought that that's what it was and I thought, well, they are getting him and shooting back, you know; I didn't know.

Mr. SPECTER. Where was the President's car at the time you thought you heard the fourth shot?

Mrs. HILL. The motorcade came to almost a halt at the time the shots rang out, and I would say it was just approximately, if not—it couldn't have been in the same position, I'm sure it wasn't, but just a very, very short distance from where it had been. It was just almost stunned.

Mr. SPECTER. And how about the time of the fifth shot, where do you think the President's car was?

Mrs. HILL. That was during those shots, I think it wasn't any further than a few feet—further down.

Mr. SPECTER. Which shots, now—you mean the fourth, and perhaps the fifth and perhaps the sixth shot?

Mrs. HILL. Yes.

Mr. SPECTER. Are you able to say what anyone was doing or what events were occurring at the time of the fourth through perhaps the sixth shots which you have testified about?

Mrs. HILL. Well, as I said, at that time she was yelling at me and on the ground.

Mr. SPECTER. Who was yelling at you?

Mrs. HILL. Mary, my friend, was yelling at me and she was down on the ground and I looked up and I could see everyone was just stunned, there was immobility all around and I just stood there looking around and I'm sure there wasn't a pause—it seemed like an eternity but I'm sure there was just a slight pause before things started moving again.

Mr. SPECTER. Were the shots over by that time when things started moving again?

Mrs. HILL. Yes.

Mr. SPECTER. Then what happened on the scene?

Mrs. HILL. Well, they say Mrs. Kennedy climbed up on the back of the car.

Mr. SPECTER. Did you observe that?

Mrs. HILL. No; I have seen pictures that show that she must have, but I ran across the street.

Mr. SPECTER. To the——

Mrs. HILL. Other side.

Mr. SPECTER. North side of Elm Street?

Mrs. HILL. That's right. I saw a man up there running, or getting away or walking away or something—I would say he was running.

Mr. SPECTER. Where was that man when you first saw him?

Mrs. HILL. He was right up there by the School Depository, just—not at the corner where they say the shots came from, at the other end, right up on the slope at the top of the slope.

Mr. SPECTER. Would that be in front of the School Book Depository Building?

Mrs. HILL. Yes.

Mr. SPECTER. At the west end?

Mrs. HILL. More to the west end.

Mr. SPECTER. Would it be between the westernmost point of the building and some other point in the building? Was he at the westernmost point or farther east than the westernmost point?

Mrs. HILL. I would say he was farther east than the westernmost point.

Mr. SPECTER. Would you draw a diagram for me in rough outline, starting with Houston Street——

Mrs. HILL. Yes; but I can't do this very well.

Mr. SPECTER. Permit me to draw an outline, then, to get your bearing here and realizing that I want your recollection, and I'll ask you the questions. Assume that Houston Street is the street which I am marking Houston. Assume that this is Main Street. Assume that Elm Street curves down in the manner that I am drawing and marking.

Mrs. HILL. All right.

191

Mr. SPECTER. Assume that the Texas School Book Depository is this large building which I will mark "TSBD." Now, would you place with the letter "A" where you were at the time the President went by?

Mrs. HILL. Well, I would have to place the President first.

Mr. SPECTER. Fine—place him with the letter "X".

Mrs. HILL. All right—if he were here——

Mr. SPECTER. Now, was he in the center of the street or on the side of the street?

Mrs. HILL. He was on the side—he wasn't just completely over there, but he was past the center of the street and we were——

Mr. SPECTER. Now, place yourself with the letter "A".

Mrs. HILL. Right there [indicating].

Mr. SPECTER. Make it a big printed "A" for us.

Mrs. HILL. Okay. [Complied with request of counsel Specter.]

Mr. SPECTER. Now, would you place the position you ran to after the President's car went by?

Mrs. HILL. By that time, I'm sure the car was here—it was on down a little way, and I ran behind here.

Mr. SPECTER. Draw a line to where you ran.

Mrs. HILL. All right—I don't know whether I've got this just right—but I ran approximately right up through here.

Mr. SPECTER. Put a "B" here where you were when you came to a stop on the other side of the street.

Mrs. HILL. These steps.

Mr. SPECTER. Now, where were you when you first noticed the——

Mrs. HILL. These steps that go up—I guess you've looked at the site, there are some steps down there that go up to that promenade, or whatever you call it.

Mr. SPECTER. That go in a generally westerly direction?

Mrs. HILL. Yes.

Mr. SPECTER. Beyond the Texas School Book Depository Building?

Mrs. HILL. Yes; and I was just on this side——

Mr. SPECTER. "This side"—you are meaning—the east of it?

Mrs. HILL. The east of it.

Mr. SPECTER. Were you beyond the westernmost point of the Texas School Book Depository Building?

Mrs. HILL. No.

Mr. SPECTER. You were still in front of that building?

Mrs. HILL. That's right.

Mr. SPECTER. Now, is the letter "B" now in the position where you were when you first saw that man?

Mrs. HILL. Yes.

Mr. SPECTER. Where was that man, indicating with the letter "C," where he was? He was very close to you?

Mrs. HILL. Well, he was at the top of this hill—you don't leave me any space in here—I mean, there's a distance in here greater than what is shown here.

Mr. SPECTER. He was between Elm Street and the Depository Building?

Mrs. HILL. Yes.

Mr. SPECTER. And where did you see him going?

Mrs. HILL. I saw him go toward the tracks, toward the railroad tracks to the west?

Mr. SPECTER. What did you observe about that man, if anything?

Mrs. HILL. That he just had on a brown overcoat and a hat.

Mr. SPECTER. Why was your attention attracted to him?

Mrs. HILL. Because he was the only thing moving up there. The other people were all grief stricken and standing there and I don't know what I would have done with him when I got up there, but I don't know why I even had the instinct to run, and I don't know that it is anything even connected with this, but since I had already—I have told it and it is part of my recollection, I am just stating it again.

Mr. SPECTER. Well, was there anything about the man that attracted your attention to him beside the fact that he was moving?

Mrs. HILL. I just thought at the time—that's the man that did it.

Mr. SPECTER. Why did you think that this was the man that did it?

Mrs. HILL. I just don't know—I mean—that was my thought.

Mr. SPECTER. Did you see any weapon in his hand?

Mrs. HILL. No; I never saw a weapon during the whole time, in anyone's hand.

Mr. SPECTER. Did you see that man from the front?

Mrs. HILL. As well as I remember, now, when I saw him he was turning and going to the west.

Mr. SPECTER. Was he in the process of turning when you first saw him?

Mrs. HILL. Yes; I would say he was turning.

Mr. SPECTER. So that you had some view of his front part of his body?

Mrs. HILL. Yes.

Mr. SPECTER. And did you see any weapon at that time?

Mrs. HILL. No, sir; he was three-fourths turned by the time I did see him.

Mr. SPECTER. Could you see both of his hands at that time?

Mrs. HILL. No.

Mr. SPECTER. Could you see one of his hands at that time?

Mrs. HILL. No; I do not even remember seeing his hands.

Mr. SPECTER. I mean, if he was turning, his hands would have been visible, wouldn't they?

Mrs. HILL. They surely would have been.

Mr. SPECTER. So, what you are saying is, you don't have any recollection of seeing his hands?

Mrs. HILL. I have no recollection—that's right.

Mr. SPECTER. But from the position of his body, his hands would have been in the position where they could have been observed?

Mrs. HILL. That's right—surely.

Mr. SPECTER. And do you have any recollection of observing any weapon in either hand?

Mrs. HILL. No; I never saw a weapon the whole time.

Mr. SPECTER. Had you moved from point "A" at the time you first saw him?

Mrs. HILL. That's the reason I ran across the street.

Mr. SPECTER. Did you see him while you were at point "A"?

Mrs. HILL. Do you mean prior to the shots? Yes; I saw him, that's the reason why I went across the street.

Mr. SPECTER. So, you saw him when you were at point "A"?

Mrs. HILL. That's right—that's the reason I left that spot.

Mr. SPECTER. And he was at point "C" when you first saw him?

Mrs. HILL. That's right.

Mr. SPECTER. Did he move before you moved?

Mrs. HILL. His moving made me start after him.

Mr. SPECTER. So, he did move before you moved?

Mrs. HILL. Yes; and as I came across the street—as I said—I never did see Mrs. Kennedy get up or anything, because when I ran across the street, the first motorcycle that was right behind her nearly hit me turning around, because I looked up in his face and he was looking all around.

Mr. SPECTER. You mean the policeman?

Mrs. HILL. Yes; and I don't think he ever did see me. I just looked at him and dodged then because I thought his wheel was going to hit me, and I don't think he ever did see me, and I ran across through there and started up the hill. When I looked down on the ground, I mean, as I was running up the hill to catch that man, I looked down and saw some red stuff and I thought, "Oh, they got him, he's bleeding," and this is embarrassing, but it turned out to be Koolade or some sort of red drink.

Mr. SPECTER. You thought they had gotten the man who was running away?

Mrs. HILL. Yes.

Mr. SPECTER. You thought that perhaps the second burst of shots you heard were being directed toward him by the Secret Service?

Mrs. HILL. I just thought, "Oh, goodness, the Secret Service is shooting back."

Mr. SPECTER. Can you describe what that man looked like?

Mrs. HILL. He wasn't——

Mr. SPECTER. How tall was he?

Mrs. HILL. He wasn't very tall.

Mr. SPECTER. Was he more than 5 feet tall, or can you give me any meaningful description of him?

Mrs. HILL. Well, yes; but I don't want to.

Mr. SPECTER. Why is that?

Mrs. HILL. Well, because I had told several people and I also said it that day down there and the person that I described, and I am fully aware that his whereabouts have been known at

193

all times, and that it seems that I am merely using a figure and converting it to my story, but the person that I saw looked a lot like—I would say the general build as I would think Jack Ruby would from that position. But I have talked with the FBI about this and I told them I realized that his whereabouts had been covered at all times and of course I didn't—at that time I didn't realize that the shots were coming from the building. I frankly thought they were coming from the knoll.

Mr. SPECTER. Why did you think they were coming from the knoll?

Mrs. HILL. That was just my idea where they were coming from.

Mr. SPECTER. Would you draw the knoll on the picture, where you mean by the knoll?

Mrs. HILL. This area in front of the Book Depository—it's right here.

Mr. SPECTER. Just draw me a circle as to where you had a general impression the shots were coming from.

Mrs. HILL. This is a hill and it was like they were coming from right in there. That's when I looked up and saw that man and all the rest of the people were stunned and not moving in that area and yet he was getting out of there—I thought that probably he had done it, and so I went to catch him, for some reason.

Mr. SPECTER. Now, did you have a conscious impression of the source of the first shot that you heard, that is, where it came from?

Mrs. HILL. Well, evidently I didn't because the only conscious recollection I have of that—I mean—until all this other came out—I had always thought that they came from the knoll.

Mr. SPECTER. Did you have any conscious impression of where the second shot came from?

Mrs. HILL. No.

Mr. SPECTER. Any conscious impression of where this third shot came from?

Mrs. HILL. Not any different from any of them. I thought it was just people shooting from the knoll—I did think there was more than one person shooting.

Mr. SPECTER. You did think there was more than one person shooting?

Mrs. HILL. Yes, sir.

Mr. SPECTER. What made you think that?

Mrs. HILL. The way the gun report sounded and the difference in the way they were fired—the timing.

Mr. SPECTER. What was your impression as to the source of the second group of shots which you have described as the fourth, perhaps the fifth, and perhaps the sixth shot?

Mrs. HILL. Well, nothing, except that I thought that they were fired by someone else.

Mr. SPECTER. And did you have any idea where they were coming from?

Mrs. HILL. No; as I said, I thought they were coming from the general direction of that knoll.

Mr. SPECTER. Well, did you think that the Secret Service was firing them from that knoll?

Mrs. HILL. I said I didn't know—I really don't.

Mr. SPECTER. You just had the general impression that shots were coming from the knoll?

Mrs. HILL. Yes.

Mr. SPECTER. And you had the general impression that the Secret Service was firing the second group of shots at the man who fired the first group of shots?

Mrs. HILL. That's right.

Mr. SPECTER. But you had no specific impression as to the source of those shots?

Mrs. HILL. No.

Mr. SPECTER. Did you get a very good look at that man, who you say was starting to run?

Mrs. HILL. Well, as I said, when I looked down at this red stuff on the ground, I said, "Oh," you know, to myself, "they hit him." You know, I was going to follow that, and when I looked up again, I looked all around and I couldn't see him anywhere and I kept running toward the train tracks and I looked all around out there and I couldn't see him—I looked everywhere and I heard someone yelling something about—it was just this voice that was yelling, "It looks like he got away," or something—I thought I had been right, you know, that he had really gone up there and he had gotten away some way in the tracks or had gone around behind the Depository, and so, I didn't know where he had gone. By that time I saw policemen—where he had gone. By that time I saw policemen—some were coming off of their motorcycles just around the curb here—just at the underpass here, and of course, the motorcade sped away and the policemen were coming from all sorts of different directions, people were closing in, and all I could think of was, "I want to get out of here fast. I don't want to be caught by anybody. I don't want to be in on anything," and everytime anybody would come toward me I would go another way until I got off of that hill back up there where the tracks were.

194

Mr. SPECTER. Did you run up toward the hill?

Mrs. HILL. Yes; I ran up toward the railroad tracks.

Mr. SPECTER. Let me draw the triple underpass there, and you ran up to what point—where? About the point of "D" here?

Mrs. HILL. Yes.

Mr. SPECTER. Why did you run up there—after the man?

Mrs. HILL. I was still looking for him. I didn't know where he had gone. I heard lots of people yelling, "Did he get away, did he get away, and which way did he go."

Mr. SPECTER. You were trying to catch him?

Mrs. HILL. Yes.

Mr. SPECTER. But you couldn't find him any more?

Mrs. HILL. No; I just couldn't find him again. When I stopped to look down at the grass, at this red stuff and when I looked back up, by that time everyone was screaming and moving around.

Mr. SPECTER. And where were you when you looked down at the ground? Point it out to me on the diagram.

Mrs. HILL. The steps that go up to this colonnade thing right there and I saw it right about here.

Mr. SPECTER. Well, mark it with the letter "E" there.

Mrs. HILL. All right.

Mr. SPECTER. Now, a moment ago you said you didn't want to say anything more about the identity of the man. Why did you tell me that, Mrs. Hill?

Mrs. HILL. Well, because I have had an awful lot of fun made of me over being a witness in this and I'm real tired of it.

Mr. SPECTER. Who made fun of you?

Mrs. HILL. Well, quite a lot of people.

Mr. SPECTER. Anybody connected with the official investigation in the case?

Mrs. HILL. No, oh, no; it was just people, but people that I know.

Mr. SPECTER. All right, and why have they made fun of you, because of your identification of who that man was?

Mrs. HILL. Yes.

Mr. SPECTER. Any other reason?

Mrs. HILL. Yes—I saw a dog in the car. They kept asking me, and I even gave that out on a radio or TV interview that I had seen a dog in the car.

Mr. SPECTER. In which car?

Mrs. HILL. Between the President and Mrs. Kennedy, and they kept asking me what kind of a dog and I said, "I don't know, I wasn't interested in what was in the seat," but I said, "It was white and fuzzy," and I said, "It was something white and kind of fuzzy and it was in the seat between them," and I said, "I just got to thinking—it must be a small dog," because I had remarked to my girl friend as they were taking us in the police station, I said, "Why?" I said, "I could see Liz Taylor or the Gabors traveling with a bunch of dogs, but I can't see the Kennedys traveling with dogs. Why would they have a dog with them on tour?" And, when we remarked about that she and I both—and I said, "Did you see it? What kind of a dog was it? Why were they taking a dog?" I found out later that it was those roses in the seat, but I knew they were looking at something and I just barely glanced and I saw this.

Mr. SPECTER. Is there any other reason people made fun of you?

Mrs. HILL. Well, basically, the people that made fun of me was my husband, and, of course, that was because—does this have to go in the record?

Mr. SPECTER. Yes; only in the sense that we are putting everything on the record. This really isn't too important but it is the best procedure to follow, that everything be written down.

Mrs. HILL. Well.

Mr. SPECTER. In a situation of this sort.

Mrs. HILL. Well, because I talked with an Oklahoma twang, and called Mrs. Kennedy "Jackie" and I said, "He pitched forward in Jackie's lap," and I just didn't rehearse it and do it right at all, because I didn't know it was going to be taken down.

Mr. SPECTER. And those are the reasons your husband made fun of you?

Mrs. HILL. Yes; and because I saw a dog and he was thoroughly hilarious when he found out that it was roses in the back seat and that I had seen a dog, and he said, "Of all people in the United States you would have to see a dog."

Mr. SPECTER. Has anybody made fun of you besides your husband?

Mrs. HILL. No; not really, but he's done enough for a whole bunch of people.

Mr. SPECTER. Now, going back to the question of the description of this man, can you describe him in any more detail than you already have?

Mrs. HILL. No; I haven't—I can't.

Mr. SPECTER. His height you said was about the height of Jack Ruby?

Mrs. HILL. That's right.

Mr. SPECTER. How about his weight?

Mrs. HILL. That's the only thing—I would say—he certainly wasn't any bigger than Jack Ruby.

Mr. SPECTER. Was he smaller than Jack Ruby?

Mrs. HILL. He could have been smaller.

Mr. SPECTER. How about—was he wearing a hat?

Mrs. HILL. Yes; I said he was wearing a hat.

Mr. SPECTER. Was he wearing a top coat?

Mrs. HILL. Yes; an overcoat.

Mr. SPECTER. And was he wearing a tie, could you tell?

Mrs. HILL. I didn't notice. It was a brown, I mean, I just got the impression of a brown hat.

Mr. SPECTER. Can you give me an estimate of his age?

Mrs. HILL. I would say the man was middle aged, or say, I would say 40.

Mr. SPECTER. Was he a white man or a Negro?

Mrs. HILL. He was a white man.

Mr. SPECTER. Can you describe him in any other way to me?

Mrs. HILL. No; I can't.

Mr. SPECTER. Do you think he was, in fact, Jack Ruby?

Mrs. HILL. That, I don't know.

Mr. SPECTER. Now, have you told me all that you can recollect about this man and your reason for moving toward him?

Mrs. HILL. Yes, as far as I know.

Mr. SPECTER. Now, you were at point "D," what did you do after being at point "D," which we have marked on the diagram?

Mrs. HILL. Well, as I said, the policemen were coming by that time from different areas, coming and closing this place off, and I was dodging them, trying to get back across the street.

Mr. SPECTER. Back across Elm Street?

Mrs. HILL. That's right.

Mr. SPECTER. And did you in fact dodge them?

Mrs. HILL. Yes.

Mr. SPECTER. And get back across Elm Street?

Mrs. HILL. Yes.

Mr. SPECTER. And what, if anything, did you do next?

Mrs. HILL. There was a man holding Mary's arm and she was crying and he had hold of her camera trying to take it with him.

Mr. SPECTER. Who was that?

Mrs. HILL. Featherstone of the Times Herald, and——

Mr. SPECTER. Dallas Times Herald?

Mrs. HILL. That's right. I ran up there and told him we had to leave. She had been impressing upon me for an hour and a half—we hadn't even gone down to see the President that day—we had been doing other things and we got down there and we just decided we would stay, but she had been impressing upon me for an hour and a half, the whole time we had been there, that we had to beat the traffic out of there, and she knows her way around real well, so I knew she could get out and we could beat the traffic, and we were just going to run for the car as fast as we could. It was parked up here on Houston. We were going to run and get out of there before the people started milling around so we wouldn't be in that traffic, and I don't know—we had been talking about it so long and she had drilled me so much, that we must get out of here, and when I came back and I found her crying and him standing there holding her camera, and holding her, I mean holding her by the arm and her camera, and telling her she had to go with him, I started trying to shake his hand loose and grab the camera and telling him that "No, we wouldn't go, we had to leave," and I guess by that time I was beginning—until then I have no conscious feeling of any scaredness or excitement or anything. I mean, you know, it is just like something that's passing in front of you, and I mean, I wasn't worried or upset in any way until I got back there and then I had a sense of urgency. I just knew I wanted to get out of there and all I could think of—and I don't think the full impact of all that had happened really hit me then, because I was just wanting to get out of there and to get away and he kept telling me—he insisted we go with him and he just practically ran us, and he got—they were throwing up a police net around that building at the time, and he just practically ran us up to the court house, I guess it is, and put us in this little room and I don't know   why we were so dumb that day unless it was just the sequence of events, that everything was just happening so fast we really didn't even think, but we couldn't leave. He kept standing in front of the door and he would let a cameraman in or someone to interview us and they were shooting things in our faces, and he wouldn't let us out.

Mr. SPECTER. Who was interviewing you—newspaper reporters?

Mrs. HILL. Newspaper reporters and radio and TV people and a man from—a man named Coker John, or John Coker.

Mr. SPECTER. From where?

Mrs. HILL. As I get it, he is a sort of freelance writer, and I think he was on an assignment then. He came out—I'm not sure—I thought it was for Life or Post, but he came in there and he was shooting pictures for—I think he was shooting them for TV, but he came out to the house about 2 weeks later with this bunch of men, about four of them, three or four came out, and that's the second time I saw him, because he said, "You remember me, I saw you in the pressroom that day."

Mr. SPECTER. Is that Miss Hill or Mrs. Hill?

Mrs. HILL. It is Mrs. Hill, and he said "I saw you in the pressroom that day," and I said, "Yes." I remembered him because I saw him more than any—now, I don't remember where I am here.

Mr. SPECTER. You were telling me about what happened to you at the county courthouse, and then you digressed from that to tell me about John coming to see you in your home.

Let's go back to the county courthouse and let me ask you if you gave an affidavit to the sheriff that day?

Mrs. HILL. Yes.

Mr. SPECTER. Now, did you talk to anybody from the Federal Government that day?

Mrs. HILL. Yes.

Mr. SPECTER. Whom did you talk to?

Mrs. HILL. I don't know.

Mr. SPECTER. What agency was the man from, if you know?

Mrs. HILL. Secret Service.

Mr. SPECTER. How many times have you talked to somebody from the Secret Service in this case altogether?

Mrs. HILL. I would say the only time I talked to the Secret Service men was when I was down at the courthouse that afternoon, just before they let us leave, and I think—now, we officially sat down and supposedly were giving a story to the Secret Service men.

Mr. SPECTER. And, did they write down what you were telling them?

Mrs. HILL. I don't think they did.

Mr. SPECTER. Did you sign anything?

Mrs. HILL. Oh, well, I signed my statement that I made over in the sheriff's office.

Mr. SPECTER. Then, how about for the Secret Service men, did you sign anything?

Mrs. HILL. No, I don't think we signed anything over there, because they just took us in a little room——

Mr. SPECTER. What did you tell the Secret Service men?

Mrs. HILL. As well as I remember, we talked to so many that day.

Mr. SPECTER. Well, did you tell everybody about the same thing you have told me here today?

Mrs. HILL. Yes, except that I didn't go into that stuff with the shots because no one ever asked me, no one ever detailed it like that, but they were interested that day in those pictures and they got them all from us.

Mr. SPECTER. Did you talk with the Secret Service men on any occasion after the events on November 22?

Mrs. HILL. No.

Mr. SPECTER. Have you ever talked to anybody else from the Federal Government?

Mrs. HILL. The FBI men.

Mr. SPECTER. On how many occasions?

Mrs. HILL. Several.

Mr. SPECTER. How many, if you remember?

Mrs. HILL. I don't recall—I was called two or three times at least after that.

Mr. SPECTER. Called on the telephone?

Mrs. HILL. Yes.

Mr. SPECTER. You discussed the matter over the phone with somebody who said he was from the FBI?

Mrs. HILL. No; I had that pulled on me and I didn't want to talk until I called back down to check to see.

Mr. SPECTER. Did you talk to somebody from the FBI when you called them back?

Mrs. HILL. Yes.

Mr. SPECTER. Over the phone?

Mrs. HILL. Yes.

Mr. SPECTER. On how many occasions?

Mrs. HILL. I think two or three times is all I had.

Mr. SPECTER. Were you ever interviewed in person by the FBI?

Mrs. HILL. Yes.

Mr. SPECTER. On how many occasions?

Mrs. HILL. After that day, I believe only once.

Mr. SPECTER. And about when was that?

Mrs. HILL. Well, it was the other day after I received this letter—no; before I received this letter, and this was last Tuesday, I think, and they came in reference to what Mark Lane had told the Warren Commission.

Mr. SPECTER. And what did they ask you when they came to see you last Tuesday, that would be a week ago today or the 16th—or the 17th?

Mrs. HILL. They just had me start over with this story again and they had Mr. Lane's copy and they asked me, you know, if I had said these things and, I read it and told them that I had said it.

Mr. SPECTER. Was Mr. Lane's version accurate?

Mrs. HILL. It was accurate in that he took down what I said. It was inaccurate in that he had taken it out of context, and the questions he asked me weren't there, nor were they given. I can see how he could have made what he made out of my statements.

Mr. SPECTER. When did you talk to Mr. Lane?

Mrs. HILL. I talked to him about—approximately 4 or 6 weeks ago.

Mr. SPECTER. Where did that take place?

Mrs. HILL. At New York.

Mr. SPECTER. Did he call you on the telephone?

Mrs. HILL. That's right, and he didn't tell me he was recording this at the time.

Mr. SPECTER. Did you ever talk to Mark Lane in person?

Mrs. HILL. No.

Mr. SPECTER. Did you ever sign an affidavit for him?

Mrs. HILL. No.

Mr. SPECTER. The only contact you had with him was this one telephone conversation?

Mrs. HILL. That's right, and he said he was coming to Dallas the next week and would I talk with him, I said, I told him then—that I guessed so. I didn't know. I mean, because I didn't fully realize what he was doing in this case.

Mr. SPECTER. And what did you tell him over the telephone?

Mrs. HILL. I told him the same story I told you, with the exception that he went further into the day's activities at the police station, and at the courthouse.

Mr. SPECTER. What else did you tell him about your day's activities at the courthouse?

Mrs. HILL. Well, he asked me, you know, he just asked me a lot of questions about that, and I told him that we didn't know that we were in a pressroom. We just knew we were in a courthouse and with police. I mean, this was to us a police station.

Mr. SPECTER. Tell me all the things that you told him, in addition to those which you have already told me, that is, tell me all the things you told Mr. Lane, in addition to that you have already testified about.

Mrs. HILL. I will, but do you realize I have had to go over this so many times that I don't know who I have told which part to? I really don't.

Mr. SPECTER. Well, I'll bear that in mind, but do the best you can in telling me all the things you told Mark Lane.

Mrs. HILL. Can't you just read my statement?

Mr. SPECTER. Feel free to smoke—just relax.

Mrs. HILL. I would except, I don't have one.

Mr. SPECTER. Just relax if you can.

Mrs. HILL. All right, if I can.

Mr. SPECTER. Off the record.

Let the record show that we were taking a brief recess to get the witness a cup of coffee so that she may be more relaxed. May the record show that we have just obtained some coffee and we are proceeding.

When we broke for the coffee, I had asked you to tell me all the things you told Mark Lane other than those which you have already testified about.

Mrs. HILL. Before we go into that—I do want to have you—because I hope that by this time I am through with it, but I do want to tell you about a camera team that came out there to my house that this John Coker was with.

Mr. SPECTER. On which occasion was that?

Mrs. HILL. That is important to me and that is the reason why I digressed and got on that.

Mr. SPECTER. This occurred, you say, about 2 weeks after the assassination?

Mrs. HILL. Say—10 days.

Mr. SPECTER. What happened on that occasion?

Mrs. HILL. They came out and brought TV cameras and were going to take, and they told me they were not going to tell me the questions that they were going to ask me, that they wanted to get my reactions to their questions, and they set up rather, I would say they set up hypothetical situations like—could he have been shot from the window, if this is the kind of wound that it would have made? Or, to make this kind of a wound, he had to have been here, now which, you know—and so I told them and from what I gathered that day, they did not think I had—I had gotten the idea from them, that there was speculation or some reasonable doubt that I—that Oswald did not do all the shooting and that all these shots did not come from the window.

Mr. SPECTER. You told the newspaper and the television cameramen that?

Mrs. HILL. That's what I got from them from the questions they asked me.

Mr. SPECTER. What answers did you give them to those questions?

Mrs. HILL. Well, when they would set up a situation, I would tell them what I thought would have had to happen in that situation.

Mr. SPECTER. Well, without formulating any questions which would lead you in any way to any conclusions, let me ask you for your best recollection as to what you think occurred, as to the point where the assassin was, if you have any idea on that question?

Mrs. HILL. Well, as I said previously, to me at the time the shot came from the knoll, you know.

Mr. SPECTER. And you have testified to that because of the sound of the shots?

Mrs. HILL. Yes.

Mr. SPECTER. And also because you saw this man running away.

Mrs. HILL. That's right.

Mr. SPECTER. Do you think perhaps that you had the impression that that came from the knoll exclusively because you saw the man running away? And your reaction that that must have been the man who did the shooting?

Mrs. HILL. It could have been very well—it could have been.

Mr. SPECTER. Now, are there any other factors which led you to think that the shots came from the knoll, factors other than those you have already told me about?

Mrs. HILL. Except that I believe these men thought so that night.

Mr. SPECTER. Well, never mind the men, but focus just on what your reaction was at the time.

Mrs. HILL. That's what I thought. At the time I thought that there was more than one person shooting, as I said before.

Mr. SPECTER. Well, you have already told me about that and you told me about the source of the knoll, and you told me why you thought that was more than one person, and now, what I'm trying to get at is why you thought they came from the knoll—was it first because the way the shot sounded and secondly, because the man ran away, and then I asked you the second question—did you think perhaps they came from the knoll exclusively because you saw the man run away, and you said you thought that might be the case.

Mrs. HILL. Could be.

Mr. SPECTER. And then I asked you were there any other findings other than those we have already talked about, which would make you think that the shots came from the knoll, based on your own personal observations, recollections or impressions.

Mrs. HILL. Nothing that comes to mind.

Mr. SPECTER. Now, is there anything else about that television interview which you consider important?

Mrs. HILL. Except for the fact it left me very doubtful and confused.

Mr. SPECTER. Because they gave you a lot of hypothetical situations, and you didn't know which was which, if you listened to them?

199

Mrs. HILL. That's right—they had some very strange ideas which I have heard here and there voiced by other people.

Mr. SPECTER. What were they doing basically, asking you to comment on those various theories?

Mrs. HILL. I asked why were they coming out here, why would they come to my home, why was that important, and they said, "Something big is going to break in a little while and we want to put it on first. We want to be ready for it."

Mr. SPECTER. Did they ever put that television interview on?

Mrs. HILL. I have never seen any, but then, I never saw myself on TV either.

Mr. SPECTER. Is there anything else about that television interview which you now consider important?

Mrs. HILL. Well, I know that it has bothered me ever since it happened, and particularly since I have been questioned these other times.

Mr. SPECTER. By the FBI last week?

Mrs. HILL. Yes; and without things of comments, and speculation that I have heard, and remarks that I've gone back over, of happenings that have happened to me that day and as to the way it happened, and frankly, I would either like to say it again or something——

Mr. SPECTER. Like to say what again?

Mrs. HILL. I would like to see this telecast or hear that questioning again because there's something about it that keeps in the back of mymind——

Mr. SPECTER. But you can't put your finger on what it is?

Mrs. HILL. No.

Mr. SPECTER. But you are annoyed or bothered or perplexed with it or confused by that?

Mrs. HILL. Yes; I have been.

Mr. SPECTER. Now, have you told me everything that you have to say about that television interview?

Mrs. HILL. Yes.

Mr. SPECTER. Now, moving on to the question about Mark Lane, what did you tell him other than that which you have told me here today?

Mrs. HILL. He asked me where we were taken and I told him in the pressroom, that we didn't know it was the pressroom at the time, and that we didn't know we couldn't leave and because they kept standing across the door, and the first time we really—we were getting tired of it, I mean, we had been down there quite a while and we were getting tired of it and we wanted to leave and this is what I told him, and so some man came in and offered Mary a sum, I think—say—$10,000 or something like this for this picture.

We realized that—they said, "Don't sell the picture." He was a representative of either Post or Life, and they said, "Don't sell that picture until our representatives have contacted you or a lawyer or something." Anyway, we realized at that time we didn't have that picture, that it had been taken from us. I mean, we had let Featherstone look at it, you know, but we told no one they could reproduce it. They said, "Would you let us look at it and see if it could be reproduced?" We said, "Yes; you could look at it," we thought it was—you know, it was fuzzy and everything, but we were wanting to keep them and we suddenly realized we didn't have that picture, and that was quite a bit of money and we were getting pretty excited about it, and Mary was getting scared——

Mr. SPECTER. Did she eventually sell the picture, by the way?

Mrs. HILL. She sold the rights, the publishing rights of it, not the original picture, but they had already—AP and UP had already picked it up because Featherstone stole it.

Mr. SPECTER. Do you know what she sold those rights for?

Mrs. HILL. I think it was $600.

Mr. SPECTER. What did you tell Mark Lane besides about the picture?

Mrs. HILL. This is it.

Mr. SPECTER. Fine, go ahead.

Mrs. HILL. Anyway, when I realized we didn't have that picture and Mary was getting upset about that—by that time I had realized we were in a pressroom and that he had no right to be holding us and he had no authority and that we could get out of there, and they kept standing in front of the door, and I told him—I said, "Get out." We kept asking him for our picture, and where it was, and he said, "We'll get it back—we'll get it back. And so I jerked away and ran out of the door and as I did, there was a Secret Service man. Now, this I was told—that he was a Secret Service man, and he said, "Do you have a red raincoat?" And, I said, "Yes; it's in yonder. Let me go." I was intent on finding someone to get that picture back and I said as I walked out, "I can get someone big enough to get it back for us." He said, "Does your friend have a blue

200

raincoat?" And I said, "Yes; she's in there." He said, "Here they are," to somebody else and they told us that they had been looking for us.

Mr. SPECTER. Who told you that?

Mrs. HILL. This man.

Mr. SPECTER. All this you told Mr. Lane?

Mrs. HILL. Yes.

Mr. SPECTER. Go ahead.

Mrs. HILL. And so, then they took us into the police station. Just about that time Sheriff Decker came out and the man was with us and we were telling him why we were in there, why we had been in the pressroom, you know, and why they hadn't been able to find us, because they had thought that Mary had been hit and they were looking for the two women that were standing right by the car with the camera. At that time they didn't know what we were doing down there and why we were right at the car. So, there followed questioning all afternoon long, and he asked me at one time—well, in fact he asked repeatedly if I was held and I told him, "Yes."

Mr. SPECTER. Who asked you that?

Mrs. HILL. Mark Lane.

Mr. SPECTER. If you were held?

Mrs. HILL. Yes; you know if I were held, if I had to stay there and I told him, "Yes," but I told him when we were in the pressroom it was just our own ignorance, really, that was keeping us there and letting the man intimidate us that had no authority.

Mr. SPECTER. That was a newsman as opposed to the police official?

Mrs. HILL. Yes; and I gave Mark Lane his name several times—clearly. I remember clearly that I gave him his name.

Mr. SPECTER. And what name did you give him?

Mrs. HILL. Featherstone of the Times Herald, and so after we got out of there and I talked with a man——

Mr. SPECTER. Now, you are continuing to tell me everything you told Mark Lane?

Mrs. HILL. That's right, and I talked with this man, a Secret Service man, and I said, "Am I a kook or what's wrong with me?" I said, "They keep saying   three shots—three shots," and I said, "I know I heard more. I heard from four to six shots anyway."

He said, "Mrs. Hill, we were standing at the window and we heard more shots also, but we have three wounds and we have three bullets, three shots is all that we are willing to say right now."

Mr. SPECTER. Now, did that Secret Service man try to suggest to you that there were only three shots in any other way than that?

Mrs. HILL. That's all he said to me. He didn't say, "You have to say three shots"—he didn't tell me what to say.

Mr. SPECTER. He didn't try to intimidate you or coerce you in any way?

Mrs. HILL. No; that's all he said.

Mr. SPECTER. All right. Go ahead and tell me what you told Mark Lane.

Mrs. HILL. I told him—I was asked by them——

Mr. SPECTER. Do you know who that Secret Service man was, by the way?

Mrs. HILL. No; I don't. I don't know—not any name that day except Decker and the President.

Mr. SPECTER. All right, go ahead and tell me everything else you said.

Mrs. HILL. Then, he asked me—I was asked did I know that a bullet struck at my feet and I said, "No; I didn't." And he said, "What do you think that dust was?" And I said, "I didn't see any dust." And I told Mark Lane that the Times Herald did run a picture in the paper of a concrete scar where a bullet had hit right where we were standing, which is evident to anybody that had an issue of the Times Herald.

Mr. SPECTER. Did you see that concrete?

Mrs. HILL. I didn't go back down there.

Mr. SPECTER. Do you know whether or not a bullet did hit that concrete?

Mrs. HILL. As I say, I saw the picture in the newspaper.

Mr. SPECTER. Aside from seeing it in the newspaper, do you know anything about that?

Mrs. HILL. No; other than what the man said he saw out of the window of the courthouse, the Secret Service man said and it struck at my feet, other than that—I don't know.

Mr. SPECTER. What else did you tell Mark Lane?

Mrs. HILL. So, he asked me, "Did you have to stay down there or did you stay of your own accord?" And I said, "No; we had stay there." He said something—he said, "Were you threatened or something?" And I told him I wasn't threatened, but—he said, "How do you know you were held?" Or something like that, and I said, "Because I tried to leave twice. At one time I

201

saw people I knew on the street and I was going to go down and talk to them and I went down and they came down and got me, and another time I went down when the evening edition of the paper hit the street and two men," and I told him, I did not tell him they were Secret Service men, but they were men from the sheriff's office. There were some kind of deputy or something that came down and took me back and they were not playing. They meant to take me back. They did take my arms and I knew I was going, because I just kept standing on the corner saying, "No; I don't want to go back yet. Please let me stay down here just a little while." They did make us go back in there.

Mr. SPECTER. Where were they from?

Mrs. HILL. They were from the sheriff's office, they were just deputies—they weren't FBI or Secret Service.

Mr. SPECTER. Was it after that that you gave the affidavit to the sheriff?

Mrs. HILL. Yes.

Mr. SPECTER. What else did you tell Mark Lane?

Mrs. HILL. Well, I told him that my story had already been given, that they had an affidavit down there, and he said, "Were you ever at any time—" I think he said, "Were you ever at any time told not to say something or this, that, and the other," and I said, "The only thing that I was told not to say was to not mention the man running," and he said, "And why?" And I said, "Well, it was an FBI or Secret Service that told me not to, but they came in to me just right after I was taken—I was in there in the pressroom, and [   ] told me in fact—I told him it was Featherstone that told me. He said, "You know you were wrong about seeing a man running." He said, "You didn't."

Mr. SPECTER. Who told you you were wrong—Featherstone or Lane?

Mrs. HILL. Featherstone. And I told him that—I told Mr. Lane that Mr. Featherstone had told me that, and I said, "But I did," and he said, "No; don't say that any more on the air."

Mr. SPECTER. Who said, "Don't say that any more on the air?"

Mrs. HILL. Featherstone; and I made it clear to Mark Lane, because I mentioned his name several times, and he said, "He has told me not to tell anyone"——

Mr. SPECTER. You mean Featherstone?

Mrs. HILL. Yes; that the shots had come from a window up in the Depository and for me not to say that any more, that I was wrong about it, and I said "Very well," and so I just didn't say any more that I ran across the street to see the man, and that's the part, as much as I can get from when the FBI men came out and talked to me the other day, that is the part mostly that I got that was out of context, because what he gave the Commission was basically true.

Mr. SPECTER. What Mark Lane gave the Commission?

Mrs. HILL. Yes.

Mr. SPECTER. Except for what——

Mrs. HILL. Except he didn't have his comments in there.

Mr. SPECTER. What were his comments?

Mrs. HILL. Well, as I said, the way he would ask me things I can see why I gave the answers I did, which to me are the truth, but I can see, taken out of context, why he or the Commission, well, not how he, because he was listening to me—how the Commission could take it to mean maybe something else?

Mr. SPECTER. Did he repeat then to the Commission how the Commission could take them to mean maybe something else?

Mrs. HILL. Yes——

Mr. SPECTER. Did he repeat them to the Commission out of context—did Mark Lane repeat them out of context?

Mrs. HILL. To me they were—to me they were—it was my comments and it wasn't everything I said.

Mr. SPECTER. Have you now related all of the ways that Mark Lane took your comments out of context?

Mrs. HILL. So far as I know.

Mr. SPECTER. Now, is there anything else about your conversation with Mark Lane which you think would be helpful to the Commission to know about?

Mrs. HILL. No.

Mr. SPECTER. Now, before getting on to Mark Lane, we were talking about the times you had been interviewed by the authorities and you had told me you were interviewed a couple of times by telephone by the FBI when you called back to verify it was the FBI and about a single interview you had with the FBI a week ago today, which would have been the 17th of March?

Mrs. HILL. Yes.

Mr. SPECTER. Now, have you had any additional interviews with any Federal authorities before today, other than those which you have already told me about?

Mrs. HILL. No; not that I remember.

Mr. SPECTER. Now, for the record, Mrs. Hill, I'm going to ask you some questions about your own background—first of all I would like you to tell me how old you are, for the record?

Mrs. HILL. Thirty-three.

Mr. SPECTER. And where is your home area—Dallas or some other part of the country or what?

Mrs. HILL. Where am I from?

Mr. SPECTER. Where are you from?

Mrs. HILL. Oklahoma.

Mr. SPECTER. And what city in Oklahoma?

Mrs. HILL. Originally Wewoka and later Oklahoma City.

Mr. SPECTER. And are you married?

Mrs. HILL. Yes.

Mr. SPECTER. And is there any unusual status with respect to your being married at this moment?

Mrs. HILL. I am in the process of getting a divorce.

Mr. SPECTER. And how many children have you?

Mrs. HILL. I have two—a boy 12 and a girl 10.

Mr. SPECTER. And what is your educational background?

Mrs. HILL. I was graduated from Wewoka High School and Oklahoma Baptist University in Shawnee.

Mr. SPECTER. And what year did you graduate from high school?

Mrs. HILL. 1948.

Mr. SPECTER. And what year from college?

Mrs. HILL. 1954, after two babies later.

Mr. SPECTER. And is that a 4-year college?

Mrs. HILL. That's right.

Mr. SPECTER. And how are you occupied at the present time?

Mrs. HILL. I taught 7 years in Oklahoma City public schools and for the past year and a half I have been doing substitute teaching for the Dallas Board of Education.

Mr. SPECTER. And what is your maiden name?

Mrs. HILL. Lollis.

Mr. SPECTER. And what is your husband's occupation?

Mrs. HILL. He is a consultant for Science Research Associates, lately IBM.

Mr. SPECTER. And is there anything else that you would care to tell me which you think might be of aid to the Commission in its investigation?

Mrs. HILL. No.

Mr. SPECTER. Thank you very much for coming and giving your deposition.

Mrs. HILL. Am I completely through with the Commission?

Mr. SPECTER. I think this will be the end of it—we have all of the records, and to the best of my expectation—yes; but you could be called anytime. You have both the pleasure and the discomfort, but the distinction of having been an eye witness.

Mrs. HILL. Well, I know, I have always been rather—I mean, it's not something you are—you are not proud to say it, but I think it was part of history and I was glad I was there, but because I got publicity, because—I think my children will be interested to know that someday that I was in it someway.

Mr. SPECTER. Well, let me say, as to the best of my knowledge there are no further plans for the Commission to call you again. This transcript will be reviewed by me in Washington and by my colleagues in Washington and it is possible that you may be contacted again. Perhaps I might talk to you again by telephone or perhaps the FBI, or it is even conceivable the Commission might want to hear from you, yourself, in Washington, but my best estimate of the situation right now is that we have the basic information from you which we need.

Mrs. HILL. I told the FBI the other day I did not want to go to Washington. I don't think I can take any more laughing at.

Mr. SPECTER. Well, we won't call on you unless it is concluded that it is absolutely necessary.

Mrs. HILL. Good. I was hoping this would do it.

Mr. SPECTER. All right. Thank you very much.

Mrs. HILL. Thank you.

Mr. SPECTER. For the purposes of the record, this diagram which was used during the deposition of Mrs. Hill will be marked Hill Exhibit No. 5.

(Instrument referred to marked by the reporter as Hill Exhibit No. 5, for identification.)

TESTIMONY OF AUSTIN L. MILLER

The testimony of Austin L. Miller was taken at 2:40 p.m., on April 8, 1964, in the office of the U.S. attorney, 301 Post Office Building, Bryan and Ervay Streets, Dallas, Tex., by Mr. David W. Belin, assistant counsel of the President's Commission.

Mr. BELIN. Would you stand and be sworn, sir.

Do you solemnly swear that the testimony you are about to give before the President's Commission is the truth, the whole truth, and nothing but the truth, so help you God?

Mr. MILLER. I do.

Mr. BELIN. Would you state your name for the record.

Mr. MILLER. Austin L. Miller.

Mr. BELIN. Where do you live?

Mr. MILLER. 1006 Powl Circle, Mesquite, Tex.

Mr. BELIN. Is that a suburb of Dallas?

Mr. MILLER. Yes; it is just a little town.

Mr. BELIN. How far out of Dallas?

Mr. MILLER. It borders the city limits of Dallas.

Mr. BELIN. How old are you?

Mr. MILLER. Twenty-six

Mr. BELIN. Married?

Mr. MILLER. Yes.

Mr. BELIN. Did you go to school in Texas?

Mr. MILLER. Yes; I did.

Mr. BELIN. How far did you go to school?

Mr. MILLER. Tenth grade.

Mr. BELIN. Then what did you do?

Mr. MILLER. I quit school and went to work.

Mr. BELIN. Where did you work?

Mr. MILLER. First worked at Titche's, and then for Robertson & King Motor Supply, and from there I went back to Titche's, and then to A. & P. Bakery Co., and then I worked for Presto Delivery Co., and then to Texas-Louisiana Freight Bureau where I am working now.

Mr. BELIN. How long have you been there?

Mr. MILLER. Ever since 1958, January 1958.

Mr. BELIN. What do you do now?

Mr. MILLER. Well, it is a combination job between mail clerk and tariff compiler.

Mr. BELIN. Where were you working on Friday, November 22, 1963, which was the day that President Kennedy came to Dallas?

Mr. MILLER. Texas-Louisiana Freight Bureau.

Mr. BELIN. Where is that located?

Mr. MILLER. 215 Union Terminal.

Mr. BELIN. Where is the Union Terminal located?

Mr. MILLER. That is down at—the address they give is 400 South Houston Street, but the book is not the correct address, but that is what they use. Because 400 is the opposite side of the block, and there is a city park there.

Mr. BELIN. What cross street? Would it be near any intersection at all, or not?

Mr. MILLER. On the corner of Houston, and I can't think of the name of that street now, right in front of the Dallas Morning News.

Mr. BELIN. Would it be north or south of Main Street?

Mr. MILLER. It would be south.

Mr. BELIN. How many blocks south of Main Street?

Mr. MILLER. Four blocks.

Mr. BELIN. Four blocks south of Main Street on Houston?

Mr. MILLER. Right.

Mr. BELIN. All right, where were you at about the time the motorcade came by?

Mr. MILLER. I was standing on the top of the triple underpass on the Main Street side.

Mr. BELIN. Now when you say triple underpass, there are actually three underpasses there?

Mr. MILLER. Yes. They are sitting side by side. It is Main, Commerce, and Elm. I was over Elm instead of Main Street. I was over Elm Street.

Mr. BELIN. Now there is a place where the railroad tracks are, and that is the first. Is it all railroad tracks, or part railroad tracks and part freeway?

Mr. MILLER. All railroad tracks go over that particular set of underpass.

Mr. BELIN. Where you were?

Mr. MILLER. Yes, sir.

Mr. BELIN. When did you get there?

Mr. MILLER. About 12:15 or 12:20.

Mr. BELIN. Do you remember what time the motorcade came by?

Mr. MILLER. No; I don't, not for sure.

Mr. BELIN. About how long after you got there did you see the motorcade?

Mr. MILLER. About 10 or 15 minutes.

Mr. BELIN. Anyone else standing around there that you knew?

Mr. MILLER. Royce Skelton, the boy I work with and an elderly man who is a building maintenance man. By name, I don't know him, but a lot of other employees I have seen in the building other than myself.

Mr. BELIN. Anyone else that you knew?

Mr. MILLER. As far as knowing, no, sir.

Mr. BELIN. You saw other people there?

Mr. MILLER. Yes, sir.

Mr. BELIN. Did you see any police officer around there?

Mr. MILLER. There was one on both sides of the bridge.

Mr. BELIN. Well, describe what happened. Did you see the motorcade come by?

Mr. MILLER. Yes, sir; it came down Main Street and turned north on Houston Street and went over two blocks and turned left onto Elm Street.

Got about halfway down the hill going toward the underpass and that is when as far as I can recall the first shot was fired.

Mr. BELIN. Did you know it was a shot when you heard it?

Mr. MILLER. I didn't know it. I thought at first the motorcycle backfiring or somebody throwed some firecrackers out.

Mr. BELIN. Then what did you hear or see?

Mr. MILLER. After the first one, just a few seconds later, there was two more shots fired or, or sounded like a sound at the time. I didn't know for sure. And it was after that I saw some man in the car fall forward, and a woman next to him grab him and hollered, and just what, I don't know exactly what she said.

Mr. BELIN. Then what did you see?

Mr. MILLER. About that time I turned and looked toward the—there is a little plaza sitting on the hill. I looked over there to see if anything was there, who threw the firecracker or whatever it was, or see if anything was up there, and there wasn't nobody standing there, so I stepped back and looked on the tracks to see if anybody run across the railroad tracks, and there was nobody running across the railroad tracks.

So I turned right straight back just in time to see the convertible take off fast.

Mr. BELIN. You mean the convertible in which the President was riding?

Mr. MILLER. I wouldn't want to say it was the President. It was a convertible, but I saw a man fall over. I don't know whose convertible it was.

Mr. BELIN. Where did the shots sound like they came from?

Mr. MILLER. Well, the way it sounded like, it came from the, I would say from right there in the car. Would be to my left, the way I was looking at him over toward that incline.

Mr. BELIN. Is there anything else that you can think of that you saw.

Mr. MILLER. About the time I looked over to the side there, there was a police officer. No; a motorcycle running his motor under against the curb, and jumped off and come up to the hill toward the top and right behind him was some more officers and plainclothesmen, too.

Mr. BELIN. Did you see anyone that might be, that gave any suspicious movements of any kind over there?

Mr. MILLER. No, sir; I didn't.

Mr. BELIN. Did you see anyone when you looked around on the railroad tracks, that you hadn't seen before?

Mr. MILLER. No, sir; I didn't. We was all standing in one group right at the rail looking over, and the police officer, he was standing about 5 or 10 feet behind us.

Mr. BELIN. Now about how many were there in that group altogether, if you can remember?

Mr. MILLER. I would say in the neighborhood of 10 or 12 people. Maybe more, maybe less.

Mr. BELIN. Apart from those people, did you see anyone else in the vicinity at all on the railroad tracks?

Mr. MILLER. There was one young man or boy. He was going to come up on the tracks, but the police officer stopped him and asked him where he was going, and he said he was going to come up where he could see, and he asked if he worked for the train station, and he said, "No," so the police officer made him go back down.

Where he went to, I don't know.

Mr. BELIN. When was this?

Mr. MILLER. Oh, before the President came along.

Mr. BELIN. About how much before, do you know? Offhand?

Mr. MILLER. I couldn't say.

Mr. BELIN. Do you know anything about this man or boy that you described? About how old he was, or anything?

Mr. MILLER. I can't think. I would say he was in his early twenties.

Mr. BELIN. Tall or short?

Mr. MILLER. I don't remember that much about him. I do recall him coming up and the man talking to him and turning him back.

Mr. BELIN. So he went back down?

Mr. MILLER. Yes.

Mr. BELIN. Where did he come up from?

Mr. MILLER. He came up from the—I am going by where I was standing. He was from our left, from around behind that parking lot.

Mr. BELIN. Did you ever see him again or not?

Mr. MILLER. No, sir; I didn't.

Mr. BELIN. Did you ever see anyone else in that area at all or anything on the railroad tracks at any time?

Mr. MILLER. No, sir; not until after the shots were fired and the police officers came up the hill and climbed over the fence and started searching.

Mr. BELIN. That was the only other people that you saw?

Mr. MILLER. That is all I recall seeing.

Mr. BELIN. Anything else that you can add that might be of help in any way to the Commission, or to the investigation into the assassination?

Mr. MILLER. Offhand, no, sir; I don't recall anything else.

My statement at the time may have some more, but I don't recall exactly what all did happen for sure.

Mr. BELIN. Well, you and I never met until just a few minutes ago, did we?

Mr. MILLER. No, sir.

Mr. BELIN. And as soon as you came in here, we started immediately taking your testimony under oath, is that correct?

Mr. MILLER. Yes.

Mr. BELIN. We never talked about the facts before then, did we?

Mr. MILLER. No, sir.

Mr. BELIN. Well, you have the right, if you like, to read this deposition when it is typewritten, and sign it, or else you can waive the signing of it and have it go directly to Washington without your signing. What would be your preference?

Mr. MILLER. If you rather it would be signed——

Mr. BELIN. We do not require it to be signed.

Mr. MILLER. It makes no difference.

Mr. BELIN. We have no preference. We do not require your signing. You can waive the signing of it to save yourself a trip coming down here again, or you have the right, if you like, to come down and read it and sign.

Mr. MILLER. I will just waive it, because it would be to my advantage to not have to take off.

Mr. BELIN. All right, we sure appreciate your coming down and thank you very much.

There is one other thing. We have a sketch. I want to ask you to put on the sketch where you were.

Mr. MILLER. Okay.

Mr. BELIN. Handing you what we call "A. Miller Deposition Exhibit A." I am going to try and get this thing oriented here.

Here is Houston Street running north this way.

There is Elm. Here is the railroad overpass, and here is the freeway overpass.

Mr. MILLER. Now where this "X" is at up here, is where we was standing.

Mr. BELIN. Where it is marked "Pos. 5," there is an arrow there which I have put there, is that right?

Mr. MILLER. Yes, sir.

Mr. BELIN. By the "X," which appears to be right over the overpass of Elm, which would be to the east side of the overpass, is that right?

Mr. MILLER. Yes, sir.

Mr. BELIN. That is where you were standing?

Mr. MILLER. Yes, sir; it was.

Mr. BELIN. All right, sir.

Thank you very much.

TESTIMONY OF FRANK E. REILLY

The testimony of Frank E. Reilly was taken at 2 p.m., on April 8, 1964, in the office of the U.S. attorney, 301 Post Office Building, Bryan and Ervay Streets, Dallas. Tex., by Mr. Joseph A. Ball, assistant counsel of the President's Commission.

Mr. BALL. Do you solemnly swear the testimony you are about to give before the Commission will be the truth, the whole truth, and nothing but the truth, so help you God?

Mr. REILLY. Yes; I do.

Mr. BALL. Will you state your name, please?

Mr. REILLY. Frank E. Reilly.

Mr. BALL. What is your address?

Mr. REILLY. 3309 Thibet, T-h-i-b-e-t [spelling].

Mr. BALL. What is your occupation?

Mr. REILLY. Electrician, Union Terminal.

Mr. BALL. You received a letter from the Commission, didn't you?

Mr. REILLY. Yes, sir.

Mr. BALL. Advising you that your deposition was to be taken?

Mr. REILLY. Yes, sir.

Mr. BALL. Where were you born and raised?

Mr. REILLY. I was born in Fort Worth.

Mr. BALL. How many years ago?

Mr. REILLY. I left over there when I was 17 and I am 70 now.

Mr. BALL. What kind of education do you have?

Mr. REILLY. Not too good—I went through the ninth grade.

Mr. BALL. What have you done since then, generally, just in a general way—you don't need to go into great detail?

Mr. REILLY. I've been with the Terminal Co. since 1916.

Mr. BALL. You have been a railroad man all of your life, then?

Mr. REILLY. Yes, sir.

Mr. BALL. On November 22, 1963, were you working for the Union Terminal Co.?

Mr. REILLY. Yes.

Mr. BALL. What were you doing that day?

Mr. REILLY. We had been working on the mail conveyor up close to the other end.

Mr. BALL. What was that?

Mr. REILLY. Mail conveyor.

Mr. BALL. Who were you working with?

Mr. REILLY. I was by myself—it was on a Friday.

Mr. BALL. About noon did you go down to someplace near Elm Street?

Mr. REILLY. I went over to Mr. Holland's shop and then we went up there together to see the parade.

Mr. BALL. You went over to Mr. Holland's office?

Mr. REILLY. Mr. Holland's shop.

Mr. BALL. What is Mr. Holland's occupation?

Mr. REILLY. He is a signal supervisor.

Mr. BALL. For the Union Terminal Co.?

Mr. REILLY. Yes, sir.

Mr. BALL. Then, where did you go?

Mr. REILLY. We taken a walk up through the overpass right there.

Mr. BALL. Where did you stand on the overpass?

207

Mr. REILLY. Well, we went over to the railing and stood there.

Mr. BALL. And with reference to what streets—were you standing over Elm, over Main, or over Commerce?

Mr. REILLY. Well, you mean when this parade came down?

Mr. BALL. Yes.

Mr. REILLY. We were between them.

Mr. BALL. Between what streets?

Mr. REILLY. Elm and Main.

Mr. BALL. I have a map here which has been used in the deposition of another witness, but it gives some idea of the location there—this is north—this shows the corner of Elm and Houston Streets.

Mr. REILLY. Yes, sir.

Mr. BALL. And it shows where Elm turns and goes under the railroad, the overpass.

Mr. REILLY. We were between the two.

Mr. BALL. Will you take this pen and this is Elm and here is Main, and make a mark and show me where you were standing?

Mr. REILLY. This is the overpass right there?

Mr. BALL. Yes; this is the overpass.

Mr. REILLY. We was between these two streets—there was big banisters up there and it was about like that, I guess.

Mr. BALL. We will put a mark there.

Mr. REILLY. (The witness Reilly marked the instrument as requested by Counsel Ball.)

Mr. BALL. And I will put on that position "7"—you were standing there when the motorcade came along?

Mr. REILLY. Yes.

Mr. BALL. Who was standing there with you?

Mr. REILLY. I believe it was Mr. Dodd and Skinney.

Mr. BALL. And what are his initials?

Mr. REILLY. Dick Dodd.

Mr. BALL. That's R. C. Dodd, isn't it?

Mr. REILLY. I think so.

Mr. BALL. And what is his position with the Union Terminal Co.?

Mr. REILLY. Foreman of the laborers.

Mr. BALL. Who else was with him?

Mr. REILLY. These two fellows here—were standing out there, but I don't know their names?

Mr. BALL. What are their names?

Mr. REILLY. I don't know their names—I don't even associate with them.

Mr. BALL. What about Mr. Holland?

Mr. REILLY. We were together.

Mr. BALL. S. M. Holland was there?

Mr. REILLY. We were together.

Mr. BALL. Holland and Dodd and you?

Mr. REILLY. And me.

Mr. BALL. Then, there were how many other men?

Mr. REILLY. Well, there were three or four—but I don't know who they were.

Mr. BALL. You have seen two of them here, haven't you?

Mr. REILLY. Yes; two of them out there.

Mr. BALL. And you know one's name is——

Mr. REILLY. I wouldn't know it—their name—I don't even know their name only by seeing them. I do go in there in the office once in a while to put in lamps.

Mr. BALL. Do you know the name of Skelton, isn't there a fellow named Skelton there?

Mr. REILLY. No; I don't.

Mr. BALL. And a man named Miller?

Mr. REILLY. No.

Mr. BALL. Were you all standing at about the same location?

Mr. REILLY. All right close together.

Mr. BALL. Were there any police officers there?

Mr. REILLY. One behind me.

Mr. BALL. One behind you?

Mr. REILLY. He was standing back close to the tracks.

Mr. BALL. That would be where?

Mr. REILLY. About 8 or 10 feet back of us.

Mr. BALL. Were there any other police officers there?

Mr. REILLY. On the far side.

Mr. BALL. What do you mean by "far side"?

Mr. REILLY. Up to the side of where the tracks are on the west side.

Mr. BALL. It would be west of where you are standing—you put a mark down and show me where the two police officers were standing, as you remember it.

Mr. REILLY. Now, this is all tracks over here.

Mr. BALL. All tracks along the railroad overpass?

Mr. REILLY. Yes; these are all tracks in here. One of them was standing behind me and one of them was standing back around here—back along here, but just how far back, I don't know.

Mr. BALL. Put a mark down there for me where the two police officers were standing.

Mr. REILLY. I have an idea one of them was standing here, and for sure, I don't know.

Mr. BALL. Where was the other one standing?

Mr. REILLY. He was on the far side, but I didn't see him.

Mr. BALL. Well, mark that "8."

Mr. REILLY. He was on the far side—and how far back—I don't know.

Mr. BALL. What do you mean by "far side"? Do you mean he was south of you?

Mr. REILLY. No; he was west of me.

Mr. BALL. You see on the map, it's marked "Elm, Main and Commerce"—this other police officer was near what?

Mr. REILLY. I wouldn't know because I wasn't facing him and there was two of them up there.

Mr. BALL. Back; by "far side" you mean that he was south of you?

Mr. REILLY. No; he was west of me—you see, this place is east and west—these streets.

Mr. BALL. But the railroad overpass goes north and south?

Mr. REILLY. Yes; north and south.

Mr. BALL. Then, if he was west of you, he would be behind you?

Mr. REILLY. Yes; behind me.

Mr. BALL. Were there two police officers behind you?

Mr. REILLY. Yes; there was two of them—both of them—one close and one here——

Mr. BALL. Listen to the question—there were two police officers there, was there?

Mr. REILLY. Yes.

Mr. BALL. Were they both behind you?

Mr. REILLY. Yes.

Mr. BALL. One was closer than the other one?

Mr. REILLY. Yes.

Mr. BALL. How close was the one that was closer to you?

Mr. REILLY. I have an idea about 8 or 10 feet.

Mr. BALL. And how far away was the other one?

Mr. REILLY. About the width of that overpass across—75 or 80 feet across there.

Mr. BALL. One was 8 or 10 feet from you, and the other one was 75 feet from you and they were both behind you?

Mr. REILLY. Yes.

Mr. BALL. Did you see the motorcade come down Elm Street?

Mr. REILLY. No; not until it turned and started to come under the underpass.

Mr. BALL. Did you see the President's car?

Mr. REILLY. Yes.

Mr. BALL. Where did you first see it?

Mr. REILLY. When it turned off of Houston Street and started around.

Mr. BALL. Onto Elm Street?

Mr. REILLY. Yes.

Mr. BALL. Is that the first time you saw the President's car, when it turned off Houston Street onto Elm Street?

Mr. REILLY. Yes.

Mr. BALL. How many people were there on the overpass at the time—at that time?

Mr. REILLY. Just what I told you.

Mr. BALL. Tell me again.

Mr. REILLY. Well, there was Holland and me and Dick Dodd and those two fellows out there and the two policemen—that's all I remember seeing out there.

Mr. BALL. Did you hear something?

Mr. REILLY. Yes.

Mr. BALL. What did you hear?

Mr. REILLY. Three shots.

Mr. BALL. Where did they seem to come from; what direction?

Mr. REILLY. It seemed to me like they come out of the trees.

Mr. BALL. What trees?

Mr. REILLY. On the north side of Elm Street at the corner up there.

Mr. BALL. On the north side of Elm—on what corner?

Mr. REILLY. Well, where all those trees are—you've never been down there?

Mr. BALL. Yes; I've been there, but you tell me—I want you to tell me because it has to go on the record here and it has to be in writing.

Mr. REILLY. Well, it's at that park where all the shrubs is up there—it's to the north of Elm Street—up the slope.

Mr. BALL. Did you see any pigeons fly?

Mr. REILLY. No; I didn't pay no attention to that.

Mr. BALL. What did you do after you heard the shots?

Mr. REILLY. I just stood there a few minutes and then I went on down to the shop.

Mr. BALL. Which way did you walk?

Mr. REILLY. South.

Mr. BALL. South?

Mr. REILLY. Toward the post office.

Mr. BALL. Your shop is down south of that place?

Mr. REILLY. Yes; it's the other side of the station.

Mr. BALL. Who walked with you?

Mr. REILLY. Nobody.

Mr. BALL. You walked alone?

Mr. REILLY. Yes.

Mr. BALL. I think that's all, Mr. Reilly. This will be written up and you can look it over and correct it if you wish, or you can waive your signature if you wish.

Which do you wish—do you want to come down and sign it, or do you want to waive your signature?

Mr. REILLY. No; I'll do anything you want me to.

Mr. BALL. Well, you do anything you want to—it's your option—what do you want to do?

Mr. REILLY. I'll sign it.

Mr. BALL. All right.

This young lady will write it up and call you and you can come down here and sign it. How is that?

Mr. REILLY. Well, will I have to come back?

Mr. BALL. Yes; you will.

Mr. REILLY. It is hard for me to get off.

Mr. BALL. It is—why don't you waive your signature, if it is inconvenient to you, and we will offer this diagram as Exhibit A to your deposition.

Mr. REILLY. All right.

(Instrument marked by the reporter as "Reilly Exhibit A," for identification.)

TESTIMONY OF EARLE V. BROWN

The testimony of Earle V. Brown was taken at 4:40 p.m., on April 7, 1964, in the office of the U.S. attorney, 301 Post Office Building, Bryan and Ervay Street, Dallas, Tex., by Messrs. Joseph A. Ball and Samuel A. Stern, assistant counsel of the President's Commission.

Mr. BALL. Would you please rise, raise your right hand and be sworn?

Mr. BROWN. All right.

Mr. BALL. Do you solemnly swear the testimony you will give will be the truth, the whole truth, and nothing but the truth, so help you God?

Mr. BROWN. I do.

Mr. BALL. Sit down. State your name and address, please.

Mr. BROWN. Earle V. Brown, 618 North Rosemont.

Mr. BALL. What is your occupation?

Mr. BROWN. Policeman.

Mr. BALL. With the Dallas Police Department?

Mr. BROWN. Yes, sir.

Mr. BALL. How long have you been a policeman?

Mr. BROWN. Fourteen years.

Mr. BALL. Where were you born and what is your education and training?

Mr. BROWN. I was born on a farm near Lyons, Nebraska, in 1917, and I completed 12 years of schooling, high school.

Mr. BALL. High school?

Mr. BROWN. Yes, sir.

Mr. BALL. Then what did you do?

Mr. BROWN. Well, I stayed on the farm until 1939, then I moved to Ohio; Lima, Ohio. I was inducted into the Army and was in there 4 years, 5 months, discharged 1945, August 15, and I was here in Dallas actually when I was discharged and then back to Ohio for about 4 years. Then, let's see, that would be August of 1949, we came back to Dallas and then February 27, 1950, I joined the police force.

Mr. BALL. Now, you are a patrolman, aren't you?

Mr. BROWN. Yes, sir.

Mr. BALL. On November 22, 1964, were you assigned to a certain post on duty?

Mr. BROWN. Yes, sir.

Mr. BALL. Where?

Mr. BROWN. That would be the railroad overpass over Stemmons Expressway service road.

Mr. BALL. Is that the one that leads off Elm?

Mr. BROWN. You mean that crosses Elm?

Mr. BALL. That crosses Elm, yes; the overpass across Elm.

Mr. BROWN. No, sir.

Mr. BALL. What does it cross?

Mr. BROWN. It's over Stemmons Expressway; in other words, they make that turn off Elm and go up.

Mr. BALL. You know where Elm, the corner of Elm and Houston is?

Mr. BROWN. Yes, sir.

Mr. BALL. Then there is a road, the highway continues on to the west, a little south, is that what you call the Stemmons Expressway?

Mr. BROWN. There's one there, too, but that overpass is actually a road. Where I was was the railroad overpass.

Mr. BALL. The railroad overpass itself?

Mr. BROWN. Yes, sir.

Mr. BALL. How far were you from the place where the continuation of Elm goes under the overpass?

Mr. BROWN. Oh, approximately 100 yards.

Mr. BALL. Let me see if we can get something in the record that will be your position. You were appointed to this particular spot?

Mr. BROWN. Yes, sir.

Mr. BALL. Was there another patrolman on the overpass also?

Mr. BROWN. Yes, sir; James Lomax.

Mr. BALL. Now, this is the place where the railroad yards run over the highway?

Mr. BROWN. Yes.

Mr. BALL. And you are on the Stemmons Freeway end of it?

Mr. BROWN. That's right; in other words, Stemmons Freeway and the service road both go under the underpass.

Mr. BALL. What is his name?

Mr. BROWN. James Lomax.

Mr. BALL. How far were you from the point where Elm Street goes under the underpass?

Mr. BROWN. I would say approximately 100 yards.

Mr. BALL. Approximately 100 yards in what direction?

Mr. BROWN. That would be—wouldn't be straight east, but it would be to easterly, kind of off at an angle—I would say about from us about a 20° angle to the right.

Mr. BALL. You would be east or west?

Mr. BROWN. We would be to the southwest of that.

Mr. BALL. You would be to the southwest of that?

Mr. BROWN. Yes, I would say that's about right.

Mr. BALL. Did you have the corner of Houston and Elm Street in sight from where you were located?

Mr. BROWN. Actually, we could see cars moving there, you know, coming and making the turn, but the intersection, that would be about all we probably could see would be cars.

211

Mr. BALL. Could you see cars going down after they made the turn and going down toward the underpass south?

Mr. BROWN. Yes.

Mr. BALL. You could see those?

Mr. BROWN. Yes.

Mr. BALL. Did you have any instructions when you were assigned to this location?

Mr. BROWN. Yes, sir.

Mr. BALL. What were they?

Mr. BROWN. Not allow anyone on the overpass whatever and walk forward and make both ends—in other words, check both ends of the overpass.

Mr. BALL. That was you and Mr. Lomax?

Mr. BROWN. That's right.

Mr. BALL. Was there an E. V. Brown?

Mr. BROWN. That's me.

Mr. BALL. That's you, and was there also a Joe Murphy?

Mr. BROWN. Joe Murphy is a three-wheeler.

Mr. BALL. Yes; where was he?

Mr. BROWN. I don't know, sir; he was, I believe he was on his three-wheeler.

Mr. BALL. On his motor?

Mr. BROWN. I believe; I wouldn't say for sure but I don't know.

Mr. BALL. Did you people keep people off the overpass?

Mr. BROWN. We made no contact with anyone except one of the railroad detectives come up there and talked to us.

Mr. BALL. Did you keep the underpass free of people?

Mr. BROWN. Underneath?

Mr. BALL. No; up above.

Mr. BROWN. Up above; yes, sir.

Mr. BALL. What about underneath?

Mr. BROWN. Well, that was roadway there; people wouldn't be able to walk.

Mr. BALL. On the top of the overpass you kept that free of people?

Mr. BROWN. Yes, sir.

Mr. BALL. Did you have the railroad yards in sight?

Mr. BROWN. Yes, sir.

Mr. BALL. They would be what direction from where you were standing?

Mr. BROWN. That would be east; that would be east of us.

Mr. BALL. East, maybe a little north?

Mr. BROWN. Yes, the whole thing kind of in that general direction, you know.

Mr. BALL. Did you see any people over in the railroad yards?

Mr. BROWN. Not that I recall; now they were moving trains in and out.

Mr. BALL. But you did not see people standing?

Mr. BROWN. No, sir; sure didn't.

Mr. BALL. Everything was in clear view?

Mr. BROWN. Yes, sir.

Mr. BALL. I withdraw the question. Was there any obstruction of your vision to the railroad yards?

Mr. BROWN. Yes.

Mr. BALL. What?

Mr. BROWN. Not the direction of the railroad yard, but at ground level we didn't have very good view. Mr. Lomax and I remarked that we didn't have a very good view.

Mr. BALL. Was that because of the moving trains?

Mr. BROWN. Yes, sir.

Mr. BALL. Did you see the President's motorcade come on to Houston Street from Elm; were you able to see that?

Mr. BROWN. Now they came down Main, didn't they, to Houston?

Mr. BALL. Yes.

Mr. BROWN. No, sir; actually, the first I noticed the car was when it stopped.

Mr. BALL. Where?

Mr. BROWN. After it made the turn and when the shots were fired, it stopped.

Mr. BALL. Did it come to a complete stop?

Mr. BROWN. That, I couldn't swear to.

Mr. BALL. It appeared to be slowed down some?

Mr. BROWN. Yes; slowed down.

Mr. BALL. Did you hear the shots?

Mr. BROWN. Yes, sir.

Mr. BALL. How many?

Mr. BROWN. Three.

Mr. BALL. Where did they seem to come from?

Mr. BROWN. Well, they seemed high to me, actually; if you want, would you like me to tell you?

Mr. BALL. Sure, tell it in your own words.

Mr. BROWN. Well, down in that river bottom there, there's a whole lot of pigeons this particular day, and they heard the shots before we did because I saw them flying up—must have been 50, 75 of them.

Mr. BALL. Where was the river bottom?

Mr. BROWN. You know, actually off to the—between us and the, this overpass you are talking about there's kind of a levee along there. It's really a grade of the railroad, is what it is; that's where they were and then I heard these shots and then I smelled this gun powder.

Mr. BALL. You did?

Mr. BROWN. It come on it would be maybe a couple minutes later so—at least it smelled like it to me.

Mr. BALL. What direction did the sound seem to come from?

Mr. BROWN. It came it seemed the direction of that building, that Texas——

Mr. BALL. School Book Depository?

Mr. BROWN. School Book Depository.

Mr. BALL. Did you see any pigeons flying around the building?

Mr. BROWN. I just don't recall that; no, sir.

Mr. BALL. Which way did you look when you heard the sound?

Mr. BROWN. When I first heard that sound I looked up toward that building because actually it seemed to come from there.

Mr. BALL. Where was it you saw the pigeons rise?

Mr. BROWN. They must have been down there feeding at that time because they just seemed to all take off.

Mr. BALL. Where were they from where you were standing?

Mr. BROWN. From where I was standing they would be about half way between—no, they would be up more toward that other overpass, what they call the triple underpass.

Mr. BALL. The triple underpass?

Mr. BROWN. Yes.

Mr. BALL. You were about 100 yards from the triple underpass?

Mr. BROWN. Approximately; yes.

Mr. BALL. Was there anybody standing on the triple underpass?

Mr. BROWN. On the triple underpass?

Mr. BALL. Yes.

Mr. BROWN. Yes, sir; they had at least two officers.

Mr. BALL. Anybody but police officers?

Mr. BROWN. Not that I know of. I didn't recall anyone.

Mr. BALL. What did you do after you heard the shots?

Mr. BROWN. Well, let me see, by that time the escort as to the motorcycles, we could see them coming, the front part of the motorcade, I don't think they probably realized what happened; they had come on ahead. And then we saw the car coming with the President, and as it passed underneath me I looked right down and I could see this officer in the back; he had this gun and he was swinging it around, looked like a machinegun, and the President was all sprawled out, his foot on the back cushion. Of course, you couldn't conceive anything that happened; of course, we knew something had happened, but we couldn't conceive the fact it did.

Mr. BALL. Did you move out of there in any direction?

Mr. BROWN. No, sir; we, well, we checked there; the area, we kept checking that area through there and, of course, there were people all over the place but we didn't allow anybody up on the railroad right-of-way through there.

Mr. BALL. Was there anybody standing on the triple underpass at the point where Elm goes underneath?

Mr. BROWN. Uh-uh, I couldn't recall; no one except police officers.

Mr. BALL. More than one?

Mr. BROWN. Yes.

Mr. BALL. Did you search any part of the area?

213

Mr. BROWN. We were instructed to stay at our posts, which we did, and later we got instructions to check the area around the Depository, Book Depository Building, and to obtain the license numbers of all those cars parked around there, which we did.

Mr. BALL. Where were any cars parked?

Mr. BROWN. Well, there's a parking lot around that building and there was several cars parked all around that building.

Mr. BALL. You took the license numbers?

Mr. BROWN. Yes; in fact, I think there must have been four or five officers taking license numbers.

Mr. BALL. How long were you around there?

Mr. BROWN. Well, we stayed and then they sent us back to the overpass and we stayed there until, let's see, I don't believe we left there until about 3:30 or 4 in the afternoon, and then we came up to the hall and Mr. Sorrels, I believe talked to us.

Mr. BALL. I think that's all, officer. This will be written up and you can take it, read it, and sign it if you wish, or you can waive your signature, just as you wish. Which do you wish?

Mr. BROWN. You mean today?

Mr. BALL. No; it will be a week or so.

Mr. BROWN. Oh, yes.

Mr. BALL. Which do you prefer?

Mr. BROWN. What preference do I have?

Mr. BALL. Well, it will be written up and you can come in and sign it——

Mr. BROWN. Yes.

Mr. BALL. Or you can waive signature and you don't need to come in and sign it. It is your option; you can do either way.

Mr. BROWN. I will be glad to come in and sign it.

Mr. BALL. She will notify you. Thanks very much.

TESTIMONY OF EARLE V. BROWN RESUMED

The testimony of Earle V. Brown was taken at 2:15 p.m., on April 8, 1964, in the office of the U.S. attorney, 301 Post Office Building, Bryan and Ervay Streets, Dallas, Tex., by Mr. Joseph A. Ball, assistant counsel of the President's Commission.

Mr. BALL. You have been sworn, so we will just continue with your deposition, and your name is Earle V. Brown?

Mr. BROWN. Right; E-a-r-l-e (spelling).

Mr. BALL. Mr. Brown, I have had a map made here which I would like to have you inspect here. The railroad overpass is shown—that runs in a north and south direction?

Mr. BROWN. Yes.

Mr. BALL. And Stemmons Freeway overpass is shown—that runs north and south, doesn't it?

Mr. BROWN. Right.

Mr. BALL. Were you on either one of those overpasses?

Mr. BROWN. Either one of those two there?

Mr. BALL. Yes.

Mr. BROWN. No, sir.

Mr. BALL. Where were you?

Mr. BROWN. On this overpass here—this TP Railroad overpass.

Mr. BALL. The overpass that runs in an east and west direction?

Mr. BROWN. Right—yes, sir.

Mr. BALL. Now, will you take this pen and draw on there your position on the overpass?

Mr. BROWN. Well, you see, on this overpass, of course, there are the tracks and then there is a railing and then there is a catwalk on each side and we walked the catwalk, and we would come around on each end and we would walk the tracks and come around there.

Mr. BALL. Where were you when you saw the President's car turn on Houston and Elm Street?

Mr. BROWN. I was on the catwalk.

Mr. BALL. Can you mark your position?

Mr. BROWN. I would be—approximately in the center. (Instrument marked by the witness, as requested by Counsel Ball.)

Mr. BALL. Have you marked the place where you were?

Mr. BROWN. Yes; it would be about the center of that.

Mr. BALL. Is that where you were when you heard the shots?

Mr. BROWN. Yes.

214

Mr. BALL. And did you see anybody out on the railroad overpass?

Mr. BROWN. No, sir; I didn't see anybody there.

Mr. BALL. You don't recall seeing anybody that would either be where Elm goes under the overpass or where Main goes under the overpass—you don't recall seeing anybody?

Mr. BROWN. No; I don't recall seeing anyone there.

Mr. BALL. You told me yesterday you saw some officers.

Mr. BROWN. Well, that would be the police officers—would be the only ones I saw.

Mr. BALL. Do you know who those officers were?

Mr. BROWN. No, sir; at the time I did, but I wouldn't know now.

Mr. BALL. Did you see any officer on Stemmons Freeway where we have positioned (1), (2), and (3) on this diagram?

Mr. BROWN. No, I didn't.

Mr. BALL. Now, the place where you marked your location—we will mark that as Brown Exhibits—the X marks the position of Brown, is that correct?

Mr. BROWN. Yes.

Mr. BALL. That's all. Thank you very much.

Mr. BROWN. All right. (Instrument marked by the reporter as "Brown Exhibit A," for identification.)

Mr. BALL. Thank you very much for coming.

Mr. BROWN. All right.

TESTIMONY OF ROYCE G. SKELTON

The testimony of Royce G. Skelton was taken at 2:45 p.m., on April 8, 1964, in the office of U.S. attorney, 301 Post Office Building, Bryan and Ervay Streets, Dallas, Tex., by Mr. Joseph A. Ball, assistant counsel of the President's Commission.

Mr. BALL. Will you raise your right hand and be sworn?

Do you solemnly swear that the testimony you are about to give before the Commission will be the truth, the whole truth and nothing but the truth?

Mr. SKELTON. I do.

Mr. BALL. Will you state your name, please, for the record?

Mr. SKELTON. Royce G. Skelton.

Mr. BALL. What is your business?

Mr. SKELTON. I am a mail clerk at the Texas Louisiana Freight Bureau.

Mr. BALL. Where do you work?

Mr. SKELTON. At the Texas Louisiana Freight Bureau.

Mr. BALL. Where were you born and where did you come from?

Mr. SKELTON. I was born in Henrietta, Tex., May 25, 1940.

Mr. BALL. And where did you go to school?

Mr. SKELTON. I attended all grade schools in Wichita Falls and I graduated from Wichita Falls High School.

Mr. BALL. Tell me where you went to school.

Mr. SKELTON. Wichita Falls through high school and I attended 1 year at Midwestern University.

Mr. BALL. And when did you go to work for the railroad?

Mr. SKELTON. February 1, 1963.

Mr. BALL. What kind of work do you do?

Mr. SKELTON. Mail clerk.

Mr. BALL. On November 22, 1963, did you watch the parade, the motorcade of the President?

Mr. SKELTON. Yes, sir; I went to the triple overpass about 12:20—I think it was 12:15, or something like that.

Mr. BALL. Whom did you go down there with?

Mr. SKELTON. Austin Miller and myself.

Mr. BALL. Where does he work?

Mr. SKELTON. He is a mail clerk also in the same company.

Mr. BALL. Where did you stand to watch the parade?

Mr. SKELTON. Well, we were directly over Elm Street.

Mr. BALL. Directly over Elm?

Mr. SKELTON. Maybe it would be to the left-hand side, if you were on the street.

Mr. BALL. Anybody else there on the overpass?

Mr. SKELTON. There were quite a few people up there.

215

Mr. BALL. Did you know any of them?

Mr. SKELTON. Well, I know by sight—I knew the electrician, an old man that's an electrician.

Mr. BALL. Frank Reilly?

Mr. SKELTON. Is that his name?

Mr. BALL. The man that was here a moment ago—his name is Reilly.

Mr. SKELTON. I know him when I see him.

Mr. BALL. Yes——

Mr. SKELTON. And Austin Miller, of course.

Mr. BALL. Did you know Dodd, the employee of the railroad?

Mr. SKELTON. No, sir; like I say, I recognized them off and on when I see them around there.

Mr. BALL. Did you see any police officers there?

Mr. SKELTON. Yes; this man right here—they say it was him—I don't recall whether it was or not.

Mr. BALL. Who—Mr. Brown?

Mr. SKELTON. The one who was in here just a while ago—they say he was the one up there, but I don't know.

Mr. BALL. You didn't recognize him there?

Mr. SKELTON. No; I didn't recognize him.

Mr. BALL. In other words, you saw some police officers up there?

Mr. SKELTON. Yes, sir.

Mr. BALL. Where were they standing?

Mr. SKELTON. There was one standing directly behind me, I think, or in the general vicinity, and there was one on the far side of the triple underpass.

Mr. BALL. By "far side," you mean where?

Mr. SKELTON. It would be back on this side.

Mr. BALL. It would be south?

Mr. SKELTON. No, sir; that would be the east side—isn't it?

Mr. BALL. Elm runs east and west.

Mr. SKELTON. It would be the west side.

Mr. BALL. It would be west?

Mr. SKELTON. Yes, sir; and then there was one back over here on Stemmons—I noticed one, at least, over there and one on the railroad overpass on Stemmons.

Mr. BALL. How many police officers were on this overpass, the railroad overpass?

Mr. SKELTON. Two, I would say, sir. That's all I saw.

Mr. BALL. And how many men did you see standing right near on the railroad overpass over Elm, just approximately?

Mr. SKELTON. Eight, including the officer—eight or nine.

Mr. BALL. Did you see the President's car turn on Elm Street?

Mr. SKELTON. Yes, sir; I saw the car carrying the Presidential flag turn.

Mr. BALL. And did you hear something soon after that?

Mr. SKELTON. Just about the same time the car straightened up—got around the corner— I heard two shots, but I didn't know at that time they were shots.

Mr. BALL. Where did they seem to come from?

Mr. SKELTON. Well, I couldn't tell then, they were still so far from where I was.

Mr. BALL. Did the shots sound like they came from where you were standing?

Mr. SKELTON. No, sir; definitely not. It sounded like they were right there—more or less like motorcycle backfire, but I thought that they were these dumbballs that they throw at the cement because I could see the smoke coming up off the cement.

Mr. BALL. You saw some smoke come off of the cement?

Mr. SKELTON. Yes.

Mr. BALL. Where did it seem to you that the sound came from, what direction?

Mr. SKELTON. Towards the President's car.

Mr. BALL. From the President's car?

Mr. SKELTON. Right around the motorcycles and all that—I couldn't distinguish because it was too far away.

Mr. BALL. How long did you stand there?

Mr. SKELTON. I stood there from about 12:15 until the time the President was shot.

Mr. BALL. How many shots did you hear?

Mr. SKELTON. I think I heard four—I mean—I couldn't be sure.

Mr. BALL. You think you heard four?

Mr. SKELTON. Yes.

Mr. BALL. How long did you stay there after you heard the fourth shot?

Mr. SKELTON. Not very long—just as soon as the cars sped away and everything was in a big commotion—we ran down to listen to the radio. We couldn't get anything off of that—we heard that the President had been shot and so we went back up there and the police officer asked us if we had seen the assassination and we told him we had. He said he would like to get a statement from us, so he took us over to the sheriff's office.

Mr. BALL. Did you see any pigeons flying or anything like that?

Mr. SKELTON. No, sir; I didn't see anything like that—any pigeons at all.

Mr. BALL. I think that's all I have. This will be written up and submitted to you for your signature, if you want to sign it, or you can waive your signature.

Which do you want to do?

Mr. SKELTON. I will waive my signature. I am sure it is all right.

Mr. BALL. That is fine. Thank you very much.

Mr. SKELTON. There's one thing I could say—you have that other report?

Mr. BALL. What is that?

Mr. SKELTON. About when I saw one of the bullets where it hit on the pavement and it hit, the smoke did come from the general vicinity of where you say Oswald was.

Mr. BALL. Wait a minute—let me ask you some questions about that.

Tell me, now, about the smoke—did you see some smoke?

Mr. SKELTON. After those two shots, and the car came on down closer to the triple underpass, well, there was another shot—two more shots I heard, but one of them—I saw a bullet, or I guess it was a bullet—I take for granted it was—hit in the left front of the President's car on the cement, and when it did, the smoke carried with it—away from the building.

Mr. BALL. You mean there was some smoke in the building?

Mr. SKELTON. No; on the pavement—you know, pavement when it is hit with a hard object it will scatter—it will spread.

Mr. BALL. Which way did it spread?

Mr. SKELTON. It spread just right in line, like you said.

Mr. BALL. I haven't said anything—tell me what you think it was?

Mr. SKELTON. Like I said—south of us—it would be southwest, you know, in a direct line from the Texas Depository.

Mr. BALL. I see. In other words, the spray seemed to go to the west; is that right?

Mr. SKELTON. Yes.

Mr. BALL. All right. Thanks very much.

I'm going to get you to mark one of these maps and show where you were standing. Here is Elm and here is the railroad underpass and pay no attention to the diagrams, but show me about where you were standing.

Mr. SKELTON. I was about right there (marked instrument referred to as requested by Counsel Ball).

Mr. BALL. By that "X" we will put the word "Skelton" and that is where you were standing with your friend?

Mr. SKELTON. Approximately—yes.

Mr. BALL. Now, did you see any smoke or anything from any place around there?

Mr. SKELTON. No, sir; I just stated to your secretary that I heard people say they did, but I didn't.

Mr. BALL. But you did see something light on the street?

Mr. SKELTON. Yes, sir.

Mr. BALL. About where?

Mr. SKELTON. A bullet—let's see—this is kind of out of proportion [referring to diagram], and I would say the bullet hit about right here [indicating on diagram].

Mr. BALL. Then, let's mark that as "Skelton (2)" and we will make the first Skelton number (1) and then Skelton number (2), and this X mark here is where you saw the bullet and which way did the spray go?

Mr. SKELTON. Just like it was going there.

Mr. BALL. Mark an arrow showing the direction that you think the spray was going.

Mr. SKELTON. (Marks the diagram with arrow.)

Mr. BALL. That's fine, and we will make that as an exhibit Shelton exhibit A and attach it to your deposition.

(Instrument marked by the reporter as Skelton exhibit A for identification)

Mr. BALL. Thank you and that is all.

217

Mr. SKELTON. Thank you.

TESTIMONY OF S. M. HOLLAND

The testimony of S. M Holland was taken at 2:20 p.m, on April 8, 1964 in the Office of the U.S. attorney, 301 Post Office Building, Bryan and Ervay Streets, Dallas, Tex., by Mr. Samuel A. Stern, assistant counsel of the President's Commission. Mr. S M Holland was accompanied by his attorney, Mr. Balford Morrison.

Mr. STERN. Would you rise please and raise your right hand so as to be sworn.

Do you solemnly swear the testimony that you are about to give will be the truth, the whole truth, and nothing but the truth, so help you God?

Mr. HOLLAND. I do.

Mr. STERN. Sit down, please.

You have recorded Mr. Morrison's presence?

The Reporter. Yes.

Mr. STERN. Mr Holland, you have received a letter from the Commission asking you to come and testify today?

Mr. HOLLAND. Yes.

Mr. STERN. As you know, the Commission is inquiring into all of the facts concerning the assassination of President Kennedy and we want your evidence concerning what you saw at the time of the assassination from the place you were standing. May we have, for the record, your name and residence address?

Mr. HOLLAND. S. M. Holland, 1119 Lucille Street, Irving, Tex.

Mr. STERN. What is your occupation?

Mr. HOLLAND. Signal supervisor for Union Terminal Railroad.

Mr. STERN. How long have you been employed by that organization?

Mr. HOLLAND. Union Terminal since 1938.

Mr. STERN. Now on Friday November 22, will you describe what you did concerning the President's visit and where you were?

Mr. HOLLAND. Well, about 11:00 o'clock, a couple of policemen and a plain clothesman came up on top of the triple underpass, and we had some men working up there, and I knew that they was going to have a parade, and I left my office, and walked up to the underpass to talk to the policemen. And they asked me during the parade if I would come back up there and identify people that was supposed to be on that overpass. That is the railroad people.

Mr. STERN. Where is your office Mr Holland?

Mr. HOLLAND. At the Union Terminal Station.

Mr. STERN. Is that within walking distance of the triple overpass?

Mr. HOLLAND. Yes, it is. About—less than a quarter of a mile, a very short distance.

Mr. STERN. And these policemen that you spoke to, there were 3 altogether?

Mr. HOLLAND. Two—there were 2 city policemen and 1 man in plainclothes. I didn't talk to him. I talked to the city policemen.

Mr. STERN. You don't know what his affiliation was?

Mr. HOLLAND. I know he was a plainclothes detective or FBI agent or some thing like that, but I don't know, and I told him I would be back and after lunch I would go up there.

Mr. STERN. Approximately what time did you arrive up there?

Mr. HOLLAND. Oh, I arrived up there, I guess, about a quarter until 12, and I would identify each person that came up there that he worked at the Union Terminal, and department so-and-so.

Mr. STERN. Whom did you see there at 11:45 when you returned, from then until 12:30?

Mr. HOLLAND. Well, I would have to try to remember who all was up there then. There was Mr. Reilly and Mr. R. C. Dodd.

Mr. STERN. Mr. Reilly?

Mr. HOLLAND. Reilly.

Mr. STERN. Who was——

Mr. HOLLAND. R. C. Dodd, and N. H. Potter and Luke Winburn.

Mr. STERN. Luke?

Mr. HOLLAND. Winburn.

Mr. STERN. And——

Mr. HOLLAND. And a fellow by the name of Johnson, he works in the car department.

Mr. STERN. Johnson.

Mr. HOLLAND. And there was another fellow who worked at the car department, tall, blond-headed boy, and I can't remember his name.

Mr. STERN. That makes six people so far. Are these all employeesof——

Mr. HOLLAND. Yes.

Mr. STERN. Of the terminal?

Mr. HOLLAND. Yes, and they were two men, one of them worked for the Katy, and one for the T. & P., that I don't know their names, but I do know that they were railroad people. They were over on business. Working on those business cars, and one of them was a Katy employee, and one was a T. & P. employee.

Mr. STERN. Could you give me their full names?

Mr. HOLLAND. Texas & Pacific, and the Missouri, Kansas, Texas Railroad.

Mr. STERN. You don't know the names of those particular men?

Mr. HOLLAND. No; I don't.

Mr. STERN. Did you see them here today?

Mr. HOLLAND. I know the policemen talked to them and got identification from them.

Mr. STERN. Yes; but they are not, as far as you know, the two gentlemen that you saw sitting in the anteroom to the U.S. attorney's office just before——

Mr. HOLLAND. No; neither one of those.

Mr. STERN. Did you recognize either of those two men?

Mr. HOLLAND. One of them is a cabdriver, and the other one is an electrician at Union Terminal. The large fellow is a cabdriver.

Mr. STERN. The electrician, do you know his name?

Mr. HOLLAND. Frank Reilly.

Mr. STERN. There were two other men out there. Perhaps you didn't notice them. I spoke to them after I spoke to you.

Mr. HOLLAND. Well, at the time the parade got started they was, I guess—Davey Cowzert was up there, too.

Mr. STERN. But, just to finish with the two, you didn't recognize either of the two people who were in the anteroom a few moments ago as being people who were on the overpass that day?

Mr. HOLLAND. No.

Mr. STERN. All right.

Mr. HOLLAND. There was two people I did recognize and that was the cabdriver and Mr. Reilly was out there and that policeman, he was up there with me.

Mr. STERN. You recognized the policeman as being the policeman who was on the triple overpass at the time?

Mr. HOLLAND. Yes.

Mr. STERN. Fine. Now, another name just occurred to you of someone else.

Mr. HOLLAND. Cowzert [spelling] C-o-w-z-e-r-t, Cowzert.

Mr. STERN. Is he also an employee?

Mr. HOLLAND. Yes; he is.

Mr. STERN. Were all the people there, as far as you know, at the time the Presidential motorcade——

Mr. HOLLAND. Yes.

Mr. STERN. Came into view?

Mr. HOLLAND. One more, if I can remember his name. One that run around the corner of the fence with me. He was right behind me—why in the world—he was one of the first ones around the fence when we run around the fence to what was happening.

Mr. STERN. Before we get to that, how about the police. How many police officers were on the overpass at the time?

Mr. HOLLAND. There were two Dallas Police officers up there at that time.

Mr. STERN. Tell me if this is correct, Mr. Holland. At the time the Presidential motorcade arrived, to the best of your recollection, on the overpass there were two uniformed Dallas Police, and the following employees of the Terminal Co.: Yourself, Mr. Reilly, Mr. Dodd, Mr. Potter, Mr. Winburn, Mr. Johnson, Mr. Cowzert, and perhaps one other man?

Mr. HOLLAND. That's right.

Mr. STERN. So, that would be eight including yourself, plus two employees of the railroad. One of the T. & P. and one of the Katy?

Mr. HOLLAND. That's right. At that time. Now, like I said a while ago, by the time they started there was quite a few come up there, but I can't remember who it was or their names, because——

Mr. STERN. Before the motorcade started?

Mr. HOLLAND. Before the motorcade started.

Mr. STERN. These were people you recognized as employees?

219

Mr. HOLLAND. Some of them, and some of them I did not recognize, but I think he was asking for credentials.

Mr. STERN. The uniformed policeman?

Mr. HOLLAND. Yes; one on that side, and one on this side to keep them——

Mr. STERN. Yes; and did you participate in identifying people as being terminal or railroad employees?

Mr. HOLLAND. When they first started arriving, yes; it was my purpose for going up there.

Mr. STERN. So, that it is fair to say that at the time the President's motorcade turned into this area, there was no one on the overpass that you didn't know either as Terminal Co. employees, or railroad employees, or as a policeman?

Mr. HOLLAND. Wouldn't be fair to say that, because there was quite a few came up there right in the last moments.

Mr. STERN. There were? Tell us about that.

Mr. HOLLAND. That I couldn't recognize. There wasn't too many people up there, but there were a few that came up there the last few minutes, but the policemen were questioning them and getting their identification, and——

Mr. STERN. Is this just about the time of the motorcade?

Mr. HOLLAND. Just about the time, or just prior to it, because there was a few up there that I didn't—that I didn't recognize myself.

Mr. STERN. Had they been, as far as you could tell, checked by the police?

Mr. HOLLAND. He was checking them as they came on top of the underpass.

Mr. STERN. Did it seem to you that everybody up there had been checked by this policeman for identification?

Mr. HOLLAND. I think everyone was checked by some person.

Mr. STERN. Yes. Can you estimate the number of people that were on the overpass immediately as the motorcade came into view?

Mr. HOLLAND. Well, I would estimate that there was between 14 to 18 people.

Mr. STERN. Now, where was the motorcade when you first saw it?

Mr. HOLLAND. Turned off the Main Street—in front of the county jail.

Mr. STERN. Turning right off of Main onto Houston?

Mr. HOLLAND. It was coming down Main and turned off of Main onto Houston.

Mr. STERN. At that time will you show me on this drawing where you were and just make a mark and put the No. 1 next to that mark. That is where you were at that time? Roughly in the middle of the overpass over Elm Street?

Mr. HOLLAND. That's right.

Mr. STERN. And where, in relation to the concrete fence that——

Mr. HOLLAND. Picket fence or concrete?

Mr. STERN. No; the concrete.

Mr. HOLLAND. Oh, the concrete banister?

Mr. STERN. The concrete banister. Were you right at the banister?

Mr. HOLLAND. I was; would you like to see the exact location?

Mr. STERN. Yes.

Mr. HOLLAND. This is my son standing in the exact location I was in [indicating].

Mr. STERN. Off the record a moment.

(Discussion off the record.)

Mr. STERN. Back on the record. Well, then, we'll mark this as Exhibit B, reserving Exhibit A for this drawing, and Exhibit B is a photograph you took on Saturday, November 23, of your son standing in the position at the banister of the triple overpass where you were at the time the motorcade came into view.

Mr. HOLLAND. That's right.

Mr. STERN. Fine. That is quite a good picture. At that time, can you indicate, to the best of your knowledge where other persons were standing on the overpass, and particularly in relationship to the two police officers who were on the overpass?

Mr. HOLLAND. Well, as well as I remember, one police officer was standing right behind me, or pretty close behind me.

Mr. STERN. Put a "2" where you believe he was standing.

Mr. HOLLAND. He was standing in close enough so that he could see, but he could also see the people, and the other policeman, I think, unless he left immediately before this happened—see, when they turned there. I didn't turn around and look back any more, but the last time I saw this policeman he was standing over here on this side, about [indicating].

Mr. STERN. Standing almost directly behind you?

Mr. HOLLAND. Yes.

220

Mr. STERN. But, on the other side of the overpass, facing west?

Mr. HOLLAND. Yes; all this way, across the tracks. See, these are all railroad tracks, and he was standing over here on this side immediately before this motorcade turned this. Now, after they turned, I don't know, but—because I was watching them.

Mr. STERN. Yes.

Would you put a "3" where you believe he was standing and can you indicate on there where you believe the other 12 to 15 or 16 people were who were on the overpass at this time.

Mr. HOLLAND. Well——

Mr. STERN. Were they all standing in one group?

Mr. HOLLAND. There was a pretty close group between this column here, and this place right in there. In other words, if I can—had a shot of it, we could find that pretty close. I don't know that I have one.

Mr. STERN. What you have indicated on the drawing is on the part of the overpass from one side of Elm Street to the other.

Mr. HOLLAND. Yes; this is one side of Elm Street, and this would be the other. If you would get over here there would be a banister or something in your way, and this is grass out here, and you couldn't get to get too good a view, and most of the people was from this right in here, over to right in here [indicating].

Mr. STERN. All right. Now——

Mr. HOLLAND. And this bench runs right along similar to that, up here to this [indicating].

Mr. STERN. That is a wooden picket fence that you are describing that runs from the end of the concrete banister?

Mr. HOLLAND. That's right.

Mr. STERN. Over to a little——

Mr. HOLLAND. Little house there.

Mr. STERN. Little——

Mr. HOLLAND. What do they call that thing?

Mr. MORRISON. I don't know.

Mr. STERN. Little pavilion? Little concrete pavilion?

Mr. HOLLAND. Yes.

Mr. STERN. Now, what did you observe from that point on, Mr. Holland?

Mr. HOLLAND. Well, I observed the motorcade when it turned off of Main Street onto Houston Street and back on Elm Street. There was two young ladies right across from this sign, which would be, I judge—would say they were standing about here [indicating].

Mr. STERN. Put No. 4 there, please. Fine.

Mr. HOLLAND. And the motorcade was coming down in this fashion, and the President was waving to the people on this side [indicating].

Mr. STERN. That is the north side of Elm Street?

Mr. HOLLAND. Yes; on the north side.

Mr. STERN. All right.

Mr. HOLLAND. And she was looking in this direction [indicating].

Mr. STERN. "She," is Mrs. Kennedy?

Mr. HOLLAND. His wife. And about that time——

Mr. STERN. Was looking in a southern direction?

Mr. HOLLAND. In the southern direction.

Mr. STERN. South side of Elm Street?

Mr. HOLLAND. And about that time he went over like that [indicating], and put his hand up, and she was still looking off, as well as I could tell.

Mr. STERN. Now, when you say, "he went like that," you leaned forward and raised your right hand?

Mr. HOLLAND. Pulled forward and hand just stood like that momentarily.

Mr. STERN. With his right hand?

Mr. HOLLAND. His right hand; and that was the first report that I heard.

Mr. STERN. What did it sound like?

Mr. HOLLAND. Well, it was pretty loud, and naturally, underneath this underpass here it would be a little louder, the concussion from underneath it, it was a pretty loud report, and the car traveled a few yards, and Governor Connally turned in this fashion, like that [indicating] with his hand out, and another report.

Mr. STERN. With his right hand out?

Mr. HOLLAND. Turning to his right.

Mr. STERN. To his right?

Mr. HOLLAND. And another report rang out and he slumped down in his seat, and about that time Mrs. Kennedy was looking at these girls over here [indicating]. The girls standing—now one of them was taking a picture, and the other one was just standing there, and she turned around facing the President and Governor Connally. In other words, she realized what was happening, I guess.

Now, I mean, that was apparently that—she turned back around, and by the time she could get turned around he was hit again along in—I'd say along in here [indicating].

Mr. STERN. How do you know that? Did you observe that?

Mr. HOLLAND. I observed it. It knocked him completely down on the floor. Over, just slumped completely over. That second——

Mr. STERN. Did you hear a third report?

Mr. HOLLAND. I heard a third report and I counted four shots and about the same time all this was happening, and in this group of trees—[indicating].

Mr. STERN. Now, you are indicating trees on the north side of Elm Street?

Mr. HOLLAND. These trees right along here [indicating].

Mr. STERN. Let's mark this Exhibit C and draw a circle around the trees you are referring to.

Mr. HOLLAND. Right in there. (Indicating.)

There was a shot, a report, I don't know whether it was a shot. I can't say that. And a puff of smoke came out about 6 or 8 feet above the ground right out from under those trees. And at just about this location from where I was standing you could see that puff of smoke, like someone had thrown a firecracker, or something out, and that is just about the way it sounded. It wasn't as loud as the previous reports or shots.

Mr. STERN. What number would that have been in the——

Mr. HOLLAND. Well, that would—they were so close together.

Mr. STERN. The second and third or the third and fourth?

Mr. HOLLAND. The third and fourth. The third and the fourth.

Mr. STERN. So, that it might have been the third or the fourth?

Mr. HOLLAND. It could have been the third or fourth, but there were definitely four reports.

Mr. STERN. You have no doubt about that?

Mr. HOLLAND. I have no doubt about it. I have no doubt about seeing that puff of smoke come out from under those trees either.

Mr. STERN. Mr. Holland, do you recall making a statement to an agent of of the FBI several days after?

Mr. HOLLAND. I made a statement that afternoon in Sheriff Bill Decker's office, and then the Sunday or the Sunday following the Friday, there were two FBI men out at my house at the time that Oswald was shot.

Mr. STERN. Did you tell them that you heard distinctly four shots at that time?

Mr. HOLLAND. Yes.

Mr. STERN. You were certain then?

Mr. HOLLAND. I was certain then and I—in that statement I believe that I——

Mr. STERN. Well, the FBI report that I have said that you heard either three or four shots fired together, and I gather the impression of the agent was that you were uncertain whether it was three or four.

Mr. HOLLAND. At the time I made that statement, of course, I was pretty well shook up, but I told the people at the sheriff's office, whoever took the statement, that I believed there was four shots, because they were so close together, and I have also told those two, four, six Federal men that have been out there that I definitely saw the puff of smoke and heard the report from under those trees.

Mr. STERN. Did you realize that these were shots then?

Mr. HOLLAND. Yes; I think I realized what was happening out there.

Mr. STERN. You did?

Mr. HOLLAND. When Governor Connally was knocked down in the seat.

Mr. STERN. What did you then do?

Mr. HOLLAND. Well, immediately after the shots was fired, I run around the end of this overpass, behind the fence to see if I could see anyone up there behind the fence.

Mr. STERN. That is the picket fence?

Mr. HOLLAND. That is the picket fence.

Mr. STERN. On the north side of Elm Street?

Mr. HOLLAND. Of course, this was this sea of cars in there and it was just a big—it wasn't an inch in there that wasn't automobiles and I couldn't see up in that corner. I ran on up to the

222

corner of this fence behind the building. By the time I got there there were 12 or 15 policemen and plainclothesmen, and we looked for empty shells around there for quite a while, and I left because I had to get back to the office. I didn't give anyone my name. No one—didn't anyone ask for it, and it wasn't but an hour or so until the deputy sheriff came down to the office and took me back up to the courthouse.

Mr. STERN. Did he know you personally?

Mr. HOLLAND. No, no; he had to find me and find where I was. He didn't know me, and I don't know who told me they wanted me over at the courthouse, so, I went back up there with him and made out the statement, and made—made out the statement before they found out the results on the shots, or before that Oswald had even shot that policeman.

I was making out the statement before that, so, it was immediately after the motorcade had passed through there.

Mr STERN. What was your impression about the source of these noises, if you had one?

Mr. HOLLAND. Well, the impression was that the shots, the first two or three shots came from the upper part of the street, now, from where I was.

Mr. STERN. East on Elm?

Mr. HOLLAND. Yes, up in here somewhere. [Indicating.] I didn't have the least idea that it was up any higher, but I thought the shot was coming—coming from this crowd in here [indicating]. That is what it sounded like to me from where I was.

Mr. STERN. You are indicating on this Exhibit C. Why don't you put a square around the area that you just pointed to. You had no idea, I take it, that the shots were coming from your area?

Mr. HOLLAND. No.

Mr. STERN. It is your impression that they did not, could not, as far as the sound was concerned?

Mr. HOLLAND. As far as the sound was concerned they did not.

Mr. STERN. Did you see anything on the overpass that seemed to you any way unusual?

Mr. HOLLAND. Oh, no; no.

Mr. STERN. All right. Off the record.

(Off the record.)

Mr. STERN. Back on the record. Now, Mr. Holland, I'm showing you a copy of an affidavit which I am marking as Exhibit D. That is the affidavit you made that you described a few moments ago?

Mr. HOLLAND. That's right.

Mr. STERN. Would you read that.

Mr. HOLLAND. "I am signal supervisor for the Union Terminal, and I was inspecting signal and switches and stopped to watch the parade. I was standing on the top of the triple underpass and the President's car was coming down Elm Street, and when they got just about to the arcade, I heard what I thought for a moment was a firecracker and he slumped over and I looked over toward the arcade and trees and saw a puff of smoke come from the trees and I heard three more shots after the first shot but that was the only puff of smoke I saw. I immediately ran around to where I could see behind the arcade and did not see anyone running from there. But the puff of smoke I saw definitely came from behind the arcade to the trees. After the first shot the President slumped over and Mrs. Kennedy jumped up and tried to get over in the back seat to him and then the second shot rang out. After the first shot the Secret Service man raised up in the seat with a machine gun and then dropped back down in the seat. And they immediately sped off. Everything is spinning in my head and if I remember anything else later I will come back and tell Bill."

That is Mr. Decker. And—brother it was, too.

Mr. STERN. I'm sure it was.

Mr. HOLLAND. Stand there and watch two or three men get killed——

Mr. STERN. Now, that statement makes clear that you heard four shots, thought you heard four shots at that time?

Mr. HOLLAND. Yes.

Mr. STERN. All right.

Mr. HOLLAND. But, two of them was rather close together, though.

Mr. STERN. So close do you think that might have been one shot?

Mr. HOLLAND. No, it was four.

Mr. STERN. You are clear there were four?

Mr. HOLLAND. No; it was different sounds, different reports.

Mr. STERN. All right. Mr. Morrison, are there any questions you would like to ask Mr. Holland to clarify any points that we discussed?

223

Mr. MORRISON. Mr. Holland, is there anything you might add to this?

Mr. HOLLAND. Well, the only thing that I remember now that I didn't then, I remember about the third car down from this fence, there was a station wagon backed up toward the fence, about the third car down, and a spot. I'd say 3 foot by 2 foot, looked to me like somebody had been standing there for a long period. I guess if you could count them about a hundred foottracks in that little spot, and also mud up on the bumper of that station wagon.

Mr. STERN. This was a car back—parked behind the picket fence? Well, why don't you put the Number "5" approximately where that car would have been.

Mr. HOLLAND. If we could call this the arcade [indicating]——

Mr. STERN. All right.

Mr. HOLLAND. And one, two, three, I think it would have been just about here [indicating].

Mr. STERN. All right.

Mr. MORRISON. That is Elm Street. It would be behind the fence, wouldn't it?

Mr. HOLLAND. Well, I have got the fence running up here, and this car would be back in there [indicating]. This is the trees out here, which would—and that is approximately the same location as—the car and the trees that I saw the smoke would probably be the same location.

Mr. STERN. All right. And this was a station wagon?

Mr. HOLLAND. Now, the reason I didn't think so much about that at the time, was because there was so many people out there, and there was law enforcement officers and I thought, well, if there is anything to that they would pick that up, or notice it, but it looks like someone had been standing there for a long time, because it was muddy.

Mr. STERN. Tracks you saw in the mud?

Mr. HOLLAND. It was muddy, and you could have if you could have counted them, I imagine it would have been a hundred tracks just in that one location. It was just——

Mr. STERN. And then you saw some mud on the bumper?

Mr. HOLLAND. Mud on the bumper in two spots.

Mr. STERN. As if someone had cleaned his foot, or——

Mr. HOLLAND. Well, as if someone had cleaned their foot, or stood up on the bumper to see over the fence.

Mr. STERN. I see.

Mr. HOLLAND. Because, you couldn't very well see over it standing down in the mud, or standing on the ground, and to get a better view youcould——

Mr. STERN. Was there anything else you noticed about this station wagon?

Mr. HOLLAND. No.

Mr. STERN. Do you recall the——

Mr. HOLLAND. They searched all the cars in that location.

Mr. STERN. Did this occur to you——

Mr. HOLLAND. It occurred to me immediately when I saw it there; yes.

Mr. STERN. And you thought about it later in the day?

Mr. HOLLAND. I thought about it that night.

Mr. STERN. I see.

Mr. HOLLAND. In fact, I went to bed—it was about a week there I couldn't sleep, much, brother, and I thought about it that night, and I have thought about it a lot of times since then.

Mr. STERN. Did you ever go back to look at that site or look at the station wagon?

Mr. HOLLAND. No; I didn't go back that afternoon, because I spent the rest of the day in the county jail office over there, but a number of your Federal Agents went out there then and Secret Service men. It was just a beehive.

Mr. STERN. Yes.

Mr. HOLLAND. In a matter of a few minutes.

Mr. STERN. Did you tell any of the Federal officers, or any of the Dallas Police officers about it?

Mr. HOLLAND. I don't think I did.

Mr. STERN. This is really the first time——

Mr. HOLLAND. This is the first time that I have discussed it, that I remember. Now, I might have told in our conversation. I don't remember that, but I don't think I did.

Mr. STERN. I am not aware of any other occasion in which you did.

Mr. MORRISON. You thought the officers there would take care of that?

Mr. HOLLAND. I thought that the officers would take care of it because there were so many there, I thought they would take care of everything, and a layman didn't have any business up there, and I went on back to my office.

224

Mr. STERN. When you ran behind the picket fence after the shots were fired, did you come near the area where the station wagon was parked?

Mr. HOLLAND. Went up to behind the arcade as far as you could go.

Mr. STERN. So, you would have passed where this station wagon was?

Mr. HOLLAND. Yes.

Mr. STERN. Or, that area?

Mr. HOLLAND. Yes; immediately, but I turned around, see, and went to searching in there for empty shells, and three or four agents there then and that is when I walked back to the car there and noticed the tracks there in one little spot.

Mr. STERN. When you first came around, that was quite soon after the shots were fired?

Mr. HOLLAND. Yes.

Mr. STERN. And did you notice anything about this station wagon?

Mr. HOLLAND. I was in front of the cars, then I went in front of the cars.

Mr. STERN. In front of the cars——

Mr. HOLLAND. The cars they were parked pretty close to the fence, and I came up in front of the cars and got over to the fence and then walked back down looking around, just like the rest of them.

Mr. STERN. And that was later you came behind the station wagon?

Mr. HOLLAND. Oh, maybe 3 or 4 minutes after I got up there, and 3 or 4 minutes after I got up to the end of the fence.

Mr. STERN. This number of cars, this is an area in which cars are regularly parked?

Mr. HOLLAND. Yes.

Mr. STERN. A parking area for the School Book Depository?

Mr. HOLLAND. No; it is a parking area for the sheriff's department and people over to the courthouse. They park in there.

Mr. STERN. I see.

Mr. HOLLAND. Sheriff's department parks in there. District attorneys' cars park in there. It is railroad property, but they let them park in there and save that 25 cents. Don't put that down. Might get in trouble.

Now, do you want to know about the two policemen that were riding in that motorcade and one of them throwed the motorcycle down right in the middle of the street and run up towards that location with his gun in his hand.

Mr. STERN. Toward——

Mr. HOLLAND. The location that——

Mr. STERN. Where you saw the puff of smoke?

Mr. HOLLAND. Where I saw the puff of smoke. And another one tried to ride up the hill on his motorcycle and got about halfway up there and he run up the rest of the way on foot.

Mr. STERN. Go ahead. This is at the time of the——

Mr. HOLLAND. At the time of the——

Mr. STERN. That the shots were fired?

Mr. HOLLAND. The shots was fired.

Mr. STERN. Two motorcycle policemen who were in the motorcade?

Mr. HOLLAND. In the motorcade, and one of them threw his motorcycle down right in the middle of the street and ran up the incline with his pistol in his hand, and the other motorcycle policeman jumped over the curb with his motorcycle and tried to ride up the hill on his motorcycle, and he—tipped over with him up there, and he ran up there the rest of the way with his——

Mr. STERN. Did you see anything further involving those two?

Mr. HOLLAND. No; I ran around, I was going around the corner of the fence.

Mr. STERN. When they were coming up the incline?

Mr. HOLLAND. When that happened.

Mr. STERN. But, nothing further came of that, that you observed?

Mr. HOLLAND. No.

Mr. STERN. Did you talk to them?

Mr. HOLLAND. No.

Mr. STERN. Anything else occur to you?

Mr. HOLLAND. No; that is about all of it. If I have been of any help, I am tickled.

Mr. STERN. You certainly have. I appreciate very much your coming here today. Our reporter, Mr. Holland, will transcribe your testimony, and you then have the opportunity of reviewing it and signing it, or if you prefer you can waive your signature and she will send it directly to the Commission. Either one, it is entirely up to you, whichever you prefer.

Mr. MORRISON. I prefer that he read it and sign it.

225

Mr. STERN. Fine. Then the reporter will get in touch with you as soon as his transcript is ready to read.

Mr. MORRISON. I would like to say—now, you will cooperate with the authorities in any way?

Mr. HOLLAND. I surely will.

Mr. MORRISON. To clear this up?

Mr. HOLLAND. I sure will.

Mr. MORRISON. And you and have—you and I have been close personal friends for over 10 years, haven't we?

Mr. HOLLAND. That's right.

Mr. MORRISON. And you wanted me to come down here because you thought you would be nervous, and if I were with you maybe you would be less nervous?

Mr. HOLLAND. That's correct, because I was real nervous when I went over to that sheriff's office that afternoon.

Mr. MORRISON. I believe that is all.

Mr. STERN. Thank you.

TESTIMONY OF J. W. FOSTER

The testimony of J. W. Foster was taken at 1:30 a.m., on April 9, 1964, in the office of the U.S. attorney, 301 Post Office Building, Bryan and Ervay Streets. Dallas, Tex., by Mr. Joseph A. Ball, assistant counsel of the President's Commission.

Mr. BALL. Do you solemnly swear that the testimony you are about to give before this Commission shall be the truth, the whole truth, and nothing but the truth, so help you God?

Mr. FOSTER. I do.

Mr. BALL. Mr. Foster, we have requested Chief Curry to have you come in and testify in this matter before the Commission. This Commission was established to investigate the facts and circumstances surrounding the assassination of President Kennedy.

Mr. FOSTER. Yes, sir.

Mr. BALL. And my name is Joseph A. Ball. I am a staff officer, staff counsel with the Commission. I would like to ask you some questions about this matter. You are willing to testify, aren't you?

Mr. FOSTER. Yes, sir.

Mr. BALL. Will you state your address?

Mr. FOSTER. 309 Cooper Street. I just moved.

Mr. BALL. What is your occupation?

Mr. FOSTER. I am a police officer.

Mr. BALL. Dallas Police Department?

Mr. FOSTER. Yes, sir.

Mr. BALL. Patrolman?

Mr. FOSTER. Yes, sir.

Mr. BALL. How long have you been on the police department?

Mr. FOSTER. Nine years.

Mr. BALL. Where were you born and raised?

Mr. FOSTER. In Hill County, town of Hillsboro.

Mr. BALL. What was your education?

Mr. FOSTER. Well——

Mr. BALL. Where did you go to school?

Mr. FOSTER. Hillsboro.

Mr. BALL. How far through school?

Mr. FOSTER. Ninth grade.

Mr. BALL. What did you do after that?

Mr. FOSTER. Service.

Mr. BALL. What branch? In the Army or Navy——

Mr. FOSTER. Army.

Mr. BALL. Then what did you do?

Mr. FOSTER. Carpenter, worked for about 9 years.

Mr. BALL. Then what did you do?

Mr. FOSTER. Come to work here.

Mr. BALL. On the police department?

Mr. FOSTER. Yes.

Mr. BALL. What kind of work were you doing in November of 1963, for the Dallas Police Department?

Mr. FOSTER. I was working in the traffic division, investigation of accidents.

Mr. BALL. Investigation of accidents?

Mr. FOSTER. Yes, sir.

Mr. BALL. Did you have a special assignment on November 22?

Mr. FOSTER. Yes, sir.

Mr. BALL. 1963. And what was that?

Mr. FOSTER. That was assigned to the triple overpass to keep all unauthorized personnel off of it.

Mr. BALL. That was the overpass, the railroad overpass?

Mr. FOSTER. Yes, sir.

Mr. BALL. Do you—the overpass runs in a north-south direction?

Mr. FOSTER. Yes, sir.

Mr. BALL. And you call it the triple overpass, why?

Mr. FOSTER. Three streets coming through there.

Mr. BALL. What are they?

Mr. FOSTER. Commerce, Main, and Elm.

Mr. BALL. I have a map that I will—just a moment. I will get it.

Mr. FOSTER. All right.

(Off the record.)

Mr. BALL. Tell me where you were standing on the triple overpass about the time that the President's motorcade came into sight?

Mr. FOSTER. I was standing approximately along the—I believe the south curb of Elm Street.

Mr. BALL. Were you on the overpass?

Mr. FOSTER. Yes, sir; at the east—be the east side of the overpass.

Mr. BALL. On the east side of the overpass?

Mr. FOSTER. Yes, sir.

Mr. BALL. Then was there another officer assigned to that same position?

Mr. FOSTER. He was assigned to the overpass with me; yes, sir.

Mr. BALL. What is his name?

Mr. FOSTER. J. C. White.

Mr. BALL. Where was he?

Mr. FOSTER. He was on the west side of the overpass.

Mr. BALL. You were on the east side?

Mr. FOSTER. Yes, sir.

Mr. BALL. He was on the west side?

Mr. FOSTER. Yes, sir.

Mr. BALL. Off the record.

(Discussion off the record.)

Mr. BALL. Let's go back on the record. Now, we have a map here which we will mark as Exhibit A for your deposition.

Mr. FOSTER. Yes, sir.

Mr. BALL. And it shows the railroad overpass running in a north and south direction, is that right?

Mr. FOSTER. Yes, sir.

Mr. BALL. Over that pass come trains into the yard, is that right?

Mr. FOSTER. Yes, sir.

Mr. BALL. And that yard is to the north and west of the Texas Book Depository Building?

Mr. FOSTER. Well, that whole thing, they have yards all over up there.

Mr. BALL. In what general direction from the Texas School Book Depository Building?

Mr. FOSTER. They have yards to the north, and some to the south of it down below the Terminal.

Mr. BALL. There are yards south?

Mr. FOSTER. They have yards here [indicating].

Mr. BALL. That is north and west?

Mr. FOSTER. Yes, sir.

Mr. BALL. And also south?

Mr. FOSTER. That's right.

Mr. BALL. Now, did you see the President's motorcade come into sight?

Mr. FOSTER. Yes, sir.

Mr. BALL. Where did you see it? Where was it when you saw it?

Mr. FOSTER. When I first saw it it was coming off of Main Street onto Houston.

Mr. BALL. And did you keep it in sight?

Mr. FOSTER. Yes, sir; it was in sight most of the time.

Mr. BALL. Now, where were you standing?

Mr. FOSTER. Standing along the east curb of—east side of the overpass over Elm Street there. About the south curb.

Mr. BALL. Over, above the south curb of Elm?

Mr. FOSTER. Yes, sir.

Mr. BALL. Will you put a mark on there? Mark an "X" where you were standing and write your initials right next to that "X".

J.—what are the initials?

Mr. FOSTER. J. W.

Mr. BALL. J. W. F. That marks where you were standing.

Mr. FOSTER. Approximately; yes, sir.

Mr. BALL. Did you keep the President's motorcade in sight after it turned?

Mr. FOSTER. Other than watching the men that were standing on the overpass there with me.

Mr. BALL. Now, you had instructions to keep all unauthorized personnel off of that overpass?

Mr. FOSTER. Yes, sir.

Mr. BALL. Did you do that?

Mr. FOSTER. Yes, sir.

Mr. BALL. Did you permit some people to be there?

Mr. FOSTER. Yes, sir.

Mr. BALL. Who?

Mr. FOSTER. People that were working for the railroad there.

Mr. BALL. Were there many people?

Mr. FOSTER. About 10 or 11.

Mr. BALL. Where were they standing?

Mr. FOSTER. They were standing along the east banister.

Mr. BALL. The east banister?

Mr. FOSTER. Yes, sir; in front of me.

Mr. BALL. In front of you. Will you make a mark there and show the general area where they were standing?

Mr. FOSTER. They were standing along this area here [indicating].

Mr. BALL. You have marked a series of X's to show where about 10 people were standing?

Mr. FOSTER. Yes, sir.

Mr. BALL. Were you looking toward them?

Mr. FOSTER. Yes, sir.

Mr. BALL. Did you have another officer with you there on that duty that day?

Mr. FOSTER. Not on that side. He was on the west side.

Mr. BALL. He was on the west side?

Mr. FOSTER. Yes, sir.

Mr. BALL. What was his name?

Mr. FOSTER. J. C. White.

Mr. BALL. Do you know exactly where he was when you were at the position you have indicated?

Mr. FOSTER. No; I don't. The only thing I know, he was supposed to be on the west side of the banister.

Mr. BALL. You were looking to the east?

Mr. FOSTER. Yes, sir.

Mr. BALL. Now, tell me what you saw happen after the President's car passed—turned onto Elm from Houston.

Mr. FOSTER. After he came onto Elm I was watching the men up on the track more than I was him. Then I heard a loud noise, sound like a large firecracker. Kind of dumbfounded at first, and then heard the second one. I moved to the banister of the overpass to see what was happening. Then the third explosion, and they were beginning to move around. I ran after I saw what was happening.

Mr. BALL. What did you see was happening?

Mr. FOSTER. Saw the President slump over in the car, and his head looked just like it blew up.

Mr. BALL. You saw that, did you?

228

Mr. FOSTER. Yes, sir.

Mr. BALL. And what did you do then?

Mr. FOSTER. Well, at that time I broke and ran around to my right—to the left—around to the bookstore.

Mr. BALL. Now, did you have any opinion at that time as to the source of the sounds, the direction of the sounds?

Mr. FOSTER. Yes, sir.

Mr. BALL. What?

Mr. FOSTER. It came from back in toward the corner of Elm and Houston Streets.

Mr. BALL. That was your impression at that time?

Mr. FOSTER. Yes, sir.

Mr. BALL. Was any shot fired from the overpass?

Mr. FOSTER. No, sir.

Mr. BALL. Did you see anyone with a weapon there?

Mr. FOSTER. No, sir.

Mr. BALL. Or did you hear any sound that appeared to come from the overpass?

Mr. FOSTER. No, sir.

Mr. BALL. Where did you go from there?

Mr. FOSTER. Went on around the back side of the bookstore.

Mr. BALL. Immediately?

Mr. FOSTER. Yes, sir.

Mr. BALL. Did you see anybody coming out of that side of the bookstore?

Mr. FOSTER. No, sir.

Mr. BALL. Backside? What do you mean by that?

Mr. FOSTER. Well, I guess you would say the northwest side of it.

Mr. BALL. Were there any people in the railroad yards around the bookstore at that time?

Mr. FOSTER. Yes, sir. There was a pretty good crowd beginning to gather back in that area.

Mr. BALL. At that time?

Mr. FOSTER. Yes, sir.

Mr. BALL. Had you seen anybody over at the railroad yard north and west of the bookstore before you heard the shots fired?

Mr. FOSTER. No; other than people that had come up there and I sent them back down the roadway.

Mr. BALL. I see. People had attempted to get on the overpass there?

Mr. FOSTER. Yes, sir.

Mr. BALL. And you had sent them away?

Mr. FOSTER. Yes, sir.

Mr. BALL. When you got over to the School Book Depository Building, what did you do?

Mr. FOSTER. I was standing around in back there to see that no one came out, and the sergeant came and got me and we were going to check the—all the railroad cars down there.

Mr. BALL. Who was that sergeant?

Mr. FOSTER. Sergeant came up there.

Mr. BALL. Did you search the railroad cars?

Mr. FOSTER. No; he sent me back down to the inspector. Told me to report back to Inspector Sawyer.

Mr. BALL. Where?

Mr. FOSTER. At the front of the Book Depository.

Mr. BALL. Did you talk to Sawyer there?

Mr. FOSTER. Yes, sir.

Mr. BALL. Did you tell your sergeant or Sawyer, either one where you thought the shots came from?

Mr. FOSTER. Yes, sir.

Mr. BALL. What did you then tell them?

Mr. FOSTER. Told them it came from that vicinity up around Elm and Houston.

Mr. BALL. Did you tell the sergeant that first, or did you tell that to Sawyer?

Mr. FOSTER. Told that to Inspector Sawyer.

Mr. BALL. You told that to Sawyer?

Mr. FOSTER. Yes, sir.

Mr. BALL. Did you tell that to the sergeant?

Mr. FOSTER. I don't know whether I told the sergeant that or not.

Mr. BALL. What did you do after that?

229

Mr. FOSTER. I moved to—down the roadway there, down to see if I could find where any of the shots hit.

Mr. BALL. Find anything?

Mr. FOSTER. Yes, sir. Found where one shot had hit the turf there at the location.

Mr. BALL. Hit the turf?

Mr. FOSTER. Yes, sir.

Mr. BALL. Did you see any marks on the street in any place?

Mr. FOSTER. No, a manhole cover. It was hit. They caught the manhole cover right at the corner and——

Mr. BALL. You saw a mark on a manhole cover did you?

Mr. FOSTER. Yes, sir.

Mr. BALL. I show you a picture here of a concrete slab, or manhole cover. Do you recognize that picture?

Mr. FOSTER. Yes, sir.

Mr. BALL. Does the picture show—tell me what it shows there.

Mr. FOSTER. This looks like the corner here where it penetrated the turf right here [indicating].

Mr. BALL. See any mark on the manhole cover?

Mr. FOSTER. No, sir; I don't. Not on the—well, it is on the turf, on the concrete, right in the corner.

Mr. BALL. Can you put an arrow showing the approximate place you saw that?

Mr. FOSTER. Should have been approximately along here [indicating].

Mr. BALL. Make it deep enough to make a mark. The arrow marks the position that you believe you saw a mark on the pavement?

Mr. FOSTER. Yes, sir.

Mr. BALL. It was not on the manhole cover?

Mr. FOSTER. No, sir.

Mr. BALL. Went into the turf?

Mr. FOSTER. Yes, sir.

Mr. BALL. Did you recover any bullet?

Mr. FOSTER. No, sir. It ricocheted on out.

Mr. BALL. Did you have the crime lab make a picture of that spot?

Mr. FOSTER. I called them to the location.

Mr. BALL. And told them to make a picture?

Mr. FOSTER. No, I didn't tell them. Called them to the spot and let them take it. Can I see the picture?

Mr. BALL. Yes, sir. Is this the picture?

Mr. FOSTER. That resembles the picture.

Mr. BALL. I offer this as "B," then. Mark it as "B" so that we have "A" and "B" now.

Officer, this will be written up and submitted to you for your signature and you can read it over and change it any way you wish, or you may waive your signature at this time, which do you prefer?

Mr. FOSTER. Well, it doesn't matter.

Mr. BALL. Suit yourself. You make the choice.

Mr. FOSTER. I would just as soon go ahead and sign it.

Mr. BALL. All right. We will notify you and you can get in here and sign it.

Mr. FOSTER. All right.

Mr. BALL. Thank you. One moment, please.

Who gave you your assignment, Mr. Foster?

Mr. FOSTER. Sergeant Harkness.

Mr. BALL. You did permit some railroad employees to remain on the overpass?

Mr. FOSTER. Yes, sir.

Mr. BALL. How did you determine they were railroad employees?

Mr. FOSTER. By identification they had with them. Identification they had and the other men that was with them verifying that they were employees.

Mr. BALL. Okay.

TESTIMONY OF J. C. WHITE

The testimony of J. C. White was taken at 11:45 a.m., on April 9, 1964, in the office of the U.S. attorney, 301 Post Office Building, Bryan and Ervay Streets, Dallas, Tex., by Mr. Joseph A. Ball, assistant counsel of the President's Commission.

Mr. BALL. All right, will you stand up and be sworn.

Do you solemnly swear that the testimony you are about to give shall be the truth, the whole truth and nothing but the truth, so help you God?

Mr. WHITE. I do.

Mr. BALL. All right.

Mr. BALL. Will you state your name, please.

Mr. WHITE. J. C. White.

Mr. BALL. What is your residence?

Mr. WHITE. 2303 Klondite.

Mr. BALL. And your occupation?

Mr. WHITE. Policeman.

Mr. BALL. Did you receive a letter from the Commission?

Mr. WHITE. No, sir.

Mr. BALL. For a request to——

Mr. WHITE. No, sir.

Mr. BALL. You were asked to come here by your——

Mr. WHITE. Captain.

Mr. BALL. Which captain?

Mr. WHITE. Lawrence.

Mr. BALL. Now, the Commission was established to investigate the facts and circumstances surrounding the assassination of President Kennedy. We want to ask you some questions about information that you might have that might aid us in that investigation.

I am a Staff officer of the Commission named Ball. Joseph A. Ball. I am authorized to administer the oath to you, to make this inquiry. During the course of our investigation in Dallas we discovered that you and the man that you were working with that day, Mr. J. W. Foster, knew of some facts that might aid us in the investigation. We asked Chief Curry if we could have you come up here and testify, and I guess that is the reason you are here.

You are willing to testify, are you not?

Mr. WHITE. Yes, sir.

Mr. BALL. Tell us whatever you know about it.

Mr. WHITE. I don't know.

Mr. BALL. Well, I can ask you.

Mr. WHITE. Okay.

Mr. BALL. I will ask you questions. Where were you born?

Mr. WHITE. Van Alstyne, Tex.

Mr. BALL. Where did you go to school?

Mr. WHITE. Van Alystyne, Tex.

Mr. BALL. How far through school?

Mr. WHITE. Ninth grade there.

Mr. BALL. Then what did you do?

Mr. WHITE. I went into the Army.

Mr. BALL. And how long were you in the Army?

Mr. WHITE. About 3 years.

Mr. BALL. And what did you do?

Mr. WHITE. Went to driving a city bus.

Mr. BALL. How long did you drive a city bus?

Mr. WHITE. 6 years.

Mr. BALL. Then what did you do?

Mr. WHITE. Joined the Police Department.

Mr. BALL. How long ago?

Mr. WHITE. 1956.

Mr. BALL. And what are you now?

Mr. WHITE. Accident investigator.

Mr. BALL. And your rank is a patrolman?

Mr. WHITE. Yes, sir.

Mr. BALL. Now, on November 22, 1963, did you have an assignment?

Mr. WHITE. Yes, sir.

Mr. BALL. Where?

Mr. WHITE. On the triple underpass.

Mr. BALL. And were you there with someone?

Mr. WHITE. Yes, sir.

Mr. BALL. Who?

Mr. WHITE. J. W. Foster.

Mr. BALL. Where were you?

Mr. WHITE. Standing on the west side of the overpass.

Mr. BALL. On the west side of the overpass?

Mr. WHITE. Yes.

Mr. BALL. Where were you with reference to Elm, Main or Commerce as they go underneath the overpass?

Mr. WHITE. Approximately at the north curb of Main Street.

Mr. BALL. Approximately the north curb of Main on the corner of the north curb of Main? That would be——

Mr. WHITE. Yes, sir.

Mr. BALL. On the west side of the overpass?

Mr. WHITE. Yes.

Mr. BALL. I'm going to get another copy of this map. Let me see. I can use this. Mark this as Exhibit A to your deposition. Now, a diagram that was drawn by a patrolman, Joe Murphy, and he has made some marks and other witnesses have, but don't pay any attention to that. I want you to look at this drawing and take a pen and mark your position on the railroad overpass in a circle, and put your initials beside it.

You have made an "X".

Mr. WHITE. Yes, sir.

Mr. BALL. And you have initialed J. C. White, is that right?

Mr. WHITE. Yes, sir.

Mr. BALL. Over the—what would be the west curb of Main?

Mr. WHITE. North curb of Main.

Mr. BALL. The north curb?

Mr. WHITE. Yes.

Mr. BALL. North curb of Main?

Mr. WHITE. Yes, sir.

Mr. BALL. And west side of the overpass?

Mr. WHITE. Yes, sir.

Mr. BALL. Is there a rail there?

Mr. WHITE. Yes, sir.

Mr. BALL. How many people were on that overpass that day?

Mr. WHITE. On the same side I was on?

Mr. BALL. Yes.

Mr. WHITE. None.

Mr. BALL. None? Any people attempt to come up on the overpass around noon?

Mr. WHITE. Not on my side.

Mr. BALL. They did not?

Mr. WHITE. No, sir.

Mr. BALL. Had you seen your partner send any people away from the overpass?

Mr. WHITE. Yes, sir.

Mr. BALL. You had certain instructions, didn't you?

Mr. WHITE. Yes, sir.

Mr. BALL. What were they?

Mr. WHITE. Not to let any unauthorized personnel on top of the overpass.

Mr. BALL. Now, you did permit some people to stay on the overpass, didn't you?

Mr. WHITE. Yes, sir.

Mr. BALL. Who were they?

Mr. WHITE. Workers of the railroad company.

Mr. BALL. Were they people you knew?

Mr. WHITE. No, sir.

Mr. BALL. Well, how did you know they were workers with the railroad company?

Mr. WHITE. Majority of them were there when we got there, working on the rails.

Mr. BALL. And you let them stay there?

Mr. WHITE. Yes, sir.

Mr. BALL. Did you see the President's car come into sight?

Mr. WHITE. No, sir; first time I saw it it has passed, passed under the triple underpass.

Mr. BALL. You were too far away to see it, were you?

Mr. WHITE. There was a freight train traveling. There was a train passing between the location I was standing and the area from which the procession was traveling, and—a big long freight train, and I did not see it.

Mr. BALL. You didn't see the procession?

Mr. WHITE. No, sir.

Mr. BALL. Before the train went by, did you see some railroad personnel over on the—would it be the——

Mr. WHITE. East side?

Mr. BALL. East side of the overpass?

Mr. WHITE. Yes, sir.

Mr. BALL. How many people?

Mr. WHITE. About 10, approximately. I didn't count them.

Mr. BALL. Did you hear any shots?

Mr. WHITE. No, sir.

Mr. BALL. Didn't?

Mr. WHITE. No, sir.

Mr. BALL. First time you saw the President's car it was going underneath?

Mr. WHITE. Yes, sir.

Mr. BALL. What did you do after that?

Mr. WHITE. As soon as the train passed I went over and on the northwest side of the Depository Building. On the northwest side of the book store up there with the rest of the officers and after about 30 minutes they told me to go out and work traffic at Main and Houston, and I stood out there and worked traffic.

Mr. BALL. All right, now, you heard no sound of no rifle fire or anything?

Mr. WHITE. No, sir.

Mr. BALL. Freight train was going through at the time?

Mr. WHITE. Yes, sir.

Mr. BALL. Making noise?

Mr. WHITE. Yes, sir; noisy train.

Mr. BALL. Mr. White, Mr. Foster was on the east side of the overpass?

Mr. WHITE. Yes, sir.

Mr. BALL. This deposition will be written up and submitted to you for your signature if you wish to sign it, or you can waive your signature. Which do you wish to do?

Mr. WHITE. You said a while ago to him it would be written up like this? Is that correct?

Mr. BALL. No, it will be written up in the form of a deposition.

Mr. WHITE. I will waive.

Mr. BALL. You waive it. Okay. Fine.

TESTIMONY OF JOE E. MURPHY

The testimony of Joe E. Murphy was taken at 9:50 a.m., on April 8, 1964, in the office of U.S. attorney, 301 Post Office Building, Bryan and Ervay Streets, Dallas, Tex., by Mr. Joseph A. Ball, assistant counsel of the President's Commission.

Mr. BALL. Will you raise your right hand and be sworn?

Do you solemnly swear that the testimony you are about to give before the Commission will be the truth, the whole truth, and nothing but the truth, so help you God?

Mr. MURPHY. I do.

Mr. BALL. Will you state your name and address for the record?

Mr. MURPHY. Joe E. Murphy, 2509 Winthrop; (spelling) W-i-n-t-h-r-o-p, Drive.

Mr. BALL. And what is your occupation?

Mr. MURPHY. Police officer.

Mr. BALL. How long have you been with the Department?

Mr. MURPHY. I am in my 21st year.

Mr. BALL. With the Dallas Police Department?

Mr. MURPHY. Yes.

Mr. BALL. Where were you born?

Mr. MURPHY. Dallas.

Mr. BALL. Where did you go to school?

Mr. MURPHY. High school—St. Joseph High School here in Dallas.

Mr. BALL. You went all through school here in Dallas, did you?

Mr. MURPHY. Yes, sir; that's right.

Mr. BALL. What did you do after you got out of high school?

Mr. MURPHY. Well, I played pro baseball for about 2 years, Class D—West Texas and New Mexico League. After that I went to work for the Humble Oil and Refining Co. in Baytown. I was down there about 2 years and came back to Dallas and then I went to work on the police force.

Mr. BALL. And you have been there ever since?

Mr. MURPHY. Yes.

Mr. BALL. You are a patrolman, are you?

Mr. MURPHY. That's right.

Mr. BALL. Do you have a three-wheeler?

Mr. MURPHY. A three-wheeler—yes.

Mr. BALL. On November 22, 1963, did they assign you to some post?

Mr. MURPHY. Yes, I was assigned to the overpass—the Stemmons Freeway overpass northbound at Elm Street—over Elm.

Mr. BALL. What instructions did you have?

Mr. MURPHY. It was to keep anyone and everyone off of the overpass and to keep traffic moving until the motorcade arrived.

Mr. BALL. Now, you have a map here which you have drawn for us to show your position, is that right? (Reporter marked instrument—Murphy Exhibit A, for identification.)

Mr. MURPHY. Yes; that's right.

Mr. BALL. And you have drawn a position there as to where you were standing, is that right?

Mr. MURPHY. That's right.

Mr. BALL. And where you parked your three-wheeler?

Mr. MURPHY. Yes.

Mr. BALL. All right, mark the place where you were standing as Position 1, using an "X".

Mr. MURPHY. All right. (Witness Murphy marked the diagram as requested by Counsel Ball.)

Mr. BALL. And your three-wheeler was beside you?

Mr. MURPHY. Yes; right on the shoulder.

Mr. BALL. Were there any other officers on that overpass?

Mr. MURPHY. Yes; there were two more about—oh, a 100 feet south of me—to slow traffic or to stop traffic whenever the motorcade entered the Stemmons Freeway north entrance.

Mr. BALL. Now where were they located—and, did they as the motorcade came down Elm Street, did they go into the highway and stop traffic?

Mr. MURPHY. Yes; they did.

Mr. BALL. Will you put their positions on the Stemmons Freeway overpass at the time the motorcade came west on Elm, and mark it (2) and (3).

Mr. MURPHY. (Marked diagram as requested by Counsel Ball.)

Mr. BALL. Do you know the names of those officers that were (2) and (3)?

Mr. MURPHY. I can't recall. I know them but I can't recall who they were.

Mr. BALL. Were they three-wheeler officers too, do they drive three-wheelers?

Mr. MURPHY. I believe both of them three-wheelers.

Mr. BALL. And as the motorcade came west on Elm, did they stop traffic on Stemmons Freeway?

Mr. MURPHY. Yes, their main job was to slow it and let the officers farther down the freeway—they would stop it, but traffic approaches pretty fast and they were to slow traffic and let the officers then stop it. They did—they—they stepped into and were slowing the traffic as the motorcade came under that railroad overpass.

Mr. BALL. Did they ever stop traffic completely?

Mr. MURPHY. Well, it stopped—it stopped itself back down when all the excitement—someone down there—they blocked the whole street and then it backed up, is what it did—backed up to our position.

Mr. BALL. On Stemmons Freeway?

Mr. MURPHY. Yes.

Mr. BALL. Now Position (1) is where you were standing?

Mr. MURPHY. Yes.

Mr. BALL. Were there any people standing on the overpass over Elm, on the Stemmons Freeway overpass over Elm, as the motorcade came down?

Mr. MURPHY. No; there was no one standing there prior to the arrival of the motorcade or after the motorcade arrived.

Mr. BALL. The only one standing there was you?

Mr. MURPHY. It was me.

Mr. BALL. Now, let's go to the railroad overpass, and first of all, as you turned west on Elm from Houston, what is the first overpass that you encounter?

Mr. MURPHY. There is a railroad overpass—all of the trains entering and leaving the Union Station cross over that overpass.

Mr. BALL. Were there any officers on that overpass?

Mr. MURPHY. There were two.

Mr. BALL. Can you mark their positions, approximately, as you saw them before the motorcade arrived?

Mr. MURPHY. As best I could see—one was on each side—one here and one over on this side.

Mr. BALL. All right, mark the position of the officer on the west side as Position (4), and the one on the east side as Position (5).

(The Witness Murphy marked the diagram as requested by Counsel Ball.) Mr. BALL. Were these uniformed officers?

Mr. MURPHY. Yes, they were.

Mr. BALL. Do you know their names?

Mr. MURPHY. No, sir; I don't.

Mr. BALL. Did they have three-wheelers?

Mr. MURPHY. No; I couldn't say.

Mr. BALL. Now, were there any other people besides the two officers on this railroad overpass?

Mr. MURPHY. There were about 8 or 10—from what I could see—about 8 or 10 men dressed in the overalls and they appeared to be railroad employees.

Mr. BALL. Can you mark in their positions, approximately?

Mr. MURPHY. Well, they were in a group right in the center of Elm Street.

Mr. BALL. They were all together?

Mr. MURPHY. Yes; it appeared that they were in a group (Witness Murphy drew circle indicating presence of persons heretofore mentioned as requested by Counsel Ball).

Mr. BALL. You have drawn a circle there?

Mr. MURPHY. Yes.

Mr. BALL. And mark that (6).

(Witness Murphy marked the diagram as requested by Counsel Ball.)

Mr. BALL. And in that circle there were about how many?

Mr. MURPHY. 8 to 10 persons.

Mr. BALL. There were 8 to 10 persons approximately, dressed in overalls?

Mr. MURPHY. Yes.

Mr. BALL. Did you see any other people on the railroad overpass?

Mr. MURPHY. No, sir; I didn't.

Mr. BALL. Could you see the motorcade on Houston from your position (1)?

Mr. MURPHY. Yes; I could.

Mr. BALL. Did you see the President's car turn the corner of Main and Houston?

Mr. MURPHY. Yes; I did.

Mr. BALL. That was in your view, was it?

Mr. MURPHY. Yes; it was.

Mr. BALL. Was the corner of Houston and Elm within your view?

Mr. MURPHY. Just a portion of it—you lose sight of it there for just a few seconds, as it makes the turn. Well, you lose sight of it. There is some kind of a—on that part there is a concrete, oh, I don't know what you would call it—kind of a framework—it appears to be.

Mr. BALL. In other words, there is an obstruction to your view?

Mr. MURPHY. Yes.

Mr. BALL. From where you were standing at Position (1)?

Mr. MURPHY. Yes.

Mr. BALL. And the corner of the intersection of Houston and Elm?

Mr. MURPHY. Yes.

Mr. BALL. Were you able to see the President's car after it had turned west on Elm from Houston?

Mr. MURPHY. Well, again there, you just get a very short view of it before it goes out of sight then, going down that hill.

Mr. BALL. You heard shots, did you?

Mr. MURPHY. Yes, I did.

Mr. BALL. Now, from the time you saw the President's car turn north on Houston from Main and until you heard the shots, what direction were you looking?

Mr. MURPHY. I was looking in an easterly direction.

Mr. BALL. Toward what?

Mr. MURPHY. Toward the motorcade—towards the President's car.

Mr. BALL. Did you keep the motorcade in sight at all times? .

Mr. MURPHY. Yes, I did.

235

Mr. BALL. Did you see anything unusual occur in this group of railroad men where you have marked Position (6)?

Mr. MURPHY. No, I didn't—I did not.

Mr. BALL. Anybody armed there?

Mr. MURPHY. No, not that I could tell.

Mr. BALL. Can you tell me what direction the policemen were looking who were at Position (4) and (5)?

Mr. MURPHY. They appeared to be looking in an easterly direction also.

Mr. BALL. The direction of the motorcade?

Mr. MURPHY. Yes.

Mr. BALL. And did you see other individuals on that railroad overpass except the ones you have described?

Mr. MURPHY. No, just that group that I have described.

Mr. BALL. Now, you say you heard something—heard shots?

Mr. MURPHY. Yes.

Mr. BALL. Describe to me your best recollection as to what you heard?

Mr. MURPHY. Well, I heard—I knew they were shots as soon as I heard them, but I thought at first it was—it sounded like a shotgun, and then I got the three shots and there were so many echoes and everything—then I did determine it sounded more like a rifle. I do quite a bit of hunting and I determined it sounded more like a rifle.

Mr. BALL. Those shots came from what direction?

Mr. MURPHY. Well, just from the direction I was looking—that's all I could tell. They came from an easterly direction, from where I was standing.

Mr. BALL. And were there echoes?

Mr. MURPHY. Yes, quite a few.

Mr. BALL. Did the men who were on the overpass at Position (5) do anything?

Mr. MURPHY. I don't recall—on that overpass—right after the shots, I did see then a group of people running up the side of this embankment on Elm and running. That would be here—right in here.

Mr. BALL. To the north of Elm?

Mr. MURPHY. To the north of Elm.

Mr. BALL. Would you put an arrow showing the direction they were running and mark that arrow as "7"—that's the direction you saw people running?

Mr. MURPHY. (Marked diagram as requested by Counsel Ball.) Yes, they were running up in this direction and then in behind this Book Depository. Oh, I could tell a lot of them were photographers, because I could see their cameras in their hands and then a number of other people, and then I did see some officers also running in that direction.

Mr. BALL. Did you see what the railroad men did who were at Position (6) on your map?

Mr. MURPHY. No; because right at that time that traffic began backing up on the freeway and I had turned in to try to keep them moving, but I found that I couldn't move them because it was blocked down below me, north of me and there was traffic just stacked up from where the other officers had it stopped there.

Mr. BALL. How long did you stay at your position?

Mr. MURPHY. Well, I stayed until, I guess, it was about maybe 3 minutes after we heard the shots and then the broadcast came over the radio that there had been a shooting—the President had been shot—and then I went towards the Book Depository.

I got on my motor and went towards the Book Depository then—off of the freeway; and then was there up around the Book Depository for the next—I would say hour or hour and a half at least.

Mr. BALL. Did you talk to any witnesses?

Mr. MURPHY. I did pick up or talk to three or four people that said they had seen things and said they heard different things, and I took them to the sheriff's office across the street.

Mr. BALL. Do you knew what their names were?

Mr. MURPHY. No, sir; I couldn't tell you. I turned them over to the investigators there with the sheriff's department—the district attorney's investigators, that's who they were.

Mr. BALL. You didn't make any notes of their names?

Mr. MURPHY. No, sir; I didn't.

Mr. BALL. Do you remember now what any of them told you?

Mr. MURPHY. Well, one man in particular—he was standing on Elm—he was standing right about here where we have marked Position (7), and he claimed that he heard two shots above him and behind him, and one shot from up around the edge of this park, and another man claimed that he had been standing nearly in this same position—he was standing here on the street and he claimed that all the shots he heard came from overhead to his rear.

Mr. BALL. That would be near the Texas School Book Depository?

Mr. MURPHY. Yes, towards that Book Depository.

Mr. BALL. Did you go on the police radio and make any announcement or statement?

Mr. MURPHY. No, sir; I didn't. It was so jammed, I didn't make any.

Mr. BALL. I would like to have this marked as Exhibit A to your deposition, which is illustrative of your testimony.

(Instrument marked by the reporter as Murphy Exhibit No. A, for identification.)

Mr. BALL. This will be written up and you can come in and look it over and sign it if you wish, or you can waive signature if you wish. It is your option—what would you like to do?

Mr. MURPHY. Well, if it's necessary, I will sign it. If it isn't, that's perfectly all right with me.

Mr. BALL. It isn't necessary.

Mr. MURPHY. Well, that's all right then.

Mr. BALL. Then, you will waive signature?

Mr. MURPHY. Yes, sir.

Mr. BALL. Thanks very much for coming in.

Mr. MURPHY. All right—certainly.

TESTIMONY OF ROGER D. CRAIG

The testimony of Roger D. Craig was taken at 2:35 p.m., on April 1, 1964, in the office of the U.S. attorney, 301 Post Office Building, Bryan and Ervay Streets, Dallas, Tex., by Mr. David W. Belin, assistant counsel of the President's Commission.

Mr. BELIN. Roger Craig, do you want to stand and raise your right hand, please?

Do you solemnly swear that the testimony that you're about to give is the truth, the whole truth, and nothing but the truth, so help you God?

Mr. CRAIG. I do.

Mr. BELIN. You can be seated.

Mr. BELIN. Will you please state your full name?

Mr. CRAIG. Roger Dean Craig.

Mr. BELIN. That's (spelling) D-e-a-n?

Mr. CRAIG. Yes.

Mr. BELIN. And where do you live, Mr. Craig?

Mr. CRAIG. 6215 Overlook Drive, Dallas.

Mr. BELIN. And what's your occupation?

Mr. CRAIG. Deputy Sheriff.

Mr. BELIN. For the Dallas County Sheriff's Department?

Mr. CRAIG. Yes.

Mr. BELIN. How old are you, Mr. Craig?

Mr. CRAIG. 27.

Mr. BELIN. Were you raised here in Texas?

Mr. CRAIG. No. I was born in Wisconsin, raised in Minnesota; and ran away from home when I was 12 and traveled all over the country.

Mr. BELIN. When you were 12?

Mr. CRAIG. Yes.

Mr. BELIN. Did you have any further schooling after you were 12—or not?

Mr. CRAIG. No; I took high school equivalent test in the Service in Japan when—uh—I was 19, and passed it and got my high school equivalent test—I mean, my diploma.

Mr. BELIN. Were you in the Service, then?

Mr. CRAIG. Yes; uh-huh.

Mr. BELIN. In what branch?

Mr. CRAIG. I was in the Army.

Mr. BELIN. And how long were you in the Army?

Mr. CRAIG. 2 years.

Mr. BELIN. Before you joined the Army, what did you do? Were you living with anyone or were you on your own—or what?

Mr. CRAIG. No; I was married to a girl who lived out in Mesquite.

Mr. BELIN. Where?

Mr. CRAIG. Mesquite. It's a suburb of Dallas. It's not a town.

Mr. BELIN. Uh-huh.

Well, let me go back a little bit. You said you ran away from home when you were 12?

Mr. CRAIG. Uh-huh.

Mr. BELIN. And then where did you live?

Mr. CRAIG. I lived in South Dakota, worked on ranches up there, and then Wyoming, Nebraska, Colorado, New Mexico, Oklahoma.

Mr. BELIN. Well, with any relatives—or were they friends, or what?

Mr. CRAIG. No, no; just jobs. Just working here and there.

Mr. BELIN. And then you were married when you were——

Mr. CRAIG. 16.

Mr. BELIN. 16. And where?

Mr. CRAIG. Here in Texas.

Mr. BELIN. Here in Texas.

And then you enlisted in the Army when?

Mr. CRAIG. I volunteered for the draft when I was 17.

Mr. BELIN. And then you went in the Service?

Mr. CRAIG. Right.

Mr. BELIN. And served overseas?

Mr. CRAIG. Right.

Mr. BELIN. You were discharged when, then?

Mr. CRAIG. In—uh—October of 1955, I believe. In September or October of 1955, sir, is when I got out.

Mr. BELIN. Was it an honorable discharge?

Mr. CRAIG. Yes.

Mr. BELIN. What did you do when you were in the service?

Mr. CRAIG. I served in the—uh—motor pool of the 92d Armored Field.

Mr. BELIN. And, after you got out of service, what did you do?

Mr. CRAIG. Well, jobs were kind of hard to get. I got a job as a dishwasher in a cafe, then cook. Then I did construction work for a while. And then I went to work for the Purex Corporation out on Storey Lane here in Dallas—2929 Storey Lane. Then I worked for them for about 3½ years. Then, I came down to the sheriff's office.

Mr. BELIN. Now, what would your job have been there with the Purex Corp.?

Mr. CRAIG. Packager. I just packaged the Purex.

Mr. BELIN. And when did you go to work for the Dallas County Sheriff's Office?

Mr. CRAIG. In October—October the 9th of 1959.

Mr. BELIN. And you've been there ever since?

Mr. CRAIG. Yes.

Mr. BELIN. Are you married?

Mr. CRAIG. Yes.

Mr. BELIN. Family?

Mr. CRAIG. Yes; I have a girl and a boy and a stepboy.

Mr. BELIN. Now, Mr. Craig, I want to take you back to November 22d, 1963, and ask you whether or not you were working at the sheriff's office that day?

Mr. CRAIG. Yes.

Mr. BELIN. Where is the sheriff's office located?

Mr. CRAIG. 505 Main Street.

Mr. BELIN. And where is 505 Main Street? Is it on the north or the south side of Main?

Mr. CRAIG. It's on the north side of Main at the corner of Houston.

Mr. BELIN. It runs from Houston east to Record Street there? Is that Record Street there?

Mr. CRAIG. No; the sheriff's office actually runs north from Main over to Elm Street. It covers that entire block.

Mr. BELIN. How far east does it go—or is it just a half-block east?

Mr. CRAIG. No; it's just a half block to—uh—well, it's divided, then the Records Building begins and goes on to Record Street.

Mr. BELIN. To Record Street.

Well, will you state what you did that day from about noon on—on November 22?

Mr. CRAIG. I stood out in front waiting for the President's motorcade. I went out there about—oh—5 minutes after 12, I guess; waited directly in front of the front door on the curb.

Mr. BELIN. That would be on the north curb of Main?

Mr. CRAIG. Right.

Mr. BELIN. All right. Then what happened?

Mr. CRAIG. Well, we waited there for several minutes—and—uh—the motorcade finally came by.

Mr. BELIN. About how fast was the motorcade going when you saw it on Main Street?

Mr. CRAIG. Oh, just barely moving. I don't know. It was just barely moving. I couldn't judge any miles per hour.

Mr. BELIN. Well, 5, 10, 15, 20—what?

Mr. CRAIG. Probably going—probably 3 or 4 miles an hour.

Mr. BELIN. All right.

You saw the President's car?

Mr. CRAIG. Yes.

Mr. BELIN. You saw the motorcade reach the intersection of Main and Houston?

Mr. CRAIG. Yes.

Mr. BELIN. And then it turned?

Mr. CRAIG. Turned north on Houston.

Mr. BELIN. About how fast was it going as it turned north on Houston?

Mr. CRAIG. Oh, about the same. They—uh—they were going about the same speed as they made the corner.

Mr. BELIN. Were there any motorcycle policemen alongside the President's car?

Mr. CRAIG. Uh—not directly beside it. They was, I believe, on the front part of it and—uh—I believe behind it—just a little ways behind the back fender there was a motorcycle officer—one on each side of the car, as I remember.

Mr. BELIN. The ones on the front—where would the back wheels of the motorcycles have been with relation to the front wheels of the President's car?

Mr. CRAIG. Uh—just in front of the bumper because they came by and moved everybody back, you know, as the car approached us.

Mr. BELIN. And what about the motorcycles that were just behind the car? Where were the front wheels of those motorcycles with relation to the back wheels or the back bumper of the President's car?

Mr. CRAIG. About equal to the back bumper.

Mr. BELIN. All right.

You saw the President's car, then, turn north on Houston?

Mr. CRAIG. Yes.

Mr. BELIN. Then, would you describe what you saw and heard and did?

Mr. CRAIG. Well, there were several other cars that came by and—uh——

Mr. BELIN. Did you watch those?

Mr. CRAIG. Some of them we watched. We watched Mr. Decker's car, of course, and a few of the others.

Mr. BELIN. Now, where was Mr. Decker's car?

Mr. CRAIG. I believe he came by just before the President's. I believe there were some dignitaries and things before that, and then we watched the President's   and—uh—oh, and then about two or three cars after the President's car had passed. And then we were just standing there looking around, you know.

Mr. BELIN. All right.

Then what happened?

Mr. CRAIG. Then I heard an explosion.

Mr. BELIN. When you heard the explosion, what did you do?

Mr. CRAIG. Well, the first—nothing. I wrestled with my mind. I knew it was a shot but—uh—I didn't want to believe it. But, a few seconds later, I heard another explosion and, this time, I knew it was a shot. And, as I began to run, I heard a third one. I was running toward Houston Street.

Mr. BELIN. How many explosions did you hear altogether?

Mr. CRAIG. Three.

Mr. BELIN. About how far were these noises apart?

Mr. CRAIG. The first one was—uh—about three seconds—2 or 3 seconds.

Mr. BELIN. Two or 3 seconds between the first and the second?

Mr. CRAIG. Well, it was quite a pause between there. It could have been a little longer.

Mr. BELIN. And what about between the second and third?

Mr. CRAIG. Not more than 2 seconds. It was—they were real rapid.

Mr. BELIN. All right.

Then what did you do?

Mr. CRAIG. I continued running across Houston Street, across the parkway, across Elm Street and, by this time, the motorcade had went on down Elm Street and I ran up to the railroad yard and—uh—started to look around when the people began to all travel over that way. So, I began moving people back out of the railroad yard.

Mr. BELIN. Where did the noises or shots sound to you like they came from?

Mr. CRAIG. It was hard to tell because—uh—they had an echo, you know. There was actually two explosions with each one. There was the—uh—the shot and then the echo from it. So, it was hard to tell.

Mr. BELIN. Did people tell you, as you ran over there, where they thought the shots came from?

Mr. CRAIG. No; as I reached the railroad yard, I talked to a girl getting her car that—uh— thought they came from the park area on the north side of Elm Street.

Mr. BELIN. Did she say why she thought they came from there?

Mr. CRAIG. No; she was standing there and it sounded real loud at that particular point— —

Mr. BELIN. Uh-huh.

Mr. CRAIG. And she thought that's where they came from.

Mr. BELIN. Did anyone say they had seen anything—such as a rifle?

Mr. CRAIG. Yes; later on. A few minutes after that—I had taken this girl to one of our criminal investigators—and was talking to some other people. I talked to a young couple and the boy said he saw two men on the—uh—sixth floor of the Book Depository Building over there; one of them had a rifle with the telescopic sight on it—but he thought they were Secret Service agents on guard and didn't report it. This was about—uh—oh, he said, 15 minutes before the motorcade ever arrived.

Mr. BELIN. Do you remember if that boy's name would have been Arnold Rowland— (spelling) R-o-w-l-a-n-d?

Mr. CRAIG. Yes.

Mr. BELIN. Does that sound like it?

Mr. CRAIG. Yes; it sounds like the name—yes.

Mr. BELIN. His wife might be Barbara Rowland?

Mr. CRAIG. Yes; I believe her name was Barbara.

Mr. BELIN. Before you talked to this couple, did you do anything else or talk with anyone before you got back with them?

Mr. CRAIG. Well, I looked around, you know, for just—after I turned this girl over to Mr. Lewis—I began looking around and talking to people to see if they'd seen anything. And that's when I ran onto this man and his wife.

Mr. BELIN. And about what time do you think this was in relation to—from when you heard the shots to the time that you talked to this young couple?

Mr. CRAIG. I don't know. 10 minutes, maybe.

Mr. BELIN. You believe you talked to this young couple 10 minutes after the shots were fired?

Mr. CRAIG. It might have been 10 minutes.

Mr. BELIN. All right.

Then, what did you do? But, first of all, let me ask you this: Did this girl say that she saw any person with a rifle?

Mr. CRAIG. No; no.

Mr. BELIN. Now, the boy—where did he say that he saw the man with the rifle?

Mr. CRAIG. On the—uh—west end of the building on the sixth floor.

Mr. BELIN. Would that be—when you say "the west end,"—you mean, the west end of the south side, or the west side?

Mr. CRAIG. The west end of the south side.

Mr. BELIN. Of the sixth floor?

Mr. CRAIG. Right.

Mr. BELIN. Did he point out the window to you?

Mr. CRAIG. Yes.

Mr. BELIN. From the west corner, where would this window have been? Right next to the west corner or two or three windows away, or what?

Mr. CRAIG. It was the—uh—the second window from the corner. They were walking, you know, back and forth.

Mr. BELIN. He said that the two men were walking back and forth?

Mr. CRAIG. Yes.

Mr. BELIN. Now, when you talk about second window, this building is located near you, is it not?

Mr. CRAIG. Yes.

240

Mr. BELIN. This is the Texas School Book Depository Building?

Mr. CRAIG. Yes.

Mr. BELIN. Each window was sort of a pair of windows. And, on the south side, there probably are around seven pairs of windows.

Mr. CRAIG. Uh-huh.

Mr. BELIN. Would this have been—when you say "the second window from the west end"—by that do you mean it was the first pair of windows but the easternmost one of that pair, or do you mean it was in the second pair of windows from the west end—or don't you remember?

Mr. CRAIG. No; I don't remember that now.

Mr. BELIN. All right.

Did he say anything else about what he had seen with this man with the rifle?

Mr. CRAIG. Yeah; he said he looked back a few minutes later and—uh—the other man was gone, and there was just one man—the man with the rifle.

Mr. BELIN. He said he looked back again and just the man with the rifle was there?

Mr. CRAIG. Right.

Mr. BELIN. Did he say how long or when the last time was that he saw the man with the rifle?

Mr. CRAIG. I believe this second time he looked was the—uh—the last time he looked up there.

Mr. BELIN. And about how long was that before the shots were fired?

Mr. CRAIG. Well, he said he first seen him—saw the two men about 15 minutes before the motorcade arrived.

Mr. BELIN. Uh-huh.

Mr. CRAIG. And he didn't say how long after that he looked back up there to just see the one man. He just said—uh—a few minutes later he looked back up.

Mr. BELIN. A few minutes later, he looked back up and he saw one man with the rifle?

Mr. CRAIG. Just the one man.

Mr. BELIN. Did he say what the one man was doing with the rifle?

Mr. CRAIG. He said he was holding it down to his side and just looking out the window.

Mr. BELIN. Did he say how far the man was from the window?

Mr. CRAIG. No; huh-uh.

Mr. BELIN. Did he say in what direction the man was looking out the window?

Mr. CRAIG. He was looking out in a southerly direction. Straight ahead. You know, straight out.

Mr. BELIN. When he said the man was holding it at his side, would this be—did he say it was, in military terminology, in any kind of a position to hold a weapon?

Mr. CRAIG. No; this I don't go into with him. I turned him over to Officer Lewis for interrogation.

Mr. BELIN. Would this be Deputy Sheriff Lemmy Lewis—(spelling) L-e-m-m-y L-e-w-i-s?

Mr. CRAIG. Yes.

Mr. BELIN. He is a criminal investigator of the Dallas Sheriff's Office?

Mr. CRAIG. Right.

Mr. BELIN. And then you left this young couple?

Mr. CRAIG. Right.

Mr. BELIN. Now, about how long would this have been after the shooting that you left them with Deputy Sheriff Lewis?

Mr. CRAIG. Well, I didn't talk with them long. I talked with them—all the time that he told me what he saw and the time that I turned him over to officer Lewis, was probably—uh—3 minutes—3 or 4 minutes.

Mr. BELIN. Uh-huh.

Mr. CRAIG. Because—uh—I took him immediately up there to him when he told me what he'd seen.

Mr. BELIN. By this time, had anyone said the shots might have come from that School Book Depository Building—do you know?

Mr. CRAIG. No. I don't—uh—I don't recall that. I don't believe so.

Mr. BELIN. At this time, do you know whether or not they had sealed off in any way the entrance or the building—the School Book Depository Building— or not?

Mr. CRAIG. No; no. I didn't notice that.

Mr. BELIN. You didn't notice that?

Mr. CRAIG. No.

Mr. BELIN. All right. Now, about how many minutes after the assassination or shooting was it that you turned this couple over to Sheriff Lemmy Lewis?

Mr. CRAIG. Oh, it was about—well, I guess, 12 minutes—10, 12 minutes. Something like that.

Mr. BELIN. Ten or 12 minutes after the shooting?

Mr. CRAIG. Right.

Mr. BELIN. Then, what did you do?

Mr. CRAIG. Well, I looked around for a little bit, you know, just observing the people and things, and Officer Lewis turned them over to someone else, as I recall, and sent them to the sheriff's office—to Mr. Decker's office. And then it was either Lemmy Lewis or Buddy Walthers—(spelling) W-a-l-t-h-e-r-s, one of our other criminal investigators, said that one of the bullets had ricocheted off the south curb of Elm Street. So, Officer Lewis and I crossed—walked down the hill and crossed Elm Street to look for the place where the bullet might have hit.

Mr. BELIN. Did he say why he believed one of the bullets ricocheted off the south curb of Elm?

Mr. CRAIG. No; he just said that someone said that one of them had. So, we checked it.

Mr. BELIN. So, you searched the south curb of Elm?

Mr. CRAIG. Right.

Mr. BELIN. Did you find anything there to indicate the ricocheted bullet?

Mr. CRAIG. No; we didn't find anything at that time. Now, as we were searching, we had just got over across the street, when I heard someone whistle.

Mr. BELIN. Now, about how many minutes was this after the time that you had turned that young couple over to Lemmy Lewis that you heard this whistle?

Mr. CRAIG. Fourteen or 15 minutes.

Mr. BELIN. Fourteen or 15 minutes?

Mr. CRAIG. Yes.

Mr. BELIN. Was this, you mean, after the shooting?

Mr. CRAIG. After the—from the time I heard the first shot.

Mr. BELIN. All right.
You heard someone whistle?

Mr. CRAIG. Yes. So I turned and—uh—saw a man start to run down the hill on the north side of Elm Street, running down toward Elm Street.

Mr. BELIN. And, about where was he with relation to the School Book Depository Building?

Mr. CRAIG. Uh—directly across that little side street that runs in front of it. He was on the south side of it.

Mr. BELIN. And he was on the south side of what would be an extension of Elm Street, if Elm Street didn't curve down into the underpass?

Mr. CRAIG. Right; right.

Mr. BELIN. And where was he with relation to the west side of the School Book Depository Building?

Mr. CRAIG. Right by the—uh—well, actually, directly in line with the west corner—the southwest corner.

Mr. BELIN. He was directly in line with the southwest corner of the building?

Mr. CRAIG. Yes.

Mr. BELIN. And he was on the south curve of that street that runs right in front of the building there?

Mr. CRAIG. Yes.

Mr. BELIN. And he started to run toward Elm Street as it curves under the underpass?

Mr. CRAIG. Yes; directly down the grassy portion of the park.

Mr. BELIN. All right.
And then what did you see happen?

Mr. CRAIG. I saw a light-colored station wagon, driving real slow, coming west on Elm Street from Houston. Uh—actually, it was nearly in line with him. And the driver was leaning to his right looking up the hill at the man running down.

Mr. BELIN. Uh-huh.

Mr. CRAIG. And the station wagon stopped almost directly across from me. And—uh—the man continued down the hill and got in the station wagon. And I attempted to cross the street. I wanted to talk to both of them. But the—uh—traffic was so heavy I couldn't get across the street. And—uh—they were gone before I could——

Mr. BELIN. Where did the station wagon head?

Mr. CRAIG. West on Elm Street.

242

Mr. BELIN. Under the triple underpass?

Mr. CRAIG. Yes.

Mr. BELIN. Could you describe the man that you saw running down toward the station wagon?

Mr. CRAIG. Oh, he was a white male in his twenties, five nine, five eight, something like that; about 140 to 150; had kind of medium brown sandy hair—you know, it was like it'd been blown—you know, he'd been in the wind or something—it was all wild-looking; had on—uh—bluetrousers——

Mr. BELIN. What shade of blue? Dark blue, medium or light?

Mr. CRAIG. No; medium, probably; I'd say medium.

And, a—uh—light tan shirt, as I remember it.

Mr. BELIN. Anything else about him?

Mr. CRAIG. No; nothing except that he looked like he was in an awful hurry.

Mr. BELIN. What about the man who was driving the car?

Mr. CRAIG. Now, he struck me, at first, as being a colored male. He was very dark complected, had real dark short hair, and was wearing a thin white-looking jacket—uh, it looked like the short windbreaker type, you know, because it was real thin and had the collar that came out over the shoulder (indicating with hands) like that—just a short jacket.

Mr. BELIN. You say that he first struck you that way. Do you now think that he was a Negro?

Mr. CRAIG. Well, I don't—I didn't get a real good look at him. But my first glance at him—I was more interested in the man coming down the hill—but my first glance at him, he struck me as a Negro.

Mr. BELIN. Is that what your opinion is today?

Mr. CRAIG. Well, I—I couldn't say, because I didn't get a good enough look at him.

Mr. BELIN. What kind and what color station wagon was it?

Mr. CRAIG. It was light colored—almost—uh—it looked white to me.

Mr. BELIN. What model or make was it?

Mr. CRAIG. I thought it was a Nash.

Mr. BELIN. Why would you think it was a Nash?

Mr. CRAIG. Because it had a built-in luggage rack on the top. And—uh—at the time, this was the only type car I could fit with that type luggage rack.

Mr. BELIN. A Nash Rambler—is that what you're referring to?

Mr. CRAIG. Yes; with a rack on the the back portion of the car, you know.

Mr. BELIN. Did it have a Texas license plate, or not?

Mr. CRAIG. It had the same color. I couldn't see the—uh—name with the numbers on it. I could just barely make them out. They were at an angle where I couldn't make the numbers of the—uh—any of the writing on it. But—uh—I'm sure it was a Texas plate.

Mr. BELIN. Anything else about this incident that you can recall?

Mr. CRAIG. No; not that——

Mr. BELIN. All right.

Then what did you do?

Mr. CRAIG. Well, then—uh, I went back up to the front of the School Book Depository—rather, I went up to it and noticed that it was sealed off. There was an officer standing guard in it with a shotgun in the doorway; several officers crowded around in front of it.

Mr. BELIN. How long would this have been after the shots were fired?

Mr. CRAIG. I'd say nearly 20 minutes.

Mr. BELIN. All right.

Mr. CRAIG. And they were calling for hand lights to search the attic of the building. At that time—uh—they thought the man was still in the building. So, they were calling for hand lights to search the building.

So, I went back across to the sheriff's office and got some hand lights and took them back over to them.

Then, I went up on the sixth floor.

Mr. BELIN. Why did you go up on the sixth floor?

Mr. CRAIG. Well, someone said that's where the shots came from. One of the city officers, if I'm not mistaken.

Mr. BELIN. All right.

Mr. CRAIG. So, we went to the sixth floor where—uh—some empty cartridges were found.

Mr. BELIN. Did you see the empty cartridges when they were found?

Mr. CRAIG. I didn't see them when they were found. I saw them laying on the floor.

243

Mr. BELIN. About how soon after they were found did you see them laying on the floor?

Mr. CRAIG. Oh, a couple of minutes. I went right on over there. I was at the far north end of the building. The cartridges were on the southeast corner.

Mr. BELIN. Well, how did you know they had been found there? Did someone yell—or what?

Mr. CRAIG. Yes; someone yelled across the room that "here's the shells."

Mr. BELIN. Do you remember who that was?

Mr. CRAIG. No; I couldn't recognize the voice.

Mr. BELIN. All right. Then, what did you do?

Mr. CRAIG. I went over there and—uh—didn't get too close because the shells were laying on the ground and there was—uh—oh, a sack and a bunch of things laying over there. So, you know, not to bother the area, I just went back across.

Mr. BELIN. Now, you say, there was a sack laying there?

Mr. CRAIG. Yes; I believe it was laying on top of a box, if I'm not mistaken.

Mr. BELIN. How big a sack was that?

Mr. CRAIG. It was a paper bag (indicating with hands)—a small paper bag.

Mr. BELIN. Well, the kind of paper bag that you carry your lunch in?

Mr. CRAIG. Yeah,—uh-huh.

Mr. BELIN. Was it more than a foot long?

Mr. CRAIG. I don't know. I think it was rolled up kind of.

Mr. BELIN. You think it was rolled up?

Mr. CRAIG. Yeah; you know, kind of crushed up.

Mr. BELIN. Was there any long sack laying in the floor there that you remember seeing, or not?

Mr. CRAIG. No; I don't remember seeing any.

Mr. BELIN. Do you remember seeing any thing there other than the shells?

Mr. CRAIG. No; not—uh—not anything that caught my eye.

Mr. BELIN. Where do you remember seeing the shells?

Mr. CRAIG. They were laying on the—uh—well, as you're facing the window——

Mr. BELIN. As you are facing the window and you're looking south?

Mr. CRAIG. The southeast corner window and you're looking south, the shells would be on your right and back away from the window, as I recall, about a foot.

Mr. BELIN. Do you recall any of the shells right up against the wall at all—or, don't you recall?

Mr. CRAIG. No; I don't; I didn't look that close.

Mr. BELIN. How many shells did you see there?

Mr. CRAIG. I saw three.

Mr. BELIN. Did anyone move any boxes in order to get in there—do you know?

Mr. CRAIG. Now, that, I don't know?

Mr. BELIN. Do you know if anyone moved any boxes in the window?

Mr. CRAIG. That I don't know either.

Mr. BELIN. Did you look very closely at the area where the shells were found?

Mr. CRAIG. Uh—no, because the identification men hadn't arrived, and we didn't want to stir up anything.

Mr. BELIN. Who was there that you remember?

Mr. CRAIG. Oh, Officer Mooney with our department—Luke Mooney; Officer Boone—Eugene Boone, with our department; myself; and some city officers that I didn't know. Those are the only that I remember. You know, there were several other people around but I didn't know them.

Mr. BELIN. All right.

Then what did you do after that?

Mr. CRAIG. They wanted to search the building for the weapon, so I went to the—I went to the northeast corner of the building and began to search west.

Mr. BELIN. Uh-huh.

Mr. CRAIG. Uh—everybody else took a different spot. And as I got nearly to the west end of the building, Officer Boone—Eugene Boone with the sheriff's office—hollered that here was the rifle.

Mr. BELIN. How far were you from Officer Boone when he hollered?

Mr. CRAIG. About 8-foot.

Mr. BELIN. What did you do then?

Mr. CRAIG. I went over to the—uh—cluster of boxes where he was standing and looked down between the boxes and saw the rifle lying on the floor.

Mr. BELIN. When you say "between the cluster of boxes," could you describe which way the boxes were?

Mr. CRAIG. There was a row going east to west on the north side of the weapon, and a box going east to west on the south side of the weapon, and—uh—if I remember, uh—as you'd look down, you had to look kinda back under the north stack of boxes to see the rifle. It was pushed kinda under—uh—or up tight against 'em—you know, where it would be hard to see. And, of course, both ends of the rows were closed off where you couldn't see through 'em. You had to get up and look in 'em.

Mr. BELIN. You are gesturing with your hand there—would you say that the boxes, then, as you gestured, were in the shape of what I would call a rectangular "O", so to speak?

Mr. CRAIG. Yes, yes, uh-huh.

Mr. BELIN. And about how high were the walls of this enclosure, so to speak?

Mr. CRAIG. Well, it—it was different heights. Now, the part where I looked in particularly was about—uh—oh, was about 5-foot.

Mr. BELIN. All right.

And you gestured there in such a way that you had to lean over and look straight down? Would that be a fair statement of your gestures?

Mr. CRAIG. Yes; yes. You had to lean over the boxes and look down.

Mr. BELIN. All right.

Then what happened? After you found this, did people come over—or what?

Mr. CRAIG. Yes; several other people came over.

Mr. BELIN. Do you remember about what time this was?

Mr. CRAIG. No; I had no idea then how long it had been.

Mr. BELIN. All right.

Do you remember who else came over?

Mr. CRAIG. Oh, Officer Mooney and—uh—several of the city officers; Will Fritz came over—Capt. Will Fritz, with the city of Dallas; some of his investigators, I didn't know them; and a criminal identification man, I believe, from the city of Dallas, then came over there to take pictures of the weapon.

Mr. BELIN. The weapon was moved by the time the pictures were taken?

Mr. CRAIG. No; no. The pictures were taken as the weapon was found lying there.

Mr. BELIN. Did you see the pictures taken of the shells?

Mr. CRAIG. No.

Mr. BELIN. You don't know whether or not anything was moved in that window before this?

Mr. CRAIG. No; no.

Mr. BELIN. All right.

Anything else happen up to that time that you haven't related here that you feel might be important?

Mr. CRAIG. No. Uh—I'm thinking it was about this time—uh—that we got the news there had been a city officer shot over in Oak Cliff.

Mr. BELIN. And then what happened?

Mr. CRAIG. Well, there was just—uh—of course, everybody stayed there, you know, and sort of mingled around and—uh—I then went back downstairs after the weapon was picked up. The identification man from the city of Dallas then, after he took his pictures, picked the weapon up and handed it to Will Fritz.

And I then went back downstairs and over to the sheriff's office.

Mr. BELIN. All right.

At this time, do you know, did any person say that any employee in the School Building was missing up until the time you left?

Mr. CRAIG. No; I don't recall anybody saying anything to that effect.

Mr. BELIN. Had any description gone out for anyone that you know of with regard to the shooting?

Mr. CRAIG. I think—uh—no description of the suspect in the shooting of the officer hadn't went out at this time, but——

Mr. BELIN. You don't know of any other that went out at that time?

Mr. CRAIG. No; no.

Mr. BELIN. All right. Then you went back over to the Dallas Sheriff's Office?

Mr. CRAIG. Yes.

Mr. BELIN. Then what did you do?

Mr. CRAIG. Well, I think I gave a statement to Rosemary Allen over there, as did all the officers, as to what they were doing at the time, you know.

Mr. BELIN. Uh-huh.

Mr. CRAIG. And—uh—then I kept thinking about this man that had run down the hill and got in this car, so—uh—it was about, oh, I don't recall exactly the time, nearly 5 or something like that, or after, when—uh—the city had apprehended a suspect in the city officer's shooting. And—uh—information was floating around that they were trying to connect him with the assassination of the President—as the assassin.

So—uh, in the meantime, I kept thinking about this subject that had run and got in the car. So, I called Captain Fritz' office and talked to one of his officers and—uh—told him what I had saw and give him a description of the man, asked him how it fit the man they had picked up as a suspect.

And—uh—it was then they asked me to come up and look at him at Captain Fritz' office.

Mr. BELIN. All right.

Then what did you do?

Mr. CRAIG. I drove up to Fritz' office about, oh, after 5—about 5:30 or something like that—and—uh—talked to Captain Fritz and told him what I had saw. And he took me in his office—I believe it was his office—it was a little office, and had the suspect setting in a chair behind a desk—beside the desk. And another gentleman, I didn't know him, he was sitting in another chair to my left as I walked in the office.

And Captain Fritz asked me was this the man I saw—and I said, "Yes," it was.

Mr. BELIN. All right.

Will you describe the man you saw in Captain Fritz' office?

Mr. CRAIG. Oh, he was sitting down but—uh—he had the same medium brown hair; it was still—well, it was kinda wild looking; he was slender, and—uh—what I could tell of him sitting there, he was—uh—short. By that, I mean not—myself, I'm five eleven—he was shorter than I was. And—uh—fairly light build.

Mr. BELIN. Could you see his trousers?

Mr. CRAIG. No; I couldn't see his trousers at all.

Mr. BELIN. What about his shirt?

Mr. CRAIG. I believe, as close as I can remember, a T-shirt—a white T-shirt.

Mr. BELIN. All right.

But you didn't see him in a lineup? You just saw him sitting there?

Mr. CRAIG. No; he was sitting there by himself in a chair—off to one side.

Mr. BELIN. All right.

Then, what did Captain Fritz say and what did you say and what did the suspect say?

Mr. CRAIG. Captain Fritz then asked him about the—uh—he said, "What about this station wagon?"

And the suspect interrupted him and said, "That station wagon belongs to Mrs. Paine"—I believe is what he said. "Don't try to tie her into this. She had nothing to do with it."

And—uh—Captain Fritz then told him, as close as I can remember, that, "All we're trying to do is find out what happened, and this man saw you leave from the scene."

And the suspect again interrupted Captain Fritz and said, "I told you people I did." And—uh—yeah—then, he said—then he continued and he said, "Everybody will know who I am now."

And he was leaning over the desk. At this time, he had risen partially out of the chair and leaning over the desk, looking directly at Captain Fritz.

Mr. BELIN. What was he wearing—or could you see the color of his trousers as he leaned over the desk?

Mr. CRAIG. No; because he never—he just leaned up, you know, sort of forward—not actually up, just out of his chair like that (indicating) forward.

Mr. BELIN. Then, did you say anything more?

Mr. CRAIG. No; I then left.

Mr. BELIN. Well, in other words, the only thing you ever said was, "This was the man,"—or words to that effect?

Mr. CRAIG. Yes.

Mr. BELIN. Did Captain Fritz say anything more.

Mr. CRAIG. No; I don't believe—not while I was there.

Mr. BELIN. Did the suspect say anything more?

Mr. CRAIG. Not that I recall.

Mr. BELIN. Did you say anything about that it was a Rambler station wagon there?

Mr. CRAIG. In the presence of the suspect?

Mr. BELIN. Yes.

Mr. CRAIG. No.

Mr. BELIN. You don't know whether Captain Fritz said anything to the suspect about this incident before you came, do you?

Mr. CRAIG. No; I don't.

Mr. BELIN. Is there anything else that you can think of involving this interrogation at which you were present?

Mr. CRAIG. No. Nothing else was said after that point. I then left and give my name to the—uh—Secret Service agent and the FBI agent that was outside the office.

Mr. BELIN. Anything else in connection with the assassination that you think might be important that we haven't discussed here?

Mr. CRAIG. No; except—uh—except for the fact that it came out later that Mrs. Paine does own a station wagon and—uh—it has a luggage rack on top. And this came out, of course, later, after I got back to the office. I didn't know about this. Buddy Walthers brought it up. I believe they went by the house and the car was parked in the driveway.

Mr. BELIN. Anything else you can think of?

Mr. CRAIG. No. That's all. I forgot about it and went back to work.

Mr. BELIN. Now, prior to the time we had your deposition taken, we chatted for a few minutes about some of these things—is that correct?

Mr. CRAIG. Yes.

Mr. BELIN. For instance, we talked about your conversation with this young couple—this Arnold Rowland and his wife?

Mr. CRAIG. Yes.

Mr. BELIN. Is there anything that we said before the deposition was taken that we haven't recorded here?

Mr. CRAIG. I don't believe so.

Mr. BELIN. Is there anything that I said or you said in our conversation that is different from anything that was recorded here—to the best of your recollection?

Mr. CRAIG. No; except you asked me before, I believe, did I talk to any of the railroad employees.

Mr. BELIN. That's right.

Mr. CRAIG. And I said, "No"—which I did not.

Mr. BELIN. Anything else?

Mr. CRAIG. (Pausing before reply.) No—nothing that I recall.

Mr. BELIN. In our conversation, did you just relate to me what your story was before we sat down to take the deposition?

Mr. CRAIG. Yes.

Mr. BELIN. Will you agree to follow or to waive signing of the deposition and leave it in the Court Reporter's hands—or do you want to sign it?

Mr. CRAIG. It makes no difference to me.

Mr. BELIN. By the way, you had notice of this, did you not, of this taking of this deposition?

Mr. CRAIG. Yes. I have the letter right here in my pocket.

Mr. BELIN. All right.

Anything else you can think of, sir?

Mr. CRAIG. No.

Mr. BELIN. Well, we want to thank you for taking your time to come down here and we appreciate your cooperation. We would appreciate your, also, thanking Sheriff Decker for us, if you would, when you get back there.

Mr. CRAIG. Okay.

Mr. BELIN. Thank you very much.

One other thing before you go, Mr. Craig. We might have covered this before, but I want to doublecheck it.

When you talked to Mr. Rowland about what he saw in the window, did he say whether or not two men he saw were white or colored?

Mr. CRAIG. Yes; I determined that right away. I asked him whether they were white or colored and he said white.

Mr. BELIN. What else did he tell you about them? Did he tell you how much of them he saw?

Mr. CRAIG. Yes. He said they—uh—walked back and forth in front of the windows there—uh—several minutes. You know, not a long time but 3, 4, 5 minutes. He did state that one of them had a rifle with a scope on it.

Mr. BELIN. Did he give you the color of the hair or the complexion or anything like that?

Mr. CRAIG. No—no; this he couldn't give.

Mr. BELIN. Could he give you the type of clothing they were wearing?

Mr. CRAIG. If I recall, he was vague on one—he thought it was khakis, but the other man he wasn't sure.

Mr. BELIN. Did he tell you anything else about these people?

Mr. CRAIG. Yes; he said he looked up a few minutes later and—uh—there was only one man up there then.

Mr. BELIN. Did he ever tell you anything about seeing any other people in any other windows?

Mr. CRAIG. Yes; he said there were people in other windows looking over the ledges—you know, leaning up against the outside of the windows, looking out.

Mr. BELIN. Did he tell you whether any of these other people were on the sixth floor?

Mr. CRAIG. No; these two men were the only ones he saw on that particular floor.

Mr. BELIN. Did he tell you that was the sixth floor he saw them on?

Mr. CRAIG. Yes. He said the second to the top floor—the next floor down; which would be the sixth floor.

Mr. BELIN. Did he tell you about ever seeing anyone else on the sixth floor—or did he say that he didn't see anyone else on the sixth floor? Or don't you remember?

Mr. CRAIG. Just the two men. That's all he saw on that particular floor.

Mr. BELIN. Did you specifically ask him if he saw anyone else on that floor, or did he say that he did not?

Mr. CRAIG. No; I asked him and he said——

Mr. BELIN. Well, what was your statement to him and what was his to you?

Mr. CRAIG. I asked him was there anybody else on the floor with these two men. And he said, "No, just the two of them."

Mr. BELIN. Did he say that he saw these two men together first?

Mr. CRAIG. Yes.

Mr. BELIN. And then he just saw one, as I understand it?

Mr. CRAIG. A few minutes later, he looked back up there and saw just the man with the rifle.

Mr. BELIN. I believe he said earlier that he saw these men around 15 minutes before the motorcade arrived? And then a few minutes later, you say that he told you he saw only one man?

Mr. CRAIG. Right.

Mr. BELIN. Did he then tell you that he saw no men—or what did he say about what he saw after that?

Mr. CRAIG. Well, then, I took him to Officer Lewis and turned him over to Lemmy Lewis.

Mr. BELIN. Anything else you can think of about that conversation?

Mr. CRAIG. No; there was not—I don't think there was anything else discussed except for the fact that he told me he thought—he said he thought he was a Secret Service agent—and that's why he didn't report it.

Mr. BELIN. All right.

Now, if you would just wait here one more minute, Mr. Craig, Mr. Ball stepped in and he's going down to pick up some clothing. And we'd like to have you take a look at this clothing and see if this looks familiar to any of the clothing that you saw on the man running toward the Rambler.

If you'll just wait a minute here please sir.

(Mr. Ball returns to deposition room with box of clothing.)

Mr. BELIN. Mr. Craig, I hand you Exhibit No. 150. Have you ever seen a shirt like this before? Does this look familiar to the shirt that the suspect might have been wearing when you saw him, or this man running toward the station wagon?

Mr. CRAIG. It's the same type of shirt.

Mr. BELIN. I believe you used the phrase, "light shirt". Would Exhibit 150 be darker than the shirt that he was wearing?

Mr. CRAIG. Uh—it looks darker in here—yes, uh-huh.

Mr. BELIN. Was this man running towards the station wagon wearing a jacket?

Mr. CRAIG. No; I don't believe he was.

Mr. BELIN. I hand you Exhibit No. 156. Did the trousers that this man running toward the station wagon had on—were they this color—lighter, darker, or a different kind of trousers—or what?

Mr. CRAIG. No. They were—uh—they were work trousers like those; but they looked blue to me.

Mr. BELIN. And this Exhibit 156 looks kind of gray?

Mr. CRAIG. Yes.

Mr. BELIN. What about Exhibit 157?

Mr. CRAIG. Well, those are more the color.

Mr. BELIN. But they still looked different from Exhibit 157, too?

Mr. CRAIG. Yes.

Mr. BELIN. Have you discussed with Sheriff Decker the fact that when Oswald was picked up they found a bus transfer in his pocket?

Mr. CRAIG. No; I knew—uh—nothing about a bus transfer.

Mr. BELIN. Do you feel, in your own mind, that the man you saw at Captain Fritz's office was the same man that you saw running towards the station wagon?

Mr. CRAIG. Yes; I feel like it was.

Mr. BELIN. Do you feel that you might have been influenced by the fact that you knew he was the suspect—subconsciously, or do you——

Mr. CRAIG. Well, it's—it's possible, but I still feel strongly that it was the same person.

Mr. BELIN. Okay. That's it. Thank you.

TESTIMONY OF GEORGE W. RACKLEY, SR.

The testimony of George W. Rackley, Sr., was taken at 11 a.m., on April 8, 1964, in the office of the U.S. attorney, 301 Post Office Building, Bryan and Ervay Streets, Dallas, Tex., by Mr. David W. Belin, assistant counsel of the President's Commission.

Mr. BELIN. Mr. Rackley, do you want to stand and raise your right hand and be sworn, please.

Do you solemnly swear that the testimony you are about to give before the President's Commission on the Assassination of President Kennedy, is the truth, the whole truth, and nothing but the truth, so help you God?

Mr. RACKLEY. I do.

Mr. BELIN. You can be seated. Your name is George W. Rackley, Sr?

Mr. RACKLEY. Yes, sir.

Mr. BELIN. Where do you live, Mr. Rackley?

Mr. RACKLEY. I live at Ferris.

Mr. BELIN. Texas?

Mr. RACKLEY. Ferris, Tex.

Mr. BELIN. Is that a suburb of Dallas?

Mr. RACKLEY. Yes, sir.

Mr. BELIN. Were you raised in Texas?

Mr. RACKLEY. Yes, sir.

Mr. BELIN. Born in Texas?

Mr. RACKLEY. No; I was born in Alabama.

Mr. BELIN. Raised in Texas? Go to school here in Texas?

Mr. RACKLEY. Yes, sir.

Mr. BELIN. How far did you get through school?

Mr. RACKLEY. Fifth.

Mr. BELIN. Fifth grade?

Mr. RACKLEY. Yes, sir.

Mr. BELIN. Then what did you do?

Mr. RACKLEY. Well, I went to farming.

Mr. BELIN. You went to farming?

Mr. RACKLEY. Yes.

Mr. BELIN. Well, I am from Iowa. We do a lot of farming up there.

Mr. RACKLEY. That is what I do here.

Mr. BELIN. All right, then what did you do?

Mr. RACKLEY. Well, at the present I am working for the Coordinated Railroad Co.

Mr. BELIN. For the what?

Mr. RACKLEY. For the Katy. It is a Katy railroad project, but it is a coordinated deal.

Mr. BELIN. What are you doing?

Mr. RACKLEY. I unload trailers.

Mr. BELIN. You unload trailers?

Mr. RACKLEY. Yes, sir.

Mr. BELIN. Let me backtrack. How old are you?

Mr. RACKLEY. I am 60.

Mr. BELIN. You said you quit school in the Fifth Grade and went to farming. How long did you farm?

Mr. RACKLEY. I farmed up to 3 years ago.

Mr. BELIN. You farmed up to 3 years ago?

Mr. RACKLEY. Yes, sir.

Mr. BELIN. What kind of farming?

Mr. RACKLEY. Well, I raised cotton and corn.

Mr. BELIN. Then 3 years ago where did you go to work?

Mr. RACKLEY. I went to work here. Well, I have been working off in spare times for about 8 years.

Mr. BELIN. For the same place?

Mr. RACKLEY. Yes; same place.

Mr. BELIN. Is that here in Dallas?

Mr. RACKLEY. That is here in Dallas.

Mr. BELIN. Where in Dallas is it?

Mr. RACKLEY. It is on Ross and Market Street, about two blocks from the courthouse.

Mr. BELIN. Now where is it with relation to the corner of Elm and Houston?

Mr. RACKLEY. Well, it is on up on Ross. Two blocks north is where our place is.

Mr. BELIN. Your place is two blocks north of the corner of Elm and Houston?

Mr. RACKLEY. Yes, sir.

Mr. BELIN. You work indoors or outdoors?

Mr. RACKLEY. Just all over town.

Mr. BELIN. Just all over town?

Mr. RACKLEY. Yes, sir.

Mr. BELIN. Where were you working around the noon hour of Friday, November 22, 1963?

Mr. RACKLEY. Well, I was there at the office.

Mr. BELIN. Were you inside or outside?

Mr. RACKLEY. Our office is just a little small place. Well, just outside, you might say, of it.

Mr. BELIN. Did you see the President's motorcade at all on that day?

Mr. RACKLEY. No, sir; I didn't.

Mr. BELIN. Were you standing with anyone there?

Mr. RACKLEY. Yes, sir.

Mr. BELIN. With whom?

Mr. RACKLEY. With James Romack. I and him had walked out.

Mr. BELIN. You had walked out?

Mr. RACKLEY. I heard the siren; the parade was coming.

Mr. BELIN. You heard sirens?

Mr. RACKLEY. Yes, sir. And I had walked out in front of the place to where I could get a better view, as a fellow says.

Mr. BELIN. Where were you standing?

Mr. RACKLEY. Well, I had walked out in the truck lot.

Mr. BELIN. In the truck lot?

Mr. RACKLEY. Yes.

Mr. BELIN. And was that——

Mr. RACKLEY. You might say would have been in the middle of the street.

Mr. BELIN. Would that have been in the middle of Houston Street?

Mr. RACKLEY. Yes.

Mr. BELIN. In what direction were you facing?

Mr. RACKLEY. Facing south.

Mr. BELIN. All right, did you see the motorcade at all?

Mr. RACKLEY. No.

Mr. BELIN. What did you see?

Mr. RACKLEY. I didn't practically see anything.

Mr. BELIN. Did you hear any sounds at all?

Mr. RACKLEY. Yes. Heard the sounds of the parade.

Mr. BELIN. Did you hear the sounds that sounded like firecrackers or shots at all?

Mr. RACKLEY. No, sir.

Mr. BELIN. Didn't hear that?

Mr. RACKLEY. No.

Mr. BELIN. About how far would you have been from the northeast corner of the Texas School Book Depository when you were standing there?

Mr. RACKLEY. I would say right at a block.

Mr. BELIN. About a block. Do you have any idea about how many feet that is?

Mr. RACKLEY. No, sir; I don't.

Mr. BELIN. Were you just standing there, or were you walking?

Mr. RACKLEY. I was just standing there.

Mr. BELIN. Did you see anything happen at all there?

Mr. RACKLEY. No, sir.

Mr. BELIN. Did you see anyone in the parade?

Mr. RACKLEY. The only thing—I told the guy, he was down there, the only thing that I saw that looked suspicious to me, there was something like a hundred pigeons flew up like you shot into them, and I noticed that, but I never heard no shots.

Mr. BELIN. Where did you see them fly from?

Mr. RACKLEY. From over the top of the building.

Mr. BELIN. Which building? The School Book Depository or over on the other side?

Mr. RACKLEY. The Trinity Building.

Mr. BELIN. Which building did they fly off of?

Mr. RACKLEY. I wasn't looking. I just seen they all flew together.

Mr. BELIN. Did it look like they were flying up from both buildings?

Mr. RACKLEY. Both buildings.

Mr. BELIN. You don't know about when this took place?

Mr. RACKLEY. No, sir; I don't.

Mr. BELIN. About what time was it that you were looking that way, do you remember, offhand?

Mr. RACKLEY. No; but it was just at the time that the parade was nearing there, I know that.

Mr. BELIN. Had any of the parade already gone by the corner of Elm and Houston?

Mr. RACKLEY. I couldn't say.

Mr. BELIN. So you don't know whether it did or didn't?

Mr. RACKLEY. No.

Mr. BELIN. But would you say it was about that time that the motorcade was to be going by there?

Mr. RACKLEY. It was between 11 and 12.

Mr. BELIN. It was between 11 and 12?

Mr. RACKLEY. Yes.

Mr. BELIN. O'clock?

Mr. RACKLEY. Yes.

Mr. BELIN. What time did you—was this before or after you had lunch?

Mr. RACKLEY. Well, I just eat just any time I get a chance.

Mr. BELIN. Do you know accurately what time it was?

Mr. RACKLEY. No, sir; I don't.

Mr. BELIN. Could it have been as late as 12:30?

Mr. RACKLEY. No.

Mr. BELIN. It was before 12:30?

Mr. RACKLEY. Yes.

Mr. BELIN. Before 12?

Mr. RACKLEY. Yes.

Mr. BELIN. Sometime between 11 and 12?

Mr. RACKLEY. Well, it was at the time that, really, that they had shot him, because I was there when the policemen covered the place.

Mr. BELIN. You were there when the policemen covered the place?

Mr. RACKLEY. Yes.

Mr. BELIN. With relation to the time that the policemen covered the place, how many minutes before that did you see the birds fly up?

Mr. RACKLEY. I saw the pigeons there 2 or 3 minutes before that.

Mr. BELIN. Now after you saw the pigeons, you saw the police covering the place?

Mr. RACKLEY. Yes, sir.

Mr. BELIN. Within 2 or 3 minutes after you saw the pigeons?

Mr. RACKLEY. Yes, sir.

Mr. BELIN. Did you see any people coming out the back door at all?

Mr. RACKLEY. No.

Mr. BELIN. Could you see the back door of the Texas School Book Depository?

Mr. RACKLEY. Yes.

Mr. BELIN. That was at the dock they have back there?

Mr. RACKLEY. Yes, sir.

Mr. BELIN. Were you looking towards that direction?

Mr. RACKLEY. Yes, sir.

Mr. BELIN. About how long did you keep your eyes fixed over there?

Mr. RACKLEY. Oh, I would say 5 minutes anyhow. Probably 10. I was looking up that way at all times.

Mr. BELIN. Five or 10 minutes, you figure?

Mr. RACKLEY. Yes.

Mr. BELIN. Did you see any people leave the Texas School Book Depository by way of the rear exit?

Mr. RACKLEY. No, sir.

Mr. BELIN. Did you see any people running north on Houston Street?

Mr. RACKLEY. No, sir.

Mr. BELIN. Did you tell your company supervisor that there had been some shooting?

Mr. RACKLEY. No; not right then.

Mr. BELIN. Later did you tell them?

Mr. RACKLEY. Yes; I imagine.

Mr. BELIN. You said you stayed there 5 or 10 minutes looking to the south?

Mr. RACKLEY. Yes.

Mr. BELIN. What did you do after that?

Mr. RACKLEY. Well, when the policemen began to crowd around and they all   over the place, well then I told him I thought that something had happened over there.

I wasn't expecting anything like that until I just, of course, seen the policemen all out there running back. They came out the back door and the side door with guns.

Mr. BELIN. Who did you tell that to that you thought something happened there?

Mr. RACKLEY. Gail George.

Mr. BELIN. Is that your foreman?

Mr. RACKLEY. Yes.

Mr. BELIN. After you said you kept your eyes on this looking south for 5 or 10 minutes, what did you do after that?

Mr. RACKLEY. Well, I went back to the office.

Mr. BELIN. Then what did you do after that?

Mr. RACKLEY. Well, I don't remember.

Mr. BELIN. During this period of 5 or 10 minutes, did you walk close to the building at all, or just stand there?

Mr. RACKLEY. Just stood out there.

Mr. BELIN. What about Romack? Did he stand with you, or did he walk closer?

Mr. RACKLEY. He walked closer.

Mr. BELIN. Anything else you can think of, whether I have asked it or not, that in any way might be relevant to this inquiry?

Mr. RACKLEY. It wasn't a thing that I knew. I didn't really know or expect what was taking place.

Mr. BELIN. Other than the pigeons?

Mr. RACKLEY. Yes.

Mr. BELIN. Sir, we thank you for your cooperation. You have a right, if you want, to come back down and read your testimony and sign it, or you can just waive doing that and have the court reporter send it directly to us without your taking another trip down here. You can do it either way.

Mr. RACKLEY. I can sign it now.

Mr. BELIN. You can either waive signing it or else you can come down again and read it and sign it. By waiving, I mean you just let it go, assuming that the court reporter will accurately transcribe it, or you have a right to come in and read it.

Mr. RACKLEY. I will just let it go.

Mr. BELIN. You waive signing it?

Mr. RACKLEY. Yes.

Mr. BELIN. That is all for now.

TESTIMONY OF JAMES ELBERT ROMACK

The testimony of James Elbert Romack was taken at 11:30 a.m., on April 8, 1964, in the office of the U.S. attorney, 301 Post Office Building, Bryan and Ervay Streets, Dallas, Tex., by Mr. David W. Belin, assistant counsel of the President's Commission.

Mr. BELIN. You want to stand and raise your right hand.

Do you solemnly swear that the testimony you are about to give will be the truth, the whole truth, and nothing but the truth, so help you God?

Mr. ROMACK. I do.

Mr. BELIN. My name is David Belin. I am actually a practicing attorney from Des Moines, Iowa. I have been with the President's Commission on the Assassination of President Kennedy for several months here, and we asked you to come down to have your deposition taken.

Mr. BELIN. Would you please state your name for the record?

Mr. ROMACK. James Elbert Romack.

Mr. BELIN. R-o-m-a-c-k?

Mr. ROMACK. Right.

Mr. BELIN. Where do you live, Mr. Romack?

Mr. ROMACK. 10825 Benbrook Drive, Dallas, Tex.

Mr. BELIN. How old a man are you?

Mr. ROMACK. I am 39 years of age.

Mr. BELIN. Were you born in Texas?

Mr. ROMACK. Yes, sir.

Mr. BELIN. Go to school here?

Mr. ROMACK. I went to school in Texas, yes, sir.

Mr. BELIN. How far did you get through school?

Mr. ROMACK. I got a couple of years of college.

Mr. BELIN. A couple of years of college?

Mr. ROMACK. Yes.

Mr. BELIN. What college?

Mr. ROMACK. East Texas State Teachers College and Technological College.

Mr. BELIN. Did you go to college right after high school?

Mr. ROMACK. It was right after the war.

Mr. BELIN. You went right after the war?

Mr. ROMACK. Yes.

Mr. BELIN. Did you go——

Mr. ROMACK. I take it back, I was going to Tech when the war broke out, and went to East Texas State after the war.

Mr. BELIN. When the war broke out, what did you do?

Mr. ROMACK. I went into the Navy.

Mr. BELIN. What did you do in the Navy?

Mr. ROMACK. I was in the Amphibious, on the Aleutian Islands, and took boot training in San Diego.

I went to the Aleutian Islands and came back and went to Pearl Harbor and stayed out there for 9 months, and boarded an LST and went through the campaigns of the Philippines and Okinawa and Japan and then returned back home.

Mr. BELIN. When did you get back to the States?

Mr. ROMACK. March 1946.

Mr. BELIN. I was stationed in Japan right after the last war. Where were you stationed?

Mr. ROMACK. I was on this LST in Pearl Harbor.

Mr. BELIN. Were you in Japan after the war?

Mr. ROMACK. Yes, I was there during the time the Treaty was signed. We were in the, I forget the name, we were riding typhoons. We rode out eight of them, and our ship came back without the two side doors. All we had was the big ramp.

Mr. BELIN. That must have been quite a voyage back?

Mr. ROMACK. They were taking water in the port and bailing it over in the back.

Mr. BELIN. When you got back to the States, what did you do?

Mr. ROMACK. Went to St. Louis and bought me an automobile, and just I was a boy. I was the boy about 6 months, I would say.

Mr. BELIN. Then what did you do?

Mr. ROMACK. Then I entered school, East Texas State Teachers College.

Mr. BELIN. You went there about a year?

Mr. ROMACK. Approximately a year, I would say, yes, sir.

Mr. BELIN. Then what did you do after that?

Mr. ROMACK. I got married once along the route, and I was married about 30 days.

Then I came to Dallas in 1947. I guess it was 1947, or 1948, I forget just when I did come to Dallas. It was along in there.

Mr. BELIN. And you have been in Dallas ever since?

Mr. ROMACK. Yes, sir.

Mr. BELIN. By the way, were you honorably discharged?

Mr. ROMACK. Yes; I surely was.

Mr. BELIN. What did you do when you got to Dallas?

Mr. ROMACK. I went to work with a motor freight carrier. They are known as ICX today. They were Miller & Miller Motor Freight at the time.

Mr. BELIN. What did you do for them?

Mr. ROMACK. Drove a truck.

Mr. BELIN. How long did you do that?

Mr. ROMACK. Approximately a year.

Mr. BELIN. Then what did you do?

Mr. ROMACK. Went back to East Texas, and my home, and piddled around for a short while.

Then I came back to Dallas. And what did I do along in there? In 1949, I went to work for the Cotton Belt Railroad.

Mr. BELIN. How long did you stay with them?

Mr. ROMACK. Until April, I believe, of 1955. I know it was in 1955.

Mr. BELIN. What did you generally do when you were with the Cotton Belt?

Mr. ROMACK. I did all the railroad work during that time. I mean, I have been a billing clerk, and I have been a foreman, and I have been checker, and assistant foreman, warehouse foreman, and I worked out in the yards, and did quite a few jobs.

Mr. BELIN. You left them in 1955, and then what did you do?

Mr. ROMACK. Went to work with—a friend wanted me to go to work with him in a service station, Conoco Service Station.

Mr. BELIN. How long did you stay there?

Mr. ROMACK. Stayed there a year, approximately.

Mr. BELIN. Then what did you do?

Mr. ROMACK. Then I went to work with Strickland Transportation Co. as a dock foreman.

Mr. BELIN. How long were you with them?

Mr. ROMACK. Oh, I would say 6 or 7 months.

Mr. BELIN. Then what?

Mr. ROMACK. Then I went to work with an air freight concern out here at Love Field Drive, driving a truck, delivering air freight and picking up air freight for, I would say, 7 or 8 months there, maybe.

Mr. BELIN. Then what?

Mr. ROMACK. Then I hired out with the Coordinating Transportation Co.

Mr. BELIN. Coordinated Transportation Co.?

Mr. ROMACK. Right, which that is where I am at today.

Mr. BELIN. What have you been doing for them?

Mr. ROMACK. Driving mostly your big van trailer-truck and bobtail trucks and pickup and delivery service.

Mr. BELIN. Where were you around the noon hour of November 22, 1963?

Mr. ROMACK. I was on lunch period, just piddling around out north by east, I would say, from the Texas School Book Depository Building.

Mr. BELIN. You were standing around Houston Street?

Mr. ROMACK. It would be just about where Houston would intersect, but the street was under construction at the time. They didn't have it, which they still don't have it opened up for through traffic.

Mr. BELIN. Were you standing with anyone?

Mr. ROMACK. Well, Lee and Mr. Rackley, we walked out there together originally to start with. We were kind of piddling around, and I kind of walked off ahead of him.

Mr. BELIN. Was that George W. Rackley you were referring to?

Mr. ROMACK. Yes, sir.

Mr. BELIN. Is he also known as "Pop" Rackley?

Mr. ROMACK. Right.

Mr. BELIN. You said you started walking away. Where did you walk?

Mr. ROMACK. Toward the School Book Depository Building.

Mr. BELIN. Along what street did you walk?

Mr. ROMACK. Well, it wouldn't be no street at the time.

Mr. BELIN. Well, if there would be a street?

Mr. ROMACK. I guess it would be just about, I don't know whether they are going to split Ross and Houston Street up.

Mr. BELIN. Would you be looking at at Houston Street?

Mr. ROMACK. More or less. I would be looking at Houston Street; yes, sir.

Mr. BELIN. All right, and what happened as you were walking?

Mr. ROMACK. I heard these three rifle shots sound out.

Mr. BELIN. Did you know they were rifle shots?

Mr. ROMACK. Yes, sir; I did. I go elk hunting in Colorado every year in October, and I just came back from this trip, and I am pretty familiar with a rifle shot.

Mr. BELIN. How many did you hear?

Mr. ROMACK. Three.

Mr. BELIN. Where did they sound like they came from?

Mr. ROMACK. It sounded, I guess, like it came from that building, but it wasn't on my side of the building.

Mr. BELIN. Did it sound like it was up high or low?

Mr. ROMACK. I would say they were high. I have never been asked that question, but it did sound like they were running out high, I would say, and the wind was blowing a little bit from the south that day, I can remember.

Mr. BELIN. The wind was blowing into your face as you walked, or was it blowing from your back, sir?

Mr. ROMACK. It was blowing into my face.

Mr. BELIN. Into your face.

How far were you from the School Book Depository Building when you heard the shots?

Mr. ROMACK. Oh, I probably was 125 yards. 100 to 125 yards, I would say.

Mr. BELIN. Would that be from the nearest corner of the building or from the front of Elm Street?

Mr. ROMACK. From the nearest corner of the building.

Mr. BELIN. From the northeast corner of the building?

Mr. ROMACK. Right.

Mr. BELIN. How close did the shots sound like they came together?

Mr. ROMACK. Oh, they happened pretty fast. I would say maybe 3 or 4 seconds apart.

Mr. BELIN. Were they equally spaced, or did one sound like it was closer than another one in time?

Mr. ROMACK. It sounded like to me that they were evenly spaced. They rang out pretty fast.

Mr. BELIN. Have you ever operated a bolt action rifle?

Mr. ROMACK. Yes, sir.

Mr. BELIN. Do you own one?

Mr. ROMACK. Yes, sir.

Mr. BELIN. Did it sound like the shots were faster than it could be operated with a bolt action rifle?

Mr. ROMACK. No, sir.

Mr. BELIN. What kind of rifle do you have now, by the way?

Mr. ROMACK. I have a—it is a—I can't answer that really.

Mr. BELIN. What caliber?

Mr. ROMACK. It is a 30-06.

Mr. BELIN. 30-06 rifle?

Mr. ROMACK. Yes, it is. And it is an old World War I mechanism. It is either an Enfleld or a Springfield.

Mr. BELIN. Bolt action?

Mr. ROMACK. Yes, sir.

Mr. BELIN. You heard those rifle shots, and you think you could shoot your rifle accurately as fast as you heard those shots?

Mr. ROMACK. I don't, wouldn't think that I would be that good a shot; no, sir; because I shot at an elk four times and I hit him everywhere and missed him one time out of four.

Mr. BELIN. How far was it?

Mr. ROMACK. He was, I would say, 350 to 500 yards away. He was quite a distance.

Mr. BELIN. Maybe I should have asked the question this way. Suppose he was 100 yards away or else 50 yards?

Mr. ROMACK. I would be more accurate with my shooting, I sure would.

Mr. BELIN. If he were, say, from 40 to 75 yards away, or not an elk, a person, do you think you could shoot 40 to 75 yards away accurately as quickly as you heard those rifle sounds?

Mr. ROMACK. I wouldn't say I could; no, sir.

Mr. BELIN. Do you think an accurate rifleman could?

255

Mr. ROMACK. Yes, sir.

Mr. BELIN. Well, you heard the shots, and then what did you do?

Mr. ROMACK. Well, I knew something was wrong. I mean, I could sense that within my own self.

Mr. BELIN. All right.

Mr. ROMACK. And I looked up and I felt kind of chilly looking down towards the—which I am facing the Houston entrance, and I looked down toward where all the people were standing along, the motorcade was passing by, and just immediately after I heard the shots, I saw a policeman running north towards me. He was running to look to see if somebody was running out of the back of this building.

Mr. BELIN. What building?

Mr. ROMACK. Texas School Book Depository Building. And he didn't stay but just, oh, he was just there to check and he runs back.

Well, sensing that something is wrong, I automatically take over watching the building for the man.

Mr. BELIN. What part of the building were you watching?

Mr. ROMACK. The back part.

Mr. BELIN. Could you see that back dock in the back part?

Mr. ROMACK. Well, I mean, they got it sealed off. I could see as much as anyone could see.

Mr. BELIN. Could you see—there are some stairs that go up to the back dock, aren't there?

Mr. ROMACK. Right here.

Mr. BELIN. You are pointing to a first floor plan of the Texas School Book Depository?

Mr. ROMACK. Yes.

Mr. BELIN. Did you watch those stairs?

Mr. ROMACK. Yes, sir.

Mr. BELIN. How long did you watch them after you saw the policeman leave?

Mr. ROMACK. Well, I watched them all the time until someone arrived, and the only time I did take my back off, turn my back to the building was Sam Pate with his KBOX news, he arrived before any of the police or anyone.

Mr. BELIN. Is that KBOX?

Mr. ROMACK. Yes.

Mr. BELIN. Is that a radio or television station?

Mr. ROMACK. It is a radio station.

Mr. BELIN. How long did you take your eyes off then?

Mr. ROMACK. He was driving up and they were having a little high—the city has a piece of wood that they use to stop traffic coming through, and I'd taken that so he could come through, drive his truck.

Mr. BELIN. How long did you leave your post?

Mr. ROMACK. I didn't leave. That was right there, even closer than what we were. But all I did was let that down for him, and then we——

Mr. BELIN. Would that have taken less than a minute?

Mr. ROMACK. Yes.

Mr. BELIN. Less than 30 seconds, do you know?

Mr. ROMACK. Yes.

Mr. BELIN. How long did you stay after that watching that back door?

Mr. ROMACK. Well, we were all there watching it then.

Mr. BELIN. How long a period of time?

Mr. ROMACK. Pardon?

Mr. BELIN. Did you see a policeman go up there?

Mr. ROMACK. I saw policemen up in there. I didn't see anyone come up the back. They came in the front, all—most of them.

Mr. BELIN. Did you see any employees walk up the back way?

Mr. ROMACK. There was two other gentlemen which I never said anything about, that taken over. They were FBI or something standing right here at the very entrance, and just stood there.

Mr. BELIN. You are pointing again to the back stairway that leads up from the street to the dock on the north side of the building?

Mr. ROMACK. Right.

Mr. BELIN. See anyone else?

Mr. ROMACK. No, sir; other than all the motorcycle officers and squad cars. They started coming in, I would say, in 4 minutes from the time that this happened. They were swarming the building, which naturally I quit watching anything particular.

Mr. BELIN. In other words, about 4 minutes after the shots came you quit watching it? Would that be accurate, or not?

Mr. ROMACK. Well, I would say somewhere in the neighborhood of 5 minutes, 4 or 5 minutes. That would probably be true. I stayed there, but I wasn't particularly watching.

Mr. BELIN. In other words, then as I understand your testimony, you said that from about the time of the shots until about 5 minutes after the shots, you watched the back door of the building?

Mr. ROMACK. Right.

Mr. BELIN. What is the fact as to whether or not you saw anyone leave the building?

Mr. ROMACK. They wasn't anyone left the building.

Mr. BELIN. What is the fact as to whether or not you saw anyone enter the building other than a police officer?

Mr. ROMACK. No one entered while I was standing there.

Mr. BELIN. Did you see anybody running down the street near you at all?

Mr. ROMACK. No, sir.

Mr. BELIN. Where were you standing? How far were you from this stairway going to this Houston Street dock?

Mr. ROMACK. Well, after this KBOX—you are asking prior to before he got there?

Mr. BELIN. Before KBOX got there first?

Mr. ROMACK. I would say I moved between 75 yards.

Mr. BELIN. 75 yards of the northeast corner of the building?

Mr. ROMACK. 75 yards of the northeast corner of the building.

Mr. BELIN. After KBOX got there?

Mr. ROMACK. He got to about, I would say, maybe 35 yards to the building, or 40. That is where he parked his car.

Mr. BELIN. How long did he stay, KBOX?

Mr. ROMACK. Oh. I would say 35 or 40 minutes. Then I went and called my wife and was telling her the sad news, and then I went back and stayed again. I ended up laying off work. I didn't even work that afternoon.

Mr. BELIN. Did you ever contact the FBI?

Mr. ROMACK. Yes, sir.

Mr. BELIN. When did you do that?

Mr. ROMACK. It was on a Saturday night after I got in from work.

Mr. BELIN. What month was it?

Mr. ROMACK. It was this past month.

Mr. BELIN. You mean March?

Mr. ROMACK. Right.

Mr. BELIN. What caused you to contact the FBI in March?

Mr. ROMACK. I was trying to pinpoint the day that I must have come in from work. It was on the weekend that I'd come home, and there was a paper up in the left-hand corner.

Mr. BELIN. You mean the newspaper?

Mr. ROMACK. Yes, sir.

Mr. BELIN. Dallas newspaper?

Mr. ROMACK. Yes.

Mr. BELIN. Which one, do you know, offhand?

Mr. ROMACK. Herald, the paper that I take.

Mr. BELIN. What did you see in the paper?

Mr. ROMACK. I saw an article that was written by a guy, which I have been   concerned about this thing all the way through, the assassination and I got to reading it, and it is a story that just don't jibe with about me sitting there and watching the building. It just kind of upset me to know there is some monkey just hatched up such a story.

Mr. BELIN. What is the story that you read that you got concerned about?

Mr. ROMACK. About a guy seeing a rifle drawn in from the building above him, and he also seen the people as the shots were being fired, and he also seen some character running toward me with an overcoat on which was brown or gray or blue, and he heard 4 shots.

Mr. BELIN. Let me ask you this. Do you remember what page of the paper this was on?

Mr. ROMACK. It was on the headlines. I don't mean the headlines. It was on the front page in the left corner of the page.

Mr. BELIN. Now you say something concerned you about the article. Was it the fact that he said he saw a rifle there that concerned you?

Mr. ROMACK. No, sir; the fact that he was running somebody over me, and that is what I was out there doing. That is what I was doing. I was watching.

Mr. BELIN. You mean the portion of the article that concerned you was that someone said that someone else was running?

Mr. ROMACK. Towards Pacific Street.

Mr. BELIN. Towards Pacific Street from the direction of the School Book Depository?

Mr. ROMACK. That is the way the article read, sir.

Mr. BELIN. What did you tell the FBI when you called them?

Mr. ROMACK. I told them, tried to tell them about the same thing that I am telling you right now today.

Mr. BELIN. Have I ever mentioned before, by the way, or talked to you before this morning?

Mr. ROMACK. No, sir.

Mr. BELIN. What is the fact as to whether or not as soon as we met, you came in here and we started taking your deposition immediately?

Mr. ROMACK. Right. Unless you called me last Saturday. I don't remember who called me.

Mr. BELIN. Well, on Saturday, what did someone do, call you and tell you to come down here?

Mr. ROMACK. Yes, sir.

Mr. BELIN. Did that person talk to you about the facts that we were talking about now?

Mr. ROMACK. No, sir.

Mr. BELIN. It wasn't I, just for the record. I believe it was the Secret Service that called you, but I am not sure.

Mr. ROMACK. It was.

Mr. BELIN. Now, I understand your testimony correctly, what you are stating is that you don't believe anyone ran out of the building towards you, at least within the first 5 minutes after the shots?

Mr. ROMACK. Right.

Mr. BELIN. You don't think anyone went out of the building during the first 5 minutes after the shots?

Mr. ROMACK. That is true.

Mr. BELIN. Is there anything else, any other information you have that you feel might be helpful to the investigation of the assassination?

Mr. ROMACK. I can't think of anything, sir.

Mr. BELIN. Well, we want to thank you very much for taking the time to come down here. We appreciate your cooperation, and certainly your cooperation particularly in volunteering to call the FBI to contact them for this information.

Mr. ROMACK. Well, I felt that—I called an attorney that I know and talked to him about the deal before I called the FBI, and I told him I wasn't doing this for a publicity thing. It was something I just didn't, after reading that article, it kind of upset me, and he said he felt it was my duty to call the FBI and let them know.

And that is when I went ahead and made my statement.

Mr. BELIN. Now, Mr. Romack, you have the right, if you want, to come back down here after these notes of the court reporter are typed, to read the typewritten transcript and sign it, or you can waive reading it and signing it and just have her send it directly to Washington, whatever you want to do. It makes no difference with us.

Mr. ROMACK. I will waive.

Mr. BELIN. You want to waive it then?

Mr. ROMACK. Yes, sir.

Mr. BELIN. Again we want to thank you very much.

Mr. ROMACK. You are quite welcome.

TESTIMONY OF LEE E. BOWERS, JR.

The testimony of Lee E. Bowers, Jr. was taken at 2 p.m., on April 2, 1964, in the office of the U.S. attorney, 301 Post Office Building, Bryan and Ervay Streets, Dallas, Tex., by Mr. Joseph A. Ball, assistant counsel of the President's Commission.

Mr. BALL. Will you stand and be sworn, Mr. Bowers?

Do you solemnly swear that the testimony you are about to give for this Commission will be the truth, the whole truth, and nothing but the truth, so help you God?

Mr. BOWERS. Yes, sir.

Mr. BALL. Will you state your name, please.

Mr. BOWERS. Lee E. Bowers, Jr.

Mr. BALL. And what is your residence address?

Mr. BOWERS. 10508 Maplegrove Lane.

Mr. BALL. Dallas, Tex.

Mr. BOWERS. Dallas.

Mr. BALL. And would you tell me something about yourself, where you were born, raised, and what has been your business, generally, or occupation?

Mr. BOWERS. I was born right here in Dallas, and lived here most of my life except when I was in the Navy, at the age of 17 to 21, and I was away 2 years going to Hardin Simmons University, also, attended Southern Methodist University 2 years, majoring in religion. I worked for the railroad 15 years and was a self-employed builder, as well as—on the side. And the first of this year when I went to work as business manager for Dr. Tim Green who operates this hospital and convalescent home and rent properties.

Mr. BALL. What railroad did you work for?

Mr. BOWERS. Worked for the Union Terminal Co. with the 8 participating railroads.

Mr. BALL. And on November 22, 1963, were you working for the Union Terminal Co.?

Mr. BOWERS. Yes.

Mr. BALL. What kind of work were you doing for them?

Mr. BOWERS. I was tower man in the north tower, Union Terminal, operating the switches and signals controlling the movement of trains.

Mr. BALL. Through railroad yards?

Mr. BOWERS. Yes.

Mr. BALL. What were your hours of work?

Mr. BOWERS. 7 to 3 p.m., Monday through Friday.

Mr. BALL. Now, do you remember what is the height of—above the ground at which you worked in the tower?

Mr. BOWERS. It is second story, it is 14 feet, 12 or 14 feet.

Mr. BALL. You worked about 14 feet above the ground?

Mr. BOWERS. Yes.

Mr. BALL. And the tower was arranged so that you could see out?

Mr. BOWERS. Yes; it is windows except for posts that—posts on each corner. It is windows on all four sides.

Mr. BALL. Where is that located with reference to the corner of Elm and Houston?

Mr. BOWERS. It is west and north of this corner, and as to distances, I really don't know. It is within 50 yards of the back of the School Depository Building, or less.

Mr. BALL. Did you say that it is built on higher ground, the base of the tower on higher ground than around Houston and Elm?

Mr. BOWERS. Approximately the same.

Mr. BALL. Same? It is higher ground than Elm as it recedes down under the triple underpass?

Mr. BOWERS. Yes, sir; considerably.

Mr. BALL. And the base of your tower is about the same height as the triple underpass, isn't it?

Mr. BOWERS. Approximately.

Mr. BALL. Now, can you tell me why you refer to that as a triple underpass? In our conversation here before you were sworn your description—you described it as a triple underpass.

Mr. BOWERS. It is just a local connotation for it since there are three streets that run under it.

Mr. BALL. I see. And how many sets of tracks do you control from your tower?

Mr. BOWERS. There are about 11 tracks in the station and 2 freight tracks.

Mr. BALL. That would be 13 tracks that is, the tracks altogether, that pass in front of your tower?

Mr. BOWERS. Yes; of course where the tracks converge and cross and split off to various railroad yards——

Mr. BALL. And the tracks are to the north and west of your tower, aren't they?

Mr. BOWERS. Well, the tracks are west, but they proceed in all directions, I mean, they are both north and south.

Mr. BALL. Now, you were on duty on November 22, 1963, weren't you?

Mr. BOWERS. That's correct.

259

Mr. BALL. Close to noon, did you make any observation of the area around between your tower and Elm Street?

Mr. BOWERS. Yes; because of the fact that the area had been covered by police for some 2 hours. Since approximately 10 o'clock in the morning traffic had been cut off into the area so that anyone moving around could actually be observed. Since I had worked there for a number of years I was familiar with most of the people who came in and out of the area.

Mr. BALL. Did you notice any cars around there?

Mr. BOWERS. Yes; there were three cars that came in during the time from around noon until the time of the shooting.

Mr. BALL. Came in where?

Mr. BOWERS. They came into the vicinity of the tower, which was at the extension of Elm Street, which runs in front of the School Depository, and which there is no way out. It is not a through street to anywhere.

Mr. BALL. There is parking area behind the School Depository, between that building and your tower?

Mr. BOWERS. Two or three railroad tracks and a small amount of parking area for the employees.

Mr. BALL. And the first came along that you noticed about what time of day?

Mr. BOWERS. I do not recall the exact time, but I believe this was approximately 12:10, wouldn't be too far off.

Mr. BALL. And the car you noticed, when you noticed the car, where was it?

Mr. BOWERS. The car proceeded in front of the School Depository down across 2 or 3 tracks and circled the area in front of the tower, and to the west of the tower, and, as if he was searching for a way out, or was checking the area, and then proceeded back through the only way he could, the same outlet he came into.

Mr. BALL. The place where Elm dead ends?

Mr. BOWERS. That's right. Back in front of the School Depository was the only way he could get out. And I lost sight of him, I couldn't watch him.

Mr. BALL. What was the description of that car?

Mr. BOWERS. The first car was a 1959 Oldsmobile, blue and white station wagon with out-of-State license.

Mr. BALL. Do you know what State?

Mr. BOWERS. No; I do not. I would know it, I could identify it, I think, if I looked at a list.

Mr. BALL. And, it had something else, some bumper stickers?

Mr. BOWERS. Had a bumper sticker, one of which was a Goldwater sticker, and the other of which was of some scenic location, I think.

Mr. BALL. And, did you see another car?

Mr. BOWERS. Yes, some 15 minutes or so after this, at approximately 12 o'clock, 20 to 12—I guess 12:20 would be close to it, little time differential there—but there was another car which was a 1957 black Ford, with one male in it that seemed to have a mike or telephone or something that gave the appearance of that at least.

Mr. BALL. How could you tell that?

Mr. BOWERS. He was holding something up to his mouth with one hand and he was driving with the other, and gave that appearance. He was very close to the tower. I could see him as he proceeded around the area.

Mr. BALL. What kind of license did that have?

Mr. BOWERS. Had a Texas license.

Mr. BALL. What did it do as it came into the area, from what street?

Mr. BOWERS. Came in from the extension of Elm Street in front of the School Depository.

Mr. BALL. Did you see it leave?

Mr. BOWERS. Yes; after 3 or 4 minutes cruising around the area it departed the same way. He did probe a little further into the area than the first car.

Mr. BALL. Did you see another car?

Mr. BOWERS. Third car, which entered the area, which was some seven or nine minutes before the shooting, I believe was a 1961 or 1962 Chevrolet, four-door Impala, white, showed signs of being on the road. It was muddy up to the windows, bore a similar out-of-state license to the first car I observed, occupied also by one white male.

Mr. BALL. What did it do?

Mr. BOWERS. He spent a little more time in the area. He tried—he circled the area and probed one spot right at the tower in an attempt to get and was forced to back out some considerable distance, and slowly cruised down back towards the front of the School Depository Building.

Mr. BALL. Then did he leave?

Mr. BOWERS. The last I saw of him he was pausing just about in—just above the assassination site.

Mr. BALL. Did the car park, or continue on or did you notice?

Mr. BOWERS. Whether it continued on at that very moment or whether it pulled up only a short distance, I couldn't tell. I was busy.

Mr. BALL. How long was this before the President's car passed there?

Mr. BOWERS. This last car? About 8 minutes.

Mr. BALL. Were you in a position where you could see the corner of Elm and Houston from the tower?

Mr. BOWERS. No; I could not see the corner of Elm and Houston. I could see the corner of Main and Houston as they came down and turned on, then I couldn't see it for about half a block, and after they passed the corner of Elm and Houston the car came in sight again.

Mr. BALL. You saw the President's car coming out the Houston Street from Main, did you?

Mr. BOWERS. Yes; I saw that.

Mr. BALL. Then you lost sight of it?

Mr. BOWERS. Right. For a moment.

Mr. BALL. Then you saw it again where?

Mr. BOWERS. It came in sight after it had turned the corner of Elm and Houston.

Mr. BALL. Did you hear anything?

Mr. BOWERS. I heard three shots. One, then a slight pause, then two very close together. Also reverberation from the shots.

Mr. BALL. And were you able to form an opinion as to the source of the sound or what direction it came from, I mean?

Mr. BOWERS. The sounds came either from up against the School Depository Building or near the mouth of the triple underpass.

Mr. BALL. Were you able to tell which?

Mr. BOWERS. No; I could not.

Mr. BALL. Well, now, had you had any experience before being in the tower as to sounds coming from those various places?

Mr. BOWERS. Yes; I had worked this same tower for some 10 or 12 years, and was there during the time they were renovating the School Depository Building, and had noticed at that time the similarity of sounds occurring in either of those two locations.

Mr. BALL. Can you tell me now whether or not it came, the sounds you heard, the three shots came from the direction of the Depository Building or the triple underpass?

Mr. BOWERS. No; I could not.

Mr. BALL. From your experience there, previous experience there in hearing sounds that originated at the Texas School Book Depository Building, did you notice that sometimes those sounds seem to come from the triple underpass? Is that what you told me a moment ago?

Mr. BOWERS. There is a similarity of sound, because there is a reverberation which takes place from either location.

Mr. BALL. Had you heard sounds originating near the triple underpass before?

Mr. BOWERS. Yes; quite often.

Because trucks backfire and various occurrences.

Mr. BALL. And you had heard noises originating from the Texas School Depository when they were building there?

Mr. BOWERS. They were renovating. I—did carpenter work as well as sandblasted the outside of the building.

Mr. BALL. Now, were there any people standing on the high side—high ground between your tower and where Elm Street goes down under the underpass toward the mouth of the underpass?

Mr. BOWERS. Directly in line, towards the mouth of the underpass, there were two men. One man, middle-aged, or slightly older, fairly heavy-set, in a white shirt, fairly dark trousers. Another younger man, about midtwenties, in either a plaid shirt or plaid coat or jacket.

Mr. BALL. Were they standing together or standing separately?

Mr. BOWERS. They were standing within 10 or 15 feet of each other, and gave no appearance of being together, as far as I knew.

Mr. BALL. In what direction were they facing?

261

Mr. BOWERS. They were facing and looking up towards Main and Houston, and following the caravan as it came down.

Mr. BALL. Did you see anyone standing on the triple underpass?

Mr. BOWERS. On the triple underpass, there were two policemen. One facing each direction, both east and west. There was one railroad employee, a signal man there with the Union Terminal Co., and two welders that worked for the Fort Worth Welding firm, and there was also a laborer's assistant furnished by the railroad to these welders.

Mr. BALL. You saw those before the President came by, you saw those people?

Mr. BOWERS. Yes; they were there before and after.

Mr. BALL. And were they standing on the triple underpass?

Mr. BOWERS. Yes; they were standing on top of it facing towards Houston Street, all except, of course, the one policeman on the west side.

Mr. BALL. Did you see any other people up on this high ground?

Mr. BOWERS. There were one or two people in the area. Not in this same vicinity. One of them was a parking lot attendant that operates a parking lot there. One or two. Each had uniforms similar to those custodians at the courthouse. But they were some distance back, just a slight distance back.

Mr. BALL. When you heard the sound, which way were you looking?

Mr. BOWERS. At the moment I heard the sound, I was looking directly towards the area—at the moment of the first shot, as close as my recollection serves, the car was out of sight behind this decorative masonry wall in the area.

Mr. BALL. And when you heard the second and third shot, could you see the car?

Mr. BOWERS. No; at the moment of the shots, I could—I do not think that it was in sight. It came in sight immediately following the last shot.

Mr. BALL. Did you see any activity in this high ground above Elm after the shot?

Mr. BOWERS. At the time of the shooting there seemed to be some commotion, and immediately following there was a motorcycle policeman who shot nearly all of the way to the top of the incline.

Mr. BALL. On his motorcycle?

Mr. BOWERS. Yes.

Mr. BALL. Did he come by way of Elm Street?

Mr. BOWERS. He was part of the motorcade and had left it for some reason, which I did not know.

Mr. BALL. He came up——

Mr. BOWERS. He came almost to the top and I believe abandoned his motorcycle for a moment and then got on it and proceeded, I don't know.

Mr. BALL. How did he get up?

Mr. BOWERS. He just shot up over the curb and up.

Mr. BALL. He didn't come then by way of Elm, which dead ends there?

Mr. BOWERS. No; he left the motorcade and came up the incline on the motorcycle.

Mr. BALL. Was his motorcycle directed toward any particular people?

Mr. BOWERS. He came up into this area where there are some trees, and where I had described the two men were in the general vicinity of this.

Mr. BALL. Were the two men there at the time?

Mr. BOWERS. I—as far as I know, one of them was. The other I could not say.

The darker dressed man was too hard to distinguish from the trees. The one in the white shirt, yes; I think he was.

Mr. BALL. When you said there was a commotion, what do you mean by that? What did it look like to you when you were looking at the commotion?

Mr. BOWERS. I just am unable to describe rather than it was something out of the ordinary, a sort of milling around, but something occurred in this particular spot which was out of the ordinary, which attracted my eye for some reason, which I could not identify.

Mr. BALL. You couldn't describe it?

Mr. BOWERS. Nothing that I could pinpoint as having happenedthat——

Mr. BALL. Afterwards did a good many people come up there on this high ground at the tower?

Mr. BOWERS. A large number of people came, more than one direction. One group converged from the corner of Elm and Houston, and came down the extension of Elm and came into the high ground, and another line—another large group went across the triangular area between Houston and Elm and then across Elm and then up the incline. Some of them all the way up.

262

Many of them did, as well as, of course, between 50 and a hundred policemen within a maximum of 5 minutes.

Mr. BALL. In this area around your tower?

Mr. BOWERS. That's right. Sealed off the area, and I held off the trains until they could be examined, and there was some transients taken on at least one train.

Mr. BALL. I believe you have talked this over with me before your deposition was taken, haven't we?

Mr. BOWERS. Yes.

Mr. BALL. Is there anything that you told me that I haven't asked you about that you think of?

Mr. BOWERS. Nothing that I can recall.

Mr. BALL. You have told me all that you know about this, haven't you?

Mr. BOWERS. Yes; I believe that I have related everything which I have told the city police, and also told to the FBI.

Mr. BALL. And everything you told me before we started taking the deposition?

Mr. BOWERS. To my knowledge I can remember nothing else.

Mr. BALL. Now, this will be reduced to writing, and you can sign it, look it over and sign it, or waive your signature if you wish.

What do you wish?

Mr. BOWERS. I have no reason to sign it unless you want me to.

Mr. BALL. Would you just as leave waive the signature?

Mr. BOWERS. Fine.

Mr. BALL. Then we thank you very much.

TESTIMONY OF B. J. MARTIN

The testimony of B. J. Martin was taken at 10:10 a.m., on April 3, 1964, in the office of the U.S. attorney, 301 Post Office Building, Bryan and Ervay Streets, Dallas, Tex., by Mr. Joseph A. Ball, assistant counsel of the President's Commission.

Mr. BALL. Will you stand up, please, and be sworn?

Do you solemnly swear that the testimony you are about to give before this Commission shall be the truth, the whole truth, and nothing but the truth, so help you God?

Mr. MARTIN. I do.

Mr. BALL. Will you state you name, please?

Mr. MARTIN. B. J. Martin.

Mr. BALL. And what is your residence address?

Mr. MARTIN. 11830 Flamingo Lane, Dallas.

Mr. BALL. What is your occupation?

Mr. MARTIN. I am a police officer.

Mr. BALL. With the Dallas Police Department?

Mr. MARTIN. Yes.

Mr. BALL. How long have you been with the Police Department?

Mr. MARTIN. It will be 11 years in June.

Mr. BALL. Tell me something about yourself, when you were born and where you were raised and where you went to school?

Mr. MARTIN. I was born in Maud, Okla., Seminole County—went to school—high school at Maud, Okla., and entered the Navy in 1948, from there and was discharged in 1952 and lived at Compton, Okla., for approximately a year, and then returned to Dallas and was employed in the Police Department in June 1953.

Mr. BALL. And were you employed as a motorcycle officer at that time?

Mr. MARTIN. No, sir; I was employed as an apprentice policeman and worked in the radio patrol division.

Mr. BALL. You are not a motorcycleman?

Mr. MARTIN. Yes.

Mr. BALL. How long have you been a motorcycle officer?

Mr. MARTIN. Let's see, 8 years in January.

Mr. BALL. On November 22, 1963, did you have some special assignment?

Mr. MARTIN. Yes, sir; I was assigned to the motorcade of President Kennedy.

Mr. BALL. And you went out to Love Field, did you?

Mr. MARTIN. Yes, sir; we made detail about 7 o'clock that morning and was assigned, I don't recall now just what time—it was about 30 minutes before his plane was to arrive at Love Field.

Mr. BALL. And in the motorcade what was your position?

263

Mr. MARTIN. I was assigned to ride on the left-hand rear side of President Kennedy.

Mr. BALL. And were you riding alone there, or was another officer riding with you?

Mr. MARTIN. There was another officer riding with me, B. W. Hargis.

Mr. BALL. He was parallel to you on another motorcycle?

Mr. MARTIN. Yes, sir; we were——

Mr. BALL. Two motorcycles abreast?

Mr. MARTIN. Yes.

Mr. BALL. As you turned onto Houston from Main, can you tell me about the speed of the President's car?

Mr. MARTIN. My estimation would be 4 to 5 miles an hour when we made the turn onto Elm Street from Houston.

Mr. BALL. From Houston?

Mr. MARTIN. Yes.

Mr. BALL. Now, did you make the turn from Main to Houston about the same speed?

Mr. MARTIN. No, sir; we were going a little faster, I would say—between probably 10 and 15 miles an hour.

Mr. BALL. And then the block between Main and Elm, did the motorcade slow down?

Mr. MARTIN. It slowed down just before we made the turn onto Elm Street.

Mr. BALL. Let's take the President's car—what do you think the speed of the President's car was as you made that turn from Houston onto Elm?

Mr. MARTIN. I believe the speed was about 4 or 5 miles an hour.

Mr. BALL. What was your speed?

Mr. MARTIN. Approximately the same—maybe a mile slower.

Mr. BALL. Were you able to maintain your position on the two-wheeler motorcycle?

Mr. MARTIN. Yes, sir; I believe I did.

Mr. BALL. What is the minimum speed at which you can maintain the position of that motorcycle?

Mr. MARTIN. About 2 miles per hour, I would imagine.

Mr. BALL. Did the President's car pick up any speed from the corner of Houston and Elm—we'll say half way down that hill?

Mr. MARTIN. No, sir; I don't recall it picking up any speed in there.

Mr. BALL. They were going fairly slow?

Mr. MARTIN. It may have picked up, gradually picked up, but not enough that I could notice.

Mr. BALL. Did you hear any unusual noise?

Mr. MARTIN. Yes, sir; I heard a shot, or what I thought at the time to be a shot.

Mr. BALL. What was the position of your motorcycle at that time with reference to the President's car?

Mr. MARTIN. Just to the rear of his car—on the left rear of his car.

Mr. BALL. How far from the car, I'll say, to the left of the car and then how far to the rear—so I can get some idea of your position?

Mr. MARTIN. I would say that my motor was 5-foot to the left and approximately 6- to 8-foot to the rear.

Mr. BALL. Of the President's car?

Mr. MARTIN. Of the President's car.

Mr. BALL. Were you anywhere near the front end of the Secret Service car?

Mr. MARTIN. Yes, sir.

Mr. BALL. The car the Secret Service men were in?

Mr. MARTIN. Yes; we were alongside the front end of their car, because one of the agents got off of the car after the first shot. The best I can remember—I was fairly close to him—he was the person riding on the fender of the car and the first agent from the front of the car, and I was fairly close to him when he jumped off of the car.

Mr. BALL. Now, where was the motorcycle driven by Mr. Hargis, with reference to your right or to your left?

Mr. MARTIN. He was to my right when we made the turn on Houston Street.

Mr. BALL. At the time you heard this shot, where was he?

Mr. MARTIN. I presume he was still to my right. I don't recall seeing him after the shots.

Mr. BALL. He would have been closer to the President's car than you would have?

Mr. MARTIN. Yes, sir—he would have been—I would say 3- or 4-foot closer than I was.

Mr. BALL. You traveled along the street about 3 or 4 feet apart from each other?

Mr. MARTIN. Yes, sir—something like that.

Mr. BALL. When you heard the first shot, did you have any idea of the direction which the shot was coming from?

Mr. MARTIN. No, sir; I didn't. I couldn't tell from which direction it was coming—any of the shots.

Mr. BALL. Did you look?

Mr. MARTIN. Yes, sir; I looked back to my right.

Mr. BALL. After which shot?

Mr. MARTIN. After the first shot.

Mr. BALL. You looked to your right?

Mr. MARTIN. I looked back to my right.

Mr. BALL. What did you look at?

Mr. MARTIN. At the building on the right there.

Mr. BALL. Is that the Texas School Book Depository Building?

Mr. MARTIN. Yes; it is.

Mr. BALL. Did you see anything?

Mr. MARTIN. No, sir.

Mr. BALL. As you turned to the right, did you turn your motorcycle also, or did you turn your body?

Mr. MARTIN. I believe I just turned my body. I don't believe I ever turned my motor. I believe I kept my motor headed down Elm Street—west on Elm.

Mr. BALL. Did you take any notice of the President after the first shot?

Mr. MARTIN. Yes, sir; I looked at the President after I heard the shot and he was leaning forward—I could see the left side of his face. At the time he had no expression on his face.

Mr. BALL. Then, did you hear some more shots?

Mr. MARTIN. Yes, sir.

Mr. BALL. How many?

Mr. MARTIN. Two more shots.

Mr. BALL. Did you see anything when you looked at the School Depository Building?

Mr. MARTIN. No, sir—just the building.

Mr. BALL. And were you able to tell—to determine or did you have any opinion, as to the direction from which the shots were coming—the last two shots—from which direction they came?

Mr. MARTIN. No, sir; you couldn't tell just where they were coming from.

Mr. BALL. Was there any breeze that day?

Mr. MARTIN. Yes; there was.

Mr. BALL. From what direction?

Mr. MARTIN. I believe it was blowing out of the southwest at that particular location. It seemed like we were going to turn into the wind as we turned off of Houston onto Elm.

Mr. BALL. The wind was in your face?

Mr. MARTIN. Yes; the best I can recall.

Mr. BALL. Now, afterward, did the motorcade pick up speed then?

Mr. MARTIN. After we turned onto Houston?

Mr. BALL. No; after the shots?

Mr. MARTIN. Yes—after the shots we picked up speed.

Mr. BALL. Did you go on to Parkland?

Mr. MARTIN. Yes, sir; I did. I rode just part of the time alongside of the President's car. At times we were forced to the rear because of the pedestrians standing out on Stemmons and there just wasn't enough room to ride in there.

Mr. BALL. Could you see the President?

Mr. MARTIN. No, sir; I couldn't see him—immediately after the first shot I saw him and after that I couldn't see him.

Mr. BALL. And did you see the Governor at all?

Mr. MARTIN. No, sir. I didn't pay any attention to the Governor.

Mr. BALL. Now, when you got to Parkland Hospital, what did you do?

Mr. MARTIN. We pulled into the emergency entrance to Parkland Hospital. The traffic had already begun to stack up and the officers ahead of the motorcade went on down into the exit and I stopped off at the first turn into the exit about 50 or 60 yards from the entrance to the emergency and began to cut traffic so they wouldn't block the roadway down into the emergency and then we had to park cars—just a lot of people got out of their cars and it was all blocked up and we had to park cars and just generally work traffic around there.

Mr. BALL. You had a white helmet on?

Mr. MARTIN. Yes.

265

Mr. BALL. Did you notice any stains on your helmet?

Mr. MARTIN. Yes, sir; during the process of working traffic there, I noticed that there were blood stains on the windshield on my motor and then I pulled off my helmet and I noticed there were blood stains on the left side of my helmet.

Mr. BALL. To give a more accurate description of the left side, could you tell us about where it started with reference to the forehead?

Mr. MARTIN. It was just to the left—of what would be the center of my forehead—approximately halfway, about a quarter of the helmet had spots of blood on it.

Mr. BALL. And were there any other spots of any other material on the helmet there besides blood?

Mr. MARTIN. Yes, sir; there was other matter that looked like pieces of flesh.

Mr. BALL. What about your uniform?

Mr. MARTIN. There was blood and matter on my left shoulder of my uniform.

Mr. BALL. You pointed to a place in front of your shoulder, about the clavicle region?

Mr. MARTIN. Yes, sir.

Mr. BALL. Is that about where it was?

Mr. MARTIN. Yes.

Mr. BALL. On the front of your uniform and not on the side?

Mr. MARTIN. No, sir.

Mr. BALL. That would be left, was it?

Mr. MARTIN. Yes; on the left side.

Mr. BALL. And just below the level of the shoulder?

Mr. MARTIN. Yes, sir.

Mr. BALL. And what spots were there?

Mr. MARTIN. They were blood spots and other matter.

Mr. BALL. And what did you notice on your windshield?

Mr. MARTIN. There was blood and other matter on my windshield and also on the motor.

Mr. BALL. Was the blood noticeable—were there large splotches?

Mr. MARTIN. No; they weren't large splotches, they were small—it was not very noticeable unless you looked at it.

Mr. BALL. Was the discoloration on your helmet noticeable?

Mr. MARTIN. Not too much—no—as a matter of fact, there were other people around there and two more officers there and they never noticed it.

Mr. BALL. At that time were you with Mr. Hargis?

Mr. MARTIN. No, sir; I don't believe that he went to the hospital with us. I believe he stopped there at the scene of the shooting.

Mr. BALL. And did you ever see his helmet or his uniform or the windshield of his motorcycle?

Mr. MARTIN. No, sir—I never recall seeing him again until the next day.

Mr. BALL. Now, was this blood on the outside or the inside of your windshield?

Mr. MARTIN. It was on the outside of my windshield.

Mr. BALL. Was it on the right or left side?

Mr. MARTIN. It was on the outside of my windshield.

Mr. BALL. And what about the fender of the motorcycle?

Mr. MARTIN. It was just in the front—right on the front just above the cowling on the motorcycle.

Mr. BALL. You say that when you first heard the first shot you thought it was rifle fire?

Mr. MARTIN. Yes, sir—the sharp crack of it.

Mr. BALL. Are you familiar with guns?

Mr. MARTIN. Yes.

Mr. BALL. Did you ever fire a rifle?

Mr. MARTIN. Yes, sir.

Mr. BALL. Do you own a rifle?

Mr. MARTIN. Yes.

Mr. BALL. You have been hunting, I suppose?

Mr. MARTIN. I just returned.

Mr. BALL. You've shot high-powered rifles, have you?

Mr. MARTIN. Yes, sir.

Mr. BALL. Now, what do you think the speed of the President's car was—give me your best estimate of the speed of the President's car when you heard the first shot?

Mr. MARTIN. I would say it was under 10 miles an hour—between 5 and 10 at that particular time, about the time of the shots.

266

Mr. BALL. You were going downhill at that time?

Mr. MARTIN. Yes, sir. The best I remember—I wasn't having any trouble keeping my motor up at that time, so that it was probably between 5 and 10 miles an hour. I don't think it was any faster than 10.

Mr. BALL. Did you at any time come abreast of the President's car in the motorcade?

Mr. MARTIN. No, sir.

Mr. BALL. Were you under certain instructions as to how far behind the car you were to keep?

Mr. MARTIN. Yes, sir.

Mr. BALL. What were those instructions?

Mr. MARTIN. They instructed us that they didn't want anyone riding past the President's car and that we were to ride to the rear, to the rear of his car, about the rear bumper.

Mr. BALL. I think that's all, Officer.

This will be written up and you can look it over and sign it if you wish, or you can waive your signature and we will send it on to the Commission without it.

It's your option.

What would you like to do?

Mr. MARTIN. It doesn't make any difference—it's the truth as I saw it that day.

Mr. BALL. You just as soon waive your signature, then?

Mr. MARTIN. That would be fine.

Mr. BALL. All right, we'll waive your signature.

Mr. MARTIN. All right.

Mr. BALL. Thanks very much for coming in.

Mr. MARTIN. Okay.

TESTIMONY OF BOBBY W. HARGIS

The testimony of Bobby W. Hargis was taken at 3:20 p.m., on April 8, 1964, in the office of the U.S. attorney, 301 Post Office Building, Bryan and Ervay Streets, Dallas, Tex., by Mr. Samuel A. Stern, assistant counsel of the President's Commission.

Mr. STERN. Will you stand, please.

Do you solemnly swear that the evidence you are about to give shall be the truth, the whole truth, and nothing but the truth, so help you God?

Mr. HARGIS. I do.

Mr. STERN. Would you state for the record your name and residence address.

Mr. HARGIS. Bobby W. Hargis, 1818 Adelaide, Dallas, Tex.

Mr. STERN. What is your occupation?

Mr. HARGIS. Police officer.

Mr. STERN. How long have you been a member of the Dallas Police Department?

Mr. HARGIS. Nine years and about 7 months.

Mr. STERN. And you are now a member of the motorcycle——

Mr. HARGIS. Division.

Mr. STERN. Division?

Mr. HARGIS. Yes.

Mr. STERN. Were you a part of the motorcade on November 22d?

Mr. HARGIS. Yes; I was.

Mr. STERN. In what position?

Mr. HARGIS. I was at the left-hand side of the Presidential limousine.

Mr. STERN. At what part of the President's car?

Mr. HARGIS. Well——

Mr. STERN. Front, or rear?

Mr. HARGIS. Oh. Rear.

Mr. STERN. Riding next to Mrs. Kennedy?

Mr. HARGIS. Right.

Mr. STERN. Will you describe what occurred or what you observed as the limousine turned into Elm Street?

Mr. HARGIS. Well, at the time that the limousine turned left on Elm Street I was staying pretty well right up with the car. Sometimes on Elm we couldn't get right up next to it on account of the crowd, but the crowd was thinning out down here at the triple underpass, so, I was next to Mrs. Kennedy when I heard the first shot, and at that time the President bent over, and Governor Connally turned around. He was sitting directly in front of him, and a real shocked and surprised expression on his face.

Mr. STERN. On Governor Connally's?

267

Mr. HARGIS. Yes; that is why I thought Governor Connally had been shot first, but it looked like the President was bending over to hear what he had to say, and I thought to myself then that Governor Connally, the Governor had been hit, and then as the President raised back up like that (indicating) the shot that killed him hit him. I don't know whether it was the second or the third shot. Everything happened so fast.

Mr. STERN. But, you cannot now recall more than two shots?

Mr. HARGIS. That is all that I can recall remembering. Of course, everything was moving so fast at the time that there could have been 30 more shots that I probably never would have noticed them.

Mr. STERN. Did something happen to you, personally in connection with the shot you have just described?

Mr. HARGIS. You mean about the blood hitting me?

Mr. STERN. Yes.

Mr. HARGIS. Yes; when President Kennedy straightened back up in the car the bullet him in the head, the one that killed him and it seemed like his head exploded, and I was splattered with blood and brain, and kind of a bloody water. It wasn't really blood. And at that time the Presidential car slowed down. I heard somebody say, "Get going," or "get going,"——

Mr. STERN. Someone inside——

Mr. HARGIS. I don't know whether it was the Secret Service car, and I remembered seeing Officer Chaney. Chaney put his motor in first gear and accelerated up to the front to tell them to get everything out of the way, that he was coming through, and that is when the Presidential limousine shot off, and I stopped and got off my motorcycle and ran to the right-hand side of the street, behind the light pole.

Mr. STERN. Just a minute. Do you recall your impression at the time regarding the source of the shots?

Mr. HARGIS. Well, at the time it sounded like the shots were right next to me. There wasn't any way in the world I could tell where they were coming from, but at the time there was something in my head that said that they probably could have been coming from the railroad overpass, because I thought since I had got splattered, with blood—I was just a little back and left of—just a little bit back and left of Mrs. Kennedy, but I didn't know. I had a feeling that it might have been from the Texas Book Depository, and these two places was the primary place that could have been shot from.

Mr. STERN. You were clear that the sounds were sounds of shots?

Mr. HARGIS. Yes, sir; I knew they were shots.

Mr. STERN. All right, what did you do then? You say you parked your motorcycle?

Mr. HARGIS. Yes, uh-huh——

Mr. STERN. Where?

Mr. HARGIS. It was to the left-hand side of the street from—south side of Elm Street.

Mr. STERN. And then what did you do?

Mr. HARGIS. I ran across the street looking over towards the railroad overpass and I remembered seeing people scattering and running and then I looked——

Mr. STERN. People on the overpass?

Mr. HARGIS. Yes; people that were there to see the President I guess. They were taking pictures and things. It was kind of a confused crowd. I don't know whether they were trying to hide or see what was happening or what—and then I looked over to the Texas School Book Depository Building, and no one that was standing at the base of the building was—seemed to be looking up at the building or anything like they knew where the shots were coming from, so——

Mr. STERN. How about the people on the incline on the north side of Elm Street? Do you recall their behavior?

Mr. HARGIS. Yes; I remember a man holding a child. Fell to the ground and covered his child with his body, and people running everywhere, trying to get out of there, I guess, and they were about as confused as to where the shots were coming from as everyone else was.

Mr. STERN. And did you run up the incline on your side of Elm Street?

Mr. HARGIS. Yes, sir; I ran to the light post, and I ran up to this kind of a little wall, brick wall up there to see if I could get a better look on the bridge, and, of course, I was looking all around that place by that time. I knew it couldn't have come from the county courthouse because that place was swarming with deputy sheriffs over there.

Mr. STERN. Did you get behind the picket fence that runs from the overpass to the concrete wall?

Mr. HARGIS. No.

Mr. STERN. On the north side of Elm Street?

Mr. HARGIS. No, no; I don't remember any picket fence.

268

Mr. STERN. Did you observe anything then on the overpass, or on the incline, or around the Depository? Anything out of the ordinary besides people running?

Mr. HARGIS. No; I didn't. That is what got me.

Mr. STERN. So, at that point you were still uncertain as to the direction of the shots?

Mr. HARGIS. Yes, uh-huh.

Mr. STERN. Then, what did you do?

Mr. HARGIS. Well, then, I thought since I had looked over at the Texas Book Depository and some people looking out of the windows up there, didn't seem like they knew what was going on, but none of them were looking towards, or near anywhere the shots had been fired from. At the time I didn't know, but about the only activity I could see was on the bridge, on the railroad bridge so——

Mr. STERN. What sort of activity was that?

Mr. HARGIS. Well, the people that were up there were just trying to get a better look at what was happening and was in a haze and running, or in a confused fashion, and I thought maybe some of them had seen who did the shooting and the rifle.

Mr. STERN. Then what did you do?

Mr. HARGIS. Then I got back on my motorcycle, which was still running, and rode underneath the first underpass to look on the opposite side in order to see if I could see anyone running away from the scene, and since I didn't see anyone coming from that direction I rode under the second underpass, which is Stemmons Expressway and went up around to see if I could see anyone coming from across Stemmons and back that way, and I couldn't see anything that was of a suspicious nature, so, I came back to the Texas School Book Depository. At that time it seemed like the activity was centered around the Texas School Book Depository, so, that is when I heard someone say, one of the sergeants or lieutenants, I don't know, "Don't let anyone out of the Texas School Book Depository," and so, I went to a gap that had not been filled, which was at the southwest corner.

Mr. STERN. And you remained there until you were relieved?

Mr. HARGIS. Yes.

Mr. STERN. Anything else that you haven't told us that you think is relevant to our inquiry?

Mr. HARGIS. No; I don't believe so.

Mr. STERN. Thank you very much, Mr. Hargis.

The reporter will transcribe your testimony and have it available for you to read and sign if you care to. Otherwise, you may waive your right to review and sign the testimony and she will mail it direct to the Commission, whichever you prefer. It is entirely your option.

Mr. HARGIS. Well; it really doesn't make any difference. It is more or less what you all think is best.

Mr. STERN. It's entirely up to you.

Mr. HARGIS. Well, how long will it be until she fixes it up?

Mr. STERN. Well, off the record.

(Discussion off the record.)

Mr. STERN. On the record.

Mr. HARGIS. All right. Well, just go ahead and I will just let you go ahead and send it in without the signature.

Mr. STERN. Thank you very much, Mr. Hargis.

TESTIMONY OF CLYDE A. HAYGOOD

Testimony of Clyde A. Haygood was taken at 9:15 a.m., on April 9, 1964, in the office of the U.S. attorney, 301 Post Office Building, Bryan and Ervay Streets, Dallas, Tex., by Mr. David W. Belin, assistant counsel of the President's Commission.

Mr. BELIN. Would you stand and raise your right hand.

Do you solemnly swear that the testimony you are about to give will be the truth, the whole truth, and nothing but the truth, so help you God?

Mr. HAYGOOD. I do.

Mr. BELIN. Would you please state your name.

Mr. HAYGOOD. Clyde A. Haygood.

Mr. BELIN. What is your occupation?

Mr. HAYGOOD. Dallas police officer, solo motorcycle section.

Mr. BELIN. How old are you?

Mr. HAYGOOD. Thirty-two.

Mr. BELIN. Born in Texas?

Mr. HAYGOOD. Yes.

Mr. BELIN. Go to school here in Texas?

Mr. HAYGOOD. Yes.

Mr. BELIN. How far did you get through school?

Mr. HAYGOOD. Finished high school.

Mr. BELIN. Then what did you do?

Mr. HAYGOOD. Went into the service.

Mr. BELIN. What branch?

Mr. HAYGOOD. Air Force.

Mr. BELIN. How long?

Mr. HAYGOOD. Four years to the day.

Mr. BELIN. What did you do in the Air Force, generally?

Mr. HAYGOOD. Ground crew chief, flight engineer.

Mr. BELIN. Do you have an honorable discharge?

Mr. HAYGOOD. Yes.

Mr. BELIN. What did you do when you got out of the Air Force?

Mr. HAYGOOD. Went to work for the Dallas Police Department.

Mr. BELIN. What year was that?

Mr. HAYGOOD. 1955.

Mr. BELIN. You have been with them ever since?

Mr. HAYGOOD. Other than 11 months in which I left the department.

Mr. BELIN. What did you do in that 11 months?

Mr. HAYGOOD. Went into a business of my own.

Mr. BELIN. Then went back to the department?

Mr. HAYGOOD. Yes, sir.

Mr. BELIN. Were you on duty on November 22, 1963?

Mr. HAYGOOD. Yes.

Mr. BELIN. What was your assignment that day?

Mr. HAYGOOD. Solo motorcycle officer on escort of the Presidential motorcade.

Mr. BELIN. You started with the motorcade at Love Field?

Mr. HAYGOOD. Yes.

Mr. BELIN. Went through town with him?

Mr. HAYGOOD. Yes.

Mr. BELIN. Where were you riding as you went through town?

Mr. HAYGOOD. Riding to the right rear of the Presidential car.

Mr. BELIN. How many cars back, if you remember?

Mr. HAYGOOD. Well, it varied. It would be hard to say as to how many cars back.

Mr. BELIN. Do you remember whether Officer M. L. Baker was riding?

Mr. HAYGOOD. He was riding in front of me.

Mr. BELIN. So you would be riding several cars back, generally, from the President's car, is that correct?

Mr. HAYGOOD. Yes.

Mr. BELIN. Did you hear any shots at all?

Mr. HAYGOOD. Yes.

Mr. BELIN. Where were you when you heard the shots?

Mr. HAYGOOD. I was on Main Street just approaching Houston Street.

Mr. BELIN. How many shots did you hear?

Mr. HAYGOOD. Three.

Mr. BELIN. Were the three spaced equally distant?

Mr. HAYGOOD. No.

Mr. BELIN. Go ahead.

Mr. HAYGOOD. No.

Mr. BELIN. Was one more close than the other one?

Mr. HAYGOOD. The last two were closer than the first. In other words, it was the first, and then a pause, and then the other two were real close.

Mr. BELIN. What did you do after you heard the sounds?

Mr. HAYGOOD. I made the shift down to lower gear and went on to the scene of the shooting.

Mr. BELIN. What do you mean by the scene of the shooting?

Mr. HAYGOOD. There on Main Street.

Mr. BELIN. On Main Street?

Mr. HAYGOOD. I am sorry, on Elm Street.

Mr. BELIN. What position of Elm Street?

270

Mr. HAYGOOD. Be just west of Houston Street.

Mr. BELIN. By the scene of the shooting, do you mean the place where you believed the President's car was when the bullets struck?

Mr. HAYGOOD. Yes.

Mr. BELIN. What did you do when you got there?

Mr. HAYGOOD. When I first got to the location there, I was still on Houston Street, and in the process of making a left turn onto Elm Street I could see all these people laying on the ground there on Elm. Some of them were pointing back up to the railroad yard, and a couple of people were headed back up that way, and I immediately tried to jump the north curb there in the 400 block, which was too high for me to get over.

Mr. BELIN. You mean with your motorcycle?

Mr. HAYGOOD. Yes.

Mr. BELIN. All right.

Mr. HAYGOOD. And I left my motor on the street and ran to the railroad yard.

Mr. BELIN. Now when you ran to the railroad yard, would that be north or south of Elm?

Mr. HAYGOOD. The railroad yard would be located at the—it consist of going over Elm Street and back north of Elm Street.

Mr. BELIN. What did you do when you got there?

Mr. HAYGOOD. Well, there was nothing. There was quite a few people in the area, spectators, and at that time I went back to my motorcycle—it was on the street—to the radio.

Mr. BELIN. Did you see any people running away from there?

Mr. HAYGOOD. No. They was all going to it.

Mr. BELIN. Did you talk to any people over there or not?

Mr. HAYGOOD. In the railroad yard, I talked to one of the people I presumed to be a railroad detective that was in the yard.

Mr. BELIN. Had he been in the yard before or not?

Mr. HAYGOOD. No. He was just coming into the area after I was.

Mr. BELIN. He was coming into the area after the shooting?

Mr. HAYGOOD. Yes.

Mr. BELIN. Did he say anything to you, that you remember?

Mr. HAYGOOD. Nothing that I remember.

Mr. BELIN. Then what did you do?

Mr. HAYGOOD. I went back to my motorcycle, which was sitting on Elm Street.

Mr. BELIN. Then what did you do?

Mr. HAYGOOD. At that time some people came up and started talking to me as to the shooting.

Mr. BELIN. What did they say?

Mr. HAYGOOD. One stated that he had seen the President when the first shot was fired, and that he definitely was hit.

Mr. BELIN. Did he say where the shot came from?

Mr. HAYGOOD. And I asked him about where the shots came from, and he stated that he didn't know, that he was looking at him when the first shot was fired, and that he slumped. And when the second shot was fired, he went completely out of sight.

Mr. BELIN. You talked to any other witnesses there?

Mr. HAYGOOD. Yes. There was another one came up who was located, at the time he stated, on the south side of Elm Street back toward the triple underpass. Back, well, it would be north of the underpass there, and said he had gotten hit by a piece of concrete or something, and he did have a slight cut on his right cheek, upper portion of his cheek just to the right of his nose.

Mr. BELIN. Would he have been to the front or to the back of the Presidential car at the time of the shot?

Mr. HAYGOOD. I don't know what you mean to the front or the back.

Mr. BELIN. When he was standing, was he to the west or to the east of the President's car at the time of the shooting?

Mr. HAYGOOD. He would be to the south of it and then west.

Mr. BELIN. Southwest of it?

Mr. HAYGOOD. Yes.

Mr. BELIN. Talk to anyone else?

Mr. HAYGOOD. And at that time, approximately, well, I was talking to him at the time this other man came up and told me that he didn't know what it was about, but he was quite sure the shot had come from this building there which he pointed out to be the Texas School Book Depository Building.

Mr. BELIN. Did he say why?

271

Mr. HAYGOOD. He said when the first shot was fired he glanced back and there was something in the building, he couldn't determine what it was, but it was just something there that he couldn't explain, but he was definite that the shots did come from there.

And after talking to him and the man that was on the other side that complained he was hit by a piece of concrete from the ricochet at that time, I called the dispatcher and asked for squads to cover the Texas School Book Depository Building off.

Mr. BELIN. Do you remember what your number was that day?

Mr. HAYGOOD. Beg your pardon?

Mr. BELIN. Do you remember what number you used for calling the dispatcher that day?

Mr. HAYGOOD. Yes. My original call number is 142.

Mr. BELIN. I have here a Sawyer Deposition Exhibit A, which appears to be a transcript of a police radio log, and I notice that at 12:35 p.m., there is a call from 142 to 531. 531 is your station headquarters?

Mr. HAYGOOD. Right.

Mr. BELIN. Do you want to read what you said?

Mr. HAYGOOD. "I talked to a guy at the scene who says the shots were fired from the Texas School Book Depository Building with the Hertz Rent A Car sign on top."

Mr. BELIN. Is that what you said?

Mr. HAYGOOD. Approximately. I don't recall the exact words.

Mr. BELIN. There was a response to you. What does it say there?

Mr. HAYGOOD. "Get his name, address, phone number and all information you can."

Mr. BELIN. Did you do that?

Mr. HAYGOOD. No, I never.

Mr. BELIN. What happened?

Mr. HAYGOOD. Because I was told to go to the School Book Depository Building. I instructed the three different people to come to the front of the School Book Depository Building and remain there until they were talked to.

Mr. BELIN. You took these people that you had with you?

Mr. HAYGOOD. I did not take them, no.

Mr. BELIN. You instructed them to go there?

Mr. HAYGOOD. Yes.

Mr. BELIN. In front of the School Book Depository?

Mr. HAYGOOD. Yes.

Mr. BELIN. And remain there until someone talked to them?

Mr. HAYGOOD. Right.

Mr. BELIN. You don't know the names of these people?

Mr. HAYGOOD. No, I don't.

Mr. BELIN. Do you know who talked to them at all?

Mr. HAYGOOD. No; I don't.

Mr. BELIN. What did you do then?

Mr. HAYGOOD. At that time I went to the School Building at the rear location of it, which would be——

Mr. BELIN. To the back door?

Mr. HAYGOOD. North side of it, yes.

Mr. BELIN. Where that door leads out there to the dock?

Mr. HAYGOOD. Yes; on the northeast corner there.

Mr. BELIN. What did you do then?

Mr. HAYGOOD. At that time I talked to the colored male that was standing at the door and asked him how long he had been there, and he said he had been there some 5 minutes or so.

And I asked him if anyone had came out that door, and he said that they had not.

Mr. BELIN. Do you remember his name?

Mr. HAYGOOD. No; I don't.

Mr. BELIN. Then what did you do?

Mr. HAYGOOD. At that time, it was people, squads and all arriving at the scene, and I went on into the building, which they stayed outside, and helped them search the building.

Mr. BELIN. Anything else?

Mr. HAYGOOD. That is about all.

Mr. BELIN. Did you search the building on the sixth floor or not?

Mr. HAYGOOD. Yes.

Mr. BELIN. Were you there when they found the rifle?

Mr. HAYGOOD. Yes.

Mr. BELIN. Were you there when they found the shells?

Mr. HAYGOOD. Yes.

Mr. BELIN. Where were you when the shells were found?

Mr. HAYGOOD. I was on the sixth floor when the shells were found. I was still on the sixth when they found the rifle—on the fifth.

Mr. BELIN. On the fifth?

Mr. HAYGOOD. Sixth floor, rather, I am sorry.

Mr. BELIN. Where on the sixth floor were you when the shells were found?

Mr. HAYGOOD. I don't recall just exactly where it was at. It was on the floor there, though. It was just a big open floor.

Mr. BELIN. Do you mean they were somewhere on that open floor?

Mr. HAYGOOD. Yes.

Mr. BELIN. Did you hear someone say they have shells, something like that?

Mr. HAYGOOD. Yes.

Mr. BELIN. Do you remember who that was?

Mr. HAYGOOD. No; I don't.

Mr. BELIN. What did you do then?

Mr. HAYGOOD. Went up to another location there.

Mr. BELIN. You saw some shells there?

Mr. HAYGOOD. Yes.

Mr. BELIN. Where did you see them?

Mr. HAYGOOD. They were there under the window.

Mr. BELIN. Which window?

Mr. HAYGOOD. On the southeast corner.

Mr. BELIN. South side or east side?

Mr. HAYGOOD. On the southeast corner facing south.

Mr. BELIN. See any paper bags or anything around there?

Mr. HAYGOOD. Yes; there was a lunch bag there. You could call it a lunch bag.

Mr. BELIN. Where was that?

Mr. HAYGOOD. There at the same location where the shells were.

Mr. BELIN. Was there a coke bottle or anything with it?

Mr. HAYGOOD. Dr. Pepper bottle.

Mr. BELIN. See any long bags which would be a foot or foot and a half or more long?

Mr. HAYGOOD. Yes; just a plain brown paper bag with tape in the corner.

Mr. BELIN. What, tape?

Mr. HAYGOOD. Yes; there was just brown paper tape on it. Just a brown paper bag with paper tape. It had been taped up.

Mr. BELIN. How long was that, if you can remember?

Mr. HAYGOOD. The exact length, I couldn't say. It was approximately rifle length.

Mr. BELIN. Would this have been right under the window, or to the east or west of the window, if you remember?

Mr. HAYGOOD. As I remember, it was directly in the corner, in the southeast corner.

Mr. BELIN. Well, as you remember, was the window directly in the southeast corner, or was the window a little bit to the west of that corner, if you remember?

Mr. HAYGOOD. The window at that location faces south, on the southeast corner.

Mr. BELIN. About how far from the east corner of the building is the window?

Mr. HAYGOOD. Well, it is just approximately like that, and then the corner here. Like the window would be there, and then it would be a corner.

Mr. BELIN. As far as the window in this room from that corner [indicating in room]?

Mr. HAYGOOD. I wouldn't even attempt to say the approximate distance of the window from the corner. I don't know.

Mr. BELIN. Well, if you don't know, that is what I want to find out.

Mr. HAYGOOD. Yes.

Mr. BELIN. Was the bag right under the window?

Mr. HAYGOOD. It was in the corner.

Mr. BELIN. Not under the window?

Mr. HAYGOOD. No; it was in the corner of the building, the southeast corner.

Mr. BELIN. Anything else you noticed up there?

Mr. HAYGOOD. That is all.

Mr. BELIN. Now, where were you when you saw the—when you heard a rifle had been found?

273

Mr. HAYGOOD. On the floor there, best as I can remember, and I went to that same location as the other one, just like I stated on the other one where the shells was found.

Mr. BELIN. Do you remember where that rifle was found, roughly, or not?

Mr. HAYGOOD. It was in a row of books back on the opposite corner. Be on the west side of the building, back to the northwest corner.

Mr. BELIN. All right, anything else you remember while you were there?

Mr. HAYGOOD. No.

Mr. BELIN. What did you do after that, after the rifle was found?

Mr. HAYGOOD. Well, it still wasn't determined whether the assailant wasn't still in the building even at that time, even after the rifle was found, and the search was continued in the building for a while after that.

Mr. BELIN. Then what did you do?

Mr. HAYGOOD. At that time after that I went to the street, went downstairs to the street.

Mr. BELIN. Did you participate in any other investigation that day?

Mr. HAYGOOD. No.

Mr. BELIN. What about on Saturday?

Mr. HAYGOOD. On Saturday I was on my way to Colorado.

Mr. BELIN. So you weren't around on Sunday either?

Mr. HAYGOOD. No. On Sunday when the other shooting was taking place, I was knee deep in snow in Colorado.

Mr. BELIN. Is there any other information you can think of, whether I have asked it or not, that in any way would be relevant to the assassination of the President or the shooting of Officer Tippit?

Mr. HAYGOOD. No, nothing; I was out of town.

Mr. BELIN. All right, sir. We thank you very much for your cooperation here. You have an opportunity, if you want to come down and read this deposition and sign it before it goes to Washington, or you can waive the reading and signing of it and just have the court reporter send it directly to us, whatever you want to do?

Mr. HAYGOOD. It makes no difference.

Mr. BELIN. It makes no difference to us either.

Mr. HAYGOOD. Just waive the signing. I don't know when I can get back over here.

(Officer Haygood was summoned back in a few minutes from across the street at the Republic National Bank Building to answer the following question.)

Mr. BELIN. Officer Haygood, I will continue your deposition with one more question, if you would, and you are still under oath.

You mentioned in your sworn deposition that you talked to about two people that you saw, and you pointed it out in your transmission at 12:35 p.m., under your Call No. 142.

Is that correct?

Mr. HAYGOOD. Right.

Mr. BELIN. I notice on there another transmission at 12:37 p.m. Could you read what the transcript has there.

Mr. HAYGOOD. Well, this part of the deposition I covered it a while ago but I gave you, is when I called to have the Texas School Book Depository covered there. That is one of the witnesses I had that believed the shot came from that location.

Mr. BELIN. Could you read what you said there?

Mr. HAYGOOD. It says, "Get men to cover the building, Texas School Book Depository, believe the shots came from there, facing it on Elm Street looking at the building it will be the second window from the end in the upper right hand corner."

Mr. BELIN. Did you say that?

Mr. HAYGOOD. Yes.

Mr. BELIN. Then the transmission made to you, 531 to 142 calling, "How many do you have there?"

And you made a response which is?

Mr. HAYGOOD. "One guy possibly hit by a ricochet off the concrete and another seen the President slump."

Mr. BELIN. Were there two more people in addition to the one that you saw?

Mr. HAYGOOD. They are still the same people I was referring to back on the transmission that I made.

Mr. BELIN. How many different people did you talk to? One that was possibly hit by a ricochet?

Mr. HAYGOOD. Piece of concrete.

Mr. BELIN. Was he the one that saw the President slump?

Mr. HAYGOOD. No.

Mr. BELIN. Was there someone that saw the President slump, and a third stated it was from the second window from the end in the upper right-hand corner?

Mr. HAYGOOD. I don't recall how many it was. There was quite a chaos there at that time.

Mr. BELIN. Do you remember if there were two or more than two?

Mr. HAYGOOD. No, sir.

Mr. BELIN. Do you remember anything about the description of the man that said that the shot came from the second window from the end in the upper right-hand corner?

Mr. HAYGOOD. No.

Mr. BELIN. Do you remember if he was white or Negro?

Mr. HAYGOOD. He was a white man.

Mr. BELIN. Man or woman?

Mr. HAYGOOD. Man.

Mr. BELIN. Do you remember whether he was young or medium or old?

Mr. HAYGOOD. That would be a guess on my part. I don't recall. He was just a medium age.

Mr. BELIN. Do you remember if he was dressed in a suit or not a suit?

Mr. HAYGOOD. Best I remember, just sports clothes. I mean, it consisted of no tie or coat.

Mr. BELIN. Okay, thank you, sir.

TESTIMONY OF E. D. BREWER

The testimony of E. D. Brewer was taken at 10 a.m., on April 9, 1964, in the office of the U.S. attorney, 301 Post Office Building, Bryan and Ervay Streets, Dallas, Tex., by Mr. David W. Belin, assistant counsel of the President's Commission.

Mr. BELIN. Would you stand and raise your right hand.

Do you solemnly swear that the testimony you are about to give will be the truth, the whole truth, and nothing but the truth, so help you God?

Mr. BREWER. I do.

Mr. BELIN. Would you state your name.

Mr. BREWER. E. D. Brewer.

Mr. BELIN. What is your occupation, Mr. Brewer?

Mr. BREWER. Police officer for the City of Dallas.

Mr. BELIN. How old are you?

Mr. BREWER. I am 32 years old.

Mr. BELIN. You go to school here in Dallas?

Mr. BREWER. Yes, sir.

Mr. BELIN. How far did you get through school?

Mr. BREWER. I graduated from high school.

Mr. BELIN. Then what did you do?

Mr. BREWER. I got married and went to work for the Dallas Power & Light. About a year later I went into the U.S. Coast Guard and stayed 3 years.

Mr. BELIN. Honorable discharge?

Mr. BREWER. Yes, sir.

Mr. BELIN. Then what did you do?

Mr. BREWER. I went to work for the Dallas Police Department.

Mr. BELIN. You have been working for them about 10 years now?

Mr. BREWER. Since December 1954.

Mr. BELIN. Were you on duty on November 22, 1963?

Mr. BREWER. Yes, sir.

Mr. BELIN. What was your assignment that day?

Mr. BREWER. I was riding solo motorcycle, in the Presidential motorcade.

Mr. BELIN. What position were you in in the motorcade?

Mr. BREWER. I was in the front.

Mr. BELIN. By which car? Near which car?

Mr. BREWER. If I remember correctly, the President's car was about—the Chief of Police was in a car immediately in front. The President's car was behind him, I believe, if I remember correctly, and I was in front of the Chief's car.

Mr. BELIN. You were in front of the Chief's car?

Mr. BREWER. Yes.

Mr. BELIN. You were in the lead part of the motorcade?

Mr. BREWER. Yes. I was the front vehicle. There was four or five of us up there in a line across the street.

Mr. BELIN. Do you remember how fast you were going as you went down Main Street there towards Houston?

Mr. BREWER. No, sir; not exactly. The speed of it would vary considerably according to the crowd of people on each side of the street as to how we could get through.

Mr. BELIN. Did you remember how fast you were going as you turned north on Houston?

Mr. BREWER. It was in my assignment to leave my position there and go ahead of the motorcade as we were approaching Houston on Main Street, and before we got to Houston Street I left. I pulled out ahead of them, and following the same route, went down to the intersection or to where the motorcade was to come onto Stemmons Freeway.

Mr. BELIN. So your speed wasn't necessarily accurate with the motorcade, is that correct, sometimes?

Mr. BREWER. Yes, sir; I had pulled away from the motorcade on Main Street and proceeded on down to the Stemmons Freeway.

Mr. BELIN. Where were you when you heard the shot?

Mr. BREWER. I never did hear any shots.

Mr. BELIN. When was the first time you learned that something was wrong?

Mr. BREWER. I was on Stemmons Freeway there where you come onto it, where the motorcade come onto Stemmons. Went under Stemmons and around to the right and onto Stemmons, and I was on Stemmons Expressway off of my motorcycle there on the expressway when I believe I heard it on the radio first about the shooting.

Mr. BELIN. Were you to stop traffic on the expressway?

Mr. BREWER. Yes. I was to assist some other officers in stopping traffic on the expressway to allow the motorcade to get onto it.

Mr. BELIN. So you were in the process of stopping traffic, waiting for the motorcade to come by, when you heard something on your motorcycle radio?

Mr. BREWER. Yes, sir.

Mr. BELIN. How far were you from the so-called underpass there, or overpass there?

Mr. BREWER. I was to the north of where the railroad track goes over. Let's see, the railroad track, where the railroad tracks go over Stemmons Expressway. I was to the north of that.

Mr. BELIN. Let me try and get a sketch. Officer, I just stepped out of the room to come back in and bring a map of Dallas, which I believe is similar to Commission's Exhibit 371, which I am going to mark here Deposition Exhibit A, which we will call it E. D. Brewer deposition Exhibit A. I have it marked in red pencil here, and on this map of Dallas, on one side of it in one corner of it is a section called, Downtown Dallas, and this is towards the top of the reverse side of the map.

I am going to ask you to look at this map. You see the place here, it looks like Dedley Plaza, Main Street runs into that, which is Houston, then you turned north on Houston and Elm, and then you take Elm?

Mr. BREWER. Left on Elm.

Mr. BELIN. Left on Elm. You went under the railroad underpass there, which appears to be in green on the map, is that correct?

Mr. BREWER. Yes, sir.

Mr. BELIN. Then I am going to ask you to take a pencil or a ball point pen, and you might just follow the route that you took. Just mark it parallel to whatever street you took to where you ended up.

Mr. BREWER. (Marks on map.)

Down Elm under the railroad tracks to Stemmons, under Stemmons to the right, headed north parallel to Stemmons on that entranceway, under that T & P Railroad, and onto Stemmons Expressway, and just north of the T & P Railroad.

Mr. BELIN. Now is that where you stopped your motorcycle?

Mr. BREWER. Yes, sir.

Mr. BELIN. I am going to put an arrow pointing to the spot that you stopped, is that correct?

Mr. BREWER. Yes, that is the spot right there.

Mr. BELIN. You have it marked kind of with an "X"?

Mr. BREWER. To the best of my knowledge, that is right where we was at.

Mr. BELIN. Was another officer there at the time when you got there?

Mr. BREWER. Yes.

Mr. BELIN. What were they doing?

276

Mr. BREWER. We all proceeded to stop the traffic northbound on Stemmons.

Mr. BELIN. Why were you going to do that?

Mr. BREWER. So that the motorcade which was headed in that direction at that time could get onto Stemmons and wouldn't be interfered with by the rest of the traffic.

Mr. BELIN. All right, where were you when you first learned of the shooting or that something was wrong?

Mr. BREWER. At that location.

Mr. BELIN. How did you learn about it?

Mr. BREWER. I believe it was on the radio, we heard it.

Mr. BELIN. What did you do?

Mr. BREWER. On the police radio. Well, when it was determined that—right after we heard that on the radio, something about it on the radio, we heard that they were enroute to Parkland Hospital, and immediately after that they came by us and came onto Stemmons Expressway and went by us in the direction of Parkland Hospital, the motorcade, part of it.

Mr. BELIN. Then what did you do?

Mr. BREWER. We heard that the shots had came from the Texas School Book Depository Building, and at that time I got on my motorcycle and proceeded back up to the Texas School Book Depository Building.

Mr. BELIN. Then what did you do?

Mr. BREWER. I went in the building.

Mr. BELIN. You went inside the building?

Mr. BREWER. Yes, sir; there was officers all around the building at the time I got there.

Mr. BELIN. What did you do when you got in the building?

Mr. BREWER. Well, with some other officers, we was part of the officers that was searching the building floor by floor.

Mr. BELIN. Now what was your call number that day?

Mr. BREWER. 137.

Mr. BELIN. Handing you what has been marked Sawyer Deposition Exhibit A, which appears to be a transcript of a police log of the Dallas Police Department, you see this exhibit here?

Mr. BREWER. Yes.

Mr. BELIN. Your call number that day was?

Mr. BREWER. 137.

Mr. BELIN. I notice here that the first time there appears Call No. 137, after 12:30 is at 12:38 p.m.

There is a call from 137 to 531. You want to read what it says there?

Mr. BREWER. "A witness says he saw 'em pull the weapon from the window off the second floor on the southeast corner of the Depository Building."

Mr. BELIN. Would that have been the second floor or the second floor from the top?

Mr. BREWER. I don't know.

Mr. BELIN. Do you remember any witness talking to you at all?

Mr. BREWER. Yes.

Mr. BELIN. Do you remember what he said?

Mr. BREWER. He said that he had saw him pull a weapon from the window from that building.

Mr. BELIN. Do you remember what window he said?

Mr. BREWER. I don't remember specifically which window he indicated, but I immediately told that to the dispatcher and proceeded on up to the building.

Mr. BELIN. I see the conversation continues on the next page. The dispatcher No. 531, to 137, "Do you have the building covered off?"

And then you reply:

Mr. BREWER. "I'm about three-fourths of a block away."

Mr. BELIN. Is that where you were when this man——

Mr. BREWER. Yes, sir.

Mr. BELIN. Now from the time you first heard that something was wrong, you had taken your motorcycle and gone where?

Mr. BREWER. Sir?

Mr. BELIN. You were on the Stemmons Freeway when you heard that something was wrong, is that correct?

Mr. BREWER. Yes, sir.

Mr. BELIN. Then you went from Stemmons Freeway where?

Mr. BREWER. Up to the Texas School Depository Building.

277

Mr. BELIN. Did you stop anywhere along the way?

Mr. BREWER. No, sir; the only time that I stopped was when this guy come up to me and told it to me, and then was gone.

Mr. BELIN. Well, you did stop then and talk to this one individual?

Mr. BREWER. Yes.

Mr. BELIN. Which street were you on when you stopped?

Mr. BREWER. I was proceeding back up Elm Street the wrong way on Elm.

Mr. BELIN. About where were you when this one person talked that said he saw him pull the weapon in?

Mr. BREWER. I was down there about the triple underpass on Elm.

Mr. BELIN. You mean right under the triple underpass?

Mr. BREWER. Or coming to it.

Mr. BELIN. Well, coming to it?

Mr. BREWER. From the west.

Mr. BELIN. Would you have been on the west side of that?

Mr. BREWER. Yes, right there about that curb.

Mr. BELIN. Before you left Stemmons Freeway, did you look up or around to see if there was anything suspicious in that area?

Mr. BREWER. We was all looking up in the railroad tracks from the west side.

Mr. BELIN. Did you see anything at all?

Mr. BREWER. No, sir; we saw some people coming up there, but they seemed to be up there looking.

Mr. BELIN. You mean you saw people up there searching?

Mr. BREWER. Yes, sir.

Mr. BELIN. Did you see anybody running away?

Mr. BREWER. No, sir.

Mr. BELIN. See anyone acting suspiciously by himself?

Mr. BREWER. No, sir.

Mr. BELIN. Then you left that area and came right down the wrong way, you say, back to retrace your route, is that correct?

Mr. BREWER. Yes, sir.

Mr. BELIN. Then somewhere in the vicinity of the railroad underpass, you were stopped by this one individual that you reported on the radio log, is that correct?

Mr. BREWER. Yes, sir.

Mr. BELIN. Do you remember whether this man that you talked to was a white male or a Negro?

Mr. BREWER. He was a white man, the best of my memory.

Mr. BELIN. Do you remember anything else about him?

Mr. BREWER. No, sir.

Mr. BELIN. Did he have any camera or anything?

Mr. BREWER. Not that I recall.

Mr. BELIN. Now after this order to report to the School Book Depository Building, what did you do?

Mr. BREWER. I went there.

Mr. BELIN. What did you do when you got there?

Mr. BREWER. Went in the building.

Mr. BELIN. Which door?

Mr. BREWER. By the front door.

Mr. BELIN. Had the building been sealed off by the time you got there?

Mr. BREWER. Yes, sir.

Mr. BELIN. Were officers blocking everyone that was coming in, to prohibit them from coming in and going out?

Mr. BREWER. Yes.

Mr. BELIN. What did you do when you got there?

Mr. BREWER. I went inside the building.

Mr. BELIN. Where did you go?

Mr. BREWER. I proceeded to assist in the floor to floor search of the building with some other officers.

Mr. BELIN. What floor did you start on?

Mr. BREWER. On the bottom floor.

Mr. BELIN. You went up to the top?

Mr. BREWER. Yes, sir.

278

Mr. BELIN. How far up did you go?

Mr. BREWER. We searched all of it before we quit.

Mr. BELIN. Well, were you ever on the 6th floor?

Mr. BREWER. Yes.

Mr. BELIN. Were you on the sixth floor when you found anything there?

Mr. BREWER. Yes, sir.

Mr. BELIN. What did you find?

Mr. BREWER. I was on the sixth floor when they found those spent cases from the rifle.

Mr. BELIN. Where were you when they found them?

Mr. BREWER. I don't know exactly. I was on the floor searching around in among some boxes that were stacked up there.

Mr. BELIN. Hear anyone say anything about cartridge cases or anything?

Mr. BREWER. Yes, sir. Whoever found them turned around and let it be known to one of the supervisor officers that he had found them, or that they had been found over there.

Mr. BELIN. What did you do when you heard the news?

Mr. BREWER. I continued searching.

Mr. BELIN. Did you go and take a look at the cartridge cases?

Mr. BREWER. Yes, sir.

Mr. BELIN. How many cartridge cases did you see?

Mr. BREWER. Three.

Mr. BELIN. Where were they?

Mr. BREWER. They were there under, by the window.

Mr. BELIN. What window?

Mr. BREWER. In the southeast corner of the building, facing south.

Mr. BELIN. See anything else there at the time by the window?

Mr. BREWER. Paper lunch sack and some chicken bones or partially eaten piece of chicken, or a piece of chicken.

Mr. BELIN. Anything else?

Mr. BREWER. A drink bottle.

Mr. BELIN. What bottle?

Mr. BREWER. A cold drink bottle, soda pop bottle.

Mr. BELIN. Anything else?

Mr. BREWER. In relation to what?

Mr. BELIN. Did you see anything else in the southeast corner?

Mr. BREWER. There was a paper, relatively long paper sack there.

Mr. BELIN. Where was that?

Mr. BREWER. It was there in the southeast corner.

Mr. BELIN. Under the window?

Mr. BREWER. No, sir. To the left of it. To the east of it.

Mr. BELIN. To the left as you faced the window?

Mr. BREWER. Yes, sir.

Mr. BELIN. Did the window come right up next to the corner there, do you remember?

Mr. BREWER. No, sir; it didn't come up next to the corner. It was offset.

Mr. BELIN. Can you remember how far at all, or not?

Mr. BREWER. No, sir; I don't remember the exact distance of it.

Mr. BELIN. Was any part of the paper sack under the window, if you remember or not? That long paper sack?

Mr. BREWER. No, sir.

Mr. BELIN. Do you remember anything about what the sack looked like?

Mr. BREWER. Well, it was assumed at the time that it was the sack that the rifle was wrapped up in when it was brought into the building, and it appeared that it could have been used for that.

Mr. BELIN. Well, you mean you assumed that before you found the rifle?

Mr. BREWER. Yes, sir; I suppose. That was discussed.

Mr. BELIN. Do you remember anything else that was found around there or not?

Mr. BREWER. Not in that particular area.

Mr. BELIN. Anything found anywhere else in the sixth floor?

Mr. BREWER. Yes, sir. The rifle was found on the sixth floor.

Mr. BELIN. Where was that?

Mr. BREWER. It was found in a northwest corner under some, in between some boxes that were stacked up there at the head of the stairs.

Mr. BELIN. Were you there when they found the rifle?

Mr. BREWER. Yes, sir.

Mr. BELIN. How far away from the area were you when you found the rifle, if you remember?

Mr. BREWER. Several feet from it. I don't remember exactly.

Mr. BELIN. Did you see the rifle?

Mr. BREWER. Yes, sir.

Mr. BELIN. Where was it located?

Mr. BREWER. It was laying down low on the door or on the floor down between some, a very narrow space where boxes were stacked up there, and there was a space between the boxes, and it was laying down there in between it, like it had been stuck in there hurriedly, and possibly just before whoever laid it there went down the stairs.

Mr. BELIN. Anything else you found of significance in the building at all or not?

Mr. BREWER. Not that I recall.

Mr. BELIN. What did you do the rest of the afternoon?

Mr. BREWER. Well, we proceeded to search the building after that, and we spent, I don't know the exact amount of time we spent in the building after that, but when Lieutenant Jack Revill was satisfied, we went back downstairs and I went back out to my motorcycle and to my immediate superior officer and received another assignment.

Mr. BELIN. Did you have anything to do with the investigation of the assassination that day?

Mr. BREWER. No, sir.

Mr. BELIN. What about on Saturday?

Mr. BREWER. No, sir.

Mr. BELIN. Sunday?

Mr. BREWER. No, sir. My primary job was traffic control.

Mr. BELIN. Did you have anything to do with the investigation of Officer Tippit's murder?

Mr. BREWER. No, sir.

Mr. BELIN. Is there anything that you can think of that might in any way be relevant to the assassination of the President or the shooting of Officer Tippit?

Mr. BREWER. Not that I can think of; no, sir.

Mr. BELIN. Sir, I want to thank you very much for coming on down here.

You have an opportunity, if you like, to come back and read the deposition and sign it, or else you can waive the signing of it and have it sent directly to Washington, whichever you prefer.

Mr. BREWER. It don't matter. Whichever you prefer.

Mr. BELIN. We have no preference.

Mr. BREWER. Okay, you send it on.

Mr. BELIN. Do you want to waive the signing of it?

Mr. BREWER. Yes, sir.

TESTIMONY OF D. V. HARKNESS

The testimony of D. V. Harkness was taken at 11:30 a.m., on April 9, 1964, in the office of the U.S. attorney, 301 Post Office Building, Bryan and Ervay Streets, Dallas, Tex., by Mr. David W. Belin, assistant counsel of the President's Commission.

Mr. BELIN. Will you stand and raise your right hand? Do you solemnly swear to tell the truth, the whole truth, and nothing but the truth, so help you God?

Mr. HARKNESS. I do.

Mr. BELIN. Your name, sir, would you please state?

Mr. HARKNESS. D. V. Harkness, Dallas Police Department.

Mr. BELIN. Where do you live?

Mr. HARKNESS. 2123 San Pablo.

Mr. BELIN. Is that in Dallas?

Mr. HARKNESS. Yes, sir.

Mr. BELIN. What position do you have with the Dallas Police Department?

Mr. HARKNESS. Sergeant of police.

Mr. BELIN. How long have you been with the Dallas Police Department?

Mr. HARKNESS. Little over 17 years.

Mr. BELIN. How old are you, sir?

Mr. HARKNESS. Forty-two.

Mr. BELIN. Did you go to school here in Dallas?

Mr. HARKNESS. Yes, sir.

Mr. BELIN. How far did you get through school?

Mr. HARKNESS. High school.

Mr. BELIN. High school graduate?

Mr. HARKNESS. Yes, sir.

Mr. BELIN. Then what did you do?

Mr. HARKNESS. One year worked for the East Texas Refining Co.

Mr. BELIN. Then what?

Mr. HARKNESS. Then I worked for the Baker Hotel in the auditing office.

Mr. BELIN. Then what did you do?

Mr. HARKNESS. Went in the service for 4 years.

Mr. BELIN. Army?

Mr. HARKNESS. Coast Guard.

Mr. BELIN. What did you do in the Coast Guard generally?

Mr. HARKNESS. I was a boatswain's mate second when I was discharged.

Mr. BELIN. Doing what?

Mr. HARKNESS. Let's see, I was on the troop transport at the time of my discharge.

Mr. BELIN. Honorable discharge?

Mr. HARKNESS. Yes, sir.

Mr. BELIN. Then what did you do?

Mr. HARKNESS. Come back and went to work for Alexander Motor Co.

Mr. BELIN. As what?

Mr. HARKNESS. Worked in the office in the purchasing department.

Mr. BELIN. Then what did you do?

Mr. HARKNESS. Went with the Dallas Police Department.

Mr. BELIN. Been there ever since?

Mr. HARKNESS. Ever since.

Mr. BELIN. Were you on duty November 22, 1963?

Mr. HARKNESS. Yes, sir.

Mr. BELIN. Doing what?

Mr. HARKNESS. Supervising the traffic officers from Main and Field along the parade route to Elm and Houston.

Mr. BELIN. Where were you around 12:30 p.m.?

Mr. HARKNESS. At Main and Houston.

Mr. BELIN. On the east or west side of Houston?

Mr. HARKNESS. West side of Houston.

Mr. BELIN. Did you watch the motorcade come by?

Mr. HARKNESS. Yes, sir.

Mr. BELIN. Where were you when you heard the shots?

Mr. HARKNESS. I had started west on Main Street to the, I don't know what they call this area here.

Mr. BELIN. Plaza.

Mr. HARKNESS. On the plaza area with the crowd to observe the President as he went west on Elm Street.

Mr. BELIN. How many shots did you hear?

Mr. HARKNESS. Three.

Mr. BELIN. What did you do after you heard those noises? Did you know they were shots, by the way?

Mr. HARKNESS. Yes, sir.

Mr. BELIN. What did you do?

Mr. HARKNESS. When I saw the first shot and the President's car slow down to almost a stop——

Mr. BELIN. When you saw the first shot, what do you mean by that?

Mr. HARKNESS. When I heard the first shot and saw the President's car almost come to a stop and some of the agents piling off the car, I went back to the intersection to get my motorcycle.

Mr. BELIN. You were in the process of doing that when you heard the second and third shots?

Mr. HARKNESS. Yes, sir.

Mr. BELIN. Where did the shots sound like they came from?

Mr. HARKNESS. I couldn't tell. They were bouncing off the buildings down there. I couldn't tell.

Mr. BELIN. You mean the reverberations?

Mr. HARKNESS. Yes.

Mr. BELIN. Then what did you do?

281

Mr. HARKNESS. I went west on Main to observe the area between the railroad tracks and Industrial.

Mr. BELIN. Why did you go down there?

Mr. HARKNESS. By the way the people, when I went into this area, everybody was hitting the ground, and someone led us to indicate that the shots were coming into the cars.

Mr. BELIN. You mean from some point in front of the cars?

Mr. HARKNESS. Yes.

Mr. BELIN. Do you know who that someone was?

Mr. HARKNESS. No, sir.

Mr. BELIN. What did that person do that indicated that?

Mr. HARKNESS. I don't remember.

Mr. BELIN. Then what did you do?

Mr. HARKNESS. I went down to Industrial to see if I could see anyone fleeing that area.

Mr. BELIN. What did you see?

Mr. HARKNESS. I didn't see anyone, so I come back to the front of the Book Depository and went around to this fence that was across the street from Elm Street.

Mr. BELIN. What do you mean across the street from Elm Street?

Mr. HARKNESS. Again, I will have to—near the railroad track.

Mr. BELIN. Behind the building?

Mr. HARKNESS. No, sir; this area right here. See, Elm Street goes down.

Mr. BELIN. What you are really saying——

Mr. HARKNESS. This area.

Mr. BELIN. You are pointing to a place between what would be the extension of Elm that doesn't go down into the parkway but the actual extension of Elm?

Mr. HARKNESS. Yes; to the plaza area.

Mr. BELIN. The plaza area?

Mr. HARKNESS. Yes, sir.

Mr. BELIN. What did you find there?

Mr. HARKNESS. I found a little colored boy, Amos Euins, who told me he saw the shots come from that building.

Mr. BELIN. Now you just picked out a little small book, one of those little pocket notebooks?

Mr. HARKNESS. Yes, sir.

Mr. BELIN. Or a notepad from your pocket here. Is that the original notation that you made?

Mr. HARKNESS. Yes, sir.

Mr. BELIN. When did you make that notation?

Mr. HARKNESS. Immediately after the shooting.

Mr. BELIN. Is that your own record that you have kept in your possession since then?

Mr. HARKNESS. Yes, sir. I turned——

Mr. BELIN. You turned what?

Mr. HARKNESS. After I took his name and address and put this information on the radio, I then took him on the back of my three-wheel motorcycle and put him in Inspector Sawyer's car.

Mr. BELIN. Now you mentioned that you put something on the radio here, and I hand you here what has been marked as Sawyer Deposition Exhibit A. Before doing that, do you remember what call number you used, you were using on that day?

Mr. HARKNESS. I believe 260.

Mr. BELIN. Well, I notice here that there is a call with a notation at 12:36 p.m., 260 to 531. 531 is your office in the main station?

Mr. HARKNESS. Yes, sir.

Mr. BELIN. What does it say there on that transcript?

Mr. HARKNESS. "Witness says shots came from fifth floor, Texas Book Depository store at Houston and Elm. I have him with me now and we are sealing off the building."

Mr. BELIN. All right, that was at 12:36 p.m.?

Mr. HARKNESS. Yes, sir.

Mr. BELIN. Had the building been sealed off at that time?

Mr. HARKNESS. Not to my knowledge. There were several officers around it, but I don't know whether it had been sealed off or not.

Mr. BELIN. In the process of sealing off the building, what did you do?

Mr. HARKNESS. Asked for a squad.

282

Mr. BELIN. How long did it take you after that to have the back part sealed off?

Mr. HARKNESS. The squad was arriving by the time I got off my motorcycle. There was already additional squads en route.

Mr. BELIN. How soon after 12:36 p.m., would you say the building was sealed off?

Mr. HARKNESS. It was sealed off then because I was back there and two other men.

Mr. BELIN. You are talking about the back part of the building?

Mr. HARKNESS. Yes, sir.

Mr. BELIN. What about the front part of the building? When was that sealed off?

Mr. HARKNESS. Inspector Sawyer and two officers were there.

Mr. BELIN. By the time you got around to the front part of the building?

Mr. HARKNESS. Yes, sir; by the time I put the witness in his car, I went immediately to the back.

Mr. BELIN. In other words, as I understand the sequence, you first went to the back of the building and had that sealed off first, or not?

Mr. HARKNESS. No, sir.

Mr. BELIN. You tell me what happened then.

Mr. HARKNESS. I had this witness with me. I didn't want to lose this witness.

Mr. BELIN. All right.

Mr. HARKNESS. So I took him to the car.

Mr. BELIN. To Inspector Sawyer's car?

Mr. HARKNESS. To Inspector Sawyer's car, which was right in front.

Mr. BELIN. Which was parked in front of the Texas School Book Depository?

Mr. HARKNESS. And left the witness there and went around to the back.

Mr. BELIN. On whose radio did you call? Did you call in before or after you left the witness in the car?

Mr. HARKNESS. I don't remember in exact sequence there, but it was in the process of going to the car there.

Mr. BELIN. Then what did you do?

Mr. HARKNESS. See, here is the thing. The radio traffic was heavy at the time, and it depended on how long you had to wait to get in.

Mr. BELIN. All right, in any event, after you made the call, what did you do on the radio? And after you got the man in the car?

Mr. HARKNESS. Well——

Mr. BELIN. The witness in the car, what did you do?

Mr. HARKNESS. Stayed at the back of the building until I was relieved by a squad.

Mr. BELIN. So you then went to the back of the building?

Mr. HARKNESS. Yes.

Mr. BELIN. When you were at Inspector Sawyer's car, did you see him there?

Mr. HARKNESS. Yes, sir.

Mr. BELIN. Was he at his car?

Mr. HARKNESS. Yes, sir; he was by his car, near his car.

Mr. BELIN. Do you know whether or not he had gone inside the building yet?

Mr. HARKNESS. No, sir.

Mr. BELIN. You mean you don't know?

Mr. HARKNESS. Don't know whether he had gone in or not. Actually, he was standing there in front taking information. All the information was being funneled to Inspector Sawyer.

Mr. BELIN. Did you tell him you had a witness?

Mr. HARKNESS. Yes, sir.

Mr. BELIN. In his car?

Mr. HARKNESS. Yes, sir.

Mr. BELIN. At that time, had the building been sealed off yet when you told him that?

Mr. HARKNESS. At that time?

Mr. BELIN. When you told Inspector Sawyer that you had a witness that said the shot came from the building, up to that particular moment, had the front part of the building been sealed off yet?

Mr. HARKNESS. Yes, sir.

Mr. BELIN. It had already been sealed off?

Mr. HARKNESS. There was two officers with Inspector Sawyer at the front.

Mr. BELIN. Were they stopping people from going in and out?

Mr. HARKNESS. I don't know.

Mr. BELIN. You don't know?

Mr. HARKNESS. No, sir; I don't know that, because I didn't go up and talk to them.

Mr. BELIN. Did you notice whether or not people were coming in and out of the building?

Mr. HARKNESS. No. I was interested in getting around to the back of the building to make sure it was.

Mr. BELIN. Then am I correct that your testimony is that you didn't notice whether people were coming in and out? Did you notice, or did you not notice whether people were coming out of the building at that time?

Mr. HARKNESS. Several officers at the area, and it was a lot of people around. I don't know whether they were going in or out or not. I couldn't say that.

Mr. BELIN. Then you went around to the back of the building?

Mr. HARKNESS. Yes, sir.

Mr. BELIN. Was anyone around in the back when you got there?

Mr. HARKNESS. There were some Secret Service agents there. I didn't get them identified. They told me they were Secret Service.

Mr. BELIN. Then did you stay around the back of the building?

Mr. HARKNESS. Yes; I stayed at the back until the squad got there.

Mr. BELIN. Then what did you do?

Mr. HARKNESS. I went back to the front, and Inspector Sawyer—helped to get the crowd back first, and then Inspector Sawyer assigned me to some freight cars that were leaving out of the yard, to go down and search all freight cars that were leaving the yard.

Mr. BELIN. Then what did you do?

Mr. HARKNESS. Well, we got a long freight that was in there, and we pulled some people off of there and took them to the station.

Mr. BELIN. You mean some transients?

Mr. HARKNESS. Tramps and hoboes.

Mr. BELIN. That were on the freight car?

Mr. HARKNESS. Yes, sir.

Mr. BELIN. Then what did you do?

Mr. HARKNESS. That was all my assignment, because they shook two long freights down that were leaving, to my knowledge, in all the area there.

We had several officers working in that area.

Mr. BELIN. Do you know whether or not anyone found any suspicious people of any kind or nature down there in the railroad yard?

Mr. HARKNESS. Yes, sir. We made some arrests, I put some people in.

Mr. BELIN. Were these what you call hoboes or tramps?

Mr. HARKNESS. Yes, sir.

Mr. BELIN. Were all those questioned?

Mr. HARKNESS. Yes, sir; they were taken to the station and questioned.

Mr. BELIN. Any guns of any kind found?

Mr. HARKNESS. Not to my knowledge.

Mr. BELIN. I want to go back to this Amos Euins. Do you remember what he said to you and what you said to him when you first saw him?

Mr. HARKNESS. I went in that crowd up there near the area there, and asked did anyone see any place where the shots come from, and there was an unidentified person pointed to him, said this boy here saw it, saw the shots, where the shots came from, and he told me it was.

Mr. BELIN. Then what did he say?

Mr. HARKNESS. He told me that the shots came from the window under the ledge.

Mr. BELIN. Of what building?

Mr. HARKNESS. Of the School Book Depository.

Mr. BELIN. Now have you since gone back to that building?

Mr. HARKNESS. Yes, sir.

Mr. BELIN. Do you know where the ledge is?

Mr. HARKNESS. Yes, sir; let's see, I have been by the place a million times. The ledge there is the one window where it came from, I believe.

Mr. BELIN. You can't right now definitely state what floor the ledge would be?

Mr. HARKNESS. Well——

Mr. BELIN. If you can't, I would rather not have you guess, but if you do know, I would like to have you state.

Mr. HARKNESS. I believe that it——

Mr. BELIN. Sergeant, now, do you know where that ledge is now?

Mr. HARKNESS. Yes, sir.

Mr. BELIN. Between what floors is the ledge?

Mr. HARKNESS. The ledge is between, over the sixth floor.

284

Mr. BELIN. All right, well here in your police report I show you Sawyer Deposition Exhibit A, you said the, "Witness says shots came from fifth floor Texas School Book Depository." Did the witness say it was from the sixth floor, or did he say it was from the fifth floor?

Mr. HARKNESS. He said it was from the fifth floor.

Mr. BELIN. What were the exact words of the witness?

Mr. HARKNESS. The exact words of the witness "It was under the ledge," which would put it on the sixth floor. It was my error in a hasty count of the floors.

Mr. BELIN. Did the witness say what particular window on that floor that he saw it on? On the floor under the ledge?

Mr. HARKNESS. Said it was the last window, which would indicate it would be the last window on the east side of the building.

Mr. BELIN. Did he say to his right as he saw it, or did he just say the last window from where he was standing?

Mr. HARKNESS. Last window from where he was standing, and at that point it would indicate that it would be the last window on the east side of the building facing Elm Street.

Mr. BELIN. Were you standing at the time, on the north or south side of Elm when you talked to this witness?

Mr. HARKNESS. I was.

Mr. BELIN. When you were with this witness, had this Amos Euins, were you standing on the north or the south side of Elm as it goes into the Parkway there?

Mr. HARKNESS. Elm as it goes under the Parkway—was between Elm where it goes under the triple underpass, and the extension of Elm there in that park area.

Mr. BELIN. So that is where you were standing?

Mr. HARKNESS. Yes.

Mr. BELIN. So that would be north of Elm as it goes into the underpass, but south of the extension of Elm?

Mr. HARKNESS. Where that building is, yes, sir.

Mr. BELIN. Would you have been west of the School Book Depository Building at that time?

Mr. HARKNESS. Yes.

Mr. BELIN. So the witness pointed to the last one on that floor? That would be the last one which would be to the east, is that correct?

Mr. HARKNESS. That's correct.

Mr. BELIN. Anything else you can remember this witness said?

Mr. HARKNESS. No, sir.

Mr. BELIN. Did he say whether or not he saw a rifle?

Mr. HARKNESS. He couldn't tell.

Mr. BELIN. Sergeant, do you remember anything else that you said?

Mr. HARKNESS. No, sir.

Mr. BELIN. Did you actually talk to any other person whose name you recorded in your little book there?

Mr. HARKNESS. Yes, sir; Arnold Rowland.

Mr. BELIN. Arnold Rowland?

Mr. HARKNESS. Yes, sir.

Mr. BELIN. What did he say?

Mr. HARKNESS. He said that he saw a man on one of those floors. He didn't clearly identify it, as he saw a man with a high-powered rifle walking around up there.

Mr. BELIN. Did he say anything else that you could have recorded there?

Mr. HARKNESS. No, sir.

Mr. BELIN. Anything else you remember?

Mr. HARKNESS. Except his address. I have his address as 3026 Hammerly.

Mr. BELIN. Did he say anything else?

Mr. HARKNESS. No, sir.

Mr. BELIN. Is there anything else that happened that day that might in any way be relevant to this investigation?

Mr. HARKNESS. No, sir.

Mr. BELIN. What did you do on Saturday?

Mr. HARKNESS. Saturday I was assigned to traffic at Elm and Houston, between Elm and Main.

Mr. BELIN. Is there anything else that you did on Saturday or on Sunday that might in any way be relevant to this area of inquiry?

Mr. HARKNESS. On Saturday had a large crowd down there, and I observed Jack Ruby at the entrance of the jail down there on Saturday.

Mr. BELIN. You saw Jack Ruby near the entrance of the jail on Saturday?

Mr. HARKNESS. Yes, sir.

Mr. BELIN. Has your statement already been taken by anyone before on the President's Commission?

Mr. HARKNESS. Yes, sir.

Mr. BELIN. But you did see Jack Ruby?

Mr. HARKNESS. I testified in Ruby's trial to that effect.

Mr. BELIN. Anyone else or anything else that might be in any way relevant here?

Mr. HARKNESS. The only thing, on Sunday I was leaving town; going to Whitesboro, and my wife and kids, we heard over the radio that Oswald had been shot.

When I arrived in Whitesboro, I called Capt. Fritz of the Dallas Police Department, and told him that I had seen Ruby near the entrance of the county jail the day before, which was a Saturday.

Mr. BELIN. Anything else?

Mr. HARKNESS. That is all.

Mr. BELIN. But did you ever talk to Ruby at any time afterwards?

Mr. HARKNESS. No, sir; not afterwards.

Mr. BELIN. Did you know Ruby at all, or not?

Mr. HARKNESS. I had met him, and being downtown traffic sergeant, I had seen him before, and I knew who he was, but other than that, that is all.

Mr. BELIN. Is there any other thing you can think of, whether I have asked it or not, that might in any way be relevant to the investigation of the assassination or the shooting of Officer Tippit?

Mr. HARKNESS. No, sir; I don't have anything on that, other than what I heard over the radio.

Mr. BELIN. By the way, did your witness ever say whether the person he saw at the window was a white man or Negro?

Mr. HARKNESS. He just told me, he just said he couldn't identify him. That is what he told me.

Mr. BELIN. Did he tell you whether or not it was a man?

Mr. HARKNESS. I don't remember, because I knew I couldn't get any information out of him, enough to put out a description on it.

Mr. BELIN. Anything else?

Mr. HARKNESS. No, sir.

Mr. BELIN. Sir, we want to thank you very much for coming down here and testifying.

You have an opportunity, if you would like, to come back and read your deposition when it is typed, and sign it, or you can waive reading and signing it and just have the court reporter send the transcript to us directly in Washington. If you have any preference, you might let us know.

Mr. HARKNESS. I have no preference. I just hope I have been able to help you on these directions, because they are complicated to give directions, especially when you try to convince.

Mr. BELIN. In any event, do you want to sign or waive signing? You have a right to sign or you can waive the signing of it and send it directly to us, whatever you want to do.

Mr. HARKNESS. Waiver is customary? It doesn't make any difference.

Mr. BELIN. Some people do one way and some the other way. Do you want to come back and read it and sign it, or do you want to waive signing it and let the court reporter send us the transcript direct?

Mr. HARKNESS. What has most of them been doing?

Mr. BELIN. Gosh, I have them doing both ways. I couldn't tell you what most have been doing, sir.

Mr. HARKNESS. I will just waive.

TESTIMONY OF J. HERBERT SAWYER

The testimony of J. Herbert Sawyer was taken at 3:45 p.m., on April 8, 1964, in the office of the U.S. attorney, 301 Post Office Building, Bryan and Ervay Streets, Dallas, Tex., by Mr. David W. Belin, assistant counsel of the President's Commission.

Mr. BELIN. Would you stand and raise your right hand.

Do you solemnly swear that the testimony you are about to give will be the truth, the whole truth and nothing but the truth, so help you God?

Mr. SAWYER. I do.

Mr. BELIN. What is your occupation?

Mr. SAWYER. Inspector of Police.

Mr. BELIN. Of what Police Department?

Mr. SAWYER. Dallas Police Department.

Mr. BELIN. You live here in Dallas?

Mr. SAWYER. Yes, sir.

Mr. BELIN. Inspector, how long have you been with the Police Department?

Mr. SAWYER. 23 years.

Mr. BELIN. That would be then you came to the Police Department around 1941 or so?

Mr. SAWYER. 1941, is right.

Mr. BELIN. You have been with them ever since 1941?

Mr. SAWYER. Except for a brief hitch in the Service during the war.

Mr. BELIN. What did you do in the Service?

Mr. SAWYER. I was a yeoman in the Navy.

Mr. BELIN. Honorable discharge?

Mr. SAWYER. Yes.

Mr. BELIN. Prior to going into the Service, what did you do?

Mr. SAWYER. Policeman.

Mr. BELIN. Before you went into the Service?

Mr. SAWYER. Yes.

Mr. BELIN. Did you go to school here in Dallas?

Mr. SAWYER. Yes.

Mr. BELIN. Graduated from high school?

Mr. SAWYER. Yes. I didn't graduate. I lacked half a year.

Mr. BELIN. Then you got out and you went in—did you go right on the police force then?

Mr. SAWYER. No.

Mr. BELIN. What did you do?

Mr. SAWYER. I worked as credit manager in a jewelry company. This was immediately prior to coming to the police department.

Before that, I was a doorman at the Mural Room of the Baker Hotel.

Mr. BELIN. When you first got out of high school, what did you do?

Mr. SAWYER. I went out to California and went to work as a clerk in a grocery store.

Mr. BELIN. What did you do after that?

Mr. SAWYER. Came back to Dallas and went to Business College, and then I went to work as a doorman at the Mural Room of the Baker Hotel.

And then from there I went to the jewelry, and later became credit manager.

Mr. BELIN. And then after that?

Mr. SAWYER. Then to the Police Department.

Mr. BELIN. You have been with the Police Department ever since except for this time in the Navy?

Mr. SAWYER. Yes.

Mr. BELIN. How old are you?

Mr. SAWYER. 47.

Mr. BELIN. You are married?

Mr. SAWYER. Yes.

Mr. BELIN. Inspector, were you on duty on November 22, 1963?

Mr. SAWYER. Yes.

Mr. BELIN. By the way, were you an Inspector at that time?

Mr. SAWYER. I was.

Mr. BELIN. Where were you stationed with reference to the motorcade? Just what were your duties?

Mr. SAWYER. I had charge of the crowd detail on Main Street from Akard to Harwood.

Mr. BELIN. After the motorcade passed, what did you do?

Mr. SAWYER. I headed west on Main Street.

Mr. BELIN. Did you immediately get in your car after the motorcade passed?

Mr. SAWYER. Well, not immediately, because the crowd was real thick and completely surrounded the car, but I did as soon as it was feasible to get back in the car.

Mr. BELIN. Do you remember where your car was parked?

Mr. SAWYER. Yes. It was parked on Ervay Street, at the intersection of Ervay and Main, but it was, well, it was on the north side of Main Street on Ervay.

It run parallel to Main Street.

287

Mr. BELIN. All right, you got in your car shortly after the motorcade passed then?

Mr. SAWYER. Yes.

Mr. BELIN. Then what did you do?

Mr. SAWYER. Well, I headed west, or tried to. I had to wait until the crowd cleared out, and as soon as the crowd cleared enough, I headed west on Main Street.

Mr. BELIN. Any particular reason why you headed west on Main Street?

Mr. SAWYER. Because that was the way the car was pointed at the time I got in.

Mr. BELIN. All right, then what did you do as you went west on Main Street?

Mr. SAWYER. I just went real slow down the street because of people crossing, and at the time, the radio broadcast came in about a lot of activity down at the lower end around Houston and Elm Street.

Mr. BELIN. Do you remember what radio broadcast this is?

Who broadcast it?

Mr. SAWYER. I heard Sheriff Decker come on the radio and tell the dispatcher to get all of his men over to, and I thought he said Texas School Book Depository, but at least that was the overall gist of the conversation. That ___ is what I gathered. He may not have said Texas School Book Depository, but the Texas School Book Depository was mentioned in the broadcasts that were made at that time.

Mr. BELIN. Was this on Channel 1 or Channel 2 if you remember?

Mr. SAWYER. Channel 2, I am sure.

Mr. BELIN. Did Sheriff Decker have any particular call number at all, or not, in your police number system?

Mr. SAWYER. No. I was wondering why he come on our radio, but then I think that he was with Chief Curry and probably using that radio.

Mr. BELIN. All right, in any event, a call was made from Chief Curry's car?

Mr. SAWYER. Well, this I don't know either. I don't know what car it was made from, but I think it was Sheriff Decker talking. I could recognize his voice, yes.

Mr. BELIN. What did you do then?

Mr. SAWYER. Then I went on down to the Texas Book Depository.

Mr. BELIN. Where did you park your car?

Mr. SAWYER. In front of the Texas School Book Depository.

Mr. BELIN. In front of the main entrance there?

Mr. SAWYER. In front of the main entrance.

Mr. BELIN. What did you do then?

Mr. SAWYER. Immediately went into—well, talked to some of the officers around there who told me the story that they had thought some shots had come from one of the floors in the building, and I think the fifth floor was mentioned, but nobody seemed to know who the shots were directed at or what had actually happened, except there had been a shooting there at the time the President's motorcade had gone by.

And I went with a couple of officers and a man who I believed worked in the building. The elevator was just to the right of the main entrance, and we went to the top floor, which was pointed out to me by this other man as being the floor that we were talking about. We had talked about the fifth floor.

And we went back to the storage area and looked around and didn't see anything.

Mr. BELIN. Now you took an elevator up, is that correct?

Mr. SAWYER. That's right.

Mr. BELIN. The route that you took to the elevator, you went to the front door?

Mr. SAWYER. Right.

Mr. BELIN. Then what did you do?

Mr. SAWYER. We got into the elevator. We run into this man.

Mr. BELIN. Well, when you say you got into the elevator, where was the elevator as you walked in the front door?

Mr. SAWYER. It was to the right.

Mr. BELIN. To the right?

Mr. SAWYER. Yes, sir.

Mr. BELIN. Was it a freight elevator or a passenger elevator?

Mr. SAWYER. The best of my recollection, it was a passenger elevator.

Mr. BELIN. Did you push for the top button in that elevator?

Mr. SAWYER. Well, I don't know who pushed it, but we went up to the top floor.

Mr. BELIN. You went up to the top floor that the elevator would go to?

Mr. SAWYER. That's right.

Mr. BELIN. You got off, and were there officers there?

288

Mr. SAWYER. There was one or two other officers with me.

Mr. BELIN. Now when you got off, you say you went into the back there into a warehouse area?

Mr. SAWYER. Storage area; what appeared to be a storage area.

Mr. BELIN. Did you go into any place other than a warehouse or storage area?

Mr. SAWYER. No.

Mr. BELIN. Was there anything other than a warehouse or storage area there?

Mr. SAWYER. Well, to one side I could see an office over there with people in it. Some women that apparently were office workers.

Mr. BELIN. Now Inspector, what did you do then?

Mr. SAWYER. Well, I didn't see anything that was out of the ordinary, so I immediately came back downstairs to check the security on the building.

Mr. BELIN. When you say check the security on the building, what do you mean by that?

Mr. SAWYER. Well, to be sure it was covered off properly, and then posted two men on the front entrance with instructions not to let anyone in or out.

Mr. BELIN. What about the rear entrance?

Mr. SAWYER. Well, I also had the sergeant go around and check to be sure that all of those were covered, although he told me that they were already covered.

Mr. BELIN. When was the order given to cover the front entrance of the building?

Mr. SAWYER. Well, they had it covered when I got there. There were officers all around the front. The only thing I don't think had been done by the time I got there, was the instructions not to let anybody in or out.

Mr. BELIN. All right, now, did you give the instructions not to let anyone in or out?

Mr. SAWYER. I did.

Mr. BELIN. Did you give those instructions before or after you came down from the fourth floor or top floor?

Mr. SAWYER. After I got down.

Mr. BELIN. So your procedure, if I understand it, was this. You were driving on Main Street when you heard Sheriff Decker on the radio?

Mr. SAWYER. Yes.

Mr. BELIN. Inspector, to try and reconstruct the time of sealing off the building, I believe you said that before you got to the building, or at about the time you got to the building, you thought that you heard something about the Texas School Book Depository over the radio?

Mr. SAWYER. Right.

Mr. BELIN. At least some time before you left your car, is that correct?

Mr. SAWYER. Yes; it would have to be, in order to hear it.

Mr. BELIN. Now, I have with me the transcript of the radio log here of November 22, and I notice that, according to the log, at 12:30, and you have examined it, there appears there is a statement by Chief Curry, and then something by Sheriff Decker concerning, well, we'd better call this Sawyer's Deposition Exhibit A, which is a transcript of the radio log, and it reads right now—we will try and restaple it later on—but right now, Page 2 and 3 are reversed insofar as the order is concerned.

You see at 12:28 p.m., on this exhibit Curry calls in that they are near the triple underpass, and then at 12:30 p.m., it says, "Station Break," is that right?

Mr. SAWYER. Yes, sir.

Mr. BELIN. Then the next thing that goes on, it is Number 1, which is Chief Curry's number, am I correct in that?

Mr. SAWYER. Right.

Mr. BELIN. Then according to the transcript, the statement is made—you might just read it here in front of you: "Go to the hospital, officers, Parkland Hospital, have them stand by. Get men on top of the underpass, see what happened up there, go up to the overpass. Have Parkland stand by."

You see these words here, Inspector Sawyer?

Mr. SAWYER. Yes.

Mr. BELIN. Then on a continuation, "Dallas-1," which is marked in by someone as Sheriff Decker says: "I'm sure it's going to take some time to get your men in there. Put every one of my men there."

Then there is a call back to Curry from 531, which is your home station, is that correct?

Mr. SAWYER. That's right.

I really didn't quite understand all of it.

289

Mr. BELIN. Then Curry is quoted as saying: "Notify Station 5 to move all men available out of my department back into the railroad yard and try to determine what happened and hold everything secure until homicide and other investigators can get in there."

Mr. SAWYER. That is Decker speaking there.

Mr. BELIN. That is Decker?

Mr. SAWYER. That's right.

Mr. BELIN. You believe that is what Decker said?

Mr. SAWYER. That is what he said, yes, that's right.

Mr. BELIN. All right.

Mr. SAWYER. His number is Dallas-1, and they are talking to 1. They have that confused.

Mr. BELIN. Well, Curry is 1 also?

Mr. SAWYER. That's right.

Mr. BELIN. But I think they were riding in the same car?

Mr. SAWYER. That might be correct, but this is actually Decker's voice here, and that is what he had to say.

Mr. BELIN. Well, then, the comment is made "Notify Station 5——"

Mr. SAWYER. That is the Sheriff's Office.

Mr. BELIN. "To move all men available out of my Department back into the railroad yard——"

And that you feel is Decker talking because of the reference to Station 5?

Mr. SAWYER. Also, my memory serves that it was his voice that made that.

Mr. BELIN. All right, then, at 12:31, is a notation there that quotes, "It looks like the President has been hit."

Then there doesn't appear to be anything pertaining to where the shots might have come from until we see at 12:34, there is a call from officer, it says No. 136, that states, "A passer-by states the shots came from Texas School Book Depository Building.

This is the first reference in the log about the Texas School Book Depository, is that correct?

Mr. SAWYER. That's correct.

Mr. BELIN. Do you feel that you heard in your car some reference to the Texas School Book Depository building?

Mr. SAWYER. I do.

Mr. BELIN. Would it be fair for me to assume then that you had not at least completely left your car by 12:34 p.m?

Mr. SAWYER. Correct.

Mr. BELIN. Then when you got to the Texas School Book Depository, well, you got out of the car and talked to some people or to some officers?

Mr. SAWYER. Officers.

Mr. BELIN. And then what did the officers tell you?

Mr. SAWYER. That their information was that the shots had come from the fifth floor of the Texas School Book Depository.

Mr. BELIN. Did any officers give you any other information about the source of the shots other than the fact that it came from the Texas School Book Depository, at that particular time?

Mr. SAWYER. I can't say whether it was officers or who, but there was a reference also made to the overpass.

Mr. BELIN. All right, in any event—pardon me, do you have anything else to add?

Mr. SAWYER. Also, there was a broadcast here in the transcript about the railroad yard.

Mr. BELIN. All right.

Mr. SAWYER. And this could be part of what I was thinking about, or what I had heard, was this broadcast on the radio about the railroad yard.

Mr. BELIN. Then what did you do? You went inside the building, is that correct?

Mr. SAWYER. We immediately went inside the building. I took—I believe Sgt. Harkness may have gone with me. I am not positive of that.

Mr. BELIN. Was the elevator on the first floor when you got there, or did you have to wait for it to come down?

Mr. SAWYER. Best of my recollection, it was there.

Mr. BELIN. You got to the elevator, went up, looked around back there.

How long did you spend up there at the top floor that the elevator took you to?

Mr. SAWYER. Just took a quick look around and made sure there was nobody hiding on that floor. I doubt if it took over a minute at the most.

Mr. BELIN. To go up and look around and come down?

Mr. SAWYER. To look around on the floor. How long it took to go up, it couldn't have been over 3 minutes at the most from the time we left, got up and back down.

Mr. BELIN. Then that would put it around no sooner than 12:37, if you heard the call at 12:34?

Mr. SAWYER. Yes, sir.

Mr. BELIN. Then you got down and what did you do?

Mr. SAWYER. I asked the Sergeant to doublecheck the security around the building, and then I took two patrolmen and stationed them at the front door and told them, with instructions not to let anybody in or out.

Mr. BELIN. Now up to the time you did this, had anyone else sealed off the building, that you know of?

Mr. SAWYER. When I arrived, the sergeant told me he had the building sealed off. There were officers all around the building.

To the best of my recollection, there was no officer actually stationed on the front door, at the front door. There was some on the sidewalk in front of the front door, and also, as far as I know, had no instructions been issued to anyone to let anybody in or out.

Mr. BELIN. So yours would have been the first instructions to stop traffic from coming in and out of the front door, am I correct in that?

Mr. SAWYER. That's right.

Mr. BELIN. All right, anybody that would have been seen leaving the building would have been stopped and interrogated by the officers that were there?

Even before you instructed them?

Mr. SAWYER. Yes, because they were looking for something or anything, and I know that anybody coming out of the back doors, from what the sergeant told me, they would have stopped them, too.

Mr. BELIN. What happened at the front door now. There were people standing out on the area of the steps, were there not?

Mr. SAWYER. No. There were some people around, yes.

Mr. BELIN. Do you know whether or not any of those would have been stopped?

Mr. SAWYER. For sure, no; I don't.

Mr. BELIN. Now after you got down and you issued these orders, then what did you do?

Mr. SAWYER. I set up a command post in front. The various officers were bringing up different witnesses who had seen various things, and I saw that this was quite an involved situation. It was so many of these people that had information, that I knew I didn't have time to take this information down, and by this time several deputy sheriffs were standing there, and one of them, I think he was a supervisor, I had his name at one time, I can't think of it now, was there, and he offered the use of an interrogation room of Sheriff Decker's office, I think he said, for interrogating these people.

Mr. BELIN. That is located down the street a little bit there?

Mr. SAWYER. Well, it is catty-corner across the street.

Mr. BELIN. All right.

Mr. SAWYER. It is southeast across the street from the Texas School Book Depository, at least from the corner, and so we set up a group of officers and deputy sheriffs who were to take charge of the witnesses and take them over to see that affidavits were taken from them.

They were more or less an escort service so the witness wouldn't get away.

And then as our detectives began to show up, I sent them over to the Sheriff's Office to assist in taking these depositions or affidavits.

Mr. BELIN. How many witnesses were there around there during this period of time that you talked to?

Mr. SAWYER. Well, during the entire period of time that I was there, I would venture to say between 25 to 50 different people had come up with information of one kind or another.

Mr. BELIN. Now, on this radio log, Sawyer's Deposition Exhibit A, do you   notice your number there for any calls at all that might have come in? What number did you use?

Mr. SAWYER. I used No. 9. That is my regular call No. 9.

Mr. BELIN. I notice here a No. 9, the first time that appears to come in here is at 12:40 p.m.; is that right?

Mr. SAWYER. That is the first one after 12:40, sir.

Mr. BELIN. The first one after 12:30?

Mr. SAWYER. The first one after 12:30, yes, that is true.

Mr. BELIN. Then at 12:40, there is a bunch of calls at 12:40, with the next call number at 12:43, so you assume sometime 12:40 and 12:43 you, as No. 9, called in, is that correct?

Mr. SAWYER. That's correct.

Mr. BELIN. Would you read what it says that you said there?

Mr. SAWYER. "We need more manpower down here at the Texas Book Depository; there should be a bunch on Main if somebody can pick them up and bring them down here."

Mr. BELIN. Was that said before or after you came down from the elevator?

Mr. SAWYER. That was after.

Mr. BELIN. Was that before or after you told the men there to guard the front door and not let anyone in or out?

Mr. SAWYER. That was after.

Mr. BELIN. Now the next time that No. 9 appears is at what time?

Mr. SAWYER. Immediately after 12:43 and before 12:45.

Mr. BELIN. What did you say then?

Mr. SAWYER. "The wanted person in this is a slender white male about 30, 5 feet 10, 165, carrying what looks to be a 30-30 or some type of Winchester."

Mr. BELIN. Then the statement is made from the home office, "It was a rifle?"

Mr. SAWYER. I answered, "Yes, a rifle."

Mr. BELIN. Then the reply to you, "Any clothing description?"

Mr. SAWYER. "Current witness can't remember that."

Mr. BELIN. Then the statement is made sometime before 12:45 p.m., and after the 12:43 p.m., call, "Attention all squads, description was broadcast and no further information at this time."

Does that mean the description you made was rebroadcast?

Mr. SAWYER. I rebroadcast that description. That is what that means.

Mr. BELIN. I then notice on this radio log—I don't see anything more under 9, at least until after the, well, it is down until we have gone as far as 1:30 p.m., I don't see anything else, do you, sir?

Mr. SAWYER. No. There is another broadcast in there somewhere, though. I put out another description on the colored boy that worked in that department.

Mr. BELIN. What do you mean the colored boy that worked in that depository?

Mr. SAWYER. He is one that had a previous record in the narcotics, and he was supposed to have been a witness to the man being on that floor. He was supposed to have been a witness to Oswald being there.

Mr. BELIN. Would Charles Givens have been that boy?

Mr. SAWYER. Yes, I think that is the name, and I put out a description on him.

Mr. BELIN. How do you know he was supposed to be a witness on that?

Mr. SAWYER. Somebody told me that. Somebody came to me with the information. And again, that particular party, whoever it was, I don't know. I remember that a deputy sheriff came up to me who had been over taking these affidavits, that I sent them over there, and he came over from the sheriff's office with a picture and a description of this colored boy and he said that he was supposed to have worked at the Texas Book Depository, and he was the one employee who was missing, or he was missing from the building.

He wasn't accounted for, and that he was suppose to have some information about the man that did the shooting.

Mr. BELIN. When you say about the man who did the shooting, did you know at that time who did the shooting?

Mr. SAWYER. No.

Mr. BELIN. Do you know about what time in the afternoon this was?

Mr. SAWYER. Somewhere along in here; let's see if we can't find it.

Mr. BELIN. This doesn't go past 1:53 p.m.

Mr. SAWYER. What about your other transcript?

Mr. BELIN. I have a transcript of another one here, at least I did have.

Mr. SAWYER. I think we caught the man in the crowd later and sent him down.

We sent him directly down to Captain Fritz's office.

Mr. BELIN. Well, just a minute now. I see here on No. 1, you have two channels there.

Mr. SAWYER. This is Channel 1, yes.

Mr. BELIN. We will call this Sawyer's Deposition Exhibit B.

I see here that you go on at 12:45 p.m., with this statement by your No. 9. You want to read it?

Mr. SAWYER. Yes.

"From this building it is unknown if he is still there or not. Unknown if he was there in the first place."

Mr. BELIN. Then it reads back here, "All the information we have received, indicates it did come from the fifth or fourth of that building."

That is the central headquarters back to you, is that it?

Mr. SAWYER. That's right.

Mr. BELIN. That is at least after 12:45 p.m., and before 12:48 p.m.?

Mr. SAWYER. Right.

Mr. BELIN. Now looking down on this log until the next time your number appears, is 1:12 p.m. What does that say?

Mr. SAWYER. "We have found empty rifle hulls on the fifth floor and from all indications the man had been there for some time."

Mr. BELIN. Then is there anything else?

Mr. SAWYER. This was reported to me by somebody inside the building.

Mr. BELIN. That was at 1:12 p.m., that the hulls were found, or at least shortly prior to that? This doesn't say anything else. It apparently doesn't go in detail much past 1:58 p.m., on Sawyer Deposition Exhibit B, and 1:53 p.m., on Sawyer's Deposition Exhibit A.

Mr. SAWYER. That's right.

Mr. BELIN. Do you still feel sometime after that you might have called out another description?

Mr. SAWYER. It was another, sometime after that, or it has been left out of this. I don't think it has been left out of this, but it must have been after 1:53.

Mr. BELIN. All right, now, sir; you did broadcast that description out of this man?

Mr. SAWYER. Yes, that's correct.

Mr. BELIN. That shows on the radio log. Where did you get that description from?

Mr. SAWYER. We are talking now about the colored man?

Mr. BELIN. No, I am talking about the one that is on Sawyer's Deposition Exhibit A, that shows you at 12:43.

Mr. SAWYER. That description came to me mainly from one witness who claimed to have seen the rifle barrel in the fifth or sixth floor of the building, and claimed to have been able to see the man up there.

Mr. BELIN. Do you know this person's name?

Mr. SAWYER. I do not.

Mr. BELIN. Do you know anything about him, what he was wearing?

Mr. SAWYER. Except that he was—I don't remember what he was wearing. I remember that he was a white man and that he wasn't young and he wasn't old. He was there. That is the only two things that I can remember about him.

Mr. BELIN. What age would you categorize as young?

Mr. SAWYER. Around 35 would be my best recollection of it, but it could be a few years either way.

Mr. BELIN. Do you remember if he was tall or short, or can't you remember anything about him?

Mr. SAWYER. I can't remember that much about him. I was real hazy about that.

Mr. BELIN. Do you remember where he said he was standing when he saw the person with the rifle?

Mr. SAWYER. I didn't go into detail with him except that from the best of my recollection, he was standing where he could have seen him. But there were too many people coming up with questions to go into detail. I got the description and sent him on over to the Sheriff's Office.

Mr. BELIN. Inspector, do you remember anything else about this person who you say gave you the primary description?

Mr. SAWYER. No, I do not, except that I did send him with an escort to the Sheriff's Office to give fuller or more complete detail.

Mr. BELIN. Do you know if he was taken there to see a lineup at the police station?

Mr. SAWYER. No.

Mr. BELIN. Did you ever see him again?

Mr. SAWYER. Not to my knowledge.

Mr. BELIN. Now, you talked to other people there that said they had some information with regard to where the shots may have come from?

Mr. SAWYER. Yes, through a number of people.

Mr. BELIN. First I am going to ask you if you talked to any other people who said they saw a rifle or part of a rifle?

Mr. SAWYER. Yes. There were a few who claimed that they had seen this.

Mr. BELIN. Where did these people that claimed they saw a rifle or part of a rifle——

Mr. SAWYER. The ones that I talked to were pointing out one of the upper floors of the Texas School Book Depository, which at that time I thought was the fifth floor.

Mr. BELIN. Do you know what portion, what side of the building it was?

293

Was it the northeast corner or west side of the building?

Mr. SAWYER. It was on the south side of the building, and in the southeast corner.

Mr. BELIN. What about this person, who I will call the primary description witness, did he say what side of the building it was on?

Mr. SAWYER. He went and pointed out the window which I now note to be the sixth floor, but when I talked to him, I thought it was the fifth floor.

Mr. BELIN. The fifth floor?

Mr. SAWYER. Yes.

Mr. BELIN. What side of the building?

Mr. SAWYER. On the south side of the building, and the southeast corner.

Mr. BELIN. Did you talk to any witness, or did any witness talk to you who claimed to see any rifle or portion of a rifle at any place other than a window of Texas School Book Depository Building?

Mr. SAWYER. No, did any——

Mr. BELIN. Did any officer give you any information about talking to anyone who saw a rifle or a portion of a rifle at any place other than a window in the Texas School Book Depository Building?

Mr. SAWYER. No, not to my knowledge.

Mr. BELIN. Did you talk to people who attempted to locate the shots on the basis of what I would call their sense of hearing, rather than their sense of sight?

In other words, what they heard rather than what they saw?

Mr. SAWYER. Correct. That is correct. Some of them claimed that they had heard shots, or thought they heard shots from over the overpass.

Mr. BELIN. Did all the people you talked to say that they heard shots over the overpass? Claim they had some knowledge about where the shots came from?

Did they all say they heard shots from the overpass, or did they say they heard some from other places?

Mr. SAWYER. No. Very few said they heard the shots come from the overpass, or thought they heard them from that area.

Mr. BELIN. Well, where did other people say they heard shots come from?

Mr. SAWYER. Most of the people that heard the shots pointed out the Texas Book Depository.

Mr. BELIN. Did some of the people that heard shots, or thought they heard shots from the Texas School Book Depository, all say they saw a rifle there?

Mr. SAWYER. No.

Mr. BELIN. Most of them say they saw a rifle there?

Mr. SAWYER. No, just a few, very few.

Mr. BELIN. Is there anything else you can think of that occurred at the Texas School Book Depository that afternoon while you were there that might have any relevancy about where the shots came from, other than what you have told thus far?

Mr. SAWYER. Well, I had heard some of the officers come to me and said there was supposed to be, somebody told them about a woman that had taken some pictures of that window, and then one of the sergeants came to me, and I am not sure who the sergeant is now, but anyway he said that there was on the building immediately west—east, I am sorry—east of the Texas School Book Depository, that a man up in one of the upper windows up there was taking some moving pictures of what had gone on.

Mr. BELIN. Did you ever contact this man? Do you know what his name is?

Mr. SAWYER. No; I don't know his name. The sergeant told me that the man would not give them the pictures, that he was waiting for the Secret Service or the FBI, I forget which now, and I sent the sergeant and two men back over there with instructions to bring that man and his pictures to me.

When they got back over there, Forrest Sorrels of the Secret Service was already there, and at least they so reported back to me, and was talking to this man.

So I told them to go ahead with their normal assignments and since Forrest was already there and talking to him, I knew that that part would be taken care of.

Mr. BELIN. You don't know what his name was or what the results of it was?

Mr. SAWYER. I don't know.

Mr. BELIN. Anything else?

Mr. SAWYER. Later that afternoon one of our colored officer detectives saw this colored man in this crowd across the street and we had previously broadcast a description on, and he took him into custody and sent him immediately down to Captain Fritz' office.

Mr. BELIN. He gave a statement, is that it?

Mr. SAWYER. This I don't know. I presume he did, but I didn't stop to talk to him or take any information.

I just sent him on down there.

Mr. BELIN. Anything else you can think of at this time?

Mr. SAWYER. No.

Mr. BELIN. You spent most of the afternoon out in front of the building there?

Mr. SAWYER. I spent most of the afternoon up until 4 o'clock.

Mr. BELIN. Then what did you do?

Mr. SAWYER. I went back down to the City Hall and checked around there to see if anything further I could do, and then I went home.

Mr. BELIN. What did you do on Saturday, the 23d? Anything that has to do with the assassination or the investigation of the Tippit murder?

Mr. SAWYER. No. I happened to be off on Saturday, and I didn't go back down. The boss didn't call me, so I stayed home.

Mr. BELIN. What about Sunday?

Mr. SAWYER. Same thing. In fact, I didn't even hear about the other thing until way late in the afternoon.

Mr. BELIN. Is there any other information that you can think of, whether I have asked it or not, that might be in any way relevant here?

Mr. SAWYER. The only other thing I can remember that I did down there, was   when the shooting on Officer Tippit came in, I released half a dozen men to go to Oak Cliff to help with that.

Mr. BELIN. Inspector, is there anything else that you can think of, whether I have asked it or not, that is in any way relevant here?

Mr. SAWYER. I can't think of anything.

Mr. BELIN. Sir, we certainly appreciate your cooperation in coming down here.

You have a right, if you would like, after this report is typewritten, to read it and sign it before it is sent to us, or you can waive the reading of it and have it sent to us directly.

It doesn't make a bit of difference to us.

Mr. SAWYER. Whichever you prefer. It doesn't make any difference to me.

I would like to read it.

Mr. BELIN. Why don't we say you read it and sign it, and it will be sent to us.

Mr. SAWYER. Okay.

TESTIMONY OF GERALD DALTON HENSLEE

The testimony of Gerald Dalton Henslee was taken at 4 p.m., on April 8, 1964, in the office of the U.S. attorney, 301 Post Office Building, Bryan and Ervay Streets, Dallas, Tex., by Mr. David W. Belin, assistant counsel of the President's Commission.

Mr. BELIN. Sergeant, do you want to stand and raise your right hand, please, to be sworn.

Do you solemnly swear that the testimony you are about to give is the truth, the whole truth, and nothing but the truth, so help you God?

Mr. HENSLEE. I do.

Mr. BELIN. Will you please state your name.

Mr. HENSLEE. Gerald Dalton Henslee.

Mr. BELIN. Your occupation?

Mr. HENSLEE. A police officer.

Mr. BELIN. For what police department?

Mr. HENSLEE. City of Dallas.

Mr. BELIN. How long have you been a police officer?

Mr. HENSLEE. 16 years.

Mr. BELIN. You are a sergeant now?

Mr. HENSLEE. Sergeant.

Mr. BELIN. What did you do before you became a police officer?

Mr. HENSLEE. I was a student in SMU.

Mr. BELIN. At SMU?

Mr. HENSLEE. Yes.

Mr. BELIN. Prior to that time?

Mr. HENSLEE. I was a dance instructor at the Arthur Murray Dance Studio.

Mr. BELIN. And prior to that?

Mr. HENSLEE. I was in the United States Army.

Mr. BELIN. Honorable discharge, sir?

Mr. HENSLEE. Yes.

Mr. BELIN. How old are you?

Mr. HENSLEE. 40.

Mr. BELIN. Married?

Mr. HENSLEE. Yes.

Mr. BELIN. Sergeant, what were your duties on November 22, 1963?

Mr. HENSLEE. I was supervising the radio dispatcher's office at the Dallas Police Department.

Mr. BELIN. Could you just describe your duties there as to what they included?

Mr. HENSLEE. Well, in this instance, I was not only supervising the channel 1 radio and the incoming radio calls, but was the police dispatcher for channel 2, covering the special event of the arrival of the President of the United States, President Kennedy.

Mr. BELIN. What were your hours of work that day?

Mr. HENSLEE. My assigned hours?

Mr. BELIN. Yes.

Mr. HENSLEE. 6:30 until 2 p.m. 6:30 a.m. until 2:30 p.m.

Mr. BELIN. Did you stay on after that?

Mr. HENSLEE. I stayed until about 5:30, as I recall, approximately.

Mr. BELIN. You mentioned channel 2. How many channels do you have?

Mr. HENSLEE. Two channels.

Mr. BELIN. Was channel 2 being used for the motorcade that day?

Mr. HENSLEE. Yes.

Mr. BELIN. I am going to hand you what has been marked Sawyer Deposition Exhibit A, and ask you to state if you know what this is?

Mr. HENSLEE. Yes. This is a transcript of the radio log of that date.

Mr. BELIN. For what channel?

Mr. HENSLEE. Channel 2.

Mr. BELIN. Covering from?

Mr. HENSLEE. From 10:25 a.m., until 1:53 p.m.

Mr. BELIN. Now I notice on the covering page it says that: "The following was recorded on channel 2, from 10 a.m. to 5 p.m. This report includes information prior to the arrival of the President's plane, progress of the motorcade, the shooting, and the escort to Parkland Hospital. Also included are events concerning the shooting of Officer Tippit."

Mr. HENSLEE. That is correct.

Mr. BELIN. Have you attempted to cover all calls that occurred that day or just the calls pertaining to the subject matter that is included in the covering paragraph.

Mr. HENSLEE. Pertaining to the subject matter, to the covering paragraph only.

Mr. BELIN. All right, I hand you what has been marked Sawyer Deposition Exhibit B, and ask you to state if you know what this is?

Mr. HENSLEE. Yes.

Mr. BELIN. What is Sawyer Deposition Exhibit B?

Mr. HENSLEE. That is a transmission pertaining to the shooting of President Kennedy and Officer Tippit on channel 1.

Mr. BELIN. All right, I notice times on Sawyer Deposition Exhibits A and B. Does this mean a time according to your police clock there when an event happened?

Mr. HENSLEE. Yes, sir.

Mr. BELIN. For instance, on Sawyer Deposition Exhibit A, I see until 12:40 p.m., a number of conversations. Then the next one is 12:43 p.m. Does that mean that all the conversations took place between 12:40 and 12:43 p.m.?

Mr. HENSLEE. That's correct.

Mr. BELIN. They took place in the order in which they are listed here?

Mr. HENSLEE. Right. There were so many, we couldn't get the time in after each transmission.

Mr. BELIN. Who prepared Sawyer Deposition Exhibits A and B, if you know?

Mr. HENSLEE. Well, I am pretty sure these are the ones I prepared. They are copies of them.

Mr. BELIN. Do you know from what source they were prepared?

Mr. HENSLEE. They were prepared from the tapes on the channel 1. We have a tape on channel 1, and we have a record on channel 2. Two separate tape records, but they are prepared from those records and tapes.

Mr. BELIN. Under your supervision?

Mr. HENSLEE. Yes, sir.

296

Mr. BELIN. I notice numbers here. For instance, I see on Sawyer Deposition Exhibit A, the No. 531 often appears. Would that be your call number?

Mr. HENSLEE. This designates the radio dispatcher.

Mr. BELIN. Then I see the number here, No. 1 sometimes appears. Who is that?

Mr. HENSLEE. That is the number assigned to Chief J. E. Curry.

Mr. BELIN. I see a No. 9. Who is No. 9?

Mr. HENSLEE. That is the number assigned to Inspector J. H. Sawyer.

Mr. BELIN. Different numbers are assigned to different people?

Mr. HENSLEE. Yes.

Mr. BELIN. If an officer is patrolling a district, does he have the number assigned to a district if he is not a high officer in the Department?

Mr. HENSLEE. That's correct.

Mr. BELIN. For instance, I see the No. 78 here. Does that appear to be the number of J. D. Tippit?

Mr. HENSLEE. On that particular day it was.

Mr. BELIN. All right, anything else you can think of, Sergeant, that might be relevant to the investigation into the assassination of the President or the shooting of Officer Tippit?

Mr. HENSLEE. No. The only thing I have is what I observed over the police radio that day. That is all the knowledge I have at all.

Mr. BELIN. All right, sir; we thank you very much for your cooperation.

One other thing, you have the right to read this deposition and sign it before it goes into Washington, or else you can waive the reading and have it go directly to Washington.

Do you have any preference?

Mr. HENSLEE. Yes, I would like to read it before I sign it.

Mr. BELIN. That is all right. It makes no difference to us. And again, we thank you.

Mr. HENSLEE. What else can I do for you?

TESTIMONY OF WILLIAM H. SHELLEY

The testimony of William H. Shelley was taken at 4:10 p.m., on April 7, 1964, in the office of the U.S. attorney, 301 Post Office Building, Bryan and Ervay Streets, Dallas, Tex., by Messrs. Joseph A. Ball and Samuel A. Stern, assistant counsel of the President's Commission.

Mr. BALL. Will you hold up your right hand and be sworn?

(Witness complying.)

Mr. BALL. Do you solemnly swear the testimony you will give here today will be the truth, the whole truth, and nothing but the truth, so help you God?

Mr. SHELLEY. Yes.

Mr. BALL. Sit down and state your name and your address.

Mr. SHELLEY. William Hoyt (spelling) Shelley, 126 South Tatum, Dallas 11.

Mr. BALL. Will you tell me something about yourself, where you were born and——

Mr. SHELLEY. I was born at Gunter, Tex.

Mr. BALL. What is your education?

Mr. SHELLEY. High school.

Mr. BALL. What have you been doing since then?

Mr. SHELLEY. I worked in defense plants a little bit during the war and started working at the Texas School Book Depository October 29, 1945.

Mr. BALL. (After leaving room for last answer, Mr. Ball returns.) Did you tell her all about yourself?

Mr. SHELLEY. You wanted to know when I was born.

Mr. BALL. You told us that, and you had your high school education?

Mr. SHELLEY. Yes.

Mr. BALL. What kind of work have you done since then?

Mr. SHELLEY. I've told her.

Mr. BALL. How long have you worked at Texas School Book Depository?

Mr. SHELLEY. She already has it, October 29, 1945.

Mr. BALL. October 29, 1945—steady since that date?

Mr. SHELLEY. Oh, yes.

Mr. BALL. In November 1963, what was your job down there?

Mr. SHELLEY. Well, I am manager of the miscellaneous department and have been for several years.

Mr. BALL. Who is your immediate superior?

Mr. SHELLEY. Roy S. Truly.

297

Mr. BALL. What is his job?

Mr. SHELLEY. He is superintendent of the place.

Mr. BALL. Did you know Lee Oswald?

Mr. SHELLEY. He worked for me.

Mr. BALL. What kind of work did he do for you?

Mr. SHELLEY. He did good work.

Mr. BALL. What?

Mr. SHELLEY. He did good work.

Mr. BALL. What was it?

Mr. SHELLEY. Order filling.

Mr. BALL. As an order filler did he have access to any more than one floor?

Mr. SHELLEY. Oh, yes.

Mr. BALL. How many floors?

Mr. SHELLEY. Just about any of them outside the offices.

Mr. BALL. Were there certain floors that he worked more upon which he worked more frequently than other floors?

Mr. SHELLEY. The first floor is where all the order filling is done; the 5th, 6th, 7th floor are used for storage and when they need stock on the first floor anybody goes up and gets it.

Mr. BALL. So he would work mostly on the first floor and sometimes on 5, 6, and 7, is that what you mean?

Mr. SHELLEY. Yes.

Mr. BALL. Did you ever talk to him?

Mr. SHELLEY. Not too much; he wasn't too talkative. If I had something I wanted him to do, I would tell him and he usually did it.

Mr. BALL. His work was satisfactory?

Mr. SHELLEY. Yes.

Mr. BALL. On the 22d of November 1963, did you see him come to work that morning?

Mr. SHELLEY. No, he was at work when I got there already filling orders.

Mr. BALL. Did you see him from time to time during that day?

Mr. SHELLEY. I am sure I did. I do remember seeing him when I came down to eat lunch about 10 to 12.

Mr. BALL. Where had you been working?

Mr. SHELLEY. I had been on the sixth floor with the boys laying that floor that morning.

Mr. BALL. What time did you go down and eat lunch?

Mr. SHELLEY. It was around 10 'til.

Mr. BALL. Did you eat your lunch?

Mr. SHELLEY. No, I started eating.

Mr. BALL. Where did you start eating it?

Mr. SHELLEY. In my office next to Mr. Truly's and I ate part of it which I do usually and finish up later on in the day but I went outside then to the front.

Mr. BALL. Why did you go to the front?

Mr. SHELLEY. Oh, several people were out there waiting to watch the motorcade and I went out to join them.

Mr. BALL. And who was out there?

Mr. SHELLEY. Well, there was Lloyd Viles of McGraw-Hill, Sarah Stanton, she's with Texas School Book, and Wesley Frazier and Billy Lovelady joined us shortly afterwards.

Mr. BALL. You were standing where?

Mr. SHELLEY. Just outside the glass doors there.

Mr. BALL. That would be on the top landing of the entrance?

Mr. SHELLEY. Yes.

Mr. BALL. Did you see the motorcade pass?

Mr. SHELLEY. Yes.

Mr. BALL. What did you hear?

Mr. SHELLEY. Well, I heard something sounded like it was a firecracker and a slight pause and then two more a little bit closer together.

Mr. BALL. And then?

Mr. SHELLEY. I didn't think anything about it.

Mr. BALL. What did it sound like to you?

Mr. SHELLEY. Sounded like a miniature cannon or baby giant firecracker, wasn't real loud.

Mr. BALL. What happened; what did you do then?

Mr. SHELLEY. I didn't do anything for a minute.

Mr. BALL. What seemed to be the direction or source of the sound?

298

Mr. SHELLEY. Sounded like it came from the west.

Mr. BALL. It sounded like it came from the west?

Mr. SHELLEY. Yes.

Mr. BALL. Then what happened?

Mr. SHELLEY. Gloria Calvary from South-Western Publishing Co. ran back up there crying and said "The President has been shot" and Billy Lovelady and myself took off across the street to that little, old island and we stopped there for a minute.

Mr. BALL. Across the street, you mean directly south?

Mr. SHELLEY. Yes, slightly to the right, you know where the light is there?

Mr. BALL. Yes.

Mr. SHELLEY. That little, old side street runs in front of our building and Elm Street.

Mr. BALL. It dead ends?

Mr. SHELLEY. There's concrete between the two streets.

Mr. BALL. Elm Street dead ends there just beyond the building, doesn't it?

Mr. SHELLEY. Well, that's also Elm that goes under the triple underpass.

Mr. BALL. That is Elm that goes under the triple underpass?

Mr. SHELLEY. Yes.

Mr. BALL. You went to the concrete between the two Elm Streets?

Mr. SHELLEY. Yes, where they split.

Mr. BALL. You went out there and then what did you do?

Mr. SHELLEY. Well, officers started running down to the railroad yards and Billy and I walked down that way.

Mr. BALL. How did you get down that way; what course did you take?

Mr. SHELLEY. We walked down the middle of the little street.

Mr. BALL. The dead-end street?

Mr. SHELLEY. Yes.

Mr. BALL. Did you see Truly, Mr. Truly and an officer go into the building?

Mr. SHELLEY. Yeah, we saw them right at the front of the building while we were on the island.

Mr. BALL. While you were out there before you walked to the railroad yards?

Mr. SHELLEY. Yes.

Mr. BALL. Do you have any idea how long it was from the time you heard those three sounds or three noises until you saw Truly and Baker going into the building?

Mr. SHELLEY. It would have to be 3 or 4 minutes I would say because this girl that ran back up there was down near where the car was when the President was hit.

Mr. BALL. She ran back up to the door and you had still remained standing there?

Mr. SHELLEY. Yes.

Mr. BALL. Going to watch the rest of the parade were you?

Mr. SHELLEY. Yes.

Mr. BALL. The Vice President hadn't gone by, had he, by your place?

Mr. SHELLEY. I don't know. I didn't recognize him. I did recognize Mr. Kennedy and his suntan I had been hearing about.

Mr. BALL. How did you happen to see Truly?

Mr. SHELLEY. We ran out on the island while some of the people that were out watching it from our building were walking back and we turned around and we saw an officer and Truly.

Mr. BALL. And Truly?

Mr. SHELLEY. Yes.

Mr. BALL. Did you see them go into the building?

Mr. SHELLEY. No; we didn't watch that long but they were at the first step like they were fixin' to go in.

Mr. BALL. Were they moving at the time, walking or running?

Mr. SHELLEY. Well, they were moving, yes.

Mr. BALL. Were they running?

Mr. SHELLEY. That, I couldn't swear to; there were so many people around.

Mr. BALL. What did you and Billy Lovelady do?

Mr. SHELLEY. We walked on down to the first railroad track there on the dead-end street and stood there and watched them searching cars down there in the parking lots for a little while and then we came in through our parking lot at the west end.

Mr. BALL. At the west end?

Mr. SHELLEY. Yes; and then in the side door into the shipping room.

Mr. BALL. When you came into the shipping room did you see anybody?

Mr. SHELLEY. I saw Eddie Piper.

Mr. BALL. What was he doing?

Mr. SHELLEY. He was coming back from where he was watching the motorcade in the southwest corner of the shipping room.

Mr. BALL. Of the first floor of the building?

Mr. SHELLEY. Yes.

Mr. BALL. Who else did you see?

Mr. SHELLEY. That's all we saw immediately.

Mr. BALL. Did you ever see Vickie Adams?

Mr. SHELLEY. I saw her that day but I don't remember where I saw her.

Mr. BALL. You don't remember whether you saw her when you came back?

Mr. SHELLEY. It was after we entered the building.

Mr. BALL. You think you did see her after you entered the building?

Mr. SHELLEY. Yes, sir; I thought it was on the fourth floor awhile after that.

Mr. BALL. Now, did the police come into the building?

Mr. SHELLEY. Yes, sir; they started coming in pretty fast.

Mr. BALL. Did you go with them any place?

Mr. SHELLEY. Yes; Mr. Truly left me guarding the elevator, not to let anybody up and down the elevator or stairway and some plainclothesmen came in; I don't know whether they were Secret Service or FBI or what but they wanted me to take them upstairs, so we went up and started searching the various floors.

Mr. BALL. Did you go up on the sixth floor?

Mr. SHELLEY. Yes, sir.

Mr. BALL. Were you there when they found anything up there?

Mr. SHELLEY. I was, I believe I was on the sixth floor when they found the gun but we were searching all parts of that floor.

Mr. BALL. Now, did you find any chicken bones up there or see any?

Mr. SHELLEY. Yes, I went up later on that day; I believe after we had gotten back from City Hall with someone, I don't remember who it was, one of the officers and they got them.

Mr. BALL. They did what?

Mr. SHELLEY. They got the bones.

Mr. BALL. Where were they?

Mr. SHELLEY. They were on the third—yeah, it would be the third window from the southeast corner.

Mr. BALL. And were they in a sack?

Mr. SHELLEY. Laying on a sack.

Mr. BALL. Laying on a sack.

Mr. SHELLEY. Yes, sir; with a coke bottle sitting in the window.

Mr. BALL. Did you see any other chicken bones anyplace around there?

Mr. SHELLEY. No, sir; that's all.

Mr. BALL. That's the only ones?

Mr. SHELLEY. That's all.

Mr. BALL. Did you see anybody eating fried chicken on that floor that morning?

Mr. SHELLEY. At one time I think I said I did but Charles Givens was the guy that was eating and he was further on over toward the west side and he was eating a sandwich so he says.

Mr. BALL. Now you say that you thought that you had seen someone had eaten fried chicken that morning?

Mr. SHELLEY. I thought I had; those colored boys are always eating chicken.

Mr. BALL. Do you think you did or do you know?

Mr. SHELLEY. I asked Charles Givens whether it was him that was eating and he said it was a sandwich.

Mr. BALL. Was that before you went down for lunch?

Mr. SHELLEY. Yes, sir; it was pretty early in the morning, about 9:30.

Mr. BALL. Where was it?

Mr. SHELLEY. It was two-thirds across the building toward the west because I didn't put plywood over there and he didn't get too far from where we were actually working.

Mr. BALL. After you heard these noises you said sounded like firecrackers this girl came up and said the President was shot?

Mr. SHELLEY. Yeah.

Mr. BALL. You were still standing there?

Mr. SHELLEY. Yes, sir.

Mr. BALL. There was still some time lapse from the time you heard the noise like a firecracker and she came up?

Mr. SHELLEY. Yes.

Mr. BALL. Then you went out across Elm?

Mr. SHELLEY. Yes, to the divider.

Mr. BALL. Between the two Elm Streets?

Mr. SHELLEY. Yes.

Mr. BALL. The one street dead ends and the other street that goes on down under the viaduct?

Mr. SHELLEY. Yes.

Mr. BALL. Did you run out to the point or walk out?

Mr. SHELLEY. I believe we trotted out there.

Mr. BALL. Did you stay very long?

Mr. SHELLEY. Oh, it wasn't very long.

Mr. BALL. How long?

Mr. SHELLEY. Maybe a minute or two.

Mr. BALL. And that's the place you saw Truly and Baker, you say, going into the building?

Mr. SHELLEY. Yes, uh-huh.

Mr. BALL. Then you went down the Elm Street that dead ends to the first railroad track?

Mr. SHELLEY. Yes.

Mr. BALL. That's about what distance?

Mr. SHELLEY. Approximately 100 yards.

Mr. BALL. Did you trot, run or walk?

Mr. SHELLEY. We were walking but it was a pretty fast walk.

Mr. BALL. Did you stay there any length of time?

Mr. SHELLEY. Not very long.

Mr. BALL. How long would you say?

Mr. SHELLEY. I wouldn't say over a minute or minute and a half.

Mr. BALL. Then you went back to the building?

Mr. SHELLEY. Yes.

Mr. BALL. Did you trot or run back to the building?

Mr. SHELLEY. We just walked back; took our good, old easy time more or less.

Mr. BALL. Then you went into the west end?

Mr. SHELLEY. Yes.

Mr. BALL. Did you see Vickie Adams after you came into the building and did you see her on the first floor?

Mr. SHELLEY. I sure don't remember.

Mr. BALL. You don't.

Mr. SHELLEY. No.

Mr. BALL. Did Oswald use a clipboard?

Mr. SHELLEY. Yes, sir.

Mr. BALL. On which he kept his orders?

Mr. SHELLEY. Yes.

Mr. BALL. Is it a clipboard you gave him to use or one——

Mr. SHELLEY. It's one he picked up.

Mr. BALL. Picked up where?

Mr. SHELLEY. Just laying around.

Mr. BALL. There are clipboards that the order fillers use there?

Mr. SHELLEY. Yeah, some of them are on bakelite and some we just use a clip and maybe a piece of cardboard.

Mr. BALL. Did he use the same one at all times?

Mr. SHELLEY. Yes; as far as I know.

Mr. BALL. Now at a later time do you remember a clipboard being found?

Mr. SHELLEY. Yes, sir.

Mr. BALL. Do you know who found it?

Mr. SHELLEY. Frankie Kaiser.

Mr. BALL. Where did he find it?

Mr. SHELLEY. He found it on the sixth floor in the corner of the stairway.

Mr. BALL. Did he show you the place?

Mr. SHELLEY. Yes.

Mr. BALL. Point it out to you?

Mr. SHELLEY. Yes; so I invited Mr. Pinkston——

Mr. BALL. Mr. who?

Mr. SHELLEY. Pinkston of the FBI.

Mr. BALL. Did he come out and get the clipboard?

Mr. SHELLEY. Yes; he got it.

Mr. BALL. But Frankie Kaiser pointed it out to you, did he?

Mr. SHELLEY. Yes, sir.

Mr. BALL. And you called the FBI and pointed it out to him?

Mr. SHELLEY. He was down there at the time and I told him about it and he and Frankie and I went up and got it.

Mr. BALL. Do you know what date?

Mr. SHELLEY. No, sir; that, I sure couldn't tell you. It was the following week though, I am pretty sure.

Mr. BALL. You mean after the 22d, the following, you say, the 22d of November?

Mr. SHELLEY. Yes, sir.

Mr. BALL. Did you examine that clipboard?

Mr. SHELLEY. No, sir.

Mr. BALL. Did you examine it to see whether or not there was on the clipboard any orders?

Mr. SHELLEY. Yes, sir.

Mr. BALL. Unfilled orders?

Mr. SHELLEY. Yes, sir; there were some invoices on it.

Mr. BALL. Were you able to identify those invoices and state to whom they had been assigned to fill?

Mr. SHELLEY. They were Scott, Foresman invoices.

Mr. BALL. Scott, Foresman invoices?

Mr. SHELLEY. Yes, sir; and he filled mostly Scott, Foresman orders.

Mr. BALL. Who is "he"?

Mr. SHELLEY. Oswald.

Mr. BALL. Oswald filled mostly Scott, Foresman orders?

Mr. SHELLEY. Yes.

Mr. BALL. That is Foresman [spelling]?

Mr. SHELLEY. Foresman [spelling].

Mr. BALL. Was there any other order filler who filled Scott, Foresman invoices?

Mr. SHELLEY. Any of the other boys would if they ran out of other publishers' orders. When I get those orders, I sort them according to publishers and during rush season like that, usually, have one guy sticking as close to one publisher as he can because skipping back and forth you have different codes and everything and it is confusing to them.

Mr. BALL. So, in the morning would you have assigned all Scott, Foresman to Oswald on that Friday morning?

Mr. SHELLEY. He already had the orders and was working when I got there.

Mr. BALL. He had?

Mr. SHELLEY. Yes.

Mr. BALL. Who would determine what orders they would get?

Mr. SHELLEY. When we run out of orders they get to one of the boxes and get orders for Scott, Foresman. He had been trained for Scott, Foresman.

Mr. BALL. Would orders be assigned the day before?

Mr. SHELLEY. No, sir; we don't definitely assign them to anyone. The boys know what they can fill best and as long as they are putting the workout——

Mr. BALL. I want to know how a man working on Scott, Foresman—suppose Oswald came to work on Friday morning, tell me what routine he would follow, where he would get the orders he was to fill.

Mr. SHELLEY. He would go over to the order desk and get them out of a box marked Scott, Foresman.

Mr. BALL. They would have Scott, Foresman on it?

Mr. SHELLEY. Yes.

Mr. BALL. Is he the only one that in the morning when he came to work would get the orders out of the box marked Scott, Foresman?

Mr. SHELLEY. No, sir; if there wasn't any orders in any of the other boxes any other order filler would take them.

Mr. BALL. Do you know whether or not he was filling Scott, Foresman orders that day?

Mr. SHELLEY. No, sir; not for sure.

Mr. BALL. Do you know whether anybody else was filling Scott, Foresman orders that day?

Mr. SHELLEY. I am sure they were; that's our biggest publishers; there's more of them.

Mr. BALL. Then you believe others besides Oswald were filling Scott, Foresman orders that day?

Mr. SHELLEY. Probably were.

Mr. BALL. Is there any way you can determine what order filler had that clipboard?

Mr. SHELLEY. No, sir.

Mr. BALL. On November 22, 1963?

Mr. SHELLEY. No, sir; it's one that looked like the one he had used.

Mr. BALL. It did look like the one he had used?

Mr. SHELLEY. Yes, sir.

Mr. BALL. There were how many unfilled orders on that clipboard when it was found?

Mr. SHELLEY. Two or three, best I remember.

Mr. BALL. Did you keep a list of them?

Mr. SHELLEY. No, sir.

Mr. BALL. Did anybody make a list of them?

Mr. SHELLEY. Not unless Mr. Pinkston did.

Mr. BALL. Mr. Pinkston of the FBI?

Mr. SHELLEY. Yes; he called in about the thing and in a little while he released it and said go ahead and fill the orders which we did because they were several days old.

Mr. BALL. You mean those orders that were on that clipboard had never been filled?

Mr. SHELLEY. No, sir.

Mr. BALL. So you went ahead and filled them?

Mr. SHELLEY. Yes.

Mr. BALL. How do you spell his name—Pinkston?

Mr. SHELLEY. I don't know how to spell it. Mr. Pinkston is all I know.

Mr. BALL. Pinkston, okay. I think that's all, Mr. Shelley. Thanks very much. This will be written up and you can come down and read it and sign it or we can waive signature; which would you rather do?

Mr. SHELLEY. I suppose it doesn't make any difference. What are the others doing?

Mr. BALL. Some waived, some insist on reading it; which would you rather do?

Mr. SHELLEY. I would kind of like to see it for curiosity.

Mr. BALL. Come down and sign it, all right. Where was the clipboard found?

Mr. SHELLEY. On the sixth floor in the far corner.

Mr. BALL. Which corner?

Mr. SHELLEY. By the stairway.

Mr. BALL. That would be the northwest?

Mr. SHELLEY. Northwest, yes, sir.

Mr. BALL. All right, fine. Thank you very much, Mr. Shelley.

TESTIMONY OF NAT A. PINKSTON

The testimony of Nat A. Pinkston was taken at 12:10 p.m., on April 9, 1964, in the office of the U.S. attorney, 301 Post Office Building, Bryan and Ervay Streets, Dallas, Tex., by Mr. Joseph A. Ball, assistant counsel of the President's Commission.

Mr. BALL. Do you solemnly swear to tell the truth, the whole truth and nothing but the truth, so help you God?

Mr. PINKSTON. I do.

Mr. BALL. State your name, please.

Mr. PINKSTON. Nat A. Pinkston.

Mr. BALL. What is your occupation?

Mr. PINKSTON. I'm a Special Agent with the Federal Bureau of Investigation.

Mr. BALL. Have you had your deposition taken before this proceeding?

Mr. PINKSTON. No, sir.

Mr. BALL. Your address is what?

Mr. PINKSTON. My residence address is 2106 Van Cleave Drive, Dallas.

Mr. BALL. And how long have you been a Special Agent for the Federal Bureau of Investigation?

Mr. PINKSTON. Be 24 years next month.

Mr. BALL. And you are assigned to what office?

Mr. PINKSTON. Dallas, Tex.

303

Mr. BALL. Now, you did not receive a letter from the Commission asking you to testify, did you?

Mr. PINKSTON. No, sir.

Mr. BALL. You were asked to come over here by Mr. Shanklin?

Mr. PINKSTON. Yes.

Mr. BALL. At my request, wasn't it?

Mr. PINKSTON. Well, I——

Mr. BALL. Anyway, you were asked to come over here by Mr. Shanklin and he advised you that your deposition would be taken at that time?

Mr. PINKSTON. Yes.

Mr. BALL. The deposition taken in the course of an investigation by the Commission to investigate the facts concerning the circumstances surrounding the assassination of President Kennedy, and I am a staff officer. My name is Joseph A. Ball. I am authorized to administer the oath to you and to ask you certain questions concerning some matters which you do have knowledge of.

Mr. PINKSTON. Yes, sir.

Mr. BALL. You are willing to testify, are you not?

Mr. PINKSTON. Yes, sir.

Mr. BALL. In the course of your investigation, were you called to the Texas School Book Depository sometimes around the 2d of December 1963?

Mr. PINKSTON. Yes, sir.

Mr. BALL. And who asked you to come down there?

Mr. PINKSTON. I was instructed by one of my supervisors to conduct an investigation there on that date.

Mr. BALL. On that date?

Mr. PINKSTON. Yes, sir.

Mr. BALL. Did you see a fellow by the name of Frankie Kaiser?

Mr. PINKSTON. Yes, sir.

Mr. BALL. And Roy Truly?

Mr. PINKSTON. Yes, sir.

Mr. BALL. What did they tell you when you came down there?

Mr. PINKSTON. To the best of my recollection I was there waiting to see Mr. Truly. He was somewhere else in the building, and I was waiting for him on the occasion in question. Frankie Kaiser came down the stairs and said that he had found something on the sixth floor. I didn't—I then accompanied him back to the sixth floor where he pointed out on the floor near the entrance to the stair well, a clipboard with some orders on it, and—pardon me a second, do you want me to testify to what Kaiser told me, which is hearsay——

Mr. BALL. That is all right, but Kaiser told you that when you were downstairs, that something—didn't he? When he was—did Kaiser come downstairs?

Mr. PINKSTON. Yes; Kaiser came downstairs and took me back upstairs with him and pointed out the clipboard which he had left on the floor.

Mr. BALL. Did he say he had left it there?

Mr. PINKSTON. He had seen it there and did not bother it.

Mr. BALL. I see.

Mr. PINKSTON. He did not put it there.

Mr. BALL. I see. Kaiser told you and you went upstairs and Kaiser pointed out the clipboard?

Mr. PINKSTON. Yes, sir.

Mr. BALL. First, the location of the clipboard.

Mr. PINKSTON. The clipboard was generally in the northwest corner of the sixth floor of the Texas School Book Depository. It was on the floor behind the books, against the wall of the stair well.

Mr. BALL. There were some book cartons in front of it, were there?

Mr. PINKSTON. Yes.

Mr. BALL. Now, did Frankie Kaiser say something? That is hearsay, but I would like to hear what it was.

Mr. PINKSTON. He told me this clipboard was the one that he had made, and had given to Oswald when Oswald went to work at the School Book Depository.

Mr. BALL. Did you examine the clipboard?

Mr. PINKSTON. I did, sir.

Mr. BALL. Did it have anybody's name on it?

Mr. PINKSTON. It had quite a bit of scribbling on it, and I believe—well, I am not in a position to say right now exactly what it had on it other than some orders.

Mr. BALL. It did have some orders on it?

Mr. PINKSTON. Yes, sir.

Mr. BALL. And did you examine the orders?

Mr. PINKSTON. Yes, sir.

Mr. BALL. Can you tell me the date of the orders and the general description of the orders?

Mr. PINKSTON. Three orders on this clipboard. Each order was dated November 22d. The first was an order from Mrs. Hazel Carroll of the Reading Clinic, SMU, for one Parliamentary Procedure at $1.40. Was published by Scott, Foresman & Co.

And this invoice bore No. 2454. The second one was an order from Dallas Independent School District from Mr. M. J. Morton, purchasing agent, at the School Administration Building, 3700 Ross Avenue, Dallas, Tex., for 10 ERS, Basic Reading Skills, for high schools, revised, at $1.12, or total of $11.20. Published by Scott, Foresman & Co.

The Invoice was No. 6057.

The third order was an order to be sent to Mr. M. K. Baker, Junior High School, Reynosa, New Mex., for one TE Basic Reading Skills. J. H. S. use. No charge. Sent at the request of Miss Mary Williams. Publisher; Scott, Foresman & Co., invoice 8291.

Each of these orders, as I say, were dated November 22, 1963.

Mr. BALL. What did you do when you—with the orders after you made these notations?

Mr. PINKSTON. I turned them over to Mr. Truly. He desired to fill the orders.

Mr. BALL. What did you do with the clipboard?

Mr. PINKSTON. I returned the clipboard to my office and made an exhibit of it, as I recall.

Mr. BALL. Is it still an exhibit? It is an FBI exhibit?

Mr. PINKSTON. I believe so.

Mr. BALL. In the possession of the FBI?

Mr. PINKSTON. I haven't seen it since then.

Mr. BALL. Will you try to determine if you still have that as an exhibit in your office, or in Washington?

Mr. PINKSTON. Yes.

Mr. BALL. All right.

Now, this will be written up and will be submitted to you for your signature, or you can waive your signature.

Mr. PINKSTON. I would like to——

Mr. BALL. See it and read it?

Mr. PINKSTON. See it and read it and sign it.

Mr. BALL. You will be notified to come to this office and read it and sign it.

(After the conclusion of the deposition and at 1 o'clock, p.m., on the same day as the taking of the deposition, Mr. Nat A. Pinkston appeared before me, Iris Leonard, stating that he wished the following statement to be incorporated with his deposition: "After reviewing my records, I am now able to state definitely that after examining the clipboard and the orders thereon, I left them at the Texas School Book Depository with Mr. Truly. The clipboard was picked up by another FBI agent at a later time and was made an exhibit.")

TESTIMONY OF BILLY NOLAN LOVELADY

The testimony of Billy Nolan Lovelady was taken at 3:50 p.m., on April 7, 1964, in the office of the U.S. attorney, 301 Post Office Building, Bryan and Ervay Streets, Dallas, Tex., by Messrs. Joseph A. Ball and Samuel A. Stern, assistant counsel of the President's Commission.

Mr. BALL. Will you please stand, hold up your right hand and be sworn?

Mr. BALL. Do you solemnly swear the testimony you are about to give will be the truth, the whole truth and nothing but the truth, so help you God?

Mr. LOVELADY. I do.

Mr. BALL. State your name, please.

Mr. LOVELADY. Billy Nolan Lovelady.

Mr. BALL. You received a letter from the Commission, didn't you?

Mr. LOVELADY. Yes, sir.

Mr. BALL. You know the purpose of the investigation?

Mr. LOVELADY. Right.

Mr. BALL. Can you tell me something about yourself, where you were born and what your education was and your experience, in general?

305

Mr. LOVELADY. Well, I was born at Myrtle Springs, Tex., 1937, February 19, and lived there for about 20 years until I went into the service and I did nursery work and that's about all there is, farm work down there and nursery and stuff like that.

Mr. BALL. When did you go to work for Texas School Book Depository?

Mr. LOVELADY. December 16, 1961, I believe it was.

Mr. BALL. What kind of work did you do there?

Mr. LOVELADY. Well, they hired me when I went there as a truck driver, drove truck until another job as stockman was open, taking care of the stock that comes in, see that it's put in the right place.

Mr. BALL. Which one of the buildings do you work in?

Mr. LOVELADY. At the one at 411 Elm.

Mr. BALL. On November 22, 1963, where were you working?

Mr. LOVELADY. At that morning, you mean?

Mr. BALL. Yes.

Mr. LOVELADY. I was working on the sixth floor putting—we was putting down that flooring.

Mr. BALL. Who were you working with?

Mr. LOVELADY. Well, there was Bonnie Ray Williams and Danny Arce and Slim, Charles Givens; we call him Slim, and let me see, well Mr. Shelley would come up every once in while, check on us. He wasn't workin' with us but he would come up see how we gettin' along.

Mr. BALL. That's Mr. Shelley?

Mr. LOVELADY. Mr. Bill Shelley.

Mr. BALL. What is his position with Texas School Book Depository?

Mr. LOVELADY. He would be under Mr. R. S. Truly.

Mr. BALL. Is he a foreman?

Mr. LOVELADY. I guess you would call it that. He takes care of most things down there, paperwork and stuff like that.

Mr. BALL. Did you know Lee Oswald?

Mr. LOVELADY. Well just to work with him.

Mr. BALL. Did you ever talk to him?

Mr. LOVELADY. Well, I never did carry on any long conversations or anything like that, maybe, you know, "Hello," or I asked him a few times how his little baby was getting along; he told me it was doing fine.

Mr. BALL. Where did Oswald work in the building?

Mr. LOVELADY. Well, he had access to all the building just like I do.

Mr. BALL. All floors?

Mr. LOVELADY. All floors.

Mr. BALL. Any floor?

Mr. LOVELADY. Any floor; I mean he didn't have no business in the office. I mean, or to if, say, like Mr. Truly would say "Okay, Lee, go up and give me a certain something from the office," he could go up there.

Mr. BALL. Did he work on one floor more than any other?

Mr. LOVELADY. No; I wouldn't say because there's different publishers on each order and he has to go to different floors to get books.

Mr. BALL. Did Oswald ever eat lunch with you?

Mr. LOVELADY. He ate two or three times in that little domino room, but not by himself, with the rest of the boys.

Mr. BALL. Did you see him come to work that morning?

Mr. LOVELADY. No, sir.

Mr. BALL. Did you ever see him carry a sack or anything in his hand?

Mr. LOVELADY. No, sir; just lunch.

Mr. BALL. Did he usually carry his lunch or did he buy his lunch?

Mr. LOVELADY. Most of the time he had fruit and stuff like that, grapes and raisins, stuff like that I noticed a few times he had.

Mr. BALL. What time did you quit work that day or knock off for lunch that day?

Mr. LOVELADY. Same time, 12.

Mr. BALL. A little before 12?

Mr. LOVELADY. Well, we came down at 10 minutes til to wash up and get ready for it.

Mr. BALL. Did you come down the elevator?

Mr. LOVELADY. Right.

Mr. BALL. Who did you go down with?

Mr. LOVELADY. Let me see, I think it was Bonnie Ray Williams on the side I was; I believe so.

Mr. BALL. Were you having a race with the other boys?

Mr. LOVELADY. Yes, sir; sure was.

Mr. BALL. Did you see anything or hear anything of Oswald on the way down?

Mr. LOVELADY. Yes; he was on the opposite side of the elevator I was on. I heard him holler to one of the boys to stop, he wanted the elevator. They said, "No; we're going down to lunch," and closed the gate I was on and come down and got ready to watch the President come by or got ready to go to lunch, and that's the last I heard of him.

Mr. BALL. You were on the west elevator?

Mr. LOVELADY. Right.

Mr. BALL. Oswald was standing in front of the east elevator?

Mr. LOVELADY. East, on back, the elevator back.

Mr. BALL. Did you see him?

Mr. LOVELADY. No; I didn't; I just heard his voice because—where those slats are in back of the elevator.

Mr. BALL. Did you ever see him again that day?

Mr. LOVELADY. No.

Mr. BALL. What did you do after you went down and washed up; what did you do?

Mr. LOVELADY. Well, I went over and got my lunch and went upstairs and got a coke and come on back down.

Mr. BALL. Upstairs on what floor?

Mr. LOVELADY. That's on the second floor; so, I started going to the domino room where I generally went in to set down and eat and nobody was there and I happened to look on the outside and Mr. Shelley was standing outside with Miss Sarah Stanton, I believe her name is, and I said, "Well, I'll go out there and talk with them, sit down and eat my lunch out there, set on the steps," so I went out there.

Mr. BALL. You ate your lunch on the steps?

Mr. LOVELADY. Yes, sir.

Mr. BALL. Who was with you?

Mr. LOVELADY. Bill Shelley and Sarah Stanton, and right behindme——

Mr. BALL. What was that last name?

Mr. LOVELADY. Stanton.

Mr. BALL. What is the first name?

Mr. LOVELADY. Bill Shelley.

Mr. BALL. And Stanton's first name?

Mr. LOVELADY. Miss Sarah Stanton.

Mr. BALL. Did you stay on the steps?

Mr. LOVELADY. Yes.

Mr. BALL. Were you there when the President's motorcade went by?

Mr. LOVELADY. Right.

Mr. BALL. Did you hear anything?

Mr. LOVELADY. Yes, sir; sure did.

Mr. BALL. What did you hear?

Mr. LOVELADY. I thought it was firecrackers or somebody celebrating the arrival of the President. It didn't occur to me at first what had happened until this Gloria came running up to us and told us the President had been shot.

Mr. BALL. Who was this girl?

Mr. LOVELADY. Gloria Calvary.

Mr. BALL. Gloria Calvary?

Mr. LOVELADY. Yes.

Mr. BALL. Where does she work?

Mr. LOVELADY. Southwestern Publishing Co.

Mr. BALL. Where was the direction of the sound?

Mr. LOVELADY. Right there around that concrete little deal on that knoll.

Mr. BALL. That's where it sounded to you?

Mr. LOVELADY. Yes, sir; to my right. I was standing as you are going down the steps, I was standing on the right, sounded like it was in that area.

Mr. BALL. From the underpass area?

Mr. LOVELADY. Between the underpass and the building right on that knoll.

Mr. BALL. I have got a picture here, Commission Exhibit 369. Are you on that picture?

Mr. LOVELADY. Yes, sir.

Mr. BALL. Take a pen or pencil and mark an arrow where you are.

Mr. LOVELADY. Where I thought the shots are?

Mr. BALL. No; you in the picture.

Mr. LOVELADY. Oh, here (indicating).

Mr. BALL. Draw an arrow down to that; do it in the dark. You got an arrow in the dark and one in the white pointing toward you. Where were you when the picture was taken?

Mr. LOVELADY. Right there at the entrance of the building standing on the top of the step, would be here (indicating).

Mr. BALL. You were standing on which step?

Mr. LOVELADY. It would be your top level.

Mr. BALL. The top step you were standing there?

Mr. LOVELADY. Right.

Mr. BALL. Now, when Gloria came up you were standing near Mr. Shelley?

Mr. LOVELADY. Yeah.

Mr. BALL. When Gloria came up and said the President had been shot, Gloria Calvary, what did you do?

Mr. LOVELADY. Well, I asked who told her. She said he had been shot so we asked her was she for certain or just had she seen the shot hit him or—she said yes, she had been right close to it to see and she had saw the blood and knew he had been hit but didn't know how serious it was and so the crowd had started towards the railroad tracks back, you know, behind our building there and we run towards that little, old island and kind of down there in that little street. We went as far as the first tracks and everybody was hollering and crying and policemen started running out that way and we said we better get back into the building, so we went back into the west entrance on the back dock had that low ramp and went into the back dock back inside the building.

Mr. BALL. First of all, let's get you to tell us whom you left the steps with.

Mr. LOVELADY. Mr. Shelley.

Mr. BALL. Shelley and you went down how far?

Mr. LOVELADY. Well, I would say a good 75, between 75 to 100 yards to the first tracks. See how those tracks goes——

Mr. BALL. You went down the dead end on Elm?

Mr. LOVELADY. Yes.

Mr. BALL. And down to the first tracks?

Mr. LOVELADY. Yes.

Mr. BALL. Did you see anything there?

Mr. LOVELADY. No sir; well, just people running.

Mr. BALL. That's all?

Mr. LOVELADY. And hollerin.

Mr. BALL. How did you happen to go down there?

Mr. LOVELADY. I don't know, because everybody was running from that way and naturally, I guess——

Mr. BALL. They were running from that way or toward that way?

Mr. LOVELADY. Toward that way; everybody thought it was coming from that direction.

Mr. BALL. By the time you left the steps had Mr. Truly entered the building?

Mr. LOVELADY. As we left the steps I would say we were at least 15, maybe 25, steps away from the building. I looked back and I saw him and the policeman running into the building.

Mr. BALL. How many steps?

Mr. LOVELADY. Twenty, 25.

Mr. BALL. Steps away and you looked back and saw him enter the building?

Mr. LOVELADY. Yes.

Mr. BALL. Then you came back. How long did you stay around the railroad tracks?

Mr. LOVELADY. Oh, just a minute, maybe minute and a half.

Mr. BALL. Then what did you do?

Mr. LOVELADY. Came back right through that part where Mr. Campbell, Mr. Truly, and Mr. Shelley park their cars and I came back inside the building.

Mr. BALL. And enter from the rear?

Mr. LOVELADY. Yes, sir; sure did.

Mr. BALL. You heard the shots. And how long after that was it before Gloria Calvary came up?

Mr. LOVELADY. Oh, approximately 3 minutes, I would say.

Mr. BALL. Three minutes is a long time.

Mr. LOVELADY. Yes, it's—I say approximately; I can't say because I don't have a watch; it could.

Mr. BALL. Had people started to run?

Mr. LOVELADY. Well, I couldn't say because she came up to us and we was talking to her, wasn't looking that direction at that time, but when we came off the steps—see, that entrance, you have a blind side when you go down the steps.

Mr. BALL. Right after you talked to Gloria, did you leave the steps and go toward the tracks?

Mr. LOVELADY. Yes.

Mr. BALL. Did you run or walk?

Mr. LOVELADY. Medium trotting or fast walk.

Mr. BALL. A fast walk?

Mr. LOVELADY. Yes.

Mr. BALL. How did you happen to turn around and see Truly and the policeman go into the building?

Mr. LOVELADY. Somebody hollered and I looked.

Mr. BALL. You turned around and looked?

Mr. LOVELADY. Yes.

Mr. BALL. After you ran to the railroad tracks you came back and went in the back door of the building?

Mr. LOVELADY. Right.

Mr. BALL. Did you go in through the docks, the wide open door or did you go in the ordinary small door?

Mr. LOVELADY. You know where we park our trucks—that door; we have a little door.

Mr. BALL. That is where you went in, that little door?

Mr. LOVELADY. That's right.

Mr. BALL. That would be the north end of the building?

Mr. LOVELADY. That would be the west end, wouldn't it?

Mr. BALL. Is it the one right off Houston Street?

Mr. LOVELADY. No; you are thinking about another dock.

Mr. BALL. I am?

Mr. LOVELADY. Yes; we have two.

Mr. BALL. Do you have a dock on the west side and one on the north side of the building?

Mr. LOVELADY. East, and well, it would be east and west but you enter it from the south side.

Mr. BALL. Now, the south side——

Mr. LOVELADY. Elm Street is that little dead-end street.

Mr. BALL. That's south.

Mr. LOVELADY. I drive my truck here (indicating) but we came in from this direction; that would have to be west.

Mr. BALL. You came into the building from the west side?

Mr. LOVELADY. Right.

Mr. BALL. Where did you go into the building?

Mr. LOVELADY. Through that, those raised-up doors.

Mr. BALL. Through the raised-up doors?

Mr. LOVELADY. Through that double door that we in the morning when we get there we raised. There's a fire door and they have two wooden doors between it.

Mr. BALL. You came in through the first floor?

Mr. LOVELADY. Right.

Mr. BALL. Who did you see in the first floor?

Mr. LOVELADY. I saw a girl but I wouldn't swear to it it's Vickie.

Mr. BALL. Who is Vickie?

Mr. LOVELADY. The girl that works for Scott, Foresman.

Mr. BALL. What is her full name?

Mr. LOVELADY. I wouldn't know.

Mr. BALL. Vickie Adams?

Mr. LOVELADY. I believe so.

Mr. BALL. Would you say it was Vickie you saw?

Mr. LOVELADY. I couldn't swear.

Mr. BALL. Where was the girl?

Mr. LOVELADY. I don't remember what place she was but I remember seeing ▢ a girl and she was talking to Bill or saw Bill or something, then I went over and asked one of the guys what time it was and to see if we should continue working or what.

Mr. BALL. Did you see any other people on the first floor?

Mr. LOVELADY. Oh, yes; by that time there were more; a few of the guys had come in.

Mr. BALL. And you stayed on the first door then?

Mr. LOVELADY. I would say 30 minutes. And one of the policemen asked me would I take them up on the sixth floor.

Mr. BALL. Did you take them up there?

Mr. LOVELADY. Yes, sir; I sure did.

Mr. BALL. Mr. Lovelady, your testimony will be written up and it can be submitted to you for your signature if you wish and you can make any changes, or you can waive signature and we will make this your final——

Mr. LOVELADY. I want this to be the final one.

Mr. BALL. All right; you waive signature?

Mr. LOVELADY. Yes.

Mr. BALL. Thanks very much.

TESTIMONY OF FRANKIE KAISER

The testimony of Frankie Kaiser was taken at 2:30 p.m., on April 8, 1964, in the office of the U.S. attorney, 301 Post Office Building, Bryan and Ervay Streets, Dallas, Tex., by Mr. Joseph A. Ball, assistant counsel of the President's Commission.

Mr. BALL. Will you hold up your right hand and be sworn, please?

Do you solemnly swear that the testimony you are about to give before the Commission shall be the truth, the whole truth, and nothing but the truth, so help you God?

Mr. KAISER. I do.

Mr. BALL. Will you give me your name, please?

Mr. KAISER. Frankie Kaiser.

Mr. BALL. What is your address?

Mr. KAISER. 5230 West Ledbetter in Duncanville.

Mr. BALL. What is your occupation?

Mr. KAISER. Warehouse workman at the Texas School Book Depository.

Mr. BALL. How long have you worked for that company?

Mr. KAISER. Oh, just about 2 years.

Mr. BALL. What time do you go to work down there?

Mr. KAISER. Eight o'clock in the morning.

Mr. BALL. What date did you go to work for them?

Mr. KAISER. It was August 24, 1962.

Mr. BALL. Where did you go to school?

Mr. KAISER. Texas—Texarkana, Ark.

Mr. BALL. Were you born there?

Mr. KAISER. No, sir; I was born in Omaha, Nebr.

Mr. BALL. And then you went to school in Texarkana, did you?

Mr. KAISER. Right.

Mr. BALL. And what did you do after you got out of school?

Mr. KAISER. I never finished.

Mr. BALL. How far did you go?

Mr. KAISER. I went to the tenth grade and quit and went in the service and went in for 6 months in the National Guards and come out and then came to Dallas and started to work and I worked for Morrises.

Mr. BALL. You worked for whom?

Mr. KAISER. Morris Warehouse.

Mr. BALL. Then what did you do after that?

Mr. KAISER. I worked there for about 3 years and then I started to work over there.

Mr. BALL. You started to work over at the Texas School Book Depository?

Mr. KAISER. Yes—then I got married.

Mr. BALL. You did—what kind of work do you do at the Texas School Book Depository?

Mr. KAISER. Drive a truck—fill orders—just about anything that needs to be done.

Mr. BALL. Did you ever know a fellow by the name of Lee Oswald that worked there?

Mr. KAISER. Not personally—I would know him when I would see him.

Mr. BALL. Did you work in the same building with him?

Mr. KAISER. Same building.

Mr. BALL. Where were you when the President's parade went by?

Mr. KAISER. At the Baylor Dental College.

Mr. BALL. Where?

Mr. KAISER. At the Baylor Dental College.

Mr. BALL. Sir, you weren't anywhere near the School Book Depository?

Mr. KAISER. No, sir; I was off Thursday and Friday with abscessed tooth. I was sitting in the chair and when I got off, we was out in the lobby watching it on TV down at the dental college there.

Mr. BALL. When did you go back to work?

Mr. KAISER. It was the following Monday.

Mr. BALL. That would be the 25th, wouldn't it?

Mr. KAISER. Yes, sir; I believe so—the 25th.

Mr. BALL. Now, one day you found a clipboard, didn't you?

Mr. KAISER. Yes; it was about a week later. I went upstairs, you see, the corner I found it in—we keep a certain teacher's edition of Catholic handbooks.

Mr. BALL. I didn't quite hear that—Catholic what?

Mr. KAISER. We keep our teacher's edition of Catholic "Think and Do" books.

Mr. BALL. I didn't quite hear that—Catholic what?

Mr. KAISER. We keep our teacher's edition of Catholic books—separated.

Mr. BALL. You do?

Mr. KAISER. Yes, sir; and I went up there to get a teacher's edition.

Mr. BALL. On what floor?

Mr. KAISER. On the sixth floor.

Mr. BALL. Now, what part of the sixth floor is this Catholic edition located?

Mr. KAISER. It was in that corner.

Mr. BALL. And in what corner is that?

Mr. KAISER. Let's see——

Mr. BALL. Without saying north or south, was it near the elevator? Or the stairway?

Mr. KAISER. Yes, it was right in front of the elevator.

Mr. BALL. Where was it with reference to the stairway?

Mr. KAISER. It was right next to the stairway—right in the corner.

Mr. BALL. Right in the corner next to the stairway, is that right?

Mr. KAISER. Yes, sir.

Mr. BALL. Now, what day did you find it, do you remember?

Mr. KAISER. I couldn't tell you. It was about a week or a week and a half, somewhere in there.

Mr. BALL. Now, this statement you gave to the Federal Bureau of Investigation on the 2d of December 1963, says you talked to an agent named Pinkston; do you remember that?

Mr. KAISER. Well, I got my boss and the FBI to go upstairs and I showed it to them.

Mr. BALL. When you saw the clipboard——

Mr. KAISER. I went downstairs and got my boss.

Mr. BALL. What is his name?

Mr. KAISER. William H. Shelley.

Mr. BALL. And then what happened?

Mr. KAISER. This FBI was standing there with me—he was standing there then and I told him I had a clipboard laying up there with the orders.

Mr. BALL. Do you think it would have been around December 2?

Mr. KAISER. I couldn't tell you, sir.

Mr. BALL. It was within a week after you went back to work, was it?

Mr. KAISER. To my best knowledge—yes, sir—somewhere in there.

Mr. BALL. How did you happen to find the clipboard?

Mr. KAISER. I was over there looking for the Catholic edition—teacher's edition.

Mr. BALL. Where did you see the clipboard?

Mr. KAISER. It was just laying there in the plain open—and just the plain open boxes—you see, we've got a pretty good space back there and I just noticed it laying over there.

Mr. BALL. Laying on the floor?

Mr. KAISER. Yes, it was laying on the floor.

Mr. BALL. It was on the floor?

Mr. KAISER. It was on the floor.

Mr. BALL. How close was it to the wall?

311

Mr. KAISER. It was about—oh—I would say, just guessing, about 5 or 6 inches, something like that.

Mr. BALL. From the wall and on the floor?

Mr. KAISER. Laying on the floor.

Mr. BALL. And were there any boxes between the wall and the clipboard?

Mr. KAISER. No, not between the wall and the clipboard—there wasn't.

Mr. BALL. Were there boxes between the stairway and the clipboard?

Mr. KAISER. No, you see, here's—let me see just a second—here's the stairs right here, and we went down this way and here's the stairs this way going up and here's the—and it was laying right in here by the cards—there are about four or five cards, I guess, running in front of it—just laying between the part you go down and the part you go up.

Mr. BALL. You mean laying between the stairway up and the stairway down?

Mr. KAISER. Yes, right there in the corner.

Mr. BALL. Did you examine that clipboard?

Mr. KAISER. I didn't touch it.

Mr. BALL. Did you later touch it?

Mr. KAISER. Yes, sir; they got me to look at it later on.

Mr. BALL. Did you see it had some orders on it?

Mr. KAISER. Yes.

Mr. BALL. And were the orders dated?

Mr. KAISER. Yes, sir.

Mr. BALL. What were they dated?

Mr. KAISER. I couldn't tell you, sir.

Mr. BALL. Take a look at this statement which you gave to Mr. Pinkston that day and read it to yourself and see if it refreshes your memory in any way?

Mr. KAISER. (Read statement referred to.)

Mr. BALL. Did you read that?

Mr. KAISER. Yes, sir.

Mr. BALL. Does that refresh your memory now as to the orders on the clipboard?

Mr. KAISER. I didn't know the date on the orders—I knew that there was some orders on there—I seen the orders on the clipboard.

Mr. BALL. Did you examine them to determine the date on them?

Mr. KAISER. Did I examine those orders? No, sir.

Mr. BALL. You didn't examine the orders?

Mr. KAISER. No, sir; I just went down and got my boss and then they took it down.

Mr. BALL. Did you make any notes of the orders?

Mr. KAISER. I didn't, sir.

Mr. BALL. Of either the names on the orders or the date of the orders?

Mr. KAISER. No, sir; now, my boss may have.

Mr. BALL. I think that's all. Did you fill the orders, then, yourself?

Mr. KAISER. No, sir; not them, I didn't.

Mr. BALL. You turned these over to your boss?

Mr. KAISER. You see, I went down and got them and they went down and got them and they handled them.

Mr. BALL. That's all, Mr. Kaiser, and thanks very much for coming up.

This will be written up and you can come down and read it over and sign it if you wish, or you can waive your signature, if you want to, and we can send it on without a signature.

Now, we will mark these pictures we've been talking about here in your deposition as Kaiser Exhibits Nos. A, B, C.

(Marked by reporter as Kaiser Exhibits Nos. A, B, C, for identification.)

Mr. KAISER. Anything else I can do, let me know.

Mr. BALL. Do you want to waive your signature to it?

Mr. KAISER. Yes, I'll waive it.

Mr. BALL. Fine. That's okay.

Mr. KAISER. All right.

TESTIMONY OF FRANKIE KAISER RESUMED

The testimony of Frankie Kaiser was taken at 3:40 p.m., on April 8, 1964, in the office of the U.S. attorney, 301 Post Office Building, Bryan and Ervay Streets, Dallas, Tex., by Mr. Joseph A. Ball, assistant counsel of the President's Commission.

Mr. BALL. Frankie, we have already taken your deposition and I just wanted to ask you a few more questions and you are still under oath.

Mr. KAISER. Yes, sir.

Mr. BALL. Now, Frankie, that clipboard you found describe it—what was it?

Mr. KAISER. It was made out of paper and tape and a little piece of pasteboard.

Mr. BALL. Who made it?

Mr. KAISER. I did.

Mr. BALL. When?

Mr. KAISER. Well, right after I started there—it had been a long time ago.

Mr. BALL. And how was it you weren't using it on this day?

Mr. KAISER. You see, when he first started there——

Mr. BALL. Who is "he"?

Mr. KAISER. Lee—when he first started to work there he got my clipboard and started using it.

Mr. BALL. Did you give it to him to use?

Mr. KAISER. No, he just picked it up and started using it and I just went and made me another one.

Mr. BALL. You recognized that clipboard when you saw it?

Mr. KAISER. Yes, because my name was all over it.

Mr. BALL. Your name was on it, too?

Mr. KAISER. Yes, sir.

Mr. BALL. You put your name "Frankie Kaiser" on it?

Mr. KAISER. You see, it don't do no good to get a clipboard around here—everybody is always running off with it.

Mr. BALL. That's the reason you put your name on it?

Mr. KAISER. He come up and got it and started using it and I just let him keep it and made me another one.

Mr. BALL. Now, here is a picture which is marked in a group of pictures as No. 36, but which I will mark as Exhibit A to your deposition.

(Instrument marked by the reporter as Kaiser Exhibit A, for identification.)

Mr. BALL. Does this show the place where the clipboard was found, or do you know?

Mr. KAISER. It wasn't found there—it was found on the floor.

Mr. BALL. Where on the floor?

Mr. KAISER. Behind these cartons—between there and the wall.

Mr. BALL. Behind which cartons?

Mr. KAISER. Right in here (indicating).

Mr. BALL. Which cartons—it was found behind—are the cartons in the picture—it wasn't found where it is circled there?

Mr. KAISER. It wasn't found where it circled—there—it was found on the floor.

Mr. BALL. Put a big "X" on the carton behind which it was found.

Mr. KAISER. I'll put it on this one—it was found between that and the wall. (Witness placed "X" on the pictures requested by Counsel Ball.)

Mr. BALL. You have marked an "X" on the carton—between that carton and the wall the clipboard was found.

Mr. KAISER. Yes, between these row of cartons right over there.

Mr. BALL. Now, did you later find clothing?

Mr. KAISER. I just found the coat there—I didn't even know it was his until somebody told me it was. I thought they were kidding.

Mr. BALL. This is Commission Exhibit 163—do you recognize that blue jacket?

Mr. KAISER. That's the one I found.

Mr. BALL. Where did you find it—tell me first.

Mr. KAISER. It was in the window sill.

Mr. BALL. In what room?

Mr. KAISER. In the domino room.

Mr. BALL. Now, I show you a picture, No. 17, this is marked—does this show the window?

Mr. KAISER. Right down in here.

Mr. BALL. There is a jacket showing in that window, is that where the jacket was found?

Mr. KAISER. Yes, sir; but it was laying behind this in the window.

Mr. BALL. It wasn't found in the position of the jacket shown in the picture?

Mr. KAISER. No; it sure wasn't.

Mr. BALL. But was it the same window?

Mr. KAISER. Yes.

Mr. BALL. And the window sill is shown there too?

Mr. KAISER. Yes; it is.

Mr. BALL. I show you a picture which is marked Exhibit 18, does this show the place where the jacket was found?

Mr. KAISER. Right over in here.

Mr. BALL. Where—put an "X" there—it's in the window sill?

Mr. KAISER. Right.

(Marked diagram with an "X".)

Mr. BALL. There is an Exhibit 17, which shows the corner of the domino room and the window and it is marked as Exhibit B and the picture marked No. 18, which shows the window sill, bearing an "X" placed there by the witness, and is marked as Exhibit "C". Will you initial that "C" please?

Mr. KAISER. (Initialed instrument as requested.)

Mr. BALL. That's "FK".

I believe we are through, now, Frankie, thank you very much.

Mr. KAISER. That's all right.

Mr. BALL. You'll waive this signature too?

Mr. KAISER. Yes.

(Instruments marked by the reporter as Kaiser Exhibits B and C, for identification.)

TESTIMONY OF CHARLES DOUGLAS GIVENS

The testimony of Charles Douglas Givens was taken at 9 a.m., on April 8, 1964, in the office of the U.S. attorney, 301 Post Office Building, Bryan and Ervay Streets, Dallas, Tex., by Mr. David W. Belin, assistant counsel of the President's Commission.

Mr. BELIN. Would you stand and raise your right hand? Do you solemnly swear that the testimony you are about to give, will be the truth, the whole truth, and nothing but the truth, so help you God?

Mr. GIVENS. I do.

Mr. BELIN. What is your name, please?

Mr. GIVENS. Charles Douglas Givens.

Mr. BELIN. Where do you live, Mr. Givens?

Mr. GIVENS. I live at 4208 First Avenue.

Mr. BELIN. In Dallas?

Mr. GIVENS. Yes, sir.

Mr. BELIN. How old are you?

Mr. GIVENS. 38.

Mr. BELIN. Married?

Mr. GIVENS. Yes, sir.

Mr. BELIN. Family?

Mr. GIVENS. No, sir.

Mr. BELIN. Where were you born, Mr. Givens?

Mr. GIVENS. Kemp, Tex.

Mr. BELIN. Have you lived in Texas most of your life?

Mr. GIVENS. All my life except I was in the Armed Forces during World War II, in the Navy.

Mr. BELIN. How long were you in the Navy?

Mr. GIVENS. About 2 years.

Mr. BELIN. Let me backtrack a little. Did you go to high school before you went in the Navy?

Mr. GIVENS. Yes, sir.

Mr. BELIN. How far did you get through school?

Mr. GIVENS. Twelfth grade.

Mr. BELIN. Did you get through the 12th?

Mr. GIVENS. No, sir.

Mr. BELIN. You got up to the 12th grade?

Mr. GIVENS. Yes.

Mr. BELIN. Then what did you do?

Mr. GIVENS. Well, I went to work.

Mr. BELIN. Doing what?

Mr. GIVENS. SMU.

Mr. BELIN. Pardon?

Mr. GIVENS. SMU.

Mr. BELIN. SMU?

Mr. GIVENS. Yes.

Mr. BELIN. What did you do out there?

Mr. GIVENS. I worked in the kitchen.

Mr. BELIN. How long did you stay there?

Mr. GIVENS. Oh, about 2 years.

Mr. BELIN. Then what did you do?

Mr. GIVENS. I went in the service.

Mr. BELIN. You went in the service for a couple of years?

Mr. GIVENS. Yes, sir.

Mr. BELIN. What did you do with most of your time in the service?

Mr. GIVENS. I was in the Steward Mate Branch.

Mr. BELIN. Were you honorably discharged?

Mr. GIVENS. Yes, sir.

Mr. BELIN. Then what did you do when you got out of the service?

Mr. GIVENS. I went back to work.

Mr. BELIN. At SMU?

Mr. GIVENS. No, sir.

Mr. BELIN. Where?

Mr. GIVENS. I worked at Central Lumber Co.

Mr. BELIN. Doing what there?

Mr. GIVENS. I was a truck helper; helper on the truck.

Mr. BELIN. You were helper on a truck?

Mr. GIVENS. Delivering lumber; yes, sir.

Mr. BELIN. How long did you do that?

Mr. GIVENS. Oh, about a year and a half, I guess.

Mr. BELIN. Then what did you do?

Mr. GIVENS. One time I got into a little difficulty. Got in a little trouble.

Mr. BELIN. You got in a little trouble?

Mr. GIVENS. Yes.

Mr. BELIN. All right, you were not working for a while?

Mr. GIVENS. Yes, sir.

Mr. BELIN. About how long was that?

Mr. GIVENS. About 13 months.

Mr. BELIN. All right, then, what did you do?

Mr. GIVENS. Well, I came back and I worked for a construction company, and then after that I got this job down here at the depository.

Mr. BELIN. At the School Book Depository?

Mr. GIVENS. Yes.

Mr. BELIN. How long have you worked there?

Mr. GIVENS. Off and on about 6 years.

Mr. BELIN. Was there any period of time that you haven't worked there?

Mr. GIVENS. Yes, sir.

Mr. BELIN. What happened then?

Mr. GIVENS. Well, I just, you know, sometimes I had some days to layoff during the slack season, like it is now, and when it is rush season he calls you back.

Mr. BELIN. So it was just a question of being laid off during the slack season?

Mr. GIVENS. Yes, sir.

Mr. BELIN. What do you do down there at the Texas Book Depository?

Mr. GIVENS. Well, I filled orders and stacked books, and you know, don't have any special job.

Mr. BELIN. On what floors do you generally work most of all?

Mr. GIVENS. Well, I work on the first floor most of the time, like we fill orders. We work out of the stock downstairs. We go upstairs. We have stock on three floors, fifth, sixth, and seventh.

Mr. BELIN. Well, do you fill orders for any particular publisher more than another, so that you might be on the fifth floor, or the sixth floor more than the seventh, or do you just spend as much time on any one of those top floors as you do on any other top floor?

Mr. GIVENS. That's right.

Mr. BELIN. Is that what you were doing on the 22d of November 1963, also?

Mr. GIVENS. No, sir.

Mr. BELIN. What were you doing on November 22?

Mr. GIVENS. We were fixing the floor, putting down some plywood on the floor.

Mr. BELIN. What floor would this have been on?

Mr. GIVENS. Sixth.

Mr. BELIN. What part of the sixth floor?

Mr. GIVENS. We were working on the west end.

Mr. BELIN. All right, do you remember what time you got to work that day?

Mr. GIVENS. Yes; I got to work around about a quarter to eight.

Mr. BELIN. Where did you go when you got to work?

Mr. GIVENS. I went in a little lunchroom that we have downstairs.

Mr. BELIN. Is that what you call the domino room?

Mr. GIVENS. Yes, sir.

Mr. BELIN. You carry your lunch with you?

Mr. GIVENS. Yes, sir.

Mr. BELIN. You put your lunch there?

Mr. GIVENS. Yes, sir.

Mr. BELIN. Did you wear a jacket to work that day?

Mr. GIVENS. I wore a raincoat, I believe. It was misting that morning.

Mr. BELIN. Did you hang up your coat in that room, too?

Mr. GIVENS. Yes, sir.

Mr. BELIN. Did you know Lee Harvey Oswald?

Mr. GIVENS. Well, I knew of him.

Mr. BELIN. Have you ever talked with him at all?

Mr. GIVENS. Well, I talked to him once in a while. I mean, just like about filling orders or something like that. Sometimes I check and he was filling orders and he make a mistake, and I call him and get the book right.

Mr. BELIN. Do you remember any conversation you ever had with him? What you said and what he said?

Mr. GIVENS. Well, he was a fellow that kept pretty much to himself. He never had too much to say.

Mr. BELIN. Did he ever say anything to you, what a nice day, or about his family, or baseball, or anything?

Mr. GIVENS. No, sir.

Mr. BELIN. Ever talk to you about any politics?

Mr. GIVENS. No, sir.

Mr. BELIN. When you talked to him about correcting an order, what did you say and what did he say?

Mr. GIVENS. Well, I just tell him he had the wrong book.

Mr. BELIN. What would he say?

Mr. GIVENS. He said, "Okay," and got the record.

Mr. BELIN. What did you call him, Lee or Oswald?

Mr. GIVENS. Called him Lee.

Mr. BELIN. What did he call you?

Mr. GIVENS. Well, he never called me anything. I never heard him call me anything.

Mr. BELIN. Did he make mistakes often?

Mr. GIVENS. Well, not too often.

Mr. BELIN. When you got to work on the morning of November 22, did you see him at all there or not?

Mr. GIVENS. 22d? That was on Friday, wasn't it?

Mr. BELIN. Friday; that is the day the President came by.

Mr. GIVENS. Yes, I saw him that day.

Mr. BELIN. Where did you see him first?

Mr. GIVENS. Well, I first saw him on the first floor.

Mr. BELIN. About what time was that?

Mr. GIVENS. Well, about 8:30.

Mr. BELIN. Now, let me ask you this. You got to work at a quarter to 8?

Mr. GIVENS. Yes, sir.

Mr. BELIN. What did you do between a quarter of 8 and 8:30? Where were you?

Mr. GIVENS. Well, I went upstairs. We went to work at 8 o'clock.

Mr. BELIN. Did you see him come into the domino room at all?

Mr. GIVENS. Not that morning, no, sir; I didn't.

Mr. BELIN. When did you leave the domino room to go up to the sixth floor?

Mr. GIVENS. 8 o'clock.

Mr. BELIN. At 8 o'clock?

Mr. GIVENS. Yes, sir.

Mr. BELIN. So you don't feel he came in the domino room before 8 o'clock?

Mr. GIVENS. No, sir; not that morning he didn't.

Mr. BELIN. How did you get up to the sixth floor?

Mr. GIVENS. On the elevator.

Mr. BELIN. The east or the west one? The west one is the one that would be nearest the railroad tracks, and the east one would be nearer the Houston Street.

Mr. GIVENS. We went up on the east one.

Mr. BELIN. Any particular reason why you took the east one rather than the west one?

Mr. GIVENS. Well, I don't know whether you call it a particular reason, but on the west, you have double gates on that.

Mr. BELIN. Was the west elevator on the first floor when you took the east elevator up?

Mr. GIVENS. It was that morning, yes, sir.

Mr. BELIN. It was that morning around 8 o'clock?

Mr. GIVENS. Yes, sir.

Mr. BELIN. Now, where did you see him at 8:30 o'clock first?

Mr. GIVENS. I came back down to use the rest room.

Mr. BELIN. Where was he?

Mr. GIVENS. He was over there in the bin filling orders.

Mr. BELIN. He was over in the bin filling orders?

Mr. GIVENS. Yes, sir; they had some bins there.

Mr. BELIN. Did you talk to him at all?

Mr. GIVENS. No.

Mr. BELIN. Did you say hello, Lee?

Mr. GIVENS. No, sir; I didn't say anything to him. I just looked at him.

Mr. BELIN. Do you remember what he was wearing?

Mr. GIVENS. Well, I believe it was kind of a greenish looking shirt and pants was about the same color as his shirt, practically the same thing he wore all the time he worked there. He never changed clothes the whole time he worked there, and he would wear a grey looking jacket.

Mr. BELIN. All right. You saw him at 8:30 on the first floor?

Mr. GIVENS. Yes, sir.

Mr. BELIN. Then what did you do?

Mr. GIVENS. Well, we went back upstairs and started to work.

Mr. BELIN. You went back up to the sixth floor to continue laying the floor?

Mr. GIVENS. Yes, sir.

Mr. BELIN. When did you see Lee Harvey Oswald next?

Mr. GIVENS. Next?

Mr. BELIN. Yes.

Mr. GIVENS. Well, it was about a quarter till 12, we were on our way downstairs, and we passed him, and he was standing at the gate on the fifth floor.

I came downstairs, and I discovered I left my cigarettes in my jacket pocket upstairs, and I took the elevator back upstairs to get my jacket with my cigarettes in it. When I got back upstairs, he was on the sixth floor in that vicinity, coming from that way.

Mr. BELIN. Coming from what way?

Mr. GIVENS. Toward the window up front where the shots were fired from.

Mr. BELIN. Just a second, where did you go? Where were you when you saw him on the sixth floor?

Mr. GIVENS. I had went and got my jacket and was on my way back to the elevator.

Mr. BELIN. All right, just a second. I am going to get a plan of the sixth floor, if I have one, and try and have you point that out to me.

Mr. GIVENS. Yes, sir.

Mr. BELIN. Well, I don't seem to have a sixth floor plan here, but perhaps we can use another plan here to help us.

Here is a diagram of the front of the building. This is the Elm Street side, and you can see the arrow pointing north.

This perhaps would be a diagram of the third floor. You notice that there are one, two, three, four, five, six, seven sets of windows, right?

Mr. GIVENS. Yes.

Mr. BELIN. On the Elm Street side, seven pairs of windows?

Mr. GIVENS. Yes, sir.

Mr. BELIN. You notice the two freight elevators toward the rear. Now did you see—when you first saw him on the sixth floor there, were you standing near any of these windows?

Mr. GIVENS. No, sir. I was over here by the elevators.

Mr. BELIN. You are pointing your finger to a spot which would be somewhat to the east of the east elevator, is that correct?

Mr. GIVENS. That's correct.

Mr. BELIN. At a spot which is about on the same line as what I call the south side of the east elevator, and about as far east of the front part of that elevator as the distance from the front of the elevator to the back of the east elevator, is that about right?

Mr. GIVENS. Yes, sir.

Mr. BELIN. You were standing at that point, and where did you see Lee Harvey Oswald?

Mr. GIVENS. Well, I was along here [indicating].

Mr. BELIN. All right, you are pointing at a spot you say along in here?

Mr. GIVENS. Yes, sir.

Mr. BELIN. That would be near the east wall of the building?

Mr. GIVENS. Yes, sir.

Mr. BELIN. You can see a scale here that is from 0 to 20 feet. Well, it would be about 30 to 40 feet north of the south wall of that building, is that right?

Mr. GIVENS. Yes, sir.

Mr. BELIN. And around 10 feet or so away from the east wall, is that about right?

Mr. GIVENS. That is about right.

Mr. BELIN. Now, did you notice whether or not there were any cartons stacked up around the southeast corner of that sixth floor?

Mr. GIVENS. Well, I didn't pay any attention about any being stacked, because we had taken all that stock from that side of the building and ran it down that side.

Mr. BELIN. You had taken stock down from the west part of the sixth floor where you were working and put it there?

Mr. GIVENS. Yes; ran it down the side right in front of the window.

Mr. BELIN. Was he between that stock and the window, or was he on the other side of the window?

Mr. GIVENS. He was between the stock and the window, coming towards the elevators.

Mr. BELIN. Coming towards the elevators?

Mr. GIVENS. Yes, sir.

Mr. BELIN. Did you see all of his body or not?

Mr. GIVENS. Yes, sir; he had his clipboard in his hand.

Mr. BELIN. He had his clipboard in his hand?

Mr. GIVENS. Yes, sir.

Mr. BELIN. Was that kind of an aisleway over there right next to the east wall that he was walking along, or what?

Mr. GIVENS. Yes, sir; they have aisles.

Mr. BELIN. Now, was there stock in back of him as well as in front of him? Were you where you had stacked it up, or not, or don't you remember?

Mr. GIVENS. Well, it was already some books stacked there.

Mr. BELIN. Were there books stacked between where you saw him and the window itself?

Mr. GIVENS. Yes, sir.

Mr. BELIN. All right, he was walking with his clipboard from that southeast corner?

Mr. GIVENS. Yes, sir.

Mr. BELIN. Where did you see him walking? What direction did you see him walking in?

Mr. GIVENS. He was coming towards the elevators.

Mr. BELIN. From the Elm Street side of the building?

Mr. GIVENS. Yes, sir.

Mr. BELIN. So that would be walking in a northerly direction?

Mr. GIVENS. Yes, sir.

Mr. BELIN. Now, you said that he had a clipboard in his hand?

Mr. GIVENS. Yes; he had his board with his orders on it.

Mr. BELIN. Did you see the orders on the board?

Mr. GIVENS. Well, yes, sir; he had it in his hand.

Mr. BELIN. Did he have any books in his hand that he was carrying?

Mr. GIVENS. No, sir.

Mr. BELIN. Did you ever fill orders in November on the sixth floor?

Mr. GIVENS. Yes, sir.

Mr. BELIN. Do you remember whether or not there were any books or book cartons over in that corner from which he might have been filling orders?

Mr. GIVENS. Well, yes, sir; it was possible.

318

Mr. BELIN. It was possible?

Mr. GIVENS. Yes, sir.

Mr. BELIN. Did you watch where he walked to?

Mr. GIVENS. Well, no, sir; I didn't pay much attention. I was getting ready to get on the elevator, and I say, "Boy, are you going downstairs?"

Mr. BELIN. What did he say to you?

Mr. GIVENS. I say, "It's near lunch time."

He said, "No, sir. When you get downstairs, close the gate to the elevator."

That meant the elevator on the west side, you can pull both gates down and it will come up by itself.

Mr. BELIN. What else did he say?

Mr. GIVENS. That is all.

Mr. BELIN. What did you say to that? Did you say you would close the elevator gate, or not say anything?

Mr. GIVENS. I said, "Okay," and got on the elevator.

Mr. BELIN. What elevator did you take down?

Mr. GIVENS. I taken this one.

Mr. BELIN. The east elevator?

Mr. GIVENS. The east elevator.

Mr. BELIN. Do you know whether or not when you got down to the first floor, the west elevator was there?

Mr. GIVENS. No, sir; it wasn't, because I looked over there to close the gate and it wasn't there.

Mr. BELIN. It wasn't there when you got down to the first floor?

Mr. GIVENS. No, sir; it wasn't.

Mr. BELIN. Do you know where it was?

Mr. GIVENS. No, sir; I don't.

Mr. BELIN. What time was this?

Mr. GIVENS. Well, I would say it was about 5 minutes to 12, then because it was——

Mr. BELIN. Now what did you do when you got down there on the first floor?

Mr. GIVENS. When I got down to the first floor Harold Norman, James Jarman and myself, we stood over by the window, and then we said we was going outside and watch the parade, so we walked out and we stood there a while, and then I said, "I believe I will walk up to the parking lot."

I had a friend that worked on the parking lot, right on Elm and Record.

Mr. BELIN. Elm and Record Streets?

Mr. GIVENS. Elm and Record Streets; yes, sir.

Mr. BELIN. That would be one block to the east of the corner of Elm and Houston?

Mr. GIVENS. That's right.

Mr. BELIN. All right, then, what did you do?

Mr. GIVENS. I stood around over there and went up on the corner.

Mr. BELIN. What corner?

Mr. GIVENS. Up on Main and Record. That is where I watched the President pass right there.

Mr. BELIN. Who else was there with you that you knew?

Mr. GIVENS. James and Edward Shields.

Mr. BELIN. Is that the same person, James Edward?

Mr. GIVENS. Edward Shields and James.

Mr. BELIN. Two other people?

Mr. GIVENS. Yes.

Mr. BELIN. You watched the motorcade together?

Mr. GIVENS. Yes, sir.

Mr. BELIN. What did you do after you watched the motorcade?

Mr. GIVENS. We turned and started back down to the parking lot.

Mr. BELIN. Then what did you do?

Mr. GIVENS. Then when we heard the shots, by the time we got along in front, right across in front of the Record Building, then we heard the shots.

Mr. BELIN. I want to backtrack a minute before we come to the shots. When did you eat lunch?

Mr. GIVENS. When did I eat lunch? I ate lunch after. Let's see, no; I ate lunch before I went up there, because I stood outside and ate my sandwich standing out there.

Mr. BELIN. You ate your lunch outside?

Mr. GIVENS. Yes, sir. Standing in front of the building.

Mr. BELIN. In front of what building?

Mr. GIVENS. Texas School Book.

Mr. BELIN. Did you ever eat any lunch inside the building?

Mr. GIVENS. Yes, sir; I eat inside the building all the time.

Mr. BELIN. On November 22, did you eat inside the building?

Mr. GIVENS. No, sir.

Mr. BELIN. Now you said you saw Lee Oswald on the sixth floor around 11:55?

Mr. GIVENS. Right.

Mr. BELIN. Did you see Lee Oswald anywhere else in the building between 11:55 and the time you left the building?

Mr. GIVENS. No, sir.

Mr. BELIN. On November 22d?

Mr. GIVENS. No, sir.

Mr. BELIN. Did you see him in the domino room at all around anywhere between 11:30 and 12 or 12:30?

Mr. GIVENS. No, sir.

Mr. BELIN. Did you see him reading the newspaper?

Mr. GIVENS. No; not that day. I did—he generally sit in there every morning. He would come to work and sit in there and read the paper, the next day paper, like if the day was Tuesday, he would read Monday's paper in the morning when he would come to work, but he didn't that morning because he didn't go in the domino room that morning. I didn't see him in the domino room that morning.

Mr. BELIN. How do you know it was the previous day paper that he read?

Mr. GIVENS. Because he would be sitting there and I would look at him, when he got through and got up to go to work, I would get it and look at it.

Mr. BELIN. Would it be a News or Times Herald?

Mr. GIVENS. Well, they bring Dallas Morning News around in the morning. Fellows bring it to work.

Mr. BELIN. You mean he would read someone else's newspaper that somebody else brought to work?

Mr. GIVENS. Yes, sir.

Mr. BELIN. Did you ever know him to buy his own newspaper?

Mr. GIVENS. No, sir; I never saw him buy one.

Mr. BELIN. Who generally brought the newspaper there?

Mr. GIVENS. Well, Harold Norman would generally bring one and James Jarman would generally bring one.

Mr. BELIN. Now you say you left the sixth floor. Well, you said you left it first to go—did you go down with the other employees on the elevator?

Mr. GIVENS. Yes, sir.

Mr. BELIN. About what time was that now?

Mr. GIVENS. That was about a quarter—I said about a quarter to 12.

Mr. BELIN. Who was on that elevator, do you remember?

Mr. GIVENS. That was Bonnie Ray Williams, and Billy Lovelady, and Danny and myself.

Mr. BELIN. That was Danny Arce?

Mr. GIVENS. Yes; a Spanish boy.

Mr. BELIN. Then you say you got down there and you say you wanted your cigarettes so you went back up?

Mr. GIVENS. Yes, sir.

Mr. BELIN. What elevator did you go down on?

Mr. GIVENS. I came down on the east elevator.

Mr. BELIN. What elevator did you take back up?

Mr. GIVENS. The east elevator.

Mr. BELIN. That day had you eaten any chicken at all, or anything on the sixth floor?

Mr. GIVENS. No, sir.

Mr. BELIN. Had you eaten any chicken or left a pop bottle on any previous days on the sixth floor?

Mr. GIVENS. No, sir.

Mr. BELIN. Did you go immediately to your jacket when you went back up to the sixth floor?

Mr. GIVENS. Yes, sir; I went straight and picked up my jacket.

Mr. BELIN. Where was your jacket?

Mr. GIVENS. It was on the west side of the building where we were working.

Mr. BELIN. Well, there are seven pairs of windows. Was it on the south wall of the building? Was it near any one of those windows on the south wall, or was it more to the center of the west side?

Mr. GIVENS. It was more to the corner on the west side. I would say along about the second window going.

Mr. BELIN. When you say the corner, do you mean the corner by the stairs or the southwest corner?

Mr. GIVENS. Southwest corner.

Mr. BELIN. You have shown the southwest corner?

Mr. GIVENS. Yes, sir; along about here [indicating].

Mr. BELIN. You have pointed to a spot which appears to be approximately, oh, 25 feet north, and about 10 feet east of the southwest corner of the sixth floor. Would that be about right?

Mr. GIVENS. Yes, sir.

Mr. BELIN. You have pointed to a spot on this floor plan here. When you walked from the east elevator to pick up your jacket, did you see Lee Oswald there?

Mr. GIVENS. No, sir.

Mr. BELIN. Did you see him anywhere on the sixth floor when you were walking off the elevator to pick up your jacket?

Mr. GIVENS. No, sir; I didn't see him until I got back along here, about in front of the elevator, fixing to get on.

Mr. BELIN. As you were walking to the first spot, which we will describe as somewhat east of the east elevator, were you standing or about to get on the elevator, or what?

Mr. GIVENS. Yes; I was fixing to get on.

Mr. BELIN. You were fixing to get on? The elevator was still there where you left it when you came up?

Mr. GIVENS. Yes, sir.

Mr. BELIN. As you were starting to get on the elevator or were turning to get on it, you saw Lee Oswald walking with his clipboard?

Mr. GIVENS. Yes, sir.

Mr. BELIN. Now, was he walking in a diagonal direction directly toward you and the elevator, or was he walking more in a direction parallel to the east wall here?

Mr. GIVENS. Well, I would say yes, sir; he was going like this.

Mr. BELIN. He was going?

Mr. GIVENS. Coming down the aisle.

Mr. BELIN. Coming down the aisle straight?

Mr. GIVENS. Yes, sir.

Mr. BELIN. Anything else in his hand other than a clipboard? Did he have a pencil in his hand?

Mr. GIVENS. No, sir; I didn't pay any attention to him.

Mr. BELIN. When you got off the elevator, as you were coming back up to get your shirt, did you have any occasion as you were walking out of the elevator to look to see if there was anyone else on the floor?

Mr. GIVENS. Well, no, sir; I wasn't thinking of that. I just happened to glance around as I was on my way back.

Mr. BELIN. Did you glance around when you got off the elevator, do you remember?

Mr. GIVENS. Well, no, sir. I just walked off and turned and went right over there and picked my jacket up and started back.

Mr. BELIN. Did you look over in the southeast corner before as you were getting off the elevator?

Mr. GIVENS. Well, I kind of glanced that way when I turned to go around the corner.

Mr. BELIN. Did you see anyone over there at that time?

Mr. GIVENS. Not at that time, no, sir; I didn't.

Mr. BELIN. Do you remember how high the books were by the southeast corner on the sixth floor?

Mr. GIVENS. Well, I would say about 10 feet from the window. In the aisle we had one pretty good stack of books there, one large stack.

Mr. BELIN. Would they have been as tall as you?

Mr. GIVENS. Well, yes, sir.

Mr. BELIN. If a man would have been standing up there, would you have been able to see him?

Mr. GIVENS. No, sir; I wouldn't unless he moved down towards the north end of the building.

Mr. BELIN. Did anyone else use any of the elevators while you were up on the sixth floor getting your cigarettes?

Mr. GIVENS. Not that I know of; no, sir.

Mr. BELIN. Did you ever tell anyone that you saw Lee Oswald reading a newspaper in the domino room around 11:50, 10 minutes to 12 on that morning on November 22d?

Mr. GIVENS. No, sir.

Mr. BELIN. Did you ever observe Lee Oswald getting the newspaper in the domino room shortly before lunch on days other than November 22d?

Mr. GIVENS. Not before lunch. It would be right at lunch time.

Mr. BELIN. Right at lunch time?

Mr. GIVENS. Yes, sir. We always ate in there.

Mr. BELIN. Would Oswald always eat in there?

Mr. GIVENS. Yes, sir.

Mr. BELIN. When you first went downstairs from the sixth floor to the first floor with the other men on those two elevators, you took two elevators, didn't you?

Mr. GIVENS. Yes; we took two down.

Mr. BELIN. Were you racing the elevators?

Mr. GIVENS. That's right.

Mr. BELIN. Who won?

Mr. GIVENS. Well, the east elevator beat the other one down, because it stopped quicker, but it had to adjust itself.

Mr. BELIN. What did you do when you got down to the first floor before you went back up to the sixth floor again?

Mr. GIVENS. Well, I got a drink of water and reached for my cigarettes and I thought about I left them in my jacket pocket.

Mr. BELIN. Did you go to the rest room at all before you went back up to the sixth floor?

Mr. GIVENS. No, sir. Yes, sir, I believe I did. I went in and washed my hands, I sure did.

Mr. BELIN. Anything else before you went back up to the sixth floor?

Mr. GIVENS. No, sir; that was it.

Mr. BELIN. Now the first time when you left the sixth floor with these other men to take the two elevators down, did you at any time look over to the southeast corner of the sixth floor?

Mr. GIVENS. Well, no, sir; I didn't pay any attention the first time I was coming down.

Mr. BELIN. Where were you laying the new floor that morning? What portion of the sixth floor would it be?

Mr. GIVENS. West side.

Mr. BELIN. How much of the west side?

Mr. GIVENS. Well, we were working, I would say, about 10 feet from Elm Street.

Mr. BELIN. Well, you were pointing to right over this point here?

Mr. GIVENS. Yes sir.

Mr. BELIN. Well, looking at the scale, it would be about 10 feet from the—it would be more than 10 feet. Here is the scale.

This would be 20 feet, so it would be more than 20 feet from Elm Street?

Mr. GIVENS. About 20 feet, maybe so.

Mr. BELIN. Do you think it was closer to 10 feet than 20 feet from the Elm Street side of the west part of the sixth floor?

Mr. GIVENS. I believe it was somewhere in that vicinity.

Mr. BELIN. How close was it to the west wall on the sixth floor?

Mr. GIVENS. Well, we were, oh, I would say about 20 feet out from the wall, we had laid.

Mr. BELIN. Did anyone else ever comment to you as having seen Oswald on the sixth floor that morning?

Mr. GIVENS. No, sir.

Mr. BELIN. All right. Now, is there anything else you can think of that happened that morning up to the time you heard the shot?

Mr. GIVENS. No, sir. Everything was all right until that.

Mr. BELIN. How many shots did you hear?

Mr. GIVENS. Three.

Mr. BELIN. What did you do when you heard them?

322

Mr. GIVENS. Well, we broke and ran down that way, and by the time we got to the corner down there of Houston and Elm, everybody was running, going toward the underpass over there by the railroad tracks.

And we asked—I asked someone—some white fellow there, "What happened?"

And he said, "Somebody shot the President." Like that. So I stood there for a while, and I went over to try to get to the building after they found out the shots came from there, and when I went over to try to get back in the officer at the door would't let me in.

Mr. BELIN. Did you tell him you worked there?

Mr. GIVENS. Yes; but he still wouldn't let me in. He told me he wouldn't let no one in.

Mr. BELIN. This was the front of Elm Street?

Mr. GIVENS. Yes. So I goes back over to the parking lot and I wait until I seen Junior.

Mr. BELIN. Is that Jarman?

Mr. GIVENS. Yes. They were on their way home, and they told me that they let them all go home for the evening, and I said, "I'd better go back and get my hat and coat."

So I started over there to pick up my hat and coat, and Officer Dawson saw me and he called me and asked me was my name Charles Givens, and I said, "Yes."

And he said, "We want you to go downtown and make a statement."

And he puts me in the car and takes me down to the city hall and I made a statement to Will Fritz down there.

Mr. BELIN. Did you ever see Lee Oswald at any time after the time you saw him carrying the clipboard on the sixth floor?

Mr. GIVENS. No, sir. The next time I saw him was on television.

Mr. BELIN. Is there anything else you can think of, whether I have asked it or not, that in any way is relevant to the assassination?

Mr. GIVENS. No, sir.

Mr. BELIN. Anything else you can think of about Lee Oswald, whether I have asked it or not, that might in any way be helpful?

Mr. GIVENS. No, sir. Other than he is just a peculiar fellow. He is just a loner. Don't have much to say to anybody. Stayed by himself most of the time.

Mr. BELIN. Did you ever notice any one person there he was more friendly with than the other?

Mr. GIVENS. Well, this boy he rode with.

Mr. BELIN. Frazier?

Mr. GIVENS. Yes, sir. Every once in a while I would see him talking to him. Bonnie Ray told me—I never saw him, but Bonnie Ray told me he talked to he and Danny sometimes.

Mr. BELIN. Anyone else?

Mr. GIVENS. Not that I know of; no, sir.

Mr. BELIN. Anything else you can think of?

Mr. GIVENS. No, sir; that is about it.

Mr. BELIN. Well, Mr. Givens, we surely appreciate your cooperation in coming down here. Now you and I didn't talk about this at all until we started taking this deposition, did we?

Mr. GIVENS. No, sir.

Mr. BELIN. You walked into the room and you raised your right hand and we started taking your testimony. Is that correct?

Mr. GIVENS. Yes, sir.

Mr. BELIN. Have I ever met you before?

Mr. GIVENS. I don't believe so. I don't believe I have.

Mr. BELIN. You have an opportunity to come back here and read this and sign it if you want, or else you can just waive signing and have the court reporter send it directly to Washington. Do you want to come back and read and sign it or do you want to just have the court reporter just send it to Washington?

Mr. GIVENS. Would it be necessary to come back?

Mr. BELIN. No, sir; it is not. You can waive it if you desire to do it. Do you want to waive it?

Mr. GIVENS. Yes, sir.

Mr. BELIN. All right, thank you. We will see you.

TESTIMONY OF TROY EUGENE WEST

The testimony of Troy Eugene West was taken at 10:30 a.m., on April 8, 1964, in the office of the U.S. attorney, 301 Post Office Building, Bryan and Ervay Streets, Dallas, Tex., by Mr. David W. Belin, assistant counsel of the President's Commission.

Mr. BELIN. Mr. West, would you raise your right hand, please.

Do you solemnly swear that the testimony you are about to give will be the truth, the whole truth, and nothing but the truth, so help you God?

Mr. WEST. I do.

Mr. BELIN. You want to sit down now, please. Will you please state your name for the record? Your name is Troy Eugene West?

Mr. WEST. Troy Eugene West.

Mr. BELIN. How old are you, Mr. West?

Mr. WEST. Well, I was born in 1907. That would be 57, I think.

Mr. BELIN. Were you born in Texas?

Mr. WEST. Yes, sir.

Mr. BELIN. You go to school at all in Texas?

Mr. WEST. Yes, sir.

Mr. BELIN. How far did you get through school?

Mr. WEST. Well, I went to the seventh grade.

Mr. BELIN. Then what did you do?

Mr. WEST. Well; I had to come out of school and go to work.

Mr. BELIN. You started working then?

Mr. WEST. Yes, sir.

Mr. BELIN. What did you do when you started working? Where did you work?

Mr. WEST. On the farm.

Mr. BELIN. On the farm?

Mr. WEST. On the farm, yes, sir.

Mr. BELIN. How long did you stay on the farm?

Mr. WEST. Oh, I stayed on the farm until way up after I got grown. I was way up past—I guess I was about 24.

Mr. BELIN. When you left the the farm, then what did you do when you left the farm?

Mr. WEST. Well, I came to town after I left.

Mr. BELIN. You came to Dallas?

Mr. WEST. No, sir; little town at Mexia, Tex.

Mr. BELIN. How long did you stay in town there?

Mr. WEST. Well, I lived there for about 7 years, I guess.

Mr. BELIN. You were in town for 7 years, and generally what did you do when you were in town?

Mr. WEST. Well, I worked the express all the time.

Mr. BELIN. For any particular company?

Mr. WEST. I was trying to think of the man's name.

Mr. BELIN. You can't remember it right now?

Mr. WEST. I just can't remember it right now. Been quite a little while.

Mr. BELIN. Well, do you remember what you did after you got through doing that? After 6 or 7 years, then where did you go?

Mr. WEST. I came to Dallas.

Mr. BELIN. Then what did you do in Dallas, generally?

Mr. WEST. Well, I worked around just different places until I started to work for the company where I am now.

Mr. BELIN. When did you start working for them?

Mr. WEST. Well, I have been with them now about 16 years.

Mr. BELIN. You have been with them 16 or 17 years? What company is that?

Mr. WEST. Texas School Book Depository.

Mr. BELIN. Are you still working for them now?

Mr. WEST. Yes, sir.

Mr. BELIN. What do you do for the Texas School Book Depository?

Mr. WEST. Well, I am a mail wrapper.

Mr. BELIN. You are a mail wrapper?

Mr. WEST. I wrap mail all the time.

Mr. BELIN. Were you doing that on November 22d of 1963, too? Were you a mail wrapper at that time back in last November?

Mr. WEST. Yes, sir.

Mr. BELIN. Did you go to work on November 22, 1963? That was a Friday, the day the President was assassinated.

Mr. WEST. Yes; I went to work that day.

Mr. BELIN. What time did you get to work?

Mr. WEST. Well, we always got to work—we were supposed to be there at 8 in the morning.

Mr. BELIN. You got there at 8 that morning?

Mr. WEST. Yes. I always, most of the time I got there a little early.

Mr. BELIN. Do you remember what time you got to work that particular morning?

Mr. WEST. It was about 10 minutes to 8. I always be 5 or 10 minutes early.

Mr. BELIN. Where did you go when you got to work?

Mr. WEST. Well, when I first got to work I always made coffee in the morning at the store. That is the first thing I do in the morning.

Mr. BELIN. Where did you make the coffee?

Mr. WEST. Sir?

Mr. BELIN. Where did you make coffee?

Mr. WEST. Well, it is down on the first floor in the same department where I wrap mail at.

Mr. BELIN. Well, I have a first floor map here of the School Book Depository. Here is Elm Street and here is the front entrance.

Here is Mr. Truly's office, and here is Mr. Shelley's office.

There is the stairway down to the basement, and there are the elevators and the back stairway. There are the toilets there. About where would you wrap mail there? Here is the domino room and the shower.

You are looking here, that is north Elm Street runs this way and Houston Street runs that way. It is shown on that diagram.

Mr. WEST. Well, my place was in the west side of the other building.

Mr. BELIN. Was it near the stairway.

Mr. WEST. No; it wasn't close to the stairway.

Mr. BELIN. Was it closer to the Elm Street side of the building?

Mr. WEST. No, sir.

Mr. BELIN. What was it close to? The west side is the side near the railroad tracks and the triple underpass. Is that what you think is the west side?

Mr. WEST. Yes, sir; that is what I would call the west side.

Mr. BELIN. Well, now, the northwest part is by the stairway, and the southwest part would be toward the corner near Elm Street. Do you mean toward the Elm or more toward the wooden dock in the back?

Mr. WEST. Well, it was about, I would say, middleways between Elm and the dock.

Mr. BELIN. Well, there are a couple of overhead doors on that west side, aren't there?

Mr. WEST. Yes, sir.

Mr. BELIN. You see where it is marked on the first floor diagram, overhead door and overhead door? Two doorways here on the west side?

Mr. WEST. Yes, sir.

Mr. BELIN. Then was it near either one of those doorways?

Mr. WEST. Well, it was near this one, pretty close to this one.

Mr. BELIN. It was close to what I would call a doorway, approximately in the middle side of the west wall of the first floor?

Mr. WEST. Yes.

Mr. BELIN. That is where you wrapped the mail?

Mr. WEST. Yes, sir.

Mr. BELIN. That is where you have the coffee machine?

Mr. WEST. Yes, sir; I have it.

Mr. BELIN. That is where you went when you got to work that morning?

Mr. WEST. Yes.

Mr. BELIN. Did you first go to the domino room and leave your lunch or hang up your coat or anything?

Mr. WEST. No, sir. I just always go right there first. Sometime I pull my coat off and lay it over on the table and go right on.

Mr. BELIN. How long did you stay about making coffee when you got there? How long did you stay around that place when you first got there?

Mr. WEST. Well, let's see, it didn't take me too long. I mean, you know, to make the coffee. After I got it made, I went right on and went right on at my work wrapping mail.

Mr. BELIN. Did you stay in that general area all the time?

Mr. WEST. Sir?

Mr. BELIN. Did you stay in that general location all the time?

Mr. WEST. That was my, all my work was right there on the first floor. I never did—

Mr. BELIN. Did you see Lee Harvey Oswald that morning?

325

Mr. WEST. I did not.

Mr. BELIN. Did you notice Lee Harvey Oswald?

Mr. WEST. Sir?

Mr. BELIN. Did you notice Lee Harvey Oswald?

Mr. WEST. Yes; I had been seeing him every morning, you know. He would come to work. Excepting the morning, I didn't see him that morning at all.

Mr. BELIN. Did you generally see him when he first came to work?

Mr. WEST. Most of the time I see him.

Mr. BELIN. Where did you see him when he first came to work?

Mr. WEST. Well, he would come in and probably I would be on my way back to the rest room, probably to get water in my percolator, or maybe wash the cups or something, and I would see him when he would come in, and I would speak and go right ahead.

Mr. BELIN. What did you say, and what did Lee Harvey Oswald say?

Mr. WEST. I would just say to him, "Good morning," and he said, "Good morning," to me, and he was going right on, and I did.

Mr. BELIN. Did he ever stop and get a cup of coffee?

Mr. WEST. I never did see him stop and get any. I don't know whether he drink coffee or not. He never did stop and get any.

Mr. BELIN. When you would see him, where would he be walking or working when he first came to work in the morning?

Mr. WEST. He would be order filler, and naturally, they have bins, all those bins down there made for stock, and he would be working around in there sometime.

Mr. BELIN. Did you see him when you walked into work, or did you see him after he started working?

Mr. WEST. Well, I would notice him times after he done started working.

Mr. BELIN. You didn't generally see him walking into work, did you, or did you?

Generally, when you would first see him, would he be just walking into work?

Mr. WEST. Be just coming in.

Mr. BELIN. What route would he take when he normally came to work? Do you know what doorway? Did he walk through the front or the back?

Mr. WEST. Well, it is through the back door. He would come in the side door next to the dock on the northeast side.

Mr. BELIN. Then what route would he take when he walked in?

Mr. WEST. Well, he would come right in, and a lot of times I would be mostly, or be passing him, and he would come right in and probably I'd go right on, and I never would see him no more than that he would be on that work, or whatever.

Mr. BELIN. When he came in, for instance, did he go right to an elevator to go upstairs, or did he go over to the domino room, or down to the basement, or where would he go when he would first come in?

Mr. WEST. He would go and pull off his jacket or coat or whatever he had on, and go on to work there.

Mr. BELIN. Well, where would he put his coat when he took it off?

Mr. WEST. Sometimes he would hang it up.

Mr. BELIN. Where?

Mr. WEST. Pretty close to the elevator, or something, or lots of times he would just lay it down on something there in the building.

Mr. BELIN. Did you ever see him take his jacket into the domino room to hang it up?

Mr. WEST. No; I never did see him.

Mr. BELIN. He would either lay his jacket or hang it up by the elevator, or lay it on these boxes where he was working, is that what your testimony is?

Mr. WEST. Yes, sir; he would lay it either close, hang it up on the elevator, or either lay it down.

A lot of times, he would just pull it off and lay it down.

Mr. BELIN. Would he ever take his shirt off and put it down there and just work in a T-shirt?

Mr. WEST. I don't believe I ever seen him working in just a T-shirt. He worked in his shirt all right, but I never did see him work in a T-shirt.

Mr. BELIN. Did you ever see him carrying his lunch inside?

Mr. WEST. No, sir; I never did see him with any lunch.

Mr. BELIN. On the morning of November 22, did you happen to see Buell Wesley Frazier? Do you remember Frazier who worked down there?

Mr. WEST. Yes.

Mr. BELIN. Did you happen to see him come in that morning on November 22, that Friday, if you remember?

Mr. WEST. Well, lots of times I seen him that day, but now I didn't see him when he came in, because I had got busy at working and I might have probably had been in, you know, a good while before I saw him. I didn't see when he came.

Mr. BELIN. Now, I believe you earlier testified you never saw Oswald on November 22?

Mr. WEST. No, sir; I didn't see him that day.

Mr. BELIN. Were you generally at your spot in the west part of the first floor there that you are talking about by the mailing place?

Mr. WEST. Yes.

Mr. BELIN. Were there many days when you would ever see him working down there in the morning near you?

Mr. WEST. No, sir. I had generally been seeing him nearly every morning, excepting that morning I didn't see him at all.

Mr. BELIN. You saw him every morning except that morning?

Mr. WEST. Practically every morning except then.

Mr. BELIN. When did you quit for lunch that day?

Mr. WEST. Well, we always quit at 12 o'clock in the day.

Mr. BELIN. Is that when you quit on November 22d?

Mr. WEST. Yes, sir.

Mr. BELIN. Then what did you do?

Mr. WEST. Well, I went in and washed my hands and face and then got ready to put my coffee on. I always make coffee at 12. Make it in the morning, and then I make it about 12, between 12 and 12:30.

Mr. BELIN. Then what did you do? Did you put your coffee on?

Mr. WEST. Yes, sir.

Mr. BELIN. In the west part of the first floor where you generally work?

Mr. WEST. Yes.

Mr. BELIN. Then what did you do?

Mr. WEST. Well, I went to get my lunch to eat a bite.

Mr. BELIN. Where did you get your lunch?

Mr. WEST. Well, I always kept my lunch right there close by my machine, by my wrapping machine that I use all the time, that I always kept my lunch. I have a little place underneath and I keep it there all the time.

Mr. BELIN. Are you the only one that wraps the books for mailing, or wraps them up for mailing?

Mr. WEST. Well, no, sir; I am not the only one, but mine is that way just every day.

Mr. BELIN. You do it all the time?

Mr. WEST. Yes; I do that.

Mr. BELIN. Are you the only one that does it all the time?

Mr. WEST. I am the only one that is steady, wraps mail all the time, although I have help, you know, when it gets stacked.

Mr. BELIN. Did Lee Harvey Oswald ever help you wrap mail?

Mr. WEST. No sir; he never did.

Mr. BELIN. Do you know whether or not he ever borrowed or used any wrapping paper for himself?

Mr. WEST. No, sir; I don't.

Mr. BELIN. You don't know?

Mr. WEST. No; I don't.

Mr. BELIN. Did you ever see him around these wrapper rolls or wrapper roll machines, or not?

Mr. WEST. No, sir; I never noticed him being around.

Mr. BELIN. Are they paper machines with the rolls of wrapping paper? You have some gum there too, for taping it? When you wrap it, would you tape it with some tape?

Mr. WEST. No, sir; I never noticed him being around.

Mr. BELIN. Did you do that? Did you put tape on the wrapping paper when it was being shipped?

When you wrap the books up with wrapping paper, did you have any gum tape that you put on it?

Mr. WEST. No, sir; I had a machine that I placed it on the machine and tied it with, and the machine tied it with a string.

Mr. BELIN. With string?

327

Mr. WEST. Yes, sir.

Mr. BELIN. Didn't you have any gummed tape by your machine?

Mr. WEST. Sir?

Mr. BELIN. Did you have any kind of a tape, sticky tape that you would put on the paper to keep it together, or was that somewhere else?

Mr. WEST. Oh, yes, sir; I used some of that wide tape.

Mr. BELIN. Is that sticky tape?

Mr. WEST. Yes, sir.

Mr. BELIN. To seal the package with?

Mr. WEST. Yes, sir; that's right.

And then I tie it, put it on the machine and then tie it.

Mr. BELIN. Is yours the only place that they have the sticky tape?

Mr. WEST. Well, that is the only place that is supposed to be, you know.

Mr. BELIN. Could other employees come and pick up some of the tape for themselves?

Mr. WEST. Yes, sir; they could come get it if they wanted to use it, but all the time it was there where it is supposed to be.

Mr. BELIN. Did other employees from time to time come and borrow some of that tape at all, or use it?

Would other employees ever use any of that tape for themselves?

Mr. WEST. Not as I know of now.

Mr. BELIN. If I wanted to use any of that tape, you know that tape that you use to seal it, is there a way to make tape wet so I don't have to lick it myself with my tongue to make it wet and sticky? Or how did you get it to be sticky and stick together?

Mr. WEST. Well, we have those machines with the little round ball that we fill them up with water, and so we set them up. In to—other words, I got a rack that we set them in, and so we put out tape in a machine, and whenever we pull the tape through, why then the water gets, you know, it gets water on it as we pull it through.

Mr. BELIN. If I wanted to pull the tape, pull off a piece without getting water on it, would I just lift it up without going over the wet roller and get the tape without getting it wet?

Mr. WEST. You would have to take it out. You would have to take it out of the machine. See, it's put on there and then run through a little clamp that holds it down, and you pull it, well, then the water, it gets water on it.

Mr. BELIN. Is this an electrical machine or is it just kind of a little apparatus for just pulling it through by hand?

Mr. WEST. Well, it is not electric, no, sir.

Mr. BELIN. Now going back to November 22, you said you quit for lunch around noon on that day on Friday, November 22?

Mr. WEST. Yes. About 12 o'clock we always quit for lunch.

Mr. BELIN. Do you remember any of the men coming down the elevator that day? Bonnie Ray Williams or James Jarman, Jr., or Danny Arce, or any one else coming down that morning? Charlie Givens?

Do you remember them coming down the elevator, or don't you remember?

Mr. WEST. I don't remember.

Mr. BELIN. Now, after you quit for lunch, you made the coffee then?

Mr. WEST. Yes, sir.

Mr. BELIN. Where did you make the coffee?

Mr. WEST. I made the coffee right there close to the wrapping mail table where I wrap mail.

Mr. BELIN. Then what did you do?

Mr. WEST. Well, I sit down to eat my lunch.

Mr. BELIN. Then what did you do?

Mr. WEST. Well, I had just, after I made coffee, I just had started to eat my lunch because I was a little hungry—I didn't eat anything that morning before I went to work—and I had started to eat my lunch.

But before I got through, well, all of this was, I mean, the police and things was coming in, and I was just spellbound. I just didn't know what was the matter. So I didn't get through eating. I had to eat about half my lunch, and that is all.

Mr. BELIN. Did you hear any shots fired?

Mr. WEST. I didn't hear a one. Didn't hear a one.

Mr. BELIN. Did you see anyone else on the first floor while you were eating your lunch? Anyone else at all did you see on the first floor?

Mr. WEST. It wasn't anybody. I didn't see anybody around at that time.

Mr. BELIN. At any time while you were making coffee or eating your lunch, did you see anyone else on the first floor?

Mr. WEST. No, sir; I didn't see.

Mr. BELIN. Who was the first person you saw on the first floor after you—while you were eating your lunch? Someone came in the building?

Mr. WEST. Yes; before I got through. The officers and things were coming in the front door.

Mr. BELIN. Who was the first person or persons that you saw coming through there while you were eating your lunch?

Mr. WEST. Well, that was police.

Mr. BELIN. A police officer?

Mr. WEST. Yes, sir.

Mr. BELIN. Anyone else?

Mr. WEST. I guess it was a bunch of them, I guess, FBI men, and just a crowd of them coming in there.

Mr. BELIN. Did you see Roy Truly coming in at all that time? Do you know Mr. Truly?

Mr. WEST. Yes, sir; that is the boss, the superintendent.

Mr. BELIN. Did you ever see him, do you remember, while you were eating your lunch, come in the building?

Mr. WEST. Yes, sir; I think he came in with the police.

Mr. BELIN. Was he one of the first people in, or did other people come in ahead of him, if you remember?

Mr. WEST. Really, I just don't know.

Mr. BELIN. That is okay if you don't remember. That is all I want you to say if you don't remember.

Did you hear anyone yelling to let the elevator loose or anything like that?

Mr. WEST. I can't remember.

Mr. BELIN. Were you working when you were eating your lunch? Were you facing the elevator or not when you were eating your lunch? Were you facing any of the elevators back there?

Mr. WEST. No, sir; I was always—I mean I would always be with my back kind of, you know, towards the elevators and facing the front side over on the side.

Mr. BELIN. The Elm Street side?

Mr. WEST. Toward Elm Street side.

Mr. BELIN. So you don't know whether anyone was using the elevators?

Mr. WEST. No, sir; I don't.

Mr. BELIN. Do you know whether anyone was going up and down the stairs?

Mr. WEST. No, sir; I don't.

Mr. BELIN. Do you know anything else about what happened on November 22, that might be helpful or relevant here?

Mr. WEST. No, sir; I don't really.

Mr. BELIN. Were you ever on the second floor on November 22?

Mr. WEST. No, sir; I never did hardly ever leave the first floor. That is just I stayed there where all my work was, and I just stayed there.

Mr. BELIN. On November 22, did you ever leave the first floor?

Mr. WEST. No, sir; I never did leave the first floor.

Mr. BELIN. Anything else that you can think of, whether I have asked it or not?

Mr. WEST. Well, I don't know anything else. I know of nothing else.

Mr. BELIN. Well, we thank you very much for coming down here, Mr. West. If you want, you can come back down again and read your deposition and sign it, or else you can just waive coming down here. You don't have to come down. You can tell the court reporter to send it directly to us, if you want to.

Mr. WEST. You mean when I get ready to sign it?

Mr. BELIN. Now you do not have to sign it if you don't want to. You can just tell the court reporter to type it up and send it directly to us, or you can tell the court reporter you would like to read it and sign it before she sends it to us in Washington.

You don't have to sign it. Or if you want to sign it, you can come back and sign it, whichever you want to do.

Mr. WEST. Well, I think—I don't know.

Mr. BELIN. Do you want to come down here again and read it and sign it, or do you want to waive?

You can waive and tell the court reporter that she can just send it after she types it up, directly to us in Washington without your reading it and signing it.

Mr. WEST. Well, I think that is what I will do, just have it waived and send it on.

Mr. BELIN. All right, that is fine.

Thank you very much, sir.

TESTIMONY OF DANNY G. ARCE

The testimony of Danny G. Arce was taken at 2:15 p.m., on April 7, 1964, in the office of the U.S. attorney, 301 Post Office Building, Bryan and Ervay Streets, Dallas, Tex., by Messrs. Joseph A. Ball and Samuel A. Stern, assistant counsel of the President's Commission.

Mr. BALL. Will you stand up and raise your right hand?

Do you solemnly swear the testimony you are about to give will be the truth, the whole truth, and nothing but the truth, so help you God?

Mr. ARCE. Yes, sir.

Mr. BALL. State your name, please.

Mr. ARCE. Danny Garcia Arce.

Mr. BALL. Where do you live?

Mr. ARCE. 1502 Bennett Avenue.

Mr. BALL. Will you tell me something about yourself, where you were born and where you went to school?

Mr. ARCE. I was born here in Dallas and I went to Stephen F. Foster Elementary school and Alex W. Spence Junior High and Crozier Tech.

Mr. BALL. Then what did you do?

Mr. ARCE. Well, I quit school and found a job and worked.

Mr. BALL. Where did you find a job?

Mr. ARCE. The first job, well, you don't want——

Mr. BALL. No; just in general.

Mr. ARCE. Oh, I worked as a cook, short order cook and busboy, and just odd jobs at this Rubenstein place on Hall—Rubenstein and Sons. I haven't had too many jobs.

Mr. BALL. What is Rubenstein and Son, a restaurant?

Mr. ARCE. No; kind of an oyster place; they pack them and send them out, I guess.

Mr. BALL. What else have you done?

Mr. ARCE. That's about all.

Mr. BALL. When did you go to work for the Texas School Book Depository?

Mr. ARCE. I started in September—September, I believe, the 6th, September 6th.

Mr. BALL. Of what year?

Mr. ARCE. 1963.

Mr. BALL. You received a letter from the Commission asking you to appear here, didn't you?

Mr. ARCE. Yes, sir.

Mr. BALL. You understand the purpose of the investigation?

Mr. ARCE. Yes.

Mr. BALL. To determine the facts surrounding the assassination of the President, President Kennedy.

Mr. ARCE. Yes, sir.

Mr. BALL. You started to work in September 1963, this last September?

Mr. ARCE. Yes; last September.

Mr. BALL. What kind of work were you employed to do?

Mr. ARCE. Order filler.

Mr. BALL. What building did you work in?

Mr. ARCE. At the warehouse.

Mr. BALL. At Houston and Elm?

Mr. ARCE. No; that's on——

Mr. BALL. Which is this?

Mr. ARCE. That's the one behind it; directly behind the Texas School Book Depository at Elm and Houston.

Mr. BALL. You worked there most of the time as an order filler?

Mr. ARCE. Yes, sir.

Mr. BALL. Did you ever work over at the building at 411 Elm?

Mr. ARCE. Yes, sir; they were short of help up there and they sent me and the other boy down there.

Mr. BALL. Who is the other boy?

Mr. ARCE. Bonnie Ray Williams.

Mr. BALL. They sent you out to do what?

Mr. ARCE. Help lay out a floor on the sixth floor.

Mr. BALL. What date did they send you down there?

Mr. ARCE. Sir, I don't remember.

Mr. BALL. October?

Mr. ARCE. I know I had been there about 4 weeks when all that happened; I believe 4 or 5 weeks. I am not too sure about that.

Mr. BALL. You mean 4 or 5 weeks before November 22, 1963?

Mr. ARCE. Yeah.

Mr. BALL. Were you laying floor at that time?

Mr. ARCE. Yes, sir; we laid floor on the fifth and then we were on the sixth when this happened.

Mr. BALL. Did you ever meet a fellow named Lee Oswald?

Mr. ARCE. Yeah, he worked with us and he didn't associate with us too much. He was kind of quiet. He didn't like to talk too much to us or anything.

Mr. BALL. You say he worked with you; did he work laying floors?

Mr. ARCE. No, he was an order filler; he just worked the same place.

Mr. BALL. Did you ever see him on the sixth floor?

Mr. ARCE. Yeah, quite a few times.

Mr. BALL. Ever see him on the first floor?

Mr. ARCE. Uh-huh.

Mr. BALL. Did you ever eat lunch with him?

Mr. ARCE. We all eat lunch together in this little domino room. We play dominoes and eat our lunch. He might walk in and lay around with us and he would walk out. He didn't stay in there too long. I guess he didn't like crowds.

Mr. BALL. On the 22d of November, what time did you go to work?

Mr. ARCE. We start at eight but I believe I was a little late.

Mr. BALL. You went to work on what floor?

Mr. ARCE. Sixth.

Mr. BALL. Did you work there all morning?

Mr. ARCE. Yes, sir.

Mr. BALL. What time did you get off work?

Mr. ARCE. That day?

Mr. BALL. At noon for your lunch hour or your lunch period?

Mr. ARCE. What time we left down for lunch?

Mr. BALL. Yes.

Mr. ARCE. We usually leave down about 5 to 12, something around there.

Mr. BALL. How did you go down stairs?

Mr. ARCE. By the elevator.

Mr. BALL. Did you have sort of a race that day, do you remember?

Mr. ARCE. Yeah.

Mr. BALL. Tell me about it.

Mr. ARCE. Well, me and Bonnie Ray and, I am not too sure, I believe it was Billy Lovelady, were on the same elevator, and Charles Givens and the other guys were on the other one and we were racing down.

Mr. BALL. Which elevator were you on?

Mr. ARCE. We have two of them that go up, the same deal and I was on the one facing east. There's an east and a west elevator and I was in the one facing east.

Mr. BALL. Did you see Lee Oswald or hear him speak on the way down?

Mr. ARCE. Yeah, he was up there and I believe someone asked if he wanted to go down.

Mr. BALL. He was there—on what floor?

Mr. ARCE. That's what I'm not too sure; I believe he was on five or the sixth floor. I am not too sure but we were going down and I believe he was on the fifth; I am not too sure.

Mr. BALL. What did you hear?

Mr. ARCE. He said "You all close the door on the elevator, I will be down," or somethin'. I didn't pay too much attention. He said to leave the elevator come down.

Mr. BALL. Did you ever see him around there after that?

Mr. ARCE. No, I didn't see him around after that.

Mr. BALL. Did you have lunch?

Mr. ARCE. Yeah.

Mr. BALL. Where?

Mr. ARCE. In that little domino room there.

Mr. BALL. Where did you go after that?

Mr. ARCE. I went outside.

Mr. BALL. With whom?

Mr. ARCE. With Billy Lovelady and Mr. Shelley and I was out there with Junior.

Mr. BALL. Who is Junior?

Mr. ARCE. I don't know his real name; I just know him by Junior.

Mr. BALL. Was Bonnie Ray Williams ever out there with you?

Mr. ARCE. No, he stayed upstairs with Hank. Junior stayed up there but he was down a little while and I guess he went upstairs.

Mr. BALL. What about Givens?

Mr. ARCE. He was down there with Shields, I guess—I mean Melvin—no, Carl, that's who he was with.

Mr. BALL. What about Jack Dougherty?

Mr. ARCE. He was on all floors; I couldn't tell you where he was.

Mr. BALL. Was he outside?

Mr. ARCE. No, he was eating lunch; me and Jack Dougherty, same time.

Mr. BALL. Dougherty ate his lunch?

Mr. ARCE. Yes, sir.

Mr. BALL. Did he go outdoors after lunch?

Mr. ARCE. I don't know; I didn't see him.

Mr. BALL. Who went outdoors with you?

Mr. ARCE. Bill Shelley and Billy Lovelady; Carl was out there and Charles Givens.

Mr. BALL. You stood there how long before the parade came along?

Mr. ARCE. I am not too sure; it was about 10 minutes, somewhere around there. I am not too sure about that.

Mr. BALL. Did you see the President go by?

Mr. ARCE. Yeah, I did. I seen him when he turned the corner and when he went down that underpass thing and I heard them shots and I couldn't see anything. There was a lot of people.

Mr. BALL. Where were you standing when you heard the shots?

Mr. ARCE. I was standing in front of the Texas School Book Depository. I was on that grassy area part in front.

Mr. BALL. You were not on the sidewalk?

Mr. ARCE. No, I was on the sidewalk, then I walked up to the grass to get a higher view and still couldn't see.

Mr. BALL. Did you hear shots?

Mr. ARCE. Yeah.

Mr. BALL. How many?

Mr. ARCE. Three.

Mr. BALL. Where did you make out the direction of the sound?

Mr. ARCE. Yeah, I thought they came from the railroad tracks to the west of the Texas School Book Depository.

Mr. BALL. When you were on the grass, were you south where you were? Where were you with reference to the entrance to the Texas School Book Depository?

Mr. ARCE. I was down to the west side, a little more to the west.

Mr. BALL. Were you west of the building itself?

Mr. ARCE. Yeah.

Mr. BALL. You were not in front of the building?

Mr. ARCE. I was directly in front, but then I walked a few steps down to the west side.

Mr. BALL. Where were you with reference to the west wall of the building?

Mr. ARCE. Oh, I was way far from it. I was across the street, I mean.

Mr. BALL. What do you mean "across the street"?

Mr. ARCE. Well, there's a little sidewalk right across the street and there's some grass and things up there and that's where I was at. I couldn't tell you exactly where I was, see, it's hard to explain.

Mr. BALL. Well, you say you were not in front of the building?

Mr. ARCE. Well, not directly, not in front; I was across the street.

Mr. BALL. And were you west of the west wall of the building?

Mr. ARCE. Well, I was, well the building——

Mr. BALL. I understand but you were to the south of the building. You had to be south of the building, didn't you?

Mr. ARCE. Well, I was south but I was, well, I guess you could say I was in front of the building but not directly in front, well, I don't know how to explain it.

Mr. BALL. Who was standing with you?

Mr. ARCE. Well, I walked away from the other guys because they were all in front of the building and I went across the street to get a closer view.

Mr. BALL. You walked which direction?

Mr. ARCE. I just—right across the street.

Mr. BALL. Right across Elm Street?

Mr. ARCE. Uh-huh.

Mr. BALL. The part of Elm that dead ends there?

Mr. ARCE. Yeah.

Mr. BALL. You crossed that and went on to the grassy part?

Mr. ARCE. Uh-huh.

Mr. BALL. Now, it sounded to you that the shots came from what direction?

Mr. ARCE. From the tracks on the west deal.

Mr. BALL. How many shots did you hear?

Mr. ARCE. Three.

Mr. BALL. Did you look back at the building?

Mr. ARCE. No, I didn't think they came from there. I just looked directly to the railroad tracks and all the people started running up there and I just ran along with them.

Mr. BALL. Did you go up to the railroad tracks?

Mr. ARCE. Yeah.

Mr. BALL. Did you see anything up there?

Mr. ARCE. No, and they told us go back there and I went back inside the building.

Mr. BALL. Where did you go then?

Mr. ARCE. Back inside the building.

Mr. BALL. How long did you stay in there?

Mr. ARCE. Oh, about 15 minutes and they took us down to city hall to make statements out.

Mr. BALL. Then you made out your statement?

Mr. ARCE. Yes, sir; to the Police Department.

Mr. BALL. Well, just I minute, let's see——

Mr. ARCE. I helped this old man, this gentleman in there.

Mr. BALL. You saw an old man?

Mr. ARCE. Yeah.

Mr. BALL. Where?

Mr. ARCE. Right in front of the Texas School Book Depository.

Mr. BALL. When?

Mr. ARCE. Right, you know, it was before it happened; I don't know.

Mr. BALL. How long before the President went by?

Mr. ARCE. I don't know. I think it was about 10 minutes, some place around there, 15 minutes; I'm not too sure.

Mr. BALL. What about the old man; what was noticeable about him?

Mr. ARCE. Well, he said he had kidney trouble, could I direct him to the men's room and I said I would and I helped him up the steps and walked him into the restroom and I opened the door for him and that's when I went inside to eat my lunch and then I seen him walk out.

Mr. BALL. Did you see him talk to anyone in there?

Mr. ARCE. No; he went straight out.

Mr. BALL. Was he in a car?

Mr. ARCE. Yeah, after I went outside I seen him driving out in a black car.

Mr. BALL. He drove away?

Mr. ARCE. Yes, sir.

Mr. BALL. Did you ever see him again?

Mr. ARCE. No, never seen him again.

Mr. BALL. Just I minute, I want to show you a picture. I show you Commission Exhibit No. 369. I show you this picture. See this man in this picture?

Mr. ARCE. Yeah.

Mr. BALL. Recognize him?

Mr. ARCE. Yes, that's Billy Lovelady.

333

Mr. BALL. Just to identify it clearly, the man on the steps—well, you see the man on the steps, do you not?

Mr. ARCE. Yes, sir.

Mr. BALL. He is a white man, isn't he?

Mr. ARCE. Yes, sir.

Mr. BALL. And you see his picture just above the picture of two colored people, is that correct; would you describe it like that?

Mr. ARCE. Yes, sir.

Mr. BALL. I am not going to mark this purposely because other witnesses have to see it.

Mr. ARCE. Yes.

Mr. BALL. Did you say that is Billy Lovelady?

Mr. ARCE. Yes, that is Billy Lovelady.

Mr. BALL. Now, there is only one face that is clearly shown within the entrance-way of the Texas School Book Depository Building, isn't there?

Mr. ARCE. Yes, sir.

Mr. BALL. And only one face of a person who is standing on the steps of the Depository Building entrance?

Mr. ARCE. Yeah.

Mr. BALL. And that one man you see there——

Mr. ARCE. Yes, that's Billy Lovelady.

Mr. BALL. When you came to work that morning, Danny——

Mr. ARCE. Yeah.

Mr. BALL. Was Oswald there at the time?

Mr. ARCE. I believe I seen him once that morning on the first floor, some place around there. I'm not too sure.

Mr. BALL. But did you see him go into the building?

Mr. ARCE. No, sir; I didn't.

Mr. BALL. Did you ever see him have in his possession any paper bag or sack that day?

Mr. ARCE. No, sir; I didn't see him.

Mr. BALL. This will be written up and you will have an opportunity to read it and sign it if you wish or you can waive signature. Which do you wish? If you waive signature, you don't have to come back. Which do you prefer? Do either one.

Mr. ARCE. I don't understand too well.

Mr. BALL. She writes this up. Then if you wish, you can come in, read it over and, if there are any changes to be made, you make them and you swear to it before this young lady, who is a notary public, or you can waive signature and we will send it on to the Commission.

Mr. ARCE. I guess you all could send it on to the Commission.

Mr. BALL. And you waive signature?

Mr. ARCE. Yes.

Mr. BALL. Thanks very much for coming in.

TESTIMONY OF JOE R. MOLINA

The testimony of Joe R. Molina was taken at 4:50 p.m., on April 7, 1964, in the office of the U.S. attorney, 301 Post Office Building, Bryan and Ervay Streets, Dallas, Tex., by Messrs. Joseph A. Ball and Samuel A. Stern, assistant counsel of the President's Commission.

Mr. BALL. Would you rise and raise your right hand, Mr. Molina?

(Witness complying.)

Mr. BALL. Do you solemnly swear the testimony you are about to give will be the truth, the whole truth, and nothing but the truth, so help you God?

Mr. MOLINA. I do.

Mr. BALL. Will you state your name, please?

Mr. MOLINA. Joe R. Molina.

Mr. BALL. What is your address?

Mr. MOLINA. 4306 Brown.

Mr. BALL. Tell me something about yourself; where were you born?

Mr. MOLINA. I was born here in Dallas.

Mr. BALL. What was your education?

Mr. MOLINA. Well, I went to Crozier Tech High School and I finished after I came back from the service and at that time my intention was to go to college but I got married and instead went to business college. Then later on after attending about 5 months business college, I had to find a job because my wife was expecting a baby, consequently, I started working on-the-job training at the Texas School Book Depository.

Mr. BALL. About what date?

Mr. MOLINA. I started working in February of 1947.

Mr. BALL. How long have you been working there?

Mr. MOLINA. 16 years.

Mr. BALL. 16 years?

Mr. MOLINA. Yes, sir.

Mr. BALL. Now, you wrote the Commission a letter asking to testify, didn't you?

Mr. MOLINA. Yes.

Mr. BALL. How did you happen to do that?

Mr. MOLINA. Well, I called in. I didn't know whether I was going to be called or not and they told me, you know, that I should write a letter and ask the Commission, you know. (Letter marked Molina Exhibit A.)

Mr. BALL. You wanted to be heard, is that right, before the Commission?

Mr. MOLINA. Yes, sir.

Mr. BALL. Did you have something particularly you wanted to tell us?

Mr. MOLINA. Yes, sir.

Mr. BALL. What is that?

Mr. MOLINA. Well, on November 23d following the assassination, I was paid a visit by the local police department at 1:30 in the morning and they sort of wanted to tie me up with this case in some way or another and they thought that I was implicated.

Mr. BALL. What makes you think they thought you were implicated?

Mr. MOLINA. Well, they were looking for something. I don't know what it was they were looking for in the house.

Mr. BALL. They came to your house here in Dallas?

Mr. MOLINA. That's right, woke up my wife and children; scared my wife half to death.

Mr. BALL. Did they search the house?

Mr. MOLINA. Yes.

Mr. BALL. Did they have a search warrant?

Mr. MOLINA. I don't know whether they did or not.

Mr. BALL. Did they tell you what they were looking for?

Mr. MOLINA. No.

Mr. BALL. Then what happened?

Mr. MOLINA. Well, they asked me questions whether I knew different persons that belong to the G.I. Forum——

Mr. BALL. To what?

Mr. MOLINA. G.I. Forum, this club I belonged to here in Dallas.

Mr. BALL. How do you spell that?

Mr. MOLINA. G.I. F-o-r-u-m [spelling].

Mr. BALL. G.I. F-o-r-u-m [spelling] in Dallas?

Mr. MOLINA. Yes.

Mr. BALL. Who was it that asked you that?

Mr. MOLINA. Well, I think it was Mr. Garroway did most of the questioning and police Lieutenant Revill, I believe—yeah, that was his name.

Mr. BALL. What did they ask you?

Mr. MOLINA. They asked me if I knew certain persons that had come into the forum when it was first initiated and if I was acquainted with them and if I associated with them, so forth and so on. I said my activities were limited to the club. I didn't have any social, you know, I wasn't intimate with them but merely a club that was started. I was asked by my pastor to go see about this particular club which I did and consequently, the club met at the church auditorium after it was founded and one of the parish priests was a chaplain.

Mr. BALL. Was it a Catholic, Roman Catholic organization?

Mr. MOLINA. The G.I. Forum?

Mr. BALL. Yes.

Mr. MOLINA. No; the forum is a veterans' club.

Mr. BALL. What else happened?

Mr. MOLINA. Well, after the police came, they didn't know whether—they were undecided what to do, whether they would take me in for questioning or not and so they decided evidently, since I told them—they asked me if they could take a look around. I said "Sure, I don't have anything to hide, look around". They looked around and did a lot of searching and my wife started to get back in bed. She didn't know that was going on. She thought they just want to question me and they told her she had to get out of bed and go into the living room and the kids were in the back room. I only have two bedrooms and the kids were sleeping out there. They woke up the kids; they were looking in their room, so they started questioning the kids, too. They started to ask me questions and ask the kids about it. In other words, to corroborate our statements. I didn't know at the time they were doing it but later on found out. They couldn't find anything. I knew they wouldn't find anything. I didn't know what they were looking for in the first place. They decided to bring me down to the Dallas Police Department for questioning.

Mr. BALL. Did you go down to the police department?

Mr. MOLINA. Well, they asked me if I would go down the next morning and I said yes, I would go down the next morning. I would rather go down the next morning than now. It was already past 2, so the next morning my wife drove me down. I got there about 11. My wife drove me down and I got there about 10:30. The place was full of television people and reporters swarming all over the place and they told me to wait in the room there and then I went into Chief Gannaway's office or whatever his name is. He said I was supposed to be questioned by Mr. Fritz down there but that he wanted to talk to me after they questioned me up there because they wanted to know more about the G.I. Forum so I said "I will come back when they get through questioning me." So I went up there and they told me to wait in an office and so I waited there for about 30, 40 minutes and, oh, must have been longer than that, they finally questioned me and they put me in a room and there was a man from the FBI or Secret Service, I don't recall which one it was. He was sitting on my right and there was a fellow from the Dallas Police Department taking a statement and a fellow from the FBI introduced himself, said I'm so and so, show me his badge and so forth. The other fellow didn't say who he was or anything, just sat there and so then they told me to wait there in that room and I did. I was there for about 45 minutes and then the fellow came back from the FBI, said "My God, are you still in here?" I said "Yes," he said "How long you been here?" Here it was about 2 or 3 o'clock. I said "I have been here since about 11; I haven't eaten lunch or haven't had a drink of water". You know, I was just there and which he told this fellow, said "Can't you let him go; he has been here. He has already given his testimony statement, whatever he is going to give; you should let him go." This fellow said "No, he got to wait in ▨▨▨ there" so I had to go back in there; about 10 or 15 minutes later, they came back and I went up to the office of Lieutenant Revill and he started asking a lot of questions about the G.I. Forum, did I know such and such fellow—some I knew, they had been in the club. Naturally, I knew them though we weren't intimate friends, some were, some weren't. Then he gave me a bunch of names, I imagine they were in their so-called subversive files that they claim they have; of course, I didn't know a lot of them. In fact, I didn't know most of them. I knew some of the names. I didn't know some of the names they mentioned are kept in their files or not. Anyhow, they asked me—I had to—they didn't ask me—I had to just ask to sign a statement I belonged to the forum and certain members were charter members of the forum and I said yes, I would sign it. I didn't see anything wrong with it so I signed it and they told me I could go home. It was 4:30 or 5 and they asked me if I had a ride home and I said no. They said "Well, we'll give you a ride home, so one of the officers there, plainclothes man, drove me home. When I got home, of course, there were about three or four cars at the house. My wife was all shook up and she said "My God" she said "Don't you know what they been saying about you?" I said "No, I don't know what they are saying about me." She said "Don't you know you been on TV and the news media across the nation saying you are on the so-called list with the Dallas Police Department claiming that you associate with persons of"—see if I can quote it right—I was known to associate with persons of subversive background.

Mr. BALL. That was on TV?

Mr. MOLINA. Oh, yes.

Mr. BALL. Who put that on TV?

Mr. MOLINA. It was a statement made by Chief Curry.

Mr. BALL. By whom?

Mr. MOLINA. Chief Curry and I says "No, I didn't know anything about it. I was just being questioned." They said "Well, did you tell them to release your name?" I said "I don't know who gave my name out, gave out the information." So, they were very concerned because at first, I didn't think it was—I figured they would make a retraction and I would be cleared, so forth and so on and nothing came out on the radio and nothing was said and I called the Police Department and told them I wanted to talk to Chief Curry and they said he was busy. I was talking to, I think someone, fellow named King. He answered the phone and he said any retraction has to come from Chief Curry. I called the Associated Press which released the statement to the news media and they wouldn't give me any satisfaction. They told me I would have to get in touch with some fellow in New York or something like that, so that was—I couldn't get any satisfaction. I was accused of something I didn't know anything about.

Mr. BALL. Did they ever give you a retraction?

Mr. MOLINA. No.

Mr. BALL. Well, now——

Mr. MOLINA. And, consequently, well, that happened on November 23d; my boss was very upset about it. He said that the vice president of the company, Mr. Campbell, they didn't say anything to me, they didn't come to me and say "Joe, we will stand by you, we don't believe it." Nothing was said for about 10 days so I went in and told them, I said, "You don't have to be afraid, I'm going to get this thing cleared. I am going to find somebody to clear me of this." They said "You better do it very fast because the president is very upset about it and we have been getting a lot of calls and several people calling in and saying he hires subversives" and so forth and so on. I saw one letter did say that. It came to them from some fellow said he wasn't going to do business with that book firm because they hired Communists. I knew they were probably under pressure. Well, on December 13, they called me in and said they wanted to talk with me and they told me that due to automation I was going to have to be replaced. That happened in December 13, about 3 weeks afterwards so I told them I said "I don't really think that's the reason why you're letting me go, it's probably because of this other thing." He said "No, we got automation here, we are taking too much business in so we have to let you go." No news was ever given to me there was no machines for replacement,   nothing, so I said—well, I didn't leave until December 30 and got all the routine work I had been assigned was gradually shifted to another person. I was there doing nothing. I finally left December 30 and I have received a letter from a friend in California saying my name was in the paper stating that I had been labeled as a communist and I got a call from Florida, from a good friend of mine saying they labeled me a communist and saying I was a friend of Oswald's.

Mr. BALL. Did you know him?

Mr. MOLINA. Oswald?

Mr. BALL. Yes.

Mr. MOLINA. No; I had seen him there in the building. I had seen him but never talked with him or been introduced.

Mr. BALL. Where are you working now?

Mr. MOLINA. I am working over here—that's another thing. I couldn't find a job. Who is going to hire me? So I called this friend of mine he belonged to the Dads Club where I go to church, Holy Trinity. His name is Mr. Redman, vice president at Neuhoff's. I called him about a job and he said "No, I don't have anything in your line of work." I happened to mention to him I used to do credit union work and at that time they happened to be looking for a man and that's the reason I found this particular job.

Mr. BALL. You are working at Neuhoff's Employees Credit Union?

Mr. MOLINA. Yes.

Mr. BALL. Are you a bookkeeper; is that what you usually do is bookkeeping?

Mr. MOLINA. Yes.

Mr. BALL. Did you pursue it any further; did you file any actions of any sort?

Mr. MOLINA. I have an attorney that is working towards something.

Mr. BALL. You went to work what date——

Mr. MOLINA. I went to work in February 1947.

Mr. BALL. For the Texas School Book Depository at that time.

Mr. MOLINA. Yes; at that time they were located at 2210 Pacific.

Mr. BALL. Now, November 22, 1963, the place you worked was in the second floor of this School Book Depository Building?

Mr. MOLINA. Yes, sir.

Mr. BALL. Did you go out on the street to see the motorcade?

Mr. MOLINA. Yes; I was standing on the front steps.

Mr. BALL. With whom?

Mr. MOLINA. Right next left of me was Mr. Williams and close to there was Mrs. Sanders.

Mr. BALL. Pauline Sanders?

Mr. MOLINA. Yes.

Mr. BALL. Did you see Roy Truly?

Mr. MOLINA. Yes; he was standing with Mr. Campbell; they were going out to lunch.

Mr. BALL. They were in front of you were they?

Mr. MOLINA. Yes.

Mr. BALL. You saw the President's car pass?

Mr. MOLINA. Yes.

Mr. BALL. Did you see anything after that?

Mr. MOLINA. Well, I heard the shots.

Mr. BALL. Where—what was the source of the sound?

Mr. MOLINA. Sort of like it reverberated, sort of kind of came from the west side; that was the first impression I got. Of course, the first shot was fired then there was an interval between the first and second longer than the second and third.

Mr. BALL. What did you do after that?

Mr. MOLINA. Well, I just stood there, everybody was running and I didn't know what to do actually, because what could I do. I was just shocked.

Mr. BALL. Did anybody say anything?

Mr. MOLINA. Yes, this fellow come to me—Mr. Williams said, somebody said, somebody was shooting at the President, somebody, I don't know who it was. There was some shooting, you know, and this fellow said "What can anybody gain ⬜ by that"; he just shook his head and I just stood there and shook my head. I didn't want to think what was happening, you know, but I wanted to find out so I went down to where the grassy slope is, you know, and I was trying to gather pieces of conversation of the people that had been close by there and somebody said "Well, the President has been shot and I think they shot somebody else", something like that.

Mr. BALL. Did you see Mr. Truly go into the building?

Mr. MOLINA. Yes.

Mr. BALL. Where were you when you saw him go into the building?

Mr. MOLINA. I was right in the entrance.

Mr. BALL. Did you see a police officer with him?

Mr. MOLINA. I didn't see a police officer. I don't recall seeing a police officer but I did see him go inside.

Mr. BALL. Did you see a white-helmeted police officer any time there in the entrance?

Mr. MOLINA. Well, of course, there might have been one after they secured the building, you know.

Mr. BALL. No, I mean when Truly went in; did you see Truly actually go into the building?

Mr. MOLINA. I saw him go in.

Mr. BALL. Where were you standing?

Mr. MOLINA. Right at the front door; right at the front door.

Mr. BALL. Outside the front door?

Mr. MOLINA. Yes, outside the front door I was standing; the door was right behind me.

Mr. BALL. Were you standing on the steps?

Mr. MOLINA. Yes, on the uppermost step.

Mr. BALL. You actually saw Truly go in?

Mr. MOLINA. Yeah.

Mr. BALL. You were still standing there?

Mr. MOLINA. Yes.

Mr. BALL. How long was it after you heard the shots?

Mr. MOLINA. Oh, I would venture to say maybe 20 or 30 seconds afterwards.

Mr. BALL. Had somebody come up and said the President was shot before you saw Truly go in?

Mr. MOLINA. No.

Mr. BALL. Do you know a girl named Gloria Calvary?

Mr. MOLINA. Yes.

Mr. BALL. Did Gloria come up?

Mr. MOLINA. Yes, she came. I was in the lobby standing there and she came in with this other girl.

Mr. BALL. What did she say?

Mr. MOLINA. She said "Oh, my God, Joe, he's been shot." They were both horrified. I said "Are you sure he was shot?" She said "Oh, Joe, I'm sure. I saw his hair fly up and I'm sure he was shot" something to that extent.

Mr. BALL. You left the building that day about what time and went home?

Mr. MOLINA. Oh, it must have been around, I would say, I would say it was about 2, maybe a little before that, I don't know.

Mr. BALL. Had you ever seen Lee Oswald?

Mr. MOLINA. I had seen him in the building, yes, sir.

Mr. BALL. Did you ever speak to him?

Mr. MOLINA. No; I never spoke to him.

Mr. BALL. Did you see him at all on November 22d?

Mr. MOLINA. I never did see him.

Mr. BALL. Did you see any strangers in the building on that day November 22d?

Mr. MOLINA. No; like I stated before, I came in at—to work at 7 in the morning because I had a key and I was on the second floor all the time, never did leave except maybe to go to the restroom, something like that. Then I ate my lunch, took my lunch and ate it and went downstairs about 12:15.

Mr. BALL. Okay, thanks very much, Mr. Molina. This will be written up for your signature if you wish; you can come in and sign it or you can waive   your signature, whichever you wish. If you wish to sign it, this young lady will notify you when it is typed and you can come in, read it, and sign it.

Mr. MOLINA. I just wanted to state in the record that I want to deny any accusations if there is any doubt in anybody's mind.

Mr. BALL. No; there is nobody I ever heard has accused you of anything.

Mr. MOLINA. I know there's a fella that I talk with that belongs to the or had worked with the FBI that knows my position in this thing.

Mr. BALL. I never heard anybody accuse you of any wrongdoing in connection with this matter.

Mr. MOLINA. In fact, Bill Lowery worked with the FBI.

Mr. BALL. You don't have to worry about that; no one is accusing you of anything.

Mr. MOLINA. Except the local people here.

Mr. BALL. Do you want to sign it or do you want to waive your signature; how do you feel about it? It's your option; you can do either way.

Mr. MOLINA. Well, I would like to.

Mr. BALL. See it and sign it?

Mr. MOLINA. See it and sign it.

Mr. BALL. She will notify you then. She will tell you when to come in.

Mr. MOLINA. Thanks very much.

TESTIMONY OF JACK EDWIN DOUGHERTY

The testimony of Jack Edwin Dougherty was taken at 10:50 a.m., on April 8, 1964, in the office of the U.S. attorney, 301 Post Office Building, Bryan and Ervay Streets, Dallas, Tex., by Mr. Joseph A. Ball, assistant counsel of the President's Commission.

Mr. BALL. Do you solemnly swear the testimony you are about to give before the Commission will be the truth, the whole truth, and nothing but the truth, so help you God?

Mr. DOUGHERTY. I do.

Mr. BALL. Will you state your name and address for the record?

Mr. DOUGHERTY. Jack Edwin Dougherty.

Mr. BALL. And your address?

Mr. DOUGHERTY. 1827 South Marsalis.

Mr. BALL. How old are you?

Mr. DOUGHERTY. Forty.

Mr. BALL. Where were you born?

Mr. DOUGHERTY. Here in Dallas.

Mr. BALL. Where did you go to school?

Mr. DOUGHERTY. Sunset High School.

Mr. BALL. You went through Sunset High School?

Mr. DOUGHERTY. Yes, sir.

Mr. BALL. What year did you get out of high school? About?

Mr. DOUGHERTY. Oh, 1937.

Mr. BALL. 1937?

Mr. DOUGHERTY. Yes.

Mr. BALL. What kind of work did you do after that?

Mr. DOUGHERTY. Well, of course, a year or so, you might say—just work in grocery stores until I was 19 and volunteered for the Armed Services in October—October 24, 1942.

Mr. BALL. How long were you in the service?

Mr. DOUGHERTY. 2 years, 1 month, 17 days, to be exact.

Mr. BALL. And you were discharged from the Service, then, after the War, was it?

Mr. DOUGHERTY. Yes, sir.

Mr. BALL. What did you do during the service—during your period in the service?

Mr. DOUGHERTY. Well, you might say just about a little bit of everything, from guard duty to——

Mr. BALL. Did you have any active service?

Mr. DOUGHERTY. Well, no—I volunteered for active service, but they said you couldn't very well volunteer—you have to be drafted, so they said, they told me at the time.

Mr. BALL. Did you ever leave the United States during the War?

Mr. DOUGHERTY. Oh, yes.

Mr. BALL. Where did you go?

Mr. DOUGHERTY. Well, I was stationed, oh, for about a year up in Indiana up there—Seymour, Ind.

Mr. BALL. Then where did you go from there in the service?

Mr. DOUGHERTY. Well, I stayed there until I got discharged.

Mr. BALL. You didn't ever go outside the country to Europe?

Mr. DOUGHERTY. Oh, no.

Mr. BALL. Or to the South Seas?

Mr. DOUGHERTY. No.

Mr. BALL. You stayed in this country all the time?

Mr. DOUGHERTY. Yes.

Mr. BALL. Now, did you ever have any difficulty with your speech?

Mr. DOUGHERTY. No.

Mr. BALL. You never had any?

Mr. DOUGHERTY. No.

Mr. BALL. Did you ever have any difficulty in the Army with any medical treatment or anything of that sort?

Mr. DOUGHERTY. No.

Mr. BALL. None at all?

Mr. DOUGHERTY. No.

Mr. BALL. What did you do after you got out of the Army?

Mr. DOUGHERTY. Well, jobs were pretty scarce about the time I got out of the service, so I just went from place to place and applied and put my application in, so I started over here at the Texas School Book Depository and put my application in there and I got it through the Suburban Employment Agency, and I been working there ever since.

Mr. BALL. And that was when—in 1940, was it, you started to work at the Texas School Book Depository?

Mr. DOUGHERTY. September 17, 1940.

Mr. BALL. 1940 what?

Mr. DOUGHERTY. Let's see, I have been with them 11 years—that would be——

Mr. BALL. That would be 1952, wouldn't it?

Mr. DOUGHERTY. Yes—that's 1952.

Mr. BALL. 1952?

Mr. DOUGHERTY. Yes; that's right, to be exact.

Mr. BALL. What did you do between the time you got out of the service and 1952?

Mr. DOUGHERTY. Well, I didn't do anything to be frank with you.

Mr. BALL. You didn't?

Mr. DOUGHERTY. No.

Mr. BALL. You didn't work?

Mr. DOUGHERTY. Oh, no.

Mr. BALL. You stayed at home?

Mr. DOUGHERTY. No, sir.

Mr. BALL. Did you live with your father and mother?

Mr. DOUGHERTY. Yes.

Mr. BALL. Have you ever been married?

Mr. DOUGHERTY. No.

Mr. BALL. And you still live with your father and mother?

Mr. DOUGHERTY. Yes.

Mr. BALL. Now, what kind of work have you been doing at the Texas School Book Depository in the last few years?

Mr. DOUGHERTY. Oh—shipping clerk.

Mr. BALL. And what kind of work is that?

Mr. DOUGHERTY. Well, that's when they bring the orders from on the second floor, and in other words, you fill them from the—they are orders, I guess you would call them orders, to fill from there, and outside of doing little odd jobs besides that—that's it.

Mr. BALL. Did you know a fellow named Lee Harvey Oswald that worked at the Texas School Book Depository?

Mr. DOUGHERTY. Well, I'll be frank with you, Mr. Ball, I don't believe nobody knew him too well. You might say he wouldn't have too much to say to anybody. He just stayed all to hisself, and I'll be frank with you, I just flat didn't know him.

Mr. BALL. Now, on November 22, 1963, that's the day the President was shot?

Mr. DOUGHERTY. Yes, sir.

Mr. BALL. What time did you go to work?

Mr. DOUGHERTY. Well, I got there—it was after 7 o'clock in the morning.

Mr. BALL. Do you usually get there in the morning at 7 o'clock?

Mr. DOUGHERTY. Yes.

Mr. BALL. Why do you get there at 7 instead of 8, when the rest of the men get there?

Mr. DOUGHERTY. Well, you might say, I have a little—extra chores to do.

Mr. BALL. You do that—you get there at 7 all the time, don't you?

Mr. DOUGHERTY. Yes, I've been doing it for 11 years.

Mr. BALL. That's what Mr. Truly told me, that you get there real early.

Mr. DOUGHERTY. Yes.

Mr. BALL. And you did get there about 7 that morning?

Mr. DOUGHERTY. Yes.

Mr. BALL. Let's see, Mr. Dougherty, you said that you have some extra chores—what are those extra chores?

Mr. DOUGHERTY. I have to see to it that the water system is pumped up. In other words, the air pressure is up to where—up to 40 pounds so that if it isn't pumped up, the alarm goes off, and the ADT runs that alarm system, and we immediately call Mr. Truly and of course they call me.

Mr. BALL. What is the ADT?

Mr. DOUGHERTY. That's that—I don't know too much about it—it has something to do with the alarm system they have got down there.

Mr. BALL. You mean the pressure, do you?

Mr. DOUGHERTY. Yes.

Mr. BALL. Is that a fire-alarm system?

Mr. DOUGHERTY. Yes—you could call it that.

Mr. BALL. Now, what else do you do there early in the morning?

Mr. DOUGHERTY. Well, let's see, I have to check and see that there is no leaks in the building, that the pipes are not leaking somewhere.

Mr. BALL. Anything else you do?

Mr. DOUGHERTY. No; I believe that just about covers it.

Mr. BALL. What time do you usually go to lunch?

Mr. DOUGHERTY. Well, usually about 12 o'clock or 12 noon.

Mr. BALL. Do you carry your lunch most of the time from home?

Mr. DOUGHERTY. Yes.

Mr. BALL. And where do you usually eat your lunch?

Mr. DOUGHERTY. Well, they have got what they call a domino room in there and I usually eat it in there.

Mr. BALL. You usually eat your lunch in the domino room?

Mr. DOUGHERTY. Yes.

Mr. BALL. And how long do you take for lunch?

Mr. DOUGHERTY. Well, from 12 to 12:45.

Mr. BALL. Forty-five minutes?

Mr. DOUGHERTY. Yes.

Mr. BALL. Do you always take a full hour?

Mr. DOUGHERTY. Yes; I usually do.

Mr. BALL. Now, do you remember the day of November 22, 1963; you do, don't you?

Mr. DOUGHERTY. Yes.

Mr. BALL. The day that the President was shot?

Mr. DOUGHERTY. Yes.

Mr. BALL. Do you remember what time you went to work that day?

Mr. DOUGHERTY. Yes—let's see—it was 12:30.

Mr. BALL. What time did you go to work that morning?

Mr. DOUGHERTY. Well, that particular morning—let's see, we didn't go back.

Mr. BALL. No; I mean, what time did you go to work the first thing in the morning?

Mr. DOUGHERTY. It was 8 o'clock when we were actually started to work.

Mr. BALL. What time did you get to the building?

Mr. DOUGHERTY. At a quarter to 7.

341

Mr. BALL. At a quarter to 7?

Mr. DOUGHERTY. Yes.

Mr. BALL. You told the FBI officers that you got there about 7 o'clock.

Mr. DOUGHERTY. Well, I mean, inside the building.

Mr. BALL. Inside the building?

Mr. DOUGHERTY. Yes—when I got inside the building it was 7 o'clock.

Mr. BALL. You parked your car?

Mr. DOUGHERTY. I don't have a car—I have to ride the bus.

Mr. BALL. Did you see Oswald come to work that morning?

Mr. DOUGHERTY. Yes—when he first come into the door.

Mr. BALL. When he came in the door?

Mr. DOUGHERTY. Yes.

Mr. BALL. Did you see him come in the door?

Mr. DOUGHERTY. Yes; I saw him when he first come in the door—yes.

Mr. BALL. Did he have anything in his hands or arms?

Mr. DOUGHERTY. Well, not that I could see of.

Mr. BALL. About what time of day was that?

Mr. DOUGHERTY. That was 8 o'clock.

Mr. BALL. That was about 8 o'clock?

Mr. DOUGHERTY. Yes, sir.

Mr. BALL. What door did he come in?

Mr. DOUGHERTY. Well, he came in the back door.

Mr. BALL. Where were you then?

Mr. DOUGHERTY. I was—sitting on top of the wrapping table.

Mr. BALL. Now, do you remember that you gave a statement to the Federal Bureau of Investigation and to a man by the name of Ellington, or a Mr. Anderton, the day after—the 23d of November?

Mr. DOUGHERTY. Yes—I talked to so many of them—it is kind of hard to remember.

Mr. BALL. And there is a statement that they took when they talked to you and in it you said, "I recall vaguely, having seen Lee Oswald, when he came to work at about 8 a.m. today."

Mr. DOUGHERTY. I did—that morning.

Mr. BALL. That seems to be dated the 22d day of November 1963.

Mr. DOUGHERTY. That's right.

Mr. BALL. The full statement is, "I am employed by the Texas School Book Depository, 411 Elm Street, Dallas, as an order filler, and reside at 1827 South Marsalis Street, Dallas, Tex."

Did you tell them that?

Mr. DOUGHERTY. Yes, sir.

Mr. BALL. "I started to work today, 11-22-63, at about 7 a.m. o'clock."

Did you tell them that?

Mr. DOUGHERTY. Yes.

Mr. BALL. The statement says, "I recall vaguely having seen Lee Oswald, when he came to work at about 8 a.m. today."

Mr. DOUGHERTY. That's right.

Mr. BALL. Now, is that a very definite impression that you saw him that morning when he came to work?

Mr. DOUGHERTY. Well, oh—it's like this—I'll try to explain it to you this way—you see, I was sitting on the wrapping table and when he came in the door, I just caught him out of the corner of my eye—that's the reason why I said it that way.

Mr. BALL. Did he come in with anybody?

Mr. DOUGHERTY. No.

Mr. BALL. He was alone?

Mr. DOUGHERTY. Yes; he was alone.

Mr. BALL. Do you recall him having anything in his hand?

Mr. DOUGHERTY. Well, I didn't see anything, if he did.

Mr. BALL. Did you pay enough attention to him, you think, that you would remember whether he did or didn't?

Mr. DOUGHERTY. Well, I believe I can—yes, sir—I'll put it this way; I didn't see anything in his hands at the time.

Mr. BALL. In other words, your memory is definite on that, is it?

Mr. DOUGHERTY. Yes, sir.

Mr. BALL. In other words, you would say positively he had nothing in his hands?

Mr. DOUGHERTY. I would say that—yes, sir.

342

Mr. BALL. Or, are you guessing?

Mr. DOUGHERTY. I don't think so.

Mr. BALL. You saw him come in the door?

Mr. DOUGHERTY. Yes.

Mr. BALL. The back door on the first floor?

Mr. DOUGHERTY. It was in the back door.

Mr. BALL. Now, that back door is the door that opens onto what? That back door would be the first floor?

Mr. DOUGHERTY. Yes.

Mr. BALL. And it opens where?

Mr. DOUGHERTY. On the back dock—on the back dock side over there.

Mr. BALL. That would be what direction from the first floor—what wall of the first floor—north?

Mr. DOUGHERTY. Well, let's see, to be frank with you—I don't know which one it would be.

Mr. BALL. Is there only one back door?

Mr. DOUGHERTY. Yes; there is only one back door.

Mr. BALL. Did you see him again that morning?

Mr. DOUGHERTY. Yes; just one more time.

Mr. BALL. Where was that?

Mr. DOUGHERTY. That was on the sixth floor.

Mr. BALL. On the sixth floor?

Mr. DOUGHERTY. Yes.

Mr. BALL. About what time of day?

Mr. DOUGHERTY. It was about 11 o'clock—that was the last time I saw him.

Mr. BALL. What was he doing up there?

Mr. DOUGHERTY. Well, as far as I could tell, he was getting some stock—as far as I could tell.

Mr. BALL. What were you doing there?

Mr. DOUGHERTY. I was getting some stock also.

Mr. BALL. And were there some other workmen up there at the time?

Mr. DOUGHERTY. Not that I know of.

Mr. BALL. Well, do you remember Shelley, Dan Arce, Bonnie Williams, Bill Lovelady, and Charlie Givens who were working up there that morning—laying floor on the sixth floor?

Mr. DOUGHERTY. Oh, yes; they were laying floor—yes, sir.

Mr. BALL. And were they there at the time you were there?

Mr. DOUGHERTY. Oh, yes, sir; they were there—yes, sir.

Mr. BALL. Is that the same time you saw Oswald?

Mr. DOUGHERTY. Yes, sir; just about that time.

Mr. BALL. And how long were you on the sixth floor?

Mr. DOUGHERTY. Well, just long enough to get some stock.

Mr. BALL. Where did you go then?

Mr. DOUGHERTY. I went to the fifth floor.

Mr. BALL. What did you do then?

Mr. DOUGHERTY. Well, I went to the fifth floor to get some stock also on the fifth floor.

Mr. BALL. Then what did you do?

Mr. DOUGHERTY. Then, just about that time—I thought I heard——

Mr. BALL. Wait a minute—did you go to lunch?

Mr. DOUGHERTY. Well, I went back downstairs to eat lunch—yes, sir.

Mr. BALL. What time?

Mr. DOUGHERTY. Oh, it was 12 o'clock.

Mr. BALL. When you talked to the FBI men, I've got a statement here dated the 19th of December 1963, a statement from Special Agent William O. Johnson, and he reports that you told him that you saw Lee Harvey Oswald at approximately 8 a.m. when he, Oswald, arrived.

Mr. DOUGHERTY. That's right.

Mr. BALL. That you saw Oswald again at approximately 11 a.m. on the sixth floor?

Mr. DOUGHERTY. That's right.

Mr. BALL. But you didn't see him again after that, is that your testimony?

Mr. DOUGHERTY. Yes.

Mr. BALL. Is that the truth?

Mr. DOUGHERTY. That's right.

343

Mr. BALL. And it also says, this report from Mr. Johnson, states that you told him that just prior to 12 noon you and five other men were working on the sixth floor. Were you?

Mr. DOUGHERTY. Yes; we were working on the sixth floor.

Mr. BALL. What were you doing?

Mr. DOUGHERTY. Well, I was getting some stock off of the sixth floor.

Mr. BALL. You weren't helping the men lay floor?

Mr. DOUGHERTY. No, sir.

Mr. BALL. Did you go down to lunch?

Mr. DOUGHERTY. Yes.

Mr. BALL. To what floor?

Mr. DOUGHERTY. The first floor.

Mr. BALL. How did you get down there?

Mr. DOUGHERTY. Well—used the elevator.

Mr. BALL. Did you go down alone or with someone?

Mr. DOUGHERTY. I went down alone.

Mr. BALL. Where did you eat your lunch?

Mr. DOUGHERTY. In the domino room.

Mr. BALL. Now, what time did you go back to work?

Mr. DOUGHERTY. Oh, at 12:30.

Mr. BALL. Did you know that the President was going to pass in a motorcade that noon?

Mr. DOUGHERTY. Well, they said something about it.

Mr. BALL. Did you intend to go out and watch him?

Mr. DOUGHERTY. Well, I would have loved to have went out and watched him but the steps were so crowded—there was no way in the world I could get out there.

Mr. BALL. Did you take a look at it—did you go out and take a look at it, or didn't you?

Mr. DOUGHERTY. Well—no, sir.

Mr. BALL. Now, you were on the first floor in the domino room when you finished your lunch, didn't you?

Mr. DOUGHERTY. Yes, sir.

Mr. BALL. And did you stay there any length of time after you finished your lunch?

Mr. DOUGHERTY. No, sir—just a short length of time.

Mr. BALL. Then what did you do?

Mr. DOUGHERTY. Well, then, I went back to work.

Mr. BALL. And where did you go to work?

Mr. DOUGHERTY. Let me see—oh, up to the sixth floor.

Mr. BALL. Did you go to the sixth floor?

Mr. DOUGHERTY. Yes, sir.

Mr. BALL. About what time?

Mr. DOUGHERTY. Oh, it was about 12:40—it was about 12:40.

Mr. BALL. Had you heard any shots before that?

Mr. DOUGHERTY. Yes—I heard one—it sounded like a backfire.

Mr. BALL. Where were you when you heard that shot?

Mr. DOUGHERTY. I was on the fifth floor.

Mr. BALL. You were on the fifth floor?

Mr. DOUGHERTY. Yes, sir.

Mr. BALL. Now, when you left your lunch, did you go to the fifth floor or the sixth floor to go back to work?

Mr. DOUGHERTY. I went on the fifth floor when I was getting ready to go down to eat lunch.

Mr. BALL. Yes; and then what happened?

Mr. DOUGHERTY. Well, at that time—I was about 10 feet away——

Mr. BALL. Wait a minute—did you hear the shots before or after you had your lunch?

Mr. DOUGHERTY. Before—before I ate my lunch.

Mr. BALL. You heard shots before you ate your lunch?

Mr. DOUGHERTY. Let's see—yes, I believe I did.

Mr. BALL. Well, now, you remember having your lunch, do you?

Mr. DOUGHERTY. Yes.

Mr. BALL. Do you remember after you had your lunch, you went back to work that day?

Mr. DOUGHERTY. Yes.

Mr. BALL. When you talked on the day this accident happened, on the 22d of November 1963, in a statement made to the Federal Bureau of Investigation and, Mr. Dougherty, you told them you went down to the first floor to eat your lunch?

Mr. DOUGHERTY. That's right.

Mr. BALL. And that you went back to work?

Mr. DOUGHERTY. Yes, sir.

Mr. BALL. And you told him on the 19th day of December, Mr. Johnson, that you went back to work on the sixth floor, and as soon as you arrived on the sixth floor, you went down to the fifth floor to get some stock?

Mr. DOUGHERTY. Yes, sir; that's right.

Mr. BALL. And while you were on the fifth floor, you heard a loud noise?

Mr. DOUGHERTY. That's right—it sounded like a car backfiring.

Mr. BALL. And did you hear more than one loud explosion or noise?

Mr. DOUGHERTY. No; that was the only one I heard.

Mr. BALL. You only heard one?

Mr. DOUGHERTY. Yes.

Mr. BALL. And where did it sound like it came from?

Mr. DOUGHERTY. It sounded like it came from overhead somewhere.

Mr. BALL. From overhead?

Mr. DOUGHERTY. Yes.

Mr. BALL. How did you get to the fifth floor?

Mr. DOUGHERTY. Elevator.

Mr. BALL. You were on the fifth floor when you heard this, were you?

Mr. DOUGHERTY. Yes.

Mr. BALL. Which elevator did you take?

Mr. DOUGHERTY. Well, you see, there's one on this side and one on this side—the one on this side is the one I took.

Mr. BALL. Well, now, "The one on this side and the one on this side," doesn't mean much when it's written down.

Mr. DOUGHERTY. Well, I know it.

Mr. BALL. Can you tell me whether it was the east side or the west side elevator?

Mr. DOUGHERTY. East side.

Mr. BALL. Is it the one that you punch a button on?

Mr. DOUGHERTY. Yes, sir.

Mr. BALL. Or the one that you use a control on?

Mr. DOUGHERTY. It's the one you push a button on.

Mr. BALL. The one you push a button on?

Mr. DOUGHERTY. Yes, sir.

Mr. BALL. I believe that is the west side, isn't it?

Mr. DOUGHERTY. Yes, I believe it is.

Mr. BALL. Now, that's the one you took up?

Mr. DOUGHERTY. Yes.

Mr. BALL. Where did you take that—to what floor?

Mr. DOUGHERTY. I took it up to the sixth floor.

Mr. BALL. Then what did you do?

Mr. DOUGHERTY. Well, when I got through getting stock off of the sixth floor, I came back down to the fifth floor.

Mr. BALL. What did you do on the fifth floor?

Mr. DOUGHERTY. Well, I got some stock.

Mr. BALL. Then what happened then?

Mr. DOUGHERTY. Well, then immediately I heard a loud noise—it sounded like a car backfiring, and I came back down to the first floor, and I asked Eddie Piper, I said, "Piper, what was that?" I says, "Has the President been shot?" He said, "Yes."

Mr. BALL. You didn't say—did you say, "Has the President been shot?"—you told the FBI agent that you went down to the first floor and you saw a man named Eddie Piper and asked him if he heard a loud noise.

Mr. DOUGHERTY. I asked him that too.

Mr. BALL. And Piper said he had heard three loud noises and told you that somebody had just shot the President; is that right?

Mr. DOUGHERTY. That's right.

Mr. BALL. Who mentioned the fact that the President had been shot first—you or Eddie Piper?

Mr. DOUGHERTY. Eddie Piper.

Mr. BALL. Did you say anything to Piper about the President being shot?

Mr. DOUGHERTY. No, sir.

345

Mr. BALL. When you talked to Eddie Piper, did you know that the President had been shot?

Mr. DOUGHERTY. No, sir; I didn't know that at the time.

Mr. BALL. When is the first time you heard that the President had been shot?

Mr. DOUGHERTY. When Eddie told me that.

Mr. BALL. Eddie told you that?

Mr. DOUGHERTY. Yes.

Mr. BALL. You told Mr. Johnson of the Federal Bureau of Investigation that when you were on the fifth floor, you heard a loud noise and it appeared to have come from within the building, but you couldn't tell where—you told him that on the 19th; did you tell him that?

Mr. DOUGHERTY. Yes, sir.

Mr. BALL. On the day that this happened, on the 22d of November, you told the FBI agents Ellington and Anderton that you heard "a loud explosion which sounded like a rifle shot coming from the next floor above me."

Now, did you tell them that it sounded like a rifle shot, coming from the next floor above you, or didn't you?

Mr. DOUGHERTY. Well; I believe I told them it sounded like a car backfiring.

Mr. BALL. Well, did you tell them it sounded like it was from the floor above you, or didn't you tell them that?

Mr. DOUGHERTY. No.

Mr. BALL. You did not tell them that?

Mr. DOUGHERTY. No.

Mr. BALL. Did it sound like it came from the floor above you?

Mr. DOUGHERTY. Well, at the time it did—yes.

Mr. BALL. Tell me this—when you heard that explosion or whatever it was—that loud noise, where were you on the fifth floor—tell me exactly where you were?

Mr. DOUGHERTY. Well, I was about 10 feet from the west elevator—the west side of the elevator.

Mr. BALL. That's the elevator that uses the push button; is that right?

Mr. DOUGHERTY. Yes.

Mr. BALL. And what were you doing?

Mr. DOUGHERTY. I was getting some stock.

Mr. BALL. And what did you do then?

Mr. DOUGHERTY. Well, I came on back downstairs.

Mr. BALL. How did you come downstairs?

Mr. DOUGHERTY. I used that push button elevator on the west side.

Mr. BALL. Did you hear Mr. Truly yell anything up the elevator shaft?

Mr. DOUGHERTY. I didn't hear anybody yell.

Mr. BALL. Or, did you see Mr. Truly?

Mr. DOUGHERTY. Well, when the FBI men—I imagine it was who it was—he showed me his credentials, but he asked me who the manager was, and I told him, "Mr. Truly." He told me to go find him. Well, I didn't know where he was so I started from the first floor and just started looking for him, and by the time I got to the sixth floor, they had found a gun and shells.

Mr. BALL. When you went up to the sixth floor, it was after they found the shotgun and shells?

Mr. DOUGHERTY. Yes, sir; and I found out later he was on the fourth floor, which I didn't find.

Mr. BALL. Did you ever see a gun around there?

Mr. DOUGHERTY. No, sir; I sure didn't.

Mr. BALL. Did you ever see anybody with a gun in the place?

Mr. DOUGHERTY. No, sir.

Mr. BALL. Did you see any strangers in the building that day?

Mr. DOUGHERTY. No, sir.

Mr. BALL. Did you ever see Lee Oswald carry any sort of large package?

Mr. DOUGHERTY. Well, I didn't, but some of the fellows said they did.

Mr. BALL. Who said that?

Mr. DOUGHERTY. Well, Bill Shelley, he told me that he thought he saw him carrying a fairly good-sized package.

Mr. BALL. When did Shelley tell you that?

Mr. DOUGHERTY. Well, it was—the day after it happened.

Mr. BALL. Are you sure you were on the fifth floor when you heard the shots?

Mr. DOUGHERTY. Yes, I'm positive.

346

Mr. BALL. Did you see any other employee on the fifth floor?

Mr. DOUGHERTY. No, sir; I didn't see nobody—there wasn't nobody on the fifth floor at all—it was just myself.

Mr. BALL. You told me that just before you heard the shots, you had been on the sixth floor?

Mr. DOUGHERTY. Yes.

Mr. BALL. And then you went down to the fifth floor?

Mr. DOUGHERTY. That's right.

Mr. BALL. Did you see anybody on the sixth floor when you were there, before you went to the fifth floor?

Mr. DOUGHERTY. Oh, yes; I did.

Mr. BALL. Who?

Mr. DOUGHERTY. Well, there was Bill Shelley, Billy Lovelady——

Mr. BALL. That was in the morning, wasn't it?

Mr. DOUGHERTY. Yes.

Mr. BALL. That wasn't after lunch, was it?

Mr. DOUGHERTY. No, sir.

Mr. BALL. After lunch, did you ever see them on the sixth floor?

Mr. DOUGHERTY. No, sir; I didn't.

Mr. BALL. Now, did you hear this shot either before or after lunch?

Mr. DOUGHERTY. It was before lunch—it was before lunch.

Mr. BALL. You think it was before lunch you heard the shot?

Mr. DOUGHERTY. I believe it was—yes, sir.

Mr. BALL. And you were alone, were you?

Mr. DOUGHERTY. Yes.

Mr. BALL. That's all I have to ask you, and this will be written up and if you would like to come down and read it and sign it, you can, or you can waive your signature.

What do you want to do?

Mr. DOUGHERTY. Well, whatever you want to do—it doesn't make any difference.

Mr. BALL. Would you like to come down and read it over and sign it?

Mr. DOUGHERTY. Well, if you've got time I'll sign it now.

Mr. BALL. Well, we have to write it up—this has to be written up and it will be so that you can read it. This young lady will notify you and you can come down and read it over and sign it.

Will you do that?

Mr. DOUGHERTY. All right.

Mr. BALL. And we will mark these statements as Dougherty Exhibits Nos. A, B, and C, and attach them to your deposition.

Thank you very much, and goodby.

Mr. DOUGHERTY. That's quite all right—thank you.

(Instruments referred to marked by the reporter as Dougherty Exhibits Nos. A, B, and C, for identification.)

TESTIMONY OF EDDIE PIPER

The testimony of Eddie Piper was taken at 10:20 a.m., on April 8, 1964, in the office of the U.S. attorney, 301 Post Office Building, Bryan and Ervay Streets, Dallas, Tex., by Mr. Joseph A. Ball, assistant counsel of the President's Commission.

Mr. BALL. Will you stand up and raise your right hand and be sworn?

Do you solemnly swear that the testimony you are about to give before the Commission will be the truth, the whole truth, and nothing but the truth, so help you God?

Mr. PIPER. Yes.

Mr. BALL. Will you state your name please, Mr. Piper?

Mr. PIPER. Eddie Piper.

Mr. BALL. And what is your address?

Mr. PIPER. 1507½ McCoy.

Mr. BALL. Tell me, Mr. Piper, where you were born and raised.

Mr. PIPER. In Travis County.

Mr. BALL. Texas?

Mr. PIPER. Yes, sir.

Mr. BALL. Where did you go to school?

Mr. PIPER. I went to school at Manor, Tex.

Mr. BALL. How far of school did you go?

Mr. PIPER. Eighth grade.

347

Mr. BALL. And what did you do after that?

Mr. PIPER. I went to work then.

Mr. BALL. Where did you go to work?

Mr. PIPER. I went to work doing harvest work, some in oil field in Chickasha, Okla., and done farm work.

Mr. BALL. Have you ever been in the Army?

Mr. PIPER. No, sir.

Mr. BALL. How old are you?

Mr. PIPER. 56.

Mr. BALL. When did you go to work for the Texas School Book Depository?

Mr. PIPER. Well, I would say I have been working for them about 4 or 5 years—I'm not sure—I don't know exactly.

Mr. BALL. What kind of work do you do?

Mr. PIPER. Janitor.

Mr. BALL. Have you been janitor ever since you were employed?

Mr. PIPER. Yes, sir.

Mr. BALL. Did you ever know a fellow named Lee Oswald, that worked there?

Mr. PIPER. Yes, sir; I know of him.

Mr. BALL. You knew of him?

Mr. PIPER. Yes.

Mr. BALL. Did you know him personally?

Mr. PIPER. No, sir.

Mr. BALL. Did you ever talk to him?

Mr. PIPER. No, sir.

Mr. BALL. Did he ever speak to you, say "Hello" or anything of that sort?

Mr. PIPER. No, sir; if he did, you hardly ever heard him.

Mr. BALL. Did you ever speak to him?

Mr. PIPER. Yes.

Mr. BALL. Did he ever reply to you that you can remember?

Mr. PIPER. If he did, I didn't ever hear him. He mumbled something and he would just keep walking.

Mr. BALL. On the 22d of November 1963, you remember that day, don't you?

Mr. PIPER. Yes.

Mr. BALL. What time did you go to work that day?

Mr. PIPER. 10 o'clock.

Mr. BALL. That was your usual time to go to work?

Mr. PIPER. Yes.

Mr. BALL. And, did you see Oswald that morning?

Mr. PIPER. Yes, sir.

Mr. BALL. Where?

Mr. PIPER. Down on the first floor filling orders.

Mr. BALL. Did you ever see him again that day?

Mr. PIPER. You mean all day—the rest of the day?

Mr. BALL. Yes, sir.

Mr. PIPER. No.

Mr. BALL. Was that the last time you saw him?

Mr. PIPER. Just at 12 o'clock.

Mr. BALL. Where were you at 12 o'clock?

Mr. PIPER. Down on the first floor.

Mr. BALL. What was he doing?

Mr. PIPER. Well, I said to him—"It's about lunch time. I believe I'll go have lunch." So, he says, "Yeah"—he mumbled something—I don't know whether he said he was going up or going out, so I got my sandwich off of the radiator and went on back to the first window of the first floor.

Mr. BALL. The first window on the first floor?

Mr. PIPER. No, not the first window—but on the first floor about the second window on the first floor. I was intending to sit there so I could see the parade because the street was so crowded with people—I didn't see anything.

Mr. BALL. You said you sat at the second window—that would be what window from the corner?

Mr. PIPER. Well, from the front door, you know where the front door is—going back right down Elm, it's the second window from the corner.

Mr. BALL. You say you sat down there?

Mr. PIPER. Yes.

Mr. BALL. What did you sit on?

Mr. PIPER. On a box.

Mr. BALL. Could you see out the window?

Mr. PIPER. Yes, I could see out the window but I couldn't see anything—too many people.

Mr. BALL. Did you eat your lunch there?

Mr. PIPER. Yes.

Mr. BALL. Where were you when the President's motorcade went by?

Mr. PIPER. Now, I don't know—I was sitting there, I'm sure.

Mr. BALL. When the President went by, where were you sitting?

Mr. PIPER. Probably sitting there in the same place.

Mr. BALL. Did you move from there from the time you had your lunch until the President went by?

Mr. PIPER. Yes, I moved—when there was a shot, I moved.

Mr. BALL. When there was a shot you moved?

Mr. PIPER. Yes.

Mr. BALL. From the time you had your lunch until the shot, did you move?

Mr. PIPER. No, sir.

Mr. BALL. You were at that window all of the time?

Mr. PIPER. All the time.

Mr. BALL. Did you ever go up on the sixth floor?

Mr. PIPER. No, sir.

Mr. BALL. Were you there at any time that day?

Mr. PIPER. No, sir.

Mr. BALL. Were you above the first floor that day up to the time of the shot?

Mr. PIPER. Before the shot?

Mr. BALL. Yes.

Mr. PIPER. Yes, sir.

Mr. BALL. Where?

Mr. PIPER. At 11 o'clock I went to the fourth floor to pick up.

Mr. BALL. You went to the fourth floor?

Mr. PIPER. Yes, at 11 o'clock.

Mr. BALL. And you worked there for how long?

Mr. PIPER. I would just take about 10 or 15 minutes to pick up—not quite that long, to pick up the mail and stuff in the fourth floor office.

Mr. BALL. Then what did you do?

Mr. PIPER. I came back down to the third floor and picked up and from there to the second and picked up and on to the first floor.

Mr. BALL. Is that what you usually did—was pick up?

Mr. PIPER. Yes, sir; every day.

Mr. BALL. Do you do that every day?

Mr. PIPER. Yes, sir.

Mr. BALL. You pick up mail?

Mr. PIPER. Yes, sir.

Mr. BALL. You pick up mail from what offices?

Mr. PIPER. From—what the name of the office is?

Mr. BALL. The different offices?

Mr. PIPER. Oh, I pick up mail first—on the fourth floor is Scott Pharmacy, and I come down on the third floor and I pick up there in the hall, you know, they have a hallway there and they put it out on the table—the packages and the mail, and I pick it up there unless they've got a name on the boards to see them in the office and then I go in the office. That's on the third floor. I come down on the second floor and I pick up for Southwestern. I goes in the office and that's the only office I go in there at Southwestern. Like I say—unless there is anything on the board that says see Lon Cunningham, and then I go in there. That's on the second floor, and from there back down to the first floor, and I unloads on the table on the first floor and that's when I'm through—I don't go back no more.

Mr. BALL. You do that every day?

Mr. PIPER. Yes.

Mr. BALL. At a certain time?

Mr. PIPER. Yes.

Mr. BALL. At what time?

Mr. PIPER. At 11 and 3.

Mr. BALL. Now, that day, November 22, 1963, you picked up the mail on the fourth floor at 11 did you?

Mr. PIPER. Yes, sir.

Mr. BALL. And then came to the third?

Mr. PIPER. Yes.

Mr. BALL. And then to the second?

Mr. PIPER. Yes.

Mr. BALL. And what time did you come to the first floor?

Mr. PIPER. Well, it was close to—around about—it must have been about 11:30—about 11:30 when I came back.

Mr. BALL. Did you leave the first floor from then on until lunch time, from 11:30 until 12?

Mr. PIPER. No.

Mr. BALL. What time was it that you spoke to Oswald and said you thought you would have your lunch?

Mr. PIPER. Just about 12 o'clock.

Mr. BALL. And do you remember exactly what he said?

Mr. PIPER. No, sir; I don't remember exactly. All I remember him was muttering out something—I didn't know whether he said he was going up or going out.

Mr. BALL. He said something like that?

Mr. PIPER. Yes—something like that.

Mr. BALL. Did you see what he did?

Mr. PIPER. No, sir; I didn't.

Mr. BALL. Did you see where he went?

Mr. PIPER. No, sir; I didn't.

Mr. BALL. You told me that you went to the window?

Mr. PIPER. That's right.

Mr. BALL. This is the second window to the right?

Mr. PIPER. Yes.

Mr. BALL. Of the front door—that would be looking toward Elm Street, is that right?

Mr. PIPER. Yes.

Mr. BALL. And were you sitting there when you heard the shot?

Mr. PIPER. That's right.

Mr. BALL. Tell me what you heard?

Mr. PIPER. I heard one shot, and then the next shot went off—the one that shot him and I got on up and went on back, back where they make coffee at the end of the counter where I could see what happened and before I could get there, the third shot went off, and I seen the people all running and in a few minutes someone came in the building, and I looked up and it was the bossman and a policeman or someone.

Mr. BALL. You say you heard one shot—you heard two shots and you got up and then what happened, where did you go?

Mr. PIPER. I came out to the end of the counter where they make coffee there by the stand.

Mr. BALL. You said you did it so you could see out better?

Mr. PIPER. No, sir; I did it to see what time it was—when all this happened—to see what time it was.

Mr. BALL. What time was it?

Mr. PIPER. It was about between 12:30—between 12:27 and 12:30—something like that, as near as I can remember.

Mr. BALL. Could you tell where the shots were coming from?

Mr. PIPER. No, sir—I couldn't, not for sure.

Mr. BALL. The direction?

Mr. PIPER. No, sir; I couldn't.

Mr. BALL. Did you look out the window later?

Mr. PIPER. No more—no, sir; I didn't go back to any window.

Mr. BALL. You mentioned you saw Truly?

Mr. PIPER. I don't know whether it was a policeman or FBI or who it was, but another fellow was with him.

Mr. BALL. And where were you?

Mr. PIPER. Standing right there where they make coffee.

Mr. BALL. What did they do?

Mr. PIPER. He ran in and yelled, "Where is the elevator?" And I said, "I don't know, sir, Mr. Truly."

They taken off and went on up the stairway and that's all I know about that.

Mr. BALL. Did you at any time go above the fourth floor on that date?

Mr. PIPER. No, sir.

Mr. BALL. Did you at any time go that day up above the fourth floor?

Mr. PIPER. No—no, sir.

Mr. BALL. You never did—either before or after the shots?

Mr. PIPER. No, sir.

Mr. BALL. Now, that day, you went over to the sheriff's office and made a statement, didn't you?

Mr. PIPER. Yes, sir—no, sir; not that day.

Mr. BALL. Did you the next day?

Mr. PIPER. Saturday.

Mr. BALL. Did you go to the sheriff's department?

Mr. PIPER. I went to the county—yes, sir.

Mr. BALL. And did you tell them at any time that you saw Lee about 12 o'clock?

Mr. PIPER. Yes.

Mr. BALL. And that Lee said, "I'm going up to eat?"

Mr. PIPER. He said either "up" or "out"—that's the way I reported it.

Mr. BALL. That's what you told them?

Mr. PIPER. Yes, sir.

Mr. BALL. Now, on that day, did you tell them that the shots that you heard seemed to come from inside the building?

Mr. PIPER. Yes, sir.

Mr. BALL. You did tell them that?

Mr. PIPER. Yes, sir.

Mr. BALL. Was that your best impression then?

Mr. PIPER. Yes; they seemed like they did come from the building, you know, by the vibration of that window—it seemed like nobody had shot in the window from the outside—it might have been coming from the building—is what I figured.

Mr. BALL. You told them that day that you thought it came from inside the building?

Mr. PIPER. Yes.

Mr. BALL. From inside the building?

Mr. PIPER. Yes.

Mr. BALL. Now, this statement you made to the sheriff's department, I'll show it to you—that's a copy there and is that your signature?

Mr. PIPER. Yes; that's my signature.

Mr. BALL. We'll attach that as Exhibit A to your deposition.

(Instrument marked by the reporter as "Piper Exhibit No. A," for identification.)

Mr. BALL. This deposition will be written up and you can come down here and look it over and sign it, if you wish.

Mr. PIPER. All right.

Mr. BALL. Or, you can waive your signature, just as you wish. Do you have any choice—which had you rather do?

Mr. PIPER. Well, what is supposed to be done—I don't really quite understand?

Mr. BALL. You can do it either way. You see, we are going to write it up—this young lady will write it up and if you want to come down and sign it, you can come down and sign it, or you don't need to sign it. You can waive your signature and we will send it on as it is written up. It is up to you which you would rather do.

Mr. PIPER. Well, I can sign it, but I don't know when I am supposed to come back to sign it.

Mr. BALL. Well, you will be notified.

Mr. PIPER. All right. I'll do that.

Mr. BALL. All right, she will call you and ask you to come back and sign it.

Mr. PIPER. All right, I'll come back and sign it.

Mr. BALL. All right, thank you very much.

Mr. PIPER. Thank you.

The testimony of Miss Victoria Elizabeth Adams was taken at 2:15 p.m., on April 7, 1964, in the office of the U.S. attorney, 301 Post Office Building, Bryan and Ervay Streets, Dallas, Tex., by Mr. David W. Belin, assistant counsel of the President's Commission.

Mr. BELIN. Do you want to stand and raise your right hand, please. Do you solemnly swear that the testimony you are about to give before the President's Commission on the Assassination of President Kennedy shall be the truth, the whole truth, and nothing but the truth, so help you God?

Miss ADAMS. I do.

Mr. BELIN. All right. Would you please state your name?

Miss ADAMS. Victoria Elizabeth Adams.

Mr. BELIN. Are you known as Vickie Adams?

Miss ADAMS. That's correct.

Mr. BELIN. Where do you live?

Miss ADAMS. 4906 Wenonah, Dallas, Tex.

Mr. BELIN. What is your occupation?

Miss ADAMS. I am employed as an office survey representative.

Mr. BELIN. By whom?

Miss ADAMS. Scott Foresman Co.

Mr. BELIN. Where do you work?

Miss ADAMS. On the fourth floor of the Texas School Book Depository.

Mr. BELIN. Where?

Miss ADAMS. 411 Elm.

Mr. BELIN. That is at the corner of Elm and Houston?

Miss ADAMS. That is correct.

Mr. BELIN. I might ask how old are you?

Miss ADAMS. Twenty-three.

Mr. BELIN. Where were you born originally? In Texas?

Miss ADAMS. San Francisco, Calif.

Mr. BELIN. Did you go to school in San Francisco?

Miss ADAMS. I attended part of my grammar school and high school in San Francisco.

Mr. BELIN. Were you graduated from high school?

Miss ADAMS. In San Francisco, that's correct.

Mr. BELIN. Then what did you do?

Miss ADAMS. Following that I entered the Ursaline Order in St. Mary's, Ohio, and I left there as a novice in 1961.

Mr. BELIN. Then what did you do from there?

Miss ADAMS. I went to Atlanta, Ga. and taught school at the Immaculate Heart of Mary School. And following that I came to Dallas and was employed by the Holiday Inn Central during the summer months, and I obtained a teaching position at St. Monica's School here.

Mr. BELIN. And you taught at St. Monica for some period of time?

Miss ADAMS. Yes; for 1 year.

Mr. BELIN. Then you went to work for Scott Foresman?

Miss ADAMS. I went to work for Scott Foresman.

Mr. BELIN. Were you at work on November 22, 1963?

Miss ADAMS. That's correct.

Mr. BELIN. Were you aware of the fact that the President's motorcade was going to go right by your building?

Miss ADAMS. Yes, sir.

Mr. BELIN. How did you learn of this information?

Miss ADAMS. Through newspaper media and also conversation.

Mr. BELIN. Do you remember when you first read about it in the papers?

Miss ADAMS. No, sir; I don't.

Mr. BELIN. Would it have been before November 22d?

Miss ADAMS. Yes.

Mr. BELIN. Where were you when the motorcade passed?

Miss ADAMS. I was at the——

Mr. BELIN. Were you inside or outside the building?

Miss ADAMS. I was inside the building.

Mr. BELIN. What floor?

Miss ADAMS. Fourth floor.

Mr. BELIN. Did you watch the motorcade through a window?

Miss ADAMS. Yes, sir.

Mr. BELIN. Sometimes that is kind of complicated to try and pick out which window if you are counting from the right or left, so I am going to count from the east side of the building to the west side of the building.

Now the windows are separate windows, but they are kind of in pairs, so to speak. Were you standing on the first pair of windows, either one of those two windows?

Miss ADAMS. No, sir.

Mr. BELIN. Counting from the east side, were you standing in the second pair of windows?

Miss ADAMS. No, sir.

Mr. BELIN. From the east side, were you standing in the third pair, of either of those windows?

Miss ADAMS. Yes, sir.

Mr. BELIN. Now of that third pair, from the east side, would it have been the east window or the west window?

Miss ADAMS. The west window.

Mr. BELIN. So another way, if you don't count in pairs, but count in single units from the east side, you would have been in the sixth window from your left as you were facing out the window, is that correct?

Miss ADAMS. That's right.

Mr. BELIN. Were you standing with anyone?

Miss ADAMS. Yes, sir.

Mr. BELIN. With whom?

Miss ADAMS. I was standing with Sandra Styles, Elsie Dorman, and Dorothy May Garner.

Mr. BELIN. Will you state what you saw, what you did, and what you heard?

Miss ADAMS. I watched the motorcade come down Main, as it turned from Main onto Houston, and watched it proceed around the corner on Elm, and apparently somebody in the crowd called to the late President, because he and his wife both turned abruptly and faced the building, so we had a very good view of both of them.

Mr. BELIN. Where was their car as you got this good view, had it come directly opposite your window? Had it come to that point on Elm, or not, if you can remember?

Miss ADAMS. I believe it was prior, just a second or so prior to that.

Mr. BELIN. All right.

Miss ADAMS. And from our vantage point we were able to see what the President's wife was wearing, the roses in the car, and things that would attract women's attention. Then we heard—then we were obstructed from the view.

Mr. BELIN. By what?

Miss ADAMS. A tree. And we heard a shot, and it was a pause, and then a second shot, and then a third shot.

It sounded like a firecracker or a cannon at a football game, it seemed as if it came from the right below rather than from the left above. Possibly because of the report.

And after the third shot, following that, the third shot, I went to the back of the building down the back stairs, and encountered Bill Shelley and Bill Lovelady on the first floor on the way out to the Houston Street dock.

Mr. BELIN. When you say on the way out to the Houston Street dock, you mean now you were on the way out?

Miss ADAMS. While I was on the way out.

Mr. BELIN. Was anyone going along with you?

Miss ADAMS. Yes, sir; Sandra Styles.

Mr. BELIN. Sometime after the third shot, and I don't want to get into the actual period of time yet, you went back into the stockroom which would be to the north of where your offices are located on the fourth floor, is that correct?

Miss ADAMS. Yes, sir; that's correct.

Mr. BELIN. When you got into the stockroom, where did you go?

Miss ADAMS. I went to the back stairs.

Mr. BELIN. Are there any other stairs that lead down from the fourth floor other than those back stairs in the rear of the stockroom?

Miss ADAMS. No, sir.

Mr. BELIN. Those stairs would be in the northwest corner of the building, is that correct?

Miss ADAMS. That's correct.

353

Mr. BELIN. You took those stairs. Were you walking or running as you went down the stairs?

Miss. ADAMS. I was running. We were running.

Mr. BELIN. What kind of shoes did you have on?

Miss ADAMS. Three-inch heels.

Mr. BELIN. You had heels. Now, as you were running down the stairs, did you encounter anyone?

Miss ADAMS. Not during the actual running down the stairs; no, sir.

Mr. BELIN. After you left the Scott Foresman office and went into the stockroom, did you see anyone until you got to the stairs on the fourth floor other than the person you were with?

Miss ADAMS. Outside of our office employees; no.

Mr. BELIN. Would these office employees that you might have seen, all be women?

Miss ADAMS. Yes, sir.

Mr. BELIN. Then you got to the stairs and you started going down the stairs. You went from the fourth floor to the third floor?

Miss ADAMS. That's correct?

Mr. BELIN. Anyone on the stairs then?

Miss ADAMS. No, sir.

Mr. BELIN. Let me ask you this. As you got to the stairs on the fourth floor, did you notice whether or not the elevator was running?

Miss ADAMS. The elevator was not moving.

Mr. BELIN. How do you know it was not moving on some other floor?

Miss ADAMS. Because the cables move when the elevator is moved, and this is evidenced because of a wooden grate.

Mr. BELIN. By that you mean a wooden door with slats in it that you have to lift up to get on the elevator?

Miss ADAMS. Yes.

Mr. BELIN. Did you look to see if the elevator was moving?

Miss ADAMS. It was not; no, sir.

Mr. BELIN. It was not moving?

Miss ADAMS. No.

Mr. BELIN. Did you happen to see where the elevator might have been located?

Miss ADAMS. No, sir.

Mr. BELIN. As you got to the third door, did you take a look at the elevator again at all, or not, if you remember?

Miss ADAMS. I can't recall.

Mr. BELIN. As you got off the stairs on the third floor, did you see anyone on the third floor?

Miss ADAMS. No, sir.

Mr. BELIN. Then you immediately went to the stairs going down from the third to the second?

Miss ADAMS. That's correct.

Mr. BELIN. As you ran down the stairs, did you see anyone on the stairs?

Miss ADAMS. No, sir.

Mr. BELIN. All right. You got down to the second floor. Did you see anyone by the second floor?

Miss ADAMS. No, sir.

Mr. BELIN. Did you immediately turn and run and keep on running down the stairs towards the first floor?

Miss ADAMS. Yes.

Mr. BELIN. When you got to the bottom of the first floor, did you see anyone there as you entered the first floor from the stairway?

Miss ADAMS. Yes, sir.

Mr. BELIN. Who did you see?

Miss ADAMS. Mr. Bill Shelley and Billy Lovelady.

Mr. BELIN. Where did you see them on the first floor?

Miss ADAMS. Well, this is the stairs, and this is the Houston Street dock that I went out. They were approximately in this position here, so I don't know how you would describe that.

Mr. BELIN. You are looking now at a first floor plan or diagram of the Texas School Book Depository, and you have pointed to a position where you encountered Bill Lovelady and Mr. Bill Shelley?

Miss ADAMS. That's correct.

354

Mr. BELIN. It would be slightly east of the front of the east elevator, and probably as far south as the length of the elevator, is that correct?

Miss ADAMS. Yes, sir.

Mr. BELIN. I have a document here called Commission's Exhibit No. 496, which includes a diagram of the first door, and there is a No. 7 and a circle on it, and I have pointed to a place marked No. 7 on the diagram. Is that correct?

Miss ADAMS. That is approximate.

Mr. BELIN. Between the time you got off the stairs and the time you got to this point when you say you encountered them, which was somewhat to the south and a little bit east of the front of the east elevator, did you see any other employees there?

Miss ADAMS. No, sir.

Mr. BELIN. Any other people prior to the time you saw them?

Miss ADAMS. No, sir.

Mr. BELIN. Now when you were running down the stairs on your trip down the stairs, did you hear anyone using the stairs?

Miss ADAMS. No, sir.

Mr. BELIN. Did you hear anyone calling for an elevator?

Miss ADAMS. No, sir.

Mr. BELIN. Did you see the foreman, Roy Truly? Did you see the superintendent of the warehouse, Roy S. Truly?

Miss ADAMS. No, sir; I did not.

Mr. BELIN. What about any motorcycle police officers?

Miss ADAMS. No, sir.

Mr. BELIN. Now what did you do after you encountered Mr. Shelley and Mr. Lovelady?

Miss ADAMS. I said I believed the President was shot.

Mr. BELIN. Do you remember what they said?

Miss ADAMS. Nothing.

Mr. BELIN. Then what did you do?

Miss ADAMS. I proceeded out to the Houston Street dock.

Mr. BELIN. That would be on this same diagram? It is marked Houston Street dock, and you went through what would be the north door, which is towards the rear of the first floor, is that correct?

And down some stairs towards the rear of the dock?

Miss ADAMS. That's correct.

Mr. BELIN. Where did you go from there?

Miss ADAMS. I proceeded—which way is east and west?

Mr. BELIN. East is here. East is towards Houston, and west is towards the railroad tracks. You went east or west? Towards the railroad tracks or towards Houston Street?

Miss ADAMS. I went west towards the tracks.

Mr. BELIN. How far west did you go?

Miss ADAMS. I went approximately 2 yards within the tracks and there was an officer standing there, and he said, "Get back to the building." And I said, "But I work here."

And he said, "That is tough, get back."

I said, "Well, was the President shot?"

And he said, "I don't know. Go back."

And I said, "All right."

Mr. BELIN. Then what did you do?

Miss ADAMS. I went back, only I went southwest.

Mr. BELIN. Well, did you come back by way of the street, or did you come back the same entrance you went out?

Miss ADAMS. No, sir.

Mr. BELIN. You went back in through the front entrance, through the front of the building?

Miss ADAMS. Well, I didn't go back in right away.

Mr. BELIN. What did you do then?

There is a street that would be a continuation of Elm Street that goes in front of the building, and Elm Street itself angles into the freeway. Did you go back either of those streets?

Miss ADAMS. Yes, sir. I went by the one directly in front of the building.

Mr. BELIN. What did you do when you got there?

Miss ADAMS. When I got there, I happened to look around and noticed several of the employees, and I noticed Joe Molina, for one, was standing in front of the building, and also Avery Davis, who works with me, and I said, "What do you think has happened?"

355

And she said, "I don't know."

And I said, "I want to find out." I think the President is shot.

There was a motorcycle that was parked on the corner of Houston and Elm directly in front of the east end of the building, and I paused there to listen to the report on the police radio, and they said that shots had been fired which apparently came either from the second floor or the fourth floor window, and so I panicked, as I was at the only open window on the fourth floor.

Mr. BELIN. Did they say second floor or second floor from the top?

Miss ADAMS. It said second floor. So then I decided maybe I had better go back into the building, and going up the stairs——

Mr. BELIN. Now at this time when you went back into the building, were there any policemen standing in front of the building keeping people out?

Miss ADAMS. There was an officer on the stairs itself, and he was prohibiting people from entering the building, that is correct. But I told him I worked there.

Mr. BELIN. Did he let you come back in?

Miss ADAMS. Yes, sir.

Mr. BELIN. Then what did you do?

Miss ADAMS. Following that, I pushed the button for the passenger elevator, but the power had been cut off on the elevator, so I took the stairs to the second floor.

Mr. BELIN. You then went all the way back to the northwest corner of the building and took the same set of stairs you had previously taken to come down, or did you take the stairs by the passenger elevator?

Miss ADAMS. By the passenger elevator.

Mr. BELIN. Do those stairs go above floor 2?

Miss ADAMS. No, sir; they didn't.

Mr. BELIN. What did you do when you got to the second floor?

Miss ADAMS. I went into the Texas School Book Depository office and just listened for a few minutes to the people that were congregating there, and decided there wasn't anything interesting going on, and went out and walked around the hall to the freight elevator meaning the one on the northwest corner.

Mr. BELIN. Would it have been the west or the east? The one nearest the stairs or the other one?

Miss ADAMS. Yes; the one nearest the stairs.

Mr. BELIN. Then what did you do?

Miss ADAMS. I went into the elevator which was stopped on the second floor, with two men who were dressed in suit and hats, and I assumed they were plainclothesmen.

Mr. BELIN. What did you do then?

Miss ADAMS. I tried to get the elevator to go to the fourth floor, but it wasn't operating, so the gentlemen lifted the elevator gate and we went out and ran up the stairs to the fourth floor.

Mr. BELIN. Then you went back to the Scott Foresman Company offices?

Miss ADAMS. Yes, sir.

Mr. BELIN. Now trying to reconstruct your actions insofar as the time sequence, which we haven't done, what is your best estimate of the time between the time the shots were fired and the time you got back to the building? How much time elapsed? If you have any estimate. Maybe you don't have one.

Miss ADAMS. I would estimate not more than 5 minutes elapsed.

Mr. BELIN. Is there any particular reason why you make this estimation?

Miss ADAMS. Yes, sir; going down the stairs toward the back, I was running. I ran to the railroad tracks. I moved quickly to the front of the building, paused briefly to talk to someone, listened only to the report of the windows from which the shot supposedly was fired, and returned to the building.

Mr. BELIN. How long do you think it was between the time the shots were fired and the time you left the window to start toward the stairway?

Miss ADAMS. Between 15 and 30 seconds, estimated, approximately.

Mr. BELIN. How long do you think it was, or do you think it took you to get from the window to the top of the fourth floor stairs?

Miss ADAMS. I don't think I can answer that question accurately, because the time approximation, without a stopwatch, would be difficult.

Mr. BELIN. How long do you think it took you to get from the window to the bottom of the stairs on the first floor?

Miss ADAMS. I would say no longer than a minute at the most.

Mr. BELIN. So you think that from the time you left the window on the fourth floor until the time you got to the stairs at the bottom of the first floor, was approximately 1 minute?

Miss ADAMS. Yes, approximately.

Mr. BELIN. As I understand your testimony previously, you saw neither Roy Truly nor any motorcycle police officer at any time?

Miss ADAMS. That's correct.

Mr. BELIN. You heard no one else running down the stairs?

Miss ADAMS. Correct.

Mr. BELIN. When you got to the first floor did you immediately proceed to this point where you say you encountered Mr. Shelley and Mr. Lovelady?

Well, you showed me on a diagram of the first floor that there was a place which was south and somewhat east of the front part of the east elevator that you encountered Truly and Lovelady?

Miss ADAMS. I saw them there.

Mr. BELIN. I mean; you saw them?

Miss ADAMS. Yes.

Mr. BELIN. Would that have been a matter of seconds after you got to the bottom of the first floor?

Miss ADAMS. Definitely.

Mr. BELIN. Less than 30 seconds?

Miss ADAMS. Yes.

Mr. BELIN. Do you know, or did you know Lee Harvey Oswald either by sight or by name?

Miss ADAMS. I didn't know Lee Harvey Oswald, per se. I didn't know his name. I recognized him after I saw him on television, as having been with some men, but I had no dealing with him.

Mr. BELIN. By that, you mean having been employed with some men by the Texas School Book Depository?

Miss ADAMS. That's correct.

Mr. BELIN. During the trip down the stairs on the way down did you ever encounter Lee Harvey Oswald?

Miss ADAMS. No, sir.

Mr. BELIN. Is there any other information that you can think of that might be relevant to anything connected with the assassination?

Miss ADAMS. At the time I left the building on the Houston Street dock, there was an officer standing about 2 yards from the curb, and about from the curb across the street from the Texas School Depository, and about 4 yards from the corner of Houston and Elm, and when we were running out the dock, going around the building, the officer was standing there, and he didn't encounter us or ask us what we were doing or where we were going, and I don't know if that is pertinent.

Mr. BELIN. No one stopped you from getting out of the building when you left?

Miss ADAMS. That's correct.

Mr. BELIN. That is helpful information. Is there any other information that you have that could be relevant?

Miss ADAMS. There was a man that was standing on the corner of Houston and Elm asking questions there. He was dressed in a suit and a hat, and when I encountered Avery Davis going down, we asked who he was, because he was questioning people as if he were a police officer, and we noticed him take a colored boy away on a motorcycle, and this man was asking questions very efficaciously, and we said, "I guess he is maybe a reporter," and later on on television, there was a man that looked very similar to him, and he was identified as Ruby.

And on questioning some police officer, they said they had witnesses to the fact that he was in the Dallas Morning News at the time. And I don't know whether that is relevant or what.

Mr. BELIN. That is all right, we want to get that information down. Was this before you got back in the front door of the building that you saw this?

Miss ADAMS. Yes, sir; while I was standing by the motorcycles.

Mr. BELIN. Is there anything else?

Miss ADAMS. That is all, I believe.

Mr. BELIN. Miss Adams, you have the opportunity if you would like, to read this deposition and sign it before it goes to Washington, or you can waive the signing of it and just let the court reporter send it directly to us. Do you have any preference?

Miss ADAMS. I think I will let you use your own discretion.

Mr. BELIN. It doesn't make any difference to us. If it doesn't make any difference, we can waive it and you won't have to make another trip down here.

Miss ADAMS. That is all right.

Mr. BELIN. We want to thank you for your cooperation. We know that it has taken time on your part. Would you also thank your employer?

Miss ADAMS. Yes, sir.

TESTIMONY OF GENEVA L. HINE

The testimony of Geneva L. Hine was taken at 2:45 p.m., on April 7, 1964, in the office of the U.S. attorney, 301 Post Office Building, Bryan and Ervay Streets, Dallas, Tex., by Messrs. Joseph A. Ball and Samuel A. Stern, assistant counsel of the President's Commission.

Mr. BALL. Please stand up and hold up your right hand. Do you solemnly swear the testimony you will give the Commission will be the truth, the whole truth, and nothing but the truth, so help you God?

Miss HINE. I do.

Mr. BALL. Will you state your name, please?

Miss HINE. Geneva L. Hine.

Mr. BALL. Where do you live.

Miss HINE. 2305 Oakdale Road in Dallas.

Mr. BALL. Can you tell me something about yourself; where you were born and raised, and educated and what kind of work you have done.

Miss. HINE. I was born and raised in Martinsville, Ind., and I graduated from elementary and junior high and high school at that same town. I attended the Ball State Teachers' College in Muncie, Ind., and I attended Metropolitan Bible Institute in Suffern, N.Y., and I received my Bachelor of Science theology degree from Assembly of God College in Waxahachie, Tex.

Mr. BALL. What did you do after that?

Miss HINE. Oh, I have always worked as a one-girl office girl until the job I have now.

Mr. BALL. When did you go to work at the Texas School Book Depository?

Miss HINE. In December 1956.

Mr. BALL. What kind of work do you do there?

Miss HINE. I have the credit desk.

Mr. BALL. Now, in November, November 22, 1963, where was your desk; in what part of the building?

Miss HINE. My desk was on the second floor, the inside wall just along by the corridor.

Mr. BALL. Did you spend most of your time at your desk?

Miss HINE. At that time?

Mr. BALL. Yes; at that time.

Miss HINE. No, sir; the girls were gone and they wanted to go out and see.

Mr. BALL. I mean did you spend most of your time in your work—it was a desk job?

Miss HINE. Yes; that's right.

Mr. BALL. Did you go in the other floors of the building any?

Miss HINE. Yes, sir; as my duties necessitated I did.

Mr. BALL. Did you ever know a fellow named Lee Harvey Oswald?

Miss HINE. Yes, sir.

Mr. BALL. When did you first meet him?

Miss HINE. I never met him to know his name but I saw him every day.

Mr. BALL. Where did you see him?

Miss HINE. Downstairs in the warehouse or stockroom whichever you want to call it.

Mr. BALL. The first floor?

Miss HINE. Yes.

Mr. BALL. Did you see him on any other floors?

Miss HINE. Yes, sir; I saw him on the second floor about noontime almost every day. He would come in and ask for change, for a dime or quarter.

Mr. BALL. Did you see him use any part of the second floor?

Miss HINE. No.

Mr. BALL. Did you ever see him spend the dime to buy anything with it?

Miss HINE. No, sir; the coke machine isn't in our room and I wouldn't have seen it.

Mr. BALL. Where is the coke machine?

Miss HINE. Out in the little lunchroom back of our office.

Mr. BALL. Did you ever speak to Oswald?

Miss HINE. Yes, sir.

Mr. BALL. Did he ever speak to you?

Miss HINE. No, sir.

Mr. BALL. He never replied to you?

Miss HINE. No, sir.

Mr. BALL. Would you say he was unfriendly?

Miss HINE. Yes, sir; I would.

Mr. BALL. Did you ever see him smile or laugh?

Miss HINE. No, sir.

Mr. BALL. What kind of an expression did he have on his face most of the time?

Miss HINE. I describe it as being stoic.

Mr. BALL. That's a pretty good description if he doesn't smile.

Miss HINE. It was just——

Mr. BALL. Did you ever mention this to any of the people around there about Oswald?

Miss HINE. Yes, sir; I mentioned it to Mr. Shelley.

Mr. BALL. What did you tell him?

Miss HINE. One day I said to Mr. Shelley, "Who is that queer duck you have working down here" and I said that just as a matter of slang because I've known Mr. Shelley for a long time and I was just talking to him, you see, and usually, all the boys that work down there speak to me because I have to go down there to pick up the little "comp" or gift slips on my desk. Every time I went by him I would speak to him, say "Good morning" and he would never catch or meet my gaze so I just made that remark to Mr. Shelley because I had spoken to him so many times and he never answered.

Mr. BALL. What did Shelley say?

Miss HINE. He said that was just his way.

Mr. BALL. On the 22d of November 1963, did you know that there was to be a motorcade or parade come by your building?

Miss HINE. Oh, yes, sir.

Mr. BALL. How did you find that out?

Miss HINE. Sir, I don't remember. I probably heard over the news but I cannot remember.

Mr. BALL. You were just aware of the fact?

Miss HINE. Yes; I knew it and the girls were discussing it in the office that morning. Many of them, probably six, had not seen the President close. You see, I had seen him on two different occasions and I had been very close to him and so they were lamenting that they couldn't go out so I spoke up and said "I will be glad to answer the telephone so you girls may go out and see the motorcade" and I had previously answered the telephone when we were in the other building before we moved in this building, so they were delighted and I thought nothing about it.

Mr. BALL. Did they all go out?

Miss HINE. Yes, sir; everyone went out.

Mr. BALL. Was there anyone left in the office part of the building on that second floor office?

Miss HINE. Only Mr. Williams and myself and he stayed with me because he was working on his desk until he thought that the motorcade was about there.

Mr. BALL. Then he went out?

Miss HINE. When he thought it was about there he said "I think I will go out for 5 minutes."

Mr. BALL. What is his name?

Miss HINE. Otis N. Williams.

Mr. BALL. He works in the office, too?

Miss HINE. Yes.

Mr. BALL. Did you have to change your desk over to another desk?

Miss HINE. Yes, sir; to the middle desk on the front row.

Mr. BALL. Was there a switchboard?

Miss HINE. No, sir; we have a telephone with three incoming lines, then we have the warehouse line and we have an intercom system.

Mr. BALL. You don't have a switchboard?

Miss HINE. Not now; we did in the other building.

Mr. BALL. Were you alone then at this time?

Miss HINE. Yes.

Mr. BALL. Did you stay at your desk?

Miss HINE. Yes, sir; I was alone until the lights all went out and the phones became dead because the motorcade was coming near us and no one was calling so I got up and thought I could see it from the east window in our office.

Mr. BALL. Did you go to the window?

359

Miss HINE. Yes, sir.

Mr. BALL. Did you look out?

Miss HINE. Yes, sir.

Mr. BALL. What did you see?

Miss HINE. I saw the escort car come first up the middle of Houston Street.

Mr. BALL. Going north on Houston Street?

Miss HINE. Yes, sir; going north on Houston Street. I saw it turn left and I saw the President's car coming and I saw the President and saw him waving his hand in greeting up in the air and I saw his wife and I saw him turn the corner and after he turned the corner I looked and I saw the next car coming just at the instant I saw the next car coming up was when I heard the shots.

Mr. BALL. How many did you hear?

Miss HINE. Three.

Mr. BALL. Could you tell where the shots were coming from?

Miss HINE. Yes, sir; they came from inside the building.

Mr. BALL. How do you know that?

Miss HINE. Because the building vibrated from the result of the explosion coming in.

Mr. BALL. It appeared to you that the shots came from the building?

Miss HINE. Yes, sir.

Mr. BALL. Did you know they were shots at the time?

Miss HINE. Yes, sir; they sounded almost like cannon shots they were so terrific.

Mr. BALL. That is when you were at the window, is that right?

Miss HINE. Yes, sir; that is when I was at the window, because the next car, you see, was coming up and turning and I looked. Of course I looked when I heard the shots. I just stood there and saw people running to the east up Elm Street. I saw people running; I saw people falling down, you know, lying down on the sidewalk.

Mr. BALL. That was on Houston Street?

Miss HINE. No, sir; Elm.

Mr. BALL. You could see—could you see any part of Elm?

Miss HINE. East, yes, sir.

Mr. BALL. You could see east on Elm?

Miss HINE. Yes, sir; I could see east on Elm. I saw them run across east on Elm away from where his car had gone and my first thought was if I could only see what happened, so I went out our front door into the foyer.

Mr. BALL. You mean the front door to the office?

Miss HINE. Yes, sir.

Mr. BALL. That opens on——

Miss HINE. The foyer, little hall, and——

Mr. BALL. Steps lead down?

Miss HINE. Yes, sir; but there is a door before the steps and the elevator is to my left and I went past the hall that goes to my right and I knocked on the door of Lyons and Carnahan; that's a publishing company.

Mr. BALL. What did you do then?

Miss HINE. I tried the door, sir, and it was locked and I couldn't get in and I called, "Lee, please let me in," because she's the girl that had that office, Mrs. Lee Watley, and she didn't answer. I don't know if she was there or not, then I left her door. I retraced my steps back to where the hall turns to my left and went down it to Southwestern Publishing Co.'s door and I tried their door and the reason for this was because those windows face out.

Mr. BALL. On to Elm?

Miss HINE. Yes; and on to the triple underpass.

Mr. BALL. I see.

Miss HINE. And there was a girl in there talking on the telephone and I could hear her but she didn't answer the door.

Mr. BALL. Was the door locked?

Miss HINE. Yes, sir.

Mr. BALL. That was which company?

Miss HINE. Southwestern Publishing Co.

Mr. BALL. Did you call to her?

Miss HINE. I called and called and shook the door and she didn't answer me because she was talking on the telephone; I could hear her. They have a little curtain up and I could see her form through the curtains. I could see her talking and I knew that's what she was doing and then I turned and went through the back hall and came through the back door.

Mr. BALL. Of your office, the second floor office?

Miss HINE. Yes; and I went straight up to the desk because the telephones were beginning to wink; outside calls were beginning to come in.

Mr. BALL. Did they did come in rapidly?

Miss HINE. They did come in rapidly.

Mr. BALL. When you came back in did you see Mrs. Reid?

Miss HINE. No, sir; I don't believe there was a soul in the office when I came back in right then.

Mr. BALL. Did you see anybody else go in through there?

Miss HINE. No, sir; after I answered the telephone then there was about four or five people that came in.

Mr. BALL. Was there anybody in that room when you came back in and went to the telephone?

Miss HINE. No, sir; not to my knowledge.

Mr. BALL. Did you see Mrs. Reid come back in?

Miss HINE. Yes, sir; I think I felt sure that I did. I thought that there were five or six that came in together. I thought she was one of those.

Mr. BALL. Mrs. Reid told us she came in alone and when she came in she didn't see anybody there.

Miss HINE. Well, it could be that she did, sir. I was talking on the phones and then came the policemen and then came the press. Everybody was wanting an outside line and then our vice president came in and he said "The next one that was clear, I have to have it" and so I was busy with the phone.

Mr. BALL. From the time you walked into the room you became immediately busy with the phone?

Miss HINE. Yes, sir; sure was.

Mr. BALL. Did you see Oswald come in?

Miss HINE. My back would have been to the door he was supposed to have come in at.

Mr. BALL. Were you facing the door he is supposed to have left by?

Miss HINE. Yes, sir.

Mr. BALL. Do you recall seeing him?

Miss HINE. No, sir.

Mr. BALL. Do you have any definite recollection of Mrs. Reid coming in?

Miss HINE. No, sir; I only saw four or five people that came by and they all came and were all talking about how terrible it was.

Mr. BALL. Do you remember their names?

Miss HINE. Yes, sir.

Mr. BALL. Who were they?

Miss HINE. Mr. Williams, Mr. Molina (spelling), Miss Martha Reid, Mrs. Reid, Mrs. Sarah Stanton, and Mr. Campbell; that's all I recall, sir.

Mr. BALL. Miss Hine, this will be written up and it will be submitted for your signature if you wish, or you can waive signature right now; which do you prefer? Do you have any choice?

Miss HINE. Well, I would prefer to see it.

Mr. BALL. Prefer to see it, all right, then this young lady will inform you to come down, read it, look it over and sign it.

Miss HINE. Okay.

Mr. BALL. Thanks very much for coming in.

Miss HINE. You are very welcome.

TESTIMONY OF MISS DORIS BURNS

The testimony of Miss Doris Burns was taken at 3:20 p.m., on April 7, 1964, in the office of the U.S. attorney, 301 Post Office Building, Bryan and Ervay Streets, Dallas, Tex., by Messrs. Joseph A. Ball and Samuel A. Stern, assistant counsel of the President's Commission.

Mr. BALL. Please stand up and hold up your right hand and be sworn.

Miss BURNS. (complying).

Mr. BALL. Do you solemnly swear the testimony you give will be the truth, the whole truth, and nothing but the truth, so help you God?

Miss BURNS. I do.

Mr. BALL. What is your name, please?

Miss BURNS. Doris Burns.

Mr. BALL. What is your address?

Miss BURNS. 2617 Shelby, Dallas.

361

Mr. BALL. What is your occupation?

Miss BURNS. I am a correspondent for the Macmillan Co.

Mr. BALL. Where is your office?

Miss BURNS. In the Texas School Book Depository Building on the third floor.

Mr. BALL. Can you tell me something about yourself, where you were born and what your education is, and what your business occupation has been.

Miss BURNS. Well, I was born in Tyler, Tex., and I graduated from high school here in Dallas and I worked many years for lawyers here.

Mr. BALL. What kind of work?

Miss BURNS. Well, I was just a legal secretary and worked for Vanette Hosiery Mills, secretary to the president. They are not here any more, I don't think. After that I worked for a geologist.

Mr. BALL. Most of your work has been secretarial, has it?

Miss BURNS. Yes, but at Macmillan I mostly compose my own letters.

Mr. BALL. When did you go to work for Macmillan?

Miss BURNS. April 19, 1955. Am I too fast?

Mr. BALL. She can write as fast as you talk.

Miss BURNS. That's wonderful.

Mr. BALL. Go right ahead.

Miss BURNS. Let's see, I've forgotten what else you wanted to know.

Mr. BALL. Well, first of all, you went to work in 1955?

Miss BURNS. Yes, sir.

Mr. BALL. Where is the office of the Macmillan Co.?

Miss BURNS. Well, at that time it was on Ross and Akard; now——

Mr. BALL. Where was it in November 1963?

Miss BURNS. At Elm and Houston.

Mr. BALL. What part of the building?

Miss BURNS. On the third floor, room 301.

Mr. BALL. Are there any windows in those offices?

Miss BURNS. Yes; they have some windows; they face the west, I guess you would say. They don't overlook the route of the President's——

Mr. BALL. Do they or do they not overlook Elm Street?

Miss BURNS. They do not overlook Elm Street.

Mr. BALL. They overlook the railroad yards, do they?

Miss BURNS. That is right.

Mr. BALL. On November 22d, what were you doing that day?

Miss BURNS. I was listening to the radio as I worked.

Mr. BALL. About noon, did you go to lunch?

Miss BURNS. Well, I had lunch at the office and then I didn't intend to go see the President, didn't have any desire to but I left about—I don't remember the exact time but, anyway, when I left they said on the radio that he—that the motorcade was coming up, I believe it was Cedar Springs; anyway, he hadn't been away from the airport long and that he was going about 5 miles an hour so everybody could see him. Well, thinking he was going that slowly, I thought I had plenty of time, so I walked up to Sanger's.

Mr. BALL. To where?

Miss BURNS. Sanger's.

Mr. BALL. Where is that?

Miss BURNS. It's about four blocks up Elm Street.

Mr. BALL. Which way on Elm—east?

Miss BURNS. East; you see, we are down at the extreme west end of the street; nothing else down there.

Mr. BALL. Then what happened?

Miss BURNS. I bought some Kleenex and came back, and everybody was out on the steps to look, but I didn't stop. I went on back to the office.

Mr. BALL. That is the third floor?

Miss BURNS. Yes.

Mr. BALL. Was anybody in the office?

Miss BURNS. Yes; Mrs. Case hadn't ever gone out. She was there. I believe she was the only one.

Mr. BALL. What did you do?

Miss BURNS. I listened to the radio, and by that time they said that he was on Main and turning at Houston or Main by the courthouse, so since he was that ▓ close, I thought, well, I guess I will go look out the window. I didn't care enough to go downstairs, but I thought I will go look out the window. So I thought I would have plenty of time, if he was just coming around Main Street, that I could still get around there, so I went around to American Book Co., which is the office closest to us that had a window looking out on Elm. There was nobody in there, so then I started down the hall to Allyn and Bacon. As I went down this hall towards the windows that looked out on Houston Street, I heard a shot, but I didn't think much about it. I didn't, of course, know it was a shot because when you hear tires backfire and all, they all sound alike to me, so I didn't think a thing about that.

I went around to Allyn and Bacon, and Mr. Wilson, the manager, was at the window looking out. He was the only one in there, so I asked him if I could look out the window with him. About that time he said "Oh, my God, there's been a shooting." I still didn't think anybody, of course, had been killed, just thought somebody had shot in the air or something, so I said "Has the President already passed? And he said "Yes," so I looked out and that big bus that had the press in it, had the word "Press" or whatever it was on the bus, was passing, so I said "Well, I guess I have missed the President then," and I started on back out of the office and I just said as I left, "Well, I hope nobody got hurt."

Mr. BALL. You heard how many shots?
Miss BURNS. One.
Mr. BALL. Just one?
Miss BURNS. It must have been the last one because I didn't hear any more.
Mr. BALL. Did you have any idea where it was coming from?
Miss BURNS. Well, it just sounded as though it was back of me. You see, I was going towards Houston Street. I was facing east and it sounded to me as if it came toward my back.
Mr. BALL. You were in the building?
Miss BURNS. Yes; I was in the building.
Mr. BALL. Walking down the hall?
Miss BURNS. Walking down the hall going towards Allyn and Bacon.
Mr. BALL. Now, what happened after that?
Miss BURNS. I came on back and listened to the radio some more and in a few minutes, why, they told it.
Mr. BALL. Did you ever know Lee Harvey Oswald?
Miss BURNS. I rode on the elevator with him one time.
Mr. BALL. That's all?
Miss BURNS. But I didn't know who he was—about a week before.
Mr. BALL. You never talked to him?
Miss BURNS. I never talked to him.
Mr. BALL. Who were you with at the time this happened?
Miss BURNS. The Macmillan Co.
Mr. BALL. Who was in the office with you?
Miss BURNS. Mrs. Case, but I couldn't see her.
Mr. BALL. She was in the same office?
Miss BURNS. I have a private office. She was around the corner where her office is.
Mr. BALL. Mrs. Case?
Miss BURNS. Yes.
Mr. BALL. Did you hear anybody running down the stairs at any time?
Miss BURNS. Yes, but I didn't know——
Mr. BALL. When?
Miss BURNS. It was after that; I went to the restroom.
Mr. BALL. How long after?
Miss BURNS. I imagine maybe it was 25 minutes. I imagine it was the policeman or somebody; of course, I don't know who it was.
Mr. BALL. I think that's all, Miss Burns. This will be written up and you can sign it; you can read it and sign it or you can waive your signature if you wish and you won't have to come back here. Which would you rather do?
Miss BURNS. I can waive signature if that is all right.
Mr. BALL. Fine, thank you very much, Miss Burns.

363

TESTIMONY OF MARY E. BLEDSOE

The testimony of Mary E. Bledsoe was taken at 9:30 a.m., on April 2, 1964, in the office of the U.S. attorney, 301 Post Office Building, Bryan and Ervay Streets, Dallas, Tex., by Messrs. Joseph A. Ball, David W. Belin, and Albert E. Jenner, Jr., assistant counsel of the President's Commission. Mrs. Mary E. Bledsoe was accompanied by her attorney, Miss Melody June Douthit.

Mr. BALL. Will you stand up, Mrs. Bledsoe, please. Will you raise your right hand. Do you solemnly swear that the testimony which you are about to give before this Commission will be the truth, the whole truth, and nothing but the truth, so help you God?

Mrs. BLEDSOE. I do.

Mr. BALL. State your name, please.

Mrs. BLEDSOE. Mary E. Bledsoe.

Mr. BALL. And your residence?

Mrs. BLEDSOE. 621 North Marsalis.

Mr. BALL. Mrs. Bledsoe, you received a letter from the counsel for the Commission asking you to be here today, didn't you?

Mrs. BLEDSOE. Yes, sir.

Mr. BALL. And you received that what date? March 26, or was it March 27?

Mrs. BLEDSOE. When? This first time?

Miss DOUTHIT. No, back.

Mr. BALL. I mean the letter your attorney just showed me. Seventeenth of March?

Mrs. BLEDSOE. Uh-huh.

Mr. BALL. And you have come down here in response to that letter, haven't you?

Mrs. BLEDSOE. Yes.

Mr. BALL. And you are here appearing with your attorney, who is present at this time?

Mrs. BLEDSOE. Yes.

Mr. BALL. You've been asked to give testimony in this matter which concerns an investigation into the assassination of President Kennedy, and certain facts which you have, which I believe that you knew of, and we are going to ask you questions about it. That is the general subject of the investigation.

Mrs. BLEDSOE. Uh-huh.

Mr. BALL. And you are willing to testify, are you not?

Mrs. BLEDSOE. Yes.

Mr. BALL. And give us as much help as you can?

Mrs. BLEDSOE. Yes.

Mr. BALL. What is your—you have given us your address, haven't you?

Mrs. BLEDSOE. Yes.

Mr. BALL. Can you tell me something, briefly, about your past life? Where you were born and what your education was and what your occupation has been?

Mrs. BLEDSOE. I was born in the country. Town of about 12 miles from Corsicanna, Tex. My father was a doctor down there, and I was a second child; I have a brother older than I am. And then I moved to Ennis, and then come to Dallas and lived here until I was a little girl, 4 or 5 years old, then I went back down to Ennis and my father practiced medicine in Ennis, Tex., and then about—I married then when I was 17, and then I moved around quite a little while I was married, but—and then my husband and I, we had trouble, and I divorced him in—oh, about in 1925, and I raised my two children by myself, and I have been in the place where I live 24 years, and over on the back, I was—I have been here 43 years in the neighborhood, and I raised both of my boys, and they are grown.

Mr. BALL. Your occupation has been that of a housewife?

Mrs. BLEDSOE. Yes. Well, I had rented rooms, but I had some money my father had given me. I had some money from him.

Mr. BALL. Your present address, you rent rooms, do you?

Mrs. BLEDSOE. Yes; I do, now. I have just started in September again. My son left home, you see, and I started——

Mr. BALL. That was September of 1963?

Mrs. BLEDSOE. Yes.

Mr. BALL. How large a house is that?

Mrs. BLEDSOE. Well, it is all on one floor. And I have four bedrooms, but I rent three.

Mr. BALL. In September of 1963, you were living there alone, were you?

Mrs. BLEDSOE. No; my son was living there.

Mr. BALL. And he left?

Mrs. BLEDSOE. Uh-huh.

Mr. BALL. Did you rent rooms before your son left your home?

Mrs. BLEDSOE. Well, let's see, now, oh, yes; uh-huh, in SeptemberI——

Mr. BALL. Except his bedroom?

Mrs. BLEDSOE. Yes; uh-huh.

Mr. BALL. When he left you rented another bedroom, did you?

Mrs. BLEDSOE. Well yes; I am trying to. Haven't got it rented.

Mr. BALL. Now, did you ever rent a room in your home to Lee Oswald?

Mrs. BLEDSOE. Yes; uh-huh.

Mr. BALL. Can you tell me about the first time that you ever saw him. What the date was?

Mrs. BLEDSOE. The first time I ever saw him or heard of him, I was in the backyard doing a lot of yardwork. I come around the house and he was standing on the porch, and he said, "Do you have a room for rent?"

I had a "for rent" sign out. I said, "Yes" and he said, "May I see it?"

And I wanted—"Yes"; and then I was trying to size him up to get in that room, and—in the house, and I said, "Are you married?"

And he said, "Yes; I am married. I just want this for a short time. My wife lives at Irving."

And then we got inside the house and he had a thing where this—pictures of his wife and baby, and he said he was in the Marine Corps, and I tried to be nice to him, and so, he paid me $7, and——

Mr. BALL. Then did he tell you what his name was?

Mrs. BLEDSOE. Oh, yes.

Mr. BALL. What did he say?

Mrs. BLEDSOE. His name was Oswald, and he put it on this thing, and my son took it and sold it.

Mr. BALL. You said he put it on this thing?

Mrs. BLEDSOE. This right here.

Mr. BALL. What is, "this thing"?

Mrs. BLEDSOE. Calendar.

Mr. BALL. Well——

Miss DOUTHIT. Mary, why don't you pull up your chair and be comfortable while you are doing this. Now, you are all right.

Mr. BALL. Now, you have a calendar here?

Mrs. BLEDSOE. That is my calendar.

Mr. BALL. That is the calendar for December 1963, and I notice it has dates and names and dates. Is that the way you keep books on your rooms?

Mrs. BLEDSOE. Yes; but I don't now. I did then, because I just had started. The first one I got was in September.

Mr. BALL. September of 1963?

Mrs. BLEDSOE. Uh-huh.

Mr. BALL. He put his name on the calendar?

Mrs. BLEDSOE. Well, got it in September. He got it, my son sold it for $5, and I didn't even know that he tore that out.

Mr. BALL. Now, let me see here in this calendar. It runs from January 1963, to December of 1963, but October of 1963, has been torn out?

Mrs. BLEDSOE. Uh-huh. And he said his name was Lee Oswald was what his name was, and I said, "Well, I can't think of that name Oswald, I will call you Lee."

So, he put it down on the 4th. Just rented for a week, you see, the 7th.

Mr. BALL. You said the 4th?

Mrs. BLEDSOE. On the 7th.

Mr. BALL. On the 7th of October? That is the first day you ever saw him?

Mrs. BLEDSOE. Ever saw him.

Mr. BALL. On the 7th of October you rented the room to him, didn't you?

Mrs. BLEDSOE. Uh-huh.

Mr. BALL. And is that the date that he put his name on the calendar?

Mrs. BLEDSOE. Yes; that is the day.

Mr. BALL. He paid you $7?

Mrs. BLEDSOE. $7 in money.

Mr. BALL. That was the rental?

Mrs. BLEDSOE. For one room.

Mr. BALL. For one room for 1 week?

Mrs. BLEDSOE. Yes, sir.

Mr. BALL. When did he move into the room?

Mrs. BLEDSOE. Right then.

Mr. BALL. Did he have his things?

Mrs. BLEDSOE. Had his things on his hand and had his bag, but after he paid my $7 he went out—I don't know, I think this YMCA, but I am not supposed to know where, and brought back another bag, and then he said, "Well, where is the grocery store?"

Well, I said, "It is down that way," but I didn't want him to use the kitchen, so, he said, "I'm going to get some milk," and so, I didn't like that much, but I didn't say anything about it because I wanted to get along with him.

Mr. BALL. Let me ask you some questions before we commence the grocery store part of it.

When you first saw him, did he have his luggage with him?

Mrs. BLEDSOE. Yes.

Mr. BALL. What did he have with him?

Mrs. BLEDSOE. A bag.

Mr. BALL. Will you describe the bag?

Mrs. BLEDSOE. I don't remember where—seemed like it was a kind of a duffelbag.

Mr. BALL. The kind the men in the service put their clothes in?

Mrs. BLEDSOE. Yes; and had some on his arm, these coathangers, you know.

Mr. BALL. Had some things on a coathanger?

Mrs. BLEDSOE. And had a clock.

Mr. BALL. Had what?

Mrs. BLEDSOE. A clock, wrapped up.

Mr. BALL. What color was this duffelbag?

Mrs. BLEDSOE. I think it was blue.

Mr. BALL. That was the only bag he had with him?

Mrs. BLEDSOE. No, he went off to town and got another one.

Mr. BALL. Then he went off to town and brought another bag back, would you describe that?

Mrs. BLEDSOE. No, I didn't pay any attention to it.

Mr. BALL. Was it leather or——

Mrs. BLEDSOE. I couldn't say.

Mr. BALL. Could you give me any idea of the size of it?

Mrs. BLEDSOE. Well, it was big. About like that [indicating].

Mr. BALL. About like that, you mean, oh, 3 feet long, 2 feet, 2½?

Mrs. BLEDSOE. No; about like that.

Mr. BALL. About——

Mrs. BLEDSOE. As well as I remember.

Mr. BALL. About 2 feet long? Was it brown?

Mrs. BLEDSOE. I just couldn't remember. I didn't pay any attention to it.

Mr. BALL. Do you remember the color?

Mrs. BLEDSOE. No.

Mr. BALL. Do you remember him carrying it into the room?

Mrs. BLEDSOE. Yes; I remember he went in.

Mr. BALL. Now——

Mrs. BLEDSOE. But, I didn't pay any attention. He rented the room, and I didn't pay any attention.

Mr. BALL. Did he carry it by a handle, or in his arms?

Mrs. BLEDSOE. I guess he carried it by a handle, but I don't know.

Mr. BALL. He brought two bags into this room?

Mrs. BLEDSOE. Yes; wasn't but one when he come in, but next time he went off——

Mr. BALL. He brought another one back?

How did he come out there, do you know?

Mrs. BLEDSOE. I don't know. I don't know whether he come here—he come and just knocked on the door. I was in the backyard.

Mr. BALL. After he moved, after he put his bags in his room, did he leave?

Mrs. BLEDSOE. No; he said——

Mr. BALL. I mean, did he leave to go downtown to get the other bag?

Mrs. BLEDSOE. Uh-huh, and come back.

Mr. BALL. Did you see him leave?

Mrs. BLEDSOE. No; I didn't see him.

Mr. BALL. The time he went to get the other bag, did you see him?

Mrs. BLEDSOE. No.

Mr. BALL. Do you know what kind of transportation he had?

Mrs. BLEDSOE. No; I guess I didn't pay any attention to him.

Mr. BALL. Did you ever see him drive up in a car?

Mrs. BLEDSOE. No, always took a bus.

Mr. BALL. How do you know that?

Mrs. BLEDSOE. Well, I saw—one time he stopped over there across the street and get the bus that is the only time I didn't—I didn't watch what he did. Of course, I had no idea he was the kind of man he was.

Mr. BALL. You say that he asked you where the grocery store was?

Mrs. BLEDSOE. Uh-huh.

Mr. BALL. Is that when he came back with this second bag?

Mrs. BLEDSOE. Yes; uh-huh, I got him something to eat.

Mr. BALL. Did you talk to him anything about his using your refrigerator?

Mrs. BLEDSOE. Well——

Miss DOUTHIT. One question. Ask her how long he was gone and you will know how far he went. That is what I wanted to know.

Mr. BALL. When he left to get this second bag, how long was he gone?

Mrs. BLEDSOE. Well, not over an hour. About an hour. It wasn't a long—I wondered then where he went, but it wasn't none of my business.

Mr. BALL. You say now not over an hour. Do you think it might have been less than an hour?

Mrs. BLEDSOE. Yes; I believe less than an hour.

Mr. BALL. How much less?

Mrs. BLEDSOE. Well, I'd say 40 minutes, anyway, at most.

Mr. BALL. This was in the afternoon, was it?

Mrs. BLEDSOE. Yes; started at 3 o'clock.

Mr. BALL. At 3 o'clock he came to your home?

Mrs. BLEDSOE. Yes.

Mr. BALL. And then he came back the second time with the second bag before 4, did he?

Mrs. BLEDSOE. Yes; I'm sure he did.

Mr. BALL. Did you talk to him any about the use of the refrigerator?

Mrs. BLEDSOE. Well, he said he was going to put something in there, and I said—I didn't have anything to say, and I hemmed-and-hawed, I said, "Well, no; I don't have a very big refrigerator."

Well, he said, "I won't use it after this time." He was very, very congenial.

Mr. BALL. Did he go down to the grocery store?

Mrs. BLEDSOE. Yes.

Mr. BALL. What did he buy?

Mrs. BLEDSOE. He bought some peanut butter and some sardines, and some bananas and put it all in his room, except the milk, and he ate there, ate in his room. I didn't like that either.

Mr. BALL. He was there how many days?

Mrs. BLEDSOE. He was there 5 days, just 5 days.

Mr. BALL. He was there—what day of the week was the day that he came?

Mrs. BLEDSOE. Monday and Tuesday he stayed home and went to bed, and stayed—I didn't pay any attention to him——

Mr. BALL. Monday night he stayed home?

Mrs. BLEDSOE. Yes; after he went to the grocery store.

Mr. BALL. What about Tuesday?

Mrs. BLEDSOE. Tuesday he went out at 9:30 and come home at 2:30. He was looking for a job, and called on the phone, wanted different ones, and I got the book, and papers, and tried to look for him a job, because he was a nice looking boy, and wanted a job.

Mr. BALL. Now, he went out at 9–9:30 in the morning and came back at 2:30?

Mrs. BLEDSOE. Let's see. 1:30. I have my nap then, and it kind of interfered, but I didn't say anything.

Mr. BALL. You say you have a what?

Mrs. BLEDSOE. I have a nap then.

Mr. BALL. You take a nap in the afternoon?

Mrs. BLEDSOE. Yes; I had a stroke, you see.

Mr. BALL. And it interfered with your nap when he came back?

Mrs. BLEDSOE. Yes; but I didn't say anything then, but then the nextday——

Mr. BALL. Let's finish Tuesday.

Mrs. BLEDSOE. All right. That's all.

Mr. BALL. Did he go out again after he came home at 1:30?

Mrs. BLEDSOE. No.

Mr. BALL. Stayed in his room?

Mrs. BLEDSOE. All the time, and stayed there that night, too.

Mr. BALL. All the time? What about Wednesday?

Mrs. BLEDSOE. He left about 9 o'clock, and went off dressed. Had a white shirt and white tie and white—white trousers, and looked very nice. Went off Monday about 2 o'clock.

Mr. BALL. This is Wednesday.

Mrs. BLEDSOE. Wednesday. Then he got back at 1:30.

Mr. BALL. Let me see, he left at 9?

Mrs. BLEDSOE. Uh-huh.

Mr. BALL. Come back at 1:30?

Mrs. BLEDSOE. Yes.

Mr. BALL. And did he go out again that day?

Mrs. BLEDSOE. No; but then he talked to somebody on the phone, and talked in a foreign language.

Mr. BALL. You mean when? Wednesday?

Mrs. BLEDSOE. On Wednesday, I guess it was Wednesday, but I am sure it must have been Wednesday. I was in my room, and the telephone is over there [indicating], and I didn't like that, somebody talking in a foreign language and, so I told my girl friend, I said, "I don't like anybody talking in a foreign language."

Mr. BALL. What time of day did he call on the phone and talk in a foreign language?

Mrs. BLEDSOE. He come home at 1:30 and talked about 2 or 2:30, talked like that.

Mr. BALL. Did he go out again that day?

Mrs. BLEDSOE. No; went to bed.

Mr. BALL. Went to bed that night and stayed there?

Mrs. BLEDSOE. And I didn't fix his room either, that is why I didn't see his luggage. I didn't go in his room at all because they take care of their own rooms.

Mr. BALL. What about Thursday?

Mrs. BLEDSOE. Thursday, he went out at 10 o'clock or 10:30, and I was out in the yard, and he come out and I said, "Oh. I thought you had gone."

"Oh, no," he said, he didn't go, but he came home a little bit early, and after I said he got into my nap, he come home at 2 o'clock, or 2:30, you see, and didn't leave until 10.

Mr. BALL. And did you tell him that he interfered with your nap?

Mrs. BLEDSOE. Yes.

Mr. BALL. What day did you tell him that?

Mrs. BLEDSOE. I told him that, I guess must have been Thursday. Thursday and then he——

Mr. BALL. You mean Thursday morning?

Mrs. BLEDSOE. Uh-huh.

Mr. BALL. Well, then Thursday morning is when he left a little later than usual?

Mrs. BLEDSOE. Uh-huh.

Mr. BALL. And you told him that he had interfered with your nap before that day?

Mrs. BLEDSOE. No; I think it was—it must have been—no; it was that day. It was after I had that call. I didn't like that and he never said a word, and then I interviewed him when he first came in and thought he was all right, and he never spoke—I had one boy on the back. He never saw him and he would run to the bathroom and go to the icebox and get some ice, and didn't like that. Went too much to the icebox, but——

Mr. BALL. Well, now——

Mrs. BLEDSOE. That was a Thursday.

Mr. BALL. When he went away on Thursday, then had you told him prior to that time that when he came in at 1:30, in the afternoon, he interfered with your nap?

Mrs. BLEDSOE. Yes.

Mr. BALL. Do you think you might have told him that on Wednesday or Tuesday?

Mrs. BLEDSOE. No; I didn't tell him until after I had that call.

Mr. BALL. When was the call?

Mrs. BLEDSOE. On Wednesday.

Mr. BALL. And who called you on Wednesday?

Mrs. BLEDSOE. He called somebody, you know.

Mr. BALL. You mean the day that he called someone and spoke in a foreign language?

Mrs. BLEDSOE. Yes.

Mr. BALL. After that, you told him——

Mrs. BLEDSOE. I didn't like that.

Mr. BALL. That he interfered with your nap?

Mrs. BLEDSOE. Uh-huh. I didn't like it, and the next day he fussed with somebody on the phone, I don't know whether it was his wife or who it was.

Mr. BALL. That was Thursday?

Mrs. BLEDSOE. Yes.

Mr. BALL. About what time of day?

Mrs. BLEDSOE. About 2 o'clock or 2:30 when he come home hereand——

Mr. BALL. Did he go out again that day?

Mrs. BLEDSOE. No.

Mr. BALL. Stayed in all day?

Mrs. BLEDSOE. Stayed in all day, and it was Friday he stayed in his room all day. Didn't eat. Ate what he had in his room. Stayed in his room all day long.

Mr. BALL. When did you next see him?

Mrs. BLEDSOE. Been—then Saturday, he started out and had his bag.

Mr. BALL. Started out with his luggage?

Mrs. BLEDSOE. Saturday morning he started out with his bag and——

Mr. BALL. Which bag did he take?

Mrs. BLEDSOE. I don't know.

Mr. BALL. Was it the duffelbag?

Mrs. BLEDSOE. I don't know.

Mr. BALL. Like you see the servicemen carrying?

Mrs. BLEDSOE. I guess it was. I didn't pay any attention.

Mr. BALL. This was Saturday morning about what time?

Mrs. BLEDSOE. About 10 o'clock, or 9:30 and I thought he was going to move and I—"Oh—" I said, "You are going to move?"

And he said, "No; I am just going for the weekend."

Well, I said, "Well, I don't know."   But he said, "And I want my room cleaned and clean sheets put on the bed."

And I said, "Well, I will after you move because you are going to move."

He said, "Why?"

I says, "Because I am not going to rent to you any more."

Mr. BALL. Not going to what?

Mrs. BLEDSOE. Not going to rent to you any more, He said, "Give me back my money." Now, $2.

I said, "Well, I don't have it."

So, he left Saturday morning and, in the meantime. I think his wife was going to have a baby——

Mr. BALL. How did you know that?

Mrs. BLEDSOE. Well, I found—I read it in the papers.

Mr. BALL. Did he ever tell you?

Mrs. BLEDSOE. No, no; he didn't ever tell me. Didn't tell me anything.

Mr. BALL. You told him you weren't going to rent to him any more on that Saturday morning about 10 o'clock. At that time did he have his bag? Was he carrying a bag?

Mrs. BLEDSOE. Yes; going out with it again. Going out to Irving.

Mr. BALL. How did you know?

Mrs. BLEDSOE. Well, said he was.

Mr. BALL. He told you he was going to Irving?

Mrs. BLEDSOE. Yes; said he was going to Irving.

Mr. BALL. Did he tell you he was going to Irving for any purpose?

Mrs. BLEDSOE. No; just said he was going to Irving. No; he didn't tell me anything.

Mr. BALL. Why did you tell him you wouldn't rent to him any more?

Mrs. BLEDSOE. Because I didn't like him.

Mr. BALL. Why?

Mrs. BLEDSOE. I didn't like his attitude. He was just kind of like this, you know, just big shot, you know, and I didn't have anything to say to him, and—but, I didn't like him. There was just something about him I didn't like or want him—just wasn't the kind of person I wanted. Just didn't want him around me.

Mr. BALL. When he left on Saturday morning do you know by what transportation he took?

Mrs. BLEDSOE. Didn't pay any attention.

Mr. BALL. Is there a bus stop near your home?

Mrs. BLEDSOE. Right in front of the house.

Mr. BALL. Did you see him take the bus.

Mrs. BLEDSOE. No; I didn't see him.

Mr. BALL. Did you see him wait for the bus?

Mrs. BLEDSOE. No; I just saw him go out the door. Didn't pay any attention. And when he left I said—oh, he was going to come back and get his things Saturday. He took it out and said, "Well, it is 2 dollars," and I—"Well, I don't have it, so, he went off."

Mr. BALL. Well, wait a minute. Did he say he would come back and get the things Saturday?

Mrs. BLEDSOE. No; he didn't say a thing.

Mr. BALL. Now, wait a minute. Saturday morning you told him you wouldn't rent to him again. What did he say about getting his money back?

Mrs. BLEDSOE. Well, he said, "Well, give me my money back and I will move now." And I said, "I don't have it."

Mr. BALL. Then what did he say?

Mrs. BLEDSOE. Didn't say anything and went on out the door.

Mr. BALL. Was there anything said about whether he would come to get his clothes?

Mrs. BLEDSOE. No; not a thing.

Mr. BALL. Did he come back Saturday night?

Mrs. BLEDSOE. No.

Mr. BALL. When did he come back?

Mrs. BLEDSOE. Monday morning.

Mr. BALL. And from Saturday morning until Monday morning you didn't see him?

Mrs. BLEDSOE. Uh-huh.

Mr. BALL. What time Monday morning did he come back?

Mrs. BLEDSOE. Between 8 and 9, 9 and 10. I mean.

Mr. BALL. When he came back did he have anything with him?

Mrs. BLEDSOE. No.

Mr. BALL. Have his bag?

Mrs. BLEDSOE. No; didn't say a word to him. He—I didn't say a word to him.

Mr. BALL. When he came back did he have anything in his hand?

Mrs. BLEDSOE. No.

Mr. BALL. Did you see him leave?

Mrs. BLEDSOE. Yes; I did.

Mr. BALL. What did he take with him?

Mrs. BLEDSOE. He had that bag.

Mr. BALL. What bag?

Mrs. BLEDSOE. The bag, you see, he had two.

Mr. BALL. Yes.

Mrs. BLEDSOE. But, I never noticed it. I don't know what kind it was or anything.

Mr. BALL. When he left, he had one bag when he left?

Mrs. BLEDSOE. One bag.

Mr. BALL. Do you know whether it was the duffelbag?

Mrs. BLEDSOE. No; I couldn't say for sure.

Mr. BALL. Do you remember what color it was?

Mrs. BLEDSOE. No; just navy blue. I don't know which one he carried, or what they were or what. I didn't pay any attention to it.

Mr. BALL. You don't know whether both bags were navy blue, or different colors?

Mrs. BLEDSOE. No.

Mr. BALL. You know one was navy blue?

Mrs. BLEDSOE. That's right.

Mr. BALL. When he left, did he say anything to you?

Mrs. BLEDSOE. No.

Mr. BALL. Or did you say anything to him?

Mrs. BLEDSOE. No. I said, "Good luck." You know, I thought to myself, "That's good riddance," and I looked in his room and it was all right, and nothing was disturbed.

Mr. BALL. Had he cleaned it up?

Mrs. BLEDSOE. No; it was dirty.

Mr. BALL. Did he leave anything around the room?

Mrs. BLEDSOE. No; somehow I saw a map. I believe he left that map.

Mr. BALL. What map?

Mrs. BLEDSOE. A map of Dallas where he could get around to get some places, jobs.

Mr. BALL. What did you do with that map?

Mrs. BLEDSOE. Throwed it in the garbage.

Mr. BALL. Threw it away?

Mrs. BLEDSOE. Yes.

Mr. BALL. Was it a map, kind of a map put out by the service stations?

Mrs. BLEDSOE. Yes; one of those kinds. I just threw it away and cleaned up the room. Just threw it away.

Mr. BALL. Did the map have any markings on it?

Mrs. BLEDSOE. Yes.

Mr. BALL. You know—do you know what the markings were?

Mrs. BLEDSOE. No; didn't pay any attention to it.

Mr. BALL. Now, did you ever see him again?

Mrs. BLEDSOE. Yes.

Mr. BALL. When?

Mrs. BLEDSOE. Well, I thought. "Well, he is gone," and forgot it.

Mr. BALL. But, before you go into that, I notice you have been reading from some notes before you.

Mrs. BLEDSOE. Well, because I forget what I have to say.

Mr. BALL. When did you make those notes?

Mrs. BLEDSOE. What day did I make them?

Miss DOUTHIT. When Mr. Sorrels and I were talking about her going to Washington, he made the suggestion that she put all the things down on paper because she might forget something, and I said, "Mary, you put everything on a piece of paper so that you can remember it and you won't forget anything, you know, what happened," and that's when she started making notes.

Mr. BALL. You have made the notes in the last week?

Mrs. BLEDSOE. Yes.

Miss DOUTHIT. At my suggestion and Mr. Sorrels.

Mr. BALL. You didn't make any notes during the week he was there?

Mrs. BLEDSOE. No; I didn't pay any attention to him.

Mr. BALL. Your address, make sure that we have this. The address where you were living on the 7th of October was 621 Marsalis—North Marsalis, Dallas, Tex.?

Mrs. BLEDSOE. That's right. Marsalis.

Mr. BALL. And you are still living there, aren't you?

Mrs. BLEDSOE. Yes.

Mr. BALL. And the foreign language that you heard Oswald using over the telephone on this Wednesday afternoon, do you know what the language was?

Mrs. BLEDSOE. No; I didn't.

Mr. BALL. Are you familiar with the Spanish language?

Mrs. BLEDSOE. No; I am not. Not familiar with any of them.

Mr. BALL. All you know it was not English?

Mrs. BLEDSOE. No.

Mr. BALL. But, you can't tell what language?

Mrs. BLEDSOE. No.

Mr. BALL. Can you make a guess?

Mrs. BLEDSOE. No; I have no idea. I do, because the girl is Spanish, but I don't know whether he called her or not.

Mr. BALL. What girl is Spanish?

Mrs. BLEDSOE. I mean—his wife was Russian.

Mr. BALL. Russian.

Mrs. BLEDSOE. I don't know.

Mr. BALL. Now, when did you see Oswald again?

Mrs. BLEDSOE. Well, I went down to the parade. Oh, when was the parade? The 22d of—the next—22d of February—when was the parade?

Mr. BALL. The 22d of November the President came to Dallas.

Mrs. BLEDSOE. And I first got off at Neiman's and I—the parade didn't come on, and I kept walking on up, and walked in front of Titche's over on that side there, and I saw the parade there. He passed—I saw the President, oh, I was happy I got to see him. And—so then I got on across and went over to the Athletic Club, and caught the bus.

Mr. BALL. What bus did you catch?

Mrs. BLEDSOE. Well, I don't remember whether it was the Marsalis or the Romana.

Mr. BALL. Both go by your house, do they? What was the last one?

Mrs. BLEDSOE. The Marsalis.

Mr. BALL. What was the second name?

Mrs. BLEDSOE. Romana.

Mr. BALL. And both go west on Elm?

Mrs. BLEDSOE. Right—so, I got on the bus, and while it was awfully crowded there——

Mr. BALL. You mean crowded on the bus?

Mrs. BLEDSOE. No; outside.

Mr. BALL. Were there many people on the bus?

Mrs. BLEDSOE. No.

Mr. BALL. How many people on the bus?

Mrs. BLEDSOE. Oh, about 10.

Mr. BALL. And what was the location on Elm where you boarded this bus?

Mrs. BLEDSOE. At the Athletic Club.

Mr. BALL. What cross street is that, do you remember?

Mrs. BLEDSOE. St. Paul.

Mr. BALL. St. Paul? You got on at St. Paul? St. Paul and Elm?

Mrs. BLEDSOE. Uh-huh.

Mr. BALL. And the bus was going in what direction?

Mrs. BLEDSOE. West.

Mr. BALL. All right, now, tell me what happened?

Mrs. BLEDSOE. And, after we got past Akard, at Murphy—I figured it out. Let's see. I don't know for sure. Oswald got on. He looks like a maniac. His sleeve was out here [indicating]. His shirt was undone.

Mr. BALL. You are indicating a sleeve of a shirt?

Mrs. BLEDSOE. Yes.

Mr. BALL. It was unraveled?

Mrs. BLEDSOE. Was a hole in it, hole, and he was dirty, and I didn't look at him. I didn't want to know I even seen him, and I just looked off, and then about that time the motorman said the President had been shot, and I sit—when I go to town I sit this way on the bus. The motorman is right there [indicating], and I sit right there so that I can get off.

Mr. BALL. You mean—where do you sit with reference to the motorman, one seat or two seats behind him?

Mrs. BLEDSOE. I don't—the motorman is here, and I sit across in the seat across the way.

Mr. BALL. Now, on this day when you boarded the bus, is that the seat you took?

Mrs. BLEDSOE. I always did.

Mr. BALL. Would that be the first seat on the right-hand side?

Mrs. BLEDSOE. Yes.

Mr. BALL. First seat on the bus?

Mrs. BLEDSOE. Well——

Miss DOUTHIT. Side seat.

Mr. BALL. Oh, it is a side seat? Was that side seat so that you were facing the motorman?

Mrs. BLEDSOE. Uh-huh.

Mr. BALL. When Oswald got on, you then weren't facing him, were you?

Mrs. BLEDSOE. No; but I saw that it was him.

Mr. BALL. How close did he pass to you as he boarded the bus?

Mrs. BLEDSOE. Just in front of me. Just like this [indicating].

Mr. BALL. Just a matter of a foot or two?

Mrs. BLEDSOE. Uh-huh.

Mr. BALL. When he got on the bus, did he say anything to the motorman?

Mrs. BLEDSOE. Oh, the motorman? I think—I don't know. I don't know.

Mr. BALL. Where did he sit?

Mrs. BLEDSOE. He sat about halfway back down.

Mr. BALL. On what side?

Mrs. BLEDSOE. On the same side I was on.

Mr. BALL. Same side? Did you look at him?

Mrs. BLEDSOE. No, sir.

Mr. BALL. Did he look at you as he went by? Did he look at you?

Mrs. BLEDSOE. I don't know. I didn't look at him. That is—I was just—he looked so bad in his face, and his face was so distorted.

Mr. BALL. Did he have a hat on?

Mrs. BLEDSOE. No.

Mr. BALL. Now, what color shirt did he have on?

Mrs. BLEDSOE. He had a brown shirt.

Mr. BALL. And unraveled?

Mrs. BLEDSOE. Hole in his sleeve right here [indicating].

Mr. BALL. Which is the elbow of the sleeve? That is, you pointed to the elbow?

Mrs. BLEDSOE. Well, it is.

Mr. BALL. And that would be which elbow, right or left elbow?

Mrs. BLEDSOE. Right.

Mr. BALL. Did he have anything on. Was the shirt open or was it buttoned?

Mrs. BLEDSOE. Yes; all the buttons torn off.

Mr. BALL. What did he have on underneath that?

Mrs. BLEDSOE. I don't know.

Mr. BALL. Do you know the color of any undershirt he had on?

Mrs. BLEDSOE. No.

Mr. BALL. Notice the color of his pants?

Mrs. BLEDSOE. Yes, they were gray, and they were all ragged in here [indicating].

Mr. BALL. Around where?

Mrs. BLEDSOE. At the seam.

Mr. BALL. At the waist?

Mrs. BLEDSOE. At the waist, uh-huh.

Mr. BALL. Was the shirt tucked beneath the belt in his pants, or outside the belt?

Mrs. BLEDSOE. No; he had it in.

Mr. BALL. Had it tucked in?

Mrs. BLEDSOE. No; it was tucked in.

Mr. BALL. So, that the belt of the pants was outside the shirt?

Mrs. BLEDSOE. Yes; uh-huh.

Mr. BALL. Now, you say the motorman said something?

Mrs. BLEDSOE. Motorman said, "Well, the President has been shot," and I say—so, and the woman over—we all got to talking about four of us sitting around talking, and Oswald was sitting back there, and one of them said, "Hope they don't shoot us," and I said, "I don't believe that—it is—I don't believe it. Somebody just said that."

And it was too crowded, you see, and Oswald had got off.

Mr. BALL. How far had he been on the bus before he got off? Until the time he got on until the time he got off?

Mrs. BLEDSOE. About three or four blocks.

Mr. BALL. Did he say anything to the motorman when he got off?

Mrs. BLEDSOE. They say he did, but I don't remember him saying anything.

Mr. BALL. Did you ever see the motorman give him a transfer?

Mrs. BLEDSOE. No; I didn't pay any attention but I believe he did.

Mr. BALL. Well, what do you mean he—you believe he did? Did you remember seeing him get on or are you telling me something you read in the newspapers?

Mrs. BLEDSOE. No; I don't remember. I don't remember.

Mr. BALL. Did you pay any attention at that time as to whether he did, or did not get a transfer?

Mrs. BLEDSOE. I didn't pay any attention to him.

Mr. BALL. Well, did you look at him as he got off the bus?

Mrs. BLEDSOE. No; I sure didn't. I didn't want to know him.

Mr. BALL. Well, you think you got enough of a glimpse of him to be able to recognize him?

Mrs. BLEDSOE. Oh, yes.

Mr. BALL. You think you might be mistaken?

Mrs. BLEDSOE. Oh, no.

Mr. BALL. You didn't look very carefully, did you?

Mrs. BLEDSOE. No; I just glanced at him, and then looked the other way and I hoped he didn't see me.

Mr. BALL. Now, are there two exits from the bus?

Mrs. BLEDSOE. Uh-huh.

Mr. BALL. The middle of the bus, and front of the bus?

Mrs. BLEDSOE. Uh-huh.

Mr. BALL. Which exit did he leave?

Mrs. BLEDSOE. Front.

Mrs. BALL. By the motorman?

Mrs. BLEDSOE. Uh-huh, by the motorman.

Mr. BALL. Did anybody else get off at that time when he got off?

Mrs. BLEDSOE. No, not then, but there was a lady sitting right across, she wanted to go to the train station.

Mr. BALL. To the what station?

Mrs. BLEDSOE. Train station, and she was worried about trying to get off, you know, trying to get there, and then we were hearing her, and I said, "Well, why don't you walk over there. It's just a little ways." Because the crowd was so bad we still didn't know the President had been killed, and finally she got off, but I think it was—it was before—I mean after Oswald did.

Mr. BALL. Did she ask for a transfer?

Mrs. BLEDSOE. Yes; she had the man give her one, because she caught the bus before she got to the train station.

Mr. BALL. How do you know that?

Mrs. BLEDSOE. Well, I saw her.

Mr. BALL. You saw her catch another bus?

Mrs. BLEDSOE. She got on when we did. She rode a block.

Mr. BALL. Did anybody get off when the lady got off? Anybody that was going to the train station?

Mrs. BLEDSOE. No.

Mr. BALL. Was there traffic? Was the traffic heavy?

Mrs. BLEDSOE. Oh, it was awful in the city, and then they had roped off that around where the President was killed, shot, and we were the first car that come around there, and then all of us were talking about the man, and we were looking up to see where he was shot and looking—and then they had one man and taking him, already got him in jail, and we got—"Well, I am glad they found him."

Mr. BALL. You were looking up at where?

Mrs. BLEDSOE. At where the boy was shot.

Mr. BALL. You mean the Texas Book Depository?

Mrs. BLEDSOE. Yes, uh-huh.

Mr. BALL. School Book Depository?

Mrs. BLEDSOE. Uh-huh, because we were right four blocks from there, you see.

Mr. BALL. Can you tell me the location of the bus with reference to a cross street on Elm where Oswald got off?

Mrs. BLEDSOE. No; I can't, because they have changed that street, so, they have torn down things and I don't go to town very much now and so I don't——

Mr. BALL. Was it in the middle of the block, or at a regular bus stop?

Mrs. BLEDSOE. Well, they said it was.

Mr. BALL. I want to know what you remember.

Mrs. BLEDSOE. No; I don't remember.

Mr. BALL. Do you remember whether it was a regular bus stop or not?

Mrs. BLEDSOE. No; I didn't pay any attention.

Mr. BALL. Did Oswald get on at a regular bus stop?

Mrs. BLEDSOE. I didn't pay any particular attention to him.

Mr. BALL. Do you remember anyone knocking on the door, and as a result, the motorman opened the front door?

Mrs. BLEDSOE. No.

Mr. BALL. You don't remember that?

Mrs. BLEDSOE. I don't remember.

Mr. BALL. You are not able to say whether Oswald got on at a regular bus stop, or at a point between blocks?

Mrs. BLEDSOE. No.

Mr. BALL. And you are not able to tell us whether he got off at regular bus stops, or between?

Mrs. BLEDSOE. That's right.

Mr. BALL. Now, had the bus gone as far as Lamar Street, when Oswald got off?

Mrs. BLEDSOE. Yes. No; I think before we got to Lamar Street.

Mr. BALL. How far?

Mrs. BLEDSOE. Well——

Mr. BALL. Close to Lamar?

Mrs. BLEDSOE. Yes, close.

Mr. BALL. How close?

Mrs. BLEDSOE. Well, I couldn't say.

Mr. BALL. Within a half block, or block?

Mrs. BLEDSOE. No; within a block.

Mr. BALL. About a block from Lamar, you think?

Mrs. BLEDSOE. Uh-huh.

Mr. BALL. It was approaching Lamar, wasn't it?

Mrs. BLEDSOE. Uh-huh.

Mr. BALL. When did you first notify the police that you believe you'd seen Oswald?

Mrs. BLEDSOE. When I got home, first thing I did I went next door and told them the President had been shot, and so she turned on the radio and I went in and called my son and said the President had been shot, and he said, "Why, he has got killed." Well, I turned on the radio—television—and we heard ambulances and going around and them, and so, I didn't pay any attention. I wanted to hear about the President and there was a little boy came in that room in the back and he turned it on, and we listened and hear about Mr. Tippen [sic] being shot, and it didn't dawn on me, and I said—told his name as Oswald. I don't—didn't mean anything to me, so, I wanted to hear about the President, only one I was interested in, so, he went on back to work and they kept talking about this boy Oswald and had on a brown shirt, and all of a sudden, well, I declare, I believe that this was this boy, and his name was Oswald—that is—give me his right name, you know, and so, about an hour my son came home, and I told him, and he immediately called the police and told them, because we wanted to do all we could, and so, I went down the next night. He took me down, and I made a statement to them, what kind of—Secret Service man or something down there.

Mr. BALL. Where?

Mrs. BLEDSOE. At the police station.

Mr. BALL. Uh-huh. Now, did you ever see Oswald in a lineup?

Mrs. BLEDSOE. No.

Mr. BALL. Did they ever show you pictures?

Mrs. BLEDSOE. Yes; showed me pictures of him.

Mr. BALL. But didn't show you Oswald?

Mrs. BLEDSOE. No.

Mr. BALL. Never did see Oswald after he was arrested?

Mrs. BLEDSOE. Not after he got off the bus; no.

Mr. BALL. But, you looked at the pictures of Oswald?

Mrs. BLEDSOE. Yes.

Mr. BALL. Showed you the pictures of Oswald?

Mrs. BLEDSOE. The man down at the police station, he had a picture of him with a gun, and said, "Do you recognize him?"

And I said, "Yes; it is Oswald." That is the one that I remember him.

Mr. BALL. Do you know the name of the man who showed you the picture of the man with the gun?

Mrs. BLEDSOE. I am so bad about names.

Mr. BALL. Was there one man or more than one man?

Mrs. BLEDSOE. Oh, about a dozen.

Mr. BALL. Oh, a dozen men?

Mrs. BLEDSOE. There sure was a lot of them. Two Secret Service men, and two to do this, and oh, I had interviewed about 9 or 10 or 12, plenty of them.

Mr. BALL. Now, I have got a piece of clothing here, which is marked——

Mrs. BLEDSOE. That is it.

Mr. BALL. Commission Exhibit 150.

Mrs. BLEDSOE. That is it.

Mr. BALL. This is a shirt——

Mrs. BLEDSOE. That is it.

Mr. BALL. What do you mean by "that is it?"

Mrs. BLEDSOE. Because they brought it out to the house and showed it.

Mr. BALL. I know. What do you mean by "this is it?"

Mrs. BLEDSOE. Well, because I can recognize it.

Mr. BALL. Recognize it as what?

Mrs. BLEDSOE. Yes, sir; see there?

Mr. BALL. Yes. You tell me what do you see here? What permits you to recognize it?

Mrs. BLEDSOE. I recognize—first thing I notice the elbow is out and then I saw—when the man brought it out and let me see it?

Mr. BALL. No, I am talking about—I am showing you this shirt now, and you said, "That is it." You mean—What do you mean by "that is it"?

Mrs. BLEDSOE. That is the one he had out there that day?

Mr. BALL. Who had it out there?

Mrs. BLEDSOE. Some Secret Service man.

Mr. BALL. He brought it out. Now, I am—you have seen this shirt then before?

Mrs. BLEDSOE. Yes.

Mr. BALL. It was brought out by the Secret Service man and shown to you?

Mrs. BLEDSOE. Yes.

Mr. BALL. Had you ever seen the shirt before that?

Mrs. BLEDSOE. Well——

Mr. BALL. Have you?

Mrs. BLEDSOE. No; he had it on, though.

Mr. BALL. Who had it on?

Mrs. BLEDSOE. Oswald.

Mr. BALL. Oswald had it on?

Mrs. BLEDSOE. Oswald had it on.

Mr. BALL. Now, what is there about the shirt that makes you believe that this is the shirt that Oswald had on when he was on the bus? What is there about it?

Mrs. BLEDSOE. Well, let's see the front of it. Yes. See all this [indicating]? I remember that.

Mr. BALL. Tell me what you see there?

Mrs. BLEDSOE. I saw the—no; not so much that. It was done after—that is the part I recognize more than anything.

Mr. BALL. You are pointing to a hole in the right elbow?

Mrs. BLEDSOE. Yes.

Mr. BALL. What about the color?

Mrs. BLEDSOE. Well, I—What do you mean?

Mr. BALL. Well——

Mrs. BLEDSOE. When he had it on?

Mr. BALL. Yes.

Mrs. BLEDSOE. Before he was shot? Yes; I remember it being brown.

Mr. BALL. You remember the shirt being brown.

Was it this color?

Mrs. BLEDSOE. Yes; it was that color.

Mr. BALL. In other words, when you remember that you have seen something before——

Mrs. BLEDSOE. Uh-huh.

Mr. BALL. In order to convince me that you did see it before you've got to tell me what there is about it that is the same, you see. Now, you try to convince me, or tell me why it is that you believe that this is the shirt that Oswald had on when you saw him on the bus?

Mrs. BLEDSOE. Well, I would say it was. That hole——

Mr. BALL. Mostly the hole in the right sleeve?

Mrs. BLEDSOE. Yes.

Mr. BALL. What about the color?

Mrs. BLEDSOE. Yes; I remember the color.

Mr. BALL. That is a similar color, isn't it?

Mrs. BLEDSOE. No; same color.

Mr. BALL. Same color?

Mrs. BLEDSOE. Uh-huh.

Mr. BALL. You think that is the shirt?

Mrs. BLEDSOE. Yes; it is the shirt.

Mr. BALL. Had you ever seen him wear this shirt before, when he was around your house?

Mrs. BLEDSOE. No.

Mr. BALL. First time you ever saw the shirt was when you saw him on the bus?

Mrs. BLEDSOE. Uh-huh.

Mr. BALL. I have two exhibits here. One Commission Exhibit 157. Exhibit 157, and Commission 156, both pants. Have you ever seen either one of those before?

Mrs. BLEDSOE. Now, is that long pants?

Mr. BALL. Yes; this is 157.

Mrs. BLEDSOE. Well, that is not the ones he had on.

Mr. BALL. That is not?

Mrs. BLEDSOE. No; it was ragged up at the top.

Mr. BALL. This other pair of pants, 156, does that look like any of the pants he had on?

Mrs. BLEDSOE. That must have been it, but seemed like it was ragged up at the top.

Mr. BALL. But, you think 156 may have been the pair of pants he had on?

Mrs. BLEDSOE. Yes.

Mr. BALL. You think 157—don't pay any attention to the fact that it is cut up—does 157 look anything like the pants he had on?

Mrs. BLEDSOE. No; I don't——

Mr. BALL. You don't think so?

Mrs. BLEDSOE. No, sir.

Mr. BALL. I have no more questions to ask you now, Mrs. Bledsoe, but Mr. Jenner will ask you some questions.

Mrs. BLEDSOE. All right.

Mr. JENNER. I will get up here close so you will hear me all right.

Mrs. BLEDSOE. All right.

Mr. JENNER. I would like to go back to the day that he came to your home on the 7th of October?

Mrs. BLEDSOE. Uh-huh.

Mr. JENNER. You were out in your backyard?

Mrs. BLEDSOE. Uh-huh.

Mr. JENNER. And did he come back there?

Mrs. BLEDSOE. No.

Mr. JENNER. Did you have a bell on your house?

Mrs. BLEDSOE. He knocked at the door.

Mr. JENNER. He knocked at the door and you heard him knock at the door?

Mrs. BLEDSOE. And I went around the front.

Mr. JENNER. And your home is all at one level?

Mrs. BLEDSOE. Yes.

Mr. JENNER. So, you walked through your house?

Mrs. BLEDSOE. No; I went through the yard and come around from the back to the front yard.

Mr. JENNER. And you saw a young man at the door?

Mrs. BLEDSOE. Uh-huh.

Mr. JENNER. How was that young man dressed on that occasion?

Mrs. BLEDSOE. I don't remember what he had on. Didn't pay any attention. He was clean and that's all you see, but I didn't know what color the pants were and what kind of shirt it was.

Mr. JENNER. Well, did he have a suit on or sportscoat, or just his shirt?

Mrs. BLEDSOE. Just the shirt. It was hot weather. October.

Mr. JENNER. Do you recall—did he have a tie on?

Mrs. BLEDSOE. No.

Mr. JENNER. The shirt, that was open at the front?

Mrs. BLEDSOE. Yes, it wasn't those short shirts. I don't know what kind it was. I didn't pay any attention to him.

Mr. JENNER. And this was a Monday morning.

Mrs. BLEDSOE. Monday afternoon.

Mr. JENNER. Monday afternoon. Did he have a hat on?

Mrs. BLEDSOE. No.

Mr. JENNER. Was he—did he have any luggage?

Mrs. BLEDSOE. Yes; had one bag, I don't know whether it was a duffel or what, but then he went on and got another one.

Mr. JENNER. Well, if you will permit me to stay with what he had when you first saw him——

Mrs. BLEDSOE. Uh-huh.

Mr. JENNER. You call on your recollection and tell me all you can tell me about the bag he had at that time, its size, its shape. In another connection, Mrs. Bledsoe, it is prior events that are important to us. If we can possibly find out or get as accurate a description as you can give us. Sit there relaxed and tell us what you remember about this bag, what size it was; what shape it was; whether it was hard; whether it was soft, what color it was.

Was it zippered? How was it fastened?

Mrs. BLEDSOE. I don't know whether it was zippered or not. But seems to me like it was, though.

Mr. JENNER. Just start from the beginning and tell us what you remember about the bag that he had when you first saw him at the door.

Mrs. BLEDSOE. Well, it was just a blue—like a canvas bag.

Mr. JENNER. Canvas?

Mrs. BLEDSOE. And, I don't know whether it was zippered or not.

Mr. JENNER. You don't recall a zippered sort of bag?

Mrs. BLEDSOE. I didn't even look. It was about that long, I guess [indicating].

Mr. JENNER. You are indicating about 26 inches?

Mrs. BLEDSOE. Yes.

Mr. JENNER. About that long.

Mrs. BLEDSOE. Then, he had some things on his back.

Mr. JENNER. Now, would you mind if we stuck with the bag?

Mrs. BLEDSOE. Well, that's all.

Mr. JENNER. Well, it was 26 inches long and you think it was canvas, and you think it was blue in color?

Mrs. BLEDSOE. Yes.

Mr. JENNER. What was its shape? Was it a round sort of soft kind of bag or was it—did it have firm, stiff sides? Was it rectangular?

Mrs. BLEDSOE. Well, I couldn't say. Couldn't say. Didn't pay any attention to it.

Mr. JENNER. Your recollection does serve you that it was not what we would call a suitcase?

Mrs. BLEDSOE. No; looked like an inexpensive bag of some kind.

Mr. JENNER. And your memory doesn't serve you that there was any sort of zipper thing, and you do seem to have a reasonably firm recollection that the color of it was blue?

Mrs. BLEDSOE. Uh-huh.

Mr. JENNER. Did it have a handle on it?

Mrs. BLEDSOE. Yes.

Mr. JENNER. When he picked it up——

Mrs. BLEDSOE. Well, that is——

Mr. JENNER. I was trying to get an idea, and well—I have a coat here, and using it for purposes of illustration, when he picked up the bag by the handles did the bag sag, or was it firm?

Mrs. BLEDSOE. I didn't pay any attention. Didn't pay a bit of attention.

Mr. JENNER. Now, I notice from your testimony that he also had, on this occasion, at this time, in addition to the canvas bag, blue in color, he had some things over his arm, or over his shoulder?

Mrs. BLEDSOE. On a coathanger.

Mr. JENNER. He had some articles of clothing?

Mrs. BLEDSOE. On coathangers.

Mr. JENNER. On coathangers?

Mrs. BLEDSOE. Yes.

Mr. JENNER. And were those draped back over the shoulder or arm, or was he holding them by the hooks or hooks on the hangers?

Mrs. BLEDSOE. I think he had them on coathangers, just—I guess—I don't know—he was standing there. I don't have no idea.

Mr. JENNER. Just how he was carrying them, you are uncertain, but you are certain that he had articles of clothing on hangers?

Mr. BLEDSOE. On coathangers.

Mr. JENNER. Were—would they be wooden coathangers or the metal?

Mrs. BLEDSOE. Metal ones.

Mr. JENNER. The type you get when you send clothes to the cleaners and they come back on these wire, metal hangers, what—was that the type?

Mrs. BLEDSOE. Well, I imagine. I couldn't tell. Now, I—no; I didn't pay any attention to him.

Mr. JENNER. Your recollection serves you now that there were hangers, but you cannot recall whether they were the wire type or whether they were wooden?

Mrs. BLEDSOE. When he left, he just carried them off. I never did look at his clothes at all.

Mr. JENNER. You impress me as a lady that wouldn't be fussing around?

Mrs. BLEDSOE. I didn't care enough about it. All I wanted him to do was rent the room.

Mr. JENNER. Now, you had a discussion, and you rented the room to him for $7 for that week?

Mrs. BLEDSOE. Uh-huh.

Mr. JENNER. And he paid you then and there?

Mrs. BLEDSOE. Uh-huh

Mr. JENNER. In cash?

Mrs. BLEDSOE. Yes; and I gave him a receipt on this book.

Mr. JENNER. Now, he then left your home?

Mrs. BLEDSOE. Uh-huh.

Mr. JENNER. Did he say anything about why he was leaving?

Mrs. BLEDSOE. He went to the grocery store. No, no; first he went to get his other bag.

Mr. JENNER. What did he say then?

Mrs. BLEDSOE. Didn't say anything.

Mr. JENNER. How did you come to know that he went to get another bag?

Mrs. BLEDSOE. He didn't say—he just went off.

Mr. JENNER. He just turned around without any leave taking?

Mrs. BLEDSOE. No; because he was not a man to talk, you know, what I got out of him, I had to get it out of him, because it was hard to—because I wanted to see what kind of a person he was, and it was hard to get, you know, to judge him in such a short time.

Mr. JENNER. When you completed the transaction about his renting the room and you got your $7, he paid it to you, so it was agreed he had the room for a week, did he go in and look at the room before he paid you the $7?

Mrs. BLEDSOE. He was in the room, and I was at the door, and he looked at it and I said, $7, so, he took it and give me the money all in ones, $7.

Mr. JENNER. Seven $1 bills?

Mrs. BLEDSOE. Seven $1 bills, and then he come over to my room and I—he wrote it down, and it is a good thing I had him write it, because I am kind of nervous, and I don't write so well, see, and he put it down on that, and that—and so, that is—this is in September, but anyway——

Mr. JENNER. Yes; I appreciate that.

Mrs. BLEDSOE. October——

Mr. JENNER. Well——

Miss DOUTHIT. Let me ask her this question about that bag, if it was puffed out, or approximately what shape it was, also, as to any further conversation that she had as to his background, how much she knows. If you are interested. You might not be.

Mr. JENNER. Mr. Robert Davis of the attorney general's office of Texas has come in, and I am not seeking to press you, but we have some problems of the highest degree of exactitude that we can obtain. And at the risk of boring you, I would like to go back to that bag again.

Mrs. BLEDSOE. Oh, that; I didn't pay much attention to it.

Mr. JENNER. When you first saw him at the door at your front of your home, he had the bag?

Mrs. BLEDSOE. Yes.

Mr. JENNER. Was it resting on the porch, or was he standing before the door with bag in hand when you first saw him?

Mrs. BLEDSOE. I come around the house, you see, and I don't know. I didn't pay—I don't know, couldn't tell you whether he was carrying it or what, but   he did have these things on his shoulder, on his hangers. It—maybe had it sitting down, I don't know. I guess he did. I didn't pay any attention to it.

Mr. JENNER. And at that point you were asking why he was there?

Mrs. BLEDSOE. No; he asked me if I had a room for rent.

Mr. JENNER. Yes.

Mrs. BLEDSOE. And I said, "Yes," and I thought, "Well, are you married?" And he said, "Yes," and——

Mr. JENNER. You asked?

Mrs. BLEDSOE. Uh-huh.

Mr. JENNER. You inquired of him as to his history?

Mrs. BLEDSOE. Yes.

Mr. JENNER. What did you inquire of him, and what did he say?

Mrs. BLEDSOE. Well, I wanted to find out something about him, and he said, "Well, I just want the room for a week or two, because I am going to get a job and then I will have my wife here."

Mr. JENNER. He told you at that time and informed you that he was unemployed?

Mrs. BLEDSOE. Yes.

Mr. JENNER. And he would be seeking work?

Mrs. BLEDSOE. Yes.

Mr. JENNER. And he said that he was going to bring his wife?

Mrs. BLEDSOE. Yes.

Mr. JENNER. And—when and if he obtained employment?

Mrs. BLEDSOE. And so, that give me a lead, something to talk about, and I said, "Well, what kind of work do you do?

379

"Oh, I do electronics," he said, and I said, "Well, there is some good jobs because you are young, and you can get a good job a young man like you."

And then went on. Then something about him being in the Marines, and I said, "Well, that is wonderful. My son was in the Navy."

And talking about him, you know, just getting to know him, and—but, "here is a picture of my wife, and picture of the girl, and the baby."

And I said, "Oh, she has got a baby, hasn't she?"

And he said, "Yes."

And everything he said, I had to pull it out of him to talk about something for him to say what it was.

Mr. JENNER. But, he volunteered the picture of his wife and child?

Mrs. BLEDSOE. Yes; he did that. Showed me that picture.

Mr. JENNER. Was that an ordinary snapshot picture?

Mrs. BLEDSOE. Uh-huh. It was in his billfold.

Mr. JENNER. Took it out of his billfold?

Mrs. BLEDSOE. No, sir; it was in the billfold. Just showed it in the billfold.

Mr. JENNER. I see. I have a billfold here. Was it this type?

Mrs. BLEDSOE. No; it was something else. Don't seem like it was like that. Seemed like it opened this other way, I——

Mr. JENNER. This?

Mrs. BLEDSOE. Yes; I think it was like that.

Mr. JENNER. Did he carry it in his trouser pocket, coat pocket?

Mrs. BLEDSOE. I didn't pay any attention where he had it.

Mr. JENNER. What other inquiries did you make of him to become better acquainted and find out about him?

Mrs. BLEDSOE. He said he had been in the Marines and I thought that was a pretty good recommendation, and I said, "Well, you won't have any trouble at all getting any job."

And so, the next morning I was helping him looking for a job.

Mr. JENNER. Now, pardon me, if you will just stick to while you're at the door now.

Mrs. BLEDSOE. Well——

Mr. JENNER. And——

Miss DOUTHIT. Just one interruption, but find out if this conversation took place at the door, or after he got in the room.

They are in this room, you see.

Mr. JENNER. You went inside the house almost immediately?

Mrs. BLEDSOE. Yes; I did.

Mr. JENNER. When he first made an inquiry?

Mrs. BLEDSOE. Yes.

Mr. JENNER. And you took him to show him the room?

Mrs. BLEDSOE. Yes.

Mr. JENNER. And your inquiries were—with respect to his history were in the room?

Mrs. BLEDSOE. Yes; uh-huh.

Mr. JENNER. And he showed you the picture while you were in the room?

Mrs. BLEDSOE. I think so.

Mr. JENNER. And I take it, am I correct, when you went into the room he had that bag, and he had the articles of clothing?

Mrs. BLEDSOE. Yes.

Mr. JENNER. And had them with him, didn't leave them on the porch?

Mrs. BLEDSOE. Yes.

Mr. JENNER. What did he do with the bag when he entered the room? Did he put it down on the floor?

Mrs. BLEDSOE. Didn't pay any attention.

Mr. JENNER. Didn't pay any attention? What did he do with the articles of clothing on the hangers?

Mrs. BLEDSOE. I wasn't paying any attention to it. I guess he hung them up. Just a young boy, and I was trying to see if he was clean, and if he was very intelligent, and he was going to go to work, so, I didn't have too much to work on. Told me he had a nice wife, so, I didn't have anything to say.

Mr. JENNER. When your son was in the Navy, did he have a duffelbag?

Mrs. BLEDSOE. No. Now, it was so long ago—it was—I don't know whether he did. I don't think he did. He didn't. He was an instructor at TI.

Mr. JENNER. Was he stationed here in Dallas?

Mrs. BLEDSOE. No, TI. Treasure Island.

Mr. JENNER. Oh, Treasure Island. How long did this discussion with him in the room take?

Mrs. BLEDSOE. Oh, I guess 10 minutes because those—he was—you know, old people, they want to get you out of the way. They don't want to listen to you, but I wanted to find out, so, I think I maybe asked him too many questions, but I wanted him to say something to me and he said something about his—I said, "Do you have a family here," and he said, "Yes, my family lives here."

Well, he wouldn't say his mother or anything, and I didn't ask him everything.

Miss DOUTHIT. Well——

Mr. JENNER. All right.

(Discussion off the record.)

Mr. JENNER. Did you notice anything in addition to the hangers with respect to these clothes? Were the articles of clothing enclosed in any kind of a bag or paper, plastic, or otherwise?

Mrs. BLEDSOE. No, just on hangers.

Mr. JENNER. Just on hangers.

Mrs. BLEDSOE. But I didn't pay any attention to what kind of—I think maybe a coat. I don't know what it was, a sweater or something.

Mr. JENNER. Did you see how many articles of clothing were there?

Mrs. BLEDSOE. Oh, about four.

Mr. JENNER. And none of them was enclosed in any kind of a container, plastic or otherwise?

Mrs. BLEDSOE. No.

Mr. JENNER. Was he pleasant during all of the conversation you had with him?

Mrs. BLEDSOE. Was the first day. Next day didn't talk any more. I didn't talk to him.

Mr. JENNER. As soon as he—recalling to mind that he paid you the $7.

Mrs. BLEDSOE. Yes.

Mr. JENNER. Did any further conversation take place after he paid you the $7?

Mrs. BLEDSOE. Yes; that is when he asked where the grocery store was.

Mr. JENNER. I see. What else?

Mrs. BLEDSOE. Well, he didn't say anything about going to get the rest of his things. I think that he must have been—said that after he came back with the other bag.

Mr. JENNER. Must have said what?

Mrs. BLEDSOE. Where was the grocery store, after he come back and got the other——

Mr. JENNER. So, your recollection presently serves you that he paid you the $7 and no further conversation took place?

Mrs. BLEDSOE. No.

Mr. JENNER. He turned and left the room?

Mrs. BLEDSOE. I—he was—I was in the room, I just walked out.

Mr. JENNER. You walked out after the transaction, financially, was complete?

Mrs. BLEDSOE. I went and he paid—he had already paid me but I wanted him to put his name on here.

Mr. JENNER. On your register?

Mrs. BLEDSOE. On this [indicating].

Mr. JENNER. He did that——

Mrs. BLEDSOE. Yes.

Mr. JENNER. In your presence?

Mrs. BLEDSOE. Yes; in the living room.

Mr. JENNER. Your recollection was that he wrote the words "Lee Oswald"?

Mrs. BLEDSOE. Lee Oswald.

Mr. JENNER. Then did he leave your home?

Mrs. BLEDSOE. Yes; huh.

Mr. JENNER. Without saying anything to you?

Mrs. BLEDSOE. No.

Mr. JENNER. And he was gone—did he return?

Mrs. BLEDSOE. Yes; within about 40 minutes, I guess.

Mr. JENNER. And he was gone about 40 minutes?

Mrs. BLEDSOE. And got the rest of his things.

Mr. JENNER. When he returned did you see him before he entered your home?

Mrs. BLEDSOE. I don't remember.

Mr. JENNER. Do you have a recollection of having seen him before he entered his room?

Mrs. BLEDSOE. No.

Mr. JENNER. When did you become aware of the fact he had returned?

Mrs. BLEDSOE. Well, I must have heard him, or he might have come in and put his milk in the icebox.

Mr. JENNER. Well, he didn't get the milk, as far as I recall, until you'd advised him where the grocery store was.

Mrs. BLEDSOE. Uh-huh.

Mr. JENNER. That was after he had returned from the——

Mrs. BLEDSOE. From the——

Mr. JENNER. After this 40-minute interval? I am just sticking for the moment to the time that he returned to your home after 40 minutes.

Mrs. BLEDSOE. Uh-huh.

Mr. JENNER. He had put his name in your register and in your presence, in the living room, and turned and left your home and returned in 40 minutes; now, is that right? It's that point that I am concentrating on. When did you become aware that he had returned on that occasion and how?

Mrs. BLEDSOE. Well, I don't know—I guess he come and put the things in the icebox. I don't even remember where I was.

Mr. JENNER. I see. So, that you didn't see him return to your home?

Mrs. BLEDSOE. I didn't see him come in.

Mr. JENNER. Didn't see him come in?

Mrs. BLEDSOE. No.

Mr. JENNER. And you didn't know what he had with him at that point?

Mrs. BLEDSOE. No.

Mr. JENNER. To the best of your ability where was he in your home when you became aware of his presence on his return after that 40 minutes?

Mrs. BLEDSOE. I must have been in the kitchen and he came back there and put the milk in, I guess.

Mr. JENNER. Did he have milk with him after he returned that 40 minutes?

Mrs. BLEDSOE. No, not the 40 minutes. That was the bag.

Mr. JENNER. See, this is what I'm trying to concentrate on for the moment, before you get the milk. And I am trying to take it sequentially. He paid the $7 and signed the register in your living room?

Mrs. BLEDSOE. Yes.

Mr. JENNER. And without any further words to you he turned and left your home, is that accurate?

Mrs. BLEDSOE. Yes; that's about right.

Mr. JENNER. He returned in 40 minutes?

Mrs. BLEDSOE. Uh-huh.

Mr. JENNER. Now, sticking right to that point, when did you become aware of the fact that he was then back in your home, that is, at that point?

Mrs. BLEDSOE. That he—he hadn't gotten the milk yet?

Mr. JENNER. No; this is when he first returned.

Mrs. BLEDSOE. Well, I don't know. I was just around the house. I didn't pay any attention to him.

Mr. JENNER. So, I take it, then, when he made that first trip back, you didn't see him?

Mrs. BLEDSOE. No.

Mr. JENNER. You don't know what he had with him on that occasion?

Mrs. BLEDSOE. Well, I guess he had the bag, didn't he?

Mr. JENNER. I want to stick with what you knew at that instant of time. What you found out afterwards, I'll go into that in a moment.

You didn't see him return?

Mrs. BLEDSOE. No.

Mr. JENNER. You don't know what he had with him when he returned?

Mrs. BLEDSOE. No.

Mr. JENNER. At that instance, because you didn't see him?

Mrs. BLEDSOE. No.

Mr. JENNER. But, you were aware; now, you became aware of the fact that he did return?

Mrs. BLEDSOE. Yes.

Mr. JENNER. Did you have a conversation with him at that point?

Mrs. BLEDSOE. No.

Mr. JENNER. When did you become aware and I gather from your earlier testimony you became aware that he had brought that into your home, or there was in your home some additional luggage. When you first saw him he had this soft canvas bag, or canvas bag, whether it was soft or not that is uncertain.

Mrs. BLEDSOE. Yes.

Mr. JENNER. And then you became aware later that day that there was another piece of luggage, and, am I correct about that?

Mrs. BLEDSOE. Now, I think he said he was going to get some more. He was going to get some more and he had some boots, too, in his hand. I—maybe he brought those the last time. I don't remember.

Mr. JENNER. What kind of boots?

Mrs. BLEDSOE. Well, they looked like they were about up to here [indicating].

Mr. JENNER. Up to the knee?

Mrs. BLEDSOE. No; about there [indicating].

Mr. JENNER. Oh,——

Mrs. BLEDSOE. There.

Mr. JENNER. Just a little above the ankle?

Mrs. BLEDSOE. Uh-huh.

Mr. JENNER. About 3 inches above the ankle?

Mrs. BLEDSOE. I don't know what they used them for.

Mrs. JENNER. Were they cowboy boots.

Mrs. BLEDSOE. No; it wasn't cowboy boots.

Mr. JENNER. Were they canvas, leather, or rubber?

Mrs. BLEDSOE. No; just leather.

Mr. JENNER. Heavy-soled?

Mrs. BLEDSOE. Heavy-soled.

Mr. JENNER. Heavy-soled. Rubber soles?

Mrs. BLEDSOE. Oh, no; leather.

Mr. JENNER. Any hobnails in them?

Mrs. BLEDSOE. No.

Mr. JENNER. Hard heel or flat heel? I mean, flat sole and heel?

Mrs. BLEDSOE. Oh, they had a heel, too. I remember them having that. He must have brought those in when he brought those the last time.

Mr. JENNER. You do not recall his having the boots at the time you first—at the first time you talked to him?

Mrs. BLEDSOE. No; I don't believe he did.

Mr. JENNER. But, you became aware of the boots afterward?

Mrs. BLEDSOE. Uh-huh.

Mr. JENNER. At, or about, or after the time he returned from this 40-minute absence?

Mrs. BLEDSOE. Uh-huh.

Mr. JENNER. And was it at the time you noticed the boots, did you also notice that he had additional items of luggage?

Mrs. BLEDSOE. Well, he went to get the luggage.

Mr. JENNER. Did he say that?

Mrs. BLEDSOE. No; I don't know whether he did or not. I know he—I don't know.

Mr. JENNER. Did you have a thought in mind when he left after he paid you the $7 and signed your register that he was going somewhere to obtain additional articles of clothing?

Mrs. BLEDSOE. Well, I thought that.

Mr. JENNER. You thought that? He didn't say anything to you about that, however?

Mrs. BLEDSOE. No; he didn't say anything. Didn't talk much.

Mr. JENNER. It is clear in your mind that he just turned around after you finished the transaction and left and returned in 40 minutes?

Mrs. BLEDSOE. I thought he said he had to get some groceries, but maybe that was after he got the luggage, I don't remember.

Mr. JENNER. You had become aware that afternoon that he had additional articles of luggage?

Mrs. BLEDSOE. Come in about 3, about 4 he got the rest of the luggage.

Mr. JENNER. Now, this additional article of luggage, would you describe it, as compared with——

Mrs. BLEDSOE. I didn't pay any——

Mr. JENNER. Please. As compared with this canvas bag, blue in color, that you just told me about?

Mrs. BLEDSOE. No; I didn't pay no attention to it at all. It was just a piece of luggage.

Mr. JENNER. Well, was it a——

Mrs. BLEDSOE. I don't——

Mr. JENNER. What I would call a suitcase or what you might call a suitcase?

Mrs. BLEDSOE. No; it wasn't a regular suitcase, but just something inexpensive, just something the boys have, and I didn't pay any attention to him.

Mr. JENNER. Was it hard-sided?

Mrs. BLEDSOE. No; it was a—you know, it was weak, you know.

Mr. JENNER. Uh-huh. It was weak. Was it strong enough so that it had a rectangular shape?

Mrs. BLEDSOE. No.

Mr. JENNER. You know what I mean by suitcase?

Mrs. BLEDSOE. Yes.

Mr. JENNER. It is reasonably firm and hard, and has a handle on it?

Mrs. BLEDSOE. No; it wasn't that way. One of those inexpensive kind of things, but I don't know whether it was canvas or what.

Mr. JENNER. Was it firmer in shape than the canvas bag you have described to me that he had earlier?

Mrs. BLEDSOE. No. Well, I think it was chuck full.

Mr. JENNER. You know it was?

Mrs. BLEDSOE. Uh-huh. It was, I remember. I don't——

Mr. JENNER. Do you remember the color?

Mrs. BLEDSOE. No. One of them was blue, and I don't know which one or anything about it.

Mr. JENNER. I see.

Miss DOUTHIT. Let me ask her something.

Mary, would it help you to remember this if you would just begin, you were out in the yard, and you went around and interviewed this man there, did you stand in the yard, or go in your room and talk? Did he put up his things then before he came across the hall to talk to you? When did he ask you about groceries? After he signed your register did he go back in his room and hang his clothes up, or what happened? Would it help if you just sit here idly without anybody asking you questions and see? Did you go back out in the yard after he paid you the money, and while he was gone—if you can, just retrace your steps without anybody interrupting you. Could you begin and go again out in the yard, and went around and saw this man here, and he told you he wanted to rent a room, whether you stood on the porch and talked to him, or whether he brought his things and you went on and showed him the room? How far is the room from where your front door was? If you go down a hall, how far? Did you go over there and talk to him and make arrangements about the rent of the room? Did he hang up his clothes while he was in the room?

Did he—if you can just trace your steps and give it to him. I ask you to do that, and I know it is confusing, but that's all he wants.

Mrs. BLEDSOE. Well, I am getting tired.

Miss DOUTHIT. All he wants is the truth, and I thought maybe you might, for the sake of the record, you know——

Mrs. BLEDSOE. Well, I would have—we have said most everything.

Miss DOUTHIT. I know it, but just do it one more time. The man was standing at your front door——

Mrs. BLEDSOE. I am getting tired, because I have had a stroke, you see.

Miss DOUTHIT. Did you go back out in the yard?

Mrs. BLEDSOE. No; I stayed in.

Miss DOUTHIT. Did he leave your house twice? Now, you said he went and got a bag and brought it back?

Mrs. BLEDSOE. Yes; he did, brought back the bag.

Miss DOUTHIT. Then he went back again?

Mrs. BLEDSOE. Uh-huh.

Miss DOUTHIT. How long was he—all I want to know is just, if you can just tell that in your own words without any questions. Could you just do that?

Mrs. BLEDSOE. Well, I'd rather they asked, because——

Miss DOUTHIT. I know, but it is hard for them to ask these particular questions, because they don't know exactly what happened. All they want to do is to say that you were in the room with him, and put this little bag down and hung up his clothes, and came across the hall and signed the register, see.

Mrs. BLEDSOE. Well, that's all. I don't know whether he put his clothes and what in the other room. I don't know whether he put his bag——

Miss DOUTHIT. Was there a closet in there?

Mrs. BLEDSOE. Yes.

Miss DOUTHIT. Well, were you with him when he put the clothes in the closet, or did you go on across the hall and leave him?

Mrs. BLEDSOE. Oh, no; I didn't pay any attention to him.

Miss DOUTHIT. Did you leave his presence—Mary, pardon me, I am not—this is not for the record.

Mr. JENNER. No; that's fine, leave it on the record.

Miss DOUTHIT. All right. When the man was on your front porch.

Mrs. BLEDSOE. Yes.

Miss DOUTHIT. He had a blue bag in there?

Mrs. BLEDSOE. Uh-huh.

Miss DOUTHIT. And you don't know whether it was round or bulging, you just don't know?

Mrs. BLEDSOE. No.

Miss DOUTHIT. You don't know whether it had a long strap or a little handle, do you?

Mrs. BLEDSOE. I think it had a handle.

Miss DOUTHIT. But, it wasn't one you sling over your shoulder?

Mrs. BLEDSOE. No.

Miss DOUTHIT. All right, can you go ahead?

Mrs. BLEDSOE. Clothes were sort of hanging over here [indicating].

Miss DOUTHIT. Uh-huh. Not covered or anything?

Mrs. BLEDSOE. No.

Miss DOUTHIT. You couldn't tell anybody about what color the clothes were, could you?

Mrs. BLEDSOE. No.

Miss DOUTHIT. Did you stand in the yard and talk to the young man? Or immediately go into the room?

Mrs. BLEDSOE. Well, I immediately—I was talking to him, but I had to go in immediately, because he wanted to see the room.

Miss DOUTHIT. All right. How far is it, Mrs. Bledsoe, from where you met this man at the front door until you showed him the room?

Mrs. BLEDSOE. Well, it is about 25 foot, and all that time I had to size him up, you see.

Miss DOUTHIT. You were talking to him as you went down the hall?

Mrs. BLEDSOE. Yes; getting——

Miss DOUTHIT. Is that where you learned that he was married, as you were walking down the hall?

Mrs. BLEDSOE. No; he told me he was married before we went in the house.

Miss DOUTHIT. All right, then, when you got to the room, did you both walk inside the room, or stand in the door and talk?

Mrs. BLEDSOE. I stood in the door, and he went in and looked at it and took it.

Miss DOUTHIT. Did he keep his clothes?

Mrs. BLEDSOE. I didn't pay any attention.

Miss DOUTHIT. When he was talking to you, you don't know what he did, just stood and talked to you?

Mrs. BLEDSOE. Uh-huh.

Miss DOUTHIT. Did you leave his presence before he came into your room and signed the register?

Mrs. BLEDSOE. Now, that, Melody——

Miss DOUTHIT. Were you with him? And took him into the room, and——

Mrs. BLEDSOE. Says, "I'll take the room."

Miss DOUTHIT. Did you leave him in the room and you go on across to your room? How far is your room from where you rented his room?

Mrs. BLEDSOE. Right next to it. No; he came on in, he came on back behind me.

Miss DOUTHIT. He never left your presence from the time you went in this room until he came over here?

Mrs. BLEDSOE. Yes.

Miss DOUTHIT. All right, did he put his things in your room—or bring them with him?

Mrs. BLEDSOE. No; he left them in the room.

Miss DOUTHIT. All right, you don't know where he put them?

Mrs. BLEDSOE. No; didn't pay any attention to him.

Miss DOUTHIT. Is there a closet in that room?

Mrs. BLEDSOE. Yes.

Miss DOUTHIT. You don't remember whether he hung his clothes in the closet?

Mrs. BLEDSOE. No.

Miss DOUTHIT. But, he left and came over where you were and signed your register, and then did he go back into his room or go down the hall and leave the house?

Mrs. BLEDSOE. Well, went back in his room.

Miss DOUTHIT. All right. You don't know how long he stayed in his room?

Mrs. BLEDSOE. No.

Miss DOUTHIT. Now, before he left your room, did he tell you anything about going and getting additional luggage, or did you know when he was leaving the room?

Mrs. BLEDSOE. Well, I didn't know. He said he was going to get some groceries but it might have been that he said that he was going, I don't know. I don't know.

Miss DOUTHIT. Was it when he signed the register that he asked you about the grocery store, or later?

Mrs. BLEDSOE. Later.

Miss DOUTHIT. All right. Then you were in your room when he went back in his room. Did you see him leave his room and go out of the house?

Mrs. BLEDSOE. Yes.

Miss DOUTHIT. Then where did you go?

Mrs. BLEDSOE. Lord have mercy. I don't know.

Miss DOUTHIT. Did you go back out in the yard?

Mrs. BLEDSOE. No; I don't think I went into the yard. I was fooling around the house.

Miss DOUTHIT. All right, how far from your room is your kitchen?

Mrs. BLEDSOE. Oh, Lord. It is a long ways. It is clear across the living room and dining room and the kitchen is right there [indicating].

Miss DOUTHIT. All right, but your room is right next to the room you rented to this man?

Mrs. BLEDSOE. Uh-huh.

Miss DOUTHIT. When did you have knowledge that he was back in his room?

Mrs. BLEDSOE. Well, when—I guess when he brought these—brought the milk in.

Miss DOUTHIT. How could he go to the grocery store and get milk unless he had already asked you where the grocery store was?

Mrs. BLEDSOE. Well, I guess he did, he had already.

Miss DOUTHIT. Okay, then, it was on his return from getting the bag that he asked you about the grocery store, is that right? Or do you remember?

Mrs. BLEDSOE. Oh, yes; it wasn't anything said about this when he rented—about eating. Just—he just rented the room, and not to eat in there.

Miss DOUTHIT. Now when you had some kind of knowledge, as you just said, could you hear him back in his room, or could you see him back in his room after he left the first time?

Mrs. BLEDSOE. Well, I heard him.

Miss DOUTHIT. Did he come in and talk to you before he left your house the second time?

Mrs. BLEDSOE. No; he never did talk to me at all. He didn't talk.

Miss DOUTHIT. The only conversation you had with this Mrs.—with this Mr. Oswald was when he came and rented the room and signed the register?

Mrs. BLEDSOE. And what I got out of him. That's all I could get.

Miss DOUTHIT. Now; did you get any information out of him after he signed the register?

Mrs. BLEDSOE. Well, the next day.

Miss DOUTHIT. I am talking about this one day.

Mrs. BLEDSOE. No; didn't get much.

Miss DOUTHIT. Then all of your conversation that you had this Monday that he rented that room took place at one time, is that correct?

Mrs. BLEDSOE. That's correct.

Miss DOUTHIT. Now, he came back, and for some reason you knew he was in there. When did he leave your house the second time?

Mrs. BLEDSOE. When he went to get the groceries.

Miss DOUTHIT. Well, when?

Mrs. BLEDSOE. Well, I don't know.

Miss DOUTHIT. Was he—when he went to leave, did he come in and say, "I'm going to get some groceries." Did he?

Mrs. BLEDSOE. No.

Miss DOUTHIT. You evidently told him about the grocery store the first time when he signed the register and your conversation with him—

Mrs. BLEDSOE. No; I didn't either.

Miss DOUTHIT. Well, you just said you had one conversation with him, and   you had no other conversation with him. Now, just remember these facts that you had no conversation with him after he paid you the money and signed the register.

Mrs. BLEDSOE. Well, I wouldn't say, because I don't know what he did. I don't remember.

Miss DOUTHIT. All right, how long after—when he brought his bag back and put it in this room, how long did he stay in that room until he left to go to the grocery store, if that is where he went?

Mrs. BLEDSOE. Was that the first when he went and got the other bag?

Miss DOUTHIT. Uh-huh.

Mrs. BLEDSOE. Well, 20 or 30 minutes.

Miss DOUTHIT. Did he go and use the telephone, or just stay in his room all that time?

Mrs. BLEDSOE. No, didn't use the phone until—I think he used it after.

Miss DOUTHIT. Did he use your telephone on Monday?

Mrs. BLEDSOE. After the, yes; after he got everything settled, I think he did. Two or three times every day. Called his wife, supposed to be.

Miss DOUTHIT. You don't know who he called?

Mrs. BLEDSOE. No; I don't know who he called.

Miss DOUTHIT. But, you don't know anything at all about when you gave him this information about the grocery store? We are just trying to get the order here in which this happened, Mrs. Bledsoe, is all, if you can just remember?

Mrs. BLEDSOE. Oh, Lord.

Miss DOUTHIT. That is the reason I asked you if you could, to write these things down.

Mrs. BLEDSOE. Well——

Miss DOUTHIT. I am sorry, but I thought in—I might help you.

Mr. JENNER. Did he make a telephone call after he became settled?

Mrs. BLEDSOE. Uh-huh.

Mr. JENNER. On the 8th of October?

Mrs. BLEDSOE. I wouldn't say for sure, but I guess he did, because he called his wife, supposedly—supposed to have been all the time, but in the morning he called some people about jobs.

Mr. JENNER. Yes.

Mrs. BLEDSOE. Because he talked on the phone and talked gruff, talked gruff to those on the phone, and talked about a job. I heard that.

Mr. JENNER. Then, one of the occasions when the gentleman interviewed you—were Secret Service and FBI people—there is a notation that you recalled that on Monday afternoon that he did call his wife?

Mrs. BLEDSOE. Uh-huh.

Mr. JENNER. Now, does that refresh your recollection, that he did call her the same day that he moved in here on——

Mrs. BLEDSOE. Well, I guess he did, uh-huh.

Mr. JENNER. And, were you aware of the fact that he was using the telephone?

Mrs. BLEDSOE. Oh, I told him he could use the phone to get him a job and call his wife.

Mr. JENNER. And were you aware of any occasion on Monday when you had your own mental conception that he was actually talking with his wife?

Mrs. BLEDSOE. Well, it didn't—I wasn't interested at all. He—I wasn't—I didn't think about it at all. When I got interested is when he called, talking in that foreign language.

Mr. JENNER. Now, the first time you heard him talking in the foreign language was when?

Mrs. BLEDSOE. As well as I can guess, it was a Wednesday.

Mr. JENNER. Wednesday?

Mrs. BLEDSOE. Wednesday afternoon, but he came on——

Mr. JENNER. Now, so you assume that the other calls he made on Monday, since he did not, I take it, did not speak in a foreign language, or you didn't hear him speak in a foreign language on Monday?

Mrs. BLEDSOE. No.

Mr. JENNER. And you didn't hear him do so on Tuesday?

Mrs. BLEDSOE. No.

Mr. JENNER. First time you heard him to do that was Wednesday?

Mrs. BLEDSOE. Yes.

Mr. JENNER. Well——

Miss DOUTHIT. Ask her if she ever heard him talk to anybody on the telephone in English. That is what——

Mr. JENNER. Well, I have assumed that you did hear him talk with people on the telephone using the English language?

Mrs. BLEDSOE. Well, was about jobs, about getting a job. He called people to get jobs, and then he would become almost mad, and sometimes he was mad.

Mr. JENNER. What did he say?

Mrs. BLEDSOE. Well, I don't know, but he was mad.

Mr. JENNER. About what?

Mrs. BLEDSOE. About what they were talking about. He would get in a bad humor, and then the day he made that call, he——

Mr. JENNER. Which call?

Mrs. BLEDSOE. That call.

Mr. JENNER. Wednesday? The call in which he spoke in a foreign language?

Mrs. BLEDSOE. He was real mad.

Mr. JENNER. He was angry with the person to whom he was speaking over the telephone?

Mrs. BLEDSOE. Uh-huh.

Mr. JENNER. But, you couldn't understand what he was saying?

Mrs. BLEDSOE. No.

Mr. JENNER. So, you don't know whether he was angry with the person, or angry with someone else and explaining it to the person on the phone about something in anger?

Mrs. BLEDSOE. I know he talked in a—he talked in a, I guess it was a foreign language, and I don't know what it was.

Mr. JENNER. Just sounded irritated?

Mrs. BLEDSOE. Uh-huh.

Mr. JENNER. Was there ever an occasion when you saw him in possession, either in his room, or carrying a long object wrapped in paper or a blanket or——

Mrs. BLEDSOE. No.

Mr. JENNER. Or something as long as 45 inches long?

Mrs. BLEDSOE. No.

Mr. JENNER. Seven or eight inches wide?

Mrs. BLEDSOE. Didn't have anything like that with him.

Mr. JENNER. Anything that you thought you could be curtain rods or——

Mrs. BLEDSOE. Uh-huh.

Mr. JENNER. Or shades that are on the spring, did he ever have any package that looked as though that sort of thing might be contained in it?

Mrs. BLEDSOE. No.

Mr. JENNER. You saw nothing of that nature in his room?

Mrs. BLEDSOE. No.

Mr. JENNER. Now, would you describe the room? Was it tastefully decorated or—shades, curtains? There was no need for him to have any—bring anything in to decorate that room, was there?

Mrs. BLEDSOE. No.

Mr. JENNER. Did he do so?

Mrs. BLEDSOE. No.

Mr. JENNER. Brought nothing in of that nature?

Mrs. BLEDSOE. No.

Mr. JENNER. And there was no discussion with you on that subject?

Mrs. BLEDSOE. No.

Mr. JENNER. You do have a distinct recollection, do you, that he was there on Friday, that would be the 11th, I think?

Mrs. BLEDSOE. Friday. That is the day that he stayed in his room all day.

Mr. JENNER. Stayed in his room all day long?

Mrs. BLEDSOE. Just went to the bathroom and came back.

Mr. JENNER. That was Friday, October 11?

Mrs. BLEDSOE. Uh-huh.

Mr. JENNER. On the 12th, that would be Saturday the 12th of October, did he receive any phone calls?

Mrs. BLEDSOE. Yes.

Mr. JENNER. Would you tell me about that?

Mrs. BLEDSOE. Well, I think he called somebody—somebody called him, and I judged it was his wife.

Mr. JENNER. Did you answer the phone, or did he?

Mrs. BLEDSOE. No; my son answered.

Mr. JENNER. Your son answered the phone?

Mrs. BLEDSOE. And he called him to the phone, and seemed like that she was going to have a child and——

Mr. JENNER. Did you gather this from what you heard him say?

Mrs. BLEDSOE. From what they said.

Mr. JENNER. From his end of the conversation?

Mrs. BLEDSOE. From him, and then I thought he was going to move, and you see, I was tickled to death, so, then said, "Well, I will meet her," or, said that he would meet her, said he would go to the hospital and meet her, see, but he didn't never get to it, I judged that is what he said.

Mr. JENNER. You heard enough of the conversation that you have the recollection that he said something about his wife possibly having to go to the hospital?

Mrs. BLEDSOE. Yes.

Mr. JENNER. For the delivery of her child?

Mrs. BLEDSOE. Yes.

Mr. JENNER. Was this the first time you had any knowledge that his wife was with child?

Mrs. BLEDSOE. Yes.

Mr. JENNER. Did you say anything about that to him?

Mrs. BLEDSOE. No; I didn't mention it. I never did mention about that man talking to him either, because it wasn't any of my business.

Mr. JENNER. Which man?

Mrs. BLEDSOE. This man who called and talked to him in the foreign language. I never did see him.

Mr. JENNER. How did you know it was a man?

Mrs. BLEDSOE. Well, I just judged that it was.

Mr. JENNER. You heard his end of the conversation? He was talking in a foreign language?

Mrs. BLEDSOE. Yes.

Mr. JENNER. You assumed from that that whoever was on the other line was likewise talking in a foreign language, and you assumed a man, though you didn't know?

Mrs. BLEDSOE. I don't know, so, I didn't say that, because I don't know, but I never did say anything about it.

Mr. JENNER. I believe that's about all I have.

Mr. BALL. All right.

Mrs. BLEDSOE. What time is it? I'm tired.

Mr. BALL. It is 5 minutes until 11.

Mrs. BLEDSOE. I guess he is going to ask something, too, and I will be up here at 12.

Mr. BALL. Mrs. Bledsoe, this deposition will be written up by the reporter, and you can take it and look it over if you wish and change it in any way and sign it, or if you wish to waive the signature we will have it written up and send it to the Commission as it is.

Do you have any preference that way? Do you want her to waive the signature?

Miss DOUTHIT. I think she can waive it. I don't see any reason for her to sign it.

Mr. BALL. Then can we, on the advice of your attorney, will you waive the signature?

Mrs. BLEDSOE. Yes.

Mr. BALL. Fine. You will know that you won't be bothered any more then.

Thank you very much, Mrs. Bledsoe.

Mr. JENNER. We do want you to know that we appreciate your coming in.

TESTIMONY OF WILLIAM W. WHALEY

The testimony of William W. Whaley was taken at 1:50 p.m., on April 8, 1964, in the office of the U.S. attorney, 301 Post Office Building, Bryan and Ervay Streets, Dallas, Tex., by Mr. David W. Belin, assistant counsel of the President's Commission.

Mr. BELIN. Would you want to stand and raise your right hand.

Do you solemnly swear that the testimony you are about to give will be the truth, the whole truth, and nothing but the truth, so help you God?

Mr. WHALEY. I do, sir.

Mr. BELIN. Would you state your name, please.

Mr. WHALEY. William W. Whaley.

Mr. BELIN. You live in Dallas, Mr. Whaley?

Mr. WHALEY. Yes, sir.

Mr. BELIN. You previously testified before the Commission in Washington, is that correct?

Mr. WHALEY. Yes, sir.

Mr. BELIN. Now before you came to Washington, did you and I ever meet?

Mr. WHALEY. Your face is familiar, sir. I still can't tell you whether I knew you here, or in Washington, or where?

Mr. BELIN. Let me ask you this.

Mr. WHALEY. You refresh my memory.

Mr. BELIN. I will try to refresh your memory here. When did you come to Washington, approximately?

Mr. WHALEY. Well, it's been about 2 or 3 weeks ago, sir. I don't remember the exact date.

Mr. BELIN. You testified before the President's Commission on the Assassination of President Kennedy in Washington, did you not?

Mr. WHALEY. Yes, sir.

Mr. BELIN. Now Mr. Ball and I were with you earlier today over the noon hour, is that correct?

Mr. WHALEY. That's correct, sir.

Mr. BELIN. Mr. Ball and I saw you in Washington, is that correct?

Mr. WHALEY. Now I don't know if that is correct or not, but your face is very familiar.

Mr. BELIN. You think you have seen me before?

Mr. WHALEY. I don't know.

Mr. BELIN. It might have been in Washington when you were there?

Mr. WHALEY. Yes, sir; it could have been.

Mr. BELIN. Mr. Whaley, today at noon there were six people including yourself that got in the car to travel that route that you drove a passenger on November 22, is that correct?

Mr. WHALEY. Yes, sir.

Mr. BELIN. One of them is sitting here in this room, Dr. Goldberg, over there. Do you see him?

Mr. WHALEY. Yes, sir.

Mr. BELIN. Then you and I got in the car, and then Secret Service Agent John Joe Hewlett. We drove in his car and he was the driver, wasn't he?

Mr. WHALEY. Yes, sir.

Mr. BELIN. Then there was Mr. Joe Ball, Joseph A. Ball, and then a Mr. Davis, this tall light-haired person?

Mr. WHALEY. Yes, sir.

Mr. BELIN. Mr. Davis is from the attorney general's office in Texas.

Now what is the fact as to whether or not we went to the Greyhound Bus Depot here in Dallas?

Mr. WHALEY. Yes, sir.

Mr. BELIN. Did you point out the place where you said you picked up this passenger?

Mr. WHALEY. I did, sir.

Mr. BELIN. We had a stopwatch, didn't we?

Mr. WHALEY. Yes, sir.

Mr. BELIN. Then you directed us to take a certain route, is that correct?

Mr. WHALEY. That's correct.

Mr. BELIN. What was the route from the Greyhound Bus Depot that you directed us?

Mr. WHALEY. On the right from the Greyhound and Lamar to Jackson; right on Jackson and left at Austin and right at Wood.

Mr. BELIN. All right.

Mr. WHALEY. Then left on Houston, which is the approach to the viaduct.

Mr. BELIN. Then what did you do when you got to Houston?

You turned left?

Mr. WHALEY. I said west to Houston.

Mr. BELIN. How far did you go?

Mr. WHALEY. You go on the approach past the Union Terminal and up the ramp which is called the Houston Street viaduct.

Mr. BELIN. Then what?

Mr. WHALEY. You run into Zangs Boulevard.

Mr. BELIN. How far on Zangs?

Mr. WHALEY. To Beckley. Beckley crosses it. We got to the intersection of Zangs and Beckley.

Mr. BELIN. Did we go about the speed you drove that day?

Mr. WHALEY. Almost. Going across the viaduct is just about the speed, but he slowed down going up Zangs Boulevard. He slowed down a little slower than I was going.

My normal rate of speed, I don't remember the exact speed I was traveling, but I assume it was normal, because that is the way I travel all the time when traffic is clear enough.

Mr. BELIN. Your normal rate of speed would be a little bit faster than the rate that he took?

Mr. WHALEY. Yes, sir. In other words, not enough to make over half a minute difference in the timing.

Mr. BELIN. Was traffic clearer on that particular day of November 22?

Mr. WHALEY. It was extra clear, for some reason. That street was clear except when I hit Beckley. When I hit Beckley, there was cars turning to the left, and I had to stop for the light.

Mr. BELIN. When we got to Beckley at noon today, or shortly thereafter, the traffic light was green, but you told us you had stopped, so we waited through the red light, did we not?

Mr. WHALEY. Yes, sir.

Mr. BELIN. Then he turned on Beckley?

Mr. WHALEY. Yes, sir.

Mr. BELIN. Heading south?

Mr. WHALEY. Yes, sir.

Mr. BELIN. Now when this man that you picked up on November 22 got into your cab, where did he say he wanted to go?

Mr. WHALEY. To the 500 block of North Beckley.

Mr. BELIN. I will take you back to November 22.

You turned south on Beckley and then where did you go as you turned south on Beckley?

Mr. WHALEY. I went right up on Beckley headed toward the 500 block.

Mr. BELIN. Then what happened?

Mr. WHALEY. When I got to Beckley almost to the intersection of Beckley and Neely, he said, "This will do right here," and I pulled up to the curb.

Mr. BELIN. Was that the 500 block of North Beckley?

Mr. WHALEY. No, sir; that was the 700 block.

Mr. BELIN. You let him out not at the 500 block but the 700 block of North Beckley?

Mr. WHALEY. Yes, sir.

Mr. BELIN. Had you crossed Neely Street yet when you let him off?

Mr. WHALEY. No, sir.

Mr. BELIN. About how far north of Neely street did you let the man off?

Mr. WHALEY. About 20 feet.

Mr. BELIN. Then you went down to the police station to identify this man?

Mr. WHALEY. Yes, sir.

Mr. BELIN. You saw a lineup?

Mr. WHALEY. Yes, sir.

Mr. BELIN. Do you remember what number he was in the lineup at all?

Mr. WHALEY. There was four of them, sir, and from the right to the left, he was No. 3.

Mr. BELIN. Starting from the right to the left, from his right or your right?

Mr. WHALEY. From your right, sir, which would have been his left. There were numbers above their heads, sir.

Mr. BELIN. Mr. Whaley, what number did you say the man was in the lineup?

Mr. WHALEY. No. 2.

Mr. BELIN. From the right or from your right?

Mr. WHALEY. From my left.

Mr. BELIN. No. 2?

Mr. WHALEY. They brought out four of them and stood them up there, and he was under No. 2. I mentioned he was the third one that come out. There were four and all handcuffed together.

Mr. BELIN. Did you sign an affidavit for the Dallas Police Department?

Mr. WHALEY. Yes, sir.

Mr. BELIN. I will hand you a document which I am calling Whaley Deposition Exhibit A, and ask you to say if your signature appears on there?

Mr. WHALEY. Yes, sir; that is my signature.

Mr. BELIN. Now I notice in the statement there it says that you traveled Wood Street to Houston Street, turned left and went over the viaduct to Zangs Boulevard. You see that statement there?

Mr. WHALEY. Yes.

Mr. BELIN. "Traveled Zangs to Beckley and turned left and traveled on Beckley until I reached the 500 block of North Beckley. When I got in the 500 block of North Beckley he said this will do and I stopped."

Now is that what you told them on that day?

Mr. WHALEY. Yes, sir; that is what I told them on that day.

Mr. BELIN. Well, was that the fact that you drove until you reached the 500 block, or not?

Mr. WHALEY. No, sir, I didn't drive until I reached the 500 block. I drove until I reached Beckley and Neely. If you would be in my place when they took me down there, when they had to force their way through the reporters to get me in the office, they wrote that up, and I signed it, because I told them that the man said he wanted to go to the 500 block of North Beckley.

Mr. BELIN. All right. Now in here it says, "The No. 3 man who I now know is Lee Harvey Oswald was the man who I carried from the Greyhound Bus Station * * *"

Was this the No. 3 or the No. 2 man?

Mr. WHALEY. I signed that statement before they carried me down to see the lineup. I signed this statement, and then they carried me down to the lineup at 2:30 in the afternoon.

Mr. BELIN. You signed this affidavit before you saw the lineup?

Mr. WHALEY. Well, now, let's get this straight. You are getting me confused.

Mr. BELIN. Now, I will put it this way. There was an FBI reporter, FBI interviewer with you?

Mr. BELIN. Yes, sir; there was.

Mr. BELIN. And there was an interview with the Dallas Police Department?

Mr. WHALEY. Yes. And Bill Alexander from the district attorney's office was there, also.

Mr. BELIN. All right, now, the last sentence.

Mr. WHALEY. Let me tell you how they fixed this up. They had me in the office saying that. They were writing it out on paper, and they wrote it out on paper, and this officer, Leavelle, I think that is his name, before he finished and before I signed he wanted me to go with him to the lineup, so I went to the lineup, and I come back and he asked me which one it was, which number it was, and I identified the man, and we went back up in the office again, and then they had me sign this. That is as near as I can remember.

My recollection for that afternoon in that office was very disturbed because everytime they would open the door, some flash camera would flash in your face and everybody coming in and out and asking you questions.

Mr. BELIN. You mean reporters?

Mr. WHALEY. I made this statement more to Bill Alexander, because I tried to talk to him more. Everybody was trying to talk to me at once.

Mr. BELIN. When you saw the statement the first time, did you see the statement before you went down to see the lineup?

Mr. WHALEY. No; I didn't see the statement. I don't think I did. I am not for sure.

I think I signed it after I came back. It was on paper. They were writing it up on paper.

Mr. BELIN. They were writing?

Mr. WHALEY. Before I left there, I signed this typewritten, because they had to get, a stenographer typed it up. I had to wait.

Mr. BELIN. But was this before or after you saw the lineup?

Mr. WHALEY. After she typed it up. It was after.

Mr. BELIN. It was after?

Mr. WHALEY. That is when I signed it, after.

Mr. BELIN. Now, when you signed it—what I want to know is, before you went down, had they already put on there a statement that the man you saw was the No. 3 man in the lineup?

Mr. WHALEY. I don't remember that. I don't remember whether it said three or two, or what.

Mr. BELIN. Did they have any statements on there before you went down to the lineup?

Mr. WHALEY. I never saw what they had in there. It was all written out by hand. The statement I saw, I think, was this one, and that could be writing. I might not even seen this one yet. I signed my name because they said that is what I said.

Mr. BELIN. Well, Mr. Whaley——

Mr. WHALEY. I know, sir, but I don't think you can understand what I had to put up with that afternoon.

Mr. BELIN. You mean with the press?

Mr. WHALEY. Yes, sir; with everything.

Mr. BELIN. Well, I do understand, sir, and I appreciate that you were under a great deal of pressure at that time, and I want to try and get at the actual facts, and that is why we asked you to come back to testify again, because we wanted to know basically whether or not the man that you drove in the cab got off in the 500 block or the 700 block.

Mr. WHALEY. The man I drove in the cab got off where I told you he got off, this morning.

I picked him up, and I showed you where I picked him up, and the trip runs 95 cents on the meter. He gave me a dollar and got off and he never spoke a word to me, except he wanted to go to 500 North Beckley.

Mr. BELIN. Do you remember a woman coming up to the cab?

Mr. WHALEY. Yes, sir; I remember that.

Mr. BELIN. What happened then?

Mr. WHALEY. The lady, I don't remember whether she was very old, but she was middle-aged. She bent down and stuck in and said, "Can I have this cab?" And he cracked the door open like he was going to get out. I thought he was going to let her have it.

I told her there would be another one, and she said, "Would you please call me one."

Mr. BELIN. Did he say anything to the woman, that you can remember?

Mr. WHALEY. When she wanted to know if she could have the cab, I don't know, but I got a faint hunch he did tell her she could have this one, or something like that. What it was, I was watching my left-hand side. I wanted to pull out when the light changed.

Mr. BELIN. Now when you saw a lineup down at the policestation——

Mr. WHALEY. He didn't have on the same clothes. He had on a white T-shirt and black pants, and that is all he had on.

Mr. BELIN. Do you remember now whether the man that you saw there was the No. 2 or the No. 3 man?

Mr. WHALEY. I will admit he was No. 2.

Mr. BELIN. No. 2 from your left, or from your right?

Mr. WHALEY. He was the third man out in the line of four as they walked out in a line. They put the first man out on the right, and the last one on my left, and as near as I can remember, he was No. 2, but it was the man I hauled.

Mr. BELIN. It says here the No. 3.

Mr. WHALEY. Well, I am not trying to mix nobody up. I'm giving it to you the best of my ability.

Mr. BELIN. Your memory right now is that it was the No. 2 man?

Mr. WHALEY. That is the way it is right now. I don't think it will change again.

But on that afternoon, all I saw was the man that I hauled up there, and they asked me which number he was, and I said No. 2. I am almost sure I did, but I couldn't get up to swear to it that I did, sir.

Mr. BELIN. Just one more minute, if you would, please?

Mr. Whaley, earlier in your testimony here you said that Lee Harvey Oswald was No. 3. Do you remember saying that?

Mr. WHALEY. Yes, sir; but I meant that he was the third one out when they walked out with him. I said from my right.

Mr. BELIN. From your right he was No. 3?

Mr. WHALEY. Yes, sir.

Mr. BELIN. What number was over his head?

Mr. WHALEY. Well, they—when they walked over the line and they stopped him, No. 2 was over his head, but he was pulling on both of the other men on each side and arguing with this detective, so he didn't stay under any certain number.

He was moving like that.

Mr. BELIN. Did you ever see him later on television?

Mr. WHALEY. No, sir; I didn't.

Mr. BELIN. You never did see his picture in the paper?

Mr. WHALEY. I saw his picture in the paper the next morning, sir.

Mr. BELIN. That would have been Sunday morning, the 24th?

Mr. WHALEY. I guess it was, if you say it was, sir.

Mr. BELIN. I don't want to——

Mr. WHALEY. I don't want to get you mixed up and get your whole investigation mixed up through my ignorance, but a good defense attorney could take me apart. I get confused. I try to tell you exactly what happened, to the best of my ability, when they brought Oswald out in the lineup of four. He was the third man out. I don't know which way they count them.

Mr. BELIN. We don't want you to be concerned about affecting the investigation one way or the other by what you say. What we want you to say is tell us what you know, to the best of your recollection.

Mr. WHALEY. That is exactly what I am doing, sir.

Mr. BELIN. Let me ask you this. What day of the week did you take this cab passenger, on a Friday or Saturday?

Mr. WHALEY. I would have to see my trip sheet.

Mr. BELIN. You don't remember?

Mr. WHALEY. No, sir.

Mr. BELIN. Was it the day of the motorcade?

Mr. WHALEY. The day of the President's parade, yes, sir.

Mr. BELIN. Now, was it that day that you went down to the police station to see the lineup?

Mr. WHALEY. No, sir.

Mr. BELIN. Was it the next day?

Mr. WHALEY. Yes, sir.

Mr. BELIN. The next day you went down to the Dallas Police Station and saw a lineup of how many people?

Mr. WHALEY. Four people.

Mr. BELIN. These men came out and there were numbers above their heads?

Mr. WHALEY. The numbers were stationary. Looked through a black silk screen at them. In other words, they were very dim, the numbers.

Mr. BELIN. What did you see as the number over the man that you identified as having been in your cab that day?

Mr. WHALEY. No. 2.

Mr. BELIN. Did you see a picture of that man in the paper at any time?

Mr. WHALEY. Saturday morning, sir; following the event on Friday.

Mr. BELIN. You saw his picture in the paper?

Mr. WHALEY. Yes, sir.

Mr. BELIN. Was that the same man that you identified as No. 2 in the lineup?

Mr. WHALEY. Yes, sir.

Mr. BELIN. Did you ever see his picture in the paper again?

Mr. WHALEY. No, sir; I take that back, sir. I saw the picture in the paper when they had, when Ruby killed him at the time between the two detectives.

Mr. BELIN. Was the man in connection with the Ruby matter with the two detectives, did it have his name in the paper as Lee Harvey Oswald? Was his name in the paper then when you saw his picture?

Mr. WHALEY. Well, I don't think they had it that way. I think they just had it Oswald. I am not sure what they had under it. I am not for sure, but I did see the picture.

Mr. BELIN. Was that the same man you carried in your cab on Friday?

Mr. WHALEY. Yes, sir.

Mr. BELIN. Was that the man you identified at the police station?

Mr. WHALEY. Yes, sir.

Mr. BELIN. It is your best recollection, if I understand it, that this was the No. 2 man in the lineup?

Mr. WHALEY. That's right, sir. That was from the left now. No. 2 from my left. I was facing him.

Mr. BELIN. Right. I mean correct. Now, your affidavit which is Whaley's Deposition Exhibit A, the last sentence says, "The No. 3 man who I now know as Lee Harvey Oswald was the man who I carried from the Greyhound bus station to the 500 block of North Beckley." Now you say it was the No. 2 man from your left, is that correct?

Mr. WHALEY. From my left. No. 3 from my right.

Mr. BELIN. What about whether or not you carried him to the 500 block of North Beckley. Did you carry him there?

Mr. WHALEY. No, sir. That is where he asked me. That is where I put on my trip sheet.

Mr. BELIN. You had it on the trip sheet the 500 block of North Beckley?

Mr. WHALEY. Yes, sir.

Mr. BELIN. When did you put it on your trip sheet, before or after you let him out?

Mr. WHALEY. After, sir; a good while after.

Mr. BELIN. Why?

Mr. WHALEY. Well, see, sometimes when you are busy you make three or four trips before you ever write one up.

394

Mr. BELIN. Why didn't you put it on your trip sheet for 700 instead of 500 North Beckley?

Mr. WHALEY. Because that is what he told me and that is what I remember when I wrote the trip up. I imagine there were hundreds of trip sheets, because people get off before they get where they are going. But I remember the thing that way.

Mr. BELIN. When did you first ascertain or start thinking about it that it was the 700 block of North Beckley where you let him off?

Mr. WHALEY. Well, when the FBI man got in my cab and he wanted to go over the route.

Mr. BELIN. When was this?

Mr. WHALEY. I don't know the exact date, sir, but it was the next week.

Mr. BELIN. In the next week you told the FBI that it was the 700 block?

Mr. WHALEY. No, sir; I don't recall. I know I took him to where I let him out.

Mr. BELIN. You did?

Mr. WHALEY. Yes, sir.

Mr. BELIN. Did you ever tell anyone it was the 700 block of North Beckley?

Mr. WHALEY. No, sir. I left it said just like I had it on my trip sheet. Nobody else asked me about it.

Mr. BELIN. When we went out there today, when we started the stopwatch from the Greyhound bus station to the 700 block of North Beckley, do you know about how many minutes that was on the stop watch?

Mr. WHALEY. A little more than 5 minutes, between 5 and 6 minutes.

Mr. BELIN. Would your trip that day, on November 22, have been longer or shorter, or about the same time as the trip we took today?

Mr. WHALEY. It would be approximately the same time, sir, give or take a few seconds, not minutes. Because the man drove just about as near to my driving as possible. We made every light that I made, and we stopped on the lights that I stopped on.

Mr. BELIN. Let the record show that the stopwatch was 5 minutes and 30 seconds from the commencement of the ride to the end of the ride, and let the record further show that Dr. Goldberg and Mr. Robert Davis from the Texas attorney general's office and I walked back from the point where the Deponent Whaley told us he let the passenger off at the residence at 1026 North Beckley, and that this walk took 5 minutes and 45 seconds.

And let the record further show that after visiting the rooming house at 1026 North Beckley—that is what I call the "long way around route,"—was walked from 1026 North Beckley to the scene of the Tippit shooting, which took 17 minutes and 45 seconds at an average walking pace, and this route would be to take Beckley to 10th Street and then turn on 10th Street toward Patton, and this is not the most direct route. Rather, the most direct route would be to take Beckley to Davis Street and then turn left or east on Davis, walking a short block to Crawford, and taking Crawford to 10th, and then 10th east to Patton, or taking Davis Street directly to Patton, and taking Patton down to East 10th, and that the more direct nature of the later route appears from the map which I believe is Commission's Exhibit No. 371, which is the Dallas street map.

Mr. Whaley, is there anything else that you care to add, or can you add anything else that might be helpful in this investigation?

Mr. WHALEY. No, sir; I can't.

Mr. BELIN. We sure appreciate all your help and taking the time to go over the route today.

Mr. WHALEY. Thank you. I still would like to know where I knew you before.

Mr. BELIN. Sir, I don't know. Now, Mr. Whaley, if you like, you can come back and read this deposition after it is typed, and sign it before you mail it to Washington, or you can waive the signing of it. You have a right to read it and sign it before it goes, or you can waive the reading of it and send it directly to us in Washington.

Mr. WHALEY. Does it make any difference?

Mr. BELIN. It does not make any difference.

Mr. WHALEY. It will all be what you said and what she took down?

Mr. BELIN. What you said?

Mr. WHALEY. Yes, sir; and what I said?

Mr. BELIN. Yes.

Mr. WHALEY. That will be all right. I will waive the signing of it.

TESTIMONY OF MRS. EARLENE ROBERTS

The testimony of Mrs. Earlene Roberts was taken at 4:10 p.m., on April 8, 1964, in the office of the U.S. attorney, 301 Post Office Building, Bryan and Ervay Streets, Dallas, Tex., by

Messrs. Joseph A. Ball and Samuel A. Stern, assistant counsel of the President's Commission. Dr. Alfred Goldberg was present.

Mr. BALL. Would you stand and take the oath?

Do you solemnly swear the testimony you are about to give before the Commission will be the truth, the whole truth, and nothing but the truth, so help you God?

Mrs. ROBERTS. Yes, sir.

Mr. BALL. Will you state your name, please?

Mrs. ROBERTS. Mrs. Earlene Roberts.

Mr. BALL. And what is your address?

Mrs. ROBERTS. 5000 Tremont, now.

Mr. BALL. You used to live at 1026 North Beckley, didn't you?

Mrs. ROBERTS. Yes; I did.

Mr. BALL. Tell me something about yourself, Mrs. Roberts, where you were born and where you have lived?

Mrs. ROBERTS. I was born in Nashville, Tenn., and my mother and father moved to Tyler, Tex., and I was raised there and married a Dallas man.

Mr. BALL. Did you go to school in Tyler?

Mrs. ROBERTS. Oh, yes.

Mr. BALL. How far through school did you go?

Mrs. ROBERTS. To my sorrows, I got married in the ninth grade.

Mr. BALL. You did—you got married in the ninth grade?

Mrs. ROBERTS. Yes, sir.

Mr. BALL. Did you get married in Dallas or in Tyler?

Mrs. ROBERTS. In Tyler.

Mr. BALL. Did you have some children?

Mrs. ROBERTS. No; to my sorrows—I couldn't.

Mr. BALL. What did you do in Tyler then—until you came to Dallas?

Mrs. ROBERTS. I was a PBX operator at the Hotel Blackstone. That's where I met my husband.

Mr. BALL. How long have you lived here?

Mrs. ROBERTS. Since 1938.

Mr. BALL. What kind of work have you done?

Mrs. ROBERTS. Well, until he passed away—I didn't work for I didn't have to. He made me a good living, but since that time I have been—well, just, I guess you would call it practical nursing or housekeeping and now I am with an elderly couple—he has cancer—the same kind that Sam Rayburn had and he's taken with leukemia.

Mr. BALL. That's at the address you have just given us?

Mrs. ROBERTS. Oh, yes.

Mr. BALL. Now, you know Mrs. Johnson, don't you?

Mrs. ROBERTS. Yes; I knew her very muchly so.

Mr. BALL. How long did you work for her?

Mrs. ROBERTS. Well, this last time I was there around 13 months—that was the third time I had went back.

Mr. BALL. When did you start working for her?

Mrs. ROBERTS. I started working for her in 1949 the first time.

Mr. BALL. You did?

Mrs. ROBERTS. Yes, sir.

Mr. BALL. And you worked for her three times altogether?

Mrs. ROBERTS. Yes; I got sick the first time—I'm a diabetic and wasn't able to do the work and one day she called me again and wanted to know if I would do it and I went back and stayed again and I went in a coma and had to leave, and the reason why I left this time, she cut me down so low and the work was too heavy—I wasn't able to do the work.

Mr. BALL. You mean she cut you down on your money?

Mrs. ROBERTS. Oh, yes; and I can't pay my doctor bill and buy my medicine at that price.

Mr. BALL. You mean, she didn't pay you enough—that's the reason you quit?

Mrs. ROBERTS. That's the reason why I quit—the work was too heavy and I wasn't able to do it and not enough pay.

Mr. BALL. And you were working there in October and November of last fall—1963?

Mrs. ROBERTS. Yes; to my sorrows.

Mr. BALL. Why to your sorrows?

Mrs. ROBERTS. Well, he was registered as O. H. Lee and I come to find out he was Oswald and I wish I had never known it.

Mr. BALL. Why?

Mrs. ROBERTS. Well, they put me through the third degree.

Mr. BALL. Who did?

Mrs. ROBERTS. The FBI, Secret Service, Mr. Will Fritz' men and Bill Decker's.

Mr. BALL. They did?

Mrs. ROBERTS. Every time I would walk out on the front porch somebody was standing with a camera on me—they had me scared to death.

Mr. BALL. When is the first time you ever saw Lee Oswald?

Mrs. ROBERTS. The day he came in and rented the room—the 14th of October.

Mr. BALL. Had you ever heard of the man before?

Mrs. ROBERTS. No, and he didn't register as Oswald—he registered as O. H. Lee.

Mr. BALL. Did he sign his name?

Mrs. ROBERTS. O. H. Lee.

Mr. BALL. Did he sign his own name that way?

Mrs. ROBERTS. O. H. Lee—that's what he was registered as.

Mr. BALL. Did you rent it to him, or did Mrs. Johnson?

Mrs. ROBERTS. I rented the room to him.

Mr. BALL. You did?

Mrs. ROBERTS. She talked to him, and she had to go back to the work and that was what I was supposed to do—I rented the rooms—she didn't know what vacancies she had.

Mr. BALL. Did you have "room for rent" sign out in the front?

Mrs. ROBERTS. Yes.

Mr. BALL. What time of day did he come in there?

Mrs. ROBERTS. Oh, it was in the early afternoon—I imagine between 1 and 2 o'clock when he came in and looked at the room; and he rented it and paid for it; and then left, and went and got his things and I don't know—it must have been around 5 or 6 o'clock when he come back in.

Mr. BALL. You say he went and got his things—what did he have with him at first when he came there?

Mrs. ROBERTS. Just a little satchel bag and some clothes on a hanger.

Mr. BALL. What kind of a satchel bag?

Mrs. ROBERTS. One of them little zip kinds.

Mr. BALL. What color was it?

Mrs. ROBERTS. It was just—don't ask me that for I can't answer that. It was just a dark bag is all I know.

Mr. BALL. How long did he stay that first time?

Mrs. ROBERTS. Oswald?

Mr. BALL. I mean before he went away to get his clothes, when he first came in—you say he rented a room?

Mrs. ROBERTS. He rented the room and paid me $8 for it and he said, "I'll go get my things and I will be back."

Mr. BALL. Did he say where he was going to get them?

Mrs. ROBERTS. No, he didn't.

Mr. BALL. Did he leave?

Mrs. ROBERTS. Yes; he left.

Mr. BALL. Did he have a car he was riding in?

Mrs. ROBERTS. I don't know—I didn't see it.

Mr. BALL. Did he take a bus?

Mrs. ROBERTS. I don't know.

Mr. BALL. You don't know?

Mrs. ROBERTS. No, I don't. I don't remember—you know in a place like that—when you rent a room—I didn't pay no attention.

Mr. BALL. And he came back about what time?

Mrs. ROBERTS. Oh, I imagine around 5 o'clock, maybe.

Mr. BALL. What did he have with him at that time?

Mrs. ROBERTS. That little zipper satchel bag and some clothes on a hanger.

Mr. BALL. The first time he came to see you he had a zipper satchel bag?

Mrs. ROBERTS. No; he didn't have nothing when he first come in and rented the room.

Mr. BALL. He didn't have anything?

397

Mrs. ROBERTS. No—he just came in.

Mr. BALL. Oh, when he came back he had the zipper satchel and the clothes on the hanger, is that right?

Mrs. ROBERTS. No—he rented the room and paid for it and said, "I'll go get my things." That's when he went and come back with his little satchel bag and some clothes on a hanger, which was a very few.

Mr. BALL. Now, did he have anything to say when he came back?

Mrs. ROBERTS. No.

Mr. BALL. Did he tell you where he had been?

Mrs. ROBERTS. No.

Mr. BALL. Did he stay there that night?

Mrs. ROBERTS. Yes.

Mr. BALL. Did you ever talk to him about anything?

Mrs. ROBERTS. No; because he wouldn't talk.

Mr. BALL. Did he say "Hello"?

Mrs. ROBERTS. No.

Mr. BALL. Or, "Goodby"?

Mrs. ROBERTS. No.

Mr. BALL. Or anything?

Mrs. ROBERTS. He wouldn't say nothing.

Mr. BALL. Did you ever speak to him?

Mrs. ROBERTS. Well, yes—I would say, "Good afternoon," and he would just maybe look at me—give me a dirty look and keep walking and go on to his room.

Mr. BALL. Did he watch television?

Mrs. ROBERTS. No—in a way—but all he did ever watch the television was if someone in the other rooms had it on, maybe he would come and stand at the back of the couch—not over 5 minutes and go to his room and shut the door and never say a word.

Mr. BALL. Did he go out any at night?

Mrs. ROBERTS. No.

Mr. BALL. Did he stay home every night?

Mrs. ROBERTS. Yes—he stayed home every night—I didn't ever know of him going out. If he did, he left after I went to bed and I never knew it.

Mr. BALL. Was he gone any weekends?

Mrs. ROBERTS. He would leave on Friday nights—he did say this much—he said, "Now, over weekends I will be out of town." He didn't say what town. He said, "I will be going out of town visiting friends." He would leave Friday morning for work and he wouldn't come back any more until Monday afternoon.

Mr. BALL. Now, was one weekend when he didn't come back on Monday?

Mrs. ROBERTS. No; there was one weekend that he didn't go out.

Mr. BALL. Which one was that?

Mrs. ROBERTS. Now, as far as—you know what?

Mr. BALL. Was that the weekend?

Mrs. ROBERTS. I think—now, if I had the books, I could tell you.

Mr. BALL. Which books?

Mrs. ROBERTS. The books that are over there on North Beckley. I believe it was on the weekend before—when was President Kennedy shot?

Mr. BALL. On the 22d of November.

Mrs. ROBERTS. What day was that—that was on Friday, wasn't it?

Mr. BALL. That was on a Friday.

Mrs. ROBERTS. Well, it was on the weekend before that.

Mr. BALL. What happened—what was that?

Mrs. ROBERTS. He didn't go nowhere.

Mr. BALL. He stayed in all weekend, is that right?

Mrs. ROBERTS. Yes, sir; and then that first Thursday, he got up Thursday and left for work and he didn't come back no more until Friday.

Mr. BALL. He left on Thursday and didn't come home on Thursday night?

Mrs. ROBERTS. He didn't spend Thursday night there and that was unusual, because he would always leave on Friday. That's the best I can do. He was just the type of person you just don't know—and I just thought he didn't like people and he would mix with nobody and he wouldn't say nothing. The only time he would ever say anything was when his rent was due and he was never behind.

I'll tell you when it was—it was when he didn't come back on Monday, you know, there was a holiday that people took off work.

Mr. BALL. That was Armistice Day.

Mrs. ROBERTS. That he said, "I have a long weekend."

Mr. BALL. He didn't come back on that Monday?

Mrs. ROBERTS. No, he didn't come back until the next day. He said he had a long weekend.

Mr. BALL. That was after his long weekend he came back on a Tuesday that week?

Mrs. ROBERTS. Yes.

Mr. BALL. Do you remember the day the President was shot?

Mrs. ROBERTS. Yes; I remember it—who would forget that?

Mr. BALL. And the police officers came out there?

Mrs. ROBERTS. Yes, sir.

Mr. BALL. Do you remember what they said?

Mrs. ROBERTS. Well, it was Will Fritz' men—it was plainclothesmen and I was at the back doing something and Mr. Johnson answered the door and they identified themselves and then he called me.

Mr. BALL. What did they say?

Mrs. ROBERTS. Well, they asked him if there was a Harvey Lee Oswald there.

Mr. BALL. What did he say?

Mrs. ROBERTS. And he says, "I don't know, I'll have to call the housekeeper," and he called me and I went and got the books and I said, "No; there's no one here by that name," and they tried to make me remember and I couldn't, and Mrs. Johnson come in in the meantime and there wasn't nobody there by that name, and Mrs. Johnson said, "Mrs. Roberts, don't you have him?" And, I said, "No; we don't, for here is my book and there is nobody there by that name." We checked it back a year.

Mr. BALL. And you didn't have that name—you didn't ever know his name was Lee Oswald?

Mrs. ROBERTS. No—he registered as O. H. Lee and they were asking for Harvey Lee Oswald.

Mr. BALL. You say that you saw Lee Oswald—you say he didn't come home Thursday night that week?

Mrs. ROBERTS. He didn't come home on Thursday night that week.

Mr. BALL. And Friday was the day the President was shot? Had you seen him at any time that Friday before the officers came up and knocked on your door?

Mrs. ROBERTS. No.

Mr. BALL. Hadn't he been home?

Mrs. ROBERTS. Oh, let's see—that was the day.

Mr. BALL. That was on a Friday——

Mrs. ROBERTS. Wait a minute, let me think of it.

Mr. BALL. That's on a Friday.

Mrs. ROBERTS. I had better back up a minute—he came home that Friday in an unusual hurry.

Mr. BALL. And about what time was this?

Mrs. ROBERTS. Well, it was after President Kennedy had been shot and I had a friend that said, "Roberts, President Kennedy has been shot," and I said, "Oh, no." She said, "Turn on your television," and I said "What are you trying to do, pull my leg?" And she said, "Well, go turn it on." I went and turned it on and I was trying to clear it up—I could hear them talking but I couldn't get the picture and he come in and I just looked up and I said, "Oh, you are in a hurry." He never said a thing, not nothing. He went on to his room and stayed about 3 or 4 minutes.

Mr. BALL. As he came in, did you say anything else except, "You are in a hurry"?

Mrs. ROBERTS. No.

Mr. BALL. Did you say anything about the President being shot?

Mrs. ROBERTS. No.

Mr. BALL. You were working with the television?

Mrs. ROBERTS. I was trying to clear it up to see what was happening and try to find out about President Kennedy.

Mr. BALL. Why did you say to this man as he came in, "You are in a hurry,"—why did you say that?

Mrs. ROBERTS. Well, he just never has come in and he was walking unusually fast and he just hadn't been that way and I just looked up and I said, "Oh, you are in a hurry."

Mr. BALL. You mean he was walking faster than he usually was?

Mrs. ROBERTS. Yes.

Mr. BALL. When he came in the door, what did he do?

Mrs. ROBERTS. He just walked in—he didn't look around at me—he didn't say nothing and went on to his room.

Mr. BALL. Did he run?

Mrs. ROBERTS. He wasn't running, but he was walking pretty fast—he was all but running.

Mr. BALL. Then, what happened after that?

Mrs. ROBERTS. He went to his room and he was in his shirt sleeves but I couldn't tell you whether it was a long-sleeved shirt or what color it was or nothing, and he got a jacket and put it on—it was kind of a zipper jacket.

Mr. BALL. Had you ever seen him wear that jacket before?

Mrs. ROBERTS. I can't say I did—if I did, I don't remember it.

Mr. BALL. When he came in he was in a shirt?

Mrs. ROBERTS. He was in his shirt sleeves.

Mr. BALL. What color was his shirt? Do you know?

Mrs. ROBERTS. I don't remember. I didn't pay that much attention for I was interested in the television trying to get it fixed.

Mr. BALL. Had you ever seen that shirt before or seen him wear it—the shirt, or do you know?

Mrs. ROBERTS. I don't remember—I don't know.

Mr. BALL. You say he put on a separate jacket?

Mrs. ROBERTS. A jacket.

Mr. BALL. I'll show you this jacket which is Commission Exhibit 162—have you ever seen this jacket before?

Mrs. ROBERTS. Well, maybe I have, but I don't remember it. It seems like the one he put on was darker than that. Now, I won't be sure, because I really don't know, but is that a zipper jacket?

Mr. BALL. Yes—it has a zipper down the front.

Mrs. ROBERTS. Well, maybe it was.

Mr. BALL. It was a zippered jacket, was it?

Mrs. ROBERTS. Yes; it was a zipper jacket. How come me to remember it, he was zipping it up as he went out the door.

Mr. BALL. He was zipping it up as he went out the door?

Mrs. ROBERTS. Yes.

Mr. BALL. Then, when you saw him, did you see any part of his belt?

Mrs. ROBERTS. No.

Mr. BALL. There is some suspicion that when he left there he might have had a pistol or a revolver in his belt; did you see anything like that?

Mrs. ROBERTS. No; I sure didn't.

Mr. BALL. Now, I show you Commission Exhibit No. 150—it is a shirt—have you seen that before?

Mrs. ROBERTS. Well, maybe I have. Now, that looks kind of like the dark shirt that he had on.

Mr. BALL. Now, when Oswald came in, he was in a shirt—does this shirt look anything like the shirt he had on?

Mrs. ROBERTS. It was a dark shirt he had on—I think it was a dark one, but whether it was long sleeve or short sleeve or what—I don't know.

Mr. BALL. Does the color of this shirt which I show you here, Commission Exhibit No. 150, look anything like the shirt he had on?

Mrs. ROBERTS. I'm sorry, I just don't know.

Mr. BALL. You are not able to testify as to that—to tell us that?

Mrs. ROBERTS. No.

Mr. BALL. Can you tell me what time it was approximately that Oswald came in?

Mrs. ROBERTS. Now, it must have been around 1 o'clock, or maybe a little after, because it was after President Kennedy had been shot—what time I wouldn't want to say because——

Mr. BALL. How long did he stay in the room?

Mrs. ROBERTS. Oh, maybe not over 3 or 4 minutes—just long enough, I guess, to go in there and get a jacket and put it on and he went out zipping it.

Mr. BALL. You recall he went out zipping it—was he running or walking?

Mrs. ROBERTS. He was walking fast—he was making tracks pretty fast.

Mr. BALL. Did he say anything to you as he went out?

Mrs. ROBERTS. No, sir.

Mr. BALL. Did you say anything to him?

Mrs. ROBERTS. Probably wouldn't have gotten no answer.

Mr. BALL. What is the only thing you said to him from the time he came in the house until he left?

Mrs. ROBERTS. "You sure are in a hurry."

Mr. BALL. Is that all?

Mrs. ROBERTS. That was all.

Mr. BALL. That's all you said to him?

Mrs. ROBERTS. That's all I said to him.

Mr. BALL. Did he say anything to you?

Mrs. ROBERTS. No.

Mr. BALL. Nothing.

Mrs. ROBERTS. He didn't say nothing—he wouldn't say nothing—period.

Mr. BALL. Did he have the same colored pants on when he left, or do you know?

Mrs. ROBERTS. What?

Mr. BALL. Did he have the same colored pants on when he came in as when he went out?

Mrs. ROBERTS. Now, I wouldn't say that because I don't remember—I didn't pay that much attention. I didn't mean to be hateful, but I didn't.

Mr. BALL. Now, did it appear to you he had on the same pants or different pants from the time he came in and when he went out?

Mrs. ROBERTS. Well, I just didn't pay that much attention. All I remember—he was zipping up a coat and I was trying to find out about President Kennedy—I was still trying to find out about President Kennedy—they was broadcasting it then—I was more interested in that.

Mr. BALL. Had you ever seen a gun in his room?

Mrs. ROBERTS. No, sir.

Mr. BALL. Had you ever cleaned up his room?

Mrs. ROBERTS. Yes; I cleaned his rooms, but I didn't see no gun.

Mr. BALL. Did you ever go through any of his effects?

Mrs. ROBERTS. Oh, no.

Mr. BALL. There was a little wooden commode or closet in there, wasn't there?

Mrs. ROBERTS. There was a chifforobe—yes.

Mr. BALL. Did you ever look in there?

Mrs. ROBERTS. No, sir; I sure didn't—that's against the rules—to ransack their things.

Mr. BALL. Were there any drawers or anything in there?

Mrs. ROBERTS. Yes; there was drawers in that chifforobe and he also had a vanity dresser with four drawers.

Mr. BALL. Did you ever look inside of that?

Mrs. ROBERTS. No; I didn't.

Mr. BALL. After he left the house and at sometime later in the afternoon, these police officers came out, did they?

Mrs. ROBERTS. Well, yes.

Mr. BALL. And they asked you if there was a man named Lee Oswald there?

Mrs. ROBERTS. Yes.

Mr. BALL. And you told them "No"?

Mrs. ROBERTS. Yes.

Mr. BALL. Then what happened after that?

Mrs. ROBERTS. Well, he was trying to make us understand that—I had two new men and they told me—Mrs. Johnson told me, "Go get your keys and let them see in" I had gone to the back and they still had the TV on, and they was broadcasting about Kennedy.

Just as I unlocked the doors Fritz' men, two of them had walked in and she come running in and said, "Oh, Roberts, come here quick. This is this fellow Lee in this little room next to yours," and they flashed him on television, is how come us to know.

Mr. BALL. Then you knew it was the man?

Mrs. ROBERTS. Yes; and I come in there and she said, "Wait," and then again they flashed him back on and I said, "Yes, that's him—that's O. H. Lee right here in this room." And it was just a little wall there between him and I.

Mr. BALL. That was the first you knew who it was?

Mrs. ROBERTS. Yes, because he was registered as O. H. Lee.

Mr. BALL. Did you ever know he had a gun in his room?

Mrs. ROBERTS. No; I sure did not.

Mr. BALL. Did you ever appear on a television interview with Mr. or Mrs. Johnson—either one?

401

Mrs. ROBERTS. Well, no; they was on and would be on and then they had me on twice.

Mr. BALL. On television?

Mrs. ROBERTS. On television.

Mr. BALL. Where were you?

Mrs. ROBERTS. I was in the living room.

Mr. BALL. And they brought their cameras into the living room?

Mrs. ROBERTS. They brought their cameras into the living room and took pictures.

Mr. BALL. Were you alone?

Mrs. ROBERTS. Well, I was then, because they was questioning me. They asked Mr. and Mrs. Johnson not to be in there at that time.

Mr. BALL. Then, they questioned you?

Mrs. ROBERTS. Yes.

Mr. BALL. Did you ever have an interview with Mr. and Mrs. Johnson being there?

Mrs. ROBERTS. Well, yes; one time, and then they would question them separate from me.

Mr. BALL. Was there any one time when they questioned all three of you together?

Mrs. ROBERTS. Yes—one time.

Mr. BALL. Just one time—were you ever on television when you and Mrs. Johnson were on it alone together?

Mrs. ROBERTS. She and Mr. Johnson would be together and then I would be at the back when they put them on television, and then they had me on two different times and I was alone. They taken me when I was standing and showed them where it was.

Mr. BALL. Now, on television did they ever ask you if Oswald had a gun?

Mrs. ROBERTS. I don't know.

Mr. BALL. You don't remember?

Mrs. ROBERTS. I don't remember.

Mr. BALL. Did they ever ask you if you knew whether Oswald had a gun in his room or not?

Mrs. ROBERTS. Yes; they asked me and I told them "No"—for I didn't.

Mr. BALL. You didn't know whether he had a gun in there or not?

Mrs. ROBERTS. No—I didn't.

Mr. BALL. You never saw one?

Mrs. ROBERTS. No, sir.

Mr. BALL. Did you tell them that?

Mrs. ROBERTS. I sure did—I didn't know he had a gun.

Mr. BALL. And when he was zipping up his jacket, his belt was covered?

Mrs. ROBERTS. Was it covered—well—I don't know. I just couldn't answer you—I don't know—I don't remember it. I couldn't any more tell you than the man in the moon whether or not the man's belt was covered or uncovered. All I know he was zipping his coat.

Mr. BALL. Let me ask you another question: Did you ever talk to a reporter from a French newspaper?

Mrs. ROBERTS. A French newspaper?

Mr. BALL. Yes.

Mrs. ROBERTS. Well, there was people in there from about everywhere, but I don't remember.

Mr. BALL. There was some French newspaperman who claims he interviewed you.

Mrs. ROBERTS. French?

Mr. BALL. Do you remember any French newspapermen interviewing you?

Mrs. ROBERTS. No, I don't remember, but there were people in there from somewhere but I don't remember where they were from.

Mr. BALL. Had you ever heard the name Lee Harvey Oswald before the Friday when the police came out?

Mrs. ROBERTS. No, sir.

Mr. BALL. And you had, of course, thought his name was what?

Mrs. ROBERTS. O. H. Lee.

Mr. BALL. He had paid you, had he?

Mrs. ROBERTS. He always paid on time.

Mr. BALL. And you made a record of it?

Mrs. ROBERTS. Oh, yes.

Mr. BALL. Now, after these police officers came out of there, did you see a gun holster in his room after they had searched it?

Mrs. ROBERTS. Yes—there was one of them little outfits—a little holster and they taken it out and where they got it—I don't know, but it was in the room. They had it in their hands, one of the men was holding it.

Mr. BALL. Had you ever seen that before?

Mrs. ROBERTS. No; I hadn't.

Mr. BALL. Let me ask you something about his habits again—how early would he leave his room in the morning?

Mrs. ROBERTS. Well, he would leave around 7 o'clock, maybe between 6:30 and 7.

Mr. BALL. And what time would he come back?

Mrs. ROBERTS. Well, he would get home about maybe 5—something around 5 o'clock.

Mr. BALL. And with the exception of the weekends that he spent away, was he home every night or was he out at night?

Mrs. ROBERTS. He was always home at night—he never went out.

Mr. BALL. Now, on one holiday that occurred on Monday—he didn't come in?

Mrs. ROBERTS. No, he didn't come in that Monday.

Mr. BALL. Was that the only Monday he didn't come in?

Mrs. ROBERTS. That was the only Monday he didn't come in.

Mr. BALL. He paid on Monday?

Mrs. ROBERTS. He paid on Monday and that was the only time he didn't pay on Monday and he wasn't there.

Mr. BALL. He paid on what day of the week that week?

Mrs. ROBERTS. Tuesday—when he came in home.

Mr. BALL. But the weekend before November 22d, he was there all weekend, was he?

Mrs. ROBERTS. Yes.

Mr. BALL. Now, I also will ask you whether or not you ever heard of a fellow by the name of Ruby—did you ever hear of a fellow by the name of Jack Ruby?

Mrs. ROBERTS. No—I didn't.

Mr. BALL. Had you ever heard his name before he was accused of shooting Oswald?

Mrs. ROBERTS. No.

Mr. BALL. You never even heard his name?

Mrs. ROBERTS. No.

Mr. BALL. You never even heard his name?

Mrs. ROBERTS. No—I never heard his name.

Mr. BALL. And had never seen him?

Mrs. ROBERTS. No, sir.

Mr. BALL. Did a police car pass the house there and honked?

Mrs. ROBERTS. Yes.

Mr. BALL. When was that?

Mrs. ROBERTS. He came in the house.

Mr. BALL. When he came in the house?

Mrs. ROBERTS. When he came in the house and went to his room, you know how the sidewalk runs?

Mr. BALL. Yes.

Mrs. ROBERTS. Right direct in front of that door—there was a police car stopped and honked. I had worked for some policemen and sometimes they come by and tell me something that maybe their wives would want me to know, and I thought it was them, and I just glanced out and saw the number, and I said, "Oh, that's not their car," for I knew their car.

Mr. BALL. You mean, it was not the car of the policemen you knew?

Mrs. ROBERTS. It wasn't the police car I knew, because their number was 170 and it wasn't 170 and I ignored it.

Mr. BALL. And who was in the car?

Mrs. ROBERTS. I don't know—I didn't pay any attention to it after I noticed it wasn't them—I didn't.

Mr. BALL. Where was it parked?

Mrs. ROBERTS. It was parked in front of the house.

Mr. BALL. At 1026 North Beckley?

Mrs. ROBERTS. And then they just eased on—the way it is—it was the third house off of Zangs and they just went on around the corner that way.

Mr. BALL. Went around what corner?

Mrs. ROBERTS. Went around the corner off of Beckley on Zangs.

Mr. BALL. Going which way—toward town or away from town?

Mrs. ROBERTS. Toward town.

Dr. GOLDBERG. Which way was the car facing?

Mrs. ROBERTS. It was facing north.

Dr. GOLDBERG. Towards Zangs?

Mrs. ROBERTS. Towards Zangs—for I was the third house right off of Zangs on Beckley.

Mr. BALL. Did this police car stop directly in front of your house?

Mrs. ROBERTS. Yes—it stopped directly in front of my house and it just "tip-tip" and that's the way Officer Alexander and Charles Burnely would do when they stopped, and I went to the door and looked and saw it wasn't their number.

Mr. BALL. Where was Oswald when this happened?

Mrs. ROBERTS. In his room.

Mr. BALL. It was after he had come in his room?

Mrs. ROBERTS. Yes.

Mr. BALL. Had that police car ever stopped there before?

Mrs. ROBERTS. I don't know—I don't remember ever seeing it.

Mr. BALL. Have you ever seen it since?

Mrs. ROBERTS. No—I didn't pay that much attention—I just saw it wasn't the police car that I knew and had worked for so, I forgot about it. I seen it at the time, but I don't remember now what it was.

Mr. BALL. Did you report the number of the car to anyone?

Mrs. ROBERTS. I think I did—I'm not sure, because I—at that particular time I remembered it.

Mr. BALL. You remembered the number of the car?

Mrs. ROBERTS. I think it was—106, it seems to me like it was 106, but I do know what theirs was—it was 170 and it wasn't their car.

Mr. BALL. It was not 170?

Mrs. ROBERTS. The people I worked for was 170.

Mr. BALL. Did you report that number to anyone, did you report this incident to anyone?

Mrs. ROBERTS. Yes, I told the FBI and the Secret Service both when they was out there.

Mr. BALL. And did you tell them the number of the car?

Mrs. ROBERTS. I'm not sure—I believe I did—I'm not sure. I think I did because—there was so much happened then until my brains was in a whirl.

Mr. BALL. On the 29th of November, Special Agents Will Griffin and James Kennedy of the Federal Bureau of Investigation interviewed you and you told them that "after Oswald had entered his room about 1 p.m. on November 22, 1963, you looked out the front window and saw police car No. 207."

Mrs. ROBERTS. No. 107.

Mr. BALL. Is that the number?

Mrs. ROBERTS. Yes—I remembered it. I don't know where I got that 106—207. Anyway, I knew it wasn't 170.

Mr. BALL. And you say that there were two uniformed policemen in the car?

Mrs. ROBERTS. Yes, and it was in a black car. It wasn't an accident squad car at all.

Mr. BALL. Were there two uniformed policemen in the car?

Mrs. ROBERTS. Oh, yes.

Mr. BALL. And one of the officers sounded the horn?

Mrs. ROBERTS. Just kind of a "tit-tit"—twice.

Mr. BALL. And then drove on to Beckley toward Zangs Boulevard, is that right?

Mrs. ROBERTS. Yes. I thought there was a number, but I couldn't remember it but I did know the number of their car—I could tell that. I want you to understand that I have been put through the third degree and it's hard to remember.

Mr. BALL. Are there any other questions?

Dr. GOLDBERG. No, that's all.

Mr. BALL. Now, Mrs. Roberts, this deposition will be written up and you can read it if you want to and you can sign it, or you can waive the signature.

Mrs. ROBERTS. Well, you know, I can't see too good how to read. I'm completely blind in my right eye.

Mr. BALL. Do you want to waive your signature? And then you won't have to come back down here.

Mrs. ROBERTS. Well, okay.

Mr. BALL. All right, you waive it then?

Mrs. ROBERTS. Yes.

Do you want me to sign it now?

Mr. BALL. No; we couldn't, because this young lady has to write it up and it will be a couple of weeks before it will be ready.

Mrs. ROBERTS. Well, will you want me to come back or how?

Mr. BALL. Well, you can waive your signature and you won't have to come back to do that—do you want to do that?

Mrs. ROBERTS. Okay, it will be all right.

Mr. BALL. All right. The Secret Service will take you home now.

Mrs. ROBERTS. All right.

Mr. BALL. Thank you for coming.

Mrs. ROBERTS. All right.

TESTIMONY OF DOMINGO BENAVIDES

The testimony of Domingo Benavides was taken at 2:30 p.m., on April 2, 1964, in the office of the U.S. attorney, 301 Post Office Building, Bryan and Ervay Streets, Dallas, Tex., by Mr. David W. Belin, assistant counsel of the President's Commission.

Mr. BELIN. You want to raise your hand and stand up and be sworn.

Do you solemnly swear to tell the truth, the whole truth, and nothing but the truth, so help you God?

Mr. BENAVIDES. I do.

Mr. BELIN. Will you state your name for our reporter, please?

Mr. BENAVIDES. Domingo Benavides.

Mr. BELIN. How old are you, sir?

Mr. BENAVIDES. I am 27, April the 9th. I am now 26.

Mr. BELIN. Single or married?

Mr. BENAVIDES. Married.

Mr. BELIN. Family?

Mr. BENAVIDES. Two children and one expected sometime this month.

Mr. BELIN. Where are you from originally?

Mr. BENAVIDES. From Dallas.

Mr. BELIN. You were born in Dallas?

Mr. BENAVIDES. Yes, sir.

Mr. BELIN. Go to school in Dallas?

Mr. BENAVIDES. Yes, sir.

Mr. BELIN. How far did you go through school?

Mr. BENAVIDES. Tenth grade.

Mr. BELIN. Then what did you do when you got out of school?

Mr. BENAVIDES. I just went to work.

Mr. BELIN. Where did you work first?

Mr. BENAVIDES. Merchants Delivery.

Mr. BELIN. What did you do?

Mr. BENAVIDES. I was helper on a truck and part-time mechanic; mechanic helper.

Mr. BELIN. How long did you work for them?

Mr. BENAVIDES. I imagine about 2 years.

Mr. BELIN. Then what did you do?

Mr. BENAVIDES. I went into the Navy.

Mr. BELIN. What did you do in the Navy?

Mr. BENAVIDES. Yeoman and seaman.

Mr. BELIN. How long were you in the Navy?

Mr. BENAVIDES. Three years.

Mr. BELIN. Honorable discharge?

Mr. BENAVIDES. No, sir.

Mr. BELIN. You did not have an honorable discharge?

Mr. BENAVIDES. No, sir.

Mr. BELIN. What did you do when you got out of the Navy?

Mr. BENAVIDES. I returned to work for Merchants Delivery.

Mr. BELIN. Then what did you do?

Mr. BENAVIDES. Well, just from there I jumped around from roofing companies. I started in roofing then and I worked for Donald Bost, which is Town & Country Roofing Co., for on up until about 4 years ago, I guess. Then I just started mechanicing.

Mr. BELIN. You started to become an automobile mechanic?

Mr. BENAVIDES. Yes.

Mr. BELIN. For whom did you work then?

Mr. BENAVIDES. I worked in Martinez, Calif., for Donley Chevrolet & Cadillac Co., and then later on I was transferred to their paint and body shop, and then I came back to Dallas and I worked for Mr. Harris.

Mr. BELIN. For whom?

Mr. BENAVIDES. Mr. Harris, at Dootch Motors.

Mr. BELIN. Dootch Motors?

Mr. BENAVIDES. Yes, sir.

Mr. BELIN. Are you still working for them now? That is, as a mechanic?

Mr. BENAVIDES. Yes, sir.

Mr. BELIN. How long have you been working for Dootch now?

Mr. BENAVIDES. Well, off and on about 3 years. During this time I went back to Merchants Delivery and worked there and then I worked for Southern Delivery, too.

Mr. BELIN. Now when was the last time you went back to Dootch Motors?

Mr. BENAVIDES. It's been a year ago.

Mr. BELIN. You have been working for them ever since?

Mr. BENAVIDES. Yes, sir.

Mr. BELIN. Taking you back to November 22, 1963, anything unusual happen that day?

Mr. BENAVIDES. On the 22d?

Mr. BELIN. 22d of November 1963?

Mr. BENAVIDES. This would be embarrassing. Was that the day of the Assassination of the President?

Mr. BELIN. Yes.

Mr. BENAVIDES. I was thinking it was the 24th. Well, nothing except it seemed like a pretty nice day.

Mr. BELIN. Do you remember what day of the week it was?

Mr. BENAVIDES. I don't remember.

Mr. BELIN. Do you remember the day that the President was assassinated?

Mr. BENAVIDES. No.

Mr. BELIN. Do you remember that he was assassinated in Dallas?

Mr. BENAVIDES. Oh, yes; I remember this.

Mr. BELIN. That day you had lunch, were you at work that day?

Mr. BENAVIDES. Yes, sir.

Mr. BELIN. You had lunch?

Mr. BENAVIDES. I had lunch. And then this man had stalled this car in the middle of the street and asked me if I would fix it. Something was wrong with the carburetor, or pump that had broken in it, and I went around to the parts house to get the part for it.

Mr. BELIN. Where had the man's car stopped in the middle of the street?

Mr. BENAVIDES. Well, on Patton Street.

Mr. BELIN. Patton and what?

Mr. BENAVIDES. Between Jefferson and 10th.

Mr. BELIN. A car stopped in the middle of the street between——

Mr. BENAVIDES. Jefferson and Tenth.

Mr. BELIN. About what time of day was this?

Mr. BENAVIDES. I imagine it was about 1 o'clock.

Mr. BELIN. You imagine it was about 1 o'clock?

Mr. BENAVIDES. It was after lunch. I had already eaten. It was after I had lunch and I had eaten around 12, somewhere around 12 o'clock.

Mr. BELIN. What did you do? You were going to get a carburetor part, so what did you do?

Mr. BENAVIDES. I was in a rush and I ran off and forgot the number of the carburetor.

Mr. BELIN. You forgot the number of the carburetor?

Mr. BENAVIDES. Then I circled back. I left down the alley.

Mr. BELIN. Which alley is this?

Mr. BENAVIDES. The one directly between 10th and Patton and Jefferson Street.

Mr. BELIN. It runs parallel to 10th and Jefferson and it runs, the alley would run east of Patton Street?

Mr. BENAVIDES. Yes, sir.

Mr. BELIN. All right. The alley runs right behind Dootch Motors there?

Mr. BENAVIDES. Yes, sir.

Mr. BELIN. What kind of vehicle were you driving?

Mr. BENAVIDES. 1958 pickup truck Chevrolet.

Mr. BELIN. All right, what route did you take? Were you headed east or west in the alley?

Mr. BENAVIDES. East.

Mr. BELIN. To what?

Mr. BENAVIDES. To Denver street.

Mr. BELIN. Which is the next street over from Patton?

Mr. BENAVIDES. Yes, sir.

Mr. BELIN. First street east of Patton, then where?

Mr. BENAVIDES. I turned right, which is east on 10th. Wait. Denver would be north, I imagine. I turned from the alley north on Denver.

Mr. BELIN. All right.

Mr. BENAVIDES. And east on 10th.

Mr. BELIN. Then you turned east on——

Mr. BENAVIDES. The parts house sets on Marsalis and 10th.

Mr. BELIN. Marsalis and 10th?

Mr. BENAVIDES. Yes; so I got almost up to the parts house and I thought about the number, so I was going to go back and get the number off the carburetor. I turned in a drive and turned around and started back.

Mr. BELIN. On what street?

Mr. BENAVIDES. On 10th Street.

Mr. BELIN. On East 10th?

Mr. BENAVIDES. I was going west on 10th Street.

Mr. BELIN. All right.

Mr. BENAVIDES. Then I got almost up to the corner when I seen the policeman. I first seen the car stop up there.

Mr. BELIN. Now, you say you got almost to a corner. What corner was that?

Mr. BENAVIDES. At Denver and 10th.

Mr. BELIN. You almost got up to Denver and 10th heading west on 10th Street when you saw something?

Mr. BENAVIDES. I saw this police car.

Mr. BELIN. You saw a police car?

Mr. BENAVIDES. Yes, sir.

Mr. BELIN. Where was the police car?

Mr. BENAVIDES. It was sitting about 4 or 5 feet from the curb and down about 2 houses from the corner of Patton Street.

Mr. BELIN. All right. Was it between Patton and Denver?

Mr. BENAVIDES. Yes, sir.

Mr. BELIN. On what side of East 10th, north or south?

Mr. BENAVIDES. On the south side.

Mr. BELIN. What direction was it headed?

Mr. BENAVIDES. It was headed east.

Mr. BELIN. What did you see then?

Mr. BENAVIDES. I then pulled on up and I seen this officer standing by the door. The door was open to the car, and I was pretty close to him, and I seen Oswald, or the man that shot him, standing on the other side of the car.

Mr. BELIN. All right. Did you see the officer as he was getting out of the car?

Mr. BENAVIDES. No; I seen as he was, well, he had his hand on the door and kind of in a hurry to get out, it seemed like.

Mr. BELIN. Had he already gotten out of the car?

Mr. BENAVIDES. He had already gotten around.

Mr. BELIN. Where did you see the other man?

Mr. BENAVIDES. The other man was standing to the right side of the car, riders side of the car, and was standing right in front of the windshield on the right front fender. And then I heard the shot. Actually I wasn't looking for anything like that, so I heard the shot, and I just turned into the curb. Looked around to miss a car, I think.

And then I pulled up to the curb, hitting the curb, and I ducked down, and then I heard two more shots.

Mr. BELIN. How many shots did you hear all told?

Mr. BENAVIDES. I heard three shots.

Mr. BELIN. You heard three shots?

Mr. BENAVIDES. Yes, sir.

Mr. BELIN. Where were you when your vehicle stopped?

Mr. BENAVIDES. About 15 foot, just directly across the street and maybe a car length away from the police car.

407

Mr. BELIN. Would you have been a car length to the east or a car length to the west of the police car?

Mr. BENAVIDES. East of the front side of it.

Mr. BELIN. So your vehicle wouldn't have quite gotten up to where the police car was?

Mr. BENAVIDES. No; it didn't.

Mr. BELIN. How fast were you going when you watched the policeman getting out of his car?

Mr. BENAVIDES. Oh, I imagine not maybe 25 miles an hour. I never did pay much attention to it.

Mr. BELIN. You say you stopped the car right away? Your vehicle, I mean?

Mr. BENAVIDES. Yes, sir. I just didn't exactly stop because—I just pulled it into the curb.

Mr. BELIN. Then you say you heard a shot and you then ducked?

Mr. BENAVIDES. Yes. No; I heard the shot before I pulled in.

Mr. BELIN. Oh, I see. You heard the shot and pulled in and then what?

Mr. BENAVIDES. Then I ducked down.

Mr. BELIN. Then what happened?

Mr. BENAVIDES. Then I heard the other two shots and I looked up and the policeman was in, he seemed like he kind of stumbled and fell.

Mr. BELIN. Did you see the policeman as he fell?

Mr. BENAVIDES. Yes, sir.

Mr. BELIN. What else did you see?

Mr. BENAVIDES. Then I seen the man turn and walk back to the sidewalk and go on the sidewalk and he walked maybe 5 foot and then kind of stalled. He didn't exactly stop. And he threw one shell and must have took five or six more steps and threw the other shell up, and then he kind of stepped up to a pretty good trot going around the corner.

Mr. BELIN. You saw the man going around the corner headed in what direction on what street?

Mr. BENAVIDES. On Patton Street. He was going south.

Mr. BELIN. He was going south on Patton Street?

Mr. BENAVIDES. Yes; do you know Dootch Motors?

Mr. BELIN. Do I know Dootch Motors?

Mr. BENAVIDES. Yes, sir.

Mr. BELIN. Was he on the east or the west side of Patton as he was going?

Mr. BENAVIDES. On the east side.

Mr. BELIN. You saw him going on the east?

Mr. BENAVIDES. Yes, sir.

Mr. BELIN. How far did you see him go down Patton?

Mr. BENAVIDES. Just as far as the house would let the view go. In other words, as soon as he went past the house, I couldn't see him any more.

Mr. BELIN. Now, the first time that you saw him, what was his position?

Mr. BENAVIDES. He was standing, the first time I saw him. The man that shot him?

Mr. BELIN. Yes.

Mr. BENAVIDES. He was standing like I say, on the center in front of the windshield, right directly on the right front fender of the car.

Mr. BELIN. He was not moving when you saw him?

Mr. BENAVIDES. No; he wasn't moving then.

Mr. BELIN. All right, after you saw him turn around the corner, what did you do?

Mr. BENAVIDES. After that, I set there for just a few minutes to kind of, I thought he went in back of the house or something. At the time, I thought maybe he might have lived in there and I didn't want to get out and rush right up. He might start shooting again.

That is when I got out of the truck and walked over to the policeman, and he was lying there and he had, looked like a big clot of blood coming out of his head, and his eyes were sunk back in his head, and just kind of made me feel real funny. I guess I was really scared.

Mr. BELIN. Did the policeman say anything?

Mr. BENAVIDES. The policeman, I believe was dead when he hit the ground, because he didn't put his hand out or nothing.

Mr. BELIN. Where was the policeman as he fell, as you saw him?

Mr. BENAVIDES. I saw him as he was falling. The door was about half way open, and he was right in front of the door, and just about in front of the fender. I would say he was between the door and the front headlight, about middleway when he started to fall.

Mr. BELIN. Did you notice where the gun of the policeman was?

Mr. BENAVIDES. The gun was in his hand and he was partially lying on his gun in his right hand. He was partially lying on his gun and on his hand, too.

Mr. BELIN. Then what did you do?

Mr. BENAVIDES. Then I don't know if I opened the car door back further than what it was or not, but anyway, I went in and pulled the radio and I mashed the button and told them that an officer had been shot, and I didn't get an answer, so I said it again, and this guy asked me whereabouts all of a sudden, and I said, on 10th Street. I couldn't remember where it was at at the time.

So I looked up and I seen this number and I said 410 East 10th Street.

Mr. BELIN. You saw a number on the house then?

Mr. BENAVIDES. Yes.

Mr. BELIN. All right.

Mr. BENAVIDES. Then he started to—then I don't know what he said; but I put the radio back. I mean, the microphone back up, and this other guy was standing there, so I got up out of the car, and I don't know, I wasn't sure if he heard me, and the other guy sat down in the car.

Mr. BELIN. There was another passerby that stopped?

Mr. BENAVIDES. Yes, sir.

Mr. BELIN. Who was he, do you know?

Mr. BENAVIDES. I couldn't tell you. I don't know who he was.

Mr. BELIN. Was he driving a car or walking?

Mr. BENAVIDES. I don't know. He was just standing there whenever I looked up. He was standing at the door of the car, and I don't know what he said to the officer or the phone, but the officer told him to keep the line clear, or something, and stay off the phone, or something like that. That he already knew about it.

So then I turned and walked off. I never did assist him after that at all.

Mr. BELIN. Then what did you do?

Mr. BENAVIDES. At the time I walked out, I guess I was scared, so I started across the street—alley between the two houses to my mother's house, and I got in the yard and I said I'd better go back, or just caught myself until I got over there, I guess, so I went back around there.

Mr. BELIN. When you went back, what did you do?

First of all, was there anything up to that time that you saw there or that you did that you haven't related here that you can think of right now?

Mr. BENAVIDES. Well. I started—I seen him throw the shells and I started to stop and pick them up, and I thought I'd better not so when I came back, after I had gotten back, I picked up the shells.

Mr. BELIN. All right. Now, you said you saw the man with the gun throw the shells?

Mr. BENAVIDES. Yes, sir.

Mr. BELIN. Well, did you see the man empty his gun?

Mr. BENAVIDES. That is what he was doing. He took one out and threw it.

Mr. BELIN. Do you remember in which hand he was holding his gun?

Mr. BENAVIDES. No; I sure don't.

Mr. BELIN. Do you remember if he was trying to put anything in the gun also?

Mr. BENAVIDES. Yes. As he turned the corner he was putting another shell in his gun.

Mr. BELIN. You saw him?

Mr. BENAVIDES. I mean, he was acting like. I didn't see him actually put a shell in his gun, but he acted like he was trying to reload it.

Maybe he was trying to take out another shell, but he could have been reloading it or something.

Mr. BELIN. Let me ask you now, I would like to have you relate again the action of the man with the gun as you saw him now.

Mr. BENAVIDES. As I saw him, I really—I mean really got a good view of the man after the bullets were fired, he had just turned. He was just turning away.

In other words, he was pointing toward the officer, and he had just turned away to his left, and then he started. There was a big tree, and it seemed like he started back going to the curb of the street and into the sidewalk, and then he turned and went down the sidewalk to, well, until he got in front of the corner house, and then he turned to the left there and went on down Patton Street.

Mr. BELIN. When he got in front of the corner, when you say he turned to his left, did he cut across the yard of the house, or did he go clear to the corner and turn off?

Mr. BENAVIDES. There is a big bush and he catty-cornered across the yard.

Mr. BELIN. He kitty-cornered across the yard?

Mr. BENAVIDES. Yes. In other words, he didn't go all the way on the sidewalk. He just cut across the yard.

Mr. BELIN. Where was he when you saw him throwing shells? Had he already started across the yard?

Mr. BENAVIDES. No, sir. He had just got back to the sidewalk when he threw the first one and when he threw the second one, he had already cut back into the yard. He just sort of cut across.

Mr. BELIN. Now you saw him throw two shells?

Mr. BENAVIDES. Yes, sir.

Mr. BELIN. You saw where he threw the shells?

Mr. BENAVIDES. Yes, sir.

Mr. BELIN. Did you later go back in that area and try and find the shells?

Mr. BENAVIDES. Yes. Well, right after that I went back and I knew exactly where they was at, and I went over and picked up one in my hand, not thinking and I dropped it, that maybe they want fingerprints off it, so I took out an empty pack of cigarettes I had and picked them up with a little stick and put them in this cigarette package; a chrome looking shell.

Mr. BELIN. A chrome looking shell?

Mr. BENAVIDES. Yes, sir.

Mr. BELIN. About how long did it take you to locate the shells once you started looking for them?

Mr. BENAVIDES. Just a minute. I mean not very long at all. Just walked directly to them.

Mr. BELIN. You saw where he had thrown them?

Mr. BENAVIDES. One of them went down inside of a bush, and the other one was by the bush.

Mr. BELIN. Did you see him after he turned the corner of the house?

Mr. BENAVIDES. No, sir.

Mr. BELIN. Do you know whether or not he threw any—you said you heard three shots. Do you know whether or not he threw other shells there?

Mr. BENAVIDES. No, sir.

Mr. BELIN. Did you look at all there?

Mr. BENAVIDES. No; I didn't bother to look there.

Mr. BELIN. Did you see him when he cut across the yard? Did he go between the bushes to get to the sidewalk on Patton Street, or do you know?

Mr. BENAVIDES. Between the house and the bush; yes, sir. He had to cut across the yard, because there was a big bush on the corner there.

Mr. BELIN. Anything else you can think of about the man after you saw him? What was he wearing? What did he look like?

Mr. BENAVIDES. Well, he was kind of, well, just about your size.

Mr. BELIN. About my size? I am standing up.

Mr. BENAVIDES. You are about 5' 10"?

Mr. BELIN. I am between 5' 10" and 5' 11". Closer to 5' 11", I believe.

Mr. BENAVIDES. I would say he was about your size, and he had a light-beige jacket, and was lightweight.

Mr. BELIN. Did it have buttons or a zipper, or do you remember?

Mr. BENAVIDES. It seemed like it was a zipper-type jacket.

Mr. BELIN. What color was the trousers?

Mr. BENAVIDES. They were dark.

Mr. BELIN. Do you remember what kind of shirt he had on?

Mr. BENAVIDES. It was dark in color, but I don't remember exactly what color.

Mr. BELIN. Was he average weight, slender, or heavy?

Mr. BENAVIDES. I would say he was average weight.

Mr. BELIN. What color hair did he have?

Mr. BENAVIDES. Oh, dark. I mean not dark.

Mr. BELIN. Black hair?

Mr. BENAVIDES. No. Not black or brown, just kind of a——

Mr. BELIN. My color hair?

Mr. BENAVIDES. Yes.

Mr. BELIN. You say he is my size, my weight, and my color hair?

Mr. BENAVIDES. He kind of looks like—well, his hair was a little bit curlier.

Mr. BELIN. Anything else about him that looked like me.

Mr. BENAVIDES. No, that is all.

Mr. BELIN. What about his skin? Was he fair complexioned or dark complexioned?

Mr. BENAVIDES. He wasn't dark.

Mr. BELIN. Average complexion?

Mr. BENAVIDES. No; a little bit darker than average.

Mr. BELIN. My complexion?

Mr. BENAVIDES. I wouldn't say that any more. I would say he is about your complexion, sir. Of course he looked, his skin looked a little bit ruddier than mine.

Mr. BELIN. His skin looked ruddier than mine?

I might say for the record, that I was not in Dallas on November 22, 1963.

Mr. BENAVIDES. No, just your size.

Mr. BELIN. Did he look like me?

Mr. BENAVIDES. No; your face, not your face, but just your size.

Mr. BELIN. Okay, well, I thank you. I was flying from St. Louis to Des Moines, Iowa, at about this time.

Is there anything else?

Mr. BENAVIDES. I remember the back of his head seemed like his hairline was sort of— looked like his hairline sort of went square instead of tapered off, and he looked like he needed a haircut for about 2 weeks, but his hair didn't taper off, it kind of went down and squared off and made his head look flat in back.

Mr. BELIN. When you put these two shells that you found in this cigarette package, what did you do with them?

Mr. BENAVIDES. I gave them to an officer.

Mr. BELIN. That came out to the scene shortly after?

Mr. BENAVIDES. Yes, sir.

Mr. BELIN. Do you remember the name of the officer?

Mr. BENAVIDES. No, sir; I didn't even ask him. I just told him that this was the shells that he had fired, and I handed them to him. Seemed like he was a young guy, maybe 24.

Mr. BELIN. How old would you say the man that you saw with gun was?

Mr. BENAVIDES. I figured he was around 25.

Mr. BELIN. When the officers came out there, did you tell them what you had seen?

Mr. BENAVIDES. No, sir.

Mr. BELIN. What did you do?

Mr. BENAVIDES. I left right after. I give the shells to the officer. I turned around and went back and we returned to work.

Mr. BELIN. Then what happened? Did the officers ever get in touch with you?

Mr. BENAVIDES. Later on that evening, about 4 o'clock, there was two officers came by and asked for me, Mr. Callaway asked me—I had told them that I had seen the officer, and the reporters were there and I was trying to hide from the reporters because they will just bother you all the time.

Then I found out that they thought this was the guy that killed the President. At the time I didn't know the President was dead or he had been shot. So I was just trying to hide from the reporters and everything, and these two officers came around and asked me if I'd seen him, and I told him yes, and told   them what I had seen, and they asked me if I could identify him, and I said I don't think I could.

At this time I was sure, I wasn't sure that I could or not. I wasn't going to say I could identify and go down and couldn't have.

Mr. BELIN. Did he ever take you to the police station and ask you if you could identify him?

Mr. BENAVIDES. No; they didn't.

Mr. BELIN. You used the name Oswald. How did you know this man was Oswald?

Mr. BENAVIDES. From the pictures I had seen. It looked like a guy, resembled the guy. That was the reason I figured it was Oswald.

Mr. BELIN. Were they newspaper pictures or television pictures, or both, or neither?

Mr. BENAVIDES. Well, television pictures and newspaper pictures. The thing lasted about a month, I believe, it seemed like.

Mr. BELIN. Pardon.

Mr. BENAVIDES. I showed—I believe they showed pictures of him every day for a long time there.

Mr. BELIN. Did you talk to anyone at all there that witnessed what was going on?

Mr. BENAVIDES. No; sure didn't. There was people that asked me what happened, came up in the crowd there and asked me what happened, and I said just the policeman got shot.

Mr. BELIN. You talked to Ted Callaway, did you?

Mr. BENAVIDES. No; afterward. You know, I told your—I told him, he asked me when we went, when Ted Callaway got around there, he opened the car door and picked up the phone and called in and told them there was an officer that had been killed. But the officer on the other side of the radio told him to hang up the phone to keep the lines clear, or something of that sort.

Then he jumped out and ran around and he asked me did I see what happened, and I said yes. And he said let's chase him, and I said no.

Mr. BELIN. Why did you say "No"?

Mr. BENAVIDES. Well, he was reaching down and getting the gun out of the policeman's hand, and I didn't think he should bother to go like that. So he then turned around and went to the cab that was sitting on the corner.

Mr. BELIN. This cab?

Mr. BENAVIDES. Yes. There was a cab sitting—oh, there isn't a sidewalk on Patton Street. I mean there is sidewalks, but not a curb, and this cab had pulled in there by the stop sign.

Mr. BELIN. Which way was the cab headed on Patton Street?

Mr. BENAVIDES. It was headed north on Patton Street.

Mr. BELIN. Was it on the south side of 10th or the north side of 10th when it was parked there?

Mr. BENAVIDES. It would be on the south side of 10th.

Mr. BELIN. Was it on the east side of Patton or the west?

Mr. BENAVIDES. It would be on the east side of Patton.

Mr. BELIN. How close to the sidewalk on East 10th would the front part of the cab have been?

Mr. BENAVIDES. The front part of the cab was, I would say, maybe 5 or 6 feet from the corner.

Mr. BELIN. From the corner?

Mr. BENAVIDES. Yes.

Mr. BELIN. All right.

Mr. BENAVIDES. He was sort of, if it had been a curb there, he would be up on the curb.

Mr. BELIN. All right.

Mr. BENAVIDES. And so Ted then got in the taxicab and the taxicab came to a halt and he asked me which way he went. I told him he went down Patton Street toward the office, and come to find out later Ted had already seen him go by there.

Mr. BELIN. Did Ted tell you later he had seen him go by?

Mr. BENAVIDES. Yes; then we had a colored porter that said he had seen him go by.

Mr. BELIN. Would this be Sam Guinyard?

Mr. BENAVIDES. Yes.

Mr. BELIN. Did Ted say whether or not he had gone down to the police station to try to identify the man?

Mr. BENAVIDES. After that—After I left that evening, I took off kind of early because I was so shookup that I couldn't work, and so when I say early, I usually work to 9 or 10 or 11 o'clock, at night. So I'd taken off early and the next day the kid told me that he went down there. I think it was the next day, or the day after.

Well, it was the next day he told me that they went down and identified him as the guy that came by the carlot.

Mr. BELIN. Ted told you the next day at work that he had gone down and identified him?

Mr. BENAVIDES. Yes; I don't know if Ted told me, but somebody told me.

Mr. BELIN. Ted worked at Dootch Motors at the same time?

Mr. BENAVIDES. Yes, sir.

Mr. BELIN. What does he do there?

Mr. BENAVIDES. General manager.

Mr. BELIN. Used-car place?

Mr. BENAVIDES. Yes, sir.

Mr. BELIN. I am going to go down and get some clothing and see if you can identify it and I will be back in 1 minute.

Mr. BENAVIDES. Okay.

Mr. BELIN. I am handing you a jacket which has been marked as "Commission's Exhibit 163," and ask you to state whether this bears any similarity to the jacket you saw this man with the gun wearing?

Mr. BENAVIDES. I would say this looks just like it. Looks like he had laundried it, but it looks like it was a newer coat than that.

Mr. BELIN. I am handing you what has been marked "Commission's Exhibit 150," and see if this looks anything like the shirt that he had on?

412

Mr. BENAVIDES. I think the shirt looked darker than that.

Mr. BELIN. The shirt was darker?

Mr. BENAVIDES. I couldn't tell at the time because he had the jacket on there. That was a waist-type jacket, wasn't it?

Mr. BELIN. Yes; anything else you can think of.

Mr. BENAVIDES. Not offhand, except later on, I don't know if I seen it on television but I believe I seen it on television where they was arresting him, the policeman from the theater. But it didn't seem like he had a jacket on there.

Mr. BELIN. When he was being arrested you say he didn't have a jacket on? Now at the time you saw him, did he have a jacket on?

Mr. BENAVIDES. He had a jacket on and it looked like that jacket there.

Mr. BELIN. Anything else?

Mr. BENAVIDES. No; I guess that is all I can think of right now.

I think there was another car that was in front of me, a red Ford, I believe. I didn't know the man, but I guess he was about 25 or 30, and he pulled over. I didn't never see him get out of his car, but when he heard the scare, I guess he was about six cars from them, and he pulled over, and I don't know if he came back there or not.

Mr. BELIN. Anything else?

Mr. BENAVIDES. That would be all. I think if anybody had seen anything really closeup, that he must have fired just as they got past him, and they must have seen him standing there, because he was right directly in front of me. And whenever you see a squad car parked like that, you think something is wrong. At least that is what comes to my mind.

Mr. BELIN. Anything else?

Mr. BENAVIDES. That is all I can think of right now that I can remember.

Mr. BELIN. Pardon?

Mr. BENAVIDES. That is all I can think of right now that I can remember.

Mr. BELIN. You and I never met before today, did we, except that one day when we were around to see Ted Callaway and he introduced you at Dootch Motors and we chatted for 3 or 4 minutes there?

Mr. BENAVIDES. Yes; you and two other men.

Mr. BELIN. Today when we met, you came up here and what is the facts as to whether I asked you before the court reporter was able to get here to just relate to me what happened, or did I start questioning you or try to tell you things as I saw them?

Mr. BENAVIDES. So; you just asked me what happened and I described to you what happened.

Mr. BELIN. Is there anything you said before the court reporter got here that is different in anyway that you said after the court reporter started taking your testimony?

Mr. BENAVIDES. Maybe now only in the change of time, or I imagine I added a little bit since she was here.

Mr. BELIN. Is there anything that would be at variance with what you told me before the court reporter got here?

Mr. BENAVIDES. Well, I don't understand.

Mr. BELIN. What I mean is, is there anything that you said before the court reporter got here that you haven't included after the court reporter got here?

Mr. BENAVIDES. No.

Mr. BELIN. Anything you have said in front of the court reporter that has been different insofar as being a fact which is opposite or different in anyway from what you told me before?

Mr. BENAVIDES. Different in wording but——

Mr. BELIN. But are the facts different?

Mr. BENAVIDES. No; I don't believe the facts are different.

Mr. BELIN. Now you have a right, if you want to, to come back and read the deposition and sign it, or you can just rely on the court reporter's accuracy and waive the signing of it. Do you want to waive it or not?

Mr. BENAVIDES. I would like to read it.

Mr. BELIN. All right.

Mr. BENAVIDES. Maybe I could add something I didn't add.

Mr. BELIN. All right, I will ask the court reporter to try and get in touch with you.

Mr. BENAVIDES. 3112 June Drive.

Mr. BELIN. She can reach you at Dootch Motors?

Mr. BENAVIDES. Dootch Motors.

Mr. BELIN. What is the address?

Mr. BENAVIDES. 501 East Jefferson.

413

Mr. BELIN. You did get notice of the taking of this deposition here today?

Mr. BENAVIDES. Yes, sir.

Mr. BELIN. You are here voluntarily appearing in front of the Commission?

Mr. BENAVIDES. Yes, sir.

Mr. BELIN. Well, we surely appreciate all of the cooperation you have shown here, sir, and if there is anything else that you think is important, we would appreciate your getting in touch with us.

Mr. BENAVIDES. That is the reason I wanted to read this, in case I might have left out something.

Mr. BELIN. Would you please thank whoever is the general manager at Dootch Motors for letting you come here and appear before us?

Mr. BENAVIDES. That is Mr. Harris.

Mr. BELIN. Thank you very much.

TESTIMONY OF MRS. CHARLIE VIRGINIA DAVIS

The testimony of Mrs. Charlie Virginia Davis was taken at 9 a.m., on April 2, 1964, in the office of the U.S. attorney. 301 Post Office Building, Bryan and Ervay Streets, Dallas, Tex., by Mr. David W. Belin, assistant counsel of the President's Commission.

Mr. BELIN. Mrs. Davis, would you stand and raise your right hand and be sworn, please? Do you solemnly swear that the testimony you give will be the truth, the whole truth, and nothing but the truth, so help you God?

Mrs. DAVIS. I do.

Mr. BELIN. Would you please state your name for the court reporter?

Mrs. DAVIS. Mrs. Charlie Virginia Davis.

Mr. BELIN. You are known as Mrs. Charles Davis?

Mrs. DAVIS. Yes, sir.

Mr. BELIN. Your first name is Virginia?

Mrs. DAVIS. Yes, sir.

Mr. BELIN. Where do you live, Mrs. Davis?

Mrs. DAVIS. Athens.

Mr. BELIN. In Texas?

Mrs. DAVIS. Yes, sir.

Mr. BELIN. How old are you?

Mrs. DAVIS. Sixteen.

Mr. BELIN. How long have you lived in Athens?

Mrs. DAVIS. Well, about 6 months. It was after the President was shot.

Mr. BELIN. Do you remember when the President was shot?

Mrs. DAVIS. On November 22.

Mr. BELIN. About how long after that did you move to Athens?

Mrs. DAVIS. It was about 2 weeks after the President was shot.

Mr. BELIN. Mrs. Davis, how long have you been married?

Mrs. DAVIS. Seven months.

Mr. BELIN. Any children?

Mrs. DAVIS. No, sir.

Mr. BELIN. The time you moved to Athens would have been sometime in December of 1963?

Mrs. DAVIS. Yes, sir.

Mr. BELIN. Prior to that time, had you always lived in Dallas?

Mrs. DAVIS. Well, after I got married we moved to Dallas and we lived there ever since.

Mr. BELIN. When you got married, you moved to Dallas. Before you got married, where did you live?

Mrs. DAVIS. Palestine.

Mr. BELIN. Is that in Texas?

Mrs. DAVIS. Yes.

Mr. BELIN. Were you raised there?

Mrs. DAVIS. No, sir; I was raised in Athens.

Mr. BELIN. You were raised in Athens. Did you go to school in Athens?

Mrs. DAVIS. No; I went to school in Palestine.

Mr. BELIN. How far did you get through school?

Mrs. DAVIS. The ninth grade.

Mr. BELIN. Have you ever been employed at all?

Mrs. DAVIS. No.

Mr. BELIN. Now, Mrs. Davis, where were you living when you were living in Dallas in November of 1963?

Mrs. DAVIS. 400 East 10th Street.

Mr. BELIN. Is that 400 East 10th?

Mrs. DAVIS. Yes.

Mr. BELIN. Do you know what cross-street runs at 10th there?

Mrs. DAVIS. Patton.

Mr. BELIN. 10th and Patton?

Mrs. DAVIS. Yes.

Mr. BELIN. What kind of house did you live in? Was it a brick or frame home?

Mrs. DAVIS. It was a frame apartment house.

Mr. BELIN. Pardon?

Mrs. DAVIS. It was a frame apartment house.

Mr. BELIN. A frame apartment house. You and your husband lived in one apartment?

Mrs. DAVIS. And my sister and her husband lived in another one.

Mr. BELIN. There were two apartments there?

Mrs. DAVIS. On the bottom floor.

Mr. BELIN. What is your sister's name?

Mrs. DAVIS. Mrs. Barbara Jeanette Davis.

Mr. BELIN. Do you know what her husband's name is?

Mrs. DAVIS. Troy Lee Davis.

Mr. BELIN. Taking you back to the afternoon of November 22, do you remember anything out of the ordinary that happened on that date?

Mrs. DAVIS. Well, the boy that was known as Lee Harvey Oswald shot J. D. Tippit.

Mr. BELIN. Well, now, did you see him shoot J. D. Tippit?

Mrs. DAVIS. No; we didn't see. Yes; we heard the shot. He had already shot him.

Mr. BELIN. You say you heard a shot?

Mrs. DAVIS. Yes, sir.

Mr. BELIN. Where were you when you heard the shot?

Mrs. DAVIS. I was over at my sister-in-law's.

Mr. BELIN. Her apartment?

Mrs. DAVIS. Yes, sir.

Mr. BELIN. Where in her apartment were you?

Mrs. DAVIS. I was in the living room.

Mr. BELIN. You were in the living room?

Mrs. DAVIS. Yes. We was lying down.

Mr. BELIN. You were lying down in the living room on the sofa bed, or what?

Mrs. DAVIS. It is a bed against the wall and a sofa.

Mr. BELIN. Who was lying down?

Mrs. DAVIS. Well, Jeanette was lying on the bed. I was lying on the couch, and Annette and James Lee were lying on the other bed.

Mr. BELIN. Are these other people children of your sister's?

Mrs. DAVIS. Yes, sir.

Mr. BELIN. About how old are those children?

Mrs. DAVIS. James will be 6 and then Annette is 5.

Mr. BELIN. Now as you were lying down, what did you see or hear?

Mrs. DAVIS. We just heard a shot.

Mr. BELIN. How many shots did you hear?

Mrs. DAVIS. We heard the first one and then we thought maybe someone had a blowout like a tire or something and we didn't get up to see. Then we heard the second shot and that is when we ran to the front door.

Mr. BELIN. Well, now, does that mean that you heard two shots?

Mrs. DAVIS. Yes, sir.

Mr. BELIN. Are you sure there were not more than two, or are you sure that you heard two?

Mrs. DAVIS. We just heard two.

Mr. BELIN. Then what did you do?

Mrs. DAVIS. Well, Mrs. Markham was trying to say——

Mr. BELIN. Mrs. Markham?

Mrs. DAVIS. Yes, sir.

Mr. BELIN. Do you know what her first name is?

Mrs. DAVIS. No, sir. I just know her by Mrs. Markham.

Mr. BELIN. Had you ever known her before?

Mrs. DAVIS. No, sir.

Mr. BELIN. How did you know it was Mrs. Markham?

Mrs. DAVIS. Well, it said in the paper that it was Mrs. Markham, and my sister-in-law said it was Mrs. Markham. My sister-in-law knows Mrs. Markham.

Mr. BELIN. Now you heard the shots. You heard, you say, the second shot and then what did you do?

Mrs. DAVIS. We was already up. We ran to the door.

Mr. BELIN. By we, who do you mean?

Mrs. DAVIS. Jeanette and I.

Mr. BELIN. You went to which door?

Mrs. DAVIS. The front door.

Mr. BELIN. That would be the front of the house facing East 10th Street?

Mrs. DAVIS. Yes, sir.

Mr. BELIN. What did you do when you got to the door?

Mrs. DAVIS. Mrs. Markham was standing at the tree.

Mr. BELIN. If we can picture the street intersection, was she standing in the middle of the street or on the sidewalk?

Mrs. DAVIS. She was on the sidewalk.

Mr. BELIN. Let me ask you this. Your house would be located at the southeast corner of the intersection, is that where it is, or not?

Mrs. DAVIS. Yes.

Mr. BELIN. Would she be standing on a corner that would be right across 10th Street but on the same side of Patton, or across Would it be catty-cornered or would it be across 10th Street but on the other side? Maybe we can draw it here on a little paper.

Mrs. DAVIS. I don't remember it too good.

Mr. BELIN. Now I have drawn on a piece of paper here a street intersection and this is Patton and here is 400 East 10th, which would be your house. Do you want to mark here where you think you saw Mrs. Markham?

Mrs. DAVIS. Well, she was standing on the sidewalk right here. Do you want to put an "X" there?

Mr. BELIN. Please put an "X" there.

Mrs. DAVIS. (Marks "X".)

Mr. BELIN. I'm going to call that Virginia Davis Deposition, Exhibit 1. What was Mrs. Markham saying, or did you hear her say anything?

Mrs. DAVIS. We heard her say "He shot him. He is dead. Call the police."

Mr. BELIN. Was she saying this in a soft or loud voice?

Mrs. DAVIS. She was screaming it.

Mr. BELIN. Did you see anything else as you heard her screaming?

Mrs. DAVIS. Well, we saw Oswald. We didn't know it was Oswald at the time. We saw that boy cut across the lawn emptying the shells out of the gun.

Mr. BELIN. All right. Now, you saw a boy. Do you know how old he was?

Mrs. DAVIS. He didn't look like he was over 20.

Mr. BELIN. Do you remember what color hair he had?

Mrs. DAVIS. Let's see, the best I recall, he had sort of light brown.

Mr. BELIN. Light brown hair?

Mrs. DAVIS. Yes.

Mr. BELIN. Was he tall or short or average height?

Mrs. DAVIS. He was about average height.

Mr. BELIN. Fat, thin, or average weight?

Mrs. DAVIS. Slim.

Mr. BELIN. Pardon?

Mrs. DAVIS. Slim.

Mr. BELIN. Do you remember what he had on?

Mrs. DAVIS. He had on a light-brown-tan jacket.

Mr. BELIN. Do you remember what color his trousers were?

Mrs. DAVIS. I think they were black. Brown jacket and trousers.

Mr. BELIN. The trousers were black?

Mrs. DAVIS. Yes.

Mr. BELIN. Do you remember what kind of shirt he had on?

Mrs. DAVIS. No, sir; I don't recall that.

416

Mr. BELIN. Was the jacket open or closed up?

Mrs. DAVIS. It was open.

Mr. BELIN. But you don't remember what kind of shirt he had on?

Mrs. DAVIS. No, sir.

Mr. BELIN. Did he look at you?

Mrs. DAVIS. No, sir; not that I remember. I don't think so.

Mr. BELIN. And where was he when you first saw him?

Mrs. DAVIS. He was cutting across our yard.

Mr. BELIN. In what direction was he walking?

Mrs. DAVIS. He was walking——

Mr. BELIN. Away from Patton or towards Patton?

Mrs. DAVIS. Towards Patton.

Mr. BELIN. When you first saw him, had he gotten up to your yard yet or not?

Mrs. DAVIS. Yes; he was cutting over across our yard.

Mr. BELIN. He was cutting across your walk that leads up to the front door?

Mrs. DAVIS. Yes, sir.

Mr. BELIN. About how far from the main sidewalk on East 10th was he?

Mrs. DAVIS. He was about 3 feet.

Mr. BELIN. About 3 feet or so?

Mrs. DAVIS. Yes; when I first saw him.

Mr. BELIN. Then he was cutting across your sidewalk about 3 feet away from the main sidewalk?

Mrs. DAVIS. Yes, sir.

Mr. BELIN. Then did you see him—how long did you see him? Where did you see him go?

Mrs. DAVIS. We saw him go around the corner of our house.

Mr. BELIN. How far did you see him go?

Mrs. DAVIS. Well, when he disappeared around that corner, that is the last we saw of him.

Mr. BELIN. Did you see him go through any bushes by your house or not? Or didn't you see him?

Mrs. DAVIS. No, sir.

Mr. BELIN. You mean you didn't see him?

Mrs. DAVIS. We saw him when he cut across our yard.

Mr. BELIN. Where was he when you last saw him? He was—was he still in your yard, or was he on the sidewalk on Patton Street?

Mrs. DAVIS. He was still in our yard.

Mr. BELIN. Then what did you do?

Mrs. DAVIS. We already called the police.

Mr. BELIN. You called the police before you saw him?

Mrs. DAVIS. When Mrs. Markham was standing across the street hollering, she told us to call the police, so Jeanette and I went in there, and Jeanette called the police and we went back and he was cutting across our yard, and we gave him time to go on because we were afraid he might shoot us.

Mr. BELIN. Did you call the police before or after you saw him cut across your yard?

Mrs. DAVIS. Before.

Mr. BELIN. In other words, to your—to the best of your recollection, you heard the shots, you ran outside, you saw Mrs. Markham—did you see anything else when you saw Mrs. Markham?

Mrs. DAVIS. No, sir; we just saw a police car sitting on the side of the road.

Mr. BELIN. Where was the police car parked?

Mrs. DAVIS. It was parked between the hedge that marks the apartment house where he lives in and the house next door.

Mr. BELIN. Was it on your side of East 10th or the other side of the street?

Mrs. DAVIS. It was on our side, the same side that we lived on.

Mr. BELIN. Was it headed as you looked to the police car, towards your right or towards your left?

Mrs. DAVIS. Right.

Mr. BELIN. Did you see any police officer in a police car when you first saw him?

Mrs. DAVIS. No, sir.

Mr. BELIN. When your sister went to call the police, did you go with her, or did you stay by the front door?

Mrs. DAVIS. I went with her.

Mr. BELIN. What did you hear your sister do?

Mrs. DAVIS. Well, she called the police and told whoever answered the phone that there had been a murder out in front of our house, to come quick.

Mr. BELIN. Then what did she do?

Mrs. DAVIS. She hung up and then we went back to the front door and told the two kids to stay indoors.

Mr. BELIN. Then what did you do?

Mrs. DAVIS. Then we went out in the front yard and right down to the police car and that is when we saw the policeman lying on the street.

Mr. BELIN. Where was the policeman lying?

Mrs. DAVIS. He was lying just, well, he was half between the front end of his car and, well, his head was lying toward the front end of it.

Mr. BELIN. Was he on the driver's side of the front or on the other side?

Mrs. DAVIS. He was on the driver's side.

Mr. BELIN. All right, now, as I understand your testimony, after you made the call, you went out to the front yard, is that it?

Mrs. DAVIS. Yes, sir.

Mr. BELIN. You then went out to see the policeman in the street?

Mrs. DAVIS. Yes, sir.

Mr. BELIN. When you went out in the front yard, were you in the front yard when the man was going by there?

Mrs. DAVIS. No, sir; he had already gone when we went outside.

Mr. BELIN. He had already gone when you went outside?

Mrs. DAVIS. Yes.

Mr. BELIN. I thought you said that when you went outside you went on the sidewalk?

Mrs. DAVIS. See, all the people had already—see, he was already gone.

Mr. BELIN. Had he gone by at that time?

Mrs. DAVIS. By the time we got back from off the phone, he had already gone. He had already disappeared behind the corner of our house.

Mr. BELIN. Did you see him going in front of your house before you called on the phone?

Mrs. DAVIS. Yes. When we heard the second shot, we ran to the front door, and that is when we saw the boy cutting across the yard.

Mr. BELIN. Well, let me see if I understand your statement now. You went to the front door after you heard the second shot?

Mrs. DAVIS. Yes, sir.

Mr. BELIN. What did you do when you got to the front door? Did you open the front door, or not?

Mrs. DAVIS. No, sir; we just looked through the front door.

Mr. BELIN. You looked through the front door?

Mrs. DAVIS. Yes.

Mr. BELIN. Was there a screen door on it or not?

Mrs. DAVIS. It was a screen door.

Mr. BELIN. Were you looking through the screen door, or was the screen door partially open, if you remember.

Mrs. DAVIS. It was closed. We was looking through it.

Mr. BELIN. You were looking through the screen door?

Mrs. DAVIS. Yes.

Mr. BELIN. Were you in front of your sister-in-law, or was she in front of you?

Mrs. DAVIS. She was in front of me.

Mr. BELIN. You were both looking through the screen door?

Mrs. DAVIS. Yes, sir.

Mr. BELIN. What did you see when you looked through the screen door?

Mrs. DAVIS. We saw a boy walking, cutting across our yard.

Mr. BELIN. Where was he when you first saw him?

Mrs. DAVIS. He was about 3 feet from the sidewalk. Not the one that comes up to our front door, but the other sidewalk.

Mr. BELIN. He was about 3 feet from the front sidewalk on East 10th?

Mrs. DAVIS. Yes.

Mr. BELIN. Had he come up to your sidewalk yet that comes up from East 10th to your front door?

Mrs. DAVIS. Yes, he had already. He was about half on the concrete, I think.

Mr. BELIN. He was half on that concrete?

Mrs. DAVIS. Yes.

Mr. BELIN. Then what did you watch this man do?

Mrs. DAVIS. We watched him unload the shells out of his gun.

Mr. BELIN. What hand was he holding this gun in?

Mrs. DAVIS. In the right.

Mr. BELIN. He was holding the gun in his right hand, if you remember?

Mrs. DAVIS. Yes, sir.

Mr. BELIN. What was he doing with his left hand?

Mrs. DAVIS. He was emptying the shells in his left hand.

Mr. BELIN. Was the gun broken open, so to speak? In other words, I don't know if you have ever seen a capgun. When you want to load the capgun, you have to kind of break it apart on a hinge.

Was the gun broken apart like that, or was the barrel straight?

Mrs. DAVIS. It was like the real gun, little one.

Mr. BELIN. What do you mean it was just like?

Mrs. DAVIS. It was just as best as I can remember, it was a little pistol, and he was emptying the shells. Where the shell was coming out, he was emptying the shells into his left hand.

Mr. BELIN. Did you see what he did with the shells when he emptied them into his left hand?

Mrs. DAVIS. After we, well, he was dropping them on the ground because we found two.

Mr. BELIN. You said that you found two? Did you see him drop them on the ground or not?

Mrs. DAVIS. No; we didn't see him.

Mr. BELIN. You just saw him emptying shells in his hand?

Mrs. DAVIS. Yes.

Mr. BELIN. You didn't actually see what he did with them when he got them in his hand, did you?

Mrs. DAVIS. No, sir.

Mr. BELIN. You are nodding your head no?

Mrs. DAVIS. No.

Mr. BELIN. Then what did you see the man do?

Mrs. DAVIS. Well, he just cut across. He disappeared from behind the corner of the house.

Mr. BELIN. Going toward what street?

Mrs. DAVIS. Well, going toward Jefferson Street.

Mr. BELIN. He was headed on Patton in the direction toward Jefferson?

Mrs. DAVIS. Yes, sir.

Mr. BELIN. Did you see him actually get to Patton Street?

Mrs. DAVIS. Yes; he was already around the corner.

Mr. BELIN. You saw him go around the corner of your home?

Mrs. DAVIS. Yes.

Mr. BELIN. What did you do or see then?

Mrs. DAVIS. Well, we just went out, because we had already called the police, notified them, and we went out in the yard.

Mr. BELIN. You notified the police. Let me ask you this. Did you notify the police before or after you saw the boy with the gun?

Mrs. DAVIS. Let's see, I think it was before.

Mr. BELIN. When you say before, what do you mean?

Mrs. DAVIS. Well, before we saw the boy.

Mr. BELIN. Before you saw the boy you notified the police?

Mrs. DAVIS. Yes, sir.

Mr. BELIN. Well, let me try and reconstruct your actions then. You heard the shots?

Mrs. DAVIS. Yes, sir.

Mr. BELIN. You ran to the door?

Mr. BELIN. What did you see when you got to the door?

Mrs. DAVIS. Well, we just saw, you know, the police car parked down there and we wondered what was going on, so we heard Mrs. Markham across the street calling.

Mr. BELIN. Then what did you do?

Mrs. DAVIS. Well, she told us to call the police, well, so went to the house. We was already in the house, and we went to the phone and called the police.

Mr. BELIN. Then what did you do?

Mrs. DAVIS. Then we went back to the front door.

Mr. BELIN. Then what did you do?

Mrs. DAVIS. We saw the boy cutting across the street.

Mr. BELIN. Then what did you do or see?

Mrs. DAVIS. After he disappeared around the corner we ran out in the front yard and down to see what had happened.

Mr. BELIN. Then is that when you saw the policeman?

Mrs. DAVIS. I saw the policeman lying on the street.

Mr. BELIN. All right. Did you see or do anything else? Did you see anyone else that you know come up to the policeman?

Mrs. DAVIS. No sir; there was a lot of people around there.

Mr. BELIN. Do you remember about what time of day this was?

Mrs. DAVIS. I wouldn't say for sure. But it was about 1:30, between 1:30 and 2.

Mr. BELIN. All right, after this, did police come out there?

Mrs. DAVIS. Yes; they was already there.

Mr. BELIN. By the time you got out there?

Mrs. DAVIS. Yes, sir.

Mr. BELIN. Then what did you do?

Mrs. DAVIS. Well, we just stood out there and watched. You know, tried to see how it all happened. But we saw part of it.

Mr. BELIN. Then what did you do?

Mrs. DAVIS. We stood out there until after the ambulance had come and picked him up.

Mr. BELIN. All right, then what did you do?

Mrs. DAVIS. And we stood out there and talked to this woman who told us that President Kennedy was shot.

Mr. BELIN. About what?

Mrs. DAVIS. This woman had told us that President Kennedy was shot.

Mr. BELIN. Then what did you do?

Mrs. DAVIS. When the police cars was circling all the blocks, about four or five blocks to see if they could find the boy, and we stayed out there all that time to see if they would locate him.

Mr. BELIN. All right, did you tell the police, that you had seen anyone with a gun?

Mrs. DAVIS. Yes, sir; we told them that we saw a boy carrying a gun.

Mr. BELIN. Then what did you do?

Mrs. DAVIS. Well, that was——

Mr. BELIN. Did you ever go down to the police station or identify him?

Mrs. DAVIS. Yes, sir; we had to identify him in the lineup.

Mr. BELIN. What day was that? This same day or another day?

Mrs. DAVIS. Same day.

Mr. BELIN. About what time of the day was it?

Mrs. DAVIS. It was probably about 5:30.

Mr. BELIN. Who went down with you?

Mrs. DAVIS. Well, let's see, my sister-in-law.

Mr. BELIN. That would be Barbara Jeanette Davis?

Mrs. DAVIS. Yes, sir; and her husband Troy Lee and myself.

Mr. BELIN. What did you do when you got to the police station?

Mrs. DAVIS. We stayed there until this detective, some man walked up to us and led us to this dark room.

Mr. BELIN. Before they led you to the dark room, did he show you any pictures of anyone?

Mrs. DAVIS. No.

Mr. BELIN. Had you seen any pictures on television of anyone that might be the man you saw walking with the gun?

Mrs. DAVIS. No.

Mr. BELIN. Had you watched television at all?

Mrs. DAVIS. No; we didn't watch television.

Mr. BELIN. Had you seen any newspapers that afternoon?

Mrs. DAVIS. No, sir; we didn't get the newspapers until that following morning.

Mr. BELIN. All right, you went with the detective to a dark room?

Mrs. DAVIS. Yes.

Mr. BELIN. What did you do when you got to the dark room?

Mrs. DAVIS. He told us to sit down.

Mr. BELIN. All right.

Mrs. DAVIS. And then these five boys, or men walked up on this platform, and he was No. 2.

Mr. BELIN. You say he was No. 2. Who was No. 2?

Mrs. DAVIS. The boy that shot Tippit.

Mr. BELIN. You mean the man—did you see him shoot Tippit? Or you mean the man you saw with the gun?

Mrs. DAVIS. The man I saw carrying the gun.

Mr. BELIN. Was he white or a Negro man?

Mrs. DAVIS. He was white.

Mr. BELIN. Were all the men in the lineup white men or some Negroes?

Mrs. DAVIS. All of them were white.

Mr. BELIN. Could you describe any other people in the lineup as to whether they might be fat or thin or short or tall?

Mrs. DAVIS. Well, one of them was sort, well, he was tall and slim. And then the other one there, he was sort of chubby and he was short. Then this other one, he was about the same height as the other one, the last one I told you about, short and chubby. And the other one was about—medium tall.

Mr. BELIN. Now you identified someone in that lineup?

Mrs. DAVIS. Yes, sir.

Mr. BELIN. Did you hear your sister-in-law identify him first, or not?

Mrs. DAVIS. No, sir; I identified him first.

Mr. BELIN. Where was your sister when you identified him?

Mrs. DAVIS. She was sitting right next to me.

Mr. BELIN. How did you identify him? Did you yell that this is the man I saw?

Mrs. DAVIS. No; I just leaned over and told the detective it was No. 2.

Mr. BELIN. Where was the detective? Was he to your right or to your left?

Mrs. DAVIS. Let's see, to my right.

Mr. BELIN. Where was your sister, to your right or to your left?

Mrs. DAVIS. Right.

Mr. BELIN. As she was to your right, so you leaned over to the detective and told the detective it was No. 2?

Mrs. DAVIS. Yes, sir.

Mr. BELIN. Anything else that you can think of that happened that day?

Mrs. DAVIS. No, sir.

Mr. BELIN. Later did you ever see a picture of Lee Harvey Oswald on television?

Mrs. DAVIS. Yes, sir.

Mr. BELIN. When did you first see it on television?

Mrs. DAVIS. When they was bringing him out of the jail out here.

Mr. BELIN. When?

Mrs. DAVIS. When they were bringing him out of the jail.

Mr. BELIN. You mean Sunday when he got shot?

Mrs. DAVIS. Yes.

Mr. BELIN. Did this look, could you tell whether this was the same man you saw running with the gun?

Mrs. DAVIS. I wouldn't say for sure.

Mr. BELIN. You mean from seeing his picture on television?

Mrs. DAVIS. Yes, sir.

Mr. BELIN. What about the man you identified as No. 2? Would you say for sure that he was the man you saw running with the gun?

Mrs. DAVIS. I would say that was him for sure.

Mr. BELIN. What you are saying is that you couldn't necessarily tell from the television picture?

Mrs. DAVIS. No, sir. Our television was blurred anyway, so we couldn't hardly tell.

Mr. BELIN. Do you remember that you signed a statement when you were down at the Dallas Police Department at all, or not?

Mrs. DAVIS. Yes, sir.

Mr. BELIN. I'm going to hand you what has been marked as Virginia Davis Deposition, Exhibit 2, and ask you to state if this is your signature on here?

Mrs. DAVIS. Yes, Sir.

421

Mr. BELIN. Would you read the contents of your deposition Exhibit 2, and I will ask you if there is anything there that is inaccurate.

(Reads statement.)

Mr. BELIN. You have read Exhibit 2?

Mrs. DAVIS. Yes, sir.

Mr. BELIN. Is there anything in that statement that is inaccurate in any way?

Mrs. DAVIS. No, sir.

Mr. BELIN. Is that what you told the police of Dallas on November 22, 1963?

Mrs. DAVIS. That's right.

Mr. BELIN. Now on this statement it says that you heard a shot and then another shot and ran to the side door at Patton Street. Was that the side door or front door?

Mrs. DAVIS. It was the front door.

Mr. BELIN. Then it says, "I saw the boy cutting across our yard and he was unloading his gun." Is that correct?

Mrs. DAVIS. That's right.

Mr. BELIN. Then it says, "We walked outside and a woman was hollering, 'He's dead, he's dead, he's shot.'" Is that right?

Mrs. DAVIS. That's right.

Mr. BELIN. Then it says, "This woman told Jeanette to call the police and she did." Is that what happened?

Mrs. DAVIS. Yes.

Mr. BELIN. It says, "I saw the officer that had been shot lying on 10th Street after Jeanette had called the police." Is that right?

Mrs. DAVIS. That's right.

Mr. BELIN. Now it says, "Jeanette found a empty shell that the man had unloaded and gave it to the police." Did you see Jeanette find that shell?

Mrs. DAVIS. Yes. I was right along behind her.

Mr. BELIN. Where did she find it?

Mrs. DAVIS. She found it beside, well, the apartment was facing this way.

Mr. BELIN. Facing Patton Street?

Mrs. DAVIS. Yes, sir. And we was already outside. We thought maybe we could find some evidence for the police. So we went through the hedge, and by my front door of the apartment where we live, right there in the grass where he dropped them.

Mr. BELIN. Had the police started to search around your house yet when they found it?

Mrs. DAVIS. Yes; they already started to search.

Mr. BELIN. Would this have been to the side of the house or the corner of the house that you found, that Jeanette found that shell?

Mrs. DAVIS. It was by the side.

Mr. BELIN. This would have been by the side of the house that is next to Patton Street.

Mrs. DAVIS. Yes, sir.

Mr. BELIN. About how far from the front of the house would it be?

Mrs. DAVIS. It was about 5 feet.

Mr. BELIN. About 5 feet. You saw Jeanette find the shell? You saw her pick it up from the ground?

Mrs. DAVIS. Yes.

Mr. BELIN. What color was it, do you remember?

Mrs. DAVIS. The best I can recall, it was gray, one of these——

Mr. BELIN. The best you can recall, it was gray?

Mrs. DAVIS. Yes.

Mr. BELIN. What did Jeanette do with it?

Mrs. DAVIS. She gave it to some detective.

Mr. BELIN. Did you see her find any other shells?

Mrs. DAVIS. I found one after Jeanette, after all the police had gone.

Mr. BELIN. When did you find yours?

Mrs. DAVIS. It was about 10 minutes after all the police had gone.

Mr. BELIN. Was that before or after you went down to the police station?

Mrs. DAVIS. It was before.

Mr. BELIN. About when before?

Mrs. DAVIS. Well, I would say it was about 2:30, or 4.

Mr. BELIN. Mrs. Davis, when did you say you found this other shell?

Mrs. DAVIS. It was about 4.

Mr. BELIN. Did you see or know of anyone else finding any other shell?

Mrs. DAVIS. No, sir; not that I remember.

Mr. BELIN. Do you remember what you did with your shell when you found it?

Mrs. DAVIS. Well, before I picked it up, this boy told me that was walking along with us helping us find, see if we could find anything for evidence, he told me the police would get me if I picked it up by my fingers, and take fingerprints, and I got scared and ran to the house and got a Kleenex tissue and brought back outside and wrapped the shell in.

Mr. BELIN. What did you do with it when you wrapped the shell up?

Mrs. DAVIS. Jeanette took it and put it in her apartment up on the mantle-board.

Mr. BELIN. Then what?

Mrs. DAVIS. Then about 5:30 the same day the police called and wanted us to come down and identify him in the lineup.

Mr. BELIN. Then what did you do with the shell?

Mrs. DAVIS. I gave it to the police.

Mr. BELIN. Did you give it to him at your house or down at the police station?

Mrs. DAVIS. They come and picked us up.

Mr. BELIN. You gave it to the officer that came to pick you up?

Mrs. DAVIS. Yes, sir.

Mr. BELIN. Do you remember what his name was, or not?

Mrs. DAVIS. No, sir.

Mr. BELIN. Now in your statement, Virginia Davis Deposition Exhibit 2, now you state that, "Jeanette found an empty shell that the man had unloaded and gave it to the police. After the police had left I found a empty shell in our yard." Is this the same shell you gave to Detective Dhority? Does the name Detective Dhority sound familiar to you now, or don't you remember?

Mrs. DAVIS. I never did hear the detective called.

Mr. BELIN. Pardon?

Mrs. DAVIS. I didn't hear the detective's name called.

Mr. BELIN. You say, "The man that was unloading the gun was the same man that I saw tonight as No. 2 man in a lineup." Is that right?

Mrs. DAVIS. Yes.

Mr. BELIN. Now, Mrs. Davis, on this statement, Virginia Davis Deposition Exhibit 2, it states that "We heard a shot and then another shot and ran to side door at Patton Street." You say that should have been the front door?

Mrs. DAVIS. That was supposed to be the front door.

Mr. BELIN. You say, "I saw the boy cutting across our yard and he was unloading his gun. We walked outside and a woman was hollering, 'he's dead, he's, he's shot'." "This woman told Jeanette to call the police and she did." Now according to this statement, you saw the man cutting across your yard before you called the police?

Mrs. DAVIS. No, sir.

Mr. BELIN. Now this statement is wrong, is that correct?

Mrs. DAVIS. That's right.

Mr. BELIN. It is your testimony now, as I understand it, that you went back in the house and you called the police, and then you went back outside the house and saw the boy cutting across the yard?

Mrs. DAVIS. That's right.

Mr. BELIN. That is your statement now?

Mrs. DAVIS. Yes.

Mr. BELIN. Now I hand you what is Deposition Exhibit 3, and ask you to state if your signature appears on Deposition Exhibit 3?

Mrs. DAVIS. That's right.

Mr. BELIN. This appears to be an affidavit dated December 1, 1963, and I would like you to read the statement if you would.

Mrs. DAVIS. (Reads statement.)

Mr. BELIN. You have now had an opportunity to read over Virginia Davis Deposition Exhibit 3, is that correct?

Mrs. DAVIS. That's right.

Mr. BELIN. Is there anything on that statement that is not accurate?

Mrs. DAVIS. As I recall, this is all right on that statement.

Mr. BELIN. Pardon?

Mrs. DAVIS. I recall that is all right on that statement.

Mr. BELIN. Is there anything on that statement that is not accurate, to the best of your knowledge?

Mrs. DAVIS. No.

423

Mr. BELIN. You are nodding your head no?

Mrs. DAVIS. Not that I recall.

Mr. BELIN. Now, in this statement it says that you and your sister-in-law were lying on the bed with the two children when you heard a loud bang, and immediately following the first report there was another loud bang and you jumped up and ran to the front door? Is that correct?

Mrs. DAVIS. That's right.

Mr. BELIN. Then it says, "When we got to the door and went out on the porch, I saw a man who I later that day identified at the Dallas Police Department." Is that correct?

Mrs. DAVIS. That's right.

Mr. BELIN. Now, according to this statement, you saw the man when you first got to the door and went out on the porch? Now, did you see him then, or did you see him——

Mrs. DAVIS. We saw him cut across after he had shot the policeman. We saw him cut across our yard, and that is the last we saw of him.

Mr. BELIN. Well, now, you actually didn't see him shoot the policeman, did you?

Mrs. DAVIS. No, sir.

Mr. BELIN. You saw——just saw the man with the gun?

Mrs. DAVIS. I just saw the man with the gun cutting across the yard.

Mr. BELIN. After you heard some shots?

Mrs. DAVIS. After I heard the two shots.

Mr. BELIN. Now, about how soon after you heard the two shots did you get to the door?

Mrs. DAVIS. Well, we didn't even put on our shoes. We just run to the front door.

Mr. BELIN. Was it a matter of seconds or a matter of minutes?

Mrs. DAVIS. A matter of seconds.

Mr. BELIN. When you got there, you opened the door, and what did you see?

Mrs. DAVIS. We saw this boy or man cut across the yard.

Mr. BELIN. All right, and he had a revolver in his hand?

Mrs. DAVIS. That is right.

Mr. BELIN. In his right hand or left hand?

Mrs. DAVIS. In his right.

Mr. BELIN. This statement goes on to say that "The man had a revolver in his left hand and was shaking the shells out of it into his right hand." Is that right or wrong?

Mrs. DAVIS. Wrong.

Mr. BELIN. It was the other way around?

Mrs. DAVIS. It was the other way around.

Mr. BELIN. You got to the door and you opened the door, and what did you see now?

Mrs. DAVIS. We saw this boy cut across our yard unloading the shells out of his gun.

Mr. BELIN. Then what did you do?

Mrs. DAVIS. Mrs. Markham, this woman, was standing across the street hollering to us to call the police. So we went back in there and called the police.

Mr. BELIN. All right. Now, this statement says, goes on to say, "This man was coming across the yard and was almost to the walk which leads directly to the porch and is in a direct line with the front door."

Is that where the man was when you first saw him?

Mrs. DAVIS. That's right.

Mr. BELIN. "The man had a revolver in his left hand and was shaking the shells out of it into his right hand."

Mrs. DAVIS. It was the other way, sir.

Mr. BELIN. But you say "The man had a revolver in his left hand and was shaking the shells out of it into his right hand. As the man passed directly in front of us, he looked up for a second or so and then continued on across the yard to Patton Street in a normal walk." Was he walking or running when you saw him?

Mrs. DAVIS. He was walking.

Mr. BELIN. Did he look up at you?

Mrs. DAVIS. No.

Mr. DAVIS. Pardon?

Mrs. DAVIS. No, sir; not that I remember.

Mr. BELIN. All right, you just remember kind of seeing him from a side view?

Mrs. DAVIS. Yes, sir.

Mr. BELIN. "At about this time, a woman directly across the intersection from our house yelled out, 'He's dead, he's dead, he shot him.'"

Mrs. DAVIS. That's right.

424

Mr. BELIN. "The man glanced up at the woman and kept on walking." Did you see the man glance up at Mrs. Markham when she was yelling?

Mrs. DAVIS. Yes; we saw when he looked over at Mrs. Markham.

Mr. BELIN. Did you see Mrs. Markham do anything when he looked at her?

Mrs. DAVIS. No; she was over there just hollering and screaming.

Mr. BELIN. Did you see her raise her hand to her face in any way?

Mrs. DAVIS. Yes, sir. She raised both her hands to her face.

Mr. BELIN. You saw her do that?

Mrs. DAVIS. Yes.

Mr. BELIN. Did you see her do anything else?

Mrs. DAVIS. No.

Mr. BELIN. You say, "He walked around the corner of the house that faces Patton Street and out of sight." Is that right?

Mrs. DAVIS. That's right.

Mr. BELIN. "Barbara Davis and I returned to the house where she called the police." Is that right?

Mrs. DAVIS. That's right.

Mr. BELIN. According to the statement then, it says that your sister Barbara Jeanette called the police after you saw the man, is that right?

Mrs. DAVIS. That's right.

Mr. BELIN. "After she called the police, we went back out on the porch but by then the man we had seen with the gun was no longer in sight."

Is that right?

Mrs. DAVIS. That's right.

Mr. BELIN. Then it says, "When the police arrived we searched the area on the side of the house that faces Patton Street, and Barbara found a gunshell that had been fired." It that right?

Mrs. DAVIS. That's right.

Mr. BELIN. "After the police left we again searched the area and I again found a gunshell that had been fired. I later turned this shell over to the Dallas Police Department." Is that right?

Mrs. DAVIS. Yes, sir.

Mr. BELIN. Then it says, "I have been given an opportunity to make additions and corrections on this statement, and it is true to the best of my knowledge and belief."

Did they give you an opportunity to make additions and corrections on the statement?

Mrs. DAVIS. No.

Mr. BELIN. They did not?

Mrs. DAVIS. No.

Mr. BELIN. Did they read the statement back to you?

Mrs. DAVIS. Not that I remember.

Mr. BELIN. They may have but you don't remember.

Mrs. DAVIS. May have but I don't remember.

Mr. BELIN. Now, Mrs. Davis, you and I never talked about this matter until the court reporter started taking your testimony, have we?

Mrs. DAVIS. No, sir.

Mr. BELIN. I never met you before, is that correct?

Mrs. DAVIS. No, sir.

Mr. BELIN. Have you ever talked with any person in connection with the President's Commission before we started taking your testimony here?

Mrs. DAVIS. No, sir.

Mr. BELIN. I want to be certain that we get this time sequence correct as to when you saw the man with the gun and when the police were called, so I am just going to ask you to sit for about 30 seconds and just think as to just what did happen, and then just tell the court reporter in your own words just what did happen there.

(Three minutes of silence.)

Mr. BELIN. Now, Mrs. Davis, you may not be able to remember just what exactly the time sequence was. You have been sitting here about 3 minutes, and if you don't remember what the time sequence was, why I would like to have you so state. But if you do remember—or do you want more time to think about it?

Mrs. DAVIS. Well, the best I can remember, it was before that we saw the boy cut across the yard that we called the police, the best that I can remember.

Mr. BELIN. In other words, it is your testimony, as I understand it now, that you heard the shot, and then what did you do?

Mrs. DAVIS. We heard the second shot and we ran to the front door.

425

Mr. BELIN. What did you see?

Mrs. DAVIS. We saw this boy cut across the yard, and we had seen this woman was coming home from work, she had on a uniform, that was Mrs. Markham—we didn't know it was at the time, but she saw all that happen.

Mr. BELIN. What did you do when you got to the door?

Mrs. DAVIS. We saw the boy cut across our yard.

Mr. BELIN. At the time you got to the door, did you also see Mrs. Markham?

Mrs. DAVIS. Yes, sir.

Mr. BELIN. Did you see both at approximately the same time? I will ask you whom did you see first, Mrs. Markham, or the boy cutting across the yard?

Mrs. DAVIS. The boy.

Mr. BELIN. You saw the boy first?

Mrs. DAVIS. That is who we saw first.

Mr. BELIN. Then you saw Mrs. Markham second?

Mrs. DAVIS. Yes, sir.

Mr. BELIN. Did the boy say anything?

Mr. BELIN. No, sir.

Mr. BELIN. Did Mrs. Markham say anything?

Mrs. DAVIS. Well, when she got across the other street, 10th, she hollered, "He's dead, he's dead, he shot him."

Mr. BELIN. Then what did she say?

Mrs. DAVIS. She was screaming. I don't know.

Mr. BELIN. Then what did you do?

Mrs. DAVIS. Well, we called the police. Notified them.

Mr. BELIN. So you called the police after you saw the boy?

Mrs. DAVIS. After we saw the boy.

Mr. BELIN. And Mrs. Markham?

Mrs. DAVIS. Yes.

Mr. BELIN. You are nodding your head yes. Is that your testimony, to the best of your recollection?

Mrs. DAVIS. That is my testimony.

Mr. BELIN. I want to ask you again, did you call the police before or after you saw the boy?

Mrs. DAVIS. It was after.

Mr. BELIN. It was after?

Mrs. DAVIS. Yes, sir; after, the best that I can remember.

Mr. BELIN. The best you can remember, you called the police before or after you saw the boy?

Mrs. DAVIS. Yes, sir.

Mr. BELIN. Before or after?

Mrs. DAVIS. After.

Mr. BELIN. After you saw the boy, you went back in the house and called the police?

Mrs. DAVIS. Yes, sir.

Mr. BELIN. Is there anything else that you can think of that we haven't talked about that might be helpful in this investigation?

Mrs. DAVIS. No.

Mr. BELIN. Did you see any ambulance come up to where Officer Tippit was?

Mrs. DAVIS. Yes; I saw the ambulance.

Mr. BELIN. You got there before the ambulance, did you not?

Mrs. DAVIS. Yes; we got there before.

Mr. BELIN. Did the ambulance get there first or the police get there first?

Mrs. DAVIS. The ambulance got there first.

Mr. BELIN. Did you see anyone making any calls over Tippit's radio?

Mrs. DAVIS. No, sir.

Mr. BELIN. When you got to Tippit's car, did you take a look at that police car?

Mrs. DAVIS. We didn't touch it.

Mr. BELIN. Did you look at it? Did you notice whether its windows were rolled up or rolled down?

Mrs. DAVIS. The one on his side was rolled down.

Mr. BELIN. What about the one on the passenger side of the front seat, did you notice that?

Mrs. DAVIS. Rolled up.

Mr. BELIN. Was that rolled up?

Mrs. DAVIS. Yes, sir.

Mr. BELIN. When you got there?

Mrs. DAVIS. Yes.

Mr. BELIN. You are nodding your head yes.

Mrs. DAVIS. Yes.

Mr. BELIN. Now the front window has kind of a little window in it. Do you know that little tiny part of the front window that opens and closes?

Mrs. DAVIS. Yes, sir.

Mr. BELIN. Do you remember whether that one on the front seat by the right side of the front seat was open or not?

Mrs. DAVIS. No, sir.

Mr. BELIN. It was not open? Or you don't——

Mrs. DAVIS. I don't remember.

Mr. BELIN. Did you hear anyone make any statements that they had seen anything other than Mrs. Markham?

Mrs. DAVIS. No, sir.

Mr. BELIN. Did you see a taxicab parked anywhere in the vicinity?

Mrs. DAVIS. No.

Mr. BELIN. You are nodding your head no.

Mrs. DAVIS. No.

Mr. BELIN. Anything else you can think of?

Mrs. DAVIS. No, sir; I think I have told it all.

Mr. BELIN. All right, Mrs. Davis, we want to thank you very much for taking the time and the effort to come here. I know that this whole episode has taken time on your part, and we certainly appreciate your cooperation with the President's Commission.

www.ingramcontent.com/pod-product-compliance
Lightning Source LLC
Chambersburg PA
CBHW051758170526
45167CB00005B/1796